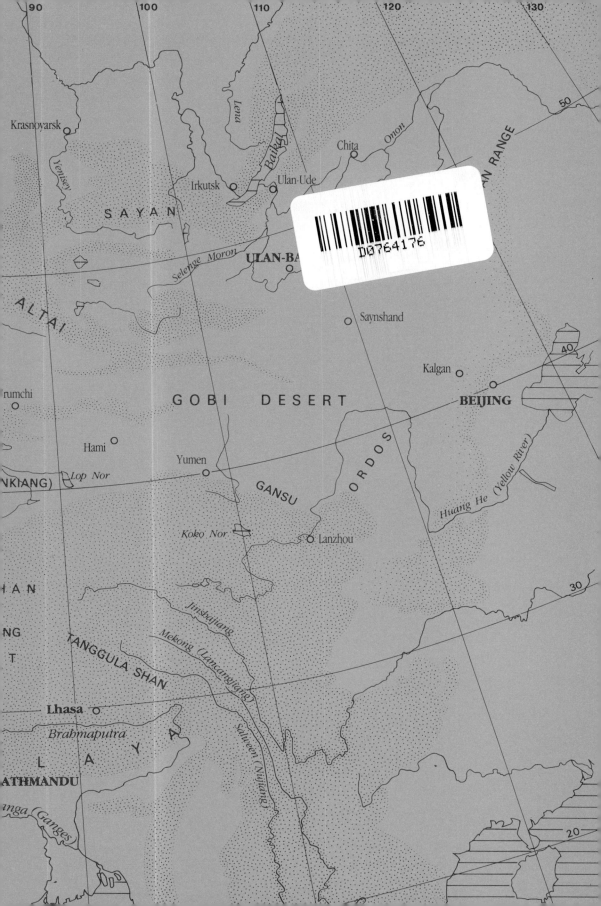

History of civilizations of Central Asia

Volume I
The dawn of civilization:
earliest times to 700 B.C.

Volume II
The development of sedentary and nomadic civilizations:
700 B.C. to A.D. 250

Volume III
The crossroads of civilizations:
A.D. 250 to 750

Volume IV
The age of achievement:
A.D. 750 to the end of the fifteenth century:
Part I:
The historical, social and economic setting
Part II:
The achievements

Volume V
Development in contrast:
sixteenth to eighteenth centuries

Volume VI
Towards contemporary civilization:
from the beginning of the nineteenth century
to the present time

History of civilizations of Central Asia

Volume I

The dawn of civilization:
earliest times to 700 B.C.

Editors:
A. H. Dani
V. M. Masson

UNESCO Publishing

The authors are responsible for the choice and the presentation
of the facts contained in this book and for the opinions
expressed therein, which are not necessarily those of UNESCO
and do not commit the Organization.

The designations employed and the presentation of material
throughout this publication do not imply the expression
of any opinion whatsoever on the part of UNESCO concerning
the legal status of any country, territory, city or
area or of its authorities, or concerning the delimitation
of its frontiers or boundaries.

Published in 1992 by the United Nations Educational,
Scientific and Cultural Organization
7 place de Fontenoy, 75700 Paris
Composed by UNESCO Publishing, Paris
Printed by Imprimerie des Presses Universitaires de France,
Vendôme

ISBN 92-3-102719-0

Printed in France

PREFACE

Federico Mayor
Director-General of UNESCO

ONE of the purposes of UNESCO, as proclaimed in its Constitution, is 'to develop and to increase the means of communication between . . . peoples and to employ these means for the purposes of mutual understanding and a truer and more perfect knowledge of each other's lives'. *The History of the Scientific and Cultural Development of Mankind,* published in 1968, was a major early response on the part of UNESCO to the task of enabling the peoples of the world to have a keener sense of their collective destiny by highlighting their individual contributions to the history of humanity. This universal history – itself now undergoing a fundamental revision – has been followed by a number of regional projects, including the *General History of Africa* and the planned volumes on Latin America, the Caribbean and on aspects of Islamic culture. The *History of Civilizations of Central Asia,* hereby initiated, is an integral part of this wider enterprise.

It is appropriate that the second of UNESCO's regional histories should be concerned with Central Asia. For, like Africa, Central Asia is a region whose cultural heritage has tended to be excluded from the main focus of historical attention. Yet from time immemorial the area has served as the generator of population movements within the Eurasian land-mass. The history of the ancient and medieval worlds, in particular, was shaped to an important extent by the succession of peoples that arose out of the steppe, desert, oases and mountain ranges of this vast area extending from the Caspian Sea to the high plateaux of Mongolia. From the Cimmerians mentioned in Homer's *Odyssey,* the Scythians described by Herodotus, the Hsiung-nu whose incursions led the Emperors of China to build the Great Wall, the sixth-century Turks who extended their empire to the boundaries of Byzantium, the Khitans who gave their name to ancient Cathay, through to the Mongols who erupted into world history in the thirteenth century under Genghis Khan, the nomadic horsemen of Central Asia helped to define the limits and test the mettle of the great civilizations of Europe and Asia.

Nor is it sufficient to identify the peoples of Central Asia simply with nomadic cultures. This is to ignore the complex symbiosis within Central Asia itself between nomadism and settlement, between pastoralists and agriculturalists. It is to overlook above all the burgeoning of the great cities of Central Asia such as Samarkand, Bukhara and Khiva, which established themselves in the late Middle Ages as outstanding centres of intellectual inquiry and artistic creation. The seminal writings of the philosopher-scientist Avicenna (a native of Bukhara) and the timeless masterpieces of Timurid architecture epitomize the flowering of medieval culture in the steppes and deserts of Central Asia.

The civilizations of Central Asia did not, of course, develop in a vacuum. The impact of Islam was pervasive and fundamental. The great civilizations on the periphery of the Eurasian continent likewise exerted an important influence on these lands. For some 1,500 years this arid inland sea – far removed from the earth's true oceans – was crucial as the route along which merchandise (notably silk) and ideas flowed between China, India, Iran and Europe. The influence of Iran – although the core of its civilization lies in south-west Asia – was particularly strong, to the extent that it is sometimes difficult to establish a clear boundary between the civilization of the Iranian motherland and that of the outlying lands of Central Asia.

To the rich variety of peoples of Central Asia was thus added a multiplicity of external influences. For century after century, the region experienced the influx of foreign art and ideas, colliding and merging with the indigenous patterns of Central Asia. Migrations and the recurrent shock of military invasion, mingling and displacing peoples and cultures, combined to maintain the vast region in flux.

The systole and diastole of population movements down the ages add to the difficulty of delimiting a region whose topology alone does not prescribe clear boundaries. Thus, when, at the nineteenth session of its General Conference, UNESCO decided to embark on a *History of Civilizations of Central Asia* the first problem to be resolved was to define the scope of the region concerned. Subsequently, at a UNESCO meeting held in 1978, it was agreed that the study on Central Asia should deal with the civilizations of Afghanistan, north-eastern Iran, Pakistan, northern India, western China, Mongolia and the Soviet Central Asian republics. The appellation 'Central Asia', as employed in this *History*, refers to this area, which corresponds to a clearly discernible cultural and historical reality.

UNESCO's call to specialists, and particularly to scholars native to the region, to participate in the undertaking met with a wide and generous response. The project was deemed by academics to be an excellent opportunity to draw back the curtain that had veiled Central Asia for so long. However, none were in any doubt as to the huge dimensions of the task.

An ad hoc International Scientific Committee was formed in 1980 to plan and prepare the work, which it was agreed should cover, in six volumes, the history of Central Asia from earliest times to the present day. The Committee's initial task was to decide where pre-eminence should be given in the very wide canvas before it. In due course, a proper balance was struck and teams of editors and authors were selected.

The preparation of the *History of Civilizations of Central Asia* is now well advanced. The best resources of research and archaeology have been used to make the work as thorough as possible, and countless annals consulted in major centres throughout the region. It is my sincere wish that this, the first volume, and those that follow will bring instruction and pleasure to readers all over the world.

It remains for me to thank the President, Rapporteur and members of the International Scientific Committee, and the editors, authors and teams of specialists who have collaborated to shed new light on Central Asia with this detailed account of its vital and stirring past. I am sure it will prove a notable contribution to the study and mutual appreciation of the cultures that are the common heritage of mankind.

CORRIGENDA

History of Civilizations of Central Asia

1. The reader's attention is drawn to the fact that Chapter 11 of Volume I was erroneously attributed to J. G. Shaffer and B. K. Thapar as joint authors.

   In fact, Professor Shaffer's contribution consisted of the text from the beginning of the chapter on page 247 up to and including the first complete paragraph on page 273 and the first paragraph of the Summary on page 281. Professor Thapar's contribution consisted of the text from the second paragraph on page 273 up to the last paragraph on page 280 and the second paragraph of the Summary on page 281.

   UNESCO wishes to extend its apologies to both authors.

2. The capital of Kyrgyzstan is now BISHKEK (formerly FRUNZE). The endpaper maps in future volumes will reflect this change.

CONTENTS

CONTENTS

DESCRIPTION OF THE PROJECT

Mohammad S. Asimov

THE General Conference of UNESCO, at its nineteenth session (Nairobi, October, November 1976), adopted the resolution which authorized the Director-General to undertake, among other activities aimed at promoting appreciation and respect for cultural identity, a new project on the preparation of a *History of Civilizations of Central Asia*. This project was a natural consequence of a pilot project on the study of Central Asia which was approved during the fourteenth session of the UNESCO General Conference in November 1966.

The purpose of this pilot project, as it was formulated in the UNESCO programme, was to make better known the civilizations of the peoples living in the regions of Central Asia through studies of their archaeology, history, languages and literature. At its initial stage, the participating Member States included Afghanistan, India, Iran, Pakistan and the Soviet Union. Later, Mongolia and China joined the UNESCO Central Asian project,[1] thus enlarging the area to cover the cultures of Mongolia and the western regions of China.

In this work, Central Asia should be understood as a cultural notion developed in the course of the long history of civilizations of peoples of the region and the above delimitation should not be taken as rigid boundaries either now or in the future.

In the absence of any existing survey of such large scope which could have served as a model, UNESCO has had to proceed by stages in this difficult task of presenting an integrated narrative of complex historical events from earliest times to the present day.

The first stage was designed to obtain better knowledge of the civilizations of Central Asia by encouraging archaeological and historical research and the study of literature and the history of science. A new project was therefore laun-

---

1. For the convenience of readers, a note prepared by Dr L. I. Miroshnikov on the meaning of the term 'Central Asia', as used in this work, is presented as an Appendix at the end of the volume.

ched to promote studies in five major domains: the archaeology and the history of the Kushan empire, the history of the arts of Central Asia, the contribution of the peoples of Central Asia to the development of science, the history of ideas and philosophy, and the literatures of Central Asia.

An International Association for the Study of Cultures of Central Asia (IASCCA), a non-governmental scholarly organization, was founded in 1973 assembling scholars of the area for the co-ordination of interdisciplinary studies of their own cultures and the promotion of regional and international co-operation.

Created under the auspices of UNESCO, the new Association became, from the very beginning of its activity, the principal consultative body of UNESCO in the implementation of its programme on the study of Central Asian cultures and the preparation of a *History of Civilizations of Central Asia*.

The second stage concentrated on the modern aspects of Central Asian civilizations and the eastward extension of the geographical boundaries of research in the new programme. A series of international scholarly conferences and symposia were organized in the countries of the area to promote studies on Central Asian cultures.

Two meetings of experts, held in 1978 and 1979 at UNESCO Headquarters, concluded that the project launched in 1967 for the study of cultures of Central Asia had led to considerable progress in research and contributed to strengthening existing institutions in the countries of the region. The experts consequently advised the Secretariat on the methodology and the preparation of the *History*. On the basis of its recommendations it was decided that this publication should consist of six volumes covering chronologically the whole history of Central Asian civilizations ranging from their very inception up to the present. Furthermore, the experts recommended that the experience acquired by UNESCO during the preparation of the *History of Scientific and Cultural Development of Mankind* and of the *General History of Africa* should also be taken into account by those responsible for the drafting of the *History*. As to its presentation, they supported the opinion expressed by the UNESCO Secretariat that the publication, while being a scholarly work, should be accessible to a general readership.

Since history constitutes an uninterrupted sequence of events, it was decided not to give undue emphasis to any specific date. Events preceding or subsequent to those indicated here are dealt with in each volume whenever their inclusion is justified by the requirements of scholarship.

The third and final stage consisted of setting up in August 1980 an International Scientific Committee of nineteen members, who sit in a personal capacity, to take reponsibility for the preparation of the *History*. The Committee thus created includes two scholars from each of the seven Central Asian countries – Afghanistan, China, India, Islamic Republic of Iran, Pakistan, Mongolia and the USSR – and five experts from other countries – Hungary, Japan, Turkey, the United Kingdom and the United States of America.

The Committee's first session was held at UNESCO Headquarters in December 1980. Real work on the preparation of the publication of the *History of Civilizations of Central Asia* started, in fact, in 1981. Those scholars selected by virtue of their qualifications and achievements relating to Central Asian history and culture should ensure objective presentation of this *History* and also the high scientific and intellectual standard of publication.

Members of the International Scientific Committee considered that the new project should correspond to the noble aims and principles of UNESCO and thereby should contribute to the promotion of mutual understanding and peace between nations.

The Committee followed the recommendation of the experts delineating for the purpose of this work the geographical area of Central Asia in accordance with the historical and cultural experience.

The first session of the International Committee decided most of the principal matters concerning the implementation of this complex project, beginning with the drafting of plans and defining the objectives and methods of work of the Committee itself.

The Bureau of the International Scientific Committee consists of a president, four vice-presidents and a rapporteur. The Bureau's task is to supervise the execution of the project between the sessions of the International Scientific Committee. The reading committee, consisting of four members, was created in 1986 to revise and finalize the manuscripts after editing Volumes I and II. Another reading committee was constituted in 1989 for Volumes III and IV.

The International Scientific Committee established the table of contents, the list of authors and the editors of the first volume. Further, it approved the plan of the chronology of the six volumes as follows:

Volume I – *The Dawn of Civilization: Earliest Times to 700 B.C.*

Volume II – *The Development of Sedentary and Nomadic Civilizations: 700 B.C. to A.D. 250.*

Volume III – *The Crossroads of Civilizations: A.D. 250 to 750.*

Volume IV – *The Age of Achievement: A.D. 750 to the End of the Fifteenth Century.*
Part 1: The Historical, Social and Economic Setting.
Part 2: The Achievements.

Volume V – *Development in Contrast: Sixteenth to Eighteenth Centuries.*

Volume VI – *Towards Contemporary Civilization: From the Beginning of the Nineteenth Century to the Present Time.*

Volume I of the *History* presented to the reader hereby was approved for publication by the decision of the Fourth Session of the Bureau of the International Scientific Committee in July 1987. It comprises chronologically a vast period of the early history of Central Asia from the appearance of Stone Age man and the Early Palaeolithic to the Iron Age. The editors and authors of various chapters of the volume are well-known experts of Central Asian archaeology and ancient history. The Editors are Professor Ahmad Hasan Dani, Honorary Director of the

Centre for the Study of Civilizations of Central Asia, Quaid-i Azam University, Islamabad, and Vadim M. Masson, Head of the Leningrad Branch of the Institute of Archaeology, Academy of Sciences of the USSR, corresponding member of the Turkmen SSR Academy of Sciences. The authors are scholars from the seven countries of Central Asia and experts from other regions. Thus, this work is the result of the regional and of the international collaboration of scholars within the framework of the programme of the United Nations Educational, Scientific and Cultural Organization (UNESCO).

It is our sincere hope that the publication of the first volume of the *History of Civilizations of Central Asia* will be the first step towards the promotion of the cultural identity of the peoples of Central Asia, strengthening their common cultural heritage and, consequently, will foster a better understanding among the peoples of the world.

MEMBERS OF THE INTERNATIONAL SCIENTIFIC COMMITTEE

(in alphabetical order)

15

LIST OF CONTRIBUTORS

BRIDGET ALLCHIN
The Ancient India and Iran trust
Brooklands House
23 Brooklands Avenue
Cambridge, CB2 2BG, United Kingdom.

A. ASKAROV
Professor
Uzbek Institute of Archaeology
Academy of Sciences
Samarkand (Uzbekistan), USSR.

A. H. DANI
Director
Centre for the Study of the
    Civilizations of Central Asia
Quaid-i-Azam University
Islamabad, Pakistan.

A. P. DEREVYANKO
Professor of History
Institute of History, Philology
    and Philosophy
Siberian Division of the Academy
    of Sciences
Prospekt Nauki 17
Novosibirsk–90, USSR.

D. DORJ
Institute of History
Academy of Sciences
Ulan Bator, Mongolia.

J. HARMATTA
Vice-President
Section of Linguistic and Literary
    Sciences
1052 Budapest, Hungary.

M. A. JOYENDA
Institute of Archaeology
International Centre for Kushan
    Studies
Kabul University
Kabul, Afghanistan.

B. B. LAL
Institute of Advanced Study
Rashtrapati Nivas, Summer Hill
Shimla 171005, India.

B. A. LITVINSKY
Professor
Institute of Oriental Studies
Academy of Sciences of the USSR
Rozhdestvenka str. 12
Moscow 103753, USSR.

S. MALEK SHAHMIRZADI
Professor of Archaeology
University of Tehran
Tehran, Islamic Republic of Iran.

V. M. Masson
Director
Institute of Archaeology
Academy of Sciences of the USSR
Leningrad Branch
Leningrad 181041, USSR.

L. I. Miroshnikov
Senior Research Fellow
Institute of Oriental Studies
Academy of Sciences of the USSR
Rozhdestvenka str. 12
Moscow 103753, USSR.

L. T. P'yankova
Institute of Oriental Studies
Academy of Sciences of the USSR
Rozhdestvenka str. 12
Moscow 103753, USSR.

V. Ranov
Head
Department of Archaeology
Institute of History
Prospekt Lenin 33
Dushanbe 734024 (Tajikistan)
USSR.

V. Sarianidi
Senior Scientific Member
Institute of Archaeology
Academy of Sciences of the USSR
Rozhdestvenka str. 12
Moscow 103753, USSR.

N. Ser-Odjav
Learned Secretary
Institute of History
Academy of Sciences
Ulan Bator, Mongolia.

J. G. Shaffer
Professor
Department of Anthropology
Case Western Reserve University
Cleveland, Ohio 44106
United States of America.

M. Sharif
Deputy Director
Department of Archaeology
Exploration and Excavation
    Branch
Government of Pakistan
Court, Sharhra-e-Faisal
Karachi–8, Pakistan.

B. K. Thapar
Chairman
Centre for Cultural Resources
    and Training
Bahawalpur House
Bhagwandas Road
New Delhi 110 001, India.

M. Tosi
Professor
Istituto Italiano per il
    Medio ed Estremo Oriente
Via Merulana, 248
00185 Rome, Italy.

V. Volkov
Senior Research fellow
Institute of History
Academy of Sciences of the USSR
Rozhdestvenka str. 12
Moscow 103753, USSR.

An Zhimin
Deputy-Director
Institute of Archaeology
Chinese Academy of Social
    Sciences
Beijing, China.

Lü Zun-E
Professor of Archaeology
Department of History
Beijing University
Beijing, China.

INTRODUCTION

A. H. Dani and V. M. Masson

NEW discoveries continue to widen and deepen our knowledge of the prehistory of mankind throughout the world. The study of ancient civilizations in Egypt and Mesopotamia considerably extended the temporal limits of history and explained the origin of some integral components in the complex evolutionary process in Europe. Archaeology in the twentieth century has once again pushed back the frontiers of our knowledge of world prehistory and brought to light numerous centres of ancient cultures and civilizations hitherto unknown. The new ideas and methods to which it has given rise have also made their contribution to a theory of world history viewed as a complex pattern linking the general with the particular. Broad similarities are reflecting global tendencies or being studied against the background of considerable regional diversities, while studies of particular regions and peoples are adding to the common store of world culture.

The need to synthesize the results obtained from the study of particular regions, macro-regions, with their comparative typological features is widely recognized and one outstanding example of this type of work is the *General History of Africa* published by Unesco.

The present publication is devoted to another macro-region of the Old World – namely, Central Asia. Situated in the very heart of the continent, this region has played a major role in the cultural–historical processes of various epochs. The role and importance of the various peoples of Central Asia are often inadequately represented in university courses, to say nothing of school textbooks. The present work is aimed at filling this gap.

As a rule, the chapters devoted to the ancient history and cultures of the particular countries belonging to the region have been written by scholars working in these countries. The editors have tried to take into consideration the contributions of different authors and present the material in a way that reflects the results of individual scholarship in an international spirit. To elucidate the history of the peoples in this area more completely, the authors of some chapters use the data in adjacent regions which have close cultural contacts, especially with Siberia, Iran and eastern Asia. Since the completion of the drafting of this first volume many new discoveries in the region have confirmed most of the suppositions made on the great role played by Central Asia in the history of world civilization and on the close links existing between different cultures inside the region.

The present volume deals with the ancient period in the history of civilizations in Central Asia, when the earliest human cultures emerged and determined to a considerable extent the later developments of local cultures and peoples. At the same time, the main trends in historical developments, namely, the steady progress in the cultural evolution as a general rule as well as regional diversities, become evident even in the case of these most ancient times.

The complex and unequal nature of the development of ancient societies was fully reflected in the Central Asian region. In studying the ancient history of Central Asia we may clearly distinguish various types of culture. In the first place, there are different stages of cultural development. One such stage, for example, was the emergence of either complex or class societies. This development was invariably accompanied by various elements, such as craft specialization, monumental architecture, systems of script and exchange. This phenomenon has manifested itself in various forms both in the Old and the New Worlds. At the same time, such general trends are locally manifested depending on the actual ecological and social setting. At this level we are dealing with the phenomena of the second order, that is, with the regional types of culture. This is clearly seen in the material of Central Asia. For example, in a number of stockbreeding cultures of the Bronze Age in Soviet Central Asia, Iran and Afghanistan, regional and subregional peculiarities combine with certain common cultural features, which enable us to integrate them into wider cultural entities. Finally, we may distinguish a basic unit of the concrete historical example, namely a local culture or a civilization reflecting the general features in the development of a group of tribes or peoples.

In this volume the authors have followed a concept of periodization, which is reflected in its structure. The lengthy Palaeolithic period is dealt with in three successive chapters, following technological and cultural developments. Local variations were either less important, or may not always be distinguished in the available data. For this reason, these chapters contain few detailed local accounts. Local variations became more obvious with the advent of food-production, manifested in various agricultural and stockbreeding societies. The presentation and analysis in these chapters follow historical and cultural subdivisions of the Central Asian macro-region. Variations in subsistence patterns increase: Neolithic agricultural communities coexisted with Neolithic predators, engaged in hunting, fishing and food-gathering, occupying the northern and eastern area of Central Asia. The development of a dynamic husbandry and, later, nomadism, increased the mobility of considerable population groups; migrations and displacement became more prevalent. The predecessors of several modern peoples emerged in this environment. The following stage in the emergence of settled civilizations arose as part of the introduction of metallurgy. The subject of the present volume covers all these important milestones in human prehistory.

The evidence related to the Palaeolithic is fairly rich, albeit limited to a series of lithic implements. No remains of Lower Palaeolithic sites, which are normally more informative, are so far known. Notwithstanding the paramount importance now attached to sites in East Africa, Central Asia retains its position if not as one of the centres of anthropogenesis then at least as an area settled by man at an early stage. As early as the Lower Palaeolithic, man effectively adapted himself to various ecological conditions. One may suggest that these lay at the root of cultural diversity and of the local peculiarities distinguished by research in the typology of lithic implements. In general terms, a hypothesis about the existence of great cultural zones, represented by hand-axes and pebble tools, was put forward by Movius[1] based mainly on the Soan assemblage from Pakistan. More recently a much more complicated pattern has emerged; everywhere local variants of Palaeolithic assemblages are distinguished, various series of pebble tools being treated as diagnostic indices. One cannot exclude the possibility of separate groups of Palaeolithic men coexisting side by side in Central Asia developing various traditions in manufacturing stone tools. This phenomenon, which is established in the eastern Mediterranean, probably occurred in Central Asia as well. The types of stone tools clearly indicate cultural links with regions of western Asia. The determination of a Neanderthal population, known from the discovery of the burial in the Teshik-Tash Cave in southern Uzbekistan, is of great significance.

How man came to build settled communities is a major question that remains to be fully answered. But it is clear that he was responding to the changing climatic conditions of the Holocene Age. Whether man himself was intelligent enough to bring about a revolution in his cultural response to the climatic change, it is difficult to say. But many have accepted the model of V. G. Childe who speaks of a 'Neolithic revolution', implying a deliberate attempt on the part of man to evolve a new technology for his survival in a new age. This model arises from the then available evidence which placed the origin of food production in western Asia and the gradual diffusion of this technology to other parts of the world. The evidence is now much more varied and Central Asia has produced definite material to show that food-producing communities developed more or less simultaneously in Iran, as evidenced by the sequences of Sialk, Hissar and Tepe Sang-i Chakmak, and also in many cave sites, in Soviet Central Asia, as evidenced by Jeitun, and also in the oases cultures; in Pakistan at Mehrgarh[2] and Kili Gul Muhammad; in Kashmir at Burzahom; in the Gangetic valley at Sarai-Nahar-Rai and Mahadaha.[3] At the same time there appears to have been a defi-

1. Movius, 1944.
2. Jarrige and Meadow, 1980.
3. Sharma, 1983.

nite change in man–animal relations. This is expressed in the terminology of nomadism, where man as a member of a nomad group builds new fraternal affinity with new kinds of animals, which not only supply him with food but serve as a source of other services. In this way these animals become subservient to man. This relational system is explained now in the contextual frame of the domestication of animals. This was certainly one of the great historical advances that man made from being dependent upon nature for his food to evolving a new socio-economic order to meet the new demands of a technology that was evolved for this purpose. The demand arose in the context of climatic change. During the Holocene new fauna and flora created new environmental conditions for man. We cannot at present illustrate the whole process of his response to this change. We only know the results. But it is clear that the change was gradual and the evidence from Central Asia shows the twin aspects of this change – one leading to settled agriculture and another to nomadism in the steppes of northern Central Asia as well as in the desert and high mountain zones.[4]

Thus, it is evident that Central Asia was part of a greater area where the emergence of a new type of economy and related mode of life occurred. This process of polycentral archaeological investigations in Central Asia has revealed the existence of several such local centres. As a rule, we may establish their relation to earlier, or Mesolithic assemblages. Thus, the change, in general terms, was of a spontaneous transformation, though in individual cases accomplished models and standards could have been used.

The first stage of historic change described above has been dubbed by some as 'barbarism' or primitive state of living, as it marked the beginning of community life, but it was certainly a great step forward in the march of humanity towards improving conditions of living by deliberate and intelligent effort. Irrigation farming by early agricultural communities produced a noticeable surplus and that stimulated the development of the economic system as a whole. It led to the exchange of experience and resource material. But the greatest change was in the development of social life. Small-scale trade in precious stones such as jade, shells and other sundries is evident in this period. Larger-scale long-distance trade appears only at the next stage when the use of metal led to mining and metallurgy. In the first stage of bronze technology land trade between sites in Soviet Central Asia is amply evidenced and at the same time trade links are noted with the sites in Iran, Afghanistan and the Indus valley. Sites such as Altyn-depe in Turkmenistan, Shahr-i Sokhta in eastern Iran, Mundigak in southern Afghanistan and Mehrgarh in Pakistan trace the beginning of Bronze Age communities and provide material for the transition stage from simple food production to a gradual growth of complex societies having multifarious craft specialization. Professional craftsmen emerged as social groups leading to a new type of socio-economic relationship. It is difficult to say what the centre of attrac-

4. Masson, 1983.

tion was for population concentration in different focuses. It may have been stimulated by craft developments, by political considerations, or by purely religious or ceremonial factors. At the same time social stratification may have resulted from particular economic relations between groups of craftsmen. Whatever may have been the motivation, the evidence is varied, as seen at Rahman Dheri in Pakistan, Mundigak in Afghanistan and Namazga-depe in Turkmenistan. Throughout this extensive area, uniformity is not apparent nor do we have any evidence of writing at this stage.

Fundamental change occurs in the nature of Bronze Age societies when alongside land-route trade, overseas commerce and communication is noted between the Indus Civilization and Mesopotamia. The Indus Civilization extended far beyond the Indus valley, and links were established from the Gujarat coast through Makran to various places on the Persian Gulf. The maturity is noted not only in the highly developed urban architecture but also in the use of writing, most probably by a sophisticated class of scribes, and increasing use of seals and sealings, probably for trading purposes. This sudden outburst reached its climax in the emergence of planned cities in the Indus Civilization. Other areas show their own peculiarities. But the Indus system with its uniform pattern is certainly unique in the civilization of the ancient world. Its extent, its richness, its influence and its wide connections present a new picture of an urban setting in Central Asia. For long it was thought that this Bronze Age development in Central Asia was due to a process of diffusion from Mesopotamia. But recent evidence has now made it abundantly clear that it experienced a long process of growth in this very environment, and its unique features prove that it did not owe its origin to western Asia. The development is not the same all over Central Asia. The patterns differ from China to the Oxus valley and from Iran to the Indus and the Ganges valleys. So far we have spoken of the 'urban revolution', of the urban centres and of their vast 'underdeveloped' neighbours who must have continued in their traditional patterns of life.

It is important to note that the development of local urban and proto-urban civilizations, as well as agriculture, are based on the stable foundation of local economic potential and cultural traditions. This was an important stage in the spontaneous transformation. At the same time, in individual cases, we may distinguish stimulated transformation, the adoption of norms and standards first established in the most ancient centres of civilization, Sumer and Elam. One significant element of this is the broad impact of Proto-Elamite culture, from cylindrical seals to tablets with Proto-Elamite scripts discovered at numerous sites on the Iranian plateau, including Hissar and Shahr-i Sokhta. We may note that the Proto-Elamite element entered at the formative stage as an integral part of the socio-cultural complex of the civilizations that developed between Mesopotamia and the Indus valley.

At the same time, the originality of local civilizations, which actively developed in the course of the third and early second millennia B.C. was remarkable.

As known from recent research, some outstanding items of artistic culture found in Elam were imported from the zone of ancient civilizations in eastern Iran and Afghanistan. If the Indus Valley Civilization, known from the early 1920s, has established itself in the literature on world history, a number of civilizations in the southern regions of Central Asia are only now appearing in the pages of archaeological publications. As a result we may distinguish a subregion of early urban civilizations taking an intermediary position between Mesopotamian on the one hand and Harappan on the other. The French scholar Pierre Amiet, stressing its original character, has labelled it as Trans-Elamic.[5] A more appropriate term may be coined later, but the existence of a separate centre of civilization in the south of Central Asia has been proved beyond doubt.

At a time when these civilizations were evolving in the south of the region, changes were under way in the steppe zone of Central Asia, which were of prime importance for world history and culture. Already in the Neolithic, the transition to farming and stockbreeding was apparent in several areas. The latter gained in importance in the course of time. From early times the dry steppes and semi-deserts were rich in fodder and contained large herds of ungulates. Then, with their domesticated animals, herdsmen inhabited this area. In all probability, the horse was domesticated in the fourth millennium B.C., while the camel spread northwards from the southern regions. In the second millennium B.C., the transition to the wide use of metals, stockbreeding and farming as the main sources of food was completed. The tribes of the steppe zone were Neolithic hunters and fishers. The use of horse-drawn light chariots was an important innovation. Warriors on chariots armed with spears with bronze heads presented an important armed force. Working tools were also made of bronze. This was a new type of culture. Mobile and warlike stockbreeders conquered the dry steppes and penetrated the mountains. Moving south they encountered the agricultural oases. Archaeological sites, cemeteries in the first place in the middle Amu Darya (Oxus) and in Pakistan, indicate the displacement of large population groups in the process of cultural assimilation and symbiosis.

The question arises of who these peoples and tribes were. Recent investigations may in some cases supply an answer. Anthropological materials from graves and cemeteries provide data on the physical appearance of this population.[6] The materials related to the Palaeolithic indicate that the population of Central Asia at that time was similar to that of Europe and the eastern Mediterranean area.[7] Based on present evidence we may conclude that the crystallization of the physical features of the population of one type in the greater part of the area was essentially complete by the beginning of the Neolithic, as it was in Europe and western Asia. Moreover, in the Altai mountains and the Minussinsk depres-

---

5. Amiet, 1986.
6. Material provided by Professor V. P. Alekseev is used here.
7. Alekseev, 1978, 1985.

sion, mixed types are recorded incorporating eastern and western physical types. Among the eastern types the so-called Mongoloid element developed initially in the forest and *taiga* regions. The evidence relating to the Late Neolithic and Bronze Ages is more complete. The northern regions of Central Asia are included in the vast area of the Andronovo culture. The skeletons of the peoples of the eastern regions of Central Asia were more massive than those of Kazakhstan, but these differences were probably local; the population as a whole was of a western character.

Anthropological records from southern Soviet Central Asia indicate the differences in the massiveness, which was an important feature in the differentiation of the western types beginning with the Late Neolithic and Bronze Age, such as the Anau-type population. Even more gracile individuals lived at Sapalli-tepe, resembling those from Mundigak in the south. In southern Tajikistan there was the same degree of gracility as in Kara-depe and Geoksiur. Thus, the establishment of the gracile varieties occurred more intensely in Afghanistan and along the Amu Darya than in Turkmenistan and south Tajikistan. The western groups spread farther to the east on the steppes of Eurasia during the great migrations at the B.C./A.D. transition. One may suggest that the Neolithic population of Altai, Tuva and Mongolia belonged also to the same population. All these areas were parts of their initial settlement. The contacts with the eastern group occurred in eastern Mongolia and in the forest-steppes of southern Siberia. The western groups spread along the northern ridges of Tibet up to Gansu province, where they came in contact with the local population.

The Harappan population was a homogeneous one, markedly gracile, apparently of the western type, making up the bulk of the population.[8] The tendency towards the broad nasal feature resembles the initial mixing with the so-called Negroid protomorphics of the Mesolithic population in northern India.

Summing up, we may note that the Pre-Indo-European speaking population of India and Pakistan belonged to the western group. The spread of this population occurred in a different environment and its anthropological manifestations may be established only if new materials belonging to later periods are found in northern India and Pakistan. Thus, Central Asia was initially settled from the west by the protomorphic mixed populations of the western and the so-called Europoid types. They survived in a slightly modified form in northern India up to the Bronze Age.

In Soviet Central Asia the assemblage of a western type based on protomorphic combinations probably evolved in the Upper Palaeolithic or Mesolithic. Tibet was originally inhabited by the Mongoloids; the contacts with the western types occurred along its confines, in Gansu province and in eastern Mongolia. The gracilization was under way beginning from the Neolithic, with various

8. Dutta, 1972.

intensity. Large-scale migrations occurred in the area of Soviet Central Asia in the Bronze Age.

Ethnicity within local populations is difficult to establish; language, being an important element of ethnicity, must have changed several times. The existing decipherment of the Indus script still exists but is generally not accepted; according to a widely held view, it belonged to the Proto-Dravidian type. Positional-statistical analysis seems to confirm indications that Dravidian languages were more widely spread in prehistory.[9] The discovery of a seal with a Proto-Indus inscription at Altyn-depe is of great significance.[10] Tablets with Proto-Elamite script from Iran suggest that its population was Elamite-oriented.

Regardless of the linguistic attribution of the most ancient groups, the population of the Central Asian area was using mainly Indo-European languages towards the end of the second and at the beginning of the first millennium B.C. Professor J. Harmatta in Chapter 15 of this volume has given his own interpretation of the spread of the Indo-Iranian tribes. The linguistic analysis shows a large proliferation of words related to stockbreeding and particularly to cattlebreeding at the stage of proto-Indo-Iranian unity. This, as well as irrefutable indications of linguistic contacts with proto-Finno-Ugric-speaking populations, seems to pinpoint the steppe zone of Eurasia as the habitation area of the most ancient Indo-European-speaking tribes. Hence it seems logical to suggest that the language of the steppe Bronze Age belonged at least partly to this linguistic family. More detailed attribution of archaeological assemblages and cultures to linguistic groups remains purely speculative. It is clear that the displacement of Bronze Age stockbreeders into Soviet Central Asia and further south, as well as related complicated cultural transformations in the second millennium B.C. are linked to the spread of Indo-Iranian and, later, of Iranian tribes.

The second millennium B.C. was a time of degradation and disintegration of local urban complexes. Such important centres as Altyn-depe in the south of Soviet Central Asia, Tepe Hissar in north-eastern Iran, Shahr-i Sokhta in Iranian Sistan fade away. This destiny was shared by the main centres of Harappan civilization including Mohenjo-daro and Harappa itself. Attempts have been made to link up these two processes, associating the decadence of the Harappan cities with an intrusion of Aryans. This explanation is a simplistic one. These changes were due to a number of factors, including the increasing aridity of the climate which undermined agriculture, the economic base of many ancient civilizations. At any rate, we may note in the second millennium B.C. a clear trend of displacement of the zone of intensive development from the Kopet Dag piedmont to Margiana and Bactria, and from the Indus valley to Gujarat and the eastern Punjab. Beginning with the second half of the second millennium B.C. the cultural transformation intensified, resulting in a complete cultural change in the first

9. Parpola et al., 1969.
10. Masson, 1981.

three centuries of the first millennium B.C. Yaz-depe-type Early Iron Age assemblages emerged in Bactria and Margiana, while painted grey ware appeared in the Indo-Pakistan subregion. Urban centres evolved inside these cultural regions, and the second cycle in the development of civilization occurred. Aryan principedoms in the Ganges valley and small kingdoms – Dahya – in Margiana and Bactria equally reflect the emergence of states and class society. New investigations indicate some similarity in this process with that of the evolution of Early Bronze Age civilization, as well as elements of heredity. Bhagwanpura-type sites are relevant in this sense in the Indian context.

Simultaneously, radical changes occurred over the vast steppe area, where early nomads replaced their direct predecessors, Bronze Age stockbreeders. This event, extremely important for world history, occurred in Central Asia. As a result, the steppe zone, initially situated outside the settled civilizations, became an area of intensive development. Steppe tribal groups moving together with herds of cattle completely changed the political situation. A new mode of life related to nomadic existence, new ideological concepts reflecting the dynamism of this life and its symbol, a winged horse, came into being. The mobility of steppe tribes and the rate of the information transmission markedly increased with the advent of wheeled chariots and, particularly, of the saddle horse. This expanded the world, new standards and models were rapidly transmitted over thousands of kilometres. Wealth in the form of easily alienable goods (cattle) was being accumulated, which provoked military conflicts and stimulated the manufacture of arms. Successful military chiefs tried to perpetuate their standing by sumptuous burial rites. By its social and cultural consequences, the transition to the epoch of the early nomads may be compared to the 'urban revolution' in settled oases where it formed an economic and cultural basis of civilization.

These are the main trends in the ancient history of Central Asia reflected in this volume. Ancient cultures and civilizations created by the efforts of numerous peoples of this area have become an integral part of world culture. We are now only beginning to study their remains; a considerable portion still awaits discovery.

EDITORS' NOTE

Changes affecting the republics of the former Soviet Union took place when this volume was at the printers. For this reason, the terms 'Soviet Central Asia', 'Soviet Union', 'USSR' appear throughout. Volume II will reflect the changes which have taken place.

I

The environment[1]

V. M. Masson

As a geographical concept, Central Asia has a long history. In 1843, the famous geographer Alexander von Humboldt published in Paris a three-volume work, in which he treated Central Asia as a separate and distinct region on account of its interior drainage system and surrounding mountain chains, in which the explorer discerned a distinct geometric system. Later the concept was redefined and the boundaries of the region were further delimited in both a wider and a narrower sense.

In the present work Central Asia is regarded as a cultural and historical concept that embraces countries joined by ancient cultural, economic and political bonds and a shared history.

It was in Central Asia that the interaction between the twin poles of the world's history – the first centres of sedentary civilizations and the pastoralists and nomads of the steppes – was played out to the full. The prerequisites for the rise of the first civilizations and of productive stockbreeding stem directly from the entire region's natural resources, because some geographical subregions are closely associated with certain types of culture and specific historical developments.

Mongolia, a land of mountains and alternating uplands, mountain valleys and depressions with plains in the south-east, has distinctive natural features. The chief mountain systems are the Mongolian Altai (Altay Nuruu), the Khangai (Hangayn Nuruu) and the Khentei (Hentiyn Nuruu), which stretch from north to south across the centre of the country. The climate is extremely continental; precipitation is concentrated in summer, and the country is predominantly arid. Two-thirds of Mongolia belong to the interior basins of Central Asia, and only in the north do the waters drain into the sea. The major rivers are the Kerulen, the Onon and Halhin *gol*, tributaries of the Amur; the Selenga flows into the deep

1. See Maps 1 and 2.

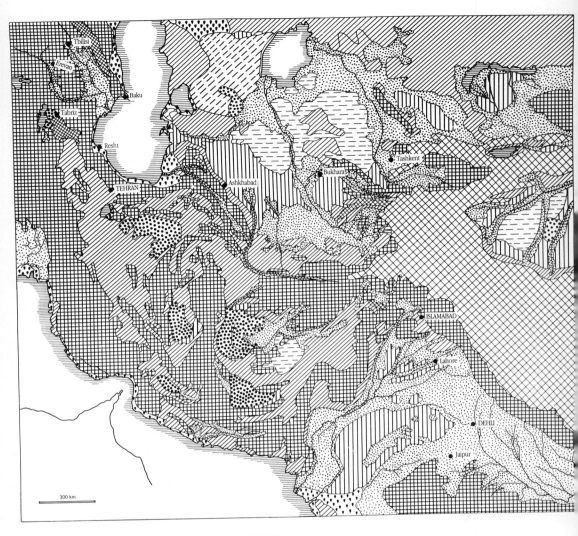

MAP 1. Geomorphic map.

 High mountains

 Medium and low mountains

Evenly tilted proluvial plains

Elevated table-lands
(structural plateaux)

Alluvial plains

Lacustrine plains

Deserts on alluvial plains

Aeolic deserts

Terraces on littoral plains

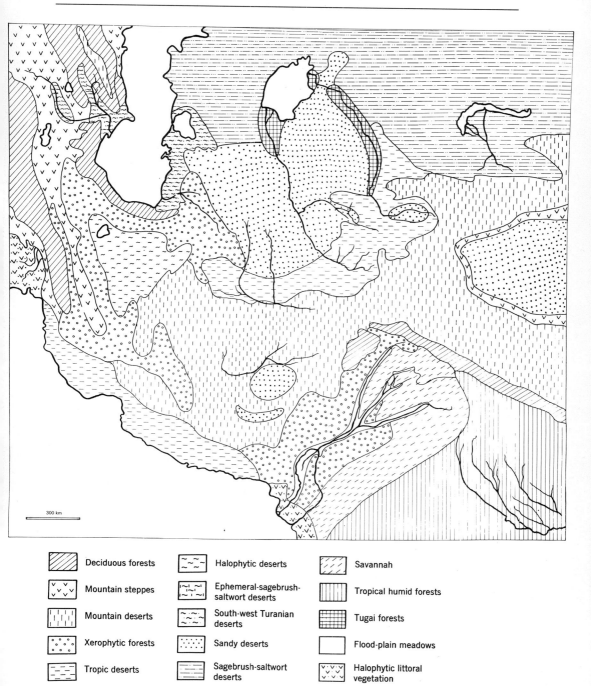

300 km

Deciduous forests	Halophytic deserts	Savannah
Mountain steppes	Ephemeral-sagebrush-saltwort deserts	Tropical humid forests
Mountain deserts	South-west Turanian deserts	Tugai forests
Xerophytic forests	Sandy deserts	Flood-plain meadows
Tropic deserts	Sagebrush-saltwort deserts	Halophytic littoral vegetation

MAP 2. Geobotanic map.

lake Baikal. Owing to the very cold winter and slight snow cover there is permafrost.

Despite these generally severe conditions, the country is suitable for herds of ungulates and the development of stockbreeding. The forest-steppes in the northern mountains have ample surface waters and are quite effective grazing lands. But the bulk of the pasture lies in the mountain-steppes on the gentle slopes of the Khangai and Khentei mountain regions at altitudes of 900 to 1,500 m, where all the principal domestic animals can be pastured.

The vegetation is sparser in the semi-desert to the south, where climatic conditions favour sheep, goats and camels. To the south again, semi-deserts gradually give way to a zone of desert, floored with gravel or rock, that borders on the Gobi and is virtually waterless. Since little or no snow falls on the grazing lands, animals can forage freely throughout the year. This set of natural conditions is largely responsible for the animal life, despite the pressure of domestic herds, the wild Bactrian camel, the Przhevalsky horse, the desert Persian gazelle and the Mongolian gazelle of the steppes may still be found.

Much the same natural conditions prevail in eastern Turkestan where the climate is admittedly still more arid. This is a land of high plateaux and mountain ranges – the Kunlun and the eastern T'ien Shan – of broad basins and vast waterless deserts, the Gobi and the Taklamakan, the latter with barely 5–10 mm of precipitation yearly. Here the eastern T'ien Shan separates two large basins: the northern is called Dzungaria and the southern Kashgaria. The greater part of the Tarim basin is occupied by the Taklamakan sand desert. Here the summer is scorching, with average July temperatures in Kashgar as high as 33 °C, and the climate as a whole is extremely dry: mean annual precipitation in the same city is only 83 mm. Extreme importance therefore is attached to water sources and groundwater springs. The most important river is the Tarim, into which flow the Kashgar, Yarkand, Khotan and Aksu. The Tarim itself has a migratory delta, one of the arms of which falls into the closed lake Lop Nor. The rivers are characteristically full in summer, fed by melted snow from the mountains and the land can be farmed only when irrigated. Desert and semi-desert vegetation predominates and woodland is found only on the mountain slopes or in the river valleys. Infertile arid deserts far outweigh lands suitable for stockbreeding. Only where mountain rivers leave their ravines or groundwater reaches the surface is the flora abundant; only there do the oases occur, stretching in a chain along the foothills north and south of the eastern T'ien Shan and north of the western Kunlun. It was water that determined the major land routes leading from east to west, from oasis to oasis, from well to well. Difficult even for camel caravans, this road was of vast importance, linking as it did the civilizations of the Mediterranean and western Asia with ancient China.

Soviet Central Asia may be divided into semi-desert, desert and mountain regions. Typical of the semi-desert and steppe zone are the expanses of Kazakhstan that form a part of the vast Eurasian steppe belt stretching from the lower

Danube to Manchuria. In orographical terms, the region is divided into the Caspian depression, the Turgai tableland – an elevated plateau – and the Kazakh uplands; the latter is a rolling or hilly area which is all that remains of a time-worn mountain chain. The continental climate, with an annual precipitation of up to 300 mm, does not prevent vegetation. In the north is a steppe of mixed feather grass with patches of pine woods; to the south the semi-desert proper sets in with drought-loving shrubs such as wormwood and annual (ephemeral) and perennial (ephemeroid) grasses. As in the Mongolian steppes, the thinness of the snow cover allows herbivores to forage easily, and the semi-desert vegetation is in winter a kind of 'hay on the root' with excellent nutritional qualities.

To the south of the semi-desert of central Kazakhstan the desert zone begins, its topography being largely due to wind erosion. The largest deserts are the Kyzyl Kum and the Kara Kum, which occupy alluvial plains made up of river deposits, chiefly sand, and frequently called the Turanian lowland. The desert zone partly extends to the loess plains at the mountain foot. Among the small hill ranges here is the waterless Ustyurt plateau, up to 340 m high and bounded by steep cliffs. The Kara Kum lowlands represent the combined deltas of ancient rivers – the Amu Darya, the Murghab and the Tedzhen/Harirud – filled with the products of wind and water erosion from the neighbouring mountains, the Pamir and Alai, the Hindu Kush and the Paropamisos. The climate in these southern deserts is characteristically subtropical with extremely low precipitation (250 mm), so that evaporation far exceeds supply. Among the sand dunes are dry lake beds – depressions filled with clay accretions – which are water catchment areas used as watering places.

The loess foothill valleys of Soviet Central Asia figured very prominently in the development of ancient cultures, particularly where water supplies were adequate. One such area was the Ferghana valley, the centre of which, with its dry or salty tracts, is virtually a desert. Scattered along the mountains that ring the valley are flourishing oases among the rolling hills or *adyrs*. The Hungry Steppe, conversely, albeit a typical foothill plain in topographical terms, because of its poor supply of water requires major irrigation before it can be farmed. In the plain to the north of the Kopet Dag are old and new alluvial fans, left either by permanent water courses or by mud-slides, and merging into a continuous hem. Farming oases lie along the small rivers and streams here.

The major waterways in Soviet Central Asia's southern deserts – the largest being the Amu Darya, Syr Darya and the Zerafshan – are fed by glaciers and melting snows. Some – the Murghab and the Tedzhen/Harirud – end in blind deltas in the deserts. A characteristic of the hydrological pattern is that atmospheric moisture is continuously accumulated in the mountains: it is then scattered on the plains, whence it evaporates back into the atmosphere. The drainage of the large Soviet Central Asian rivers, the Amu Darya and the Syr Darya, makes them difficult to tap for irrigation purposes without a major technological effort. Particularly indomitable is the Amu Darya which, because it falls sharply as it leaves the hills and because of the local slopes, has a rapid flow whose power far exceeds the resistance of the banks. Consequently, the 'mad river' constantly changes course; within hours it can literally wash away its banks and entire settlements, while its troubled waters carry a vast quantity of suspended particles.

A characteristic of Soviet Central Asia is the geographical orientation of main ranges running from west to east and having very high altitudes. The Khan Tengri in the T'ien Shan, for instance, has a height of 6,995 m and is the tallest in the entire system. Of the intramontane basins, mention may be made of the Naryn depression and that of the Issyk-kul with its eponymous 702-m-deep lake, the Ili and the Ferghana valleys. Among the high-altitude valleys mention should be made of the Altai with its mountain steppes producing vast quantities of fodder. The Pamir mountains fall distinctly into two natural areas – the western and the eastern. In the western Pamirs there is complex fracturing of the terrain with clear-cut contours, pointed peaks and deeps, steep-sided valleys and ravines: here the climate is relatively mild, warm and moist. In this area the mountains end at the western Tajik or Tajik-Afghan depression. The fertile valleys of the Amu Darya's right-bank tributaries, the Surkhan Darya, the Vakhsh and the Kafirnigan, are protected by the mountains from the cold northerly airstreams. The landscape of the eastern Pamirs is more generally glacial and less rugged. The prevailing climate is that of Central Asian high-altitude deserts. The major icefield is the Fedchenko Glacier. Similar to the cold desert of the eastern Pamirs are the *syrty* of the central T'ien Shan.

The southern border of the Kara Kum desert is formed by the Kopet Dag, which is part of the Turkmen-Khorasan mountains. The Kopet Dag is steep-sided, flat-topped and, particularly in the outer or north-eastern chain, which is cut by the ravines of small rivers, markedly rectilinear. This is due to the synchronized tectonic movements that during the orogenic period moved the Kopet Dag on the Kara Kum shield. The mountains are not high, ranging from 2,500 to 3,100 m and no more than 1,000 to 1,700 m in the outlying spurs. The high-altitude zones change from mountain desert to mountain steppes with sparse juniper shrubs. Trees still grow plentifully in the moist ravines, including wild nut and fruit trees such as the plum.

The dominant environmental feature of Iran is the Iranian highland, the eastern part of which extends into Afghanistan and Baluchistan. The highland itself is a vast and frequently waterless tract of high deserts and steppes which are hot in summer and cold in winter. It is framed, and in parts intersected, by broad and formidable chains of inaccessible hills that are themselves chiefly steppe and desert; only the narrow band of the outer slopes is clad with woods. As in Soviet Central Asia, the oases lie in the foothills, basins and mountain valleys that have adequate water supplies.

The mountains are generally moderate in height, with few summits exceeding 3,000 m. The southern peripheral hills form a chain of the Zagros, the Makran and the Sulaiman mountains, the last two in Pakistan. There are two humid zones of mountain forests in this system: one to the west in the Zagros, where a Mediterranean landscape prevails, and one in the east which has a tropical monsoon climate. Along the southern coast the mountains drop away to the arid *garmsir* desert. To the north the Iranian highland is framed by the Elburz and Turkmen-Khorasan mountains, a chain that is continued in Afghanistan by the Paropamisos (Hindu Kush). The Elburz is an important store of moisture and its rivulets and springs feed many Iranian oases. The Caspian coastal line, to the north of Elburz, is a humid region with precipitation of up to 1,000 to 1,600 mm yearly. This area, which geographers treat separately as the Hyrcanian region after the ancient province of that name, has relic broadleaf forest on its heavily and constantly watered mountain slopes. During the cool episodes of the Quaternary period, the region served as a kind of haven for heat-loving plants.

The Turkmen-Khorasan mountains comprise a number of east–west oriented ranges, the northernmost of which is Kopet Dag. Between the ranges lie bands of flat or hilly plains. Particularly fertile is the moist Gorgan-Mashhad belt of depressions which, at its far west, includes the Gorgan valley around the Caspian, watered by the Gorgan river. Eastward along the upper Atrek lies the Kushan-Shirvan basin, and further east again the Mashhad valley watered by the river Kashafrud, a tributary of the Harirud. The foothills of this mountain system are characteristically deserts of wormwood and ephemerals with their luxuriant meadow-like growth. Higher in the hills groves of junipers and pistachios are to be found.

On the whole, eastern Iran combines, with minor exceptions, an extremely continental climate with the high temperatures typical of the subtropics. Another feature of this area is its pronounced aridity. Many rivers are consequently intermittent, flowing regularly only during the rainy period, or even spasmodic, filling up whenever downpours occur. The vegetation is predominantly of desert or mountainous xerophytic type, and this is particularly obvious on the Iranian highland itself – a hot plateau overlaid with accumulations of sand and gravel. There are two large deserts: the Dasht-i Lut and the Dasht-i Kavir. The latter, occupying an area of some 400 × 250 km and consisting of a number of salt basins, is particularly oppressive: even the temporary water courses are salty. It is among the world's largest absolute deserts. During the spring rains many parts of it become lakes of liquid mud in which entire caravans may perish during the sudden downpours. The major east–west transport routes therefore run along the peripheral hills, following the chains of oases, while north–south movement uses passes in the Elburz and the Turkmen-Khorasan mountains which are generally fragmented and comparatively accessible.

Afghanistan is to a large extent a land of mountains, four-fifths of its territory being mountainous. Almost in the centre, the Paropamisos and Hindu Kush ranges run from west to east, presenting a formidable barrier that protects the basin of the Amu Darya and its left-bank tributaries – most of which now lose themselves in the sands – from the south. The Paropamisos consists of a number

35

of latitudinal chains, the chief of which, the Sefid Kuh rises up to 4,200 m. The northern foothills are a desert of ephemeral sedge and meadow-grass. The more humid southern slopes support steppes of mixed couched-grass which burn out in summer, in places giving way to a typical desert. In the basin of the Tedzhen/ Harirud lies the fertile Herat valley, an eastward extension of the Gorgan-Mashhad depressions; safely protected by the mountains from the cold northerly airstreams, it can be harvested twice yearly. The lowlands between the Hindu Kush and the Amu Darya are part of the Afghan-Tajik valley, which was subjected to protracted sinking and is filled with thick layers of crumbly rock. These lowlands are the natural extension of the Kara Kum desert, and a narrow belt of sands stretches parallel to the river's channel. Between them and the rolling foothills reminiscent of the *adyr* of the Ferghana lie fertile oases watered by streams that run down from the hills and sink into the sand and clay plain with its extensive dry lake beds and salt-flats. Only the Surkhab or Kunduz flows permanently to join with the Amu Darya. When in flood the Band-i Baba river is a major watercourse that carries water deep into the Kara Kum far to the north-west.

The Hindu Kush, which forms the watershed between the Aral and the Indus basins, is among Asia's highest mountain ranges. it includes the Kuh-i Baba range, 5,100 m high, and one of Afghanistan's key orographic and hydrographic complexes, where the country's main rivers – the Harirud, the Helmand and the Kabul – all rise. The characteristic landscape of the Hindu Kush is much fragmented with majestic ravines, vast glaciers and many mud-slides. The east–west routes across use the high passes – the Shibir pass (2,987 m) on the road from Kabul to Mazar-i Sharif and the Unai pass (3,444 m) between Kabul and Herat. The eastern Hindu Kush is a high-altitude desert. On the southern slope lie wormwood and ephemeral deserts, while higher there are forests similar to those of the western Himalayas. This area is open to the Indian monsoons, and is thus more humid than the lands north of the mountains with their sharply continental climate. Where mountain valleys meet the desert plains there are oases.

In the Kabul river valley lie the flourishing basins of Kabul and Jalalabad. On its way towards the Indus, the river cuts through the Spinghar range in a deep, impenetrable ravine. The road to Pakistan and India here leads through the Khyber pass to the south, which appears to have been widely used only in the Middle Ages.[2]

The deserts of south-western Afghanistan are divided by the Helmand river, along which lie *tugai* forests and farming oases. Where the river reaches its delta lakes, which fluctuate in size, there are many reed marshes, and north of the Helmand is the clay and gravel Dasht-i Margo, while to the south stretches the sandy desert of Segistan (Sistan). These regions have a sub-tropical desert climate.

Pakistan and northern India are also related to Central Asia in many ways. Pakistan borders on the eastern edge of the Iranian upland, while the Himalayan

2. Dani, 1975, p. 18.

mountains have direct orographical connections with the Hindu Kush and the Pamirs.

Two low mountain systems – the Kirthar and the Sulaiman mountains – separate Baluchistan from the Indus valley. The highest (up to 3,300 m) is the Quetta group with the passes of Bolan and Harnai, apparently used since ancient times. Quetta still preserves its importance as a major crossroads commanding the routes northwards to Afghanistan and beyond it to Soviet Central Asia, and eastwards to the Indus valley. Baluchistan has at its centre the Kalat highland and the fertile valleys of the Zhob and Loralai rivers in the north. The climate is generally hot and dry, and xerophytic vegetation consequently predominates. Precipitation usually falls in the shape of downpours leading to flash floods; at other times, the rivers are mere streamlets in stony beds.

The valley of the Indus and its tributaries fall into several natural zones. West of the river at its upper reaches is the fertile and well-watered Peshawar valley, which represents the lower reaches of the Kabul river. It contains both fields and many groves of osier, tamarisk and mulberry. The Indus itself, which rises in southern Tibet and flows north of Kashmir, is noted for its full waters but also for its sharply varying flow. Leaving the mountains, it cuts through a number of lesser chains, including the Salt range which separates the foothills from the fertile Punjab plain. It is between the Salt range and the edge of the Himalayan foothills that the critically important road runs from India to Iran and Soviet Central Asia.

The Punjab is a vast region of alluvium washed down both by the Indus and its five main tributaries, Jhelum, Chenab, Ravi, Beas and Sutlej, that gave the country its name, which means 'five rivers'. The areas between the rivers are called *doabs* and are, when irrigated, extremely productive farmlands, though the climate is markedly continental and arid.

To the south the Indus flows through the hot and arid lowlands of Sind. Gallery forest still remains along its banks, and to the east and west are valleys of alluvial sand and clay crossed by many old channels of the river including the Nara. In addition to providing water for irrigation, the river is a major longitudinal transport artery. The arid coast of Sind and Baluchistan with its many havens is suitable for coastal shipping.[3] Along the eastern valley of the Indus, the Thar desert stretches from east to west.

The second great farming region in northern India is watered by the Ganges and its tributaries, the most important being the Jamuna. The Delhi district, which figures prominently as a junction on the major transport routes running from the west to this, the heartland of India, stands in the Ganges-Jamuna *doab*: movement along the chief communication systems was crucial to the development of India's ancient cultures.[4]

3. Subbarao, 1958, p. 10.
4. Ibid., p. 15.

The flora and fauna of the Central Asian region are noted for their variety, but above all for their adaptation to the local environment and for thriving as though in optimal conditions. Characteristic of the vegetation of this area is a group of desert flora of the Central Asian type, comprising xerophilized migrants, primarily alpine and sub-alpine groups, from various mountains countries. From these there evolved permanent associations of steppe and desert plants adapted to the markedly continental, dry and chiefly hot climate. A current example is Mongolia, where steppe and desert flora is invading the Khangai, turning it to steppe and displacing mesophytic Siberian elements.[5] Much the same steppe, semi-desert and desert associations of xerophilous plants are represented in equal measure in Xinjiang (Sinkiang), Middle Asia, the Iranian plateau and Pakistan which forms the border of the vast zone of dry steppes and Central Asian type deserts. Another common feature is the marked zonality, with the flora of semi-deserts and dry steppes gradually giving way to sub-alpine meadows. In Afghanistan, for instance, below 1,500 or 1,800 m, wormwood, saltwort, vetches and camel thorn are common: above that level they give way to the wormwood and the cereals of the dry steppes.

In these vast tracts of grass and scrub, woods are something of an exception. In the deserts and semi-deserts groves of leafless *saxaul* may be found here and there: more common are the *tugai* forests which stretch along the humid river valleys and consist of maple, poplar, tamarisk and various shrubs. On the arid slopes of the low mountains in Soviet Central Asia, Iran and Afghanistan there are pistachios and more occasionally sparse savins. Where the humidity is higher the woods are more abundant. The mountain forest-steppe of northern Mongolia, for instance, has many Siberian tree species. Further south in the Zagros, Elburz, the Turkmen-Khorasan mountains and the Hindu Kush, broadleaf woods of oak, beech, horn-beam or plane predominate. As the moist southern slopes of the Hindu Kush climb higher, the broadleaf woods gradually give way to coniferous deodars, firs and pines.

A great adaptability to natural conditions is shown by animal life, and western Asian species again figure prominently. In the Holarctic region zoogeographers treat the Central Asian subregion somewhat separately as a land of high mountains and far-flung deserts. But a close connection with its faunal assemblage may clearly be sensed both in Iran and Pakistan.

In the main the desert and steppe animals are of a clear biological type and the characteristic forms are highly specialized. All the evidence suggests that Central Asia in the broad meaning of the term was a mighty and ancient centre of species formation. Such animals as the yak and the *saiga* antelope of the steppes are endemic, as are many birds – particularly mountain species – and rodents. Among the desert animals, for instance, the aridity of the climate has engendered such adaptations as aestivation.

5. Murzaev, 1952.

The steppes and semi-deserts are rich in vegetable food, and a wide variety of rodent species consequently abound. The fauna of the open ranges is characterized by a large number of fast-moving animals which can rapidly travel great distances in search of waterholes. Examples are the wild horse, the wild ass or *kulan* and various species of antelope, ranging from the *saiga* to the Mongolian steppe gazelle or the Persian desert gazelle. The last-mentioned lives in widely differing types of desert and can range quite high into the foothills. Fleet of foot, sharp of eye and hearing, camouflaged by its sandy-yellow colouring, able to survive with even bitter or brackish water, the Persian gazelle is almost ideally adapted to the hot, dry deserts of both western and eastern Central Asia. Another of the region's oldest species is the Bactrian camel, still to be found running wild. The herds of wild herbivores in the desert and steppe zone do not have many predators: the chief of them are wolves and, in the more southern parts, the cheetah. The striped hyena is nature's scavenger.

In the *tugai* scrub along the rivers are wild boar, deer and roe. Predators too are common – the jackal, the jungle cat and the now almost extinct tiger. Typical of the mountains is the wild sheep or *arkhar*, which inhabits open, smooth-worn hills but readily comes down to the lower lands: it is sometimes found on high ground in the desert and steppe zone. The moufflon, a relative of the wild sheep, is commonly encountered in the Kopet Dag and the Iranian highland. One very distinctive animal is the mountain ibex, which zoologists classify, with less than complete accuracy, as the Siberian ibex (*Capra ibex siberica*): other specialists comment that this species should more correctly be called the Central Asian ibex.[6] A typical mountain animal grazing in small bands, it is admirably suited to the steep slopes in which this much fragmented mountain region abounds. A representative mountain predator is the snow-leopard or *irbis,* while bears are also common in the hills. In ancient times, both in the Iranian highlands and, apparently, in southern Central Asia, the Iranian maneless lion, as it was called, was commonly found; however, it is now completely extinct, surviving only in heraldry.

All this domestic plant and animal life formed resources that human society has used in different ways and in different degrees at the various stages of its development. The fact that there were herbivores in virtually every natural zone made intensive hunting possible, though it also required that specific techniques and, to some extent, special hunting weapons be devised for each specific case. The drive technique of hunting would not have been developed but for, *inter alia*, the presence of large herds of ungulates in the steppes.

Viewed as a cultural and historical concept, the Central Asian region and its natural resources were also a potent force in the development of stockbreeding and agriculture. It offered both the original varieties of wild animals and plants and the appropriate conditions for the further progressive evolution of these methods of obtaining foodstuffs. There is every indication that Central Asia was

6. Dolukhanov, 1979.

the region where the Bactrian camel was domesticated and possibly, in the west of the region, the horse, which zoologists are now inclined to think descended from the tarpan rather than Przhevalski horse. Also found here were: the wild goat, the acknowledged ancestor of the domestic goat; the boar, which may have been domesticated in several regions; and the wild bull and buffalo, of which at least the latter was, in the area in question, developed into the domestic strain.

Regardless of where this or that animal was originally domesticated, the dry steppes and semi-deserts are extremely favourable for the subsequent development of stockbreeding. Dry air is thought to stimulate the metabolism, while damp air acts as a depressant. Dry air and the bright light of the steppe and semi-desert created the best possible conditions for the rearing of stock which by and large support cold and heat better than damp.[7] In this regard the relevant areas of Mongolia and Middle Asia provided the best possible environment. The dry steppes with their xerophilous woody cereals and feather-grasses (12–15 tonnes per hectare) have outstanding nutritional value, a further important factor being that they can be used for grazing through the spring, early summer and autumn, which is a large part of the year. The semi-deserts, having a high incidence of saline soils with shrubby vegetation – wormwood, prostrate summer cypresses and ephemerals – are also reliable grazing ground yielding 0.7 to 1.5 tonnes per hectare. The proximity of uplands and mountain systems to the desert and steppe zone enable the grazing cycle according to the season. The mountain steppe areas are estimated to provide 0.5 to 0.8 tonnes of fodder per hectare, while higher up are alpine and sub-alpine meadows whose fodder resources vary from 0.2 to 0.8 tonnes per hectare. Because of the thinner air, however, cattle thrive far less well here than at lower altitudes. Thus the desert and steppe zones held out enormous potential for the flowering of pastoral cultures, and this may be observed from the Bronze Age to the period of the early nomads and the Middle Ages, when these were the regions where the basic centres of the active and warlike steppe societies sprang up.

No less important, however, were the resources for the origin and development of arable farming, the invariable economic basis of the ancient and medieval civilizations. The fact that among the floras were wild forms of the chief cereals on which man feeds – wheat, barley and rice – provided all the requisites for the development of specialized gathering cultures which, even if not the first to discover the secrets of selection and domestication, were quite capable of absorbing and developing these agronomical innovations. N. I. Vavilov[8] grouped Soviet Central Asia, Afghanistan, Iran, Pakistan and India together with south-western Asia as one of the original homelands of cultivated plants. He considered that soft and club wheats, fine-seeded flax, peas, lentils, horsebeans, chick peas and Asia cotton were cultivated there. At the same time he underlined that cul-

---

7. Ryabchikov, 1976, p. 384.
8. Vavilov, 1967*b*, p. 193.

tivated plants had originated in the mountainous areas bordering on the Central Asia type deserts, where the extremes of precipitation were moderate, temperatures changed dramatically and the soils were varied, all of which provided optimal conditions for breeding different strains. Symptomatically, however, the marked impoverishment of the range of cultivated plants in Kashgaria points clearly to the function of the Himalayas, the Pamirs and the T'ien Shan as barriers and filters. Vavilov comes to the conclusion that the selection of genetically recessive strains to be observed there is characteristic of the periphery of the main centres of development form.[9]

But the region's natural conditions also emphasized the value of irrigated agriculture, in most places the only possible way to farm or at any rate the most profitable, given the arid climate and the usual additional complication of a particular distribution of precipitation. The potential of irrigated agriculture is assessed on the basis of three factors: temperature, topography and water supply.

Of great importance to the developing cultures in ancient times was the availability of roads. In the case of India and Pakistan, this problem has been studied by B. Subbarao,[10] who identified three types of region: focal or central, relatively isolated and completely isolated regions. The problem has also been specially examined in relation to Bronze Age cultures by A. H. Dani.[11] In Central Asia the major routes for cultural and commercial contacts, the dispersal of tribal groups and subsequently the movement of military forces generally circumverted the harsh mountain countries and the waterless deserts. Of the large rivers, the Indus in Pakistan and the Amu Darya in Soviet Central Asia were used for transport in various parts. With its convenient anchorages, the coastline of southern Iran and the adjacent part of Pakistan prompted the development of interregional sea commerce, which is attested even during the Harappan civilization and which figured prominently both in Roman times and in the Middle Ages. But the chief role in all periods was played by the overland roads, and, from the early agricultural period, caravan paths threaded their way along the mountain systems that frame the Iranian plateau. For archaeologists they are mapped by the settlements of the early farming tribes that were dispersed along them. Harder to overcome was the barrier of the Paropamisos and the Hindu Kush with its high passes that lay across the way from Soviet Central Asia to Pakistan and India. Yet they too, like the southern coastal shipping route, were conquered no later than the period of the Harappan civilization, as indicated by the discovery of a Harappan trading post at Shortugai on the middle course of the Amu Darya, which confirmed the close links between the cultures of the Bronze Age Indus valley and of the northern Kopet Dag plain that had previously been established from close parallels in their material cultures and finds of imported artefacts: for

9. Vavilov, 1967*a*, pp. 207–9.
10. Subbarao, 1958.
11. Dani, 1975.

instance, the distribution of stone vessels with artistic reliefs, some of which were made in Tepe Yahya in south-eastern Iran, the Indus valley and Mesopotamia.[12]

Natural conditions in Central Asia were not stable but have changed even within the time-span of human history, identified by geographers as a separate period in the earth's history, the Quaternary, embracing the last 3– 3.5 million years. The general characteristics of the Quaternary Period are an increasingly dry climate and a universal cooling. In Central Asia, meanwhile, the process known as alpine orogeny continued, forming the present-day mountain topography of the Hindu Kush, the Himalayas, the Pamirs and the T'ien Shan. The trend towards aridity in Central Asia appears, on all the evidence, to have set in even before the Quaternary Period: even in the Cretaceous and Tertiary Periods the former sea basin there gradually shrank, apparently leaving only a gulf in the southern part of what is now the Tarim basin. The formation of the desert and steppe terrains similarly dates from the Tertiary Period. But there were then no completely lifeless deserts: Xinjiang contained many lakes and rivers along the banks of which wandered rhinoceroses, bisons, antelopes, ostriches and crocodiles. The alpine orogeny, during which the mountain systems that ring Central Asia rose by 600 to 1,000 m, increased the region's isolation and aridity with a consequent expansion of the deserts and the shifting sands.

Among the key natural phenomena of the Quaternary were the glacials, the periodization of which has been accurately established in western Europe, chiefly in the Alps, and in North America. The chain of events in Central Asia has been less well studied. Mountain glaciation here was less than in Europe and North America, and the periodicity of glaciation appears to have differed from mountain system to mountain system.

Intensive deposition has also been discovered in the western Tajik-Afghan depression, where high-grass savannah and temperate pine and broad-leaf woods began to spread during the interglacials. The bones of a close relative of the Przhevalski horse have been found in northern Afghanistan in caves inhabited by Stone Age man, indicating that the region contained tracts of humid grassland.

During the pluvials there were extremely active river systems in the Turan depression which had gigantic rivers – the forerunners of the Amu Darya and the Syr Darya. These deposited vast layers of sediments that subsequently became eroded into the sands of the Kara Kum. During the cooler periods there were also considerable changes in the animal world, the so-called Early Dushanbe assemblage including, in addition to wild goat, deer, boar and horse, the woolly rhinoceros. But the general trend towards greater aridity led to the early establishment of desert and steppe landscapes and the flora and fauna that go with them. The Quaternary Period flora of the Turan depression has invariably been that of a predominantly steppe and desert ecology. Changes in the fauna have been quite

12. Kohl, 1975.

definitely established through the evidence found in Kazakhstan.[13] At the start of the Quaternary the region had an Ili fauna assemblage including the mastodon, the southern forest elephant, the Stenon horse and two species of camel, the early Bactrian and the giant camel. The later Kosh assemblage is close to the fauna of the famous reference monument of the Chinese Palaeolithic, Choukoutien. This again contains the southern elephant, the bison, the camels and two species of horse. Everything suggests that the steppe expanses alternated with woodlands and thick scrub. During the coldest periods the landscape was a periglacial steppe where herds of woolly mammoths, *kulans* and elk (the Khazar assemblage) grazed. The time of the Würm Glacial Stage, which was Europe's severest, was that of the Upper Khavalynsk transgression when the eastern gulf of the Caspian sea stretched as far as Balkany. This was when the Aral sea formed as a large fresh-water basin. At the same time the mammoth group, the mammoth itself, woolly rhinoceros, the lesser bison and the cave bear moved southward. In the steppes and high meadows *saiga* antelopes, roe deer, the *arkhar* and the maral deer were common. The Baikal yak and the kudu are known to have inhabited the Altai. Palaeogeographical research in the Zagros of western Iran has established that some 22,000–14,000 years ago cold dry steppe predominated there, followed by a warmer period in which forest spread.[14]

Climatic variations in the post-glacial period were less abrupt, though they too may have had some impact on the fragile economic systems of the primitive communities. In some cases, the change may have been local; furthermore, as human society gained experience in changing its environment, the anthropogenous factor became increasingly important. Recent research in the region of the Thar desert has shown that although until 8000 B.C. its climate was dry with much movement of sand dunes, precipitation increased in the years 8000–7500 B.C. and water flowed freely in the river valleys.[15] The subsequent slight diminution in precipitation in the years 7500–3000 B.C. had no effect on the lakes, where the fresh water remained. According to some data, the amount of precipitation in the Indus valley between 3000 and 1800 B.C. was almost 500 mm more than it is now, after which a more arid phase set in.[16] These climatic changes are thought by some authorities[17] to have played a decisive role in the demise of the Harappan civilization, although reservations have also been expressed over this.[18] It must be said that many scholars have thought it probable that in Middle Asia the rise in aridity and xerothermic conditions climaxed in the late third and early second millennia B.C., and this appears to be borne out by research in the Kyzyl Kum,

13. Kostenko, 1963.
14. Van Zeist, 1967.
15. Ghosh, 1977.
16. Singh, 1971.
17. Dales, 1965a, p. 18.
18. Raikes and Dyson, 1961.

where hunting and fishing camps emptied in that period.[19] However, as technology and society advanced, man discovered ever greater inner potentials both for maximizing his use of natural resources and for withstanding natural forces in extreme situations.

19. Vinogradov, 1981, p. 23.

LOWER PALAEOLITHIC CULTURES[1]

V. A. Ranov, D. Dorj and Lü Zun-E

F OR the study of the earliest stages of human history in Central Asia, the most important researches have been carried out in Pakistan and north-western India,[2] Mongolia[3] and south-eastern Soviet Central Asia.[4] Unfortunately, only at isolated spots in the first of these regions, and at a limited number of places in the loess districts of the Tajik-Afghan depression, is archaeological material presented in clear stratigraphical order. Elsewhere we have only typologically archaic artefacts which are ascribed to the Lower Palaeolithic, hypothetically on the basis of general considerations or of geomorphological information.

Of all the mountain regions of Central Asia, the best studied is southern Tajikistan. Here the complex Late Cenozoic deposits (conglomerate sands, silts and gravels) are covered by a layer of loess up to 200 m thick which in the foot-hill zone regulary alternates with ancient palaeosols. Most scholars think that the periods of loess formation coincided with the onset of the surface glacial stages in more northerly latitudes and the development of mountain glacial stages in Central Asia, though the glaciers there did not descend below 2,000 m above sea-level. Conversely soils, or rather soil assemblages consisting of several superimposed layers of soils at different stages of development, correspond to the warmer and more humid climatic conditions of the inter-glacials.

The loess sediment lies like a mantle over low watersheds less than 1,500–2,000 m above sea-level and the flanks of the foothills or *adyrs,* and fills out the surface of the intramontane valleys, thereby embracing every topographical feature.

The totality of palaeogeographical information indicates that during the

1. See Map 3.
2. De Terra and Paterson, 1939.
3. Okladnikov, 1978.
4. Ranov and Davis, 1979, pp. 252–6.

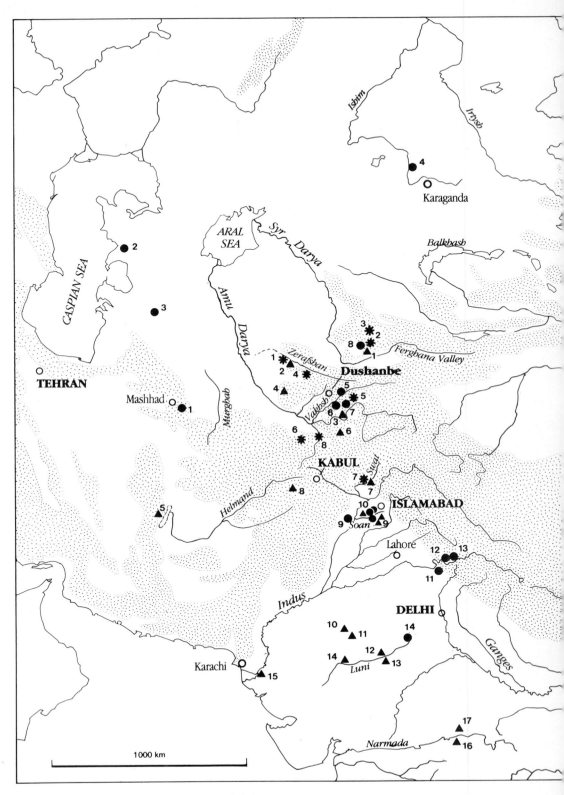

MAP 3. Palaeolithic sites of Central Asia.

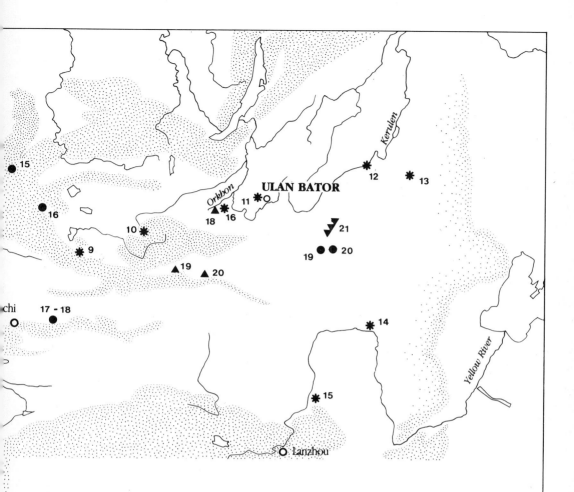

● Lower Palaeolithic sites	▲ Middle Palaeolithic sites	* Upper Palaeolithic sites
1 Keshef-rud	1 Kulbulak	1 Kuturbulak
2 Shahbagata	2 Kuturbulak	2 Kulbulak
3 Alam-Kul	3 Ogzi-Kichik	3 Obi-Rahmat
4 Semizbugu	4 Teshik-Tash	4 Amankutan
5 Kuldara	5 Khunik	5 Shugnou
6 Karatau	6 Dara-i Kur	6 Ak-Kupruk
7 Lakhuti	7 Sanghao	7 Sanghao
8 Kulbulak	8 Dasht-i Nawur	8 Kara-Kamar
9 Morgah	9 Soan	9 Khoist-Tsenker-Agui
10 Soan	10 Bharidani	10 Sangino
11 Chandigarh	11 Nagri	11 Zausan Tolotoi
12 Guler	12 Hokra	12 Choibalsan
13 Sisra	13 Pushkar	13 Tamsagbulag
14 Udaipur	14 Mogra	14 Dayao
15 Ulalinka	15 Jerruk	15 Shuidonggou
16 Bojan-Ulga	16 Adamgarh	16 Moiltyn-am
17 Sidaogou	17 Bhimbetka	
18 Erdaogou	18 Moiltyn-am	
19 Yarkh	19 Ikh-Bogd	
20 Saynshand	20 Arts-Bogd	
	21 Valley of Sirdzhi	

Pleistocene the landscape here was high-grass savannah in the climatic optimums of the interglacials (temperate coniferious and broadleaf woods combined with steppe assemblages) and sparse xerophytic woods with large areas of arid steppes in the periods of loess formation.

It must be emphasized that the bulk of the archaeological finds relates to the middle strata of palaeosols or soil assemblages, or in other words, to the climatic optima. This suggests that there were periods, each of which is thought to have lasted from 6,000 to 10,000 years, that were most favourable to primitive man. During the loess-formation periods, which coincided with a reduction in precipitation and the drying up of springs on the watersheds, people either left the region altogether or went lower down into the valleys; at the same time, the number of hunting and gathering groups diminished markedly. It should be borne in mind that when Lower Palaeolithic man lived there the terrain was gentler and flatter than it is now, since the intensive tectonic lifting and the carving of the rivers that reshaped it occurred during the Middle and to some extent the Late Pleistocene.

A total of forty-eight palaeosols have been identified in the Tajik-Afghan depression. Of these soils 1–9 have been ascribed, by stratigraphy, geological methods, palaeogeography, thermoluminescent dating and palaeomagnetic survey, to the Pleistocene; soils 10–19 to the Eneopleistocene, and the remainder to the Late Pleistocene.

Up to the end of 1986, three Lower Palaeolithic sites, yielding significant archaeological material, had been excavated in southern Tajikistan, and isolated artefacts had been found in more than twenty different places.

Over 60 per cent of the finds concerned palaeosols 5 and 6, which is where the two biggest sites were located. These discoveries suggest that the period from 250,000 to 130,000 years ago was the most favourable for primitive man in this region.

Excavations in recent years have produced evidence that fossil man appeared in southern Central Asia at a much earlier date. An isolated artefact was found in palaeosol 9, the date of which corresponds to the European Cromerian (some 50,000 years ago according to thermoluminescent dating). The relatively small site of Kuldara (Khavaling region of southern Tajikistan) produced forty artefacts scattered in palaeosols 11 and 12, which have been dated by the palaeomagnetic method to 75,000–80,000 years ago.

The industry of Kuldara is characterized by very small stone artefacts (generally measuring less than 5 cm), along which it is possible to identify cores and tiny scraping tools, including side scrapers with a fine serrated finish. Although small in scale, the industry of Kuldara preserves certain features of the stone-splitting technique characteristic of the pebble culture.

Relatively large-scale excavations, involving the removal of a sterile layer of loess 15 m thick, have been carried out at two sites uncovering 500 m² at Karatau I and 216 m² at Lakhuti I (Figs. 1 and 2). At the first site, about 1,000 artefacts and stone manuports were found in palaeosol 6 (200,000 years ago) at a depth of 64 m. Similarly 1,100 pieces were discovered at the second site, in palaeosol 5 (300,000 years ago) at a depth of 55 m.[5]

These objects give an excellent picture of the Karatau pebble culture, which represents the Lower Palaeolithic in the mountains of Soviet Central Asia.

In either case the stone artefacts, which were found in varying concentrations in both vertical and horizontal sections,[6] were scattered in the palaeosol stratum that corresponds most exactly to the climatic optimum, the usual thickness of the vividly coloured soil being 2.7 to 2.3 m. No traces were found of a genuine cultural stratum combining living quarters, fireplaces, culinary remains, etc., and the animal remains were almost negligible. To all appearances, these were temporary hunting camps rather than long-term settlements.

The stone tools of the Karatau culture have a number of specific features stemming both from an enduring technical tradition and from the poor quality of the raw material, most of which was brittle, unworkable magmatic or sedimentary rock that ancient man gathered as pebbles from the river beds. Their chief peculiarity is that they include none of the bifacially-worked axes characteristic of the Lower Palaeolithic in other regions and, indeed, no bifacial tools whatsoever. Only in the Riss-Würm period (Lakhuti I) do more or less distinct rectangular and disc-shaped cores appear; flake-tools are very few in number, and most of the flakes are irregular in shape. The 'citrus' technique and *quartier d'orange* artefacts, conversely, are comparatively well represented. Most of the flakes and debris result from the dressing of the pebble's edge or from its cutting: specially prepared cores were not required for this purpose. The tools include choppers of various shapes, rare chopping tools, irregularly-edged scrapers, small scrapers of dissimilar shapes, roughly-worked small points and serrated and concave tools. By and large the tools are very irregular and individual with no fixed patterns (Figs. 1 and 2).

The Karatau culture is thus a distinctive phenomenon in the Lower Palaeolithic of Central Asia, resembling in its fundamentals the Lower Palaeolithic industry of the Soan and Beas valleys and the loess regions of China, but differing considerably in many technical and typological aspects from the traditional Acheulean culture. A similar technical tradition that may be described as a 'pebble culture' existed in the Lower and Middle Pleistocene over most of the mountainous parts of Soviet Central Asia.

There have been individual finds of Acheulean-type bifaces in Middle Asia – on the Krasnovodsk peninsula and in the Ferghana valley – but their geological dating is not definite. An Acheulean culture of still undetermined typology, initially estimated to be 700,000 to 500,000 years old, has been found in good stra-

---

5. Ranov, 1980.
6. Ibid., pp. 202–7.

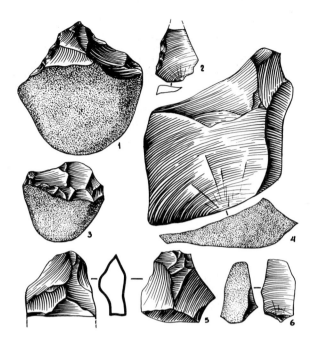

FIG. 1. Stone tools from the site of Karatau I (1–3: choppers; 2: scraper; 4: flake; 5: bifacial tool; 6: waste).

tigraphic order near the town of Angren, at the site of Kulbulak where there are several strata.

In the steppes of Kazakhstan and the desert regions of Soviet Central Asia, a large quantity of bifacial tools have been found among which the traditional Acheulean hand axes may be distinguished. The more patinated and rounded examples (all the collections consist of excavated items) found near the Semiz-bugu hills, at the village of Vishnevka near Tselinograd, on the Mangyshlak peninsula and elsewhere, may belong to the Lower Palaeolithic and correspond to the Riss-Würm or an earlier geological period. No final verdict can be given until sites are found with clear stratigraphic horizons and dates obtained through multidisciplinary methods. In view of a number of circumstances pertaining to the accumulation of sediment in these regions, no great hopes can be placed on this.

The best-known Palaeolithic culture of Central Asia is generally accepted as that of the Soan valley. Identified, following the work of H. de Terra and T. T. Paterson on the Potwar plateau in Pakistan, this culture has become a standard model and provided the impetus for the development of the still-topical theory of the 'Asian Palaeolithic'.[7]

7. Movius, 1944.

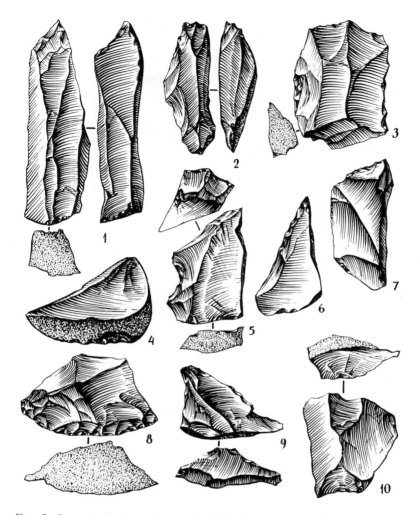

FIG. 2. Stone tools from the site of Lakhuti I, south Tajikistan (1, 2, 9: carinated; 3, 4, 6, 7, 8: scrapers; 5: notched; 8: Mousterian-type scraper; 9, 10: flakes).

The age of the culture was determined on the basis of the supposed geo-morphological location of the Palaeolithic finds on the Punjab river terraces, which vary in height. The archaeological data are based on Palaeolithic industry complexes which differ markedly among themselves. Work subsequent to that of H. de Terra and T. T. Paterson has until recently made only partial amendments to this model, according to which the earliest of pre-Soan industry, which is represented only by a few crudely fashioned implements in the boulder conglom-erates of the watershed plateaux, is contemporary with the second or Mindel Gla-cial Stage of the Himalayas. This industry is known only in Pakistan (Makhad,

51

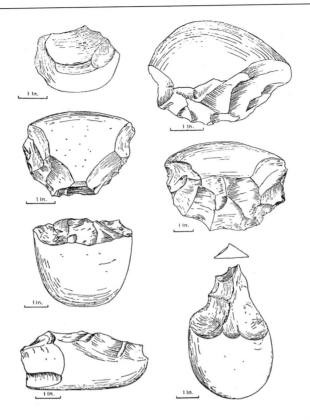

FIG. 3. Early Soan pebble tools (Potwar Plateau, Pakistan).

Adiala et al.); terrace T1 – the uppermost of the river terraces in the Himalayan foothill region, corresponding to the Mindel-Riss Interglacial Stage – contains finds of the early or Lower Palaeolothic Soan culture (Shadipur, Jalwal, etc.) (Fig. 3).

In both western and eastern Punjab, the bulk of the early Soan tools were taken from the top or flanks of these terraces. In rare cases artefacts were excavated from pebble beds or the loess-type soils that cover them, but no proper geological study of these finds has yet been carried out. To this, one might add a number of finds made by H. D. Sankalia in moraine deposits near Pahalgam in Kashmir, which that author considers the oldest on the southern Asian subcontinent and ascribes to the first or Günz-Mindel Interglacial Stage – in other words to the Lower Pleistocene – while the pre-Soan and early Soan industries correspond to the Middle Pleistocene in Himalayan chronology.[8] Implements

8. Sankalia, 1974.

52

ascribed to the early Soan have been found at several places in the eastern Punjab, examples being the upper terraces at Guler and Nalagarh in the state of Himachal Pradesh.

In typological terms, the pre-Soan is represented by large, heavily rounded quartzite flakes with a broad, flat, unfaceted struck crest set at an angle of 100 or 125 degrees to the flaked surface, and by a few unifacial pebble-core tools. The early Soan is more complex; it is subdivided, on the basis of the tools' surfaces and the degree of weathering, into two and sometimes three groups which none the less contain completely identical types of artefact. Many specialists have pointed out that the chief peculiarity of the Soan industry was, from the early phase of its development, the use of rounded pebbles for tool-making, with the additional feature that most tools were made in such a way that part of the pebble was left intact.[9] As in the Karatau culture, there was a very long-lasting tradition of pebble tools that changed little in type until the very last stages of the Palaeolithic.

Tools of the Soan industry were made of flat-based or rounded pebbles. In the first case, the working edge was shaped with a series of large chips running up from the base at an angle varying from 45 to 60 degrees; in the second, both sides were worked. Additionally, the edges were retouched to some extent. That was how the two chief tools of the Soan industry, the chopper and the chopping tool, were produced: in quantitative terms, the former unquestionably predominate. The working edge could run around the entire perimeter or only part of it. Other categories – cores, flake-tools and flakes – are very summarily described. Some cores were reminiscent of the Clactonian and others of the Levalloisian types. The commonest category is relatively large flakes with an angle of spallation of 95 to 130 degrees and straight-struck crests. Only occasionally is the spine cut correctly, retouching is rarely recorded, and there is an absolute lack of well-defined flake-tools such as points or scrapers. On the whole, early Soan artefacts demonstrate a distinctive pebble technology in the traditional typological shapes.

In recent years, however, there has been mounting evidence that the old hypothesis, according to which the Soan culture developed independently and was set against the hand-axe industry of the Madrasian culture that was common in non-Himalayan regions, requires further proof. While pebble tools undoubtedly dominated the early discoveries, with only occasional finds of hand-axes, tools such as hand-axes, bifaces and cleavers are now being found in such places as Morgah in Pakistan, the Kangra river valley and near the town of Chandigarh in the state of Himachal Pradesh (Fig. 4).

Since 1980 an interdisciplinary team, consisting of the British Archaeological Mission to Pakistan working in collaboration with the Pakistan Government Department of Archaeology and the Geological Survey of Pakistan, has come to

9. Paterson and Drummond, 1962.

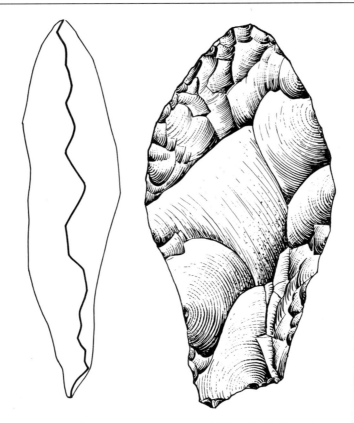

FIG. 4. Hand-axe from the site of Morgah (Pakistan).

a new understanding of the geology of the Potwar plateau.[10] This provides a basis for understanding the context and chronology of the Palaeolithic cultures represented there. The impact of peninsular India on the main land mass of Asia which has been taking place for the last 20 million years as part of the worldwide process of plate tectonics has been steadily forcing up the Himalayas, Tibetan plateau and other major mountain formations. This has led to massive erosion, rivers and streams carrying gravel, silt and other material out of the mountains. This material has been laid down on the plain below the mountains, forming what are known as the Siwalik deposits. Laid down horizontally the Siwaliks were in turn progressively folded, particularly during the period between 1.6 and 0.4 million years ago. During this time man and his hominid ancestors were already present in the region, making stone artefacts. The artefacts were incorporated into the Siwalik material, and when the Siwalik folds were planed off and dissected by further erosion, artefact-bearing layers were exposed.

10. Dennell, 1984; Rendell, 1984; Rendell and Dennell, 1985, Stiles, 1978; Allchin, 1986.

A programme of palaeomagnetic and fission-track dating of the Siwalik strata recently completed by a joint Pakistani-American team has provided a framework of dates to which the archaeological material has been related. Further programmes of thermoluminescent and palaeomagnetic dating undertaken by the British Archaeological Mission to Pakistan have extended and refined this. Hand-axes have been found in strata dated to 700,000 years ago. Scrapers and small chopping tools are associated with a sandstone stratum rich in fossil fauna dated to between 1.2 and 1.4 million years ago. A group of artefacts including a core and a number of flakes were found in a context for which a date of 2 million years has been recently obtained.

At the time of writing, work is still in progress on the Potwar plateau and in the adjoining Pabbi hills. The area is clearly one of great immediate and potential importance for the study of early man and his hominid ancestors. It is particularly interesting because of the scope it provides for the study of past environments, which is currently taking place, and will make it possible to understand the context in which the makers of the stone tools lived. Throughout, the Potwar industries are based on quartzite pebbles and cobbles, the only good quality raw material readily available. Choppers and chopping tools are frequently found alongside other artefacts. The nature of the raw material has placed certain controls upon the methods of stone working practised and the tool types produced. There can be little doubt that the use of cobbles and pebbles has favoured the production of simple choppers and chopping tools.

In the 1970s there were simultaneous discoveries of comparatively large collections of pebble tools, primarily choppers and allied tools made of flakes and various chippings, at several places in Iran.

In Iranian Baluchistan, G. Hume discovered, in the valleys of the Ladiz and Mashkid rivers, a new industry comprising seven sites which he ascribed, on the basis of geomorphology, roughly to the interval between the Riss and Early Würm glacial maxima. Its raw materials were in part pebbles and in part fragments of quartzite, flinty shale and jasper. The artefacts were collected from the surface of river terraces. This is a well-defined complex of pebble technology, chiefly choppers, the bulk of which may be compared with the late Soan and the oldest part with Acheulean.[11]

Near Mashhad in the north-eastern corner of Iran, A. Arari and C. Thibault collected from the valley of the Keshef-rud a noteworthy series of pebble tools, choppers, serrated and concave flake-tools, bill-shaped instruments and Clactonian flakes. Some of these were collected on the slopes in pebble spillages fron Middle and Upper Pleistocene formations, and some on the pebbly surfaces of the highest terraces, which relate geomorphologically to the Lower Pleisto-

11. Hume, 1976.

cene. This definitely entitles the discoverers to consider them to be the earliest in Iran and to estimate their age at 800,000 years.[12]

A small quantity of choppers, cores and the accompanying flakes were found between Tabriz and Mianeh in the region of the Sahand hills. Found on the surface, these objects were most probably remains of small hunting camps in the Lower Palaeolithic.[13]

Hence various parts of Iran reveal the traces of fossil man using pebble tools and other similar to the early and late Soan complexes. But none of these finds are stratified, and in these circumstances their geological date cannot be considered definitive. They therefore remain of merely general historic and cultural interest, and their significance cannot yet be viewed as incontrovertible.

There is very slight evidence of another culture, the Acheulean, most probably of the West Asian type, relating to the production of bifacial tools. Thus an Acheulean-type axe was found by R. Braidwood on the surface of a mount near Kermanshah, and a similar artefact is known from the region of Tabriz where it was found on a low terrace and had clearly been disturbed.

The great paucity of Lower Palaeolithic finds in Iran is due, in our view, to two main factors: (a) the country has been little studied by archaeologists and (b) the topography was restructured in the Upper Pleistocene, as were many mountain parts of Central Asia.

Where Afghanistan is concerned, the only place where crude flakes, cleavers, choppers and chopping tools have been collected is on the former banks of Lake Dasht-i Nawur in Ghazni province. But neither their typological character nor their geological environment inspire complete confidence that the collection really belongs to the Lower Palaeolithic.[14]

The interior of Central Asia is a large and geographically complex land of predominantly desert and mountain terrain. Only in the north is there an upper layer of loess-type soils, chiefly of recent, Upper Pleistocene origin. In the north tracts of taiga may be encountered, and in the south the scorching badlands and sand-dunes of the Gobi Desert.

Despite the fact that the search for Palaeolothic cultures in Mongolia was started by A. P. Okladnikov in 1949, and in southern Siberia even earlier, the region's Lower Palaeolithic sites have been very little studied. With one exception, all the finds ascribed with varying degrees of reliability to the Lower Palaeolithic were taken from the surface and consequently, like H. de Terra and T. Paterson's Soan collections, they have no stratigraphic substantiation: their antiquity was determined from technical and typological features and can be accepted only with reservation.

The site of Ulalinka, within the town of Gornoaltaisk in the northern

12. Arari and Thibault, n.d.
13. Sadek-Kooros, 1976.
14. Davis, 1978.

Altai, gives rise to considerable controversy among specialists. Discovered in 1961, it was excavated over several seasons by A. P. Okladnikov. Beneath a four-metre layer of alluvial loam lies a stratum of multicoloured clays resting on boulder deposits. In the lower part of the clay, which geologists ascribe to the Kochorka Eneopleistocene suite, a series of hand-worked pebbles is to be found in a seam of yellow-ochre-coloured clay, containing quartzite boulders and pebbles. Palaeomagnetic analysis suggests that the yellow-ochre is in the Matayama zone of negative magnetization. The thermoluminescent date of the layer that contains the tools is 1.48 million years.[15]

The archaeological material is restricted to quartzite tools scattered among the pebbles in the clay. Okladnikov identifies several groups: crude pebble 'proto-axes', 'tools with an extended nose', crudely made choppers and crude scrapers. Particular attention was paid to laterally split quartzite pebbles with dressed edges and tips. Although these artefacts are comparable in period with the Olduvan industry, their general appearance does not allow direct analogies to be drawn with that site or its typological series. The reason is that Ulalinka lacks both stable designs and, most importantly, the usual signs of deliberate working – the struck crest, surface cutting, precise spalling facets and so on. Okladnikov overcomes this difficulty by explaining that the Ulalinka finds are unusual in that the pebbles were split not by striking but by being heated in a fire and then dropped in water.[16] Analysing the formation about this site, it should be noted that until more convincing evidence is available, Okladnikov's conclusions cannot be unreservedly accepted.

Another group of Lower Palaeolithic finds in this region comprises pebble tools of Palaeolithic appearance – choppers, chopping tools and 'nosed' tools – whose surface is covered with a thick patina (Fig. 5a).In appearance these quartzite artefacts recall similar products from the Lower Palaeolithic period in Africa and Asia, and there is every justification for seeing them as the earliest indigenous stratum of Palaeolithic cultures. Such objects have been found in south-eastern Mongolia in the vicinity of the town of Saynshand, and in the west, near Bojan-Ulga, Kobdo-Zhargalang, Dalai-Dzagada and elsewhere. They are generally found on the surface of ancient, possibly Lower Pleistocene, pebble beds scattered among the remnants of former terraces.

Quite different in appearance are the artefacts encountered in the foothills of the Yarkh mountains at the site of an enormous Palaeolithic workshop located on outcrops of a yellow, jasper-like rock, west of Saynshand. Okladnikov, who discovered them, suggests that these are clearly-defined Acheulean tools – hand-axes of classic design: oval (amygdaloid) or roughly triangular in shape, carefully worked on both sides and with the slightly curved longitudinal edges typical of the Acheulean. The collection includes unifacial core tools of a proto-Levalloi-

15. Ragozin, 1982, pp. 119–21.
16. Okladnikov, 1972*b*, pp. 7–12.

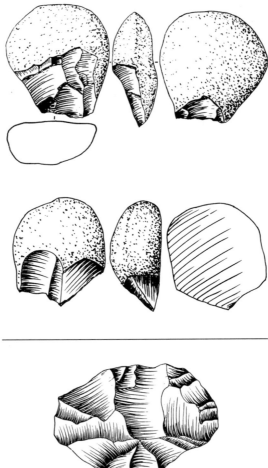

(a)

(b)

FIG. 5. Stone tools from Mongolia: (a) pebble tools from Mongolia; (b) biface tool from Yarkh.

sian type, massive, roughly triangular flakes and rare flake-tools of a Levalloisian appearance, shaped in an extended triangle but without retouch on the struck crest. These designs, particularly the bifacial hand-axes, have no parallels in other parts of Central Asia or the adjacent lands. Okladnikov draws the following conclusion that 'there are reasons to believe that not only the Acheulean technique but its carriers had penetrated from the areas of the classic Abbevillian and Acheulean cultures of Afro-European origin to the central regions of Asia'.[17]

The discovery of Lower Palaeolithic relics near the Yarkh mountain (Fig. 5b) at Erol-Gobi in central Mongolia has a direct bearing on the peopling of Mongolia by the ancestors of Neanderthal man and throws considerable light on the indigenous nature of the Palaeolithic culture. It presents 'local variations' of the Lower Palaeolithic cultures of Asia and Europe and emphasizes their importance in the early Stone Age of Central Asia. Great significance can be attached to the techniques for working stone and their own set of durable and typical two-sided tools or bifaces, very similar in type and design to those of western Europe. The biface was a wholly new technical variation or device hitherto not found in Lower Palaeolithic remains in Central Asia in general and Mongolia in particular.

In our view, the similarity between Mongolian and European hand-axes is to be explained by conditions affecting two cultures separated from each other. The similarity is purely external and arises from the fact that at a certain stage of Early Palaeolithic development, the inhabitants of Asia like those of Europe were confronted by the same problems.

There is yet another reason why the occurrence in the Lower Palaeolithic complex of central Mongolia of tools similar to those of Acheulean type (according to European periodization) cannot be linked with the cultures of western Europe, that is to say the tools, if not earlier, are at least of the same time. Consequently, the emergence and development of the techniques for making bifaces was an independent process.

A. P. Okladnikov observed that 'such a site [Yarkh] with such clear-cut evidence of Acheulean industry as that found in Europe, the Caucasus, India and Africa is the *first and only one in East Asia*' (my italics). In any case, by their presentation of Acheulean techniques and form, the tools found on Mount Yarkh have nothing in common with the occasional and, in fact, haphazardly designated 'bifaces' of northern China and Korea.

Indeed, in neither central nor northern Asia, nor in other territories are any tools to be found that bear even an indirect resemblance to the hand-axes and sharp-pointed tools of central Mongolia. Accordingly, everything described above points first of all to the fact that in the early Stone Age in Mongolia, that is, in the Middle Acheulean period, there existed an independent area of Acheulean-type development distinguished by stable and favourable conditions; and,

17. Okladnikov, 1978, p. 321.

secondly, it indicates that at one and the same stage of their early development, people came to make the same discoveries and developed similar techniques for the working of stone and did so in isolation from one another.

Finally, the techniques and methods of producing hand-axes made of high-grade local materials provide evidence that the peopling of Mongolia originally took place on precisely that territory; that is to say, in the Lower Palaeolithic period of Mongolia the Yarkh settlement emerged and developed independently, as we now know from the discovery of the first and only flint works in the whole of Central Asia.

In conclusion, let us note that in respect of both the volume of artefacts it produces and the quality of their archaeological and geological substantiation, this region of Mongolia and southern Siberia is markedly inferior to the two previous regions.

In many parts of China such as the provinces of Yunnan, Guizhoi, Hubei, Shaanxi Hebei and the Autonomous Region of Inner Mongolia human fossils and cultural remains of this age have been found. The physical type of this period was still very primitive.

Peking man represents the most important evidence of the initial stage of China's Palaeolithic era, but the site lies outside Central Asia. However, because of its importance to the cultural study of this area, a brief account is included here. The source of the Peking Man fossils is at Dragon Bone (Longgu) Hill, Choukoutien, 45 km south-west of Beijing.[18] A palaeogeomagnetic test determined the date of Peking Man as about 200,000 years old, corresponding to the Middle Pleistocene epoch in geology.

The skull of Peking Man is markedly primitive whereas the limb bones are fairly advanced. The skull for instance is squat and its brow-ridge is very coarse, jutting forward and continuing to the left and right. The wall of the skull is twice as thick as that of contemporary man, whilst the brain capacity is an average 1,043 cm^3, placing it between the hominids and contemporary man.

The site of Peking Man has produced at least 100,000 items including stone tools and flakes, pieces of raw materials and half-made artefacts. But the quantity of finished tools is rather small. The primary material for making tools is quartz and quartz crystal; flint and sandstone are secondary materials.

Chopping tools (Fig. 6) are the most common, and great numbers of oblate sandstone or quartz pebbles are struck from one or two sides to produce a sharp cutting edge, while the side opposite to the edge often preserves a section of pebble surface which can be conveniently grasped in the hand. Scrapers were widely used by Peking Man and are found in great numbers. They are often made of quartz, quartzite or flint. The great majority are made by chipping the edge from either one or two sides.

18. Jia, 1950; Li and Ji, 1981; Pei, 1962; Pei and Zhang, 1979; Teilhard de Chardin and Wen, 1932; Weidenreich, 1934, 1941; Woo and Jia, 1954.

Fɪɢ. 6. Chopping tools and scrapers from Choukoutien.

In the caves occupied by Peking Man many layers of ash were discovered. In the ash there were many burnt animal bones and stones and also a piece of charcoal of the Chinese redbud tree and seeds of Chinese hackberry tree. The stones had been burnt to a black colour and the surfaces bore irregular crackmarks. The animal bones had been burnt to a black or grey-blue colour and on the surface there were also crackmarks even to the extent of metamorphosis of the bone. The ash was found to be distributed in piles limited to particular areas, and wood had been used for the fire. Evidently this was not wild fire but is sufficient to prove its purposeful use by man.

The animal most frequently hunted by Peking Man was deer. Among the wild-animal bones discovered, 70 per cent were broken and burnt deer bones and deer horns. There were from two species of deer, the thick-jawed and the sika, both of them very numerous. There were over 2,000 fossil pieces of the thick-jawed deer alone. It seems that the hunters hunted these two species at particular seasons.

The activity of hunting had a very great influence on many aspects of the life of Peking Man. Not only did it directly supply him with meat, but also, thanks to the development of hunting and the processing of the quarry (as, for example, skinning and jointing), it undoubtedly gave a considerable impetus to the manufacture, use and improvement of tools. Not everybody could take part in the hunting and there was perforce an increase in the division of labour, differing division of the spoils between the sexes and different age-groups of the community. Hunting also strengthened social organization and caused it to develop.

The Palaeolithic material of Inner Mongolia is primarily limited to the discovery of stone implements. While surveying at Sidaogou in Nanshan Province in October 1977, many stone flakes and fragments were found in red clay deposits of the Middle Pleistocene epoch. Stone implements of the Late Palaeolithic period were also found in 1973 at Erdaogou, Nanshan. Subsequently excavations were undertaken and quantities of blades were found as well as flint flakes and fragments of waste material.

There is very little evidence on which to base a reconstruction of the lifestyle and economy of the Central Asian population in the Lower Palaeolithic. Even in well-stratified sites such as the loess camps of Tajikistan, finds are still restricted to stone tools, while such important elements for a sociological reconstruction as the overall area of the site and the remains of dwellings of fauna assemblages stay completely unknown.

It may be supposed that in the Central Asian Lower Palaeolithic groups of fossil man came together and lived within the same framework of the laws of general development as governed the same stage of anthropogeny in many parts of the Old World: in China (Choukoutien), Africa (Olduvai, Orlegezai, Ismila and elsewhere), Europe (Terra Amata, Ambrona, etc.) and the Near East (Ubaidiya and Latamna). The essential point about these processes is that they led to more advanced and socially united communities than was previously the case.

The existence of permanent settlements, the organization of residential space, the construction of the first primitive dwellings, the production of different tools, the collective hunting of large animals: all this is the sign of well-established social bonds, the basis of which had been laid at the *Homo habilis* stage and shaped as long ago as the pre-Neanderthal period. The pebble cultures that are particularly characteristic of Central Asia were contemporary with the Acheulean of Europe and Africa. It is now thought that even Acheulean man lived in cohesive communities rather than herds, while human groups that may be described as the forerunners of tribes appeared in the Mousterian period. Work was already divided along sexual lines, and certain bans or taboos governed life within Palaeolithic communities particularly relations between the sexes. This fairly complex social life, and particularly the collective practice of the drive method of hunting large animals, could not have existed without articulate speech which presumably arose long before the appearance of Cro-Magnon man.

It is hard to say what were the important features of life and social structure in the Lower Palaeolithic communities of Central Asia or how they differed from similar associations of Acheulean tool-makers in the regions listed above. This question will be answered only by future research. But one thing may confidently be said: the ascent of contemporary man, once the primeval and early stages were past, was a single process throughout all the continents of the globe.

MIDDLE PALAEOLITHIC CULTURE[1]

Bridget Allchin

T HE region we shall discuss is one of varying degrees of aridity, ranging from parts of Upper Sind and the Thar desert which have an annual average rainfall of less than 130 mm (in many years they may have no rain at all), to areas such as the northern Punjab, eastern Rajasthan and the mountainous regions of Tajikistan which enjoy a relatively high rainfall. Throughout the Holocene the greater part of the whole region must have been relatively arid, the general pattern of rainfall distribution being similar to that we see today with slight overall and local variations from time to time. In recent decades widespread pressure of human activity, previously confined to limited areas, has tended to affect all marginal areas. As a result a major environmental change is being brought about which makes the countryside of much of the region appear rather as it must have done during the driest phases of the Holocene, or perhaps during the final Pleistocene arid phase.

There is abundant evidence that, during the latter part of the Pleistocene, this region was subject to several significant changes of climate that radically altered the environment. The region was subject to worldwide changing patterns of climate and also to massive tectonic activity associated with the uplift of the Himalayas, Hindu Kush and other mountain ranges. How far these two sets of factors coincided in their effects upon the environment, and how far they ran counter to one another to produce conditions unlike the rest of the world we are not yet in a position to estimate. There is a certain broad parallelism in the patterns of change seen in the Indian Desert and in arid regions of Africa,[2] but it also appears highly probable that conditions in the proximity of the major mountain ranges were profoundly affected by other factors,[3] and it is here that unique local

---

1. See Map 3 on pages 46 and 47. Material presented by D. Dorj and A. Z. Yusofzay has also been used in this chapter.
2. Allchin et al., 1978.
3. Agrawal, 1982.

conditions may be expected to produce patterns at variance in some respects with those pertaining elsewhere.

What do we mean by the 'Middle Palaeolithic' of this vast climatically and topographically diverse region? In the simplest terms, we mean the stone industries, and the cultures of which they were a part, that succeeded the Lower Palaeolithic and preceded the Upper Palaeolithic. This designation assumes that the technological and typological factors we regard as characteristics of the Middle Palaeolithic follow sequentially, and therefore chronologically, after the hand-axe industries of the Lower Palaeolithic, and are in turn followed by the characteristic blade technology and artefact types of the Upper Palaeolithic. In western Europe this sequential development of technology and typology is more or less clear cut and tends to be taken for granted. In the past, prehistorians dealing with those parts of the world that we are considering have tended to assume that the same situation must be found there also. Therefore they have looked for the established artefact types of the European and western Asiatic Mousterian: edge-trimmed points and scrapers made from flakes struck from prepared cores, denticulate scrapers and various types of burins, accompanied in some cases by small hand-axes, or by blades and blade-flakes anticipating the Upper Palaeolithic.

During the last three decades it has become increasingly clear that while broadly comparable sequences of lithic technology and typology can be traced in various parts of the region, none correspond exactly to that of western Europe. Some indeed differ radically, and this is one of the factors that have held up research in some cases. All that can be said by way of a technological or typological definition of the Middle Palaeolithic of the region is that the manufacture of stone tools is based upon flakes struck from prepared cores of a wide variety of types; that scrapers, again of wide variety, are the predominant artefact type throughout and are made largely upon flakes and blade flakes. Most industries include edge-trimmed points and simple burins. Some also include a varying proportion of choppers and chopping tools.

Throughout the region physical dating for Middle Palaeolithic cultures is almost non-existent, and such dates as there are, are all now subject to serious reservations of one kind or another. Attempts at dating by analogy with culturally or technologically similar sites in adjacent regions, while helpful in giving a general time perspective to the Middle Palaeolithic of certain parts of the region, are of little use for any sort of more precise dating. In particular the very interesting questions of the beginning and end of Middle Palaeolithic or Mousterian cultures in the various parts of the region and their relations in time to one another are at present too vague and problematic to discuss here. In Iraq, C14 dates of around 30,000 years ago have been obtained from Shanidar and other Mousterian sites. There is every expectation that some Middle Palaeolithic sites may be much earlier, and also that some technologically Middle Palaeolithic industries in all parts of the region may belong to cultures of a much later date, perhaps in some cases almost to the end of the Pleistocene.

The search for anticipated artefact types has sometimes diverted attention from the main issue, namely the study of the development through time of human culture in as many of its aspects as the evidence will allow. This is linked to another of the fundamental problems of the Palaeolithic archaeologist, which is that stone artefacts are frequently all that survive as a cultural record. It is all too easy therefore to over-emphasize their significance or to give it the wrong emphasis. Stone artefacts are of great importance because they are primary indicators of human presence and activity, and because they must have been a fundamental element in the economy and daily life of many of the cultures to which they belonged, but their study is not an end in itself, merely a means to an end. First and foremost, stone artefacts demonstrate the working of the human mind. The choice of suitable stone, and the various stages of core preparation, followed by removal of a suitable flake, for example, secondary trimming of the flake and, ultimately in some cases, giving it a suitable haft or incorporating it into a more complex tool or weapon, all require forethought and conceptual thinking of a high order.

Ethnographic records and archaeological research in relatively recent non-metal-using communities in Australia and Africa show that the degree of dependence upon stone varies greatly. They show that the same artefact type, such as, for example, a bifacially worked or edge-trimmed point, may serve a totally different function in different communities within the same region. Conversely, the same function may be served by totally different lithic artefacts. The situation becomes further complicated when we recognize that the same basic, and sometimes long established, artefact form can be used as a component part of several different composite tools. Sections of microlithic blades, for example, either untrimmed or trimmed to 'geometrical forms', in combination with suitable mastics, have been recorded as forming the points, barbs and cutting edges of missiles; and they also have been recorded as the component parts of composite sickle blades. Likewise, edge-trimmed flakes (scrapers) are known to have been used for a variety of purposes, again combined with mastics, either held directly in the hand or mounted on wooden shafts or handles, in both instances by Australian Aborigines. All these observations combine to show how careful we must be in making deductions about further technological processes on the basis of stone technology alone; how necessary it is to consider every cultural situation in all its aspects; how rash to attempt detailed or exclusive interpretations based only upon stone artefacts.

Problems of the kind referred to in the preceding paragraphs are encountered particularly when we attempt to define culturally the Middle Palaeolithic of the regions we are considering or to analyse and interpret in broader terms assemblages of Middle Palaeolithic material. Middle Palaeolithic culture and lithic practice show great variation throughout all parts of the Old World where attempts have been made to study them. Where they are preceded by a long sequence of hand-axe industries their contrasting diversity is striking. Soviet

Central Asia, north-west India and Pakistan are on the frontier, albeit a fairly broad and flexible frontier, where the hand-axe complex of the Old World loses some of its regularity and universality. Other industries, at present less well known and apparently lacking distinctive formal artefact types, including the so-called chopper/chopping-tool industries of eastern Asia, appear to predominate in certain areas. Therefore we may expect the Middle Palaeolithic tradition of the region to perpetuate and carry on something of a more broadly based tradition. The material we are dealing with is not only intrinsically varied in all kinds of ways, but the sites are very different, and so is the way they have been dealt with. Therefore it is not possible to compare like with like in any systematic way. For the purpose of this chapter we shall confine ourselves to simple, brief descriptions of the available evidence of Middle Palaeolithic cultures in each major sub-region, drawing such inferences of a wider cultural nature as we can from time to time.

Describing the Middle Palaeolithic of Soviet Central Asia, Ranov and Davis write:

> Middle Palaeolithic (Mousterian) sites are numerous in Central Asia, and they exhibit great variability in terms of geographical location, stone-tool typology and technology, and preservation of features. Present are industries with and without Levallois technique, pebble choppers and chopping tools, and other Palaeolithic blade elements. Although some industries share some features with the south-western Asian Middle Palaeolithic, it is not at all correct to conclude that they developed as a result of a simple diffusion.[4]

This applies to virtually the whole region under consideration. Throughout there is a marked tendency to technological and typological overlap with the Upper Palaeolithic. In Afghanistan and eastern Iran this appears to take the form of alternating levels of predominantly Mousterian and Upper Palaeolithic artefacts in occupied caves and rock shelters. In north-west Pakistan the two sets of techniques appear to have been practised side by side, and this seems to be the case in Sind and the Punjab too. Throughout we have indications of the increasing predominance of the blade element as time goes on. In southern Asia as a whole the flake tradition seems never to have been wholly lost until the advent of the highly specialized blade industries of the Urban Chalcolithic cultures of the Indus plains in the third millennium B.C. In north-west India, the Thar desert and the arid zone on its south-eastern margins, and indeed most of peninsular India, the distinction between the two technological and cultural stages is rather clearer than in northern Pakistan, but the Middle Palaeolithic tradition of flake production is a persistent minor element throughout the Upper Palaeolithic and even the succeeding microlithic blade industries.

4. Ranov and Davis, 1979, p. 249.

Northern India

The Middle Palaeolithic of northern and north-west India is probably more easily defined chronologically than that of other parts of the region. But as yet no human remains have been found in association with Indian Middle Palaeolithic artefacts, and only in one instance, in the Bhimbetka group of rock shelters in central India, have Middle Palaeolithic occupation deposits been systematically excavated. The great majority of Middle Palaeolithic sites are in the open, or are geologically stratified within the valley fill laid down by the major rivers of central India and the northern Deccan and between the sands of two arid phases on the margin of the Thar desert during the latter part of the Pleistocene.

The increasing tendency during recent centuries for the rivers, particularly in their middle courses, to cut down earlier alluvial deposits has resulted in the cutting of sections through the valley fill. In general these show later Lower Palaeolithic material (i.e. hand-axes, cleavers, discoids, cores, flakes, pebble choppers, etc.), in a much rolled and weathered condition, incorporated into gravels or conglomerates at the bottom of the section on or near bedrock. Above this is usually found an alluvial deposit of varying depth, frequently 30 m or more, consisting chiefly of fine silts with lenses of sand and gravel, spanning the development of both the Middle and Upper Palaeolithic. Microliths are frequently associated with top-soil formed on the surface of the valley alluvium. Concentrations of Middle Palaeolithic material, usually in a rolled and weathered state, occur incorporated into gravels and conglomerates associated with a major break in aggradation about half-way up the section. Artefacts in gravel lenses below this horizon in certain rivers provide evidence of the local development of the Middle Palaeolithic from the preceding Lower Palaeolithic.[5] Sporadic finds in the upper alluvium above the break, and another concentration associated with a thin gravel layer in some north Indian rivers, indicate a further development towards an Upper Palaeolithic blade and burin industry, and thence to a microlithic blade industry on the modern surface.[6]

First defined by Allchin[7] the Indian Middle Palaeolithic industries were further described and designated 'Nevasan' by Sankalia five years later. Further research has shown the Middle Palaeolithic industries of northern and central India and the peninsula as a whole to have a remarkably homogeneous character, in spite of certain local variations, and the term 'Nevasan' has been retained, other terms being coined for the Middle Palaeolithic industries of the arid regions north-west of the Aravalli range.

Technologically the Nevasan industries are based upon flakes struck from prepared cores, the methods of core preparation, etc., as already pointed out,

5. Joshi, 1966.
6. Sharma et al., 1980, pp. 88–97.
7. Allchin, B., 1959.

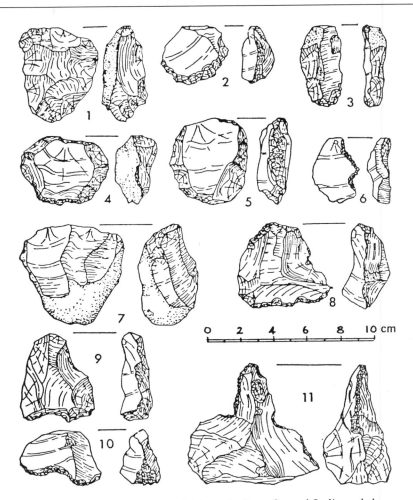

FIG. 1. Nevasan: Middle Palaeolithic tools from Central India and the Deccan: 1 – core unstruck; 2, 6, 8, 9, 10, 11 – scrapers of various types on flakes; 3 – blade-flake; 4, 5, 7 – struck cores. (After Allchin, 1952.)

being a development of Lower Palaeolithic technology. But the characteristic artefact types of the Lower Palaeolithic, with the exception of occasional small hand-axes, have disappeared and the overall size of the artefacts is reduced. The predominant Nevasan artefact type is a scraper made from a flake. There is a remarkable absence of formal artefact types such as characterize the Mousterian industries of Europe and parts of western Asia. Instead Nevasan artefacts give the impression that their shape was primarily dictated by that of the best available flake, modified to suit the requirements of the job in hand. Scraper edges range from those on thick heavy flakes produced by steep retouch, capable of sustaining forceful use as adze blades or planes, to knife-like edges on thin flakes produced by delicate shallow retouch. The forms include straight, convex, concave and

ARTEFACTS	STRATIGRAPHY	CLIMATIC INTERPRETATION

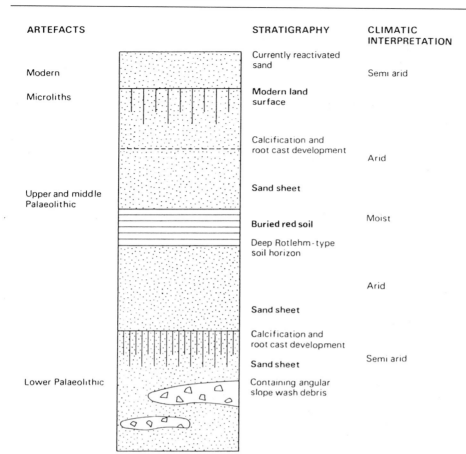

Modern — Currently reactivated sand — Semi arid

Microliths — Modern land surface

Calcification and root cast development — Arid

Upper and middle Palaeolithic — Sand sheet

Buried red soil — Moist

Deep Rotlehm-type soil horizon

Arid

Sand sheet

Calcification and root cast development

Sand sheet — Semi arid

Lower Palaeolithic — Containing angular slope wash debris

Fig. 2. Schematic diagram of Late Pleistocene stratigraphic and cultural sequence at Pushkar. (After Allchin, Goudie and Hegde, 1978.)

nosed types, and combinations of two or more of these on the same flake, but are not constant (Fig. 1). Middle Palaeolithic material from a series of stratified gravels on the Belan river, a southern tributary of the Ganges system, shows a steady development from the lowest level with 10 per cent of cleavers and 90 per cent of scrapers, through a stage where scrapers are virtually the only artefact, to the top where blades and burins are added to the tool kit. There is a steady swing from quartzite to chert as the predominant raw material.[8]

The Middle Palaeolithic factory sites have been recorded in the same area, the valleys of the Belan and Son rivers in southern Uttar Pradesh. In both cases they are situated on old fans and on the lower slopes of the hills overlooking the river. The material, being *in situ* and therefore unrolled but somewhat weathered, bears out the observations made earlier. The siting of these working, and perhaps living, areas to which some of the stone at any rate was carried from the river gra-

8. Sharma et al., 1980, p. 95.

vels, adds a certain cultural dimension to the artefact record. These were selected places within reach of water and raw material providing a good view of the surrounding country. Here the tool-makers could watch the movements of game, the activities of other men or the approach of predators. Of the many rock shelters in central India a considerable proportion were occupied by microlith-makers and some also by Upper Palaeolithic man, but few were regularly inhabited during Middle or Lower Palaeolithic times. The Bhimbetka group of rock shelters mentioned above are an exception having been regularly occupied by late Lower Palaeolithic and Middle Palaeolithic communities. Publication of the Middle Palaeolithic material is eagerly awaited as this should shed further light on the ecology and daily life of the Middle Palaeolithic inhabitants of the area.

The Thar desert of north-western India and Pakistan

There are no perennial rivers in the north-west of the Aravalli range, in the Thar desert and the arid or semi-desert zone along its south-eastern margin. The only river system is that of the Luni (meaning salty), and this flows only briefly, following rare heavy rains. Throughout the region there are 'dead' drainage systems which can be observed both from the air and the ground. These must have taken shape under conditions of greater humidity than at present, when somewhat more rain fell and the rate of evaporation was considerably less. Middle Palaeolithic sites are found associated with the courses of dead streams in areas where today people can only maintain life with the help of deep wells. Middle Palaeolithic material is also associated with an ancient fossil soil, which has a deeper and better developed soil profile than modern soil. Both the fossil and contemporary soils are formed upon deep, widespread sand-drifts. The upper, more recent sand sheet has been stripped off by wind action in places, re-exposing the fossil soil (Fig. 2). In certain places Middle Palaeolithic sites including factory areas have been exposed in this way. The archaeologist lucky enough to find a place where this has happened, can study the disposition of cores, flakes, hammerstones, etc., and see Middle Palaeolithic artefacts in a fresh and unweathered condition little changed from that in which their makers left them, as, for example, at Hokra near Ajmer.[9]

The pattern of alternating sands and soils has been interpreted as showing a sequence of two arid phases, each represented by a sand sheet, divided by a humid phase represented by the fossil red soil.[10] Middle Palaeolithic man inhabited the Thar region during the humid phase, living on the banks of streams that no longer flow, and the shores of old lakes, as at Hokra and Bharidani in Rajasthan. Lower Palaeolithic artefacts occur in detritus from the hills stratified below the sands of the penultimate arid phase. Middle Palaeolithic assemblages on the sur-

9. Allchin et al., 1978.
10. Ibid.

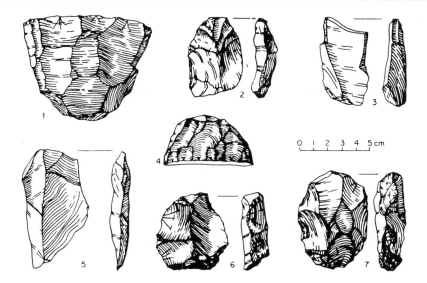

FIG. 3. Hokra: Middle Palaeolithic artefacts: 1 – struck core; 2, 5 – flakes from prepared cores; 3 – burin; 4 – carinated scraper; 6 – scraper made on flake from prepared core; 7 – unstruck core. (After Allchin et al., 1978.)

face of the old red soil range from those that appear to be transitional from Lower to Middle Palaeolithic to those showing a distinctly Mousterian character. Upper Palaeolithic sites also are found on the same horizon. Microlithic sites are associated with the modern soil formed on the sand of the final arid phase. Working floors of several periods from early Middle Palaeolithic to microlithic are sometimes found in close proximity to isolated outcrops of suitable rock in the desert as for example at Mogra, near Jodhpur, and Nagri, between Jodhpur and Bikaner.

The Middle Palaeolithic tradition of the arid Thar region is quite distinct from Nevasan. This was first pointed out by Misra.[11] This group may be called the Luni industries. As in the Nevasan, scrapers are the predominant artefact type, but, as hand-axes, cleavers and other characteristic Lower Palaeolithic forms decline or disappear, other artefacts make their appearance. These include edge-trimmed points; smaller cleavers of a particular type with a greatly reduced butt suggesting that they were intended for mounting as adze blades; side scrapers and choppers, some with denticulate edges. A further range of type, including burins, carinated scrapers and blades, are found with what appear to be the later Middle Palaeolithic industries. The manner in which these artefact types recur leaves no doubt that they were being deliberately created in accordance with preconceived formulae, as in the Mousterian tradition of Europe and western Asia, or in that of the hand-axe industries (Fig. 3).

11. Misra, 1968.

These more formal artefacts must have been produced at factory sites and perhaps incorporated into composite tools serving as missile heads, knife blades, adze blades, etc. They were being prepared in advance to meet a whole series of both predictable and unknown situations. On the other hand, many of the scrapers made on flakes struck from prepared cores and utilized flakes were probably produced 'on site' to serve the job in hand and discarded on the spot. Indeed, many of the smaller sites in the desert positively suggest this. We have here side by side two approaches to tool-making expressed in the artefact record; two expressions of the working of the human mind. One indicates conceptual thought and forethought of a complex and sophisticated kind; the other represents improvisation. Taken together as part of the same culture, as they appear to be, these two demonstrations of thinking and tool-making represent a wide range of mental competence. No occupied caves or rock shelters and no skeletal remains of Stone Age man so far have been found in the Thar region.

The lower Indus plains

In its lower course through the province of Sind, in Pakistan, the Indus flows in a shallow channel on or even above the surface of the plain. It is contained by low banks or levies through which the water formerly broke out to inundate large areas of the plain each year (it is now contained by barrages, etc.). The main channel has changed its course on a number of occasions during historical times, and, seen from the air, the plain is covered with old river courses and cut-off meanders. Silt brought down and deposited each year by the flood-water has caused the plain to be built up by an estimated 1–2 m per millennium for the last 5,000 years, and the process has probably been going on for a much longer period. Therefore there is no means of knowing exactly where in its trough the main course of the Indus flowed in Middle Palaeolithic times. A significant part of the dead drainage system of the Thar, with which Middle Palaeolithic sites are associated, mentioned in the last section, is directed towards the Indus trough and disappears beneath the silts of the plain: this indicates that a major river must have flowed there in Middle Palaeolithic times. There is also a well-established drainage pattern along the north-western margins of the valley. Some tributaries from this direction reach the Indus today, but others do not, becoming lost on entering the plain. Whether the main river of the time carried as much water from the mountain regions of the north and north-east as the present Indus is uncertain, as many changes in the drainage pattern of the Himalayan region have taken place in the Late Pleistocene and even perhaps in recent geological times.

As a result of the accumulation of silt in the plain all the observable Palaeolithic sites in Sind are located either on its edges or on outlying hills that emerge from it. Middle Palaeolithic artefacts have been found in the southern part of Lasbela district on the Sind/Baluchistan border, on a limestone plateau that extends into the plain at Jerruk on the west bank near Hyderabad and on the flat tops of the Rohri hills, also limestone, through which the Indus flows in Upper Sind. In both the latter areas the limestone hills are capped by a layer of large flint nodules which have been used by man for tool-making at many periods, and factory sites cover almost the entire hill-top, an area of many square kilometres in each case. At Jerruk there is a great deal of Lower Palaeolithic material; in Upper Sind this is less in evidence and Middle Palaeolithic material predominates in the Rohri hills. Neither locality has been studied in detail, both groups of sites having been investigated and briefly described in 1975.[12]

The Middle Palaeolithic industry of the Rohri hills shows a similar range of types to that seen in the Luni industries, the principal difference being that the average size of the artefacts appears to be somewhat larger and the proportion of reworked scrapers markedly smaller in the Rohri industry. But these differences could be attributed to the flint occurring in large nodules which were used as cores with only minimal trimming. The shape of some is such that after removal of any major irregularities, flake after flake could be struck off in the same direction without further core preparation, rather like slicing bread or salami. The flakes sometimes appear to have been trimmed to improve the working edge, but more often seem to have been used as they were.

The vast area covered by working floors and debris indicates that each of these hill-top or plateau factories must have supplied a wide area up and down the course of the Indus, far into what is now desert, over a long period of time. This means that there must have been a network of trade and exchange covering the territories of many groups and families in all directions. Such indications as we have of environmental conditions at this period suggest that the climate of Middle Palaeolithic times was somewhat less severely arid than at present. Several factors point in this direction. The distribution of Middle Palaeolithic factory sites in the Rohri hills, where they are often many kilometres from the Indus, the only source of non-saline water today, suggests that local sources of potable surface water were then available. Associated with the flint layer capping the limestone hills is a reddish soil. H. de Terra[13] described this as 'ancient soil of "terrarosa" type which does not form under present arid conditions'. The final and perhaps most cogent argument is the evidence of more humid conditions, throughout the Thar desert immediately to the south-east, noted in the previous section. There is some evidence that blade cores and blades characteristic of the Upper Palaeolithic were made alongside the Middle Palaeolithic artefacts at least at one and probably several sites in the Rohri hills.[14]

A major river (the Indus today carries approximately twice as much water as the Nile) flowing through either a desert or through relatively dry open

12. Allchin, B., 1976.
13. De Terra and Paterson, 1939, p. 332.
14. Allchin, B., 1976.

TABLE I. Modified relative chronology of the Siwalik and Pleistocene deposits of the middle Soan valley

		Tentative dates
———————— erosion/deposition ————————		
Loess deposition		
———————— erosion/warping ————————		– Middle Palaeolithic
Lei conglomerate complex (valley fill) includes deposition of loess/uplift partly contemporaneous		(0.4 mya)[1]
———————— uplift/folding/start of erosion ————————		0.7-0.5 mya
	Upper Siwalik conglomerates	1.9 mya
Soan		
formation	Pinjor beds	2.5 mya
	Tatrot beds	
———————— diconformity ————————		
Dhok Pathan formation		
Nagri formation		
Chinji formation		

SWALIK GROUP {

1. Mya = million years ago.
Source: Rendell, 1982.

country, such as we envisage in Middle Palaeolithic times, would provide a rich environment for hunter-gatherers. Today the river provides fish and water birds, and many wild animals inhabit the gallery forest along its banks. A more humid environment would mean that the surrounding savannah too would be rich in game. Therefore this was a favourable environment within which Middle Palaeolithic communities could expand and develop new cultural features.

In the Karachi area, the extreme south-eastern corner of the Baluchistan mountain region, a long sequence of Palaeolithic industries, some related to a sequence of Pleistocene deposits, have been recorded.[15] These include Middle Palaeolithic material, very widely distributed on the surface and said to resemble the Nevasan and to be heavily sand-blasted. Its distribution suggests that it was produced during a period of rather more humid conditions than at present and the sand-blasting indicates that arid conditions have prevailed since.

15. Khan, 1979.

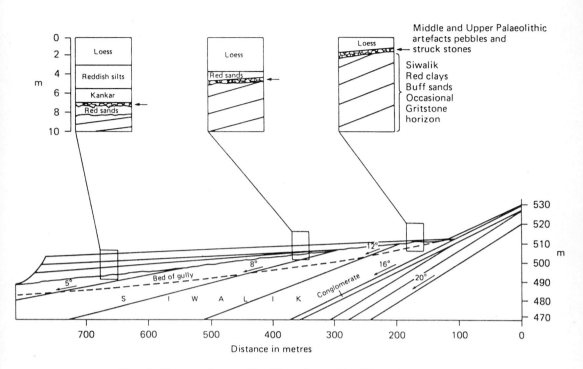

FIG. 4. Potwar plateau, Siwalik and post-Siwalik sections, Rawat. (After Rendell, 1984.)

The Potwar plateau, Punjab

The association of the Soan industries with a series of terraces as proposed by de Terra and Paterson[16] has recently been shown to be incorrect.[17] The Middle Palaeolithic industries of the Soan valley can now be related to geologically stratified deposits of the final phases of the Pleistocene. The Siwalik silts laid down in the earlier phases of the Pleistocene and preceding geological periods were subject in the later Pleistocene to violent uplift and folding (see Table 1). This was followed by a massive outwash and erosion of material from the Himalayas which resulted in planing off of the folded and uptilted Siwalik strata and deposition of gravels, silts, etc. On the surface of the final layer of material deposited in this way Middle and Upper Palaeolithic sites are found in the Potwar plateau, in association with the present course of the Soan river, and elsewhere. The eroded surface with which the Palaeolithic sites are associated is overlain by a mantle of loess of varying thickness (Fig. 4).Artefacts and associated factory debris can be

16. De Terra and Paterson, 1939.
17. Allchin, B., 1981; Rendell, 1984.

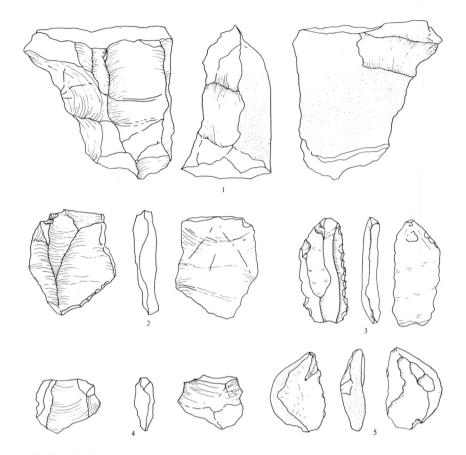

F<small>IG</small>. 5. Middle Palaeolithic of the Soan valley, Pakistan: 1, 2, 4 – prepared core and flakes from group at locality 55; 3, 5 – blade flake with scraper edge and pebble segment from locality 2. (After Cilletus, 1981.)

seen in sections exposed in gulleys and also on the surface where the overlying loess has been stripped off by erosion, accelerated in recent years by the pressure of agriculture, road-building, quarrying and other activities on the land.

Concentrations of artefacts including Middle and Upper Palaeolithic material, suggesting other activities in addition to tool-making, commensurate with regular temporary or semi-permanent habitation over considerable periods of time, are found extending more or less continuously over many square kilometres in localities that provide water and a supply of raw material. The relationship of Middle and Upper Palaeolithic typology and technology remains to be worked out. Both are present on the same horizon and it is not yet clear whether they are contemporary as appears to be the case in the Rohri hills for example, or represent a chronological sequence. The Soan Middle Palaeolithic material has not yet been fully analysed and described, but it appears to be based upon flakes struck from prepared cores and to include a range of scrapers, trimmed points, small cleavers or axes, larger cleavers or choppers made from split quartzite pebbles and other artefacts, comparable to the range seen in the Luni and Rohri industries (Fig. 5). The source of water for these sites was the Soan river and its tributaries, probably more accessible and flowing more regularly then than they do today. The raw material was almost exclusively quartzite, in the form of pebbles, cobbles and small boulders derived from the underlying uptilted Siwalik strata. Sites occur where this material was available on the surface.

The results of a detailed investigation into the climatic and general environmental conditions prevailing during Middle and Upper Palaeolithic times are awaited. The loess deposits above the horizon with which the factory sites are associated have been dated by thermoluminescence to between 20,000 and 60,000 years ago. The implications of the extensive sites in the Potwar region once again point to larger communities or more complex inter-community relations than we have been accustomed to infer in the case of Middle Palaeolithic cultures based only upon occupied caves and rock shelters and surface sites of limited dimensions.

Hindu Kush: the mountain region between the Indus and the Oxus

This region, which extends from the north-west frontier province of Pakistan and eastern Afghanistan to the borders of eastern Iran and Baluchistan, is less fully studied and understood in terms or early prehistory than either the plains and hills of the Indian subcontinent or the mountains and valleys of Soviet Central Asia. Due to the nature of the terrain, organized programmes of prehistoric research and thorough investigation of excavated sites have so far not been possible. The region appears to be relatively rich in occupiable and occupied caves and rock shelters, a number of which have been excavated in haste and somewhat cursorily described. Middle Palaeolithic material has been reported from caves and rock shelters in Afghanistan, from one rock shelter, Sanghao, in the Northwest frontier province of Pakistan and from open air sites on the shores of saline lakes in the Dasht-i Nawur plateau in Afghanistan.

There is no doubt that Middle Palaeolithic artefact types and technology are present at Sanghao, along with characteristic Upper Palaeolithic blade cores, blades and burins. But the material from the excavation was recorded in such a way that it is impossible to ascertain whether the two sets of stone-working techniques were practised side by side, as they appear to have been in Sind, for example, or have a sequential relationship. While it is unlikely that one totally replaced the other, as there appears to be no absolute break or hiatus in the sequence as seen in the section cut through an occupation deposit of over 3 m by

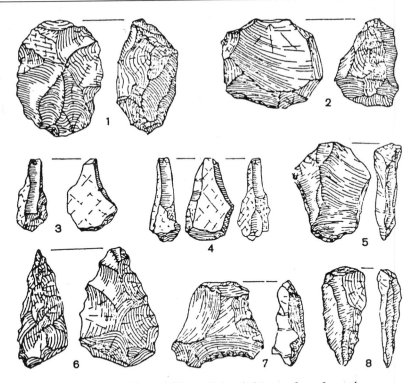

Fig. 6. Sanghao: Middle and Upper Palaeolithic artefacts from the excavation: 1 – unstruck discoidal core; 2 – struck core; 3, 4 – burins; 5 – flake struck from prepared core; 6 – hand-axe; 7 – hollow scraper made on flake; 8 – pointed flake struck from prepared core.
(After Allchin and Allchin, 1982.)

the excavators, it would be interesting to know which element was the dominant one at any stage, and, if change or development took place, where this was most evident.[18]

Sanghao cave is situated in a remote valley with a southern aspect on a minor tributary of the Swat river, providing a sheltered local environment in an otherwise harsh mountain region. The stream provides a perennial supply of excellent water within a few yards of the large rock shelter in which artefacts were made, suggesting winter occupancy and perhaps a colder climate than at present. Analysis of the cave deposits should yield information on the climate and environment, and numerous bones visible in the section should yield dating material and further information regarding diet, environment and possibly human skeletal remains. The material is exclusively milky quartz throughout, and the source of supply is clearly visible within 100 m of the rock shelter. Over 3 m of occupation deposit must represent a considerable period of time throughout

18. Dani, 1964.

which the rock shelter was regularly, if not continuously, occupied; it also indicates cultural if not actual ethnic continuity. The only changes noted by the excavators were expressed in terms of twelve layers or levels numbered from the top downwards: levels 12 to 10 were the richest in terms of quartz artefacts; 9 to 5 yielded similar artefacts but not in such profusion; in levels 3 and 4 the character of the industry changed and quartz microliths predominated and graded into early historic material in levels 1 and 2.[19]

The Middle Palaeolithic artefacts from Sanghao are considerably smaller than those from other regions. This is dictated by the nature of the quartz which tends to break up into nodules, the size of which is dependent upon the natural planes of fracture along which the material tends to break. Therefore it cannot be taken as a factor of chronological or cultural significance. The range of artefacts from levels 12 to 5 is as follows: flake cores, flakes from prepared cores, scrapers (predominantly concave) awls, burins and one small hand-axe; in addition there are blades and blade cores which appear to represent an Upper Palaeolithic tradition (Fig. 6). Although certain minor changes are observable there is a remarkable consistency of size and style throughout levels 12 to 5, further reinforcing the hypothesis of local cultural continuity.

The first Middle Palaeolithic artefact to be found in Afghanistan in 1950 was a Mousterian point in the spoil from a deep irrigation canal on the Oxus plain.[20] In 1954 the caves of Kara Kamar and others were excavated by C. S. Coon[21] who claimed to find both Middle and Upper Palaeolithic artefacts in alternating layers. During the following years Dupree, McBurney, Vinogradov and others all worked on the Palaeolithic of Afghanistan, and each made a contribution to the subject. In a recent survey of the Palaeolithic in Afghanistan, Davis, one of the very few people to have examined all the available material, says that although claims have been made to have identified Middle Palaeolithic material in five excavated caves or rock shelters and on other sites, in the case of only one cave, Dara-i Kur, could he really endorse this.[22]

Dara-i Kur is a large rock shelter high up on the side of a valley with a good view of the surrounding country in Badakhshan province, eastern Afghanistan.[23] The upper levels yielded remains of the 'goat cult Neolithic' including stone blades, grinding stones, incised pottery and human burials with goat remains. Immediately below came the Middle Palaeolithic levels in which over 800 artefacts were found, all made of a local basalt which fractures somewhat irregularly. Circumstances prevented the excavators from making a complete analysis of the finds, but they drew up a brief but clear illustrated description of them. The pre-

19. Allchin, B., 1973.
20. Allchin, F. R., 1953.
21. Coon, 1957.
22. Davis, 1978.
23. Dupree and Davis, 1972; Davis and Dupree, 1977.

dominant artefact technique was that of striking flakes from a prepared discoidal core and using them as tools, with or without further trimming. Multi-platform and 'Levallois' type cores and flakes (i.e. blade flakes and pointed triangular flakes) were in a minority and edge-trimmed points and scrapers were rare. There were no hand-axes and only one or two rather doubtful burins. The same levels produced remains of sheep or goat – both animals would seem to have been of paramount importance to man in this region from that time onwards – and possibly also bovid remains. There was also a fragment of a human skull which has been described.[24] In summary it was said that it 'would fit into a partly Neanderthal population like that of Skhul (Palestine) just as well as a modern one'. This is the only human skeletal material found so far in a Middle Palaeolithic context in Afghanistan. A C14 date of 30,300 + 1900–1200 B.C. has been obtained for Dara-i Kur Middle Palaeolithic but is regarded as possibly too young on account of the probability of slight contamination by later material.

Among the Middle Palaeolithic artefact assemblages reported elsewhere in Afghanistan are some from caves where they are claimed to occur alongside or in alternating layers between Upper Palaeolithic blade and burin industries, which appear to be relatively plentiful in Afghanistan. These are described by Davis as being either amorphous collections lacking formal artefact types or parts of Upper Palaeolithic assemblages. The same goes for artefacts and waste materials found on the Dasht-i Nawur plateau in association with old lake shorelines, and in the Dara Dadil and Dara Chakmak valleys where they occur in the gravels of the streams, the source being seams of flint in the surrounding limestone rock. On the basis of illustrations, the present writer is inclined to accept this with regard to the cave material but to differ regarding that from the river gravels. In any case the question is at present little more than a semantic one, as it depends upon the definition of Middle Palaeolithic we apply. In the Afghan context this is still rather unclear.

The terrain and environmental conditions found in Afghanistan extend into eastern Iran; here also there are occupied caves and rock shelters and remains of Mousterian, Middle Palaeolithic industries. Khunik cave on the western side of the Helmand basin (excavated by Coon in 1950) showed clear evidence of a brief Mousterian presence and, as in Afghanistan, there is every expectation that further research will lead to the discovery of more sites, both occupied caves and open stations. The less arid region of northern Iran between the desert and the Caspian Sea and especially the escarpment falling away to the Caspian is said to be rich in caves. Some, like Ghar-i Kamarband and Hotu[25] were only occupied in later times. This area is part of another region in any case, outside the one we are discussing here. Likewise, Bisitun in the Zagros mountains; Shanidar

24. Angel, 1972.
25. Coon, 1951.

excavated by Soleki in 1971,[26] with a Mousterian industry and a spectacular Neanderthal burial accompanied by red ochre, ibex horns and flowers; the many other
sites of this region and of the Crimea are all part of the major geographical and
environmental regions. They do however form part of a continuum of associated
Mousterian industries and Neanderthal physical remains that stretch from T'ien
Shan through central and western Asia, southern Russia, eastern and western
Europe and north Africa to the Atlantic.

Soviet Central Asia

The Palaeolithic of Soviet Central Asia has been very ably discussed and the current state of knowledge summarized by Ranov and Davis.[27] They emphasize the
diversity and local character of the Mousterian or Middle Palaeolithic industries
in the region. This parallels the sort of diversity seen in Pakistan and northern
India, but is perhaps more readily understandable in view of the great variation
in relief as well as other aspects of environment. By 1979 five Mousterian cave
sites and thirteen large surface collections had been recorded in addition to fifty-
four minor-find spots. They divide the Middle Palaeolithic sites into four varieties and a possible fifth on the basis of typology and technology as follows:
1. Levallois, with single and multiple striking platform cores; triangular and sub-
     rectangular blades and blade flakes; simple edge-retouched pieces predom-
     inating and few formal tool types.
2. Levallois-Mousterian, similar to the above but with more platformed and dis-
     coidal cores; marginally retouched blades predominating.
3. Typical or Mountain Mousterian, which differs significantly from the first two
     in having more formal tools of several distinct types, some, such as scrapers
     and to a lesser extent points, resembling those that characterize western
     European assemblages.
4. Mousterian of Soan tradition, also including scrapers and points of traditional
     Mousterian forms, but with them are found a high proportion of choppers
     and chopping tools made on pebbles.
5. The possible fifth variant is a denticulate Mousterian assemblage from one site,
     Kulbulak.
As yet there is no traceable developmental link between the Lower and the Middle Palaeolithic of Soviet Central Asia and the way in which the typological variants are related chronologically is also not yet clear. There is, however, a certain
regional pattern of distribution. The Levallois and Levallois-Mousterian groups
occur in the Ferghana valley and the foothills of the T'ien Shan range in the
northern part of the region. The Mountain Mousterian has been found further
south in the valleys and spurs of the Hissar range and other mountains, notably at

26. Soleki, 1971.
27. Ranov and Davis, 1979.

the caves of Teshik-Tash and Ogzi-Kichik, in the former of which it is associated with a Neanderthal burial. The Mousterian of Soan tradition is found only along the course of the Vakhsh river in southern Tajikistan.

The lithic assemblages from many Soviet Central Asian Mousterian sites include Upper Palaeolithic features and for this and other reasons the Middle Palaeolithic has been considered by some to extend forward in time, perhaps even to the end of the Pleistocene. The present writer is inclined to agree with this point of view and also to see the Mousterian of Soan tradition as an adaptation to the utilization of available material (i.e. river pebbles and cobbles) as appears to be the case in the Potwar region of the Punjab. Thus it might be seen as having a fairly direct relationship to the Mountain Mousterian of the adjacent mountains, as both these groups include formal artefact types not found to any significant extent in the Levallois and Levallois-Mousterian groups of industries further north. It seems possible that the two groups in this case may be part of a single complex of which each forms a local occupational facies. This is at present mere speculation, but might be a topic of future research.

There is some evidence regarding the environment of Middle Palaeolithic man in Soviet Central Asia derived from Pleistocene loess and palaeosols and from cave deposits. In general this points towards somewhat more humid conditions than those at present prevailing. Palaeobotanical evidence in particular demonstrates this and faunal remains found in cave deposits lend support to it. Modern species were already much in evidence, especially various kinds of sheep and goats, and certain now extinct animals, such as the hyena for example, were also present. A clear example of the general pattern of change is seen at Ogzi-Kichik.

The caves occupied by Middle Palaeolithic man in Uzbekistan and Tajikistan have been found to be rich in cultural material and remains of many kinds. The cave of Teshik-Tash is situated in a limestone escarpment on a spur of the Baisun mountain range on a southern extension of the Hissar mountains overlooking the valley of the Surkhan Darya in Uzbekistan. It was excavated by Okladnikov and others in 1938 and yielded the first conclusive evidence of Mousterian or Middle Palaeolithic culture in Central Asia.[28] Here, in five occupation layers, were found not only an extensive Mousterian artefact assemblage including some worked bones, but animal bones, hearths and other evidence of regular occupation.

Associated with the final occupation layer was the burial of a Neanderthal child surrounded by six pairs of horns of a Siberian mountain goat (*Capra sibirica*). The stone industry, now seen as belonging to Ranov and Davis's typical Mountain Mousterian, shows little change throughout. The cave was totally excavated and 329 tools and 2,520 trimming flakes and chips were recovered (Fig. 7). The main artefact types are scrapers of various kinds with steeply trimmed working

28. Gremyatsky, 1979.

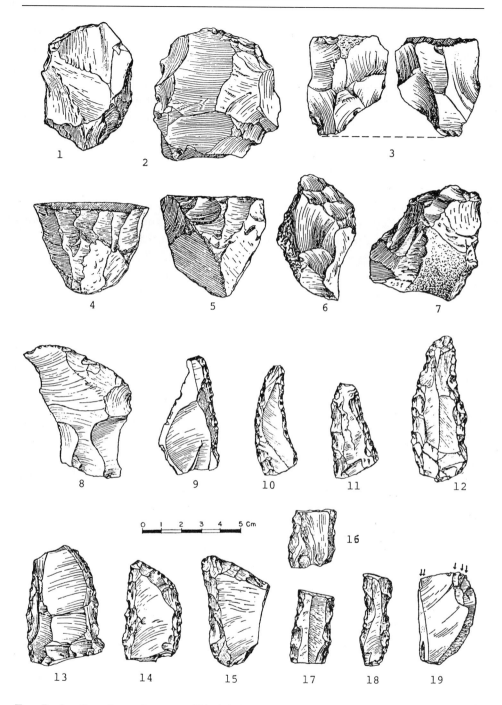

FIG. 7. Artefacts from the cave of Teshik-Tash, Uzbekistan: 1–7 – cores; 8–18 flake, scrapers and points; 19 – burin.

edges including long blade flakes worked on one or both edges, some almost large enough to be classified as chopping tools made on flakes; characteristic Mousterian points and a small number of simple burins. A variety of locally available types of rock were used, none of the best quality for tool-making. Among the bones of animals evidently used for food those of the Siberian mountain goat predominated forming 83.79 per cent of the total. The wild horse (*Equus caballus*), leopard, brown bear, hyena, and many small mammals and birds were also found. In the same area, also in steep inaccessible valleys, the caves of the Amir-Temir assemblage suggested a brief or occasional occupancy, rather as did that from Khunik cave in eastern Iran. Okladnikov suggested that in the foothills of the Baisun mountains open settlements might be found, which were more continuously occupied by goat-hunters. Perhaps the cave culture represents only one, seasonal, aspect of the life of the Middle Palaeolithic inhabitants.

The cave of Ogzi-Kichik, excavated by Ranov in 1979, is situated in a small sheltered valley on the southern slopes of the Vakhsh range in Tajikistan. It is at the foot of a limestone escarpment in close proximity to what must formerly have been a spring which now no longer flows. Palaeolithic and faunal remains both point to more humid conditions during Mousterian times and there was probably a pool below the cave. The animal remains include those of turtle which probably lived in the pool, horse (*Equus caballus*), red deer and rhino, and are more or less constant throughout the Middle Palaeolithic occupation. Remains of turtles were found in hearths, suggesting that they were roasted in their shells.

The stone industry is similar to that of Teshik-Tash, belonging to the same typical Mountain Mousterian, but has its own local character. Here again it is based upon a range of locally available types of rock. In contrast to Teshik-Tash the best occupation layers were in the talus slope immediately outside and below the cave (which was perhaps larger in the past). Approximately 10,000 artefacts, including finished pieces, cores and trimming flakes etc., were recovered from the excavation. Throughout there were fragments of bone, evidently broken by man, and large hearths. There was also an oval arrangement of stones approximately 1.5 m across with a pair of ibex horns at one end. As this was not associated with the burial there seems to be little doubt that is was a shrine.

Mongolia

Along with the regions discussed above, we may include some newly discovered materials from Mongolia that throw light on the Middle and Upper Palaeolithic of that area. They have been found at Otstonmaint and Gurvan-Sikhan in the southern Gobi, Ikh-Bogd in the Gobi-Altai *aimak,* and in the Arts-Bogd area of Uburkhangai *aimak* in Bogd Somon. In the first site typically Levalloisian cores and flakes were discovered. The neighbouring site produced numerous Mousterian tools. A similar Mousterian culture, with implements made of igneous rock, was identified at Ikh-Bogd. Arts-Bogd has revealed a factory site where tools of great variety have been found. Particularly those of red jasper appertain to the Upper Palaeolithic period. Surface materials have also been found in the valley of Sirdzhi in the Gobi-Altai area and at three sites in eastern Mongolia between the towns of Barun-urt and Saynshand in the vicinity of the Somon of Delgerekh as well as at the Moiltyn-am site on the Orkhon river. This last site presents a continuous sequence from the Upper Palaeolithic to Mesolithic. The Levallois-Mousterian material of this region appears to be related to that from the Altai region and Siberia, while the Upper Palaeolithic shows similarity to that from northern Asia.

Conclusion

The mountain cave sites of Soviet Central Asia thus tell us more about the nature and culture of their occupants than any of the other Middle Palaeolithic sites in the whole region we have covered in this brief survey. We started by pointing out what can be inferred about the working of the human mind from stone artefacts alone. We then saw how the distribution and varying nature of surface sites can add a further cultural dimension to the stone industries, and how the picture obtained by analysis of the nature and distribution of surface sites is extended and given greater meaning by relating it as far as possible to the environmental context of its time. This allows us to comprehend aspects of the life and economy of the communities who made the tools. Once we have reached the stage of considering the culture of Middle Palaeolithic man in these terms the vast factory sites and open living sites of Sind and other parts of the region can be seen to pose some very interesting problems of community relations. They raise the question as to how far networks of exchange were developed during Middle Palaeolithic times in South and Central Asia.

The cave sites we have looked at, particularly Sanghao, Teshik-Tash and Ogzi-Kichik, give a more intimate insight into the day-to-day cultural life of their occupants and demonstrate interdependence and mutual respect between members of a group, an interest in an after-life and perhaps also indicate religious practices. They also show a quite remarkable local continuity throughout what appear to be long periods of regular or continuous occupation. This in itself suggests stable communities living permanently in these very choice spots, or returning regularly to them in the course of seasonal migrations, making use of different sources of food, such as present-day hunter-gatherers practice. How the conflicting ideas generated by examining the evidence of Middle Palaeolithic cultures in various parts of the region we have covered are to be resolved, and what total picture they will finally enable us to reconstruct of the life and culture of Middle Palaeolithic man in South and Central Asia, are among the outstanding wider problems for future research. One thing is certain, we are only at the beginning. There is a great deal of research and fieldwork to be done and much discussion and controversy lie ahead. The picture that emerges will be a complex one in both ethnic and cultural terms.

4

UPPER PALAEOLITHIC CULTURES[1]

A. P. Derevyanko and Lü Zun-E

THE Upper (or Late) Palaeolithic of Soviet Central Asia has not yet been thoroughly studied. Throughout this territory little archaeological material has been collected as yet, and Late Palaeolithic remains appear to occur as isolated groups. About fifty sites have provided material which has been ascribed to Upper Palaeolithic and most of these ascriptions are provisional.[2] So far considerably more Mousterian sites have been discovered in Soviet Central Asia. Various explanations have been put forward for this; for example that some Late Palaeolithic sites have been mistaken for Mousterian;[3] that the weather has destroyed many;[4] and that many Late Palaeolithic sites are buried under loess.[5]

An important feature of Upper Palaeolithic sites in Central Asia is the similarity of the material to the Mousterian. In the cave of Obi-Rahmat only a gradual increase in the number of types distinguishes the Late Palaeolithic layers from the Mousterian. R. K. Suleymanov has established the following relationship between Mousterian and Late Palaeolithic types:[6]

Site horizon	Mousterian (%)	Late Palaeolithic (%)
Obi-Rahmat (D)	148	86
Obi-Rahmat (C)	15	85
Obi-Rahmat (B)	20	80

Links with the Mousterian stone-working tradition are also in evidence at

---

1. See Map 3 on pages 46 and 47. Material presented by A. Z. Yusofzay has also been used in this chapter.
2. Ranov and Nesmeyanov, 1973, p. 17.
3. Lazyukov, 1981.
4. Ranov, 1972, pp. 275–97.
5. Ibid., 1972, p. 282.
6. Suleymanov, 1972, p. 134.

the sites of Boz-Su (C14 date 38,000 years),[7] Kulbulak,[8] Shugnou[9] and Samarkand[10] (Fig. 1). This relationship suggests that the Late Palaeolithic stone technology of Central Asia was not introduced from outside but is a development of the indigenous Mousterian industry. This is supported by V. A. Alekseev's suggestion that the Teshik-Tash child may be an example of a pre-Asiatic type, and this in turn may lead to the conclusion that Central Asia may now be considered part of the primordial homeland of modern man.[11]

The Late Palaeolithic sites of Central Asia are usually associated with the surface deposits of the Golodnaya Steppe (Hungry Steppe) and Dushanbe terrace levels of the Upper Pleistocene. Shugnou, the Samarkand site and Kulbulak are among these. Some well-known finds were made on the Krasnovodsk peninsula at the Khazar and Khvalyn terraces (Yangaja and others). They have, however, been removed from their original site.

Since there is very little Central Asian Late Palaeolithic material available, all attempts to present its culture have been provisional. V. A. Ranov[12] has put forward a most sophisticated scheme based on A. P. Okladnikov's concept of two separate lines of development of Palaeolithic cultures in Soviet Central Asia. According to this scheme Group A cultures developed from a Levalloisian/Mousterian basis (e.g. the cave of Obi-Rahmat). The line of development of this group, which resembles the Late Palaeolithic of western Asia, has so far been traced only in its general outlines, especially because there is a gap in time between Obi-Rahmat, Yangi and Kaj-Gor. Group B is traced from the Karasu site in southern Kazakhstan through the Samarkand culture to the post-Palaeolithic Hissar culture. Ranov points out the traditional features of 'Asian Palaeolithic' in this line of development – a clear pattern of evolution influenced by the Asia Minor (Mediterranean) province.

Within these two groups Ranov distinguishes three basic technical variants of Late Palaeolithic culture: (a) Kara-Kamar (Aurignacian) type; (b) Khoja-i gor (Asia Minor) type (Khoja-i gor, Kizil-lai); and (c) the Samarkand variant (the Samarkand site, Siabsai, Khoja-mazgil, Neiza-tash, etc.).[13] After these groups come Shugnou[14] and Ak-Kupruk[15] (northern Afghanistan). The creation of the Kara-Kamar variant was evidently premature, since the material available is insufficient.[16]

7. Okladnikov and Islamov, 1961, pp. 51–60.
8. Kasymov, 1972, pp. 111–19.
9. Ranov, 1973, pp. 42–61.
10. Dzhurakulov et al., 1980, p. 92; Kholyushkin, 1981, p. 21; Taskenbaev and Suleymanov, 1980.
11. Alekseev, 1981.
12. Ranov and Nesmeyanov, 1973, p. 31.
13. Ranov, 1965, p. 10.
14. Ranov, 1973, pp. 57–9.
15. Dupree and Davis, 1972, pp. 14–28.
16. Ranov, 1960, pp. 145–50.

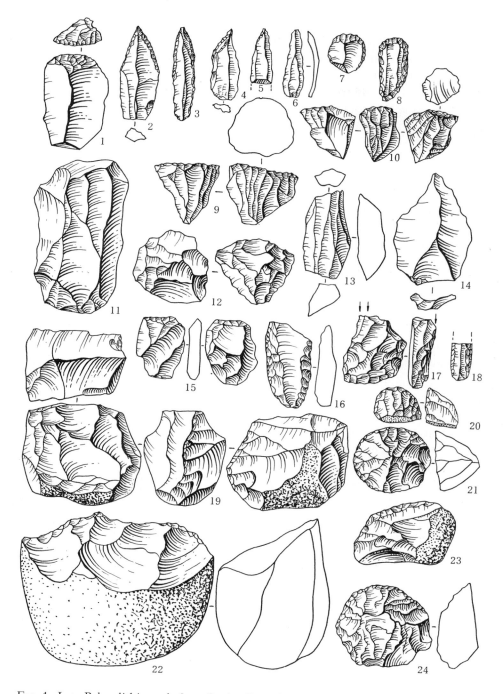

Fig. 1. Late Palaeolithic tools from Soviet Central Asia: 1–14 – Shugnou site;
15–24 – Samarkand site.

One of the most thoroughly researched sites in Central Asia is Kulbulak in the valley of the river Angren, north-west of the T'ien Shan mountains. It is an open site by a stream that is still intact today. M. R. Kasymov has identified nine cultural layers.[17] The top three layers may, in his opinion, date from the Late Palaeolithic. These show a continuing tradition of denticulate tools. There are miniature scrapers, often with toothed, retouched edges and wedge-shaped and prismatic cores. A better finish distinguishes the Mousterian tools in the Late Palaeolithic levels from those in the layers below. The objects found in these layers lie in deposits of the Golodnaya Steppe cycle.

Five layers have been identified at Shugnou, which is situated in the upper reaches of the river Yaksu, in the upper part of a 10 m (third) section of the early Dushanbe terrace.[18] The site has an excavated area of 500 m². The excavator considers all the layers to be remnants of temporary hunting camps, and that the top layer is Mesolithic and the four lower layers Late Palaeolithic. Some 4,700 stone implements were found at the site. All five cultural horizons present the same pattern: accumulations of worked stone, a few bones clustered together and the remains of heavily eroded camp-fires.

The same kind of fauna, with a few exceptions, is found in all layers: horse, ox or bison, ram or goat, marmot and tortoise. The cultural levels also contain a considerable amount of tree-pollen, including birch, pine, fir, cedar, alder, willow, poplar, plane, walnut, ash and other varieties. Only a few objects were found in the third and fourth horizons. Most of them appear to be Mousterian and are strongly reminiscent of material found in the upper layers of Obi-Rahmat. Many of the elements found are post-Mousterian, like the oblong core typical of Late Palaeolithic found in the third horizon.[19]

The second horizon yielded the largest quantity of material. There is a preponderance of heavy blades, often Mousterian in appearance, many with lateral ribs, which seem to be picks. There are several basic categories of tools. One of these is the scraper: end-scrapers are made from either heavy, elongated blades or wide, truncated blades; there are instances of round scrapers retouched along the entire perimeter of the disc; and there are simple flake scrapers. Points constitute another large group. They include awls with sharpening retouch along one or two edges, pierced points with blunted edges, Gravettian and 'Tutkal' points.

Smaller, curved blades characterize the industry of Horizon I. The most noteworthy tool type is a core scraper with a well-defined 'nose', which is common to Kara-Kamar, the workshop on the Krasnovodsk peninsula, and the Samarkand site. With the core-scrapers, there are blade scrapers with meticulously finished points and edges, and coarser flake scrapers. The C14 date of this horizon is 10,700 ± 500 years (GIN 590).

17. Kasymov, 1972.
18. Ranov and Nesmeyanov, 1973, p. 83.
19. Ranov, 1973, p. 57.

Horizon 0 is Mesolithic. The cores found here are closely related to those of the Markansu culture of the eastern Pamirs.[20] The tools include unusual hollowed, scraper-like implements. The commonest tool is the scraper made from either flakes or sections of blades, more often from heavy flakes.[21] The Samarkand site, located in the centre of the city, was discovered in 1939 by N. G. Kharlamov, and has been studied more thoroughly than the others. The main excavations were carried out between 1958 and 1967 by D. N. Lev.[22] Cultural layers have been noted on both the lower (10 m) and upper (13–17 m) terraces. V. A. Ranov and S. A. Nesmeyanov consider that the deposits containing the cultural layers were formed after the late Golodnaya Steppe (Samarkand) terrace of the Siabsai and Zerafshan river,[23] that is, around 16,000 years ago. The results of the statistical analysis of the stone industry corroborate such a conclusion.[24] D. N. Lev distinguished three cultural levels. The variety of fauna is poor, thirteen species in all, including eleven species of mammal, birds of the sparrow family, and one species of reptile – the tortoise. The mammals are as follows: elephant or rhinoceros, horse, Pleistocene ass, wild donkey, camel, boar, deer, a type of gazelle, sheep of the steppe, aurochs and wolf.[25]

Lev has pointed to organic links both between the three layers themselves and between them all and the Mousterian industry of Amankutan. In establishing this hypothesis, he has attempted to highlight indirect lines of evolution in the typology and methods of fashioning the tools. He sees evidence of such lines of development in both the vaguely Mousterian form of tools from the Samarkand site, and in individual analogies between the knife-shaped and hollowed tools of the two industries under discussion.

However, in the absence of any concrete demonstration of a transformation of the Amankutan industry into an industry such as that of Samarkand, and in view of the small number of artefacts found at the former site, such assertions carry no conviction unless based on a comparison of the local roots of that industry with possible external influences.

The material found at Kuturbulak is very similar to that found at Samarkand.[26] We find the same retouched flakes and blades, hollowed tools and core tools, scrapers, burins and pebble tools. At Kuturbulak, most of the mentioned are smaller in size and more delicately fashioned. The relationship between the different types of tool is also different.

The spatio-temporal relations between the industry of the Samarkand site and the Late Palaeolithic industries of Soviet Central Asia to those of surround-

20. Ibid., p. 52.
21. Ibid., p. 52.
22. Lev, 1964, pp. 102–7.
23. Nesmeyanov, 1980, p. 46.
24. Dzhurakulov at al., 1980, pp. 51–95.
25. Ibid., pp. 54–95.
26. Tashkhenbaev, 1975, pp. 5–15.

ing territories present a problem that is no less complex. In speaking of the special features of the 'Asiatic' line of development of the Samarkand site – of the 'provenance' of the Mousterian forms and pebble tools, we must bear in mind a number of features common to the Palaeolithic of Europe and Asia Minor. The first is the presence of core-scrapers and high-profile scrapers, and often well-defined nose scrapers; this allows us to speak of definite links with industries such as those of Asia Minor and East Asia. These types of tools have direct counterparts in Mugaret-el-Wadi and Kara-Kamar. The two human lower jaws found on the Samarkand site are of great interest; they have been described as being of Mediterranean type.[27] In terms of tool typology, the Samarkand site is closely related to two others: Khoja-mazgil and Siabsai situated at a distance of 70 and 2 km respectively.

Upper Palaeolithic tools were found at the Yangaja sites, on the Krasnovodsk peninsula: as well as coarse, prismatic cores and Upper Palaeolithic blade and flake tools, there was a series of core-scrapers with high profiles.[28] The site of Khoja-i gor, on the right bank of the river Isfar, in the Ferghana depression, dates from the closing stages of the Upper Palaeolithic.[29] Geomorphological dates put it near the end of the Upper Pleistocene. The prevalent type of tool is the end-scraper, in both rounded and double-edged variants. The presence of small points with blunted edges relates this site to West Asia.

The site at Kara-Kamar bears a ressemblance to Upper Palaeolithic complexes in Afghanistan.[30] Keeled core-scrapers predominate here (Fig. 2). The industry also contains numbers of end-scrapers of the grooved and toothed variety. 21 per cent of the finds are blades and retouched flakes. Kuhn's opinion is that these scrapers give Kara-Kamar an Aurignacian character. Ranov holds that the second horizon at Kara-Kamar is a variant of Late Palaeolithic culture fairly common in this part of Asia, developed from archaic Mousterian traditions.[31] The basic implement here is the Mousterian blade with retouched edges, and occasionally with a retouched platform. Horizon I has a C14 date of 10,580 $\pm$ 720 years. It is characterized by the appearance of the microblade technique, and also has keeled scrapers. The lamellar flakes and end-scrapers are completely Palaeolithic in nature. The industries of this horizon are analogous to those of Oshkhon in the eastern Pamirs and to the third horizon of Tutkal.

Ak-kupruk sites II and III in Afghanistan, are of great help in understanding the general character of the Late Palaeolithic of this part of Central Asia.[32] Ak-kupruk is dated around 16,615 $\pm$ 215 years ago. Taking the material of complexes A and B together, Dupree and Davis discern two components. The first

27. Ginzburg and Gokhman, 1974, pp. 5–11.
28. Ranov and Nesmeyanov, 1973, p. 17.
29. Okladnikov, 1959, pp. 158–84.
30. Ranov, 1978, p. 233.
31. Ranov, 1960, pp. 145–50.
32. Dupree and Davis, 1972.

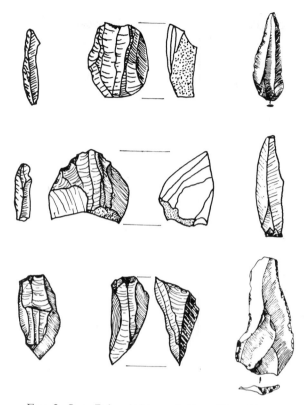

F<small>IG</small>. 2. Late Palaeolithic tools from Kara-Kamar,
Afghanistan: bladelets, bladelet-cores and blades.

consists of heavy items, cores, flakes, blades, denticulate scrapers, sharpening chips and ribbed blades. The microlithic component includes prismatic micro-cores and microblades. There are two further types of scraper; keeled and end-scrapers. Burins from the second largest category, consisting mainly of simple burins on the end of blades or flakes. There are also angle burins, combined burin-knives, shouldered points, cleavers and bifaces. The presence of micro-lithic cores in this complex shows that it is possible that material from different periods has been mixed together. We should take special note of the limestone pebble found in the cave of Ak-kupruk II which bears the carved outline of a human face.[33]

Recent studies by the British Archeaeological Mission in Pakistan have made a definite contribution to the study of the Upper Palaeolithic in the Potwar

33. Marshack, 1972, pp. 66–70.

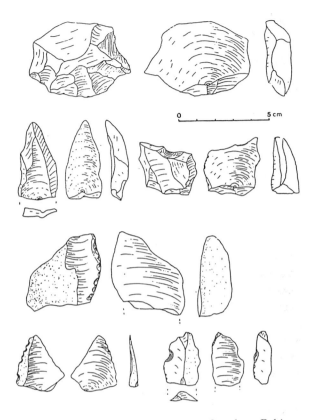

Fig. 3. Upper Palaeolithic tools from Sanghao, Pakistan:
Levallois flake and point, scrapers, etc.

region of Punjab. The tools associated with Lei Conglomerate fall mostly into the Middle to Upper Palaeolithic bracket. An important excavation has been carried out at the open-air site of Riwat and an intensive survey has been done in the surrounding area of nearly 2 km². This appears to be a temporary working site and is dated approximately 40,000 years ago by the thermoluminescence method. The excavation revealed 'a low stone wall and post sockets which appear to have been the base of a small windbreak or shelter and a small stone-lined pit of unknown purpose. With these were associated Upper Palaeolithic type cores, blades, etc., of fine grained quartzite, in fresh condition comparable to those found earlier on the edge of the loess'. This was probably a camping place.[34]

Sanghao cave is the most extensively studied Palaeolithic site in Pakistan. It was discovered and excavated by A. H. Dani and described by B. Allchin (1973).[35]

34. Allchin, 1986, pp. 78–81.
35. Dani, 1964.

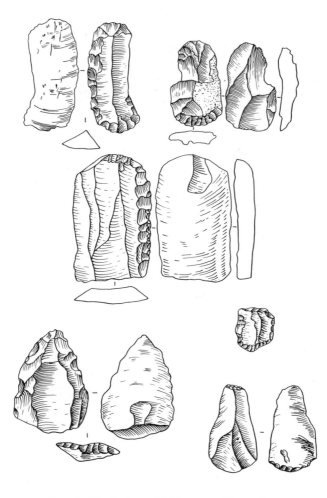

FIG. 4. Tools from Moiltyn-am, Mongolia.

The deposit consists of twelve cultural horizons, the lower ten of which include artefacts made in both Mousterian and Upper Palaeolithic traditions (Fig. 3). The basic raw material used in making the tools is quartz. A small proportion of the tools were made from bone. Uneven flakes, many of them elongated, lamellar flakes, served as blanks for tools. The flakes were struck from prepared cores, some of the striking platforms were at right angles to the flake surfaces and some were faceted. This shows that the technique of working stone was fairly well developed and reminiscent of the late Soan and the Middle Palaeolithic in India. Some of the flake cores were discoidal, and there were Levalloisian and tortoise cores; a few prismatic blade cores were also found. A number of cores had been turned into choppers and chopping tools by means of secondary flaking. Layers 3 and 4 (Period III) contain a significant number of narrow, attenuated blades, straight and symmetrical in form, blades with burin facets make their appearance here, and the Mousterian tradition continues.

It is still difficult to correlate all the ancient sites in the region, to show all the lines of development, because the Upper Palaeolithic in Central Asia and the adjacent areas of Afghanistan and Pakistan have not yet been sufficiently studied.

Writing of the obvious similarity between Indian Palaeolithic and the culture of Group B in Soviet Central Asia, V. A. Ranov notes also the influence of Group A sites on Indian Palaeolithic – this on the evidence of Sanghao and other Upper and Middle Palaeolithic sites,[36] but the development of ancient cultures in this territory followed its own individual course. In contrast, the Samarkand site and others with a similar stone-tool typology are akin to Siberian and Mongolian localities. All this testifies to great complexity in the development of the Upper Palaeolithic cultures in Central Asia.

The discovery of Late Mousterian sites in southern Siberia has added a new aspect to the problem of sources and lines of development of Late Palaeolithic cultures. The Ust-Kansk site in the Altai Mountains is a case in point.[37] Analysis of its inventory of stone tools has established that it belongs to the Mousterian/Levalloisian tradition.[38] Whether there are examples of Levalloisian is a difficult question. Researchers at first put Shuidonggou and Sjara-osso-gol at the end of the Mousterian period. Now it has been established that all these materials relate to the Upper Palaeolithic. The earliest of them are of the Shuidonggou type. The sites of Chzhiyui and Sjara-osso-gol relate to the final stage of the Upper Palaeolithic.

Insufficient attention has been devoted to the Upper Palaeolithic in the region of Mongolia. At present, several sites can be singled out which, in their general make-up, afford an impression of the final stage of the Palaeolithic in this area (Fig. 4). In the east of the region, the first find of Palaeolithic tools were made in 1967, 20 km north of Choibalsan in the locality of Ulbi Nuur.[39] A further find of Palaeolithic implements was made at the source of the Khuitin-Bulak river, 100 km from Choibalsan in the direction of Halhin-gol, where the road passes through a depression, bounded to east and west by clearly defined terraces, 30–40 m high, their edges indented with gullies of some depth. Towards the middle of the depression, a further terrace, 2–3 m in height, can be seen. Several hundred broken pebbles were found here in a fairly small area, and they can be divided into a number of basic shapes. The majority are pebble tools, chopping-tools and denticulates, made from basalt and andesite pebbles, edge-formed by repeated blows to one side of the pebble. The resultant working edge could be

36. Ranov, 1972, p. 291.
37. Rudenko, 1960, pp. 104–25.
38. Anisyutkin and Astakhov, 1970.
39. Derevyanko and Okladnikov, 1969.

straight, convex or pointed, occasionally with secondary flaking. The butt of the tool retains its pebble cortex. Bifacial chopping-tools, too, were made from heavy pebbles. At one end a wedge-shaped blade was made by chipping both sides and subsequently retouched. This cutting edge of a chopping-tool was carefully fashioned; half, or even two-thirds, of the surface of the tool was hewn and the butt was left intact. Denticulates, too, were made from pebbles, but unlike the chopping-tools, they were formed by chipping not the narrow but the broad end of the pebble; furthermore, the denticulates are rather smaller and are chipped over the entire surface, some on one side only, some on both. Their working edge, which may be straight or oval is retouched.

There are more than twenty cores among the worked pebbles. It is difficult to divide them into distinct categories, though there are Levalloisian cores to be found – discoidal and roughly prismatic. Only one Levalloisian core is well formed and finished. As usual in the Levalloisian tradition, the perimeter of one side has been flaked off. Its striking platform is particularly well formed. This core was prepared for subsequent removal of blades. Some of the discoidal cores could also have been used as denticulates. A few of them had relatively well-prepared striking platforms. The flakes detached were small. Prismatic cores were made from long pebbles one of whose sides was made by transverse chipping into a striking platform which is always slightly askew. Heavy, lamellar flakes were detached from such cores. Among the tools found here there were several picks. Almost all the tools found near the streams were heavily patinated – indirect evidence of their antiquity.

Judging by the finds at Choibalsan and at the source of the Khuitin-Bulak, the formation of the Palaeolithic culture of eastern Mongolia was influenced by two regions: western Mongolia, with its Levalloisian/Mousterian pebble industry; and, as the presence of denticulates of the Siberian type shows, the region of the Yenisey and the Angara.

The Upper Palaeolithic sites of central Mongolia have been studied more thoroughly. One of the most important sites for the surrouding area as well as for Mongolia itself is the many-layered settlement of Moiltyn-am (Cheryomukho-vaya ravine) on the left bank of the Orkhon river (Fig. 4). The settlement is situated opposite the ruins of Karakorum, ancient capital of the Mongol khans. The settlement was discovered in 1949 by A. P. Okladnikov.[40]

The stone tools found are of the same period as the loess deposits in the second terrace of the Orkhon valley.[41] The terrace has two levels. The lower level (10–12 m) was formed without significant interruption or change in conditions. The distinctive features of this level of the terrace are its great width and flatness and the composition of the river deposits.

40. Okladnikov, 1962, 1964, 1981; Okladnikov and Larichev, 1963.
41. Okladnikov and Troitskiy, 1967.

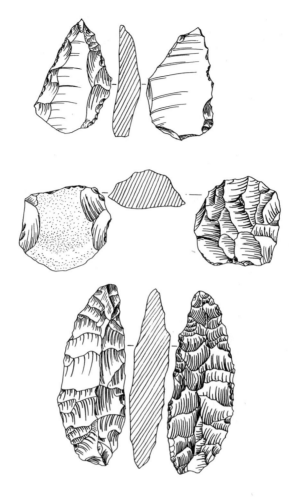

FIG. 5. Stone tools from Sangino, Mongolia.

The second level of this terrace extends from 20 to 14 m above the level of the river. The base of the terrace consists of heavy, alluvial deposits of shingle covered with a series of further deposits. Man first settled the diluvial-proluvial strip alongside the old channel – this strip was the foundation of the second level of the terrace – before its flat surface was covered by the floods.

Excavation has uncovered five cultural horizons, and this allows us to follow the process of development in the form and manufacture of stone tools from the first to the last stage of the Upper Palaeolithic. Okladnikov concluded that an overall conformity and a single line of development ran through all the cultural horizons of Moiltyn-am. This continuity is to be seen in the fact that all layers contain cores of the Levalloisian tradition – discoidal, pebble and prismoidal – as well as scratchers, scrapers, awls and other implements.

Notwithstanding this stability in form and formation of stone tools, significant changes can be observed. The first and most important phenomena are the appearance in the fourth layer of the oblong core, and its subsequent development, as well as the appearance of scratchers with a convex working edge. It is highly significant that the number of items made from knife-shaped blades increases as we move from the lowest cultural horizon to the highest. The blades themselves take on a regular shape and progressively diminish in size. Thus the stone tool inventory tends to become microlithic. Furthermore the upper cultural horizons show an increase in the number of items with delicate retouch and secondary flaking to improve the shape.

The earliest horizons of Moiltyn-am evidently belong to the very beginning of the Upper Palaeolithic and their stone tools and cores are typologically very close to the Mousterian. The third layer shows the formation of a system of forms which were common to a large part of Mongolia and are also similar to Upper Palaeolithic remains in the Altai and southern Siberia. The topmost horizon belongs to the last phase of the Upper Palaeolithic, and Okladnikov dates it to between 15,000 and 12,000–10,000 years ago.

Roughly contemporaneous with the lower layers of Moiltyn-am are sites such as Zausan Tolotoi near Ulan Bator, Sangino, the lowest horizon on the Uliastai river and on the heights of Bulun-Khujin. The Levalloisian/Mousterian tradition is typical of all these sites, though stone tools characteristic of the Upper Palaeolithic already prevail (Fig. 5).

The subsequent stage in the history of the ancient peoples of Mongolia is connected with the finds on the lower level of the second terrace. The cultural level of these sites is connected not with the yellow, diluvial stratum of sandy soil and loam left by the Ice Age (which relates to the low layers at Moiltyn-am), but with the brown-soil horizon. This latter stage is also associated with the upper horizons of the Moiltyn-am settlements, as well as with Sangino sites similar to Sharakho I, and other sites.

The last phase of the Palaeolithic and the transition to Mesolithic are represented by the material excavated at Khere-Uul Mountain in eastern Mongolia.[42] The settlement is situated on an eminence next to a terrace of up to 60 m in height which rises from the Halhin-gol river valley. On the western slope of the eminence there are eroded patches which have now become largely covered in turf. Excavations were conducted on this western slope. Discoveries were made at a depth of 40–60 cm beneath the present surface in a layer of sandy loam containing small amounts of humus.

The Khere-Uul settlement displays a new phase in the development of human culture: the evolution of the blade techniques. Most of the tools were made from fairly small, regular, knife-shaped blades. These were generally detached from oblong or wedge-shaped cores. Blade techniques were widely used

42. Okladnikov, 1974.

throughout Central, East and North Asia at the end of the Pleistocene and the beginning of the Holocene. This coincided with profound changes in the natural environment.

The atmosphere was becoming warmer, and the mammoth and animals associated with it retreated northwards and finally became totally extinct. At the same time man was advancing from south to north, going as far as America; this is demonstrated by the diffusion over a vast area of many common elements in the stone-tool culture and techniques of ancient peoples.

The discovery of paintings in the cave of Khoist-Tsenker-Agui was of great importance in determining the cultural level of the tribes in Mongolia at the end of the Palaeolithic. The cave is situated 23 km south-west of Monhhaan somon in the Mongolian Altai.[43] It formed within impressive deposits of limestone and gypsum. The floor at the entrance is piled high with massive blocks of the entrance arch which, at some stage, partially collapsed. The cave floor drops steeply away from the entrance. The roof rises like the gigantic dome of some underground cathedral, and its steep cornices hang down like stalactites.

The paintings were found in peculiar niches. The artists apparently had to draw while lying down in an awkward position. Most of the paintings were done on even rock surfaces and, because these were not extensive, the paintings partly overlap. In some places there is a complete interweaving of strangely stylized animal figures: horses, goats, bulls and birds. One composition, done in red, attracts special attention. It portrays several mountain goats in the most varied attitudes. Some running headlong, others preparing for a vertiginous leap, while others still are resting in calm, relaxed postures. The horns of the animals, too, are shown in different ways; some beasts with barely noticeable horns drawn in short, sparse lines, others with proudly uplifted, convoluted spirals. The most striking things in this Stone Age gallery are the images of large birds with enormous bodies and long, curved necks, as well as the pictures of powerful beasts with a clearly drawn long trunk. The birds bear a striking resemblance to ostriches. The animal with the trunk is either an elephant or a mammoth.

The cave paintings of Khoist-Tsenker-Agui show a cultural, historical and artistic world that is bright and completely individual. They express the different aesthetic traditions of the art of ancient Mongolia. The most significant feature of western Mongolian cave paintings taken as a whole is the absence of representation of human beings. This art is completely and exclusively devoted to the depiction of animals. The artists were confronted with a world of wild, undomesticated animals that inhabited the steppe and the desert of Central Asia, and they regarded this world whose life supported theirs not with detachment but with the passionate eye of the hunter.

The manner in which the particular animals are represented in the various cave paintings of Khoist-Tsenker is especially important when we come to

43. Okladnikov, 1972, p. 75; Derevyanko, 1980.

consider themes common to both Mongolian cave paintings and the Palaeolithic art of the distant west. Among the animals depicted in cave painting in western Mongolia an elephant-like beast, understandably, occupies a special place. Two Khoist-Tsenker drawings of an animal with a trunk are, in all probability, drawings of an elephant: the typical eastern namadicus elephant rather than the northern mammoth. On one of the drawings, tusks as well as a trunk are distinctly visible.

The horse, a classical subject occurring frequently in western Palaeolithic painting, is to be found in only one drawing at Khoist-Tsenker, and even then its aspect is strange: it has no head, and two tails. Although many of the same animals are depicted both in western European Palaeolithic art and in the paintings at Khoist-Tsenker, one marked discrepancy is obvious: among all the paintings in France and Spain, there is not one depicting a camel. Yet the two-humped, or bactrian, camel of the Khoist-Tsenker cave is a natural, almost necessary subject, for this area was its home. Since the Tertiary period this animal had inhabited the dry, arid wastes of Central Asia. It fits as naturally into the basic selection, the repertoire of wall paintings in Central Asia and southern Siberia as the one-humped camel, or dromedary, 'the ship of the desert' and features in wall paintings scattered over a wide area of the Sinai peninsula and North Africa.

In Inner Mongolia and Ningxia Muslim Autonomous Regions, during the Late Pleistocene epoch, the weather gradually became colder and drier, and loess deposits were formed. There are many deposits of fine sand and much low-lying land, and rivers and marshes. It is particularly in the general area of the southern foothills of the Yin mountain range that rivers and lakes were formed which attracted animals and men.[44] Of the human fossils and cultures of the Late Palaeolithic era found in this region the most important are: Hetao man, the Shuidonggou site, the Sjara-osso-gol river site and the Dayao culture.

Hetao man is the term used for the human fossils of the initial stage of the Late Palaeolithic era.[45] Teilhard de Chardin and E. Licent discovered a human upper-left outer incisor in a layer of gravel on the bank of the Sjara-osso-gol river in the Yikezaho league of Inner Mongolia. The tooth is very well preserved, the crown has not been eroded and the root has not reached maturity; it is similar to that of a modern child. Because of the protrusion of the two sides of the lingual surface of the molar, the centre of this surface is concave, or shovel-shaped and bears the charateristics of present-day Mongolian teeth. D. Black has done preliminary research on this tooth and named it Hetao man. In 1957 the Inner Mongolian Museum found a fossil human parietal bone and a section of a femur in terrace deposits near the village of Dishaogouwan, again on the Sjara-osso-gol river in the Yikezhao league of Inner Mongolia. The thickness of the parietal

44. Pei, 1960; Zhou, 1955.
45. Jia, 1953; Wo, 1958.

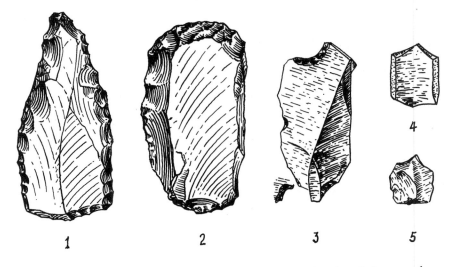

FIG. 6. Stone tools from Shuidonggou, China: 1 – pointed tool; 2 – round-top scraper; 3–5 – burins (original size).

indicates that it approximates to that of Neanderthal man and is larger than that of contemporary man. Traces of pressure of the artery branches on the inside of the parietal bone were greater on the back branch than on the front, further indicating primitivity. The wall of the femur is thick and the marrow cavity small, representing only a third of the diameter. It seems that the characteristics of the femur and the parietal bones must belong to the category of *Homo sapiens* and are human fossils of the early part of the Late Palaeolithic era.

The Shuidonggou site is in Lingwa county 45 km south-east of Yiunchuan city in Ningxia.[46] This site was first excavated in 1922. In 1957, 1963 and 1980 there have been geological surveys and fairly systematic excavations in this area. From top to bottom the local deposits divide into red soil, loess, and gravel deposits of the post-loess period. The culture stratum is in the loess layer at a depth of about 12 m from the surface and is about 50 cm thick.

Cultural remains are a layer of ashes, chipped stone implements and burnt fragments of bone, together with mammalian fossils including the Asian wild ass (*Equus hemionus*), the hyena (*Crocuta ultima*), rhinoceros (*Coelodonta antiquitatis*) and gazelle (*Gazella sp.*).

The stone implements of Shuidonggou, which are considered to belong to the early part of the Late Palaeolithic, are numerous; the principal material of which they are made is red quartzite. This material comes from the gravel layer at the base of the loess. By working at the stone core it was possible to produce regularly formed stone flakes, and the implements made were very fine. They

46. Wang, 1962; Jia et al., 1964.

104

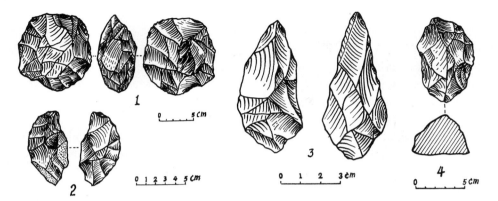

FIG. 7. Stone tools of the Dayao Culture, China: 1 – chopping tools;
2 – scrapers; 3 – pointed tools; 4 – turtle-back shaped scraper.

include points, scrapers and choppers, and clearing tools. Pointed tools of very uniform quality were made with stone flakes. All are made by running the two edges of the stone flakes from the broken face towards the back face, the tip being thus formed into a sharp point. The working is of high quality. These are standard artefacts of the Shuidonggou culture (Fig. 6). The scrapers are for the most part made from stone flakes and various forms of straight, concave, convex and hull-shaped blades. There are also a few which are made from small pebbles. The material for the chopping-tools is always quartzite pebbles using a technique of chipping from both sides to form a curved blade, with the butt being preserved in its pebble cortex to facilitate holding. Cutting implements are made with stone flakes and they are all very small. However, they are very numerous and of uniform manufacture. There are two forms, beak-shape and ridge-shape.

The Sjara-osso-gol river valley used to be very deep, around 65 m below the present ground surface. The two banks of the river are formed from deposits of fine yellow and light-blue sand, with earth in between. This layer of thick sand is situated directly upon a red Mesozoic sandstone. At about 45 m below the surface, stone implements and many animal fossils have been discovered. Stone artefacts found on the Sjara-osso-gol river site were not numerous. The material is largely quartzite, with a small amount of black flint. These tools are very small, and there is a characteristic range of microlithic forms, including pointed implements, many kinds of scrapers and cutting implements.

Forty-five species of animal fossils have been found. The more important include the hyena, rhinoceros, Asian wild ass, Mongolian wild horse, wild boar, camel, deer, including the Hetao flat-antler giant deer, gazelle, twisted-horn gazelle, water buffalo, primitive ox, elephant and ostrich. The presence of this range of animals indicates that the Sjara-osso-gol river area was not then as dry as it is now; it suggests a grassy and wooded environment. From the extent of the lake deposits it appears that the lake of that time was larger than at present, and in the light-blue sand layers there is a large quantity of shell fossils, which indicates a proliferation of water plants. The two banks of the Sjara-osso-gol river encompassed a wide stretch of grassland, and by the lakes there grew grass and trees forming the habitat of the water buffalo and the primitive ox. The Hetao flat-antler giant deer, the deer *Cervus canadensis*, the wild boar, gazelle, wild ass and wild horse would have lived on the grassy plains, and this environment must have been an excellent hunting-ground for primitive man.

The Dayao culture includes the stone tools (Fig. 7) of the Late Palaeolithic era found in 1973 in the eastern suburbs of the city of Huhhot in Inner Mongolia. One site is on the Nanshan at Dayao village of Baoheshao commune, 33 km north-east of Huhhot. The second site is at the Naobao bridge of the Qian Nai-moban village, Yulin commune, 30 km east of Huhhot. Both sites are in the foothills of the Daqing mountain and are separated by 10 km on a north–south axis.

The Nanshan of the Dayao village is formed by granite gneiss of the Archean group: it is 1,420 m above sea-level and rises about 200 m above the river-bed. On the summit and half-way up the hill are scattered flint fragments. On the northern slope at a height of 1,330 m above sea-level loess begins to appear and these deposits increase in thickness as the slope descends, to link up with the plain below the hill. There are two large ravines on the southern slope of the Nanshan: the northern one is called the Tuershan ravine, the southern the Nanliang ravine. The deposits of the two ravines are similar. At both the base and upper-middle part of the loess there is a layer of flint flakes, chips, implements and half-made tools, the products of human labour. At the base it is fairly thick reaching a maximum of 1 m, while the upper layer is rather thin, 5–20 cm. In the loess there were found animal fossils of gazelle, species of deer, and finally hyena and rhinoceros: they are of Late Pleistocene period, which coincides with Late Palaeolithic.

On the slope and summit close to the head of the Nanliang ravine there stand a great number of huge blocks of flint (the largest of them is 4 m high, 3 m broad, and 2 m thick). Virtually all of them bear evidence of stones being chipped against them. Wherever blocks of flint appear the slope around is strewn with pieces of flint, large and small stone flakes, stone chips and broken stone implements, all the result of human work. This is to be found all over a very large area; from a preliminary survey the area is about 3 million m². On the slope between the Nanliang ravine and the northern Tuershan ravine, in the last years of the Qing dynasty and the early years of the Republic the local people opened pits and dug trenches to collect flints of good quality from the culture layers to sell as fire flints and marketed them as far away as Beijing. Today there remain over thrity pits, and their perimeters are strewn with blocks of flint, stone flakes, and broken stone implements dug from the layers. Dayao village became known through the cutting of pits to collect flints.

At another factory site – Naobaoliang at Naimoban – apart from a layer of purple clay which appeared between the red clay and the base-rock, the geo-morphology, stratigraphy and typology of the stone artefacts and their characte-ristics are otherwise very similar to the Dayao industry.

The Nanshan at Dayao village and the Naobaoling at Qian Naimoban are both ridges extending from the Daqing mountain to the foothills. These face the wide flatlands, and the Dahei and Xiaohei rivers both flow near by. From the loess deposits and an analysis of the spores we can deduce that the climate of that time was comparatively dry and cold, and the environment one of grasslands with grassy marsh and scrub. There was a profusion of forest on the Daqing mountain, while on the foothills there were small patches of forest and woody scrubland, and on the whole area of upland and plain, wild grasses grew thickly. There is no doubt that this environment was suitable for human habitation. In the Dayao culture the numbers of chopping tools and scrapers are greatest: they may have been used to cut down trees, and by hafting on a wooden club they may have become instruments to aid hunting. The stone ball could be a throwing implement to catch wild animals. Every shape of turtle-backed scraper with its thick back and flat base may have served to process animal hides. The Dayao stone tools are lacking in large pointed implements: possibly the gathering economy occupied a secondary position. An analysis of the totality of cultural remains suggests that men of that period lived mainly by hunting and that gather-ing was a supplementary activity.

The two stone implement factories are separated by 10 km: the breadth of this area and the depth of the cultural strata tell us that the human population of that period was considerable and that they lived in this district for a long time. From the continuity of the cultural strata, which both the base and middle-upper section of the loess have cultural relics of the Late Palaeolithic, and where there is a rich microlithic culture distributed in the topsoil and on the surface, it can be seen that, in this region, from Late Palaeolithic to Neolithic times man was cut-ting primary rock to make stone artefacts.

From 1963 stone implements and large quantities of animal fossils of the Late Palaeolithic have also been found at Loufangzi, Quzi commune, Huan county, and at Jujiayuan, Wenquan commune, Qingyang county, both places being in Gansu province.

Cultural relics of this period have not yet been found in the Xinjiang Uighur Autonomous Region. However at the time of writing it was learnt that recently, at Agu in Atusha county, Xinjiang, there has been found a human skull and several fragments of skull. A preliminary estimate has assigned these to the Late Palaeolithic era. There has not yet been any proper survey or research.

At Kekexili in Zhiduo county, Qinghai province, and at Dingri county in Tibet stone implements of the Late Palaeolithic era have also been found. Owing to the paucity of material the question of their cultural origin still awaits further research.

Conclusion

The materials described in this chapter testify to the development of the Central Asian region in Upper Palaeolithic times. Technical progress is very noticeable in methods of production of flint tools, such as thin blades of accurate contours capable of being inserted in handles made of horn or wood. Working edges of such tools were very effective. The cultural particularity of Central Asia manifests itself, where a new technology of tool production combined with the archaic traditions of the Middle Palaeolithic epoch. The development of arts testifying to the noticeable intellectual achievement of humanity was an important feature of the new era. The main sites of cave painting of the Upper Palaeolithic are concentrated in western Europe, but now, as it becomes clear, they are also found in the territory of Central Asia. Soviet archaeologists discovered cave painting in the Urals. The Khoist-Tsenker cave paintings in Mongolia also form an important site in terms of Upper Palaeolithic art. The increasing economic and cultural potential of the ancient inhabitants of Central Asia allowed them to create such outstanding works of art.

Food-producing and other Neolithic communities in Khorasan and Transoxania: eastern Iran, Soviet Central Asia and Afghanistan[1]

V. Sarianidi

C LIMATIC changes on the boundary of the Pleistocene and Holocene periods produced a somewhat warmer, moister climate in the greater part of western Asia. The different ecological conditions provided prehistoric man with more stable food supplies and led to a sharp increase in his numbers. The regular collection of wild cereals led to the empirical breeding and selection of types that could be cultivated artificially, and the domestication of animals to stockbreeding.

The global climatic changes of the Late Pleistocene and the first half of the Holocene were not without local incidence in the Caspian region. Here the early Holocene coincided with the deep Mangishlak regression of the tenth and ninth millennia B.C. Since palynological, palaeontological, geochemical and palaeo-graphical evidence bears out the postulate that the Caspian regressions were arid periods, these two millennia must be considered unfavourable to the develop-ment of an economy of production in these parts. By and large the change to ara-ble farming and livestock rearing that goes with it is associated with lasting periods of moist, warm weather. Neither, on the whole, do Mesolithic remains in the south and western of the Caspian region provide incontrovertible proof that elements of the new economy developed in that period. And that accords well with palaeogeographical suppositions.

An equally direct coincidence may be seen in the subsequent epoch. In the eighth millennium B.C. the Mangishlak regression gave way to the neo-Caspian transgression. In the Caspian region, this was the Atlantic Interval, that part of the Holocene when the climate reached its optimum: moisture was markedly more abundant, and the semi-desert or desert landscapes of the Mangishlak period gave way to areas of arid steppe covered with mixed grass, cereals and some clusters of trees. It is clearly no mere chance that the earliest known

---

1. See Map 4.

remains of an economy of production in this region relate to the sixth millennium B.C.

In the early phase of the change to a production-based economy, it was essential that wild plants of a kind suitable for domestication should be available. One area where this was so is approximately that part of western Asia which, long before the term 'Neolithic revolution' came into use, N. I. Vavilov[2] identified as a main source of cultivated plants.

The change to farming and stock-keeping, in other words, the change to an economy of production, played a critical role in the history of the rise of human society. In the case of western Asia, this theory was first formulated by R. Braidwood,[3] whose work was seminal to the development of V. G. Childe's concept of the 'Neolithic revolution'.[4] It postulates a dramatic leap in the development of the prehistoric economy from reliance on gathering and hunting to working the soil and rearing animals. From merely commandeering the products of nature, man moved on to producing them. Early farming and stockbreeding became the principal methods of producing food, that essential first step that was in the long run to lead mankind to civilization.

The advent of the production-based economy entails two indispensable prerequisites: favourable natural conditions and a highly developed society, implying a sophisticated technology, great density of population and an advanced economy of the commandeering type. These two categories merge and interact, and only through a combination of social and natural factors was the new type of economy brought about. At the initial phase, the greatest importance attached to the availability of the original wild animals and plants for domestication, and likewise to a numerical increase in population, so that the older commandeering kind of economy could no longer meet its needs. In other words, acute necessity prompted the economic breakthrough, and only the enormous impact of land and animal husbandry could guarantee that individual groups would survive.

The triumph of the economy of production does not exclude gathering, hunting and fishing, it presupposes them, though their role becomes secondary to that of land and animal husbandry. Starting some 10,000 years ago, this process signalled a crucial shift in the development of mankind.

Seasonal camps, caves, rock shelters and grottoes gave way to the first permanent settlements with houses built of sun-baked bricks, ushering in the final triumph of the sedentary life-style over nomadism. The gradual domestication of sheep and goats and the growing of cultivated wheat and barley provided the reliable food resources needed for a settled way of life. Because of the more varied diet there was need for storage supplied by pots, made first of stone but shortly afterwards of clay. Their manufacture denotes more sophisticated techniques for

2. Vavilov, 1967.
3. Braidwood, 1952.
4. Childe, 1941.

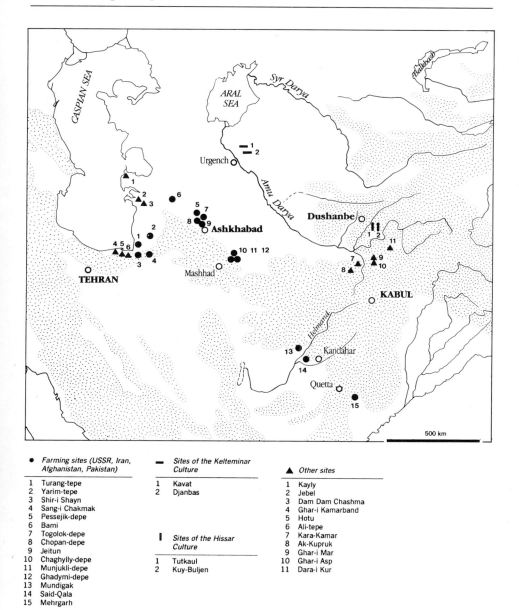

	Farming sites (USSR, Iran, Afghanistan, Pakistan)		Sites of the Kelteminar Culture		Other sites
1	Turang-tepe	1	Kavat	1	Kayly
2	Yarim-tepe	2	Djanbas	2	Jebel
3	Shir-i Shayn			3	Dam Dam Chashma
4	Sang-i Chakmak			4	Ghar-i Kamarband
5	Pessejik-depe			5	Hotu
6	Bami			6	Ali-tepe
7	Togolok-depe		Sites of the Hissar Culture	7	Kara-Kamar
8	Chopan-depe			8	Ak-Kupruk
9	Jeitun	1	Tutkaul	9	Ghar-i Mar
10	Chaghylly-depe	2	Kuy-Buljen	10	Ghar-i Asp
11	Munjukli-depe			11	Dara-i Kur
12	Ghadymi-depe				
13	Mundigak				
14	Said-Qala				
15	Mehrgarh				

Map 4. Early agricultural sites of Central Asia.

111

the preparation, processing and storage of food. The increased cultivation of the soil led to a wide range of farming implements, stone hoes, flint sickle blades, or querns.

There was a marked growth in intercommunal links, commerce expanded, economic and cultural relationship and even the concepts of productive techniques or specialized implements were carried ever further afield. Land and animal husbandry sharply reduced the amount of labour spent on producing foodstuffs, leading to the appearance of additional or surplus produce: together, these factors enabled man to make more use of his intellectual faculties and develop them. Consequently, there was a widening of ideological horizons that gained physical expression in the applied arts, while the structures of society also became more complex. Contacts between communities and cross-cultural influences caused bodies of men to unite in larger groups – a movement that was subsequently to play a great part in the ethnic history of mankind.

There were several centres in western Asia where the transition to a Neolithic economy is traceable – primarily in northern Iraq and western Iran. Similar centres have now been identified in Asia Minor and Jordan/Palestine, where elements of the production-based economy may be traced back to the Mesolithic cultures of the tenth to eighth millennia B.C.[5] The earliest evidence of these changes in Central Asia comes from Mehrgarh in Pakistan (see Chapter 6). Somewhat later, in the sixth, if not the seventh, millennium B.C., clear evidence of that system is revealed in the archaeological remains of the area.

We shall start our survey with north-eastern Iran, where the trend towards an economy of production set in as early as the Mesolithic period, and where a particular Caspian centre of that economy is felt to have existed. In the mountain caves and rock shelters of this region, the detritus of past cultures still lies in strata several metres thick, a testimony to the presence of hunters and fishermen since the Early Mesolithic. A case in point is Ghar-i Karmarband (Belt cave), where the Early Mesolithic strata dating from the tenth to eighth millennia B.C. have preserved geometrical flint tools, including large assymetrical trapezes whose sides are frequently concave. It is supposed that some, if not all, of the flint tools may have been used as parts of composite arrow – or javelin – heads, and this is borne out by the animal remains which include the bones of Persian gazelles, wild bulls and reindeer.[6] Apparently the Mesolithic hunters went down to the plains for game, and they are thought to have already made good use of hunting dogs.

Sophisticated ideological concepts are revealed by the tomb of a girl whose body, found in the Middle Mesolithic strata, was sprinkled with red ochre. As in the preceding period, the game was the Persian gazelle, bull and reindeer. Judging by the prevalence of gazelle bones, particularly in the Late Mesolithic strata, this

5. Mellaart, 1975.
6. Coon, 1951.

was probably the main quarry. The ornaments found include pendants of polished stone or animal teeth and pierced shells. Of particular interest is the discovery of clay cones, providing documentary evidence of the fact that the people of Ghar-i Kamarband were familiar with this soft and pliable material at an early stage. The lack of clay vessels, however, is also telling, since it shows that these were the first experiments in the use of chemically transformed material, shortly to lead to the invention of the earliest pottery.

Indirect evidence and the kind of bone remnants found suggest that in the late period of settlement at Ghar-i Kamarband the hunters were already making their first attempts to domesticate sheep and goats. In Hotu, another cave in the Caspian region, the Mesolithic strata were similarly found to contain flint tools bound up with hunting, but also small clay cones and what may be a schematic sculpture of a woman. Excavations in a further cave, Ali-tepe,[7] have shown that wild goats and sheep were hunted in the southern Caspian region even earlier, in the twelfth and eleventh millennia B.C., and that climatic changes in the level of the Caspian Sea affected quite considerably the kind of game pursued. Evidence has been unearthed which shows that man was forced to alter his hunting methods and quarry, for instance at the start of the Holocene, when seals, gazelles, goats and sheep were the chief quarry, though in Ghar-i Kamarband, gazelles account for 70 per cent and sheep and goats just 4 per cent of the Late Mesolithic bones, indicating that the bulk of the meat in the cave-dwellers' diet came from the gazelle.

Although there is no direct proof that animals were domesticated in the Mesolithic period, there are weighty reasons for supposing that in the Neolithic period this process was complete. This necessarily implies a previous phase starting in the Late Mesolithic. Be that as it may, in north-eastern Iran the change from a commandeering economy to one of production may quite definitely be dated if not to the seventh then to the sixth millennium B.C. The first indirect evidence was found during excavations of the Turang-tepe settlement in the Gorgan valley. Although the high level of groundwater placed the Neolithic cultural remains in the lowest strata of Turang-tepe beyond reach, the excavator J. Deshayes, succeeded in identifying the earliest complex, Turang-tepe I,[8] from tiny ceramic fragments found in the raw brick of later structures. This he quite rightly compared with the remains of the Neolithic culture of Jeitun in neighbouring Turkmenistan rather than that of Sialk in central Iran. One can only add, for the sake of accuracy, that the ceramic samples rather correspond to the later phase of the Jeitun culture.

Another settlement in the Gorgan valley, Yarim-tepe, near Gonbad-i Kavus, also contains at the base of the mound strata of material typical of the Jeitun culture. The similarity is so obvious that the existence of a Neolithic

7. McBurney, 1968.
8. Deshayes, 1967.

settlement of the prehistoric agricultural type, with a production-based economy, can no longer be in doubt.

Turang-tepe and Yarim-tepe provide indirect evidence that in the sixth millennium B.C. the Gorgan valley contained scattered early agricultural settlements that were based fully on production, and in very recent years similar evidence has been found at the settlement of Sang-i Chakmak (flint stone).[9] This evidence comes from several mounds in the fertile alluvial plain of Gorgan near the southern slopes of the Elburz mountains. Only two have been investigated, and of these, the western, some 3 m high with five cultural strata, is specially relevant to our study. In all the strata, floors of former buildings have been found, covered with a lime plaster sometimes stained with red, or made of plain beaten earth. There were two distinct types of structure; some had a raised fireplace and frequently smoke-blackened walls, while others, with no fireplace, took the shape of small rooms with carefully rendered floors. In one such small building in the second stratum, heavily stylized clay figurines were discovered. Additionally, excavations have revealed small bone fibulae and pins, flint flakes, microliths and cores. Most importantly, however, obsidian blades were found. Only three ceramic sherds were unearthed: two on the surface of the mound and one in the third stratum. When it is realized that as much as 300 m² of this stratum has been cleared, it is obvious that the people of western mound, if indeed they knew how to make pottery, were at the very first stage of this discovery.

The eastern mound, 150 m from the western, is far larger, from the excavations of the second to fifth strata, the settlements of that period consisting of dwellings and ancillary buildings, often with a small work area and stove. Most of the buildings were rectangular and made of clay blocks 70 × 20 cm, bringing to mind the similar techniques used in the Jeitun culture in southern Turkmenistan. In the upper stratum, three tombs containing the bodies of women and infants were discovered, while the skull of a further young woman was covered with a decorated pot of a type known from the central Iranian settlement of Sialk II.

Quite large quantities of ceramics were found in the eastern mound, indicating that clay vessels were widely used in everyday life. The bulk of the decorated samples bore geometrical patterns, including criss-crossing, horizontal and vertical parallel lines, painted red or dark brown against a cream or reddish background. On the pottery of the upper (later) strata for instance, animal motifs, of which there are none in the lower strata, were used to decorate vessels. Additionally, there were what may be described as personal requisites made of bone or stone, together with clay cones, spindles, clay or stone animal statuettes, bone pins, polished stone axes, flint flakes and microliths. Of particular interest are wooden sickle handles decorated with animal pictures found in the fourth and fifth strata. The entire stock of finds from the eastern mound bears most direct and telling analogies with the evidence of the lowest stratum at Yarim-tepe

9. Masuda, 1974.

and especially with the Neolithic Jeitun culture.[10] The western mound seems to be older than the eastern, and may well reflect a transitional period in the rise of the production-based economy in the Gorgan valley.

For all its meagreness and partiality, the evidence cited incontrovertibly shows that this fertile valley held a large number of prehistoric agricultural settlements. In this regard, the material from the settlement of Shir-i Shayn near the east Iranian site of Hissar is revealing, containing as it does ceramics that closely resemble and possibly predate those in the lower strata of Hissar.

All this pottery is hand-made, and some is decorated with simple line patterns such as zigzags, to some extent reminiscent of the pottery of Jeitun. Exploratory digs have unearthed no prehistoric structures. This does not, however, necessarily imply a temporary encampment, but may be explained by the limited scale of the excavations. At the same time, the absence of any trace of metal is very significant, since it identifies Shir-i Shayn as an early agricultural site previous to the oldest periods of Hissar.

Be that as it may, the fact that one and the same historical and geographical region contained both Late Mesolithic caves of hunters and gatherers and sedentary villages whose population had already acquired an economy of production is suggestive. Most of the animals pursued by the Mesolithic hunters lived on the plains, and this permits us to suppose that man regularly moved from the upland grottoes, shelters and caves to the foothills and lesser river valleys and then to the Gorgan plain. In this regard particular note is due to the material of the western mound at Sang-i Chakmak, where the small clay cones suggest a link with the Mesolithic caves of the Caspian region, while the same cones and individual pots point to a change from the pre-pottery to the pottery Neolithic, the archaeological complex of which is most fully and vividly represented in the Jeitun culture, as it is called. Thus the material itself leads us from north-eastern Iran to southern Turkmenistan, with the Gorgan valley as the natural geographical link between the two.

Although the settlements of the Jeitun culture stretched in a chain of almost 700 km along the northern foothills of the Kopet Dag, it is revealing that the earliest sites lie close to the Caspian region where, as in north-eastern Iran, there are also Mesolithic caves. The Kayly, Jebel and Dam Dam Chashma caves, were used by hunters as seasonal shelters even in the Early Mesolithic period (tenth to seventh millennia B.C.). Their quarry was chiefly smaller animals such as goats, sheep or Persian gazelles. In the earliest strata of Kayly, a bone needle with an eye was found with which the local hunters may have sewn clothing or footwear from dressed hides.

In both the Jebel cave and in Dam Dam Chashma II, however, domesticated animals appear comparatively late, possibly suggesting that they arrived here in a fully domesticated form. In Dam Dam Chashma, for instance, the bones

10. Masson, 1971.

of a domesticated goat or sheep may be found only in Stratum IV and in Jebel only in Strata III–IV of the Neolithic period. And although wild goats and sheep had roamed these parts since time immemorial, the domesticated varieties appear to have descended, as several biological features show, not from the local strains but from those of western Asia. These and certain other archaeological observations suggest that domesticated animals reached the Caspian region together with people spreading northwards from regions closely involved in the early stages of domestication.

Although the initial phases of the economy of production in the Caspian centre of prehistoric agriculture are still not fully known, the remains of the Jeitun culture, already mentioned several times, paint a vivid picture of the Neolithic economy of the sixth millennium B.C. in the extreme south-west of Soviet Central Asia, in southern Turkmenistan (Fig. 1).

The settlements of this ancient farming culture stretch in a long, if broken, chain along the northern foothills of the Kopet Dag, with the result that over twenty sites are now known, divided into three geographical groups. The western group includes the settlement of Bami, Naysa-depe and the ceramics at the Baga well. The central group is more numerous, including eponymous Jeitun, Chopan-depe, Togolok-depe, Pessejik-depe, New Nisa and isolated finds of pottery at the wells of Kelyata, Kepele, Kantar and Yarty Gumbaz. The eastern group is made up of sites such as Chaghylly-depe, Munjukli and Ghadymi.

These settlements are located in a region with a predominantly dry desert climate and little precipitation. Significantly, most of them were built along the banks of small but permanent water-courses, chiefly mountain streams, which alone could enable settled farming communities to survive. Special palaeographical studies have proved that in prehistoric times this arid zone could not have been farmed without irrigation, most probably by what is called the catchment technique, which uses simple banks to retain flood-water, or channels to divert it as required. It has long been argued that this method involves a minimum of labour, since the seed is sown when the earth is still moist and hence sinks by itself into the liquid alluvial silt. The simplicity of the agricultural technology practised by the people of this culture may well explain their limited range of farming implements. It may be seen at its fullest in the completely excavated settlement of Jeitun. With an area of 5,000 m², it stands on a sand-dune in the Kara Kum desert, 30 km north of Ashkhabad. It is made up of free-standing houses strikingly uniform in ground plan.

Generally speaking, the houses were rectangular, with a large fireplace on one wall and a niche facing it; the floors were often covered with a lime plaster, and traces of a black or red rendering were sometimes found. Outside were small ancillary structures completely surrounded with walls, most probably used as farmsteads. These were less carefully and painstakingly built than the houses. All the structures were built of cylindrical clay blocks up to 70 cm long and 20–25 cm thick. The clay was mixed with finely chopped straw, and the cylinders them-

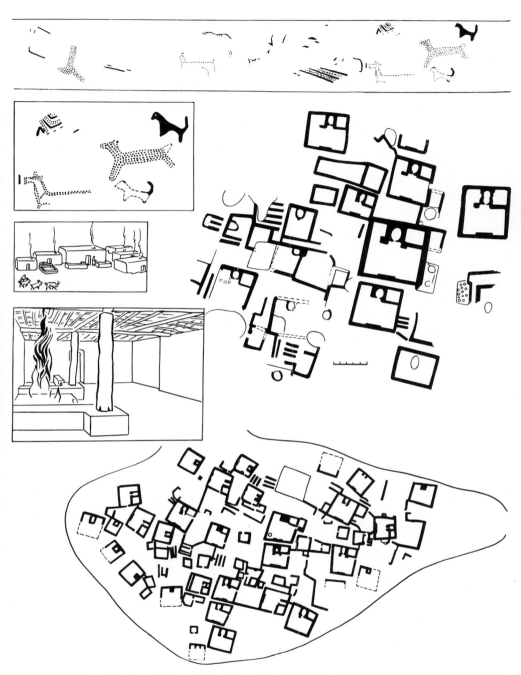

FIG. 1. Jeitun culture: plan of settlements and reconstructions.

selves were bonded together in the walls with a clay mix. The settlements contained a total of 30–35 single-roomed homes with their ancillary premises, and in all some 160–200 people lived there at any one time. It is further thought that each house was the home of a nuclear family of five to six members, and that together they may have formed a tribal settlement. None the less, the economy appears to have been communal rather than individual.

This layout is repeated with striking similarity at the other sites, even the settlements of the eastern group such as Chaghylly, more than 300 km from Jeitun. Here too, the Neolithic settlement was built of one-roomed houses with a wall fireplace within and ancillary structures outside. Although the buildings were made of cylindrical clay blocks, at a later stage, rectangular bricks came into use and in the subsequent Chalcolithic period, were used to the exclusion of all other techniques.

A particular place among the lesser settlements of southern Turkmenistan goes to Pessejik-depe,[11] which had, in the middle of its standard one-roomed houses, a special building larger than the rest. It was set apart, and its overall area was some 65 m². Everything – the massive walls, the careful white alabaster screening of the floor and the almost total absence of the usual household objects – emphasizes its special purpose. As in the other houses, there was an enormous fireplace on one wall while the facing wall, from which a lunar moulding protruded, was covered with mural paintings. One can still see the geometrical patterns combined with animal figures (thought to be snow leopards) painted in black or red against the snow-white stucco. It has been quite plausibly suggested that this was a public building, a kind of communal or tribal centre intended for the needs of the entire settlement. Here we have some of the oldest mural paintings, pointing not only to the greater ideological sophistication, but also to the high cultural standard of the local tribes, reminiscent in some degree of the Çatal-hüyuk frescoes in southern Turkey.

The people of the Jeitun culture were arable farmers, growing two-rowed barley (*Hordeum distichum*), soft wheat (*Triticum vulgare*) and club wheat (*Triticum compactum*) in their fields. Making use of natural water courses and often practising catchment irrigation the population would till the soil for their crops with digging-sticks. In all probability, stone hoes of the kind found here in the subsequent Early Chalcolithic period were used.

Wheat and barley were harvested with wooden or bone reaping knives or sickles with inset stone blades like those found at Chopan-depe. At Jeitun, almost every house was found to contain such blades, implying that virtually the entire population took part in farming work. The early forms of comparatively recently domesticated cereals had a hard husk, and were probably roasted to help separation before being ground in a stone quern or pounded with a pestle. Although hunting was still practised, the wild goat and possibly the sheep are thought to

11. Berdyev, 1969.

have been domesticated, and somewhat later cattle. The animals were grazed around the settlements in herds tended by shepherds and possibly dogs.

The animals hunted were first Persian gazelles, followed by wild sheep, boars, foxes, cats, wolves, hares and onagers. The absence of flint arrowheads suggests that composite points were used in their stead, made up of the geometrical microliths so widely found in settlements of this culture. That home-based crafts were practised is shown by the manufacture of flint implements which also indicate that leather dressing was practised, while the absence of clearly identifiable spindles might suggest that clothing and footwear were made primarily of leather. Considerable progress had also been made in pottery: vessels were built up in strips of clay heavily mixed with chopped straw, their surface was carefully smoothed and they were fired in primitive ovens or stoves. The majority of them were plain, and those that were decorated frequently bore patterns of curving stripes winding round the body of the pot, rows of arabesques or a simple red latticework against the creamy background. Indeed, Jeitun pottery is on the whole distinguished by its conservatism, the limited range of forms, the simplicity of decorative patterns and the prevalence of crude, thick-walled vessels. The complete lack of cauldrons and the small number of smoke-blackened vessels, together with the discovery of splintered stones around the fireplaces, strongly suggest that food was cooked by placing red-hot stones in vessels rather than by boiling.

These people were not without a sense of beauty and adorned themselves with bone or stone beads, often made by cutting the hollow bones of animals or birds into pierced segments (Fig. 2). For amulets they used stone figurines of humans or animals, while the small cones were presumably used for cosmetic purposes. The first attempts to make small terracotta mouldings may be seen, and the find of one clay head suggests that comparatively large statuettes were produced. Animal figurines of clay quite often bear tiny 'stab wounds', most probably the result of magic hunting rites. The dead were buried within the settlement, in a doubled-up position and often sprinkled with red ochre.

The qualitative changes in the economy of the time, inevitably brought social changes in their wake. Here the prime source of information is again the fully excavated settlement of Jeitun, the ground plan of which shows beyond question that it was built up of one-roomed houses. It has very plausibly been suggested that each was the home of a nuclear family, and the useful area of the houses, varying as it does from 15 to 30 m² would tend to bear this out. Also revealing is the fact that each had only one fireplace, designed for a single family but not for collective meals. It is now becoming clear that the same layout designed for the nuclear family, is to be found at other Neolithic settlements in western Asia. Indeed, it has convincingly been argued that the small family existed in Upper Palaeolithic societies and survived into the Mesolithic period. These observations would suggest that the social structure of the Jeitun culture was derived from Palaeolithic traditions, though the old forms were given a new

FIG. 2. Jeitun culture: flint, stone, bones, clay artefacts and clay figurines.

content. The difference is that nuclear families were still at the initial phase of a development that called for the collective management of the economy and team-work. It has already been remarked that the Neolithic settlements consisted of several dozen one-roomed houses, revealing a tendency for nuclear families to come together in larger units, prompted in the first place by economic necessity arising from the partial use of irrigation. The same tendency could lie behind the public building such as that found at Pessejik-depe, which were intended for a large group rather than an individual family. Clearly, the society of Jeitun consisted of nuclear families living in kinship settlements that together formed small tribes.

As we have seen, settlements of the Jeitun culture exhibit all the characteristics of a production-based economy. It is logical to inquire where that culture originated and in what specific ways the Neolithic economy came about in this part of Asia. It has been suggested that its origins were purely local, and that the forefathers of Jeitun may have been the Mesolithic hunters and gatherers of the southern Caspian or the uplands of Turkmenistan and Khorasan. But no wild ancestors of barley or wheat are known in this region, while soft and club wheat are cultivated strains requiring millennia of evolution from wild forebears in other regions.

Similarly, the hypothesis that first goats and subsequently sheep were domesticated locally would – biologists consider – require additional proof, since the bones found in Jeitun are related to the wild sheep of western Asia rather than the local species. At the present time, a more probable theory is that the local Late Mesolithic hunters and gatherers of the Caspian were moving towards an economy of production, but that the completion of that process resulted from the arrival of new tribes that had already in their former homelands wholly taken up the new way of life. Apart from the long-established parallels between the Jeitun culture and the early agriculture sites of western Asia, previously unknown sites have now been unearthed in northern Iran which may well mark the routes by which the more advanced economic methods spread. One such site might be the settlement of Zagheh at the southern tip of the Caspian Sea, the culture of which in its material aspects largely recalls that of Jeitun. Clearly, it may very plausibly be supposed that by the sixth millennium B.C. at the latest, the transition to an economy of production was already complete in this part of Central Asia, and that its inception may even be rooted in the seventh millennium B.C. Thus northeastern Iran and southern Turkmenistan emerge as one of those few regions in which, together with the advanced western Asian centres, that economy had already become established.

In contrast with the narrow belt along the foothills of the Kopet Dag where the Neolithic people of the Jeitun culture had already acquired an economy of production, the vast region to the north comprising the greater part of Soviet Central Asia was populated by the hunters and fisherfolk of what is called the Kelteminar culture (sixth to fourth millennia B.C.), whose main tools and weapons were made of flint and to some extent bone. Flint was mined in quarries, the traces of one such having been detected near the spurs of the Sultan-Uisdag mountains. A characteristic of these flint implements is the extent to which they employ microliths calling to mind the flint-working techniques of the Jeitun culture : evidence of this is the wide dispersal of various kinds of piercers that doubled as augers. Unlike Jeitun however, the Kelteminar culture is completely lacking in flint sickle blades but abounds in arrowheads specifically shaped as such, with hollowed sides and a cut-off base. Later more sophisticated arrowheads appear, leaf-shaped or rhomboid and finished on both sides (Fig. 3). Clearly, these people pursued a primarily hunting life-style and that is indeed why projectile weapons figure more prominently among the finds than other flint artefacts. Querns, fishing-net weights, axes and adzes were made of various kinds of stone, and arrowheads were also made of bone.

Generally speaking, their homes were seasonal encampments or resting grounds where the cultural strata are slight. Most are small, though, along the course of the now dry Uzboy, sites lie close together and may be 5–6 hectares in size. The people are thought to have lived in frame shelters up to 300 m² in size and 8 to 10 m high, or in domed mud-huts half buried in the ground, no more than 3–4 m high. They made clay pottery of simple hemispherical shape, generally with a rounded base, which they decorated lavishly by painting, drawing or incision. The patterns themselves were quite simple – small holes, zigzags, rhomboids or triangles frequently filled with curling lines.

The archaic aspect of the Kelteminar culture is in all respects that of a prehistoric society still at the stage of the commandeering economy based on hunting, fishing and, to a lesser extent, gathering. This is suggested not only by the range of typical hunting-and-fishing implements described above but also by the fact that sites were located along the banks of rivers and lakes in the desert and steppe regions. Judging by osteological discoveries, the quarry was the onager and Persian gazelle: such steppe fauna of those times as the boar, roe and red deer were more common in the *tugay* scrub. Found with them were the bones of camels, cattle and wild horses whose true role in the lives of the Kelteminar people is not yet fully clear.

Evidence of fishing is provided by the bones of pike, sazan carp and sheatfish which were caught either with nets or, apparently, with stone-tipped fishing-spears. Remains of fresh-water molluscs and eggshells complete with crushing-stones suggest that gathering supplemented hunting and fishing. The complete absence both of cultivated cereals and domestic animal bones, other than those of dogs, proves that the Kelteminar tribes had not yet advanced to a production-based economy. It is with every justification supposed the specific natural conditions in which they lived necessitated no dramatic change in their economic habits.[12]

12. Vinogradov, 1981.

FIG. 3. Kelteminar culture: flint, stone tools and pottery.

Ecological conditions favourable to hunting and fishing and a vast territory with virtually unlimited wild fauna presented optimal conditions for a commandeering economy, so that in this region the change to production did not occur before the Chalcolithic Age, at the same time as Bronze Age sites became widespread.

A distinctive picture emerges in the wooded foothill districts of the Tajikistan region where new elements of economic development are bound up with the Hissar culture sites and might point to the first stages in the rise of a production-based economy in western Tajikistan, though the limited range of sickle blades makes hasty conclusions ill-advised. All authors, however, agree that the domestication of animals had long been completed here, and the view that this is a case of an economy of production that developed through stockbreeding would appear to be correct. It remains doubtful, however, whether the domesticated animals came here from elsewhere or whether the local people themselves moved from hunting to stockbreeding.

A similar picture emerges from the known sites of Afghanistan, especially in the northern foothills of the Hindu Kush where they emerge with the plain of Bactria. The caves and rock shelters such as Kara-Kamar and Ak-Kupruk reveal if not a more sophisticated way of life, then at least new economic trends. The ninth millennium B.C. Mesolithic strata at Kara-Kamar, for instance, contained, in addition to painstakingly prepared and often finished flint flakes, a wealth of animal remains including those of wild sheep, gazelles, foxes and birds, indicating that life still revolved around hunting. It has been suggested that like the Ghar-i Kamarband and Hotu caves, Kara-Kamar reflects the spread of Mesolithic people from the Zagros mountains to the northern foothills of the Hindu Kush via the Caspian coast.

Far more information about the different ways in which the production-based economy developed is contained in the caves of Ghar-i Mar and Ghar-i Asp at Ak-Kupruk. In the former, two strata designated A and B have been identified, separated by a layer of sterile sand. The A stratum, which is the earlier, has been ascribed by C14 dates to 6610 ± 100 B.C. Tools consist of flakes used as reaping blades, scrapers – some made of flakes – piercers and chisels, there are also bone awls and burnishers. Animal remains include those of domesticated sheep or goats. The upper or B stratum is similar, but contains stone hoes, querns and steatite and stone vessels. By and large, comparable objects may be found in the Ghar-i Asp cave in strata dated by C14 to 8260 ± 235 B.C. The presence of domesticated animals, of plants which were at least partially if not fully domesticated, of reaping flakes – possibly from simple sickles – stone hoes and querns, all point to the arrival of a new type of economy more typical of sedentary farming communities. It has been suggested that northern Afghanistan within the latitudes of 30 and 40 degrees (500–750 m above sea-level) may have been one of the centres where plants and animals were first domesticated, subsequently spreading through central Afghanistan to Anatolia and the Aegean, though this requires confirmation by new evidence. Despite all this, hunting still figured prominently, as is proved by the discovery of the bones of red deer, gazelles and wild sheep.[13]

The subsequent period at Ak-Kupruk has been identified on the basis of the objects found as 'pottery Neolithic'. These strata are best represented in the same caves of Ghar-i Asp and Ghar-i Mar, the youngest having a C14 date of 2550 ± 60 B.C. Flint tools include sickle blades, flakes, scrapers and chisels as well as bone artefacts, awls, needles, piercers and burnishers. Additionally, slate hoes, querns, pestles, axes and fragments of steatite vessels have been found: scratched tortoise shells were apparently used as ornaments. Together with domesticated sheep and goats, there is a wide range of wild animals: onagers, gazelles and cattle. Of particular significance is the appearance of pottery made of brittle paste mixed with chopped straw. The chronology of the pottery Neolithic strata in Ghar-i Mar is demonstrated by their C14 dates: 4815 ± 85, 4360 ± 70 and 5005 ± 75 B.C.

The stratigraphically earliest pottery, found together with flint tools, was made of plain, soft, brittle black paste. It should immediately be pointed out that one and the same stratum probably contains pottery from different periods, so that vessels made on the wheel must be approached with extreme circumspection. Pottery of this age is unknown even in the foremost centres of prehistoric agriculture, implying that the higher stratum of Ghar-i Mar, said to be Chalcolithic – where microlithic tools are found side by side with ceramics, some with scratched zigzag patterns, and with copperware – must be treated with great reserve. The strata themselves are contradictory, giving C14 dates of 5270 ± 100 and 5080 ± 110 B.C., which is earlier than the lower strata said to be Neolithic. At the Dara-i Kur cave in Badakhshan, the 'Neolithic' remains designated as the 'sacred goat' stratum require further verification. They were found to contain a small number of stone tools (including reaping blades), polished axes, a slate knife and scrapers, a basalt hammer, pebble tools and fragments of copperware. Black and red pots decorated with zigzags, chevrons, triangles and finger-pressing were found. Three pits containing buried goats together with the dismembered bones of children were excavated and identified as sacred goat burials. The C14 dates are relatively recent: 1830 ± 130 and 1485 ± 125 B.C.

As will be seen there is definite evidence, adequate albeit fragmentary, of the establishment of an economy of production in northern Afghanistan. And yet, here, on the Bactrian plain at the foothills of the Hindu Kush, no trace remains of the growth of a settled farming life-style, for reasons that are not yet wholly clear. It is thought that, as biologists have rightly pointed out,[14] ecological conditions were not conducive to the development of early irrigation farming. In this regard, it should be noted that on the left bank of the Amu Darya, where the sands and the alluvial plains come together, Mesolithic and Neolithic encampments have recently been found whose flint artefacts are akin to the Central

13. Dupree, 1972.
14. Vavilov and Bukinich, 1929.

Asian Stone Age rather than to the caves of the Hindu Kush. Unfortunately, there is no direct evidence of the economy of those who left these camps. If an economy of production did develop here, then it must have been highly individual in form, a consequence of the distinctive ecological conditions in northern Afghanistan.

Southern Afghanistan, conversely, reveals an earlier development of agricultural economy, represented by the lower strata of such sites as Mundigak and Said Qala. Of particular interest are the finds at Mundigak I, where in the earliest period there were first adobe and later brick house-walls, indicating that sedentarism and a production-based economy had long been established. Graphic proof of this is given by the wheel-turned pottery and copperware, which denotes a society already far advanced in its economic and cultural development.[15]

Conclusion

The culture of Neolithic agricultures and of cattle-breeders of Iran, Afghanistan and Soviet Central Asia shows that a transition to the forms of economy, usually termed the 'Neolithic revolution', took place here almost simultaneously with similar developments in western Asia. A new way of life is clearly represented here by comfortable houses with accurate trimming of interiors, bright ceramics and wide use of ornaments. This qualitative leap in social development prepared the necessary base for the creation of ancient civilizations. At the same time inequalities in the course of historical development become clear: the ancient tribes of Iran and southern Turkmenistan passed to the new forms of economy, while in other areas of Soviet Central Asia and northern Afghanistan the transition was delayed. Tribes of hunters, fishers and food-gatherers, maintaining many archaic features in their culture, were contemporary with sedentary communities in oases. The lines of cultural links that emerged during the Palaeolithic epoch not only keep their importance but also become stronger – a fact which played an important role in the diffusion of cultivating cereals and of cattle-breeding.

15. Casal, 1961.

FOOD-PRODUCING COMMUNITIES
IN PAKISTAN AND NORTHERN INDIA[1]

M. Sharif and B. K. Thapar

RECENT archaeological discoveries in this region have produced sufficient evidence to reconstruct the various stages in the evolution of the food-producing communities on the basis of local developments. The old model of diffusionism from west to east and its consequent effect on the regional developments in Baluchistan and the Indus valley needs to be modified in the light of the new cultural data that have provided very early dates comparable with those found in western Asia.[2]

The cultural material is not only varied in time but also extensive, covering the northern, central and southern parts of the Indus valley. From the north, the excavated material comes from Swat, Dir and Sarai Kala (Saraikhola) near Taxila; from the central area the excavations at Jalilpur and Gumla have supplied the data; from Baluchistan Kili Gul Muhammad provided the first reliable date; and more recently Mehrgarh, at the foot of the Bolan pass in the north of the Kachi plain, has proved to be a classic site showing a full sequence of the development of Neolithic and Chalcolithic cultures in this region.[3] Mehrgarh is situated on one of the main routes connecting the high inland plateau of Central Asia to the alluvial plains of the Indus system. The Kachi plain, where it is located, is a transitional area between two different worlds, the arid inland plateaux of Baluchistan, Afghanistan and Iran on one side and the Indo-Gangetic plains on the other.[4]

Mehrgarh has been in the course of excavation for the past decade by the French Archaeological Mission to Pakistan led by J. F. Jarrige. The Neolithic site, called MR3, covers an area of several hectares characterized by the presence of flint tools etc. on the surface. It has been cut to the east by the Bolan river and

1. See Map 5.
2. Jarrige, 1984, p. 21.
3. The description of sites from Pakistan in this section mainly follows Allchin and Allchin, 1982, Chapter 5, q.v., and quotes extensively without further reference.
4. Jarrige and Lechevallier, 1974, pp. 463–4.

to the north by a wide and deep gully. At one point the Bolan river has carved a deep channel through the site, creating a straight cliff over 10 m high, showing a continuous series of archaeological layers from top to bottom.[5]

In different parts of the main Neolithic site at Mehrgarh eight periods have been defined. Period I (site MR3) covers the aceramic Neolithic phase; Period II covers the ceramic Neolithic and Chalcolithic phases represented at site MR4, which spreads around the nuclear site of MR3. Period III is found at the site of MR2, covering an area of about 900 m². Periods IV to VII are observed at the original site, MR1, and Period VIII is evidenced at the cemetery to the south of MR1 at Sibri, 8 km away.[6]

Period I, which is aceramic, the first phase of settlement, is marked by plant and animal domestication, craft activities and burial practices – features which fit into a western Asian context. In absolute chronology this period is dated to around 7000 B.C. It is followed by a Neolithic phase whose deposits are associated with a few coarse chaff-tempered sherds. This is dated between 5500 and 6000 B.C. and is referred to as Period IIA. Its cultural assemblage is still very similar to that of the aceramic Neolithic Period I, but in addition to a few stone vessels and fragments of thick bowls in alabaster, there are a very restricted number of potsherds in a chaff-tempered ceramic, occasionally with a red slip. On the other hand Jarrige notes:

> There are so far no remains reported from this region which could be connected to a proto-Neolithic stage which, as in Palestine or the Zagros area, from 12,000 B.C. onward, corresponds to a phase of incipient cultivation. . . . But one must not exclude the possibility of further discoveries.[7]

Period IIB, which is dated to 5000 B.C., includes the archaeological remains on the tops of the cliff that overlies two palaeosols and thick strata of alluvium. Evidence from Period II does not show any major innovation. The tool-kit in bone and stone derives from the earlier Period and metallurgy is limited to the 'discovery of a ring and a bead in copper, plus a small ingot also in copper from an early level of Period IIB'. Pottery, which is a new element, is found in very limited quantity.[8] Period III, which is dated around 4000 B.C., shows the mass-production of pottery, a high density of population, many industrial activities 'showing the skill of the artisans using fine micro-drills in phtanite, suggesting the use of bow-drills, working and engraving ornaments in shell. The discovery of a few crucibles containing traces of copper indicates some developments in metallurgy'.[9] Such an impressive complex of developments in all these fields

5. Lechevallier and Quivron, 1981, pp. 73–4.
6. Lechevallier, 1984, p. 41.
7. Jarrige, 1984, pp. 22–3.
8. Ibid., p. 24.
9. Ibid., p. 27.

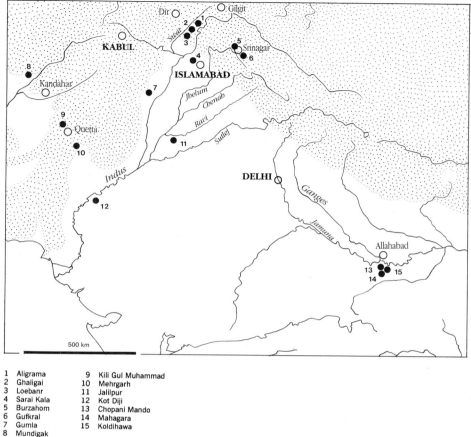

MAP 5. Food-producing communities in Pakistan and northern India.

1	Aligrama	9	Kili Gul Muhammad
2	Ghaligai	10	Mehrgarh
3	Loebanr	11	Jalilpur
4	Sarai Kala	12	Kot Diji
5	Burzahom	13	Chopani Mando
6	Gufkral	14	Mahagara
7	Gumla	15	Koldihawa
8	Mundigak		

bears witness to a process of evolution that ultimately culminated in the highly complex socio-political organization seen later in the Indus Civilization.

Right from the ceramic level of Period I architectural discoveries have been made: a rectangular room of a house has walls built of mud-bricks of regular size, the bricks showing finger impressions on their surfaces. On its floor of packed clay a small grindstone and reed impressions were found. On a higher level of Period I one complete structure, with its walls built with three rows of mud-bricks and making four small compartments, measured 1.5 × 1.0 m. In the upper level several complex buildings have been excavated. These buildings are divided into six or ten rectangular rooms. Such large rectangular buildings of various plans, proportions and types of construction were apparently designed for different purposes.[10] In Period II similar compartmented buildings are found which have been identified as granaries. In Period IIA alone three such buildings have produced coarse ware, a grooved elephant tusk and seeds of barley.[11] In Period III five further compartmented buildings representing three building phases have been exposed.

Side by side with architectural activity human burials have also been found. In the lower levels the burials are characterized by the lack of built structures: red ochre covers the skeletons and the ornaments placed among them. Only stone, shell and bone were used to make these ornaments. In the northern part of the site graves belonging to the upper level were found associated with structures. These burials attest to elaborate funeral rites. Numerous traces of red ochre have been observed with the bones stained red. The skeletons are all in a flexed position. No regular burial structure or pit has been observed. The deceased are buried with many ornaments and offerings such as hexagonal shell pendants, a stone pendant, stone and shell necklaces, bone rings, the bottom of an asphalt-coated basket, and, in addition, one skeleton showed traces of a textile. In the eastern burial ground, pit burials with remains of mud-brick structures have been found. The grave goods include a complete basket, a necklace of turquoise and steatite beads, a stone and shell bracelet, a stone chisel and a textile impression.[12]

The faunal remains from Mehrgarh are highly significant in that they demonstrate the progression from a hunting-and-collecting to a food-producing economy. In the aceramic Neolithic the predominant animal remains are those of wild species, particularly gazelle, while sheep or goat are markedly less numerous and cattle – whether wild or domesticated – are still less frequent. Thereafter, in successive stages, the position changes: gazelle becomes less and less common, while sheep and goat and later zebu cattle increase in frequency, until these three domesticated species assume proportions in the economy comparable to those which they hold to this day. From MR3 twelve species of big game have been identified. They include gazelle, swamp deer, nilgai, black buck, onager, spotted

10. Lechevallier and Quivron, 1981, pp. 72–7.
11. Jarrige, 1984, pp. 24–5.
12. Lechevallier and Quivron, 1981, pp. 79–85.

deer or chital, water buffalo, wild sheep, wild goat, wild pig and elephant. R. H. Meadow draws the following conclusion:

> First, a shift during the aceramic Neolithic from the hunting of wild animals to the keeping of domesticated sheep, goats and cattle; second, an increase in the importance of zebu cattle in relation to sheep and goats during the course of the aceramic and early ceramic periods; third, a revival of this trend during later occupations at the site; and, fourth, a decrease in the size of the individual domestic animals through time.[13]

Evidence of cultivated plants has been obtained from impressions of straw and grain in mud-bricks. These impressions show various kinds of barley and wheat. The barley shows characteristics of a local variety. Naked six-row barley seems to have been the principal crop. Naked wheat is present in restricted quantities together with typical hulled varieties. Other floral remains from this period include *zizyphus* fruit, grape and date palm. Cotton seeds have also been found.[14]

As regards the flint industry, houses in general contain very few flint artefacts. But in tombs, particularly in the upper levels of MR3, some artefacts are recorded which are interesting for their quality and freshness. A total of 32,000 artefacts have been collected, of which over 20,000 belong to Period I, 4,000 to Period II and 4,000 to Period III. The remainder belong to later periods. Various types of flint arfetacts have been found from Periods I to III. They include cores, hammer-stones, blades, bladelets, flakes, geometric microliths, sickle blades, burins, borers and end-scrapers. Among the blades are truncated, notched, backed and retouched varieties. Axes/adzes have also been found but arrowheads are seen only in the later periods. M. Lechevallier concludes:

> Periods I and II form the first unit; there is a great homogeneity in the blade production. The assemblage is on the whole Neolithic, with certain Epipalaeolithic characteristics like the varied, unstandardized geometric microliths. Period III has its own characteristics: the disappearance of microliths and the exclusive use of new types (large triangles and obliquely truncated blades), and a large number of retouched flakes such as scrapers, notches and denticulates.[15]

Pottery, which is a new element in Period II, is found in very limited quantities. The number of sherds increases in Period IIB when pottery becomes much finer with vessels shaped on a turntable and rounded with a dabber. At the site of MR4 above the filling of rooms of the early phase and in the loose deposit above two burials an enormous amount of potsherds were recovered. Half of them, which show a mixture of straw and clay pressed by hand, are fragments of bowls and flat circular dishes with a grooved surface; it is a yellowish ware. A small number of

13. Meadow, 1984, p. 34.
14. Costantini, 1984.
15. Lechevallier, 1984, p. 50.

vessels, which are also hand-made but of better quality, have their lower part moulded in a basket. The other half of the sherds belong to fine wheel-turned ware, consisting of open bowls and medium-sized globular vessels with a collared rim in buff, often decorated with simple geometric motifs, criss-cross and oblique lines, dots or hatched squares. Sometimes the decoration is bichrome. Many bangles, rectangular in section, made out of the same buff ware, have also been found.[16] Period III shows the mass-production of pottery with heaps of sherds, 40 per cent in a fine fabric with geometric or animal motifs. This is a great technical advance over the hand-made and basket-marked pottery of the earlier period. The pottery of this period evidences an intensive use of the wheel, improved quality of paintings, mostly geometric in the early phases and later consisting of rows of caprids and birds.

Among the exceptional finds of Period III are five figurines made from unfired clay. Three represent human beings and two animals. One human figure is conical in shape and has a necklace of appliqué clay lozenges. The second is in a seated position. They are similar to the early human figurines of western Iran.[17]

The evidence from the first two periods of Mehrgarh has opened a new chapter in the Neolithic of this region.

> The cultivation of cereal crops and the husbandry of animals were practised in addition to hunting and gathering in Period I, and to their exclusion in Period II. Specialized crafts existed, and a network of long-distance contacts brought to Mehrgarh turquoise from Iran or Soviet Central Asia, lapis lazuli from northern Afghanistan and shells from the coast of the Arabian Sea.[18]

In the light of the finds from Mehrgarh it becomes abundantly clear that we are dealing with a pattern common to the whole Central Asian area. The artefactual assemblage of Mehrgarh is of an archaic aspect; it is a Neolithic-type industry, similar in many respects to that of Jeitun in south Turkmenistan. We may distinguish there elongated blades, geometric microliths (trapezes and, more seldom, lunates). We may also note bone awls, axes and adzes made of polished stone. Particular attention was given to the trimming of implements, as in the case of a bone polisher, which is adorned with a carved ornament. Stone blades were used in most cases as inset blades in sickles, the principal implement of early farmers. The earliest complexes of Mehrgarh may perhaps be dated to the sixth millennium rather than to the seventh millennium B.C. as is often hypothesized. In the course of their existence, a gradual emergence of a new type of economy occurred. At Mehrgarh, along with flint implements, which soon achieved a high degree of perfection, pottery was being made on the potter's wheel and decorated with picturesque painted patterns. Hence a local artist school emerged, being part of the pattern of prehistoric Indus valley cultures in India and Pakistan.

16. Jarrige and Lechevallier, 1979, pp. 477–8.
17. Jarrige and Meadow, 1980, p. 108.
18. Ibid., pp. 107–8.

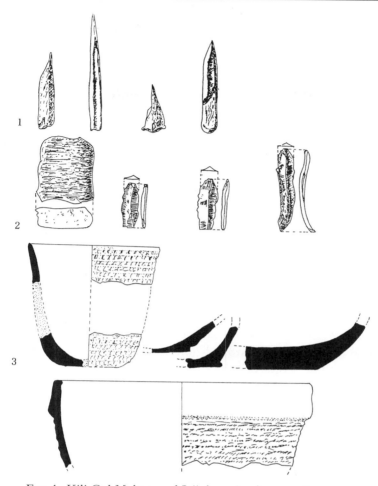

FIG. 1. Kili Gul Muhammad I (1: bone implements; 2: stone artefacts; 3: hand-made wares).

Another settlement of considerable antiquity, though not as ancient as Mehrgarh, is Kili Gul Muhammad[19] located about 3 km north of the modern city of Quetta in the plains near the Zarghun mountains (Fig. 1). It is a small mound approximately 90 m long by 55 m wide. Here in 1950, W. Fairservis carried out a small exploratory excavation, only 3.5 m², reaching virgin soil at a depth of 11–14 m. Hence in the lower levels the area excavated was very small indeed. Period I, the lowest of the four cultural phases revealed at the site, produced C14 samples from a hearth in its uppermost levels. These have given dates of 4900 and 4300 B.C. (MASCA corrected). Below, there is a further deposit of nearly 4 m in thickness, doubtless representing a considerable time duration. These earliest date indicate that the inhabitants kept domestic sheep, goats and oxen, and were

19. Fairservis, 1956.

probably nomadic. However, by the end of the period they had houses of mud-brick or hard-packed clay. Their material equipment included blades of chert, jasper or chalcedony, and a fragment of rubbing or grinding stone, but no metal objects. Awls or points of bone were also found, but no pottery was discovered, and hence the excavator treats the period as pre-ceramic. There followed two further periods, II and III, the earlier yielding crude hand-made and basket-marked pottery. These levels contained further house walls of mud-brick, and a material culture otherwise little different from that of the preceding period. The predominant pottery had a red or yellow-red surface with a yellowish body, and a coarse ware with a sandy body was also found. In Period III the first copper was found along with distinctive pottery, both wheel-thrown and hand-made, decorated with black or painted designs including simple geometric motifs.

A third early settlement is at Sarai Kala[20] (Fig. 2). It stands in a prominent position on the southern bank of the Kala Jala (stream) near the Grand Trunk Road at a distance of about 3 km south-west of Taxila. The mound which rises in four successive terraces measures about 610 m north–south and 300 m east–west. The depth of the cultural deposits is more than 4 m. Of the four periods only the first relates to this chapter. This may be described as Neolithic on account of the material culture. Subsequent investigations have revealed the presence of several pit-dwellings in this period. Ground-stone axes, a stone-blade industry, bone points and burnished pottery formed the material culture. This period is now dated by C14 to 3000–3160 B.C. Only a very small part of the blade industry came from Period I, the majority of the finds arising from the second period. The same is true of the ground-stone axes, which are of simple kind, generally with median ground edges and rounded butts. The pottery is coarse red-brown and frequently burnished. There is a limited range of types, all hand-made or built on a simple turntable. Some of the pottery shows the addition of a coarse gritty sand to the outer surface while the clay was still soft. Painted pottery is notably absent. There is no evidence of any metal in this period, though later it becomes relatively common. This excavation provides evidence of a period which, though in many respects differentiated from its successor, none the less has many continuing traits, suggesting that there was no complete abandonment of the settlement or change in population.

Period I at Sarai Kala belongs to the Late Neolithic, assignable to the late fourth and early third millennia B.C. Outstanding features of the pottery of Period I are that it is all hand-made, slipped with dark-red colour, and the vessels are burnished on both sides or only externally. The fabric is generally fine but some examples are also present in which tempered clay has been used. The body is generally thick and the bases show basket or coiled-mat impressions. However, there is no evidence to show that the hand-made wares of Period I were moulded in baskets and then surface smoothed. It seems more likely that the vessels were

20. Halim, 1972*a*, 1972*b*; Thomas and Allchin, 1986.

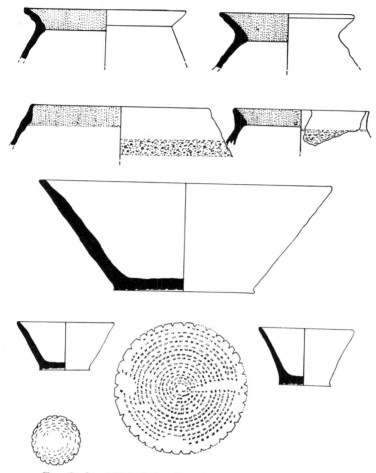

FIG. 2. Sarai Kala I: hand-made and burnished wares.

made either resting on a mat or placed on a mat for drying after they had been made. As regards the burnishing technique, it seems that a red slip was applied and then the surface was rubbed with a dabber or stone so as to produce a glassy surface. In some examples a thick coat mixed with mud was applied on the exterior surface on which sand was dusted. These wares also occur at Gumla, Mehrgarh and in the fourth and early third millennia B.C. levels of Jalilpur.

At Sarai Kala, basket impressions occuring on the bases and the technique of scratching the external surface with a straw brush are reminiscent of the Neolithic pottery of the Yangshao horizon in northern China and the Neolithic pottery of Burzahom in Kashmir. There are, however, local differences in the colour of the pottery. It is also significant to note that the earliest levels of Sarai Kala and Burzahom yielded bone tools and ground-stone celts which are also strikingly similar to those associated with the Yangshao horizon of the Neolithic period.

The prehistoric site of Jalilpur[21] is located about 5 km south of the left bank of the Ravi river and at a distance of 65 km south-west of Harappa in the central Indus valley. The mound covers an area of 360 × 400 m with a maximum height of 5 m above the surrounding cultivable fields. The excavations revealed an accumulation roughly 2 m thick which represented two culturally distinct but interrelated occupational periods. The earlier, which is labeled Jalilpur I, consists of three main occupational levels above the natural soil. Here too the early Period may be called Neolithic, in that no copper or bronze has been reported, and the stone-blade industry and the bone points recall Period I at Kili Gul Muhammad, Gumla and Sarai Kala.

The occupational levels assigned to Period I did not reveal any substantial structural remains in the excavated area but mud-brick and mud-floors are attested. The pottery of the period is hand-made of bright red clay, with a soft crumbling surface. A most distinctive feature is the roughening of the surface by the application, before firing, of a thick coating or slurry made up of clay mixed with fragments of crushed pottery, providing an equivalent to the granular sand-roughening of pottery from the early level of Sarai Kala. From the mud floor laid on a layer of lime 'Kankar', one rectangular bead of sheet gold, with tabular per-foration, and several barrel-shaped cylindrical beads were found. Other finds include terracotta net-sinkers, chert blades, numerous bone points and a large number of bones of cattle, sheep, goat and gazelle. The presence of terracotta net-sinkers indicates that fishing formed an element of the economy. However, many animal bones that were either burnt or cut suggest that the inhabitants of this period depended on slaughtered animals for a major part of their diet.

Another settlement of considerable antiquity, though not as ancient as Mehrgarh, is Gumla,[22] north-west of Dera Ismail Khan. The location of this site is in some ways similar to Mehrgarh. Gumla lies to the west of the Indus river, where the alluvial plain of the Indus meets that of the tributary Gomal river. It is a small mound, and was excavated by A. H. Dani. A sequence of six periods was discovered, of which only the first concerns us here. It is claimed in the report that the earliest stratum contained no structural remains and no pottery but only hearths, community ovens, animal bones and stone tools (microliths) and goes back to the Neolithic. It is stated that pottery of the subsequent Period falls into two classes, of which one, consisting of coarse hand-made sherds, was only found at the bottom of the deposit, while the other, of better made pottery, including painted wares, occured in pits dug during the second period. The coarse pottery can be fairly assigned to the first period. The relative lateness is almost confirmed when we compare the blade and microlith industry with that of Mehrgarh. None the less, as Gumla seems to be the first of the whole series of sites in the neigh-bourhood of Dera Ismail Khan its importance is obvious.

21. Mughal, 1972.
22. Dani, 1970/71.

The Ghaligai[23] rock shelter is located at the foot of a limestone hill near the road from Mingora to Barikot in the former state of Swat. The excavation in the rock shelter has furnished important evidence about the prehistoric cultures of Swat and the north-west regions of the subcontinent. As many as seven major periods have been established of which the earliest, the pre-ceramic level, is considered to be of Neolithic Age.

The cultural component from the lowest level comprises pebbles and flakes. This earliest phase is overlain by a level containing pottery. The pottery is all hand-made, tempered with coarse sand and with a surface colour varying usually from red-brown to grey-brown. Most of the vases show traces of slip and some even have their inner surface burnished. The partially reconstructed shapes include jars with everted rims, hemispherical bowls, and biconical vases, and certain shapes can be compared to common types in the Chalcolithic Period sites of Soviet Turkmenistan. Three C14 dates give 2970–2930 B.C. The stone artefacts are all made from pebbles, primarily with pyramidal points, half-moon flakes and flakes with wide flat bodies, some showing a shouldered hoe profile. There are also tools made from animal bones. Animal remains include antler and boar tusks, and lead us to think that in this period those who frequented the shelter practised hunting.

The coarse burnished grey and brown wares of the early level recall in general terms those of Burzahom in Kashmir and Sarai Kala, and lead us to believe that all belong to a single complex. Although not yet securely dated we may expect this interesting site to belong culturally if not chronologically to the broad Period of the early occupation at both the above-mentioned archaeological sites in Kashmir and near Taxila.

On the basis of the present evidence certain broad conclusions can be drawn. The earliest settlements not only in Pakistan but in the entire subcontinent have been found west of the Indus, on the borders of the Iranian plateau. At Mehrgarh there is a pre-ceramic Neolithic which may have lasted for a long period, perhaps for as long as two millennia (7000–5000 B.C.). At the close of this period there were already developed mud-brick structures; wheat and barley were cultivated; cattle and sheep were domesticated. This was followed by a period of ceramic Neolithic, when comparable settlements were found at Kili Gul Muhammad, Sarai Kala, Jalilpur, Ghaligai rock shelter and Gumla. One of the most striking things about this early Period is that trade links with the Arabian coast and with Soviet Central Asia seem already to have been established. The main similarities of Neolithic material cultures are bone points, stone tools commonly found on all the contemporary Period sites, and hand-made pottery with basket-like impressions on their bases. Such affinity in artefactual remains in three areas, mixed with other materials, has suggested to some an outward contact with northern China and Soviet Central Asia.

23. Stacul, 1967, 1969.

Evidence for food-producing communities in northern India has come from Kashmir and the Ganges valleys. Both areas have their own peculiarities. While the Kashmir Neolithic shows a development in the colder region, the material from the Ganges valley shows a pattern in the plains of north India. The period following the close of the Pleistocene in Kashmir still remains inadequately understood as the transition or transformation from the terminal hunter/forager stage to the farming economy and the adaptation to Post-Pleistocene environmental changes has not so far been fully identified in these areas. Current investigations into this admittedly complex problem have, however, revealed at Sombur in the Kashmir valley, a lithic industry, based on jasper, siliceous limestone and trap, and represented in such tool types as burins, points and borers.[24] This industry, being the first find of its kind in the valley, may perhaps indicate a particular stage in this long-drawn process of the transformation from the exploitive to productive economies. It may be recalled that H. de Terra and Paterson also found some thin indeterminate flakes near Sombur in the lowest Jhelum terrace which they had postulated as representing a Late Palaeolithic or Proto-Palaeolithic culture.[25] Understanding of the origins and early spread of farming in the valley, therefore, is still very insecure and fragmentary.

The Neolithic culture in the Kashmir valley is represented by nearly three dozen sites, all located on the elevated flats of the Karewas, often overlooking streams and lakes. As regards depositional environment SEM (scanning electron microscopy), studies have shown that the deposit preceding the Neolithic occupation at different sites is a wind-borne silt called loess, the deposition of which ceased before the advent of Neolithic culture in the valley.[26] Pollen diagrams constructed from the Harwan deposits not very far from Srinagar have furnished evidence for a three-stage disturbance of natural vegetation as shown by the decline and appearance of pine-forests. The clearance of these at one stage is thought to be related to the farming experiments of the Neolithic settlers in the valley.

Of the explored Neolithic sites, only two, namely Burzahom and Gufkral, have been systematically excavated. The former, literally meaning the place of birch, and situated 16 km north-east of Srinagar, was initially excavated in 1935, albeit in a summary fashion, by H. de Terra and Paterson, who laid bare the potentialities of the site by recording a succession of three cultural strata.[27] It was not until 1960, however, that a large-scale excavation extending to 1971 was undertaken by T. N. Khazanchi of the Archaeological Survey of India.[28] Gufkral, literally meaning the cave of the pottery and situated 41 km south-west of Srinagar, was initially explored by Khazanchi in 1966 and is currently under excava-

24. Pant et al., 1982.
25. Paterson and Drummond, 1962; de Terra and Paterson, 1939, p. 233.
26. Pant et al., 1978.
27. De Terra and Paterson, 1939, p. 234.
28. Khazanchi, 1976.

Fig. 3. Burzahom: pit-dwelling – Period IB.

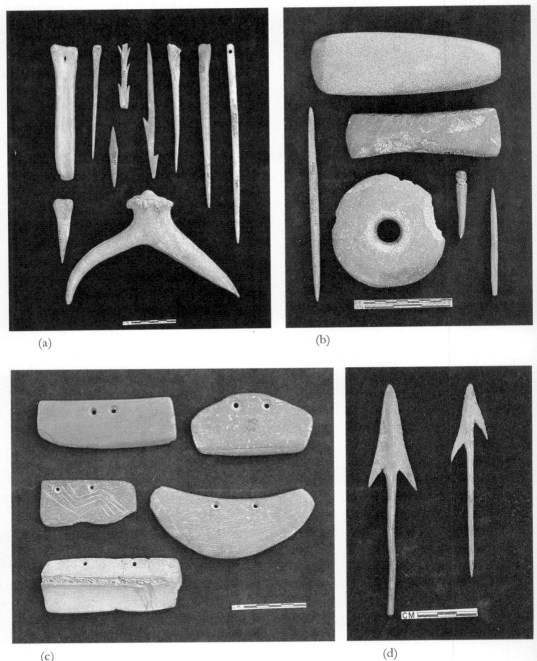

FIG. 4. Burzahom: (a) representative bone tools; (b) representative stone tools; (c) harvesters, stone and bone; (d) copper arrowheads.

tion by A. K. Sharma of the Archaeological Survey of India.[29] The excavations at these sites have yielded a three-phase evolving sequence of the Neolithic culture followed by the Megalithic and historical cultures. The scope of the present study, however, concerns itself only with the Neolithic culture and unless otherwise stated the data furnished below relate to the excavated remains at Burzahom.

Of the three phases of the Neolithic culture, the earliest, labelled as IA, is ceramic. During this period the subsistence economy of the people seems to have been both specialized in food-gathering and cereal-farming, including stock-raising, as evidenced by the finds at Gufkral of bones of both wild (ibex, bear, sheep, goat, cattle, wolf and Kashmir stag) and domesticated (sheep and goat) animals and grains of wheat, barley and lentils. So far as it goes confirmatory evidence in respect of domesticated animals is also available at Burzahom. As regards cereals no direct evidence of their discovery has so far come forth from that site, but palynological studies carried out near the site have revealed the existence of weeds, usually associated with the cultivation of wheat and barley.[30] The analysis of the bones of domesticated goats reveals the absence of very old animals and a predominance of immature ones, suggesting herd management.

The inhabitants lived in underground pits which on plan were mostly circular or rectangular and less frequently oval or squarish, the former variety being usually narrow at the top and wide at the base (Fig. 3). The pits were cut into the natural loess soil by means of long stone-celts, the tell-tale marks of which are still present on some of their sides. The floors were found to be painted in red ochre. The size of the pits, including the depth, varied according to the needs of the family. As protection against the weather, the pits had a birch-cover supported on wooden posts as indicated by the presence of post-holes along the periphery of the mouth. In close proximity to these pits were also found smaller-sized shallower pits which were used by the dwellers as storage-bins and hearths. The floors of the storage-pits at Gufkral were also treated with a red ochre paint. The floors of the storage-pits or chambers were likewise cut in the loess soil and had post-holes at the corners for supporting a roof. For their daily occupation, they used both bone and stone tools, the former consisting of points, needles and scrapers (Fig. 4a), and the latter of axes, drills, picks, pounders, querns and mace-heads (Fig. 4b). Besides, tools were also made of antler-horns. The stone tools were made of the Himalayan trap while the bone ones came from various animals including goat, sheep and stag when the bones were at the green stage.

In the succeeding phase, labelled as IB, pottery came to be used. Among animals, cattle and dogs, and among plants, common peas, also began to be domesticated in addition to those already known in the earlier phase. During this period, as also in the following, the percentage of domesticated animal bones shows a progressive increase and those of wild animals a corresponding decrease.

29. Sharma, 1967.
30. Singh, 1964; Vishnu-Mittre, 1968.

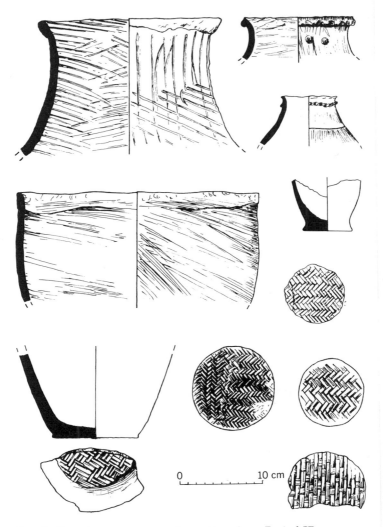

FIG. 5. Burzahom: representative pottery from Period IB.

It is interesting to note that with the exception of the wolf all the animals hunted during the various phases of the Neolithic Period belong to the herbivorous group. The other items of cultural equipment of the previous phase continued during this phase with an increasing variety in tool-kit – harpoons, needles with or without eyes, awls, and arrowheads in bone, hoes, chisels, adzes, etc., in stone. In view of the restricted extent of the excavation in the aceramic levels (Period IA) no emphasis need be laid on the presence or absence of a particular bone or stone tool in the deposits of Periods IA and IB, the distinguishing trait between the two periods being only the use of pottery in the latter. The inhabitants continued living in subterranean pits and chambers. Examples are not wanting where pits of the previous period have been reused by widening the sides, the pit-floors showing different levels of occupation. At Burzahom as many as thirty-seven circular pits and forty-five pit-chambers have been exposed. Of these, the latter were found mostly in the central part of the settlement and the former in the peripheral, suggesting perhaps a planned layout with clan type of kinship grouping. The largest of the circular pits measures 2.74 m at the top, 4.57 m at the base and 3.95 m in depth. Although steps were provided in the deeper pits, these do not reach the bottom, access to which would presumably be by direct descent beyond the step level. The excavated pit-chambers had depressions on all four sides and storage-pits and hearths in the centre, the hearths being either of stone or earth.

Coming to pottery, three principal fabrics, all hand-made, were in use during this phase (Fig. 5): thick coarse grey ware; fine grey ware; gritty dull red ware. Among these, the thick coarse grey ware predominated over the other two fabrics. Made by strip or coil technique, the ware shows irregular marks of brushing on the surface, resulting from the rubbing of twigs or grass bundled together. It is uniformly fired to a dull grey colour but shows an irregular fracture due to the presence of coarse grains of sand in the paste. The main shapes represented in this ware are the globular jars and basins, both of which show disc bases, often bearing mat-impressions, suggesting a high level of development of fabric and mat technology. It is certain that people wove mats and twined baskets for domestic use. The fine grey ware, potted with coil or strip technique, is comparatively thinner in section and has a finer matrix tempered with crushed rock. Fired to a uniformly ash grey colour, its surface shows marks of brushing and scraping. It is represented mainly in vase forms showing incised nail-tip decoration on the rim. The third fabric, namely the gritty dull red ware, is made of a coarse paste containing pieces of quartz, the technique of potting being the same as that of previous fabrics. Indifferently fired, showing unoxidized core-portions, it is represented in jars, deep bowls and basins.

The last phase of the Neolithic culture in the valley, Period IC, marks a distinct change from the preceding phases.[31] The underground dwelling pits and chambers of the earlier periods were no longer used. Most were filled up and covered with a mud-plastered floor having a thin coat of red ochre. The dwelling units now began to be built above ground either from mud or mud-bricks. At Burzahom, the presence of numerous post-holes, in one instance as many as forty-nine in an area of 3.96 × 1.31 m, indicates timber structures as well. A few mud-platforms with remains of walls were also exposed at Burzahom. Associated with these structures were various floors carefully made of rammed earth coated with red ochre, as well as hearths and storage-pits. The basis of subsistence seems to have undergone progressive changes. The period saw a further diversification

31. Khazanchi, 1977.

0 _____ 10 cm

Fɪɢ. 6. Burzahom: painted pot of Kot Diji
affiliation, Period IC.

in material equipment, perhaps through contacts with other regional and extra-
regional cultures. Not only did the tools begin to be made to a better finish and in
larger number indicating craft specialization, but some new types were also added
to the kit, such as the large-sized bone needle with or without eye, the small-sized
bone points, the double-edged pick, spindle whorl and harvester (rectangular or
semi-lunar knife with holes) (Fig. 4c). The last was made both from stone and
bone and was probably fastened to the hand with strings through the holes for
cutting, scraping and harvesting.

In ceramics, another fabric termed burnished grey ware was added to the
already existing range. Made by the coil-and-strip technique it was fired to variegated shades of grey and black and shows a burnished surface. The core-sections
show a fine-to-medium paste with fillers. The principal shapes represented in this
ware are high-necked globular jars, dishes with hollowed stands and stems with
triangular perforations, bowls and basins. Although the ceramic industries of the
preceding Period continued in use, the fine grey ware and the burnished grey
ware became the dominant industries of the period.

Noteworthy among the finds of pottery, however, is the occurrence, in the
lower levels of the period, of a wheel-made vase of orange-slipped ware, painted
in black with a horned figure (Fig. 6), in a panel between the neck and shoulder
bands. The pot is further decorated with multiple incised wavy lines at the level
of the painted figure and with close parallel corrugations on the lower part of the

body. Both in shape and in painted design the pot resembles the pre-Harappan Kot Diji fabric[32] and obviously must have been imported from the nearest site of that genre, namely Sarai Kala.[33] In the upper levels of the period was also found a wheel-made red ware pot containing as many as 950 beads of agate and cornelian, which again seems to be out of context with the existing assemblage. Metallurgy as such does not seem to have been practised by these early farming communities of the Kashmir valley. But a few copper arrowheads (Fig. 4d), a ring, bangle fragments and a pin were found in the deposits of Period IC at Burzahom and a pin with flattened head in the corresponding levels at Gufkral. Their occurrence, however, seems to be as intrusive as that of wheel-made painted pottery and agate beads etc., and as such did not alter the basic Neolithic subsistence economy and technology of the period.

Other finds which deserve special attention are the two engraved stone slabs found fixed in a rectangular structure, forming some sort of tank. Of these, one was upside down, while the other was in a damaged condition, indicating that both were out of their original context. The former slab is slightly broken towards the top but retains the original width of 70 cm, with the result that the upper part of the scene is partly lost. The engraving depicts a hunting scene showing a stag being pierced from behind with a long spear and struck from the front by an arrow by two hunters. The upper part of the scene shows two suns and a dog. The ritualistic value for a successful hunt notwithstanding, the two suns may perhaps signify that the hunting was done during the daytime.[34] The other stone slab, broken along the edges and originally perhaps rectangular in shape, depicts an incomplete pattern identified as a tectiform. The design on the slab seems to be a highly stylized and abstract representation of a hut with a domed roof, the body portion of the anilmal and its tail. These engraved stone slabs 'are the only indubitable examples of Neolithic art in India, found from a regular, stratified dig'.[35]

Evidence relating to the burial practices was provided by six human internments exposed at Burzahom,[36] which indicate that both primary and secondary interments were in vogue. Of the six burials excavated, four showed primary interments, two adult bodies were found, placed in a crouching position, oriented respectively north-east to south-west and south-east to north-west; one body of a child in foetal position, oriented west to east; and one other adult in an extended, articulated position, oriented south-west to north-east. The two secondary burials had no fixed orientation. In fact, one was partially articulated, and oriented south-east to north-west.

Three of these human interments (one secondary and two primary, includ-

---

32. Dani, 1970/71; Khan, 1965.
33. Halim, 1972*a*, 1972*b*.
34. Pande, 1973.
35. Pande, 1972.
36. Sharma, 1967.

TABLE 1

Laboratory No.	Period	C14 date half-life value 5730 years (B.C.)	MASCA calibrated dates (B.C.)
TF–123	IB	2225 ± 115	2650–2780
TF–127	IC	2100 ± 115	2550
TF–14	IC	2025 ± 350	2340–2460
TF–13	IC	1850 ± 125	2160
TF–129	IC	1825 ± 100	2120–2140
TF–15	IC	1535 ± 110	1720–1760
TF–128	IC	2375 ± 120	2920–2940

ing that of the child) had no grave-goods while the remaining three (one secondary and two primary) contained respectively such items as a small barrel-shaped paste bead, animal bones, a skull and fragments of antler, a soapstone circular disc and five cornelian barrel-beads. A distinctive feature of these burials was the application of red ochre on the interred human and animal bones (excepting the child). A special feature of one of the primary burials was the existence, on the left parietal bone of the skull, of eleven trephined areas – six complete circular holes, varying between 8 and 13 mm, and five shallow depressions, being unsuccessful attempts at treatment, none of them showing any signs of healing. Opinions, however, differ about the purpose of these trephinations. One view holds that they are *ante mortem*, made perhaps to treat apparent anomaly of the skull, while the other view asserts that the perforations are a clear case of *post mortem* operation, undertaken for ritual purpose rather than for medical treatment.[37] Dental wear patterns reveal that the Neolithic population of Burzahom had a very coarse and rough diet, which is consistent with their subsistence economy. On the ethnic side, an analysis of the values of the absolute measurements and indices shows that the Burzahom skulls are closer to mature Harappan skulls from Cemetery R-37 than to those of the Neolithic people of southern India.[38]

Examples of animal burials were also found in the deposits belonging to Period IC. In one such burial fragmentary bones of wild dogs along with two antlers of *barasingha* were found. The bones of wild dogs comprise five skulls with vertebral columns in articulated position. From the condition of the bones it may be inferred that the dogs were first sacrificed, then stripped of their flesh and finally buried ceremonially. There are seven C14 determinations from Burzahom as indicated in Table 1. There is only one sample from Period IB and none from Period IA. All the remaining samples belong to Period IC, and except for one aberration, namely. TF–128, these are found to be consistent, showing a time bracket of 2100–1500 B.C. ± 100 MASCA calibrated to 2250–1720 B.C. Using the MASCA calibration, it seems reasonable to assign the following dates to the

37. Basu and Pal, 1980, pp. 15-19.
38. Ibid., pp. 73–80.

respective three periods of the Neolithic culture in the Kashmir valley: Period IA, 3000–2850 B.C., Period IB 2850–2550 B.C. and Period IC 2550–1700 B.C.

Coming to inter- and extra-regional relationships, we find that the Kashmir Neolithic culture shares certain traits with the Neolithic cultures of Sarai Kala in the Potwar plateau,[39] Ghaligai and Loebanr Swat valley[40] all in Pakistan, and Yangshao far away in the Yellow River valley in China[41] which calls for an analytical study.

The similarity extends only to the technique of potting to produce mat-impressions on the bases and straw scratchings on the body, and to the use of celts and bone objects, irrespective of their small number. Admittedly, these are only rudimentary similarities. The distinctive elements of the Kashmir Neolithic culture remain unparalleled. This is not to deny the existence of contacts, however tenuous, with other regions. The occurrence, in the levels of Period IC at Burzahom, of a typically Kot Dijian globular vase,[42] which is one of the dominant types of the pottery of Period II at Sarai Kala dated to 2800–2400 B.C., is illustrative of such an inter-communication. The painted pots from Sarai Kala could have been brought to Burzahom at any time during Period II at the former site, possibly in the latter half when their frequency rises to 13 per cent,[43] but not later. At any rate the linkage invests the sequences at both sites with some measure of near contemporaneity.

As regards Ghaligai and Loebanr, the reported similarities with the Neolithic culture of Burzahom, in the case of the former, are principally the occurrence, in Strata 17, 16 and 15, of grey or grey-brown drab ware and burnished

TABLE 2

Laboratory No.	Period level	C14 date half-life value 5730 years (B.C.)	MASCA calibrated dates (B.C.)
R–377	Ghaligai III Stratum 17	1505 ± 50	1920–1950
P–2583	Leobanr III Pit 1, Layer 5	1430 ± 90	1650
P–2584	Leobanr III Pit 1, Layer 6	1280 ± 60	1500
P–2585	Leobanr III Pit 1, Layer 7	1400 ± 60	1600–1640
P–2856	Leobanr III Pit 1, Layer 5	1510 ± 60	1690–1730
P–2152	Aligrama Layer 13	1400 ± 60	1690–1710

39. Halim, 1972*b*, pp. 3–32; Mughal and Halim, 1972.
40. Stacul, 1967, 1969, 1976, 1977.
41. Chang, 1977, pp. 91–142.
42. Mughal and Halim, 1972, Fig. 12.
43. Ibid., pp. 41–2, Tables 9 and 10.

black ware, sometimes with mat impressions on the vases and bone implements; in the case of the latter, the presence at Loebanr III of underground dwelling pits and the use of black-grey burnished ware and gritty drab ware, with basket or mat-impressions and of stone (celts and mace-heads), and bone objects (points, awls, etc.). A closer analysis of the Neolithic assemblages from each site would show that the similarities are only generic. At Ghaligai, the Neolithic culture is associated with a flake-tool industry and at Loebanr with a wheel-made painted ware, terracotta human and animal figurines and objects of copper and iron.

It may be recalled that the above-mentioned traits, but for the intrusive copper objects, are conspicuously absent in the Neolithic culture of the Kashmir valley. Furthermore, the appearance in Swat of the black-grey burnished ware, with characteristic types like bowl-on-stand, is probably connected with the influences originating from northern Iran (Shah-tepe, Tepe Hissar, etc.). The dates in Table 2 indicate the chronological horizon of the Neolithic phase in the Swat region, which demonstrably is a later manifestation than that of Kashmir (Burzahom). The occupational phase of Loebanr III is related to Period IV in the sequence of proto-historic cultures in the Swat valley. The C14 date from Ali-grama (P–2152), ascribable to this period, confirms the range indicated by the Loebanr dates.

To recapitulate the contacts of the Neolithic cultures of these two regions with that of China, we find unmistakable examples of two items of material equipment of the Yangshao culture of north China, namely the harvester (semi-lunar knife with holes) and jade beads which were included in the inventory of the Neolithic cultures, the Kashmir and Swat valleys respectively. Besides, the occurrence of semi-subterranean dwellings and of mat, or basket, impressions on the bases of some of the pots is common in all the three regions. For a proper appraisal of this inter-relationship or nexus we may take into consideration both the temporal horizon and the form or identity of the Yangshao culture. The spread of the Yangshao culture in Chung Yuan region is ascribed to 6000–3000 B.C. and in Gansu to 3000–1800 B.C.[44] In respect of material equipment, the Yangshao culture in both regions presents a different cultural style to that of the Kashmir (Burzahom) or Swat Neolithic cultures, as revealed by the range and forms of ceramics, including especially tripods with solid legs, the painted ware, terracotta human figurines, horse models and separately located cemeteries *vis-à-vis* the habitation area.[45] The mechanism of diffusion or borrowing of only two characteristic items of equipment of this culture by the Neolithic cultures of the Kashmir and Swat valleys still remains inadequately understood. Meanwhile, a significant addition to our knowledge on the subject has been made by the recent explorations undertaken in northern Sikkim where typical harvesters have been found with other Neolithic tools like celts (some with single and double

44. Chang, 1977, p. 119.
45. Ibid., p. 105.

perforations), adzes, etc., from a number of locations in the Djangu area. Single perforated celts have also been reported from the Neolithic assemblages of Hunan province in northern China. Such close affinity in artefactual remains in these areas would suggest a southward penetration of the cultural influences from China some time in the early part of the third millennium B.C. or a little later, perhaps through Lungshenoid cultures,[46] some of which were characterized by the use of burnished grey-black pottery. The possible route of this penetration into Kashmir and the Indus valley was through a series of passes which link the Gilgit valley with Xinjiang (Sinkiang). In the absence of identifiable sites located between northern China and the Kashmir, Potwar and Swat regions, it would be premature to consider the manifestations of the Neolithic cultures in these regions 'as separate extensions from one long cultural tradition of Yangshao Neolithic cultures'.[47] The antecedent stages of these cultures still remain to be fully ascertained.

In the Belan valley and the Vindhyan plateau the findings at Chopani Mando, Koldihawa and Mahagara indicate a continuous sequence of transition from the stage of intensified food-gathering and selective hunting (Epi-Palaeolithic) through incipient food-producing (Advanced Mesolithic or proto-Neolithic) to settled village farming (Neolithic). This admittedly is the first evidence of its kind in India which seeks to dispel notions of diffusion of the Neolithic way of life either from western or south-eastern Asia, and to establish the primacy of the proposed chronology (seventh–fifth millennia B.C.) for the latter and the existence of antecedent stages thereof.

Chopani Mando is located within a former meander on the left bank of the Belan, 77 km east-south-east of Allahabad. The excavation revealed a threefold sequence of cultures, extending from the Epi-Palaeolithic, through Early Mesolithic to advanced Mesolithic or proto-Neolithic. The first two cultural periods are distinguished largely by the occurrence of particular tool types such as blades, non-geometric and geometric microliths, their gradual reduction in size and the change in raw material. In the proto-Neolithic period, significant additions to the repertory of tools and other cultural equipment were: (a) tranchets; (b) groundstone tools like hammer-stones, anvils, querns, mullers and ring-stones; and (c) use of hand-made pottery (red ware and khaki or brownish-grey ware), sometimes decorated with impressed designs. Of special importance at this site was the discovery of a number of hut foundations and hearths, which began to appear from the Early Mesolithic period onwards. Thirteen such huts belonging to the proto-Neolithic were exposed. These were either round or oval in plan with an average diameter ranging between 5.7 and 3.5 m. The floors were littered with a large number of microliths, anvils, hammer-stones, sling balls, mullers, querns, fragments of burnt clay, animal bones, potsherds, etc. These huts were

46. Dikshit, 1982.
47. Mughal and Halim, 1972, p. 37, n. 7.

close together in a beehive fashion. The economy of the settlement was that of gathering and hunting. There is no evidence for the domestication of animals or plants. From the presence of querns and mullers, however, we may infer some sort of incipient cultivation; perhaps the people were on the very threshold of effective food-production. The excavation yielded remains of wild rice (carbonized, embedded in lumps of burnt clay) and bones of wild cattle and goat/sheep. The Mesolithic period at Chopani Mando is ascribed to around the ninth to eighth millennia B.C.

The other notable sites in the region which deserve our attention are Koldihawa and Mahagara, situated on the opposite banks of the Belan river, the former on the left bank and the latter on the right, only 3 km from Chopani Mando, and about 85 km south-east of Allahabad. The excavation at Koldihawa revealed a threefold sequence of cultures covering the Neolithic, Chalcolithic and Iron Age. The Neolithic culture was distinguished by the occurrence of ground stone tools, including celts, microliths and hand-made pottery represented by cord-impressed, rusticated and burnished wares. Palaeobotanical analysis of the rice-husks used in the paste of the pottery showed that the rice belongs to the domesticated variety, which on the basis of C14 dates obtained for the Neolithic deposit (seventh–fifth millennia B.C.) provides the earliest known evidence so far for rice cultivation in the subcontinent.[48]

Mahagara is a single culture (Neolithic) site with a 2.6 m thick occupation-deposit, indicating six structural phases. As many as twenty huts, represented by floors and post-holes were exposed in the excavated area. Of these, eighteen belonged to the last structural phase (VI). The sides of these huts were perhaps retained by wattle-and-daub screens as evidenced by the presence of burnt fragments of daub-bearing impressions of reed or bamboo. These eighteen hut-floors are reported to constitute the remains of houses situated in a nucleated ring-like fashion. On these hut-floors lay scattered Neolithic blades and microliths, pottery, querns, mullers, sling balls, celts, bone arrowheads, terracotta beads and bones of animals. An interesting feature of the excavation was the discovery of a cattle pen, irregularly rectangular in plan, measuring 12.5 × 7.5 m, with the longer axis oriented north–south. The cattle pen seems to have been fenced by twenty post-holes with wider spaces left for the openings, of which three can be surmised, two on the eastern and one on the western side. Within the fenced area no pottery or other finds were found, instead a large number of hoof-impressions of cattle, belonging to different age-groups and occurring in clusters, were recorded. From the number of hoof-marks, it is estimated that the cattle pen would accommodate about forty to sixty animals. Outside the pen, near the hut clusters, hoof-marks of sheep or goats were found situated almost in a straight line, suggesting the movement of the animals. The Neolithic pottery is represented by four wares, called cord-impressed, rusticated, burnished-red and

48. Sharma, 1980.

burnished-black, all hand-made and ill-fired. Among these, the cord-impressed ware is the most distinctive. The subsistence economy of the people was based upon both hunting and farming, as attested by the occurrence of both wild and domesticated cattle, sheep, goat and horse, and rice. The simultaneous existence of skeletal remains of wild and domesticated cattle is indicative of the process of transition from a hunting to a food-producing economy.[49]

Hence, important changes both in culture and in subsistence activities occurred in the north Indian subcontinent in the course of the Neolithic period. The long epoch related to hunting and food-collecting came to an end, and a new epoch based on food-production started. The great number of new sites discovered by archaeologists from India and Pakistan make it possible to study this process as a complicated and concrete phenomenon, as separate tribal groups were developing following their own courses and at different rates. Hence, a characteristic feature of the Central Asian region gradually emerged, that of inequality in historical development. The Mehrgarh settlement in southern Pakistan features an early stage in the transition to an agricultural-pastoral economy with a mode of life of its own, and particularly with a well-established everyday life pattern. Neolithic culture developed in the mountainous regions particularly in Kashmir. A lengthy survival of pit dwelling and retardation in a transition to food-production were typical of that area. The archaic traditions in some cases survived up to the time when the process of emergence of the urban type civilization was well under way in the Indus valley. Broad cultural links, particularly within Central Asia persisted and developed in the course of the Neolithic period. Thus, the Mehrgarh materials find close analogies in the Jeitunian of southern Turkmenistan, as well as in several sites of northern Iran (Tepe Sang-i Chakmak). Several features of the Neolithic cultures in the mountainous regions (e.g. semi-lunar knives) may be placed within the area of eastern Asian traditions. These may be seen as a reflection of cultural links, as well as common cultural traditions with the Xinjiang Neolithic cultures (see Chapter 13). However, the discovery in the Gangetic valley has produced sufficient evidence for accepting the primacy of food-production in this region.

49. Thapar, 1984, pp. 195–7.

Neolithic communities
in eastern parts of Central Asia[1]

An Zhimin

THE Neolithic cultures of the eastern parts of Central Asia developed in close contact with neighbouring areas. To the north and west there roamed hunters and food gatherers, using flint microliths – some geometric in shape – as tools. We see a transition to food-production, particularly cattle-raising and agriculture, only in isolated pockets. But to the south and east the pattern was primarily that of sedentary farming which had moved away from the technical tradition of microlith manufacture and adapted to different cultural traditions. This latter cultural complex, of which the best known is the Yangshao culture, belongs entirely to the early agricultural zone with its characteristic features such as well-constructed dwelling houses and rich and varied painted pottery.[2]

The remains of various cultures in the vast area of the west or parts of China are divided in terms of production activity into two types – farming communities and those dependent on hunting and animal husbandry.

Farming communities in this area were found mainly in river valleys on the loess plateau. These communities belonged to the same system as the Neolithic culture and economy in the Yellow river valley. Their remains have been discovered in the oases in Xinjiang (Sinkiang), but they were sporadic and dated generally to late periods. The exact nature of their culture and economic activities is not fully known.

The Dadiwan culture was discovered at Dadiwan in Qin'an, Gansu province in 1979. It is scattered mainly in the valleys of the Weihe and Jingshui rivers in Gansu and Shaanxi provinces. The actual distribution is probably wider. At Dadiwan itself and at the sites of Beiliu, Weinan, Shaanxi province, the Dadiwan culture was superimposed by the Yangshao culture. Specimens of the former have been dated by C14 to 5200 ± 90 B.C. and 4780 ± 90 B.C., while specimens

1. See Map 6.
2. An, 1979*b*.

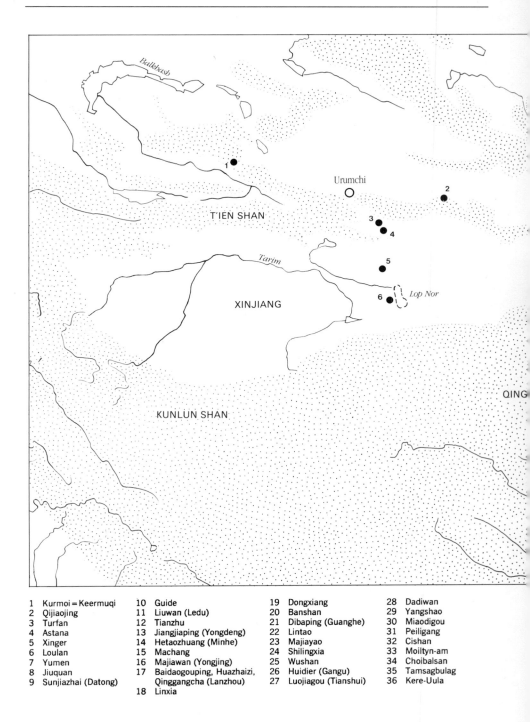

MAP 6. Neolithic communities in eastern and northern parts of Central Asia.

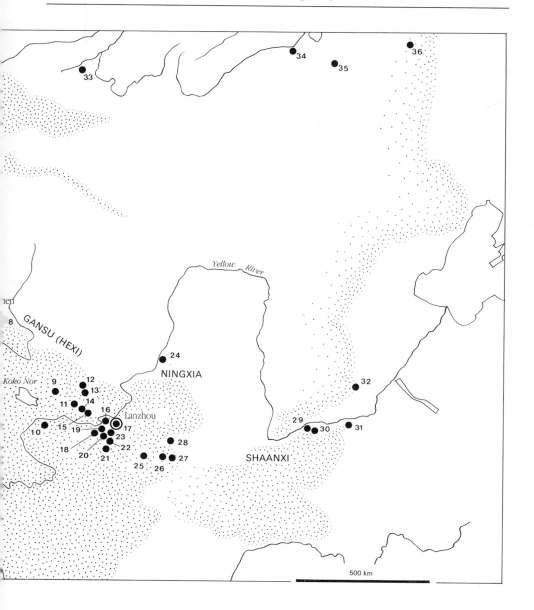

FIG. 1. Painted pottery vase from Dadiwan, Qin'an
County, Gansu. Yangshao culture.

of the latter have been dated to 5010 ± 120 B.C. They all prove that the Dadiwan
culture is representative of earlier Neolithic sites.

The sites are generally not large, but they suggest the existence of settled life
in villages. Also found were storage pits and burial grounds. There were stone
shovels, stone knives and other farm tools. Among the funerary objects there
were the lower jawbones of pigs. All this points to the considerable development
of an agricultural economy. In addition, the discovery of a quantity of deer bones
shows that hunting remained an important factor of subsidiary production.

The stone tools found here were well chipped or polished. They include
choppers, scrapers, axes, spades and knives. Bone instruments such as arrowheads, awls and chisels were finely polished. Spindle whorls, made of pottery, testify to the emergence of weaving. The pottery is rather coarse and its colour is not
even (Fig. 1). The pottery vessels, dominated by red and greyish-brown pot-

FIG. 2. (a) pottery *bo* vase with three legs from Dadiwan, Qin'an County, Gansu;
(b) painted pottery *pen* basin from Majiagua in Yuzhong County, Gansu – Majiayao type;
(c) painted pottery *guan* vase from Dibaping in Guanghe County, Gansu – Banshan type;
(d) painted pottery *hu* vase from Shanwanjia in Qin'an County, Gansu.

tery, are decorated with a crosscord pattern. Some are polished or plain. It is worth noting that there was a small amount of painted pottery. The rims of the pots were occasionally painted in red. In some cases, the vessels were painted inside with simple double zigzag patterns. Painted pottery seemed to be in the embryonic stage. The shape was simple. The vessels mainly include bowls with a round bottom or three legs, and three-footed *guan* vases with deep bodies. There were also round-bodied *guan* vases with round bottoms and bowls with a ring foot. These vessels possessing striking characteristics were rather primitive when compared with those of the Yangshao culture that came into being later.

The newly discovered Dadiwan culture has yet to be studied. It lies on the loess plateau, bordering the Peiligang culture and the Cishan culture on the north China plain. These cultures share a general character to a certain degree; for instance, they were all agricultural communities and contained three-footed pottery *bo* vessels (Fig. 2a). Even the painted potsherds decorated with a zigzag pattern found at Cishan were similar to those found at Dadiwan. Their C14 dates are quite close to one another, representing earlier Neolithic sites. What is more important, they had direct ties with the Yangshao culture with respect to stratigraphic succession and cultural factors, offering grounds for the origin of the Yangshao culture. From the discovery of these three early cultures we know pretty well that 7,000–8,000 years ago, the Yellow river valley was dotted with developed agricultural communities marked by different cultural features. Earlier sites have yet to be found.

Remains of Majiayao culture are scattered mainly in Gansu, Qinghai and Ningxia in the upper reaches of the Yellow river. It was once known as the Gansu Yangshao culture, so as to be differentiated from the Yangshao culture in the middle reaches of the Yellow river. As a local variant of the Yangshao culture, it was represented by the Majiayao sites at Lintao, Gansu province and thus called the Majiayao culture.

Most remains of communities have been found on the second terrace of the river valley. They are similar to those of the Yangshao culture in scope and economic life. The Majiayao culture can be divided into four types, the Shilingxia, the Majiayao (Fig. 2b), the Banshan (Fig. 2c) and the Machang, representing different stages of development. Generally speaking, it originated in the upper reaches of the Weihe river in eastern Gansu and developed on the basis of the Miaodigou type of the Yangshao culture.

The remains of the Shilingxia type are scattered mainly in the upper reaches of the Weihe river in Gansu province. It also extended to the valleys of the Xihan, the Hulu and Taohe rivers. Its western boundary reached the eastern end of the Hexi corridor. Remains of Shilingxia type have also been found in the vicinity of Tianzhu. Stratigraphic evidence has been discovered explicitly at Shilingxia in Wushan county, Luojiagou in Tianshui county and Majiayao in Lintao county. The lower stratum belongs to the Miaodigou type and the Majiayao type, which shows their relationship.

The most distinct characteristics of the pottery indicate a transition from the Miaodigou to the Majiayao type. Most of the vessels are red, but some are orange. The decorations are painted basically in black, consisting of geometric and zoomorphic designs. The former made up delicate patterns of lines, curves, triangles, dots and impressed checks. The latter form stylized bird heads in vivid lines. There are also cord impressions and applied decorations. The major types of pottery vessels, such as bowls, basins and small-mouthed vases with pointed bottoms, followed the basic forms of the Yangshao culture. Small-mouthed and high-necked pots, however, were a new creation, followed by the Majiayao culture. An analysis of its designs and of the shapes of pottery vessels indicates that the Shilingxia type, which spanned the preceding and the following phases, probably belongs to the early stage of the Majiayao culture.

Few remains of stone and bone instruments have been found. Their characteristics are not striking. At Huidier in Gangu county a square-shaped pottery house was unearthed with a square cone-shaped roof and a rectangular door, which was probably representative of actual buildings on the site. At least it can help us restore the house construction of the Majiayao culture and its basic form. Remains of the Majiayao type have a fairly wide distribution, extending from the upper reaches of the Jingshui and Weihe rivers in eastern Gansu, to the upper reaches of the Yellow river in the Guide basin in Qinghai province in the west, to the Qingshui river in Sichuan province in the south. In the Hexi Corridor, they are limited to Yongchang, Wuwei and the surrounding areas in the eastern section of the corridor. Their distribution is wider than those of the Shilingxia type. Besides the relative age, which can be determined by the aforesaid stratigraphic evidence, the six C14 dates give a range of about 2700–2300 B.C. The Majiayao type is therefore later than the Shilingxia type but earlier than the Banshan type.

The size of settlements was from 10,000–100,000 m². More than thirty dwelling sites have been excavated at Linjia in Dongxiang county and Jiangjiaping in Yongdeng county, both in Gansu province. Houses built in the earlier period were usually marked by square semi-subterranean structures. Each house had two kitchen ranges, which were linked together, and a doorway with steps. However, houses built in the later period were usually square or rectangular surface structures. Foundations were dug and walls were built. Each house had one kitchen range. In some cases, a house was separated into two or more rooms. In other cases, a smaller hut was built beside the door of a bigger house. Storage pits were found near the houses. Remains of carbonized grains of millet were found in one storage pit, indicating that millet was the principal crop in those days. Remains of kilns were discovered at dwelling sites. Dug out of the undisturbed earth, the kiln chamber had a hole in front and three flues slanting inwards. The top of the kiln was made of straw and earth, about 1 m in diameter. They belong to the more advanced vertical kind of kilns designed to ensure the quality of pottery.

159

Tombs are generally found in the vicinity of dwelling sites. A total of more than twenty vertical tomb pits and a dozen pottery urns for small children have been unearthed. This discovery proves that it is groundless to regard the Majiayao type as a dwelling site, and the Banshan types and the Machang type as burial grounds. The manner of burial was different. In Gansu, the dead usually lay in an extended supine position, while in Qinghai, secondary burials were popular. Traces of a wooden coffin were found in a large tomb at Hetaozhuang in Minhe county, Qinghai province. Among over seventy pottery vessels unearthed, one-third are painted. In ordinary tombs only a few vessels were found, most of which were painted. It is interesting to note that in the two tombs of a couple unearthed at upper Sunjiazhai, Datong county, Qinghai province, was found the mouth and neck of a painted pot in the husband's tomb, while the body and bottom were in the wife's tomb. Put together, they form a whole vessel. Obviously, the pot was broken on purpose and its pieces were then placed in separate tombs. They suggest a special burial custom.

The production instruments consisted mainly of stone tools. The polished tools include spades, adzes, knives and discs. Among the finds are typical micro-blade tools and bone knives, indicating the continuation of the tradition of microlithic technology. There are also bone implements such as spades, awls, arrowheads, needles, pottery, knives and spindle whorls. The art of pot-making attains a fair degree of excellence. Coarse vessels are usually decorated with cross-cord impressions and applied decoration similar to those of the Shilingxia type. The clay is orange in colour. The vessels are finely polished, and are painted in black. In a few cases, white paint was applied between black designs. The decorations consist of parallel lines, garland borders, triangles with curved lines, spirals, circles, dots and checks, forming rich and varying patterns. With the regular layout, elegant and symmetrical, the new designs are unique. The decorations also include stylized frogs, fishes and birds, and even a design of five people joining arms dancing – a rare work of art from life. Pots, vases and jars are usually painted from top to bottom, while in some cases, only the upper part of these vessels is painted. The inner part of bowls and basins is painted in general; their rims are also painted. In design and shape, the painted pottery of the Majiayao type inherited the traditions of the Shilingxia type and made new progress.

The extent of the Banshan culture was slightly smaller than that of the Majiayao type. It was confined generally to certain parts of Gansu, Qinghai and Ningxia, basically in the upper reaches of the Yellow and Weihe rivers and their tributaries, and in the Hexi corridor they extended only to areas east of Yong-chang. Some tombs were intruded by remains of the Machang type, offering explicit stratigraphic evidence. The six C14 dates available give a range of 2200–1900 B.C.

Remains of the Banshan type were formerly regarded as representative of cemeteries, but this is clearly a mistake. It is a fact that from that period onwards, dwelling sites and cemeteries were universally separated. Dwelling sites could be found near cemeteries. For instance, cultural deposits of the Banshan type were discovered from the plain adjacent to Banshan burial grounds. Three square-shaped semi-subterranean houses were discovered at Qinggangcha in Lanzhou, Gansu province, their doors facing east. Remains of fireplaces were visible. The eight post holes were found in the walls and in the centre of each of the three houses, reminiscent of a wooden structure with its roof and walls plastered with a mixture of straw and clay. Storage pots and sites of kilns were also found near the houses.

More than 4,000 tombs have been found over the past thirty years or so, most of them being rectangular shaft tombs. In some cases burial furniture was used, for instance, oblong or trapezoid wooden coffins made of planks or logs. For stone coffins, the sides were formed by whole stone slabs, while the cover and the bottom were made of a number of small stone slabs. The burial rites are varied. In most cases, the body lay on its side in a flexed position; sometimes the body had been reburied. In some cases, the body lay in an extended, supine position. There were also a number of collective burials, each tomb containing the bodies of two to seven persons, and joint tombs of two or three were commonly encountered. Most funerary objects were pottery vessels, 80–90 per cent of which were painted. Each tomb had seven or eight vessels, and in some cases, the number rose to twenty or thirty. They were found in rows by the side of the skeletons. Small pottery vessels were usually placed near the skulls. As regards other funerary objects there is a slight difference between the male and the female. For example at Dibaping in Guanghe county, Gansu province, stone axes, adzes, chisels and other tools of production were found in men's tombs, while spindle whorls made of stone or pottery were unearthed from women's tombs. This probably suggests a division of labour in society, with men engaged in farming and women specializing in weaving. Rich burials for women were customary. For instance, buried in Tomb No. 48 at Dibaping was a middle-aged woman. The funerary objects there include 17 pottery vessels, a spindle whorl of stone and 250 bone beads. Buried in Tomb No. 235 at Huazhaizi, in Lanzhou, was an adult female. Among the funerary objects were 18 pottery vessels, a spindle whorl of stone and 448 bone beads. The rich burial was a sign of respect for women, and indication of a matriarchal clan community.

Stone tools unearthed from the dwelling sites are chipped discs and scrapers and polished stone axes, chisels and knives. There were also knives of pottery and other farm tools. These indicate that farming was the main occupation. However, microblades and bone knives inlaid with microblades were also found in the tombs. There were also considerable numbers of stone balls, bone arrowheads and a bone quiver, which shows that hunting still occupied a significant place in economic life.

Beautifully shaped pottery vessels were marked by a rich variety of designs and unique styles. Coarse pottery vessels generally bear applied ornaments, but some are cord-marked or undecorated and simple in form. The clay of the painted pottery was fine and the surface was burnished. Both black and red paints are found in the Hexi corridor. Some remains of the Machang type were found even at Jiuquan and Yumen. Stratigraphically the Majiayao is superimposed on the Machang type which intruded into the tombs of the Banshan type in numerous cases. Seven C14 dates give a range from 2000 to 1700 B.C., indicating that the Machang type belonged to the late stages of the Majiayao culture.

A total of fourteen houses have been unearthed at Majiawan in Yongjing county and Jiangjiaping in Yongdeng county, both in Gansu province. Most of them are round or oblong semi-subterranean buildings. Some consist of two or more rooms. Inside the houses, the flat, hard floor is plastered with a mixture of straw and clay and red clay, on which there is the base of a circular fireplace. Generally speaking, storage pits were found inside or near the houses. Pottery kilns were usually found in groups of two or three at a single dwelling site. At Baidaogouping in Lanzhou, archaeologists have discovered twelve kiln sites, all built in the undisturbed soil. About 1 m in diameter, each of the kilns had nine fire holes which entered the kiln chambers through flues. They are similar in structure to those of the Majiayao type, but improved.

Tombs of the Machang type discovered are most numerous, totalling 1,200. They are usually clan cemeteries (for collective burials). Small children were also interred there. Most of the tombs are shaft pits. Some are oval with a ramp, set up with a vertical plank or a stone slab. A well-made coffin was unearthed at Liuwan in Ledu, Qinghai province. Oblong in shape, it was made of planks or semi-circular slabs of wood, linked together by three horizontal planks, dovetailed with mortises and tenons on both ends. In some cases, planks or twigs were found beneath the skeletons. The burial rites varied in different places, including extended supine position, flexed burial on the side, secondary burials, prone burial and adult joint burial. Funerary objects ranged from one or two dozens of pieces. This is probably an indication of difference between the rich and the poor. Take Tomb No. 564 at Liuwan: among the ninety-five funerary objects, ninety-one pieces are pottery vessels, the rest being stone tools and turquoise ornaments. However, there are not many funerary objects in ordinary tombs. Pottery vessels were usually laid near the skulls or on one side of the tomb, but large-sized pottery was put near the entrance. Shells and imitation shell *guan* vases of stone were also used as funerary objects. At least they serve as witnesses to the ties of communication and trade with the south-eastern coastal areas.

Of the stone tools unearthed from dwelling sites the polished stone instruments such as axes, adzes, chisels, knives, sickles, querns and pestles predominate; all are finely polished. There are also microblades, scrapers, and bone knives with notches. Among the ornaments are bone beads, stone balls and turquoise objects. The only exception is an incomplete bronze knife found at Jiangjiaping. This shows that bronze was rare in the Machang culture.

Most of the pottery vessels are coarse, only a very few being well made. Designs of painted pottery became simpler. Most coarse pottery vessels are

Fig. 3. Microliths from Astana in Turfan County, Xinjiang.

undecorated and simple in form. There are still cord impressions and applied ornaments. Some vessels are coated in red and painted in black and red. Chevron designs are rare. Designs marked by four large circles are common. There are also varied designs of human images, broken lines, triangles, and rhombric, check and coil designs, but they are slightly simpler than those of the Banshan-type pottery. A painted pot unearthed at Liuwan features a lifelike image of a female nude which was a combination of painted pottery and sculpture – a great work of art. Over 100 varied marks are found on the lower part of the painted pottery. The *hu* vase (Fig. 2d), *guan* vase, *pen* basin, *dou* vessel and cups are most common. A rare cooking vessel like a tripod was unearthed at Hualinping. It is probably a result of further cultural exchanges with the central plains. Both the shapes and the designs of the Machang pottery manifest close ties with the Banshan. However, the technology of painted pottery was in decline. Eventually, the Majiayao culture was replaced by the new and developing Qijia culture which belonged to the Chalcolithic Age.

Neolithic remains in Xinjiang were first found at the turn of this century, but they were collected mainly from the surface.[3] Generally speaking, no clear picture has been obtained of the sites, cultural strata and their associations. In southern Xinjiang, according to the finds which have been collected so far, the remains are distributed mainly in hillside fields around the Tarim basin. Remains have also been found near the Lop Nor and the Kum river. In northern Xinjiang, they have been found mainly at the northern and southern foot of T'ien Shan. These finds are all limited to oases. As a result of changes in natural conditions, however, some places have become desolate.

Finds have been divided into three categories represented by microliths, tools and painted pottery, all being regarded as the Neolithic culture. However, the latest study proves that they belong to different eras. They possess their own

3. Ibid.

characteristics in terms of culture and the type of economy. Remains represented by microliths are scattered extensively (Fig. 3). They persisted for quite a long period and largely belonged to the Neolithic period. Animal husbandry and hunting were the main sectors of economy. Traces of farming were not very clear. Remains represented by pebble tools and painted pottery date from the Chalcolithic Age or the Bronze Age. Farming was the chief sector of production and economy. But there are still missing links of Neolithic agricultural communities.

It is worth noting that Xinjiang lies in the hinterland of Asia marked by a dry climate. The farmland has to be irrigated by water from melting snow or drawn from wells. No similar measures of irrigation dating from the Neolithic Age have been discovered yet. Of course, we cannot conclude that there were no farming activities at all in the area in the Neolithic Age. At least the natural conditions and the cultural remains represented by microliths are sufficient to prove that it is likely that farming activities emerged in the area at a later stage.

Sites of Neolithic agricultural settlements on the Tibetan plateau have been found only in river valleys in the south and east of the country. The climate in these low-lying areas is fit for the development of agriculture. Today, they are still the principal farming areas in Tibet. Neolithic sites and relics have been discovered in the suburbs of Lhasa, Nyingchi county and Medog county in the Tsangpo (Brahmaputra) river valley. The area can be divided into two parts. Nyingchi county is the centre of the northern part, including Lhasa, and relics there have been collected from the surface. Cultural deposits have also been found in individual cases, but they are neither deep nor connected. Though agricultural settlements were formed, they were far less developed than those on the loess plateau. The stone tools include discs, choppers and net weights as well as polished axes, chisels and knives. Elongated stone knives with perforations used for harvesting are identical to those found on the loess plateau. Pottery vessels consist mainly of coarse brown ware, and only a few of unburnt clay. There were also black pottery vessels with a burnished surface, decorated with cord impressions, incised patterns and open work. The shapes include bowls, *guan* vases and *pan* vessels. Fragments of spouts have also been found. The quantity of finds is small and their cultural character is not altogether clear, but they are similar to the Qijia culture in Gansu and Qinghai.

The southern region has Medog county as its centre. Here have been found, at seven sites, a number of polished stone tools, including axes, adzes, chisels and spindle whorls. Polished with great care, they are certainly tools for cutting trees, tilling the land and weaving. Coarse postsherds with cord impressions and incised patterns have also been discovered. Marked by its subtropical climate, the low-lying area here is ideal for farming.

A well-preserved settlement site has been discovered at Karuo in Qamdo, in the Lancang river valley in eastern Tibet. It lies on the second terrace at the confluence of the Lancang and the Karuo rivers. Being 3,100 m above sea-level, the site is about 10,000 m² in area and the cultural layer is over 1 m thick. Both semi-subterranean and surface houses have been discovered. Judging from the existing post-holes they were wooden structures with earthern or stone walls. The commonest finds are chipped stone tools such as choppers, discs and scrapers. Polished stone tools are more rare, and include axes, chisels, knives and arrowheads. There was also a considerable quantity of microliths and bone hafts inlaid with microblades. They are basically identical in shape with those found in the Yellow river valley and in the north. Most pottery vessels consist of coarse ware, and are only of unburnt clay, incised patterns are predominant, but cord impressions are also seen. There are a small number of painted pottery vessels. Marked by simple shapes, the vessels include *pan* basins, *bo* vessels and *guan* vases. The C14 dates range from 3300 to 1800 B.C., indicating that the sites covered a long period of development. The stabilization of a settled life and the emergence of farming tools and domesticated pigs prove that farming was the foundation of the economy. The discovery of a good many bones of wild animals confirms that hunting still played an important role in the economic life. The pottery vessels found here are in shapes and designs similar to those found at the site of Dadunzi in Yuanmou county, Yunnan province, in the middle reaches of the Lancang river. However, the painted pottery, elongated stone knives with multiple perforations and microliths prove that they had certain ties with the Neolithic culture of the Yellow river valley.

Microliths have a wide distribution in the western part of China. Strictly speaking, microliths were chipped in an indirect way, involving special craft and skill, and they were limited to microcores and blades as well as certain artefacts processed from microblades. In the past, small stone tools apart from microcores and blades were habitually known as microliths and even imprecisely called a 'Microlithic Culture'. This is not appropriate. Microliths made on microblades can be called microliths for short. It is likely that this tradition originated in the Yellow river valley during the Late Palaeolithic and prevailed into the Mesolithic. With the development of farming microliths in the Yellow river valley declined abruptly. Apart from a number of semi-husbandry and semi-farming sites, there were only a few microlithic sites, but in the desert and pasture areas to the north, microliths were still in use after the emergence of metal tools and vessels. This shows that microliths continued to be used for hunting and animal husbandry for a fairly long time in these parts.

In the western part of Inner Mongolia more than eighty microlithic sites have been found in the vast desert or semi-desert areas extending from the Helan mountain ranges[4] to the east of the Tarim basin. Most of the cultural relics were exposed in shifting sand-dunes. Trial diggings have been conducted at certain places, but no cultural deposits have been unearthed. Therefore, it is rather difficult to give a date to these localities in this area. The distribution of remains

4. Maringer, 1950; Teilhard de Chardin and Young, 1932.

proves that Neolithic people had temporary settlements along rivers and lakes and lived by hunting and livestock breeding. Today, however, most of these lakes have dried up or become saline. For instance, quite a number of Neolithic sites are distributed on the shores of Sogho Nor lake. The extent of the lake remains unchanged, but the water is now too salty to drink. This indicates that the environmental conditions in this area were much better than today. Therefore, we can assume that the dwelling sites were scattered in oases, not in desert areas as today.

The majority of cultural relics are of stone. Most common are microliths including stone cores in the shape of cylinders, cones and wedges. microblades are unusually plentiful. Traces of retouch or use can be seen on one or both sides. Many were probably hafted in bone knives. Some microblades were worked on both sides and shaped into drills. There are also plenty of end-scrapers and round-scrapers. However, stone arrowheads are few. As a striking feature, there was a quantity of large chipped stone tools such as choppers and scrapers. There are also stone axes and adzes retouched on both edges, and a small number of querns and pestles. Potsherds are also scarce, they are plain and cord-marked, and probably belong to a later stage. In some places archaeologists have discovered a small number of beads made of ostrich egg-shells, which are believed to be characteristic of the Mesolithic.

The well-made stone drills and the rich range of large polished stone artefacts are local features. Stone arrowheads and pottery vessels are rare. This has something to do with the constant movement of tribes for hunting and livestock breeding. The great majority of remains belong to the Neolithic. It is also possible that remains at certain places may be dated earlier – to the Mesolithic. These chipped-stone tools, which were roughly associated with microliths, cannot be dated to earlier times.

Remains represented by microliths are also scattered quite extensively in Xinjiang.[5] More than thirty sites have been found at the southern and northern foot of the T'ien Shan, the border of the Tarim basin, in southern Xinjiang and even on the shores of Lop Nor and the Kum river. They have also been collected from the surface. A clear picture of their cultural deposits and settlements is not yet available. The distribution of sites is similar to that of the western part of Inner Mongolia. Some (those in the vicinity of Lop Nor, for example) have become desolate areas today. As a result of wind erosion, sites are unusually exposed on the surface. Cultural deposits are absent. Well-preserved dwelling sites, however, will probably be discovered at the southern and northern foot of the T'ien Shan and the northern foot of the Kunlun.

The sites here are strikingly characterized by microliths. They can be divided into at least two types. For the first type, microliths have been found without pottery. So far only one site has been discovered at Qijiaojing. For the

---

5. An, 1978; Bergman, 1939; Huang, 1948, 1958.

second type, microliths have been found with pottery. But in most cases, the associated pottery is scarce. Furthermore, one cannot exclude the possibility that the microliths constitute a separate group. In addition, there are numerous finds of stone laurel-leaf points which are unique to Xinjiang. The sites are scattered fairly widely, probably representing a later date. Now, we shall illustrate the situation with a few typical sites.

The site of Qijiaojing lies to the north of the Lanzhou–Xinjiang highway in the vicinity of Hami, eastern Xinjiang. In the surrounding areas there are plenty of fixed sand-dunes covered with Chinese tamarisks. The stone tools that have been collected in the area can be divided roughly into three categories:

1. Microliths, which are fairly plentiful, including stone cores shaped like the keel of a boat, cone-shaped stone cores and microblades.

2. Flake tools, which are most plentiful. Flakes chipped directly from stones are shaped into side-scrapers and end-scrapers. There are also many large-sized, thick, heavy stone flakes which are processed on one side to serve as choppers. There are also plenty of ordinary unprocessed rectangular flakes, but which bear traces of use.

3. Core stone tools. Only a pointed stone axe has been discovered. It is massive and 31 cm in length. Here, pottery is absent, but microliths are quite typical. The large-sized flake tools are more or less primitive in nature. In particular, the stone core shaped like the bottom of a boat is representative of early microlithic traditions, whose date probably ranges from the Meso-lithic to the Early Neolithic Age.

The site of Xinger lies at the northern foot of the Kuruktag mountains on the north-eastern border of the Tarim basin. From the surface one can see grey traces of dwellings which are 1–5 m in diameter. Also visible are remains of two fire-places hardened by fire which are slightly higher than the ground. One of the dwelling sites contains cultural deposits 10 cm thick. As man led a settled life on a semi-stable basis, hunting and animal husbandry seemed to be the principal source of economy. But it did not exclude the possibility that farming had taken shape already. Remains of the same character are scattered quite extensively at Loulan, on the banks of the Konqi (Kum) river, at Astana in Turfan, and in other places. Although quite a lot of remains have been collected, their stra-tigraphic relationships have not yet been ascertained. The polished stone axes and adzes collected around Lop Nor are rarely seen at other sites, but they are likely to be remains of a later period.

The traditions of microliths in Xinjiang are basically identical with those of Inner Mongolia. However, they possess a certain regional character. The early remains represented by Qijiaojing share, to a greater extent, the general character of those in the eastern part of China. For example, the absence of stone cores shaped like the keel of a boat. However, the plentiful stone points in the shape of laurel-leaves are unique to Xinjiang. As for the triangular stone arrowheads which were common in eastern Inner Mongolia, only two examples have been found in the vicinity of Lop Nor. They were far less common than the laurel-leaf arrowheads. Such stone arrowheads were in use for a long period, probably lasting up to the second–fifth centuries B.C. For instance, they have been unearthed from tombs at Kurmoi, Altay Xian, and at Loulan, near Lop Nor. They are flat-based and roughly made, but they have virtually inherited the form of the laurel-leaf arrowheads. Since typical microliths are rarely seen at Bronze Age sites, the tradition of microliths in the area is not later than the Neolithic.

Conclusion

Up to now the western regions of China have produced very limited material for correctly assessing the cultural tradition. Whatever information is known shows a cultural link with the neighbouring areas to the north and west but as we go eastwards, particularly to the Gansu area, the influence from the culture of the Yellow river did produce some results. While the relations of the flint industry and of the microliths in Xinjiang and Inner Mongolia show local variants, the Gansu cultural zone presents an adoption of the cultural features of the east.

Neolithic tribes in northern parts of Central Asia[1]

A. P. Derevyanko and D. Dorj

THE development of the Neolithic cultures of Mongolia, southern Siberia and Kazakhstan took place as modern faunal and floral complexes and landscapes were taking shape. In the early stage the Neolithic tribes inhabiting this great expanse of territory had a mobile way of life which involved frequent contacts between ancient populations belonging to differing historico-cultural groups and which implied mutual cultural enrichment. At the same time each area remained highly distinctive, as is evidenced by the mosaic-like character of the cultures and complexes identified and investigated so far.

There was also very great variety in productive activities. The Neolithic cultures in the northern areas of Central Asia generally inherited the Upper Palaeolithic traditions of hafted blade technology for work tools. One innovation that had already begun to appear in the Mesolithic period was the wide-scale use of microliths, particularly of geometric forms. Various economic systems involving different combinations of hunting, fishing and gathering were developed and perfected on the basis of this range of tools. The Mesolithic and Neolithic hunters chiefly hunted the large herds of hoofed animals of the steppes and semi-arid lands. Economic differences were intertwined with cultural differences, and a more detailed and specific description can therefore be given of individual regions.

Two such regions are readily identifiable within the enormous area of the steppes and central Mongolia, where Neolithic cultures developed in large measure following the tradition of more ancient Palaeolithic and Mesolithic cultures. Of particular significance are sites of the Kere-Uula type with their flake technology. A major influence was likewise exercised by tribes from the Lake Baikal region to the north and from the eastern regions of Manchuria and the Far East. Hence, in discussing the origins of the Neolithic of eastern and central Mongolia,

---

1. See Map 6 on pages 154 and 155.

two major factors must be stressed, namely the local basis and the influence of contiguous territories.[2]

The sources of the Neolithic cultures of Mongolia can be seen in the Mesolithic epoch. The expanses of present-day Mongolia are rich in Mesolithic remains. In particular, they have been discovered on the slopes of Kere-Uula, on the left bank of the Halhin-gol river in the eastern *aimak*, along the right bank of the Kerulen river across from the city of Choibalsan (Site No. 9), at Moiltyn-am (Layer I) on the Orkhon river in the *aimak* of Kentei, in the southern Gobi *aimak*, as well as at various locations in the Bain-Ugli, Kobdo, Gobi-Altai, central Gobi, and Sukhe-Bator *aimaks* of Mongolia.

The above sites are best exemplified by the purely Mesolithic settlement at Kere-Uula, Site No. 9 on the Kerulen and by the extremely well-preserved and representative multi-layered settlements of Rashan-Khad and Moiltyn-am, which exhibit with utmost clarity and in a highly unified manner all the characteristic features of the Mesolithic culture of Mongolia.

Excavations of the Kere-Uula tepe over a total area of 75 m² yielded numerous stone tools. These included Gobi cores and core blanks of brown flint; tongue-shaped convex-blade scrapers, fashioned out of flakes of lamellar chips; single-blade knives, side-scrapers of the Kere-Uula type, worked from flat pieces of black shale; Kere-Uula type angle and medium burins made from knive-shaped flakes; edge chips constituting a by-product of core shaping and ski-shaped flakes struck from the long sides of cores, larger triangular flakes, struck from Gobi cores, which were either trimmed or else unretouched along their edges; microflakes, likewise struck from Gobi cores; and, finally, some individual chopper-like artefacts as well as relatively shapeless pebbles and flints that might have served as cores after careful working.

In fact, the principal function of the Gobi cores was to yield knife-shaped micro-blades. In individual instances the cores may also have been used as scrapers. The angle of Kere-Uula tepe burins are knife-shaped flakes with retouched long edges and slanting transverse cleavage faces struck diagonally from the flake vertex. Their chief use was in fashioning hafted composite tools, that is, making grooves in bone and wooden blade holders. Tools of a similar type found in Japan are known as 'Araya' burins after one of the sites in northern Japan.

The second and third cultural layers of the Rashan-Khad settlement were also found to contain Gobi and boat-shaped cores, together with larger and smaller cores of the subprismatic and Levallois types with either one or two striking platforms.

Other tools included burins with a diagonal cutting edge, angle and median burins formed from a cleavage face perpendicular to the longitudinal axis of the

---

2. Derevyanko and Okladnikov, 1969; Okladnikov and Derevyanko, 1970; Dorj and Derevyanko, 1970; Dorj, 1971.

implement. Whatever their type, these burins were made from flakes and flake-shaped chips retouched along their edges.

Also present were ski-shaped flakes, end-scrapers fashioned out of chips and some of rounded shapes with high-relief spines and steeply retouched working edges, large, roughly worked side-scrapers and knives of the Kere-Uula type. The principal material used to make all these implements collected at the Rashan-Khad settlement are fully identical with those of the Kere-Uula inventory. Gobi cores were also found at the settlement of Moiltyn-am in the first cultural horizon, together with various pebble-tools including small scrapers, fine piercing tools and projectile points.

Site No. 9 in the Kerulen area was of entirely different character as regards both its artefacts and the culture which they represented. The Neolithic finds which turned up in the course of excavating some 50 m² at the site included a significant array of arrowheads made out of grey, light yellow and green flint flakes. All of these were finely retouched at the sharpened tip; some of the arrowheads were likewise retouched along the edges, more often than not from the ventral surface.

Similar flake arrowheads were found in the Gurmiin-nor area of Bayan-obo *somon* (Kentei *aimak*) and by mount Bat-Khan in the same *somon*. Here they were accompanied by Gobi cores, as well as (in the case of the early complexes of the Neolithic site of Dulany-gobi in the eastern *aimak*) by Kere-Uula knives.

This completes our brief account of the principal pre-ceramic sites in Mongolia. Some of them date back to the Late Pleistocene, i.e. 17,000 to 12,000 years ago (in the case of Moiltyn-am and Rashan-Khad, whose early artefacts show a marked tendency towards Levallois forms of stone chipping), or else to the Early Holocene, i.e. 12,000–10,000 years ago (Kere-Uula).

Site No. 9 and other contemporary sites belong to the final stages of the Mesolithic, that is, to the fifth millennium B.C. as is evidenced by their bifacially retouched flake arrowheads reflecting perfect mastery of stone-working technique.

A distinctive clue to the cultural identity of the Mesolithic population of Mongolia is afforded by the Gobi core, which begins to occur in the territory of present-day Mongolia towards the end of the Upper Palaeolithic, developing during the Mesolithic and surviving until the Early Neolithic.

Independently of the Gobi core, the presence of other individual items from the above list of Mesolithic cultural artefacts found in Mongolia at sites situated in the above-mentioned territories also points to a clear picture of the routes taken by specific ethnic groups migrating outwards from the heart of Central Asia. Eloquent testimony of this may be seen in the fact that in Mongolia all the elements of the Mesolithic are present as a unified complex (as at the settlement of Kere-Uula and Rashan-Khad), rather than in the scattered fashion in which they occur in the neighbouring parts of northern Asia. This establishes beyond doubt the stability of the local forms of stone-artefact assemblages, while at the same time providing solid ground for supposing that such a stable source culture might well originally have been that of a fully formed and unified ethnic group with an Upper Palaeolithic tradition behind it. According to all available evidence, the Mesolithic population of Mongolia constituted precisely such a group.

Among the earliest of the Neolithic finds in Mongolia are the settlement-type sites by Lake Yamat-Nuur some 10 km from the station of Khovirga. The lake is shallow and is gradually drying up. Its width is 250–300 m. The water line is now 300–400 m away from the old lake shore.

Most of the finds were made on the northern and north-western shores of the lake as well as along the rim of the ancient terrace adjacent to the high southern shore. The material collected in the area around the lake has certain highly distinctive features, the cores being chiefly of the flake type. Of these, the majority are either prismatic or quasi-prismatic, with flakes struck off from three or four sides. Wedge-shaped cores and scraper cores are also present.

Most of the collection consists of primary flakes and flake tools. Particularly noteworthy among the finished implements are end-scrapers made from both chips and flaked stones as well as invert blades and cutters. The end-scrapers were fashioned by high-angle oblique retouching. The invert blades were worked largely out of knife-shaped flakes. The fine retouching was done on the ventral face, with some of the items finished by retouching on the dorsal face as well. Distinctively shaped adze or scraper-like tools constitute a special group. These are quasi-triangular in plan. One whole face of these tools was worked in broad scaling strokes.

The settlement in question exhibits numerous archaic features. Its scraper cores, cutters, and composite implements are analogous to those found in such early sites as that of Mount Kere-Uula. The adze or scraper-like tools are also of early date. Moreover, no potsherds were found at the Lake Yamat-Nuur site. Both of these considerations suggest that sites of this type date back to the fifth or fourth millennium B.C.

One important Neolithic site in Mongolia is the settlement of Tamsagbulag. It is situated on a high terrace above a flood plain and consists of large semi-subterranean dwellings having an area of roughly 40 m².

All the stone objects discovered in the Tamsagbulag settlements are characteristic of a fairly clearly defined stage in the history of the ancient tribes of the Tamsagbulag culture. The stone implements consisted of cores of various shapes (with one notched lateral edge; sub-prismatic pebble-shaped), including core scrapers of both the classical and Tamsagbulag type. The latter are so named because of their highly distinctive features peculiar to this culture alone, that is, a bevelled striking surface fashioned by making transverse chips. The flakes were removed from only one side and the shoulder was cut into a point or wedge shape. Cores were usually fashioned from flint, jasper, tuff and, occasionally, chalcedony. The finished cores were often later converted into different types of

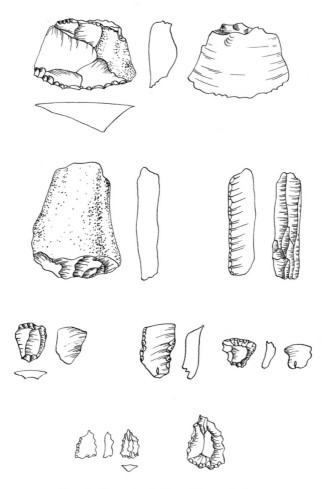

FIG. 1. Stone tools from Tamsagbulag.

implements – hammers, cutters, draw-knives and planes for making bone and wooden objects. It is possible, in fact, to use almost all 'Tamsagbulag' cores as tools of this kind since, after a slight modification by chipping, their final surface constitutes a good notched blade.

A large number of knife-like flakes – and tools made from them – were found. In fact, they constitute the majority of all such finds, and include cutters, knives, knife-blades, awls and scrapers. The scrapers are of several kinds: end-scrapers with a straight or rounded blade, lingulate scrapers and scrapers made of flat flakes of siliceous tuff or, as they are called, Tamsagbulag scrapers, since they are characteristic of that culture alone. The working blade is at the broader end, the edge of which was first roughly hammer-dressed and then finished off by fine chipping (Fig. 1).

Among other objects were hammer-dressed and carefully polished adzes, oval in cross-section with slightly narrowed lateral faces; arrowheads with chipping on both faces; quite large scrapers made of flakes or other special fragments; and adze and scraper-like implements used as chopping tools.

Besides stone implements, the Tamsagbulag inhabitants also used bone tools on a large scale. They used bone for making arrowheads, knives and blades for composite knives and daggers. Without working them, they also made use of the ribs of animals, the ends of which were worn and polished through long use.

Some fragments of pottery were also found, thick-walled, grey in colour and decorated with deeply cut parallel lines. This pottery was unquestionably of local manufacture in as much as nothing like it has been found among remains from the same period in other parts of Central, North and East Asia. Thus, we have here features in the working of stone and earthenware that are specific to the Tamsagbulag culture alone, and distinct from the Neolithic cultures around it.

One of the most important problems in studying the history of the tribes of the Tamsagbulag culture is that of agriculture and cattle-breeding. Striking evidence of the emergence and full development of agriculture in the region in question is provided by the numerous specimens of pestles, grinders and graters for grinding grain; hoes for loosening the soil; millstones (with biconical centre holes having a diameter of between 10 and 15 cm) and weighting material for digging sticks.

Agriculture, the new branch of economic activity, played a tremendous role in the further development and advancement or the material culture of the Tamsagbulag inhabitants and in their economic life in so far as it provided man with new, continuous and inexhaustible supplies of food and in the methods of economic management. V. G. Childe quite aptly termed the emergence of agriculture and cattle-breeding and the technical innovations it brought with it the 'Neolithic revolution', which, for the peoples of Tamsagbulag, occurred in the middle of the third millennium B.C.

All available information indicates that agriculture in eastern Mongolia emerged independently and had its origins in the active practice of food-gathering. The agricultural implements mentioned above are clear evidence of the fact that the inhabitants of Tamsagbulag engaged in primitive hoe agriculture. Consequently, the favourable climatic conditions and the presence of local varieties of wild plants that might have been the forerunners of later cultivated plants, such as paniculate and capitate millet, all provided the preconditions for the independent development of agriculture in the Tamsagbulag region. Agriculture combined with both food-gathering and hunting, evidence of this being provided by flint and bone arrowheads of various forms, and implements for working the wool of animals and animal bones found at the Tamsagbulag settlement. According to A. P. Okladnikov, hunting even had a specialized character.

To all this must be added fishing, and when we remember that, with agriculture, the most important feature of the Tamsagbulag economy was cattle-raising, there can be no doubt that this economy was a complex one. That fishing constituted a subsidiary element of the economy is evidenced by the finds of fish bones, while the presence of the bones of domesticated animals indicates that cattle-breeding was a fully developed activity.

Further study of the osteological material is required before we can positively identify the particular types of domestic animals, but there is sure evidence that among the large animals, horses and cattle had already been domesticated at that time (a whole ritual heap of bulls, for example, was discovered at Tamsagbulag). Nevertheless, we cannot exclude the possibility that many other kinds of domestic animals were bred, given the particularly favourable natural conditions that then existed in eastern Mongolia – endless stretches of steppe with excellent grazing lands and watering places.

The combination of agriculture with hunting, food-gathering and, to some extent, fishing was conducive to a sedentary way of life in sturdy dwellings sunk halfway into the ground. In addition, a whole ancestral 'microregion' grew up at Tamsagbulag, something that was unknown to the tribes who had settled in neighbouring territories. The Tamsagbulag dwellings were rectangular in plan and the ground around them, in which large numbers of animal bones and various tools were discovered, was usually very dark, almost jet black, in colour. To judge from one dwelling that survived completely intact, the Tamsagbulag house consisted of a foundation trench dug 50 to 80 cm into the ground, two connected rows of posts (one row abutting the walls of the trench and serving as the foundation of the wall frame and supporting the exterior binding, and the other placed in the centre of the dwelling and serving as a support for the internal binding) and a pyramidal roof. The dwelling had no door (apparently, a smoke hole or a special opening in the roof into which a notched log was inserted took the place of a door).

The presence of durable, semi-subterranean houses, is eloquent testimony to the establishment of a settled mode of life within the tribal community of Tamsagbulag (one of the five dwellings excavated there was 35 m² in area). This

175

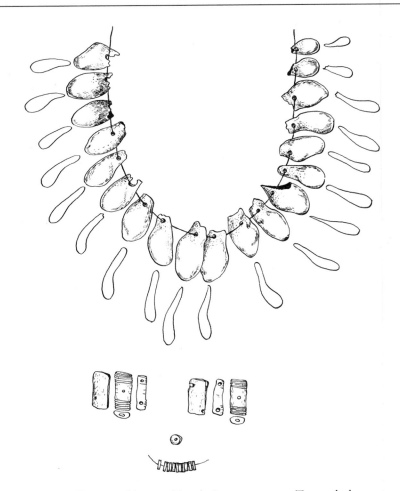

FIG. 2. Bone necklace and beads from a grave at Tamsagbulag.

is evidence of the fact that the tribes of Mongolia were not all itinerant hunters or permanent nomads throughout the long history of that country.

It is interesting to note that under the floor of one of the dwellings the grave of a young woman was found. It contained ornaments made of mother-of-pearl, stag's teeth that had been bored and strung on a thread and two bone daggers (one of them with interchangeable flint blades). The mother-of-pearl beads (some 200 were found) were fashioned from thin, flat, round wafers, pierced at the centre. A store of unfinished pieces, discovered in the inhabited parts of the dwelling, indicates that the beads were of local manufacture (Fig. 2). The woman was buried in a sitting position in a narrow pit. In general, one of the typical features of the Neolithic tribes of the Tamsagbulag and other regions of the Kerulen valley was the manner of burial. All corpses without exception were found in a contracted, sitting position, their face turned towards the west or east. The burial pit was so small and constricted that there was room for only one body.

Compared with burials found in other Neolithic cultures, those of the Tamsagbulag region are highly distinctive and nothing like them has been found in neighbouring territories or, at best, extremely rarely. In other words, the custom of burying the dead in a narrow pit, in a contracted sitting position was peculiar to this region and the fact that there was just this one burial site in our view testifies to the specific ethnic unity of the population of that period.

Thus, the Tamsagbulag culture is intrinsically different from contemporaneous cultures, from the standpoint both of the remains left of its economy and the way of life of its members, and therefore occupies a prominent and distinctly original place in the ancient history of this part of Central Asia.

The third stage, lasting from the end of the third to the beginning of the second millennium B.C. is represented in eastern and central Mongolia by sites at which flake trimming had been supplanted by bifacially retouched artefacts. Some sites of this type may be dated to the Early Bronze Age. This would be the case, for example, with the finds at Lake Khuityn-Bulag at a distance of 130 km from the town of Choibalsan along the road to Halhin-gol. Here the area between a string of lakes and their sources is straddled by a row of low *solonchak* hills thickly overgrown with dersen grass (*Lasiagrostis splendens*). The eroded slopes of these hills were found to contain accumulations of debris in the form of large fired and cracked pebbles. Scattered about these accumulations were large quantities of animal bones, chips, knife-shaped flakes and finished artefacts. Certain patches were found to contain calcinated reddish-coloured loamy sand dash, the remains of hearths.

The stone artefacts collected from around the hearths and at a small distance away from them were largely finished tools. The implements are mostly of chalcedony, flint items being much less common. The arrowheads are of three types: with a straight tang, with asymmetrical barbs and with a rounded base (laurel-leaf arrowheads). The arrowheads are quite similar in shape and fabrication technique to the Glazkovo arrowheads of the Lake Baikal region. All the arrowheads were worked by very fine retouching. In addition to arrowheads, the find included some ten scrapers and fitted knife blades. Some of the hearth-midden slag included baked copper droplets. The slag in question was definitely part of the find as a whole. The advent of these new materials, namely copper and bronze, is associated with the almost complete disappearance of flake cores and knife-shaped flake artefacts.

The other extensive area of north-eastern Central Asia with its own distinctive features as regards the development of Neolithic cultures is the southern part of Mongolia and the Gobi desert, where man was obliged to adapt to certain special conditions imposed by nature and the landscape. This region also exhibits three principal stages in the development of Neolithic cultures. The earliest complexes – those of the Late Mesolithic and Early Neolithic – are characterized by an advanced flake-tool technology and a large number of artefacts fashioned out of knife-shaped flakes. This enabled Nelson and later Maringer to refer to the microlithic character of the Mesolithic and Neolithic cultures of this region.[3]

The best-known of the sites discovered in the 1920s by the members of the United States expedition to Central Asia led by R. C. Andrews are those in the region of Baindzak or Shabrak-Usu in the central Gobi, where two cultural horizons were unearthed. The lower of these contained no pottery but was characterized by an abundance of wedge-shaped cores which have come to be called 'Gobi cores' by virtue of the Baindzak find. These and other types of cores (prismatic, conic, etc.) had been struck to yield knife-shaped flakes which were then transformed into a wide range of implements: scrapers, cutters, knives, and multipurpose tools. The layer contained small disc-shaped ostrich eggshell beads. The same area was subsequently revisited by a Soviet/Mongolian archaeological expedition which refined the previously available findings as regards stratigraphy and collected new material.

Early site complexes in this area are associated with a range of ancient dunes covering the floor of what was once a depression of enormous size. The culture-bearing stratum is exposed in areas where the dunes have been blown away by the wind. The finds occurred in the form of hearth-centred clusters and smallish individual groups. Two horizons were identifiable, each of them reflecting a particular stage in the development of the Neolithic cultures in the region.

The more ancient of these was the Neolithic horizon extending below the dune base layer. This was characterized by stone implements and ceramics with parallels in the Early Neolithic cultures of the Lake Baikal region. Links with the preceding stage are present in the form of cores for the striking off of kniveshaped flakes as well as flake-type implements. In shape and production technique, these are very similar to their more ancient antecedents. The tools in question are scrapers, cutters, etc. Major changes in the culture are evidenced by the advent of pottery. The vessels are of semi-oval shape with a pointed bottom. The outer surfaces bear textile-imprints, some of the artefacts bearing the woven net impressions typical of the ceramic wares of the Lake Baikal region and Transbaikalye. Specimens of a similar type have been unearthed in other *taiga* and forest-steppe regions of Siberia, as well as at sites in Manchuria and all the way to the Great Wall in northern China.

Links with cultures of the north are also evident from the presence of arrowheads, knives and hafted blades typical of the Neolithic of the Lake Baikal region and Transbaikalye. The Neolithic culture in question apparently took shape on the basis of the culture of peoples who had wandered out over this area during the Mesolithic, as well as that of the incoming hunters and fishers from the *taiga* and forest-steppe parts of Siberia.

The next stage in development of the Neolithic culture of southern Mon-

3. Nelson, 1926*a*, 1926*b*; Maringer, 1930.

golia is less complex. The cultural horizons of this stage lie within the body of the dune deposits and are associated with fairly deep sand-covered burial grounds. Items fashioned from knife-shaped flakes continue to occur at this time, but are to a large extent superseded by bifacially retouched artefacts. The ceramics, too, are of an entirely different aspect: the vessels are thin-walled, well profiled with flat bottoms. Painted ceramics likewise make their appearance. The outer surfaces of pottery were often ornamented in black paint. Also present are sherds bearing traces of black ornamentation against a red background. In some settlements a dark paint was applied to a yellow background. Painted ceramics are fairly common in the Neolithic sites in the southern Gobi desert.

The period in question is also marked by important changes in economic life and activity. The settlements investigated yielded large numbers of grinding stones, mullers and pestles. Also significant is the fact that cultural artefacts of this time were often included in burials. Such finds were made with particular consistency in the case of the site near the Darigangi *somon* in the western Gobi. To the south of the *somon*, several kilometres away from a large freshwater lake, are some extensive ranges of dunes. The depressions between the dunes were found to contain numerous Neolithic complexes. Differentiating between them stratigraphically and chronologically proved a very difficult task. The ceramic wares found at the wind-exposed sites were of three types: cord-impressed; smooth-walled with an evenly flared slightly thicker lip; and thick-walled vessels decorated with incised horizontal lines and appliqué torus moulding ('cordons'). The stone items included both objects fashioned out of knife-shaped flakes and bifacially worked implements.

Another group of Neolithic complexes was discovered between the above-mentioned lake and the Darigangi *somon*. The Neolithic finds here occur in clusters scattered over a fairly wide area. Stratigraphically these are bedded in well-composted ancient buried soil containing large amounts of vegetational residue and covered over with sand. Remains of dwellings have been found here. The finds include grinding stones, mullers, pestles, and hoe-like tools used to work the soil. no ceramics were found, even though the stone items were typologically close to contemporaneous finds from the southern Gobi.

Studies of Neolithic sites in Mongolia have made it possible to answer some of the questions concerning the beliefs and arts of the ancient population. All the graves found in eastern Mongolia testify to the unity of burial customs over a considerable area, and therefore to a certain ethnic unity of the people in question. Skeletons were found in a seated position, facing either westward or eastward. The burial pit was of small size and so narrow that it could contain only one sitting body. The graves for the most part yielded very little, and only the one in dwelling No. 1 at Tamsagbulag contained ornaments and bone daggers with inset blades.

The Neolithic tribes of eastern Mongolia have left traces of animal worship. Tamsagbulag yielded a cluster consisting of the skull of some smaller animal, beads of decorated bone, and the canines of a maral, or Asiatic red deer (*Cervus elaphus*). Another cluster contained the bones of a large animal gathered and packed into a special shallow pit. This burial probably related to an animal cult.

Knowledge about the arts as practised by the Neolithic tribes of Mongolia is still rather meagre. Decorations found in the eastern areas include maral canine pendants and shell beads, while those from southern Mongolia have been known to contain ostrich eggshell beads, some of them with geometric ornamentation. The peoples of Mongolia used tens and even hundreds of thousands of ornamental patterns. Chronologically these belong largely to the Bronze and Iron Ages. On the other hand, reliably dated Neolithic rock pictures are virtually unknown, even though it remains highly likely that any number of ancient rock-face 'art galleries' were in fact created in Neolithic times. It is apparently to this period that the rock pictures at Ulzit-Somon in the central part of the Gobi may be attributed. The sand-scoured, flat shale surfaces are covered with dozens of chiseled representations of animal and human figures. Many of the pictures are coated with the same dense patina of 'rust' as the rock surfaces on which they were executed. The most ancient subjects show wild stallions with exaggerated genitalia. These images no doubt express the ancients' notion of the fertility of animals – the chief source of sustenance of the hunting tribes of the distant past.

The question of the economic activity of the Neolithic tribes of Mongolia is an exceedingly interesting yet difficult one. Students of the ancient cultures of eastern and Central Asia have for a long time thought of Mongolia as having been a land of nomads. But materials collected over the past few years point to more complex processes. Already in the Early Neolithic, and possibly as early as the Mesolithic, ancient tribes in Mongolia were actively engaged in gathering vegetable foods, which logically should have led to the cultivation of plants. Climatic conditions were certainly conducive to such a development, as in the past Mongolia received much more rain than it does today. Well preserved traces of erosion provide clear evidence of this fact. Further testimony of the erstwhile abundance of water in the Mongolian steppes is afforded by the large number of dried-out stream beds, traces of ancient shore-lines, and saline lakes. The increasing aridity of the climate appears to have proceeded at different rates in various periods, but it is certain that in the fourth and third millennia B.C. the climate of eastern Mongolia was more humid than at present. One piece of evidence for this is the ancient bed of the Tamsagbulag river, which once flowed into Lake Buir-nor at its south-western extremity. The width of this dry bed is 100 m, and abundant waters once flowed along it.[4]

The very prevalence in Mongolia of large and long-lived settlements with semi-subterranean habitations allows us to state with confidence that agriculture was destined to become the basis of the economy of such settlements, since, apart from agriculture, Mongolia offers no source of food which could be relied upon

4. Murzaev, 1952, p. 128.

to provide sustenance for a sizeable settled community. Both hunting and fishing in Mongolia were associated with periodic nomadic migrations, and it was agriculture alone which could have provided a constant and reliable supply of food. Another indication of agricultural pursuits is provided by the agricultural implements such as grinding stones, mullers, pestles, hoes, digging-stick weights found at the Tamsagbulag and other settlements of eastern and southern Mongolia. Despite its relatively unsophisticated character, agriculture in the Middle and Late Neolithic was, it seems, a more effective source of food than hunting and fishing.

Needless to say, agriculture was not practised throughout the territory of Mongolia, and some tribes continued to live by other appropriate economic systems. However, the transition to agriculture constituted an important step towards the further progressive development of the material culture of the tribes of Stone Age Mongolia. It is even conceivable that along with the advent of agriculture, animal raising began at this time in Mongolia, although the formation of an animal-raising society proceeded at a greater pace in the next stage, that is, during the Bronze and Early Iron Ages. The shift was probably linked to increasing aridity of the territory, as well as the arrival in Bronze Age central and eastern Asia of mobile pastoral tribes from the west. It was only in the second millennium B.C. that the nomadic way of life, which eventually would bring about such major changes in the day-to-day existence and activities of the peoples of Central Asia, began to take root in Mongolia.

The tribes of Kazakhstan constitute a distinctive cultural-historical milieu which had little to do with either the Neolithic people of Central Asia to the south or the tribes of the southern Urals and Siberia to the north. The Mesolithic period in Kazakhstan is known only through isolated finds. These finds indicate that microlithic flint industries, practised by tribes hunting herds of large game, occurred there at that period as they did in Mongolia. A considerable number of Neolithic sites have been unearthed and investigated in southern Kazakhstan.[5] One of the most thoroughly investigated Stone Age sites in this area is the Karaungur cave located on the right bank of the small river of the same name. The site is multi-layered, its upper horizons belonging to the Mesolithic and Neolithic. The industry of the Neolithic inhabitants was based on flake tool-making.

Knife-shaped flakes were used to fashion elongated end-scrapers, points, arrowheads, and other articles. Flakes with lateral indentation and blunted edges have also been found. Microlithic flakes with worked and unretouched blades which fitted into bone or wooden hafts are present in abundance. Other implements worthy of mention are axe or adze-type tools, pestles and scraper knives.

A material in common use by the Neolithic tribes was bone, of which they fashioned awls, piercing tools, eyed needles (the prototypes of modern needles), scrapers, and other implements for working animal hides. Among the rare items, both from the point of view of purpose and of the care taken in finishing, is a

5. *Istoriya Kazakhskoy SSSR*, Vol. I, 1977.

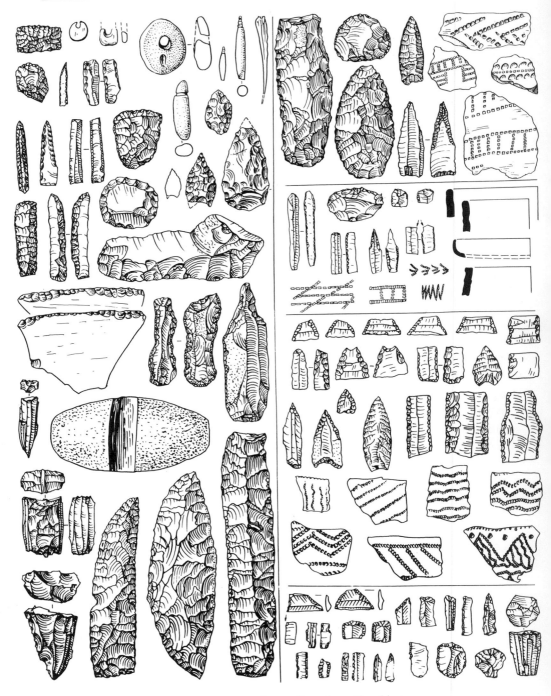

FIG. 3. Kelteminar culture of southern Kazakhstan.

calibrated bone gauge, adornments made of drilled shell, tooth ornaments with short scratches, bone pendants and beads, and sculptured figurines carved from animal phalanges.

The clay vessels found in the Neolithic horizon had rounded bottoms and weak profiles. The upper portions of the vessels were decorated with incised points, pits and figures applied with a serrated die.

Neolithic sites in southern Kazakhstan have been studied along the Berkutta river, as well as along lake-shores and in the vicinity of springs. Most of the Neolithic sites are characterized by the extensive use of knife-shaped flakes for the fabrication of implements. The Neolithic sites of southern Kazakhstan generally have much in common with the Kelteminar culture (Fig. 3).

Another somewhat distinct group is comprised of the Neolithic tribes of central and western Kazakhstan. The most abundant finds have been made in the valleys of the rivers Karaturgai and Kenzebaisai, by springs, as well as along the shores of ancient lake basins. As in other parts of Kazakhstan, the most characteristic feature of the Neolithic in this region is the extensive use of knife-shaped flakes as primary work-pieces coupled with the persistence of microlithic forms. The most widespread cores are prismatic or wedge-shaped, well prepared for the striking off of knife-shaped flakes. Multiple flake scars are evident over the cleavage front.

The Neolithic sites of the Karaturgai river valley are characterized by smaller-sized thin, narrow flakes. Most of the struck fragments bear traces of secondary working. The finds include flakes sharpened by retouching from the dorsal side and along the edges and bevelled ends. Flakes with one or more lateral indentations are also not unknown. The scrapers are mostly of the end type. Wide use was made of sectioning, flakes being used to produce inserts for composite implements with a bone or wooden haft as the basic element. On the other hand, classical implements of geometric shape are relatively few in number. In addition to flaking, the stone workers of the sites in question made wide use of chips (primary flakes) for fashioning implements. Chips were used to make scrapers, points, cutters, drills and other articles. Arrowheads were made of flakes with only their points finished by retouching, as well as of special billets. The latter were retouched on both faces. Bifacial retouching was also employed in making dart- and spearheads.

The sites also contained ceramic items. These are largely sherds of vessels of parabolic shape with a slightly flared lip and a smoothly widening body. They are decorated with a comb die, as well as by scoring imprinting (pitting), and gouging.

Neolithic sites unearthed in the vicinity of springs and ancient lacustrine basins in the Kenzebaisai river valley contained not only the products of the flaking technique, but also implements fashioned out of chips (primary flakes) and special billets; in fact, 43 per cent of the scrapers were made out of flakes and 54 per cent out of chips. In the case of sites in the Sari-su river basin and by Lake

Sari-zen, the proportion of splinter-based scrapers reaches 88 per cent, while at Karaganda–15 site with its clear-cut stratigraphy Layer VI contained scrapers 93 per cent of which were fashioned out of chips. All the sites in this area are also characterized by the common occurrence of microlithic implements, including trapezoidal shapes and inserts.

A distinct group of Neolithic finds is constituted by the sites situated in the ancient valley of the Syr Darya and the Aral Sea region. Many of these were situated in wind-blown areas, while quite a few others lay buried under sand. The sites of this region may be thought of as occupying an intermediate position between the Neolithic of the northern steppe regions of Central Asia and the Trans-Uralic region. They have features in common both with the Kelteminar culture, and with the cultures of the southern Trans-Uralic and the eastern portion of the Aral Sea region. Many of the artefacts of the Neolithic sites of the Aral Sea region were made out of knife-shaped flakes; such articles included scrapers, cutters, piercing tools and arrowheads. Knife-shaped flakes were also used to fashion hafted blades. Flakes with one or several lateral indentations and flakes with a blunted spine and bevelled edge are also present.

Scholars concerned with the Aral Sea region have distinguished between two chronological stages, the Neolithic and the Eneolithic. The artefacts found at the Neolithic sites of Saksaul'skaya I and Agispe do not number among them bifacially worked arrow and dart heads; on the other hand, they include trapezoidal inserts and numerous small regular knife-shaped flakes. Later sites such as Saksaul'skaya II are the first to include bifacially flaked arrowheads.

The ceramic wares at the Neolithic sites in question are varied. Neolithic discoveries in the Zhalpak area have been found to contain large vessels with clearly distinguishable necks, as well as hemispherical cups. Their bases are either flat or rounded. Decoration was applied with a serrated die or by incision. The Kosmola 4 and 5 sites included thin-walled vessels made of well-fired paste with an admixture of gravel. The wares were ornamented by scoring, pocking, reed impression and incising. The ornamentation was applied sparingly and in several rows. Smaller vessels with flat or rounded bases have been found at later sites such as Saksaul'skaya II. The lips are well profiled and flattened along the top. Ornamentation takes the form of serrated die impressions, straight and wavy incised lines, and pocking to produce various geometric figures.

Interesting materials relating to the Neolithic of northern Kazakhstan and the area bordering the upper reaches of the Irtysh river have been collected in recent years. It is very important to note that the preceding Mesolithic stage has been studied more thoroughly in this area than in the adjoining regions.[6] The Mesolithic in northern Kazakhstan, just as in the central part of the Trans-Uralic region and western Siberia, was not characterized by the production of asymmetric, geometric trapezoids and segments. Such inserts as occur take the form of

6. Zaybert and Potemkina, 1981.

blunted-spine flakes or the less common parallelograms and endface-worked artefacts. Sites in this region are characterized by long rounded chip scrapers and end-scrapers which predominate over flake-type implements. Many of the features characteristic of the previous stage survived into the Neolithic of eastern and northern Kazakhstan.

The recently discovered settlement of Boatai in the Petropavlovsk *oblast'* region in northern Kazakhstan is of particular interest for the study of the dynamics of the cultural and economic development of the steppe tribes. It was a permanent settlement of semi-subterranean dwellings having an area of 40–70 m² and wooden roofs smeared with clay daub. On the basis of the large number of flint tools present, including microliths, Boatai may be dated to the end of the Neolithic, possibly to the fourth–third millennia B.C. An examination of the remains of animal bones indicated a clear form of economic specialization; 99 per cent of the bones were the bones of horses. These people were possibly hunters specializing in wild horses and may even have begun to domesticate them, though no indication of this has yet been found in the osteological evidence. However, as a result of an expert analysis carried out in Leningrad by G. F. Korobkova, primitive cheek pieces, which constitute clear evidence of the bridling of horses, were identified among the bone artefacts. At all events, the economy of the steppe pastoralists and nomads who played such an important role in the history of Central Asia originated in communities precisely of the type living in Boatai.

The best-studied sites of eastern Kazakhstan are the settlements of Ust'-Narym, Trushnikovo, Malo-Krasnoyarskaya, etc.[7] Of these, the one to have received most attention is the Ust'-Narym settlement, where excavations have yielded the remains of an elongated light habitation, roundish midden and debris pits, twenty-five hearths and fires, two burials, and large numbers of stone and bone artefacts, ceramic wares, and fauna.[8]

The stone industry at the site involved primary and secondary core preparation and core cleaving. Most of the cores are of the types from which knife-shaped flakes were struck (prismatic, cone-pencil, edge-like, etc.). The implements found here were fashioned largely from knife-shaped flakes. Artefacts of geometric shape (trapezoids and segments) were entirely absent. The implement types include scrapers, knives, knife inserts, small saws, sickle inserts, drills, piercing tools, arrow- and spearheads as well as other items. The ancient inhabitants of the settlements also used a wide selection of chopping instruments, including adzes, axes and chisels.

The small number of bone articles unearthed included awls, eyed needles, and a needle-case with a herring-bone ornament. The bone dagger, whose longitudinal grooves still held unretouched flint blades, was a unique find. The handle

7. Chernikov, 1959.
8. Korobkova, 1969.

of the dagger was ornamentally carved. The same settlement likewise yielded a fragment of a knife or dagger with a single groove.

In addition to hunting weapons, the Ust'-Narym collection also includes artefacts related to fishing, among them the fragments of a composite fishhook made of a soft grey stone of the steatite type with annular incisions at both ends. Such hooks were widespread among the Neolithic tribes of Siberia.

Several inserts for sickles, which were important tools for ancient gatherers and agriculturalists, were identified by expert analysis among the flint tools at Ust'-Narym. The preconditions for the transition to new forms of economy were being established also in eastern Kazakhstan.

The artefacts found at the Ust'-Narym settlement have much in common with those of the Neolithic period in Siberia. There are close similarities in the fact that stones were split directly and in the shapes of many core types, as well as in implements such as scrapers, shaving-knives, bifacially worked arrow and dart heads, knives and daggers with inserted blades, fish-hook shafts, and numerous other items.

The Ust'-Narym complex nevertheless has many distinctive features of its own which set it apart from the Neolithic sites of Siberia and reflect a kinship with the sites of south-eastern Soviet Central Asia, and especially with those of the Kelteminar culture. This is evidenced by arrowheads and bifacially worked microflakes blunted by fine counter-retouch, as well as flakes with bevelled upper edges. Some of the Ust'-Narym vessels are ornamented in a way that is characteristic of the later complexes of the Kelteminar culture.

The foregoing attributes point to the very distinctive status of the Ust'-Narym complex. While preserving some of the features already found at more ancient sites, it was strongly influenced by two extensive ethno-cultural domains – that of southern Siberia and that of the Kelteminar people.

The best-known of the northern Kazakhstan sites are Pen'ki 1 and Pen'ki 2, located 200 km north-east of Pavlodar bordering the present Omsk region.[9] The more ancient of these sites is Pen'ki 1. Most of the cores here are wedge-shaped. Knife-like flakes were used to fashion scrapers, drills, shaving knives, inserts for composite implements, knives and arrowheads. The extensive use of the flake-splitting technique and the presence among the collected materials of trapezoids, indented flakes, and flakes with a blunted spine and an end bevelled by retouching, renders this complex similar to the inventory of Layer IV at Jebel. However, the bifacially worked arrowheads, miniature disc-shaped scrapers, and knives with bifacial edge-retouching suggest that the site in question is of more recent date. In contrast to Jebel, the finds do not include either arrowheads of the Kelteminar type or tanged arrowheads fashioned out of flakes. Typologically these arrowheads are closer to those of the Neolithic sites of Siberia and the southern part of the Ural region.

9. Chalaya, 1972.

The site likewise contained potsherds. The thick-walled vessels had pointed bottoms and were decorated largely by pocking and comb-scraping to produce various ornamental compositions. With respect to both vessel shape and ornamentation the ceramic wares resemble those of the Neolithic period in the Urals to the north and of the Kelteminar culture to the south. The site contained the remains of a dwelling 15 m long and 7 m wide with its longitudinal axis lying in a north–south direction. At the centre of the dwelling was an oval hearth of 2.5 m diameter. Two smaller hearths were placed by the north and south walls.

The stone inventory of the Pen'ki 2 site, corresponding to the end of the Neolithic and beginning of the Eneolithic, reflects continuity in the stone tool-making tradition. But at the same time some differences are apparent. The fact is that this stage is marked by a considerable increase in the number of chip (prim-ary flake) based implements, with a corresponding decrease in the use of knife-shaped flakes. The vast majority of the arrowheads were bifacially worked. Inserts were rarely employed.

The vessels here are largely thick-walled and flat based. They are orna-mented with pock and comb marks to produce composite triangular motifs. Both Pen'ki 1 and Pen'ki 2 contained artistic artefacts and adornments. Interesting items found at Pen'ki 1 include two well-polished fangs (probably pendants) and two beads. One of these latter was fashioned from half of a mother-of-pearl bi-valve shell and the other out of stone. A 14 cm long representation of an elk's head was found at Pen'ki 2. The animal is shown with jaws open and ears laid back. Such artefacts are most typical of the Neolithic of the Urals and southern Siberia.

A small number of burial sites have been discovered within the territory of Kazakhstan. Those that have been studied are located largely in the northern part of this region. None of these graves had any external signs by which they might have been recognized. The most interesting grave investigated is located near the village of Zhelezinka, 100 km from the Pen'ki site. Burial was preceded by crema-tion of the deceased. Besides these remains the grave contained a sickle-shaped frontal piece of a head-dress fashioned out of bone, and a necklace consisting of animal teeth and large shell beads. Implements included an adze, an awl, arrow- and spearheads of bone, and three jar-shaped clay vessels with rounded bases. The same grave contained two phalanges of a kulan (a kind of wild ass) stained with red ochre. The burial rite bears witness to the complex notions about an after-life which must have been held by the tribes in question, and affords evidence con-cerning their beliefs.

Questions of the genesis of the Neolithic cultures of Kazakhstan, their local variations and their relations with adjacent regions are indeed complex. This being the case, it is important to bear in mind that the preceding Mesolithic stage had not been studied with any thoroughness, the total absence of carefully inves-tigated multi-layered reference complexes compounding the difficulty of the issues raised. It is clear, however, that the shaping of these cultures was influenced in a major way by the tribes of the Kelteminar culture. Links with Kelteminar are most palpable in the sites of southern and especially western Kazakhstan. A considerable effect on Neolithic cultures there was also exercised by tribes from the north, that is, from the southern Ural Mountains and western Siberia. The links stand out with particular clarity in the Neolithic complexes of northern and eastern Kazakhstan. Important parallels in the production technique and shape of stone implements are also apparent in the Mesolithic and Neolithic complexes of the Caspian Sea hunter-fishermen. Thus, the Neolithic in Kazakhstan was far from being homogeneous. Most of the Neolithic tribes of the large region encompassing Soviet Central Asia, Kazakhstan and adjacent territories, led a mobile way of life, and the ancient complexes incorporate numerous elements testifying to their stability and extensive contacts with neighbours.

The economic life of the Kazakhstan tribes was likewise differentiated. In the earlier stages the tribes in this territory were mobile and engaged in hunting and fishing. The advanced Neolithic in eastern Kazakhstan shows the beginnings of agriculture. It is highly likely that animal raising became widespread among them in the Late Neolithic-Eneolithic period. In time, with the coming of the Bronze and Iron Ages, pastoralism was to evolve into the major economic activity.

Conclusion

The Neolithic period in the northern part of Central Asia witnessed the prodigious development of cultures that made extensive use of microlithic techniques for the manufacture of some tools. Groups of tribes using these techniques occupied areas in differing kinds of terrain and practised a mixed form of economy based on different combinations of hunting, fishing and gathering, depending on their ecological environment. A stable economy encouraged the people to put down roots, and we find a whole series of permanent settlements in this area.

But changes, particularly in methods of procuring food, were beginning to take place among the Neolithic tribes in the northern part of Central Asia. The settlement of Boatai in northern Kazakhstan and the Tamsagbulag culture in eastern Mongolia are particularly interesting and important in this connection. At Boatai, tribes hunting herds of hoofed animals were specializing in the capture of horses and had possibly begun to domesticate them. These were vital preconditions for the transition to pastoralism in the steppes and, in a sense, Boatai is a precursor of the renowned nomadic cultures of Asia.

Recent studies show that the eastern part of Mongolia, by virtue of its favourable geographical position and climatic conditions, was the birthplace of one of the sedentary agricultural cultures of Central Asia. The discovery of the Neolithic culture in Tamsagbulag is significant because it provides evidence that the inhabitants of this particular region changed over, at the same time as other cultures in neighbouring provinces, from a food-gathering to a food-producing economy. Until quite recently, in fact, apart from the collections of stone arte-facts, which had been found on the surface, there had been virtually no evidence of the existence of early purely agricultural settlements in the full meaning of that term. The discovery is also significant because it throws a good deal of light on the complex historical evolution of Neolithic man in Mongolia in the period be-tween the fifth and third millennia B.C. The study of the Tamsagbulag culture shows that a vital role in that culture was played by the numerous settlements with their characteristically constructed dwellings, burial practices and other features.

THE BRONZE AGE IN IRAN
AND AFGHANISTAN[1]

M. Tosi, S. Malek Shahmirzadi and M. A. Joyenda

THE agricultural economy and the stable mode of life connected with it were firmly established on Iranian territory in the Neolithic Age. During the following period cultures of a new type arose, solidly based in all eco-logical niches suitable for a food-producing economy. This period, which intro-duced copper implements into the culture, is usually referred to as Eneolithic or Chalcolithic. Its age on Iranian territory roughly corresponds to the time-span between 5500–5000 and 2900 B.C. The occurrence of rich mineral deposits favoured an early spread of metal objects; ore was not only processed by the local population but, equally, exported to neighbouring countries, into Mesopotamia and to the north of the Kopet Dag range.

We may distinguish several cultural centres among the early agricultural communities in Iran. The central regions, including Kashan and Tehran, are best-known from the excavations at Tepe Sialk (Sialk I–III).[2] Copper pins and beads are reported from the lowermost layers of the site, which also include a developed painted pottery with decorative patterns gradually becoming more complicated (Fig. 1). Ornaments of Sialk III pottery are particularly rich; apart from geometric patterns, they include animal figures. One may distinguish goats, birds, snakes, horses, bulls, panthers (Fig. 2). Human figures are also present in rare cases. On some vessels there are complicated scenes which include several human figures; these probably illustrate intricate mythological stories. A finite, stable, ornament-oriented style shows the artistic pattern of the early agricultural age, as represented by Sialk pottery. Specialized industries are typical of the mate-rial production of Sialk III; copper implements increased in number, and at least some were cast in closed moulds. Similar technical progress occurred in pottery production, where the potter's wheel was introduced. A closely comparable cul-ture is represented in the lower strata of Tepe Hissar.

1. See Map 7.
2. Ghirshman, 1938.

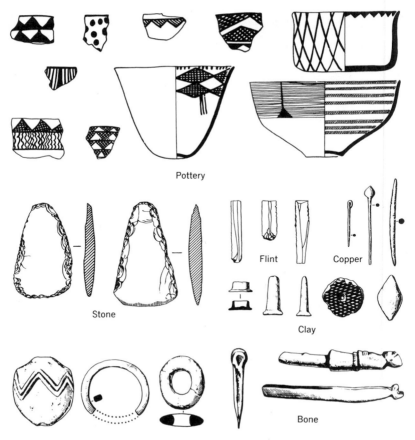

Pottery

Stone

Flint

Copper

Clay

Bone

FIG. 1. Sialk I.

A distinct centre of early agricultural communities was established in Fars; Tal-i Bakun is the best-known site there.[3] Colourful geometric ornament, combined with stylized animal figures is typical of the local artistic style. The cultural ties in the course of the Eneolithic Age were mostly oriented towards the west, to the areas of highly developed cultures of Mesopotamia and Elam. The spread of early agricultural tribes to the east by the end of the Eneolithic Age resulted in the establishment of a clear interaction with the communities in southern and northern Baluchistan. Judging from preliminary reports, the Khorasan Eneolithic was in many respects similar to Namazga type Eneolithic assemblages in southern Turkmenistan.

The specialized production which universally occurred in the early agricultural communities led to greater complexity of the socio-economic pattern, while the stable production of food stimulated population growth. The division of communal groups into classes resulted in the establishment of a settled hierarchy,

3. Zangsdorff and McCorn, 1942; Egami and Masuda, 1962.

192

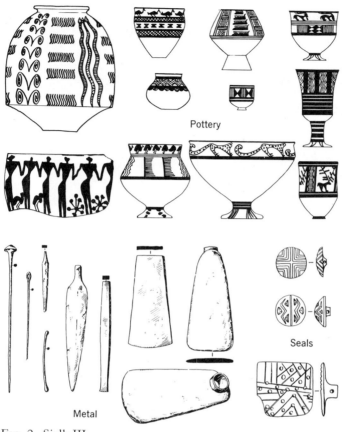

Pottery

Seals

Metal

FIG. 2. Sialk III.

which could be politically related to tribal or supra-tribal organization. These trends were reflected in the most spectacular way in the emergence of large urban or proto-urban settlements. This process, which already occurred in the final stages of the Eneolithic, was particularly characteristic of the following Bronze Age.

The early agricultural culture dating from the end of the fifth to the third millennia B.C. is the best known in southern Afghanistan. The main settlements were situated inside the fertile and sufficiently irrigated province of Kandahar (Mundigak,[4] Said Qala,[5] Deh Morasi Ghundai[6]). The three features of an early agricultural mode of life, namely, solid mud-brick houses, developed painted pottery and terracotta figurines representing a female fertility goddess or various ungulates, are present in the local material culture. Occurrence of rich copper deposits favoured the development of metallurgy on the territory of Afghanistan.

4. Casal, 1961.
5. Shaffer, 1971.
6. Dupree, 1963.

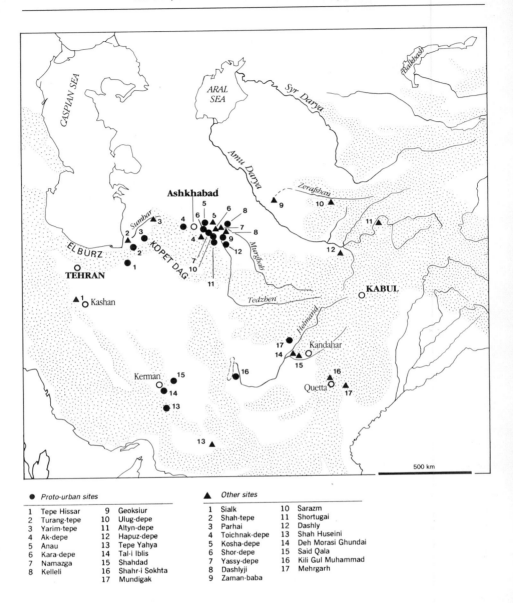

•	Proto-urban sites				▲	Other sites		
1	Tepe Hissar	9	Geoksiur		1	Sialk	10	Sarazm
2	Turang-tepe	10	Ulug-depe		2	Shah-tepe	11	Shortugai
3	Yarim-tepe	11	Altyn-depe		3	Parhai	12	Dashly
4	Ak-depe	12	Hapuz-depe		4	Toichnak-depe	13	Shah Huseini
5	Anau	13	Tepe Yahya		5	Kosha-depe	14	Deh Morasi Ghundai
6	Kara-depe	14	Tal-i Iblis		6	Shor-depe	15	Said Qala
7	Namazga	15	Shahdad		7	Yassy-depe	16	Kili Gul Muhammad
8	Kelleli	16	Shahr-i Sokhta		8	Dashlyji	17	Mehrgarh
		17	Mundigak		9	Zaman-baba		

MAP 7. Settled Bronze Age sites of Central Asia.

The technique of a closed moulding was mastered not later than the mid-third millennium B.C. As in Iran, the economic pattern favoured the concentration of population and the emergence of large proto-urban settlements.

The northern coast of the Persian Gulf is strongly affected by tectonic uplift. A compact series of orographic ridges narrows where the easternmost extensions of the Zagros mountains merge with the Makran, linking the Iranian plateau to the Indian subcontinent. The Zagros-Makran coastal chain isolates the whole region from any marine influence so that, in spite of its proximity to the ocean, the climate is an arid or continental steppe. Human settlements can be located either on the better watered sections of the piedmont escarpments or along the water-courses; however, they mostly cluster like a bunch of grapes around the deltaic fans.

The scarcity of water and soil has kept the size and distribution of agricultural settlements within very narrow limits, and deviations from the norm have required very high energy expenditure to redirect the flow of water and resources. Periodically in the history of the Central Asian countries, no matter how great and radical the labour investment and technological innovations, sudden, total interruptions in the water supply have always occurred. Urban life has been ephemeral throughout their history. Archaeological evidence clearly indicates that the process involved in the formation of proto-urban societies, albeit displaying a fairly uniform cultural pattern throughout the vast region, was characterized by highly autarchic economic regimes articulated in many small territorial cells across large stretches of desert. The average distance between deltaic enclaves and along the desert margins is about 70 km, that is, a good two-day journey for a loaded camel caravan; this distance is much greater in the southern basins, for example, Sistan lies some 350 km away from the Arachosian plain to the east along the Helmand and about 300 km from the oasis belt of Dasht-i Lut to the west. The large stretches of desert wasteland separating each river system from its neighbour probably stood in the way of any attempt to integrate the isolated ecosystem cells into larger political entities until late protohistoric times. These environmental constraints could hardly have been overcome before the introduction of animal transport to reduce time/distance ratios of transport, so increasing economic interdependence. Only in the second half of the third millennium B.C. were camel figurines found in southern Turkmenistan depicted as drawing wheeled vehicles.[7] This followed a period of increasing occurrence at human settlements where they were probably first used as a source of meat and fur.[8]

In earlier periods local societies may be assumed to have operated their production systems in conditions of isolation, making do with little or no dependence upon foreign goods to meet their subsistence requirements. Quite unlike

7. Masson, 1981.
8. Compagnoni and Tosi, 1978.

the vast, largely coherent, alluvial plains of western Asia, all the deltaic oases were close to a variety of mineral and biological ressources, mainly as a result of their wide variety on environments.[9] Full functioning of early state economies during the third millennium B.C. would have been physically feasible only within a range of 50–250 km. The archaeological evidence suggests that, following a period of steady, low-profile economic growth, from 3200 B.C. almost every local society underwent radical social transformation, reaching its peak in about 2500 B.C. when the centres of each enclave had attained their maximum physical expansion and were marked by all the effects of increasing hierarchical complexity.[10]

The social and economic development of the local society was not however slowed down by the geographical isolation of the individual enclaves, nor by the irregular water supplies. Like Baluchistan in the southern regions of Central Asia, eastern Iran also became the scene of urban and proto-state formation no later, nor less complex, than those emerging around 3000 B.C. along the great alluvial corridors of Mesopotamia and the Nile. Indeed, in the light of our present knowledge, it could be claimed that the protohistoric civilizations of eastern Iran were the third corner of one and the same triangular area of primary development of a state society, lying between the Nile valley, Anatolia and the Hindu Kush.

Lack of resources, even of water, is not enough in itself to prevent a region from developing economically. In most cases it speeds up the selective trends towards more sophisticated systems of social organization. The technical and political tools required to ensure survival and material prosperity grow with the communities, generation after generation, in a process of adaptation expected to last thousands of years. The control over the desert margin economic complexes of eastern Iran was thus made possible, at least as far as the main branches of its economy were concerned, as early as the Chalcolithic, that is, between 5500–5000 and 3500 B.C. During this time-span, not only were the material bases of the Neolithic economy consolidated through the selection of the first domestic mutants of wheat and barley in the whole of Central Asia but the pattern was one of sedentary, intensive peopling of rural villages linked to land tenure. There is no doubt that the urban societies of the third millennium B.C. in Central Asia are the result of an evolution deeply rooted in local adaptation and that the material tools had been completely acquired by the end of the fifth millennium B.C. Large-scale investment is evident at this time in the form of extensive copper-mining in central and south-eastern Iran[11] and in complex waterworks designed to make even the outlying areas fertile. The most significant evidence consists of the ter-

9. Costantini and Tosi, 1977, pp. 277–93, map on p. 334; Jarrige and Tosi, 1981, pp. 118–20.
10. Masson, 1967; Tosi, 1977.
11. Caldwell, 1967.

races of Rud-i Gushk near Tepe Yahya[12] and the canals on the Tedzhen delta, near the oasis of Geoksiur.[13]

In Greater Mesopotamia the period of gestation was equally long and was brought to an end in about 3200 B.C. by the profound changes accompanying the Uruk period. There was such a radical change in the material culture that the entire social structure may be assumed to have been shaken by a rapid acceleration in the mechanisms of production, exchange and accumulation. The emerging stages appear to have been fully operational right from middle Uruk, that is, about 3300 B.C., while all the elements of centralization of the ceremonial and administrative functions defining the urban configuration of a territory appeared together within the following century. The formation of the state and urbanization thus largely coincided in western Asia.

In eastern Iran the process was somewhat different and was characterized by a greater degree of detachment; here the urban society took several centuries longer to reach maturity with respect to the appearance at about 3300–3200 B.C. of the first signs of state emergence. These may be identified in the instruments of administration and redistribution of agricultural produce: proto-Elamite writing tablets, cylinder seals and their clay impressions, counters fashioned out of clay and certain ceramic types such as bevelled-rim bowls. They were found either collectively or singly in all the explored sites of this period, for example, Sialk IV, Yahya IVC, Iblis V, Shahr-i Sokhta I and Hissar II.[14] However, these new classes of objects were developed earlier only in Susiana, while they appear in eastern Iran as imports, albeit without the various Late Chalcolithic cultural complexes undergoing any other changes. In fact, unlike Mesopotamia or Susiana, the archaeological evidence seems to indicate that the acquisition of elements so closely related to the emergence of a new order of economic relations was not accompanied by any dramatic social upheavals. However, both the above considerations point to a direct interference extending from Susiana towards the Plateau, the underlying causes of which seem more complex and more closely related to peculiar regional circumstances than had been originally believed, giving rise to speculation about colonization.[15] In fact, although tablets and seals were identical, the way they were introduced in each region varied considerably.

At Sialk IV and Yahya IVC, both situated on the more exposed western boundaries of the Turanian basin, the inventory of proto-Elamite materials is one of the most complete. Tablets and seals (Fig. 3) are associated inside individual architectural complexes in which discontinuity of occupation is combined with the continuity of the tradition dominating the rest of the cultural complex.[16]

---

12. Prickett, 1976.
13. Lisitsyna, 1970, 1972.
14. Lamberg-Karlovsky, 1978; Lamberg-Karlovsky and Tosi, 1973, pp. 34–7; Amiet, 1983; Amiet and Tosi, 1978.
15. Ghirshman, 1938; Weiss and Young, 1975.
16. Lamberg-Karlovsky, 1978, p. 117.

FIG. 3. Tepe Yahya: proto-Elamite seals and tablets.

At Shahr-i Sokhta they are found at the earliest levels of Phase 10, with no connections with the west emerging even from the extremely abundant pottery inventory.[17] The same has been detected at Hissar II.[18] The general impression is one of a slight influence on the cultural terrain, upon which the response of the local populations was immediately grafted. This was particularly apparent in the more central and densely populated regions of the basin, such as the Helmand valley and the eastern Elburz piedmont. This dominant influence of local traditions is particularly apparent in the seal inventory, the only discriminant element present in the Chalcolithic complexes preceding the proto-Elamite interference. Rare seal impressions have been found in Sialk III and the seals themselves are of the stamp type whith concentric crosses and other geometric compositions.[19] Seals of the same type made of limestone and soap-stone (gypsum) have frequently been found in Layers IB and IC at Hissar[20] and have recently been dated to about the mid-fourth millennium B.C.[21] Following the proto-Elamite period, after 2800 B.C., the stamp seal returned to favour and continued to be the most characteristic feature of the whole of eastern Iranian and middle Asian sphragistics until the second millennium B.C.

In conclusion, what probably happened was that a management model was exported in the framework of an intensified exchange of resources, already highly developed during Chalcolithic times. This is indicated also by the kind of texts written on the sixteen tablets from Sialk and the twenty-seven from Yahya. They record the delivery of foodstuffs and receipts referring exclusively to agricultural products and involving several agencies and their dependants.[22]

The final Chalcolithic is thus characterized by proto-state structures in which elements of the new social organization remain confined to specific functions, while the structure of the population still shows no strong signs of tension caused by disparities between the larger centres and the smaller rural areas. Although the effect seems to be delayed with respect to western Asia, the break with tradition was nevertheless a radical one.

Already in the first two centuries of the third millennium B.C. there was a considerable increase in the size of each regional centre, a phenomenon conventionally denoted as proto-urbanism. The span of maximum expension corresponds to the Early Bronze Age. The most striking example is the rapid development of the Helmand valley. Urbanization was completed between 2600 and 2500 B.C., as is attested by the construction of monumental architectural complexes at Mundigak and Shahr-i Sokhta, by the grassroots expansion of the rural architectural villages and by the layout of the craftsmen's quarters in the sub-

17. Amiet and Tosi, 1978.
18. Dyson and Howards, n.d.
19. Ghirshman, 1938; Deshayes, 1974.
20. Schmidt, 1937, pp. 54–6, 359, Plate XV.
21. Dyson and Howards, 1989.
22. Meriggi, 1971/72.

urban environment. After the year 2200, that is, at the beginning of the Middle Bronze Age, the urban system begins to deteriorate and there is a radical and rapid decline of the large centres in all the enclaves of Central Asia. None of the explanations proposed so far successfully link up the numerous conditions of the archaeological evidence over such a wide area. It was certainly a very complex political phenomenon, which does not necessarily mark the end of the state of supertribal organization.[23] Unlike the western Asian Mediterranean and historical Indian civilizations, in the Central Asian world the state as a suprafamiliar hierarchical system developed with structures that did not necessarily depend on the concentration of people and services allocated in regional centres.

In the archaeology of prehistoric Iran, the shapes and decorations of the painted pottery have represented the main diagnostic elements for defining the variability in time and space of the different cultural traditions. During the two millennia preceding the advent of the first proto-state entities at the end of the fourth millennium B.C., pottery vases were not used merely as containers. By means of the richness of the composite painted decorations, with their geometric or naturalistic themes, the surfaces of the vessels were transformed into a symbolic and representational system. They were projected inside the community as bearers of coded information. In the many villages on the strips of irrigable soil around the large eastern Iranian deserts between the end of the sixth and the beginning of the fourth millennia B.C. the complex patterns covering almost the entire surface of bowls and jars became an instrument for representing and transmitting an ideological heritage common to very large areas. It is thus to be expected that, despite the size of the areas involved, this transformation helped for a long time to maintain a substantial cultural homogeneity in the production of such ordinary instrumental goods. This dual nature of pottery products was shared by the earliest agrarian societies to be found in the whole of western Asia. With the rise of social stratification in the fourth millennium B.C., pottery lost this symbolic and representational function, replaced by more expandable information processors, up to and including the universal medium of writing. Meanwhile, painted decoration became increasingly cursive and schematic until it ultimately disappeared.

Inversely, in the whole of eastern Iran painted decoration persisted until the mid-third millennium B.C., that is, until nearly 1,000 years after its decline in the western Asian regions. This persistence enables us today to evaluate the continuity and spread of the various cultural traditions included in the more mature phases of the urbanization process.

On examination of the situation prevailing in about 4000 B.C., for which the archaeological evidence is more reliable, there can be seen to be three main cultural traditions in eastern Iran and Baluchistan. North of the great Iranian desert, the area of integration coincides with the distribution of red-slipped pot-

23. Biscione, 1977; Biscione and Tosi, 1975.

tery with black or bichrome black-and-brown decoration, which was identified for the first time at Anau IA[24] and subsequently at Hissar I on the Gorgan plain. With only a few variants, it extends along the Elburz and Kopet Dag ridges, over an area roughly coinciding with that of the early agricultural culture of Jeitun.[25] It extends southwards as far as the oasis of Kashan, where this pottery is characteristic of the Sialk Periods I–II. In contrast with this cultural complex is the buff ware that, south of the 32° N. parallel, defines the area of expansion of the southern tradition, which spread along the whole extent of the southern Zagros. McCown[26] had already remarked on the opposition between these two traditions, and subsequent research has not so much changed the terms of this generic dialectic as shed more light on particular situations and different formative processes. Since recent research has shown that agriculture in the eastern Iranian countries is based on the domestication of local cultivars, the origin of such a marked opposition probably lay in the first agrarian communities that arose between the seventh and the sixth millennia B.C. and developed in relation to separate centres of primary domestication.

It is no coincidence that a third cultural tradition was identified as early as 1945 in northern Baluchistan, in the Quetta pottery.[27] Its area of distribution actually corresponds to a third centre of agricultural origins which grew up around barley cultivation, and cattle, sheep and goat grazing as early as the seventh millennium B.C., which was identified thanks to recent discoveries at Mehrgarh on the Bolan river.[28] The Baluchistan tradition of the early millennia B.C. is characterized by buff ware with geometric decorations rigidly organized into panels often with pronounced two-tone colours. The area of distribution covers at least the whole of central-northern Baluchistan and the middle Helmand valley where Layers II–III of Tepe A of Mundigak[29] are to be found. The Baluchistan pottery tradition is followed in reverse until Period IB–IA of Mehrgarh, and very soon emerges as the technologically most highly advanced of the whole of eastern Iran. The use of the potter's wheel became generalized by the end of the fifth millennium B.C., that is, at a time the large production centres such as Mehrgarh were being set up. In the rest of eastern Iran the introduction of the fast wheel took place much later, around 2600–2500 B.C. and corresponds to the production standardization of full urbanization.[30]

Of the three cultural traditions, only the southern one seems to have consistently embodied influences stemming from south-western Iran and Mesopota-

24. Pumpelly, 1908; Masson, 1962.
25. Masson, 1971; Masuda, 1976.
26. McCown, 1942.
27. Piggott, 1947; Fairservis, 1956.
28. Jarrige and Meadow, 1980; Lechevallier and Quivron, 1981; Costantini, 1984a.
29. Casal, 1961, pp. 128–34.
30. Vidale, 1984.

mia, mostly in the Ubaid period.[31] However, here also, the palaeobotanical scenario concerning agriculture during Period VI (6000–5000 B.C.) of Tepe Yahya and surroundings seems to suggest that the production processes were quite autonomous well before these influences were felt,[32] proto-state structures developed early towards the end of the fourth millennium B.C., the relative urban centres being concentrated in the fertile plain of Gorgan at Turang-tepe[33] and in the piedmont strip of the Etek at Namazga and Altyn-depe.[34]

The boundary line in the southern piedmont zone corresponds to the course of the Halil-rud along the Jiroft valley, westward from which lies the Kerman region, while to the east there are the longitudinal valleys of the Makran leading into Baluchistan. In the cultural complexes of Iblis and Yahya to the south of Kerman as well as of the Bampur valley to the east, there are marked differences in pottery production as early as the first half of the fourth millennium B.C., that is, the earliest documentation of the Bampur valley through the site of Shah Huseini.[35] In general, the whole region has not developed into forms of urbanization, but is structured into a system of small oases at the bottom of the mountain valleys, and into a semi-nomadic population of the steppe highlands accompanied by an early intensification of sheep and goat grazing.

There were very strong links with the coast which in the second half of the third millennium B.C. led to a very high degree of integration in the whole of the Oman peninsula, as is documented by the convergences between the pottery of Yahya IVB and that of Bampur IV–VI towards the Umm an-Nar culture.[36] Also the complex of Baluchistan tradition can roughly be divided into a western area, including the Quetta and the Helmand valleys, on the one hand, and an eastern-southern one extending from the Kalat plains to the piedmont strips between the Sind and the Kirthar mountains. The Helmand valley was the most important pole of urban development and was to play the role of a culture hinge between the three different traditions of eastern Iran during the Chalcolithic period. For the whole of the fourth millennium B.C., pottery production remains characterized by painted decoration, which in any case is enriched by the addition of naturalistic themes, mostly zoomorphic in nature. The gradual cultural integration into smaller regional organizations does away with the north–south contrasts expressed in terms of red and buff ware. This transformation is made more evident by the emergence of new pottery types related to the improved control over the manufacturing processes, and of firing in particular. The introduction of reduction kilns afforded higher temperatures and the production of the earliest

31. Kamilli and Lamberg-Karlovsky, 1979.
32. Costantini, 1984*b*.
33. Deshayes, 1977.
34. Masson, 1967, 1968, 1981.
35. Stein, 1937.
36. De Cardi, 1970, pp. 268–9; Lamberg-Karlovsky and Tosi, 1973, pp. 42–4; Tosi, 1974*b*, pp. 147–62.

grey ware, first appearing in Baluchistan during the Togau A Phase, about 3800 B.C.[37] This particular black-painted grey ware actually consists of *porcelaine grès* fired at a temperature exceeding 1,000 °C, as a result of the amalgam between the clay and high percentages of ferrous oxides.[38] It was to continue to be used for another 1,500 years, spreading throughout Baluchistan both over the Indus plain and westward to take in the whole of the Helmand valley, Bampur and Kerman. In the northern enclaves, grey ware appeared later, towards the end of the fourth millennium B.C. at Hissar II and Sialk IV, though only in the region between Elburz and Gorgan. It consists of an undecorated pottery class with finely burnished, almost metallic surfaces more or less in the Caucasic-Anatolian tradition. With the advent of the first elements of state formation, the only change undergone by pottery production consisted of an increased reciprocal borrowing of shapes and decorations between the more rapidly developing regions. This is the case of Shahr-i Sokhta, where the ordinary pottery production about 3000 B.C. included southern Turkmenian, Baluchi and southern Iranian types.[39]

The more radical transformations occurred when the pottery ultimately lost its symbolic and ideological value at the time that an urban order became fully internalized in about 2600 B.C. The behaviour of the urban enclaves in north-eastern Iran and the Helmand valley can now be clearly distinguished from those having remained at the level of oases composed of rural villages with market tendencies towards nomadic animal husbandry throughout the southern strip. While painted decoration virtually died out in the former, or else was reduced to a few summarily executed motifs, it persisted in the south and in Baluchistan throughout the third millennium B.C. At Shahr-i Sokhta III the sharp drop in painted decoration coincided with the introduction of the fast wheel and the structuring of pottery production into large centres composed of 50–100 kilns. Furthermore, the reorganization of production on a semi-industrial scale paved the way for the technological improvements that were to make third-millennium pottery a standardized and fully functional product.

The production of all the southern countries during the second half of the second millennium B.C., from Shahdad to Yahya IVB, from Bampur IV–VI until the Kulli culture in Pakistan Makran, continued with the naturalistic motifs of the fourth millennium B.C., albeit by then perhaps highly stylized. The vast majority consists of friezes depicting running goats and stylized representations of plants. The painted decoration pottery tradition was nevertheless approaching the end and, in about 2000 B.C., seems to coincide with the appearance of direct interference from the Indus civilization. A rearrangement of the economy of the population structure also appears to have occurred as an effect of such upheavals.[40]

37. De Cardi, 1965.
38. Lamberg-Karlovsky and Tosi, 1973, pp. 39–40.
39. Amiet and Tosi, 1978, pp. 21–3; Biscione, 1984.
40. Lamberg-Karlovsky, 1973, p. 43. Costantini, 1984*a*.

During the Early Bronze Age, the territorial organization of the proto-urban societies of eastern Iran was characterized by very powerful tendencies towards demographic concentration which had no equivalent in other western Asian regions. The disparity between rural villages and the centre in each enclave increased during the first half of the third millennium B.C. While the average size of the smaller villages remained that of the Chalcolithic settlements of the fifth and fourth millennia B.C. (between 0.8 and 1.2 ha), the hegemonic centres increased out of all proportion. The most typical case is certainly that of Sistan, where Shahr-i Sokhta grew from the 15–17 ha, of Period I (3200–2800 B.C.) to 150 ha in Period III (about 2400 B.C.) At this time the next settlement in the Helmand delta in order of size was barely 4 ha in area, while the other forty so far located range between 0.5 and 2 ha. During the same time-span, the increase in size of Mundigak was equally astonishing, rising from 6–8 ha in Period III to 55–60 ha[41] in Period IV despite its highly excentric position with respect to the Kandahar plain, where most fertile farmland is found.[42] In the two enclaves on the Helmand, the maximum increase in area achieved by the main centres by the mid-third millennium B.C. is thus almost identical, that is, seven to eight times their area at the end of the Chalcolithic, some 400 years earlier. The growth of Shahdad was equally great, at least according to the preliminary observations of the few surface reconnaissances carried out so far.[43] The development that took place in the Damghan plain at the turn of the third millennium B.C. reflected a third type of situation: Hissar declined from the 12–15 ha reached in Period I during the fourth millennium B.C. to 7–8 ha immediately after the mid-third millennium. However, this decrease in area was accompanied by a marked tendency to demographic concentration. In a recent survey only two protohistoric settlements were located, both of which were no greater than 1 ha in area.[44] As in all piedmont oases in eastern Iran and southern Turkmenistan, the urban agglomeration here was even stronger, achieving the concentration of both population and non-rural activities into a single centre capable of directly managing also most of the agricultural resources over a radius of 10–12 km.

However, there is no need to explain all settlement growth in terms of population density, considering that our object of archaeological observation concerns surfaces and not people. Growth in the size of urban centres is not solely related to the concentration of rural populations but also to the increase in the number of specialized functions. Ceremonial infrastructures, administration organization, the stockpiling of agricultural produce, and craft activities are but some of the more apparent in the archaeological record. Each one called for the allocation of new areas to be added to or superimposed on the existing residential quarters, thus materially characterizing the hegemony of the centre over the ter-

41. Casal, 1961, p. 76, Fig. 3.
42. Snead, 1978; Jarrige and Tosi, 1981, pp. 118–21.
43. Meder, 1979, pp. 80-1, Fig. 27; Salvatori and Vidale, 1982, pp. 5–10, Fig. 1.
44. Dyson and Howards, 1989.

ritory. In the case of Shahr-i Sokhta, the process continued for the whole of the first half of the third millennium B.C. Until 2600 B.C. the craft activity production centres were scattered throughout the residential areas and agricultural villages. Five hundred years later the latter occupied 30–39 ha in the western and southern quarters of the city. At the same time, the area of the graveyard, which was always kept rigidly separate from the inhabited part, grew by some 21 ha. If we consider also the ceremonial and palace structures, still somewhat incompletely identified, as well as the gaps left in the gradually abandoned blocks, the alleged population increase would be reduced considerably. Hissar is an even more striking example of such a segregative use of space at the beginning of the third millennium B.C. In Period II, almost a third of its total area was allocated to craft production, particularly the smelting of copper from the nearby deposits in the Damghan hills. A similar pattern has been observed at Shahdad where copper-smelting and bead-making surface spreads account for nearly a quarter of the whole site.[45]

The numerous craft activities involved the manufature of ornaments, instrumental goods and domestic commodities. Pottery production and copper-smelting are therefore found side by side with large areas covered with wasters from the production of beads and other ornaments made of lapis lazuli and turquoise at Shahr-i Sokhta and Hissar,[46] soap-stone at Tepe Yahya,[47] chalcedony, quartz and flint at Shahr-i Sokhta,[48] limestone and soap-stone again at Hissar. It is interesting to observe how the production areas of the more exotic semi-precious stones such as lapis lazuli and turquoise were rigidly separate from those in which ornaments made of local materials were produced. At Shahr-i Sokhta this separation continues also in the burial context, with graves of stone-cutting craftsmen buried with their tools and specimens of their products.[49] On the basis of the surface spreads of wasters, most of these workshops can be assumed to have occupied no more than one or two rooms or courtyards with comparatively few infrastructures in which a set of stone and wooden tools differing very little from the Neolithic tradition were used almost exclusively. The innovation lay not so much in the technology as in the organization of the production forces, reaching the definitive separation of specialities from the domestic sphere. Only the pyro-technological activities, mostly pottery-making and metal-working, were destined to become actual factories with large numbers of workmen organized in several hierarchical levels. With the advent of urbanization, this gave birth to the craftsmen's quarters at Hissar, Altyn-depe, Shahdad and Shahr-i Sokhta[50] and

45. Salvatori and Vidale, 1982, Figs. 1–2.
46. Tosi and Piperno, 1973; Bulgarelli, 1979; Tosi, 1974*b*.
47. Kohl, 1975.
48. Bulgarelli and Tosi, 1977.
49. Piperno, 1976.
50. Tosi, 1977, p. 57; Mariani, 1984; Tosi, 1984.

also to sites of 1–2 ha in areas dedicated more specifically to individual activities detached from the hegemonic centres.

The organization of craft activities during the period of the early eastern Iranian state therefore shows a tendency towards a level of territorial integration that breaks with the normal microregional patterns of the Chalcolithic enclaves. That this areal expansion of craft activities should be evaluated more in terms of a shift of functions than population growth emerges also from a second consideration: an over-extended transplant of farmers from the rural hinterland would have entailed a reduction in the number of labourers generating primary surpluses just when economic take-off was about to be boosted to the full.

The process of urban expansion is assumed to have taken place in two stages. In the earliest stage (3000–2600 B.C.), a pre-existing trend towards the reorganization of certain manufacturing processes accelerated the reallocation of specialists outside the confines of the house. Craftsmen's workshops in eastern Iran and Afghanistan contributed to dwelling settlements that had already developed into centres of riverine enclaves during the fourth millennium B.C. and where the volume and quantity of commodity production had been high throughout the Chalcolithic period. Essentially it originated as a change in the distribution of activities and took place in those enclaves in which the majority of the population was already concentrated in the primary centre (e.g. Hissar, Shahdad or Mundigak) and where no further demographic expansion was possible without full integration into larger systems. Each of these sites had been a main regional centre all through the fourth millennium B.C. on the same scale as Altyn and Namazga in southern Turkmenistan. V. M. Masson has determined the area extension of Altyn-depe during the Namazga II period as around 12 ha towards the end of Period I, and in Mundigak during Period III. In conclusion, the changes in the proto-state societies in eastern Iran took place gradually throughout the first half of the third millennium B.C., basically remaining the same as the models having developed inside the pre-state Chalcolithic institutions. The effects of accumulation and of the new social order have been seen to emerge in the subsequent phase between 2600 and 2400 B.C., which corresponds to Period III of the Shahr-i Sokhta sequence in Sistan, to Mundigak IV in Arachosia and to Namazga V in southern Turkmenistan.

In addition to the areal increase in the central parts of each regional system, and to the reorganization of the production forces, these effects are found in the rise of monumental architecture according to the requirements of the new urban élites. The few monumental buildings of the Bronze Age so far found in eastern Iran have features in common that, besides allowing them to be distinguished from domestic architecture, are not found in any other cultural area in western Asia. Generally speaking, they were more than 1,000 m² in area, compared with the 80–150 m² of contemporary private houses. Probably in order to ensure that they would dominate the rest of the city, the monumental buildings were situated on high ground. In the specific context of a protohistorical settlement, the most suitable sites are the elevations left by the accumulation of structures and debris from earlier periods. By means of buildings made entirely of mud-bricks and articulated into scalar blocks redefining the slopes, whole hillsides were incorporated in a solid retaining construction. Such terrace substructures have been identified in Tepe A at Mundigak[51] and in the 'temple' in Sector 7 of Altyn-depe,[52] while the largest is possibly the one at Turang-tepe, which has a front 80 m long.[53]

Their construction can be dated between 2500 and 2300 B.C. and is in the phase of most rapid expansion of the urban centres and of the most extensive territorial integration corresponding to the latter part of the Early Bronze Age. The internal part of the platforms consisted of a close-knit network of large blocks of masonry that, by relieving the counterthrusts, enabled the structure to fit in with the uneven ground morphology of recently accumulated soils. The foundation masonry actually penetrated inside pre-existing buildings, so that the new substructure cut across the buried walls. The same type of anchoring system is found at Shahr-i Sokhta during the second half of the third millennium B.C., both in the Phase 5 'House of the Foundations' of the East Residential Area[54] and in the large enclosured building of Phase 4–3 in the Central Quarters (Fig. 4).[55]

The use of mud-bricks was exclusive, with the sole exception of the building on Tepe G at Mundigak, laid on rough limestone foundations.[56] It could conceivably be a more peculiarly 'Baluchi' feature not only for reasons of geographical proximity, but also because of the abundant stone available in the narrow valley of the Kushk-i Nakhod.

The characteristic by means of which the monumental architecture of the Bronze Age can be identified most easily nevertheless consists of the way the façades were treated, which more than anything else set these stately buildings above the rank of common dwellings. This treatment consisted of elaborate mud-brick relief decorations in a masonry cladding laid over the façade of the terraces or on the front of the building. In Tepe A at Mundigak the remaining façade consists of two low stepped platforms. The decoration on the front of both of these consists of a sequence of circular half-pillars, standing 1.6 m above ground-level and surmounted by a frieze of bricks arranged in step-side triangles. The same step-sided triangle motif, so common in prehistoric iconography reappears in the shapes of the pilaster strips decorating the platforms of the temple of Altyn-depe.[57] At Turang-tepe the elements were square pilasters. Also at Mundigak, the

51. Casal, 1961.
52. Masson, 1970, 1981, pp. 56–64.
53. Deshayes, 1975, 1977, pp. 108–11.
54. Tosi, 1983, pp. 112–15.
55. Salvatori, 1979.
56. Casal, 1961, p. 63, Fig. 36, Plate XXI A.
57. Masson, 1981, Plate III 2.

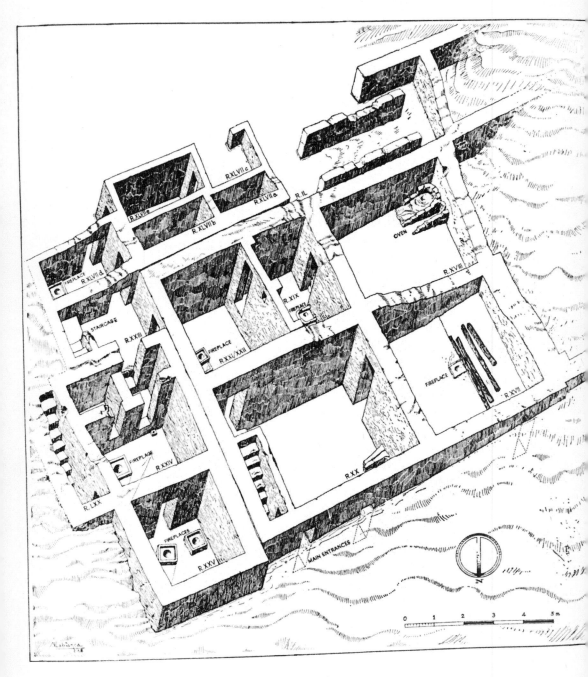

FIG. 4. Shahr-i Sokhta: isometrical view of a house.

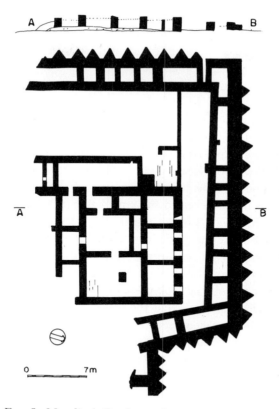

Fɪɢ. 5. Mundigak G, plan and section of a temple.

large building on Tepe G (Fig. 5) has a façade decorated with a tight network of triangular pilaster strips.

In terms of relative cultural sequence the construction of these monumental compounds may well have coincided with a new stage in socio-political development. While the first state structures emerged between 3200 and 2800 B.C., and are visible in specialist sectors such as information and administration, a later phase (between 2800 and 2400 B.C.) saw the construction of the actual urban structures themselves in small territorial cells some 500–100 km² in area, that is, only slightly larger than the pre-urban concentrations of the fourth millennium B.C. The large public buildings constructed in roughly the same period in larger centres, whether shrines or palaces, were most likely the effect of one or more extensive political projects by some of the ruling élite. The need for a sumptuous ceremonial organization reflects that increased control over the rural resources and production forces which also becomes visible in the contemporary foundations of the craftsmen's quarters and the repopulation of the deltaic plains in Sistan and Arachosia.

It is possible that in the second half of the third millennium B.C. larger political systems were coming into being throughout eastern Iran and Afghanistan as evidenced by new aspects of cultural identity between distant enclaves of the same region. The strong cultural connections of the reduced town of Hissar III A–B with the rich Gorgan plain 80 to 150 km to the north suggest that the Damghan valley might have been integrated around the mid-third millennium B.C., as an enclave mediating between the larger centres in the Gorgan farmlands and the copper, lead and gold ore sources around the edge of the Kavir desert. Perhaps the most striking case of political integration possible occurred in the Helmand valley between the two population poles of Sistan and Arachosia. A correspondence test carried out on the natural resources of the two centres of Shahr-i Sokhta and Mundigak has revealed the emergence of a higher degree of interdependence about half-way through the third millennium B.C.,[58] when Phases 5–3 at Shahr-i Sokhta are morphologically the same as those of Mundigak IV 1–3. This is the period of greatest territorial expansion in both regions and the first monumental structures to see the light of day all belong to this period. The process of integration probably took place during the third quarter of the third millennium B.C., with the result that the embryonic Iranian and middle Asian states of the Early Iron Age were set up between Kerman and Bactriana, from the Caspian to the Helmand. Furthermore, the timing and stages of this process apparently corresponded to, or just preceded, those of the Indus civilization. The latter, towards the end of the third millennium B.C., achieved the greatest degree of territorial integration of the whole pre-Achaemenid world with the entire north-western plainland of India and Pakistan being united in a single material complex.

Nothing is yet known about the town-planning aspects of the cities of the Bronze Age. Not enough excavation work has been carried out in these vast agglomerations of dwellings to be able to define the structures of the quarters or even the organization of the street networks. They all share the absence of perimeter walls and fortifications so characteristic of those of the Syro-Mesopotamian region. A city gate with a partitioned carriage way has been found in Area 8 at Altyn-depe dating back to the period of greatest expansion,[59] though it is still doubtful whether there were any continuous city walls. The majority of the streets consisted of narrow, winding, unpaved lanes whose level was rapidly raised by accumulated refuse from the houses. The settlement of population was virtually uncontrolled and the residential quarters emerge from the excavations as a somewhat heterogenous system. The impression is that the organization of the urban space was influenced by pre-existing buildings and social relations of the Chalcolithic Age. Turang-tepe, Hissar, Shahdad and Mundigak developed according to the fabric of the fourth millennium B.C. Obviously planned inter-

58. Jarrige and Tosi, 1981, p. 139; Ciarla, 1981, pp. 55–8.
59. Masson, 1981, p. 33, Fig. 10.

ventions are evident only after 2500 B.C. with the setting up of the first monumental structures.

The third millennium B.C. dwellings consisted of mud-brick buildings formed by rather asymmetrical groups of square rooms. The basic ground-plan was rectangular in shape and covered an area of 90–150 m² laid out around a courtyard from which the only door providing access to the exterior opened towards the east. The roofs were flat and supported by a frame consisting of five or six parallel poplar trunks built into the tops of the walls and covered with interwoven tamarisk branches on which the roof itself was laid. The latter was composed of woven rush matting covered with a layer of clay mixed with large quantities of straw. At Shahr-i Sokhta access to the ground floor was through the external wall or from one side of the internal courtyard.

Furthermore, all the service structures inside the dwellings were made of unbaked clay and bricks – box containers, hearths, square raised fireplaces, horse-shoe-domed ovens for breadmaking, sloping bases of grindstones. The same forms were used in eastern Iran throughout the Bronze Age and certainly until the Achaemenid period.[60] The dwellings had virtually no wooden furniture or wall niches. The problem of food preservation was solved by using mobile containers of all shapes and sizes: fibre baskets, cloth or leather bags, and pottery, stone and wooden vessels. The exceptionally good preservation of Shahr-i Sokhta has often allowed the discovery of vessels still with their contents of perishable material *in situ*. Grain, which formed the staple diet, was preserved in large pottery jars with a capacity of up to 20 kg of seeds. Store-rooms packed with jars are rare and it is quite possible that from around 3000 B.C. the long-term storage of foodstuffs was mainly provided for by the central administration who removed them from the control of individual families and concentrated them in centralized stores in which they were subject to written registration for the purpose of redistribution.

In the autarchic regime prevailing in all the early stages in eastern Iran, food supply was naturally based on the consumption of local products. Generally speaking, the agricultural production of the third millennium B.C. was based on wheat and barley species that had been selected locally during the Neolithic or in any case prior to 5000 B.C. During the accelerating pre-state phase of the fourth millennium B.C., the palaeobotanical finds of Tepe Yahya V and Hissar I attest to a definite increase in hexaploid grain forms compared with both barley and the tetraploid form. This points to a gradual reorganization of agriculture towards the selection of higher yield species.[61] Although the date palm was apparently used from the sixth millennium B.C. (cf. Yahya VI and Mehrgarh II: Costantini, personal communication), the first capital-intensive fruit-tree cultivation dates back to the end of the fourth millennium B.C. The earliest and main representa-

60. Genito, 1982.
61. Costantini, 1984*a*.

tive is the grapevine, which appears in the archaeological record during the final Chalcolithic at the same time as the first proto-Elamite tablets.

At Shahr-i Sokhta, the vegetable foodstuffs consisted of both wild and cultivated plants.[62] The latter obviously included the domestic species of wheat (*Triticum aestivum*) and barley (*Hordeum vulgare* var. *nudum*), though fruits such as grapes and melons (*Cucumis melo*) were also eaten. Evidence of wild plants consists of the identification of seeds of two Polygonaceae and one Chenopodiaceae species (*Chenopodium album*), which could also be used for making low-quality flour, while the abandoned remains of swamp rushes point to the use of cat-tail shoots (*Typha angustifolia*). The staple diet presumably consisted of graminaceous plants eaten in the form of bread and porridge, which every dwelling had the necessary equipment to prepare, that is, ovens, hearths and grindstones with collecting basins of clay. The large quantities of grape seeds found indicate that grapes were normally consumed in the cities. Although there is no direct evidence, it may reasonably be assumed that there was a flourishing production of grape wine and barley beer. The smart-looking balloon goblets used at Mundigak and Shahr-i Sokhta during the period of maximum urban expansion were presumably designed for drinking fermented beverages.

Vegetable oil could be extracted from linseed and even grape seeds, although the main source of protein was animal husbandry, hunting and fishing. Niche-packing conditions allowed the simultaneous exploitation of several different environments and gave access to a broad spectrum of natural resources. Sheep, goats and bovines in different proportions together always accounted for more than 90 per cent of animal bones in the Early Bronze Age sites. During the third millennium B.C., hunting on the alluvial plain was restricted to a few types of gazelle and the onager (*Equus Hemionus*), by now restricted to the edges of the desert.[63] The wild-animal remains found at Tepe Hissar were more abundant owing to the vicinity of the highland forests of the Elburz mountains. At Sistan a considerable contribution to the food supplies was nevertheless made by hunting owing to the abundance of bird life in the swamps. As many as forty-one bird species have been identified among the osteological finds at Shahr-i Sokhta, more than 95 per cent of which are, however, marsh birds such as the coot (*Fulica atra*) and anseridae.[64] Moreover, thousands of eggshell fragments belonging to six different species have been gathered and identified; marsh birds are by far the most frequent.[65]

This state of equilibrium between the various ecological niches inside each proto-urban enclave is not representative of a new order but marks the final expansion of the Chalcolithic economy. Towards the end of the third millen-

62. Costantini, 1977.
63. Compagnoni and Caloi, 1977; Compagnoni, 1978*a*, pp. 105–18, 1978*b*, pp. 119–28.
64. Cassoli, 1977.
65. Spröde, 1977.

nium B.C., at the same time as the crisis affecting the whole basin, new cultivars and domestic animals developed in other regions of Asia and Africa and were introduced into Baluchistan, Oman and eastern Iran. These consisted of new summer-crop cereals, rice, sorghum and millet[66] and the first pack animals, such as horses, asses and camels.[67] From this stage on, the countryside began to resemble the present-day one. As far as the primary economy is concerned, the proto-urban societies, though perhaps partly preparing the well-ordered and more flexible agriculture of the second millennium B.C., still had their material bases determined by the same range of Neolithic resources as had been expanded during the Chalcolithic.

The best-known protohistoric graveyards in the area are to be found at Shahr-i Sokhta and Tepe Hissar. Smaller groups of graves and isolated burials have been explored also at Mundigak, Turang-tepe and in various parts of southern Iran. In the general forms of the funerary ritual a fairly high degree of uniformity exists throughout all these regions, including Baluchistan and southern Turkmenistan. Burials always consisted of inhumation without any prior exposure, the body being laid on one side with arms and legs flexed. The offerings consisted mainly of personal ornaments, pottery and other objects of everyday use, arranged around the body starting from the head and the feet. While at Hissar graves were dug in uninhabited areas of the settlement, between the ruins of abandoned dwellings, in the Helmand area they were kept quite separate from the other areas of the city and confined to cemetery areas of ever-increasing size. The Shahr-i Sokhta graveyard, for instance, reached an area of 21 ha.[68]

Graves often contain mud-brick masonry structures dividing them into two halves: one half for the body and the other for the offerings. There are also fairly frequent cases of actual circular or square chambers. The former are better-known as *tholoi* and were used in southern Turkmenistan from the beginning of the fourth millennium B.C., mostly for multiple burials.[69] At Shahr-i Sokhta the same structures were used in the early third millennium B.C., reaching a diameter of 3 m with thirteen burials arranged in successive depositions. Also square chambers were built as multiple tombs to accomodate successive depositions.[70] The most typical examples are the Period III graves of Tepe C at Mundigak[71] identical to the somewhat later grave 11 of Altyn-depe.[72] The graves partitioned by a small brick wall are perhaps the reflection of an even older morphology of Baluchistan, and not of middle Asian, origin. In fact, specimens identical to

66. Cleuziou and Costantini, 1981.
67. Meadow, 1983.
68. Piperno and Tosi, 1975; Tosi, 1976.
69. Sarianidi, 1959; Masson, 1977, Fig. 3.
70. Piperno and Salvatori, 1983, p. 175, Fig. 3a–c.
71. Casal, 1961, pp. 44–5, Plate X 13D.
72. Masson, 1981, p. 52, Fig. 16.

those of the third millennium B.C. have been found in the earliest aceramic Neolithic layers of Mehrgarh, more than 3,000 years earlier.[73]

A more complex type of grave has a pit opening into an underground chamber dug in the clay. At Shahr-i Sokhta it has been found to have been used for multiple burials accompanied by richer grave goods.[74] The shape closely recalls that of the later catacomb graves of southern Siberia and Soviet Central Asia, though it is too early to say whether there is a common ideological background behind this convergence. The good state of preservation of the organic remains at Shahr-i Sokhta has made it possible to analyse the contents of vases found in the graves, much of which consisted of the remains of both cooked and raw food. Kids and lambs had also been well documented as early as the Neolithic at Mehrgarh.[75]

The variability of burial types recorded in the Helmand valley graveyards is related neither to the wealth of furnishings nor to age or sex. In view of the presence at Shahr-i Sokhta of morphologies typical of both the southern Turkmenian Chalcolithic and the Baluchi Neolithic-Chalcolithic, the new urban configuration of cultural tradition is more likely to have been influenced by a convergence of customs and traditions flowing from the two poles. On the other hand, the signs of economic inequality are clearly expressed in the differing degrees of richness of the grave goods. A recent comparative analysis carried out on a sample of 300 Period I–III graves (3200–2300 B.C.) at Shahr-i Sokhta has indicated that the furnishings can be divided into three main groups according to number and quality of objects.[76] This other variability axis is not determined by differences in sex or age, but on both a chronological factor and on an assumed social stratification. The richer graves are those mostly dated around Phases 4 and 3. This 'richness' is evaluated according to the number of pottery vases and metal objects, two aspects of the technology in rapid expansion after 2500 B.C., and the reorganization of the production forces that coincides with the maximum expansion of the urban areas. This increased availability of goods at all levels is particularly apparent in the extremely rich graveyard of Shahdad, dated to the second half of the third millennium B.C.[77] The evidence accumulated here from hundreds of graves points to a high-level metal-working industry with much in common with the quality productions of Hissar IIIB and Bactria in the Middle Bronze Age.

It is still not possible to define the political entities in eastern Iran which governed one of the largest centres of civilization in Asia during the second half of the third millennium B.C. Elements of social complexity are all present in the

73. Lechevallier et al., 1982.
74. Piperno, 1977, p. 123.
75. Lechevallier et al., 1982.
76. Piperno, 1977, 1979.
77. Hakemi, 1972.

archaeological record, even though systematic research has been carried out for only a few decades. The most impressive discoveries will be made in the future. What is certain is that this congeries of centres and states had a considerable and lasting effect on the whole of southern Central Asia and along the coasts of the Indian Ocean, as is attested by the extensive convergence linking eastern Iran to the Oman peninsula throughout the third millennium B.C. To what extent they influenced the social development of the ancient world is a question that cannot be answered until systematic research has also been carried out on the second millennium B.C. linking the Early Bronze Age civilizations. Unfortunately, in the light of what has been discovered so far, we know only that after reaching its peak the urban civilization suddenly collapsed. It lost all its features of centrality and most of the cities were sharply reduced or abandoned in the space of a few years. However, the disappearance of cities does not necessarily imply the dissolution of the state organization. We have seen how the process of state formation began at least five centuries before the phase of rapid expansion of the cities. This gap indicates that some caution must be observed in considering the two phenomena as interdependent. Urbanism is one but not the only outcome of a social order based on the state, which appears to hold for Central Asia. Its success in the Early and Middle Bronze Ages nevertheless had lasting effects and we should soon be able to examine them in the historical context of the earliest Iranian and Indian societies.

Our knowledge of the Chalcolithic and Bronze Ages in Afghanistan is confined to the excavation of three sites in southern Afghanistan: Mundigak, Said Qala and Deh Morasi Ghundai. Mundigak is situated in a mountainous region about 55 km north-west of modern Kandahar located in the upper drainage of the Kushk-i Nakhod river, which is roughly parallel to the Arghandab river near Kandahar. As with most areas of Afghanistan, this region is arid. The site of Mundigak comprises a series of mounds.

Casal's[78] sequence at Mundigak remains the primary reference point for the Bronze Age in Afghanistan. This sequence has been supplemented by limited excavation of Said Qala-tepe[79] and Deh Morasi Ghundai.[80] The results of excavation clearly indicated seven major occupation periods. From a chronological point of view these represent a time-span of approximately 3,000 years, from the beginning of the fourth to some time in the second millennium B.C. During this time Mundigak developed from a small agricultural village (Periods I–III) to a major urban centre (Periods IV–V), to be abandoned during the Iron Age.

The first mud-brick habitations were encountered in Phase I 4–5. At the end of Period I foundations made of *pisé* and sometimes mixed with stone were started. In Period II the notable features are deeper foundations, mud-brick walls

78. Casal, 1961.
79. Shaffer, 1971.
80. Dupree, 1963.

and rectangular rooms, divided into two rooms, one smaller than the other. Period IV is basically different from the previous periods, being very impressive and without parallel in the prehistory of Afghanistan as described earlier.

From the point of view of architectural structures there is no greater change between Periods IV and V than there was between IV and III. However, some difference can be traced in the ceramics of the two periods.

Among all the materials which have been found at Mundigak, the ceramics are of prime importance. The pottery is buff-red ware predominantly wheel-made (90 per cent). However, in Phase I 5 wheel-made pottery had decreased significantly in frequency (80 per cent, I = 70 per cent). Vessel forms were limited to straight-angular or curved-wall bowls in Phase I 2–3, and to only straight-sided vessels in Phase I 4–5. Painted globular jars appeared for the first time. The basic decorative pattern for Period I consisted of black geometric motifs on a red background. All pottery in Period II was made of a buff-red paste; however, hand-made pottery had coarse tempering materials added.

Period III also had two variants in wheel-made pottery, undecorated and decorated. The vast majority of decorated pottery is of a single basic type with two variants. Both variants are of buff-red paste with self- or sand-tempering. Zoomorphic and anthropomorphic figurines are represented in Period III. All figurines found at Mundigak are highly stylized, in a standing position and predominantly female with prominent breasts.

Period IV had the final occurrence of figurines in any significant quantity. It is necessary to note here two points about the Period IV figurines. First, considering the horizontal area of excavation in contrast to that of previous periods, the quantity of figurines seems very small. Secondly, according to available data, these figurines are clearly absent from both 'Palace' and 'Temple' structures. Most zoomorphic figurines were highly stylized representations of humped cattle and several were found with painted decorations including a polychrome or appliqué collar. Anthropomorphic figurines were highly stylized with pinched faces, prominent breasts, appliqué eyes, winged arms, broad lips and a rather flat profile. Two very fine examples of female figurines modelled in the round in the style usually referred to as 'Zhob' were located in Period IV.

For the first time, metal artefacts were found in Phase I 2 and increased in frequency and variety throughout the sequence. The earliest example was a flat blade which might have had a hafting tang. The most frequent metal artefact found throughout the Mundigak sequence was a simple type of bronze point or punch with a circular cross-section. This was first identified in Phase I 4 and easily replaced the bone awl/punch in Period IV. In Period III, a tanged lozenge-shaped point and, in Period IV, a tanged oval-shaped point were introduced. Among the rare metal artefacts of Mundigak were a large lance head and knife.

The first examples of 'luxury' metal artefacts were located in Phase II 3. These included pins, one with a double-voluted end while the other had a flattened, perforated end. The greatest number and variety of 'luxury' type objects were found in Phase IV 1. These are as follows: concave discs (mirrors), double-voluted, lozenge-shaped and broad, flat-headed pins, handles for disc-mirrors and buckles. It is important to mention that in two instances smelted iron decorative buttons were found on objects of Period IV. Three important metal artefacts have been found in Phase III 6, being the only examples, two socket-hole axes and an adze; from analysis of some of these metal artefacts it is clear that the metal of the early Mundigak period was a very low-tin bronze. Tin accounted for only about 1 per cent, iron 0.15 per cent, the remaining material being copper. The artefacts had a tin content of almost 5 per cent, the highest recorded at Mundigak.

Sheep, goat, cattle, ass, horse and dog are among the domesticated animals, and ibex, gazelle and lynx were the wild animals identified initially in Period I. The remains of domesticated and wild animals, with the addition of wild birds of prey, were found in Period II. The first cereal remains identified at Mundigak come from the same period with the addition of domesticated wheat.

The second Bronze Age site, Said Qala, is located approximately 96 km south-east of Mundigak near Kandahar city, very close to Deh Morasi Ghundai. The site was first tested by Fairservis; however, the major excavations were conducted by J. G. Shaffer some twenty years later. Four prehistoric occupations were identified at Said Qala, all being contemporary with Mundigak III 5 to IV 1. The initial occupation at the site, Period I, is known only from the lowest 3 m of the deposit. Small rectangular mud-brick house structures, similar to those at Mundigak, were found throughout the first three occupations. Three C14 dates for Said Qala are basically contemporary with the end of the third millennium B.C., and all recovered cultural materials indicate that all occupations at Said Qala are essentially equivalent to those of Mundigak Phases III 5–6 to IV 1.

The ceramics of Said Qala recorded by Casal are equivalent to Phase III 5 to IV 1 of Mundigak except for a complete absence of zoomorphic motifs. Two varieties of hand-made pottery can be distinguished on the basis of their surfaces, though both have chaff tempering and the same vessel forms as those described for Mundigak hand-made pottery. From the site of Said Qala only rarely were a few sherds of Quetta ware found. A few sherds of a black-on-red slipped pottery of Kili Gul Muhammad and Faiz Muhammad grey ware were also found from the same area. A small percentage of hand-made pottery with chaff or crushed rock temper was found in all occupations, and it occasionally occurred with basket impressions. In Period II there was little change in the wheel-made pottery, and such changes as occur parallel those of Mundigak III 5 to IV 1. Bowls change from angular-wall to an S-shaped wall form. Floral motifs are found on Said Qala pottery, but zoomorphic motifs as mentioned above completely absent. Cattle figurines are found throughout Periods I–IV. These figurines are similar to the types occurring at Mundigak. A single example of a possible bird figurine was also found.

Bronze artefacts are confined to the end of Periods II–IV. Among the functional artefacts sickles, blades, lozenge-tanged points and punches were identified. Luxury items in the form of pins were found in Periods II–IV. A single example of a bronze handle was also located. In general the artefacts are very similar to those found at Mundigak. The samples of fauna and flora have not been analysed so far, but there is no doubt that Said Qala exploited domesticated sheep, goat and cattle as well as wheat and barley.

The third Bronze Age site is Deh Morasi Ghundai, situated 16 km to the south-west of Said Qala, and about half its size. Deh Morasi is later than Said Qala and represents a Mundigak IV type occupation.

The major occupation at Deh Morasi occurred in Period II which is divided into three phases. The only significant architectural feature found in Period II was a small (45 × 28 cm) mud-brick structure, trapezoidal in shape, directly associated with a terracotta female figurine, a copper tube and seal, goat bones and horn, a utilized magnetite nodule and pottery. The entire feature was surrounded by prepared clay floor. L. Dupree interpreted this structure as a 'household shrine'.

Prehistoric pottery has been located in all subsequent occupations at the site, all of which are comparable to that identified in Mundigak IV 1. But Period I contained only crude hand-made chaff-tempered pottery, samples of which were found at both Mundigak and Said Qala throughout most occupations. With the exception of crude hand-made pottery, all are wheel-made in a buff-red paste with sand or self temper. Decorated motifs are almost entirely confined to geometrics which are very similar in their overall style to those of Mundigak III 5–6 to IV 1. Bowls and beakers are predominant vessel forms. From the point of view of form, they are confined primarily to vessels with S-shaped walls, and some beakers have pedestal bases. Special-function or intrusive-type pottery was located at Deh Morasi Ghundai. The zoomorphic motif of Deh Morasi IIb is the same as in the Quetta ware. Zoomorphic figurines were confined to leg fragments in Period IIb. The female figurine found in association with the 'shrine complex' of Period II is a classic example of the 'Zhob'-style figurine found in a Period IV context at Mundigak.

Deh Morasi metal artefacts were limited to copper (Periods IIa–IV). In Period II two hollow tube and handle fragments associated with the 'shrine complex' were found. Several fragments of simple pins were located in IIb–c and one fragment of a copper seal with a geometric motif was found in Period IV.

As indicated above, an establishment of proto-urban and early-urban culture occurred in southern Afghanistan and in neighbouring Iran in the third millennium B.C. In all probability, the largest settlement, Mundigak, served the function of a regional capital. A monumental building with a façade consisting of a sequence of semi-circular pilasters is tentatively regarded as the residence of a local ruler. There exist clear indications of cultural links with areas of early agricultural tribes in the south of Soviet Central Asia and, particularly, with the neighbouring communities in northern Baluchistan and the Indus valley where the formative process of the Harappan civilization was actively under way. There are reasons to suggest that the large centres in the Indus valley imported copper ore and lapis lazuli from Afghanistan; the semi-precious stone was cherished throughout the Ancient East for the magic properties ascribed to it. Lapis lazuli was imported into Mesopotamia and Egypt from the beginning of the second half of the fourth millennium B.C., reaching Troy in Asia Minor. Lapis lazuli from Afghanistan reached areas far to the west through multiple exchanges; whereas direct cultural and economic links existed with neighbouring communities in eastern Iran, Soviet Central Asia and Baluchistan. This is probably related to the emergence of the settlement of Shortugai on the southern bank of the Amu Darya (Oxus) river.

The site contains typical elements of the Harappan Civilization ranging from pottery to seals. In all probability, this was a trading factory situated along the meridional trade route, which held its importance down to the Middle Ages. The concentration of population, specialization of production, regular trade and exchange greatly facilitated the development of urban tendencies. In the course of the third millennium B.C. Mundigak, the largest centre in southern Afghanistan, turned into an urban-type settlement.

Important changes occurred in this area during the second millennium B.C. At that time, as in other centres of Central Asia, there was a general decline of the proto-urban culture. By contrast, a highly developed culture appeared at the same time in the north; it was studied in detail by the Soviet-Afghan expedition in the 1970s. Dozens of sites belonging to settled agriculturalists and stock-breeders clustering in five or six oases were discovered in a limited space between Daulatabad and Mazar-i Sharif. The sites were situated along the beds of small rivers. They clustered inside the deltaic plains in the areas flanking the desert where the flood-water could be easily used for irrigation. One may suggest that small canals were used for the same purpose. Tilling was carried out by wooden ploughs; a picture of a bull drawing a carriage was engraved on the surface of a silver vessel. Each oasis possessed a centre distinguished from common villages by the presence of a rectangular or square fortress up to 1 ha in size. The fortress was surrounded by mud-brick walls with towers, circular at the corner, and semi-circular along the perimeter (Dashly I, Gardai I).

High standards both in culture and technology were typical of these Bronze Age examples. Pottery of uniform shapes was made on the wheel and fired in vertical kilns situated near the settlements. The prehistoric potters produced vessels of austere shapes with no ornamental patterns. As in other regions, the painted pottery disappeared with the advent of the period of craft specialization and with a decline in the early agricultural tradition of applied art. There are indications of various activities performed by metallurgists, smiths and jewellers. We may distinguish various axes, sickles, mirrors and pins, with heads depicting various animals. The considerable number of arms is noteworthy; there are swords, spears and battle-axes. The occurrence of fortresses and arms indicates an uneasy epoch of hostilities and conflicts. This was a factor that accelerated an institutional-ization of power and a crystallization of a military élite.

Probably, production of bronze filigree seals, often anthropomorphic or therimorphic, became an independent branch of industry. There exist also stone seals with various figures, some with wings, a theme obviously of Mesopotamian origin. Seated female figurines, with bodies carved in a dark serpentine and heads in a light-coloured marble, are seen as masterpieces of prehistoric art. These figu-rines bear an unmistakable reflection of artistic standards which originated in distant Mesopotamia (Fig. 6).

This culture from the north of Afghanistan spread equally to south Uzbe-kistan and to south-west Tajikistan, where its local variant (Sapalli-type com-plexes) was represented. Its numerous features go back to the Altyn-depe civil-ization in south Turkmenistan, whence communities belonging to a highly developed urban-style civilization were spreading to the east in the course of the second millennium B.C. At the same time, this culture reveals unmistakable Mesopotamian and Elamite elements. Grey ware pottery, not typical of Altyn-depe indicates connections with the Iranian Hissar culture. Glyptics seem to denote links with both western Asia and Harappan traditions. The time-span in question featured an amplification of cultural contacts and of intraregional links.

Up to now no large sites that could be interpreted as remains of urban set-tlements have been found in northern Afghanistan. The prevailing settlement pattern indicates small communities, each one representing an independent social unit, situated at short distances from one another. At the same time, we should note the occurrence of isolated large monumental structures which, beyond any doubt, performed specific functions common to a cluster of sites or even for northern Afghanistan as a whole. Two such structures were excavated at Dashly 3. A circular fortress was situated in the centre of a square structure, each side of which was 130–150 m long. The occurrence of a shrine inside the fortress with an altar against the wall, validates a suggestion that this was a ceremonial centre, probably a temple with numerous services, repositories, granaries, dwell-ing-houses for priests and auxiliary personnel. The second rectangular structure, 84 × 88 m, features a central courtyard, which contained various repositories and a small house with altar niches. Numerous pilasters decorated the outer walls. It was suggested that this was of a ceremonial temple character but, judging by its planning the residential portion of the hypothetical temple was not present. Probably, it was a temple devoted to a different divinity, as in Mesopotamia, where temples devoted to a supreme god and to his divine spouse were often sit-uated side by side. At any rate, there is no doubt that we are dealing with a clearly indicated ceremonial and administrative centre of the Bronze Age. We may sug-gest that the supreme power was of a theocratic nature as was often the case in the formative stage of emerging civilizations, where the supreme military chief also performed priestly functions.

The possibility cannot be ruled out that among prehistoric burials exca-

FIG. 6. Female figurine in stone. (Courtesy of P. Amiet.)

vated, not by professional archaeologists but by amateurs, there were tombs that belong either to the priesthood or to a civic élite. It was not by chance that numerous artistic items, among them objects in bronze, silver and gold, originated from these tombs. The Fullol hoard, which contained a variety of gold and silver vessels with highly artistic decoration, is representative in this respect. Hence, one may conclude that the development of a civilization of an ancient oriental type was actively under way in northern Afghanistan in the course of the second millennium B.C. None the less, the natural and cultural environment here was different from that in the south of the country in the third millennium B.C. This cultural stratum was of principal importance for the ultimate development of the areas referred to in written sources as Bactria.

Conclusion

The Bronze Age was an important stage in the history of Iran and Afghanistan. In the aftermath of a decisive leap forward in food-production which took place in the Neolithic, there occurred an active accumulation of economic, cultural and intellectual potentialities. Several centres of early agricultural cultures arose, inside which there occurred an intensive development of exquisite painted pottery, samples of which may be seen as first-class masterpieces of prehistoric applied art. The stable surplus product obtained by irrigated culture, and the technical progress primarily due to the development of metallurgy, metal-processing and thermotechnics, led to a concentration of population and the emergence of large proto-urban and early-urban type settlements. As a result, a proto-urban civilization emerged in Iran and Afghanistan in the course of the Bronze Age. Among its regional centres, the best-explored are Hissar in north-western Iran, Mundigak in southern Afghanistan and Shahr-i Sokhta in Sistan (which is sometimes labelled by its explorers as the Helmand civilization). The discovery of highly developed centres of Bronze Age proto-urban civilization in Iran, Afghanistan and southern Soviet Central Asia was an outstanding achievement of archaeology from the 1950s to the 1970s. As a result, it has been proved that great urban civilizations of Mesopotamia and the Indus valley were separated not by backward tribes, but by local proto-urban and early-urban civilizations, which contributed in their own way to the development of world culture. This was an important achievement of the peoples of the pre-Achaemenid Age, and it was archaeology that brought to light these brilliant cultures.

At the same time, the Bronze Age illustrates an active development and strengthening of cultural ties, which was one of the prerequisites of its outstanding accomplishments. Intraregional interactions amplified. Results of these interactions are clearly indicated in the spheres of production, material culture and the arts of all important centres: in Shahdad, Hissar and Shahr-i Sokhta (Iran), in Mundigak (southern Afghanistan), and in Altyn-depe (southern Soviet

Central Asia). Traditions common to the whole subregion came into being. This took shape in the production of elegant and varied vessels carved in marble and chlorite, as well as of flat metal button seals with an eye on the back. An independent origin of several traditions proper to this subregion, and to Bactria in particular, became obvious only recently; earlier they were erroneously regarded as imported from Elam or Mesopotamia. At the same time, there are irrefutable proofs of links with these ancient civilizations of western Asia, as well as of a creative use thereof, often on a selective base, by means of adoption of cultural models and standards. Propagation of these items was much facilitated by the spread in Iran of proto-Elamite communities featured by a specific cultural assemblage which included cylindrical seals and clay tablets with pictographic inscriptions. None the less, we should clearly stress that these links, which enriched the local traditions, were not the determinants of the development of local Bronze Age civilizations of early urban type.

THE BRONZE AGE IN KHORASAN
AND TRANSOXANIA[1]

V. M. Masson

T HE transition to a production economy gave decisive impetus to cultural and social progress. The results of this change are particularly clear in the Metal Age, when copper (Eneolithic) and subsequently bronze (Bronze Age) implements heralded major increases in production efficiency. This was paralleled by the further territorial spread of new types of economic activity. Whereas in the Neolithic only a few tribes in the foothill oases of Kopet Dag had switched to agriculture and animal husbandry, in the period in question outward-bound agricultural communes extended more advanced forms of securing a livelihood to regions lying further east, namely to the Murghab valley and later to Transoxania. Gradually the hunters, fishermen and gatherers of the steppes saw the emergence of cattle-raising as a way of life, a complete transition to a cattle-raising and agricultural tribal existence occurring in the course of the second millennium B.C.

Southern Turkmenistan went through the final stages of the formation of an agricultural and cattle-raising economy, coupled with a corresponding type of culture, in the fifth and fourth millennia B.C. Archaic elements still much in evidence in the Jeitun culture now disappear entirely.[2] Extensive excavations of ancient settlements north of Kopet Dag have made it possible to delimit roughly the periods of development of local society in that period.

The Early Eneolithic (fifth and early fourth millennia B.C.) was marked by a growth in the population of the foothill belt at Kopet Dag. Along with smaller settlements 0.5–1 ha in area (Anau, Dashlyji, Yassy-depe),[3] some major centres covering more than 10 ha sprang up (Kara-depe, Namazga-depe).[4] Fanning out over still unsettled areas, the early agrarian tribes wandered eastward as far as the

1. See Map 7 on page 194.
2. Korobkova, 1981.
3. Khlopin, 1963; Pumpelly, 1908.
4. Masson, 1962.

ancient delta of the River Tedzhen (Harirud), the site of the Geoksiur oasis.[5] The early stage, corresponding to the creation of the archaeological complex of the Anau IA[6] type, is characterized by the penetration into the oases of southern Turkmenistan of tribal groups from central Iran – a migration accompanied by several cultural and technological innovations, including the advent of metallurgy. However, the newcomers were soon fully assimilated by the descendants of Jeitun tribes; this development is clearly evidenced by the next archaeological complex, namely that of Namazga I. The settlement of related tribal groups over a sizeable territory meant the emergence of certain local cultural differences, particularly marked in the case of ornamental motifs on clay pottery. But by and large the cultural unity of the region remained intact.

The twin pillars of the economy were agriculture and cattle-raising, the latter activity providing over four-fifths of the meat consumed. Along with cattle and sheep, pigs were also domesticated. The soil-working implements of the Anau IA complex include massive stone hoes, while the Namazga I complex contains ring stones once fitted to the ends of digging sticks. At the same time flint implements practically fell into disuse, the Stone Age giving way to the Metal Age. The Anau IA period supplies the first instances of cast copper objects including awls, punches and knives. Among the household crafts, weaving achieved a fairly advanced state of development: excavations of ancient settlement sites have yielded conical terracotta yarn spindles in large numbers.

To judge by their size, the single-chamber houses making up the settlements were built to lodge single small families, which must have represented the primary-level societal unit. At the same time, the collective character of the basically agrarian economy made it necessary to preserve clan groupings. The fully excavated settlement of Dashlyji, whose population must have numbered forty to fifty persons, possibly belonged to just such a single-clan community. The typical ideological centres of these communities were sanctuaries with walls adorned with painted red and black geometric patterns.

The culture of the Early Eneolithic testifies to improved standards of everyday life and well-being. The applied arts underwent considerable development: almost a third of the clay pottery is decorated in black paint against a red or yellowish background. The dominant style is a quiet ornamentalism consisting of large geometric elements, mostly triangles. A lively realism finds its reflection in terracotta figurines of stout women. The art of the early agricultural communities was still in its infancy.

During the Middle Eneolithic dating back to the middle of the fourth millennium B.C., the unitary culture of the early agrarian communities of southern Turkmenistan split into two distinct local variants – the western and the eastern. The western variant is distinguished by its colourful painted pottery vessels dec-

5. Khlopin, 1964.
6. Khlopin, 1963.

FIG. 1. Female figurine from Yalangach-depe
(beginning of fourth millenium B.C.).

orated with geometric ornaments subdivided into two colours – red and black (Anau, Kara-depe, Namazga-depe). In the east, on the other hand, the ornaments become simpler and more austere, the dominant motifs being straight parallel lines running along the lips of cups and pots (Altyn-depe and settlements of the Geoksiur oasis). This distinction very likely reflects a process of ethnocultural differentiation with the formation of two tribal groups. The Geoksiur oasis in the ancient delta of the Tedzhen is likewise typified by settlements surrounded by natural brick walls, with the perimeter including circular-plan structures which also served as dwellings (Yalangach-depe, Mullali-depe). This development may have owed much to the location of the oasis, which constituted the easternmost limit of the area peopled by settled agriculturalists whose immediate neighbours by this time would have been Neolithic hunting tribes ranging the steppe and semi-desert regions.

The agriculturalists continued to grow the principal grains already consumed during the Neolithic, namely wheat and barley. But the preferred cereal was certainly the latter: excavations at Mullali-depe[7] have yielded 9,100 barley seeds as against just 250 seeds of wheat. But the salient fact was the progress achieved in irrigation agriculture. The Geoksiur oasis excavations have exposed a contemporaneous artificial reservoir, while a study of barley seeds from Altyn-depe[8] has revealed that they had germinated in conditions of multiple-field irrigation. Copper implements were cold-forged and annealed, which improved the durability of the working edge considerably. Also noteworthy are the gold and silver decorative pieces pointing to the further refinement of metallurgy. Finds include decorative items, among them semi-precious stones, such as carnelian, turquoise and lapis lazuli. It was then that the last-named stone came into systematic use, not only by the inhabitants of the oases around Kopet Dag but also throughout the ancient East. Efforts to ensure a regular supply of this beautiful blue stone, whose chief deposits lie in the mountains of north-eastern Afghanistan, played a significant role in the establishment of lasting trading and cultural ties over a large territory. The arts evolved remarkably. In addition to painted vessels, particularly richly decorated in finds of the western group, art works discovered include terracotta statuettes representing the ample-bodied protectress of fertility. In the Geoksiur oasis such figurines are of several types, including massive seated statuettes with arms and shoulders supplanted by plump breasts and thighs bearing various magical symbols (Fig. 1). In accordance with the principle of *pars pro toto* the sculptors of this period thus emphasized in their representations of the patroness of agriculture features germane to motherhood and fecundity.

The settled communities of southern Turkmenistan achieved a particularly significant level of development in the Late Eneolithic, that is, from the late

7. Khlopin, 1969.
8. Masson, 1981*a*.

fourth to the early third millennium B.C. At that time they found themselves included in a system of increasingly close cultural ties and ethnic shifts which encompassed an extensive area in Iran, Afghanistan and north-western India/Pakistan. The Kopet Dag communities continued to migrate eastward, with small settlements appearing in the Murghab delta. On the evidence of discoveries by archaeologists in Tajikistan, the settled agrarian culture had by now reached Transoxania (Sarazm near Pendjikent). At the same time, judging by changes in certain objects of material culture and in the physical type of the population, southern Turkmenistan was penetrated by individual tribal groups coming from Iran. Although they were assimilated comparatively quickly by the native population, they brought with them certain specific cultural traditions. The Kopet Dag oases bear traces of differentiation into two cultural zones – a western and an eastern. The western zone contains extensive finds of painted pottery in the Kara-depe style, characterized by fine geometric patterning and representations of various animals – goats, spotted snow leopards and birds. To the east we see the formation of a new style of ornamented ceramics, namely the Geoksiur style with its large bright polychrome figures of crosses and half-crosses. On the other hand, other features – house types, statuettes, metal objects, burial rites – clearly indicate that the two groups must have constituted a single cultural entity.

The gradual development of irrigation agriculture is evident from the sizeable and extensive irrigation systems discovered in the Geoksiur oasis. Excavations in the vicinity of the principal settlement of the oasis, Geoksiur I,[9] have revealed man-made channels approximately 3 km in length and 2.5–5 m in width. These channels were used to irrigate fields, the water being distributed by shallow ditches. By permitting the multiple watering of crops, irrigation agriculture ensured stable harvests and was a major factor in economic and cultural progress.

The camel became domesticated and some small clay wheels found in the excavations possibly belonged to model carts, testifying to the development of transportation and the use of animals for draught purposes. The metallurgical remains reveal a significant variety of technological devices used in the fashioning of various objects, a fact suggesting the existence of permanent metal workshops. Pottery was fired in special furnaces that ensured uniform temperatures and at the same time required considerable technical skill on the potter's part. The fashioning of vessels out of marble-like limestone also required a high level of artistic ability. Very probably by this time the agrarian communes had evolved a special category of professional craftsmen, first and foremost potters and metal workers. These craftsmen laboured to satisfy the needs of their kinsmen not through buying and selling, but rather by virtue of membership in the community, which is why they are referred to as 'communal craftsmen'.

All these developments acted to ramify the social structure, to stimulate

9. Sarianidi, 1965; Lisitsyna, 1978.

FIG. 2. Painted pottery from Kara-depe (3300–3000 B.C.).

differentiation in respect of social status and property. The larger settlements now consisted of multichambered houses of twelve to fifteen rooms, including a kitchen, common grain-storage enclosures and a common household yard. Most likely such houses belonged to multi-family communes in which smaller family units were grouped by family relationship and joint household activity. The multi-family community became the basic unit of society. Parallel to this we have the advent of collective tombs often containing the remains of twelve to twenty persons, which probably constituted the family tombs of such multi-family communities. There are also richly furnished graves. Whereas ordinary graves included one or two painted pots, one Kara-depe grave was found to contain eight splendid painted pots and a large, carefully executed terracotta statuette. Another grave, in a very damaged state, may have housed a group of fifteen painted vessels and a terracotta figurine of a standing male with a long beard. Altyn-depe has yielded up the grave of a woman accompanied by five clay and two stone vessels, together with several copper objects, which were particularly prized in Turkmenistan, which has little or no copper. In all probability such burials are to be associated with the upper stratum of Late Eneolithic society – its chiefs, priests and priestesses whose position in society required special distinction in the matter of burial customs. It may be that warlords are represented by the terracotta figurines of warriors in finely wrought helmets with elongated earpieces. The residences of such leaders may well have been situated in major settlements of the Kara-depe[10] or Altyn-depe[11] type. The extent of the latter increased considerably at that time, reaching an area of 25 ha. The entire settlement was surrounded by natural brick walls roughly 2 m thick reinforced by rectangular buttresses along the outer perimeter.

Economic prosperity was accompanied by a flowering of culture. An exceptional richness of artistic expression was to be found in the smaller forms, particularly in painted ceramics and small carved objects. The designs on vessels are devoid of the primeval archaism typical of the painted ceramic of the Early Eneolithic. The variegated, carpet-like and strictly symmetrical designs adorning vessels are characterized by a wealth of ornament (Fig. 2), spontaneous decoration, and a symbolism somewhat akin to abstract art. Not infrequently, particularly at Kara-depe, refined ornamentation becomes an end in itself, lending a flavour of festivity and sophistication to the everyday life of the ancient farmers. Certain features in the figurative structure of the ornaments suggest an imitation of carpet or other textile motifs that might have been used on real objects which have not survived, as would be true of many items fashioned from organic materials.

To a certain extent the same features of decorativeness and refinement are evident in the small terracotta sculptures. The stout matrons are supplanted by

10. Masson, 1960.
11. Masson, 1981*a*.

231

figurines of more slender shape and smooth, delicate lines. A richly detailed decorative approach characterizes the treatment of hairstyle and head-dress; plaits and S-shaped pendants are meticulously rendered. Some of the material figures carry a child, which points to the further development of the notion of a patroness of fertility, now clearly manifest in images of motherhood. The thigh of another female statuette bears a creeping-snake design. The figurine in question was found next to a collective tomb and may represent a Clithonic deity of the beyond. We likewise witness the emergence of larger sculptural works in mamoreal limestone. The finds in question include a human torso and the figure of a bull. A painted ceramic item features two human figures standing before a similar larger statue placed in a central sanctuary.

The Kopet Dag oases constituted a major centre of ancient cultures whose influence extented far beyond its confines. Moving out from the Geoksiur oasis, a population group entered the Murghab delta, where a recent find exposed several widely scattered settlements with ceramics typical of the Geoksiur style. Still more important is the discovery of a typical Geoksiur ceramic complex in the Zerafshan valley of Transoxania. In the hilly banks of one of its ravines was the site of an ancient settlement with houses of mud-brick.

There was also a sanctuary among the houses, with a centrally located oval altar and walls covered with polychrome paintings. The decorated ceramics of Sarazm with polychrome ornamentation in the form of crosses and half-crosses are practically identical to the Geoksiur ware, but there are many distinctive features in the culture as a whole. For example, a seashell bracelet was found in one of the burials; this is typical of sites in Baluchistan but not of those in southern Turkmenistan.

Decorated ceramics made on the potter's wheel and clearly following Baluchistan models subsequently appear at Sarazm. This is a remarkable indication of the cultural interaction within Central Asia during the period of the early agriculturalists. It is possible that the upper reaches of the Zerafshan river proved attractive because of their proximity to the ore deposits of Ferghana. At all events, there are quite large quantities of metal artefacts at Sarazm and evidence of the accumulation of wealth is provided by the burial of a woman with many beads of gold, carnelian and lazurite on her neck, arms and legs. Thus, the migration of the Geoksiur communities to the north-east gave an impetus to the formation of a new centre of highly developed culture in Soviet Central Asia.

But along with the eastward and north-eastward migration, which resulted in the gradual colonization of Transoxania by a settled agrarian community yet another line of links extending southward and south-eastward is clearly discernible. Thus, in the Sistani settlement of Shahr-i Sokhta almost a third of the painted pottery in the lowest layers, that is, those corresponding to its foundation, can be classed among the southern Turkmenian specimens.[12] It is likely that

12. Biscione, 1973; Lamberg-Karlovsky and Tosi, 1973.

people from the Altyn-depe/Geoksiur region accounted for some part of the original population of Shahr-i Sokhta, and at least initially retained their age-old traditions. Such ties with the culture of Kara-depe and Geoksiur, manifested both in the painted ceramics and in the statuette types, are notable in a variety of other remains in southern Afghanistan and Pakistan. This is yet further evidence of the close ties that united the settled agrarian tribes.

Achievements in the cultural and economic domains in large measure opened the way to further progress, which became particularly evident in the middle of the third millennium B.C., when the Kopet Dag oases begin to exhibit complexes of the Namazga IV type, ascribed by scholars to the Early Bronze Age. The subsequent evolution of the culture of that time is best evidenced by the excavations at Altyn-depe,[13] which even then was a major centre with features of incipient urbanism. It was then that the central gate was conceived in the form of monumental pilaster-adorned pylons. The width of the entryway was approximately 15 m; it was divided by longitudinal walls into two alleyways for pedestrians and a broader central avenue paved with stones and large pottery shards designed to accommodate wheeled traffic. Eastern Altyn-depe exhibits a complex associated with religious edifices, with an outer border of natural brick walls roughly 2 m thick. Just outside the walls were sanctuaries and houses possibly belonging to priestly families. Initially the sanctuary constituted a large enclosure with a vestibule. At the centre of the principal chamber was a rectangular hearth-stone or podium, while the walls had niches in the shape of small pyramids. Likewise linked with religious rituals were the square-shaped terracotta censers with sides richly embellished with carved ornaments consisting of alternate forms of stepped crosses and little pyramids painted black and red. A later development is evident in the special architectural style of a small temple consisting of a suite of three or four chambers on one side of a long corridor. The traditional hearth-stone-podium was situated at the centre of the largest of these chambers.

Camels were already being used as draught animals. This is evidenced by finds of terracotta models of four-wheel carts drawn by camels. In addition to the older crops, the inhabitants of the Kopet Dag oases were by now growing grapes. Particularly significant progress was achieved in metallurgy and pottery production, both of which were advanced by improved technology and implements. The potter's wheel was used on an increasingly wider scale; towards the end of the Early Bronze Age almost all clay pottery was produced with its aid. Casting technique also exhibits a number of innovations, including the early use of artificial alloys and the moulding of hollow items using a mandrel. Settlement sites have yielded the remains of copper-foundry furnaces.

The presence of multichambered houses at both the larger (Hapuz-depe) and smaller (Ak-depe) settlements, together with the preservation of the tradition of collective-tomb burials, suggests that the multi-family commune conti-

---

13. Masson, 1981*a*.

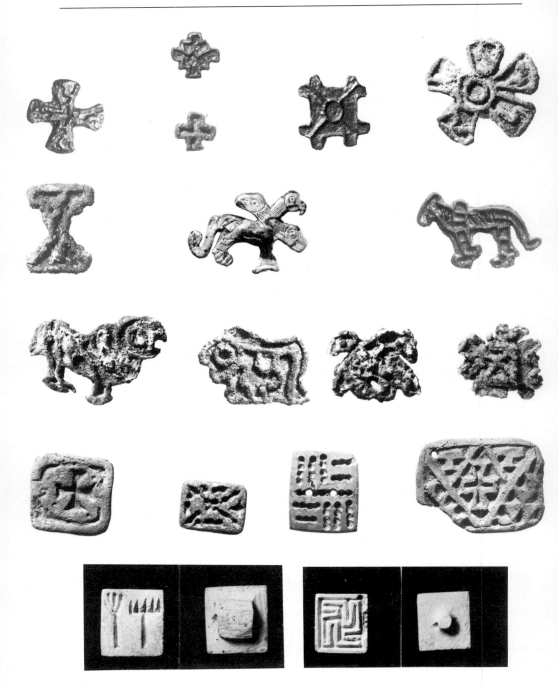

FIG. 3. Native and Harappa-like seals from Altyn-depe (2300–2000 B.C.).

nued to be the fundamental unit of society.[14] Close to the sanctuary at Altyn-depe we find not only collective graves, but also individual burials distinguished by fairly rich grave-goods, including not only ceramic vessels, but also stoneware, bronze pins and other ornaments. It is possible that such offerings marked the burials of priestly personages, an interesting sidelight in this connection being the predominance of female burials among such tombs. A new custom was the inclusion in the tombs of cylindrical stone lamps. Also characteristic of the Early Bronze Age are bronze and terracotta stamps with a loop eyelet on the reverse side (Fig. 3). The geometric, predominantly cruciform figures carved on the faces of these stamps practically reproduce the ornamentation of the painted-clay vessels and the carving adorning the censers. It is not impossible that the stamps were used by that time not simply as amulets, but also as signs of ownership.

Local differences in the culture of the communes persisted. Ceramic finds enable us to distinguish three distinct cultural provinces in southern Turkmenistan at the time in question. The westernmost of these is represented by the Parhai II burial excavated near Kara-kala in the Sumbar valley. To judge by the material uncovered, this is closest to the culture of north-eastern Iran, familiar from the Shah-tepe and Tepe Hissar excavations. In the Sumbar valley no actual settlements of the ancient agrarian people of that period have yet come to light; on the other hand, collective tombs have been uncovered in the form of oval graves approximately 2 m across dug in the soil. The entrances to such tombs were often covered with a stone slab. The funerary objects placed in the tombs provide an idea of the material culture of the tribes concerned. Dominant among the finds are hand-made black or grey dishes occasionally ornamented with fine lines applied by carving or even by polishing. One such design constitutes an entire composition, depicting a goat standing among spreading trees. Particularly striking decorative items include large copper pins with multiple-twin double-helical heads. Remarkably original too are the rectangular four-legged vessels with goblets (possibly incense burners) and ram's heads in appliqué on their sides. Similar material originates from a number of small settlements in the foothill region west of Ashkhabad, where statuettes as well as vessels were commonly executed in black and grey ceramic. The close cultural relationship of remains of this type with material from Hissar, particularly Hissar II, is beyond doubt. Perhaps in Antiquity these were settlements belonging to a single cultural community.

The second cultural province encompasses the central portion of the foothill region, its typical monuments being Ak-depe near Ashkhabad and Namazga-depe. Here we find grey ceramics in relative abundance, but coloured ceramic objects also occur. In particular, there is a ceramic vessel found at Ak-depe on which is depicted a large goat among trees, a direct replica of a similar subject from the Sumbar valley, but here executed in colour. Along with this,

14. Sarianidi, 1976.

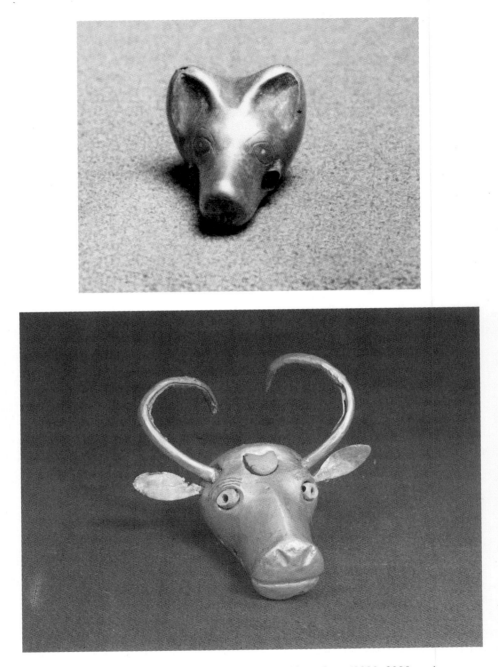

Fig. 4. Gold heads of bull and wolf from Altyn-depe (2300–2000 B.C.).

terracotta figurines of people and animals, as well as ceramic stamps, are grey. To a lesser extent this is characteristic of Namazga-depe, but here too grey dishes are fairly frequent.

Finally, the third ceramic province of the Early Bronze Age is constituted by eastern monuments where Geoksiur-type ceramics had previously been prevalent (Altyn-depe, Hapuz-depe and others). Here we are clearly faced with a continuance of local traditions: painted pottery is intermingled with, and gradually gives way to, increasingly fine ornamentation retaining the motifs of an earlier period. The same tendency is evident among the terracotta objects which, it must be said, become heavier and clumsier compared with those of the Late Eneolithic. Technical progress and the slow decline of traditional cultural standards were a fundamental feature of the Early Bronze Age.

The establishment of new standards in virtually all realms of culture signified the dawning of a new age in the history of the ancient agrarian population of southern Turkmenistan. This was a middle or advanced Bronze Age period characterized by complexes of the Namazga V type and constituting the pinnacle of local culture. The traditional dating of this complex in the archaeology of Central Asia is from the end of the third to the first quarter of the second millennium B.C., which corresponds to the short chronology of Hissar. However, the recalculation of radiocarbon dates using the MASCA correction enables us not only to revise the traditional Hissar datings[15] but also to refine the chronology of Harappa,[16] which can be synchronized with Altyn-depe on the basis of a variety of objects. This is the reason for suggesting setting the dates of the Namazga V type layers back to 2300 B.C.[17] The centres of cultural and economic progress at that time were the larger settlements, most completely and systematically studied in the case of Altyn-depe.[18] By its structure alone, Altyn-depe differs from earlier settlements. Here we find clear evidence of individual districts or quarters of differing functional significance. Thus to the north we find a specialized craftsmen's quarter occupying an area of nearly 2 ha, where we find no fewer than fifty pottery kilns. Here and in other quarters we see a prevalence of multichambered houses separated by narrow curving passageways. Dinstinguishable from such commonplace structures is the 'quarter of the nobility', which is marked by the regularity of its plan, by its streets intersecting at right angles, and by its spacious, carefully finished houses. An important structural unit was the centre of cult worship consisting of a stepped tower-like building 12 m high, spacious storage areas and household structures, as well as a burial ensemble which apparently was the place of interment of members of a priestly commune, and where many valuable objects were uncovered, including the golden heads of a bull and a wolf (Fig. 4).

15. Dyson, 1965; Bovington et al., 1974.
16. Agrawal, 1971, p. 280.
17. Masson, 1981*a*, p. 95.
18. Masson, 1981*b*.

Altyn-depe was situated on high mounds formed by the cultural remains of earlier ages. Its hillsides were faced with mud-brick walls topped by continuous house walls joined in places by additional surrounds. Over certain segments the walls were further reinforced with rectangular tower pylons. The central entryway was designed with particular care, the surrounding walls being 6 m thick, while the entrance gate proper was flanked by two massive rectangular towers. Clearly, the structure of Namazga-depe was a complex one, its excavation revealing a number of multichambered houses within the residential quarter, as well as several pottery workshops.

A characteristic feature of the developed Bronze Age economy was the considerable variety of its crafts. There are grounds for stating that in the major centres of the time the crafts became distinct from agriculture, and that the social division of labour had progressed significantly. In the realm of metal-working[19] a variety of independent forms of manufacture emerged, including the specialized production of artistic stamps. Finds include maces with sculptured heads in the shape of an animal or animal head. In addition to copper, silver and gold, wide use was made of copper-arsenic and copper-lead alloys, that is, of arsenic and lead bronze. Tin bronze occurs much more rarely. Bronze was used as a material for both weapons and implements: finds include daggers, blowpipe darts, various types of knives and sickles. Silver objects (rings, bracelets, pins, mirrors and even massive adzes) were fairly common. In the production of pottery,[20] use was made of a high-speed potter's wheel, which led to the standardization of pot shapes. The standard mass-produced vessels issuing from professional pottery workshops were now entirely devoid of the painted designs applied by the earlier pottery artists. The sheer productivity of the pottery craft increased considerably. Vessels were fired in two-level kilns which made it possible to achieve uniform temperatures. One pottery kiln at Altyn-depe could fire 16,000–20,000 vessels annually, which, given enough workers within the quarter to service several dozen such kilns, affords some idea of the marketability of the wares in question. The range of agricultural crops was augmented by the chick-pea (*Cicer arietinum*). Clay models of four-wheeled vehicles show that some of them were probably intended to carry heavier loads than before and were drawn by a pair of camels.

All these important changes in the economic basis could not fail to influence the social order. The materials excavated at Altyn-depe show how the prior state of primeval equality came to be supplanted by social differentiation entailing the emergence of social groups with distinct living standards and way of life, probably in accordance with their respective status in the system of production. Thus, the multichambered houses in the craftsmen's quarter are similar to the houses of multi-family communes discovered in the Late Eneolithic settlements. The collective tombs discovered here contain merely a few clay pots, the

19. Kuz'mina, 1966.
20. Masimov, 1976.

deceased having been wrapped in rude cane matting. Those concerned are representatives of a lower social and property group, that is, ordinary members of a commune. The second population group likewise resided in multichambered dwelling units, but these did not form a single household-type entity, but rather were grouped into individual 'apartments' consisting of five or six rooms and a separate kitchen. In tombs situated in the vicinity of these houses we find not only ceramic objects, but also bronze rings, bead necklaces, terracotta statuettes and metal stamps. This was a quarter of well-to-do city-dwellers apparently living in individual families, each with its own household. Finally, the third type of residential area at Altyn-depe consists of large and spacious houses of the 'quarter of the nobility' situated near tombs with particularly rich and varied contents, including stamps, statuettes and many bead bracelets and necklaces. Often the latter were placed not only around the necks of the dead, but encircled their hips as a kind of a belt. The deceased were placed in their graves wrapped in fine woollen shrouds. In addition to rich collective tombs, we also have individual burials remarkable for the outstanding variety of objects accompanying the deceased. Thus, the grave of one man, in addition to the usual beads and vessels, was found to contain a massive 'column' of white marmoreal limestone (an object of undoubted religious significance) and a long carved grey stone staff probably betokening his special social position. In another case, a younger woman of 30 to 35 years had been placed in her grave not only with her jewellery and ornaments, but along with a rich toilet ensemble including, in addition to smaller clay vessels, a double marble dish, a metal awl, a pin, a flat spatula, a short-handled silver mirror, and an ivory stick with an incised circular ornemental motif. No doubt the persons buried in the priests' tomb, whose funerary furnishings were, as already noted, especially opulent, belonged to the same prosperous class. They were most probably members of the lay and sacerdotal aristocracy which gradually became a distinct class within the social structure. It is notable that along with the collective tombs of the 'quarter of the nobility', but outside their confines, we find individual graves completely devoid of any funerary accoutrements. These may represent burials of servants or patriarchal slaves. But whatever the truth of the matter, we are dealing here with a fairly developed society with a complex internal structure.

In Antiquity, Altyn-depe constituted a major central social organism: its population, given the different housing densities of its various quarters, must have numbered 6,000 to 7,500. Its complex structure, the variety of activities engaged in, and the fact of social and property-related differentiation suggest that Altyn-depe must have become something more than just a major agricultural centre. However, given the presence of its religious complex, it can be described as a proto-urban or early urban organism. Possibly it constituted a temple town where a theocratic form of rule restrained the development of a secular power as such. At present there is no evidence of smaller settlements in the immediate vicinity of Altyn-depe, but these are most probably covered over by alluvial-

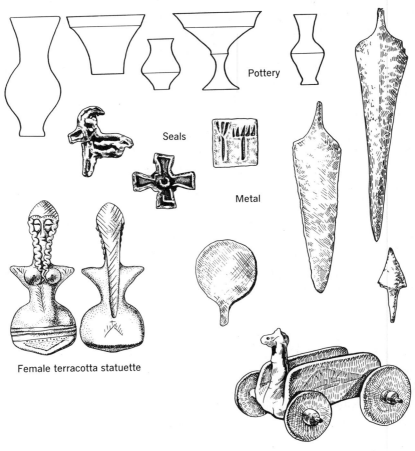

Pottery

Seals

Metal

Female terracotta statuette

Four-wheeled vehicle in clay

FIG. 5. Culture of Altyn-depe (2300–2000 B.C.).

diluvial sediments which during the period following the fall of the ancient town accumulated to a depth of 2 m. New investigations in the vicinity of another major centre of the Kopet Dag plain, that of Namazga-depe, have revealed a fairly extensive urban area. Namazga-depe was clearly the focus of attraction for three smaller rural settlements situated 40–50 km to the west: Toichnak-depe, Shor-depe and Kosha-depe. It is quite probable that these two formations embracing the Kopet Dag oases, namely Namazga and Altyn, provided the context for the emergence of the city-state which was a feature of Antiquity. However, at the time in question this process had hardly progressed very far. In any event, neither rich princely burials nor any building resembling a palace has been uncovered at either site.

Considerable changes occurred in the ideological sphere as well. During the developed Bronze Age period a female deity was still worshipped widely.

Terracotta female figurines were kept in every house and included in collective burials. But now the statuettes displayed symbolic signs scratched on their thighs and shoulders, whereas the figurines themselves differ from one another in various details of hairstyle, head-dress and adornment.[21] This most likely testifies to the differentiation of a once-unitary image of the female deity. What we see forming is a whole female pantheon, with a special deity of the heavens (the star sign), a water deity (the zigzag), a plant deity (the ear-of-corn or branch sign) and certain others. On the other hand, the religious complex at Altyn-depe did not yield a single female statuette. But here the religious objects of the priests' tomb did include a stone plaquette with astral symbols of the moon and stars; moreover, the golden bull's head exhibits a crescent-shaped turquoise inlay on its forehead. All this leads us to suppose that the religious centre of Altyn-depe was dedicated to the divine patron of the town, probably a moon god, who in ancient Mesopotamia likewise often appears in the guise of a sacred celestial bull. The changes occurring in the realm of ideology are also reflected in the spread of a new style in the production of female terracotta statuettes, that traditional object in the cultures of the early farming communities. The realistic style of the Eneolithic period in regard to volume, notwithstanding its conventionality in the depiction of individual details in accordance with the dictates of a system of magical notions, was on the whole close to that of the initial prototype of the opulent matron. During the developed Bronze Age this manner was supplanted by a conventionally flattened style testifying to the development of abstraction. The flattened clay art on which the statuette was then based had nothing in common with three-dimensional modelling. Ressemblance to the female figure was achieved largely through the fashioning of a frontally developed silhouette. Much attention was given to the depiction of the head surmounting a long neck and crowned with an intricate head-dress. Particularly noteworthy are the exaggeratedly large eyes executed in low relief which have a hypnotic all-seeing quality. The new age had brought with it new aesthetic notions (Fig. 5).

On the whole the culture of the Kopet Dag oases of the developed Bronze Age period is characterized by a continuity of cultural and artistic traditions and by the formation of new standards and models using prototypes evolved by the ancient civilizations of Sumer and Elam. The introduction of new models was often linked with advances in technology. Thus, the increasingly wide use of the potter's wheel resulted in a virtually total replacement of the traditional forms of clay vessels. Now it was no longer colourful painting that served to emphasize their aesthetic aspect, but rather the delicacy of refined shape. Continuity is observed in the maintenance of the magical significance of figures executed in stepped crosses and their components. Precisely such figures are most frequently encountered in stamps of the developed Bronze Age. A special group of stamps bear the image of various animals – a goat, a snow leopard, a spread eagle – which

---

21. Masson and Sarianidi, 1973; Masson, 1976.

are likewise encountered in Eneolithic ceramic ornament. However, we also find new images of fantastic monsters clearly suggested by mythological subjects. Such, for example, is the four-legged animal with a bill and a claw on its front paw. Particularly striking is a three-headed dragon with the body of a feline predator, two of whose heads are reptilian, possibly ophidian, and the third that of a bird of prey. There are also crescent-shaped stamps bearing the likeness of a creeping snake.

Considerable advances were achieved in building construction, where architectural canons of sorts begin to appear. Judging by the proportions of buildings and gate towers, the basis of the ancient modulus was a 52 × 26 cm rectangular brick, which these structures repeat on increased scales. This most probably represents the same unit of linear measurement, the cubit, that we see throughout the ancient East. There is also a tendency to give shape to the space within a settlement, which is evident in the building of the 'quarter of the nobility' in regular blocks and in the development of monumental structures (the religious complex, the design of the central entryway). At the same time, the device of enlivening walls with evenly spaced and particularly three-step pilasters is directly related to Mesopotamian architecture. Mesopotamian ziggurats must also have suggested the idea of a stepped tower-like structure. The signs scratched on the statuettes bear a clear parallel to proto-Sumerian, and especially to proto-Elamite writing. A number of details characterizing the terracotta figurines, including the large 'all-seeing' eyes, find their analogies in terracotta items from Mesopotamia.

But particularly close are the links with the ancient civilization of Harappa. The influence of Harappa prototypes is evident in a variety of ceramic and metal objects from Altyn-depe.[22] Finds even include imported specimens, primarily ivory carvings, invariably occurring in the richer troves or the funerary inventories of wealthier burials. Thus, a treasure found immured in the wall of one of the houses of the 'quarter of the nobility' includes divination sticks made of ivory and flat square chips, used in some unknown game, fashioned of the same material. Ivory beads formed part of the offerings found in the priests' burial-vault. Of particular interest are two Harappa-type stamps found at Altyn-depe – one bearing a swastika, the other two signs of proto-Indus writing regarded by most scholars as appertaining to some proto-Dravidian language. It is well known that there existed a southern sea route linking the Harappan civilization with ancient Mesopotamia. Today there is every reason to posit the existence of another international route, an overland route in this case, leading from the Indus valley to the north and north-east. In addition to the Altyn-depe finds, striking evidence of the existence of such a route is supplied by the discovery of the Harappan settlement of Shortugai in northern Afghanistan on the banks of the Amu Darya. In all likelihood, at least initially, this settlement existed as a trading station.

22. Masson, 1981*a*.

Towards the end of the developed Bronze Age period the Kopet Dag oases began to feel the winds of change. At Altyn-depe the settled territory diminished in area, with the abandonment of the major urban formation represented by the religious centre. Concomitantly we see a lively eastward migration of early agrarian tribes into the Murghab valley, attempts at whose colonization had been made by Late Eneolithic communities.[23] By now its settlement had become a well-organized enterprise resulting in the founding of an entire oasis of eleven settlements along one of the arms of the ancient Murghab delta. Its centre was the settlement of Kelleli I covering an area of approximately 8 ha. Here there is as yet no unified mound massif, but component elements include a regularly planned rectangle measuring 280 × 230 m. Most probably this constituted the original fortified core of the newly founded centre. Adjacent to the fortified area was a fairly large plot with numerous remains of pottery production, forming a kind of crafts suburb. The other settlements of the oasis are not large: their overall area generally did not exceed 1 ha, and they were scattered at varying distances about the basic monument, forming a compact cluster. The total population of the oasis has been roughly estimated at 2,900 to 3,600 persons.

The material culture of the Kelleli oasis is practically identical with the culture of the uppermost layers of Altyn-depe. The similar items include ceramics, terracotta statuettes with plant symbols scratched on certain of their parts, and the cloisonné-work stamps. Apart from stamps, metal objects found here include knives, mirrors and pins with double-helical heads.

The origin of the settlers leaves no room for doubt: they arrived with a ready-made culture from the foothill plain, which had entered on a period of stagnation and decline. The very structure of the new oasis seems to replicate the system that had evolved in the mother country: we have here a major centre with developed craft industries surrounded by agrarian suburbs. It appears that the corresponding political organization of this agglomeration of communes assisted it in becoming established at the new site and in turning a new page in the history of the early agricultural tribes.

While settlements in the Kopet Dag oases saw the formation of a local civilization of the ancient eastern type, considerable economic and cultural changes were also taking place in Transoxania. Whereas in the fourth millennia B.C. Sarazm as a settled farming area was a unique focal point for Neolithic hunters and fishermen, by the late third and early second millennia B.C. the situation had radically altered. The formerly primitive tribes intensively developed new ways of securing their food, first and foremost through animal husbandry. Links were strengthened with the Kopet Dag oases, whose influence became a major stimulus to progressive development. The inhabitants of Altyn-depe and Namazga-depe may well have travelled very far in a north-easterly direction. At any rate the Ferghana valley has yielded up a rich store of bronze and silver

23. Masimov, 1979; Masson and Sarianidi, 1972; Masson, 1964.

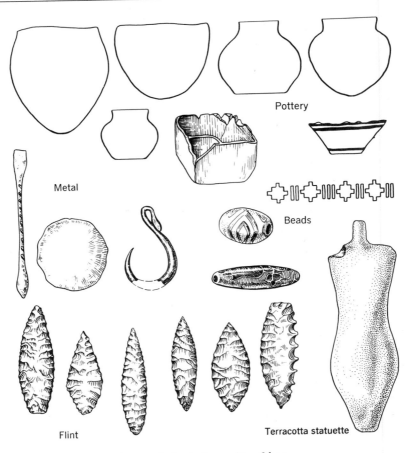

Pottery

Metal

Beads

Flint

Terracotta statuette

FIG. 6. Culture of Zaman-baba in lower Zerafshan.

objects of clearly southern origin. The trove includes a pin with a double-helical head and a mace with a sculptural group representing the milking of a cow and the suckling of a calf. The residents of the southern oases may have been attracted to the Ferghana valley by its tin deposits so vital for metalworking in the Bronze Age.

Highly representative of the changing culture of the cattle-raisers and agriculturalists of the lower reaches of the Zerafshan was what is known as the Zaman-baba culture, which is dated to the late third and early second millennia B.C.[24] Here a zone of small channels and lakes in the delta area of a major watercourse is the site of an ancient settlement and burial ground. The settlement itself consisted not of the *pisé* houses typical of settled farming communes, but rather of large adobe half-cottages elongated in plan. Situated next to the cottages were two-tier pottery kilns, the entire settlement being surrounded by a *pisé* wall. The

24. Gulyamov et al., 1966.

pottery was mostly of high quality, but fashioned without the aid of a potter's wheel. Metallurgy had attained a high state of development, all the metal items being of bronze. Agricultural pursuits are evidenced by imprints of wheat and barley seeds, flint sickle inserts, pestles and seed-grinders. Over 80 per cent of the animal bones were those of domesticated species: cows, sheep and goats. Near the settlement was a burial ground in which the dead were placed in small cata-combs, mostly individually. Also found were paired burials of men and women, which are generally taken as one sign of stable marriage, and perhaps the exis-tence of the individual family unit. The male burials usually included flint arrow-heads, whereas the female graves were typified by the presence of ornaments and cosmetic items – bits of ochre and antimony hair-dye, beads of turquoise, carne-lian and other semi-precious stones, as well as gold. One grave was found to con-tain a flattened female statuette (Fig. 6).

From all the evidence available, the origin of the Zaman-baba culture was fairly complex. Here we have traces both of traditions attributable to a native Neolithic culture, which probably constituted the original stratum, and of the indisputable influence of the settled farming communes to the south. Thus, the construction of two-tier pottery kilns was clearly of southern origin. It was from the Kopet Dag oases that the lower reaches of the Zerafshan valley received ves-sels turned with the aid of the potter's wheel, including one specimen bearing a design of the late Namazga IV type; southern traditions too are evident in the ter-racotta statuettes and certain metal objects. Many of the beads found in the Zaman-baba burial ground are probably also of southern origin. On the other hand, the highly specific type of grave represented by the catacombs and at least two types of modelled vessels are closely matched in the cultures of the Eurasian steppe. While southern influences can be directly related to the outward migra-tion of settled farming communes then taking over the Murghab delta, the anal-ogies with the steppe regions might serve as evidence of the incipient migration of groups of wandering cattle-raisers. At all events, cultural links and the growth of trade prompted by the need to secure raw materials for more sophisticated metal-working, together with tribal movements, tended to increase the interac-tion of tribal groups belonging to different cultures. This was the start of an age of active contacts so important in the emergence of the peoples of Central Asia.

PRE-INDUS AND EARLY INDUS CULTURES
OF PAKISTAN AND INDIA[1]

J. G. Shaffer and B. K. Thapar

B ALUCHISTAN and the Indus valley are adjacent geographical regions with strikingly different characteristics. Baluchistan consists of north-east–south-west mountain ranges separated by narrow alluvial valleys. It has some perennial rivers, but receives most of its moisture from summer and winter rains (sometimes snow). The Indus valley, on the other hand, is a broad, fertile alluvial valley watered by major perennial rivers and summer monsoons. With such environmental variations, it is not surprising that the two areas saw the development of similar yet distinctive cultural traditions.

To aid discussion of archaeological data for these regions, two cultural concepts will be used – 'tradition' and 'phase'.[2] A tradition[3] refers to persistent patterns of basic technologies and cultural systems within the context of spatial and temporal continuity. This concept allows grouping stylistically diverse archaeological assemblages in an analytical unit, but limits the need for establishing precise cultural and chronological relationships linking assemblages. Although definition of such relationships is the ultimate research goal, it is currently prevented by limited data (small stratigraphic tests and sporadic C14 dates). A phase represents 'an archaeological unit possessing traits sufficiently characteristic to distinguish it from all other units similarly conceived, whether of the same or other cultures or civilizations, spatially limited to the order of magnitude of a locality or region and chronologically limited to a relatively brief interval of time'.[4] At present, a diagnostic ceramic style located at one or more site is the major characteristic of a phase.

1. See Map 8.
2. For similar applications of these concepts, see Flam, 1981a, pp. 16–23; Possehl, 1980, pp. 13–21.
3. Willey and Phillips, 1958, p. 37.
4. Ibid., p. 22.

The Baluchistan Tradition[5]

The adaptive strategy of this tradition was food-production based on domesticated plants and animals. The Mehrgarh excavations[6] indicate that the most important plants were barley and wheat, while the important animals were cattle, sheep, goat, water buffalo and possibly camel (in later periods). This economic strategy is reflected in numerous settlements ranging from small agricultural villages to large urban centres located throughout Baluchistan. Although conclusive evidence is lacking now, it is likely that pastoral nomadism was also an important part of this adaptive strategy.[7]

Habitation structures were constructed with mud-brick, *pisé*, stone and combinations of all three depending upon local circumstances. Large, or public, architectural units have been defined at only a few sites, but with the large size of many sites numerous types of public architecture must be present.

The most common stone tools found from earliest periods include non-diagnostic milling stones, ground stone balls, and flint blades, scrapers and microliths. Stone projectile points, axes, adzes, celts or maces are rare. In general, the lapidary industry was well developed as evidenced by a variety of semi-precious stones (lapis lazuli, turquoise, alabaster, carnelian), beads and pendants as well as alabaster bowls. Steatite/chlorite was used for beads, pendants, stamp seals and, more rarely, bowls. Shell was used to make beads, bangles and pendants. The identification of chlorite and shell workshop areas at Mehrgarh suggests at least part-time craft specialists, and indicates that such activities were culturally important. Metallurgy appears to have reached a comparable level of development. Bronze, or copper, objects include pins (decorative examples are present), points, blades, beads and mirrors. The metal objects associated with the recently discovered Mehrgarh cemetery indicate that metallurgical skills were more highly developed than current evidence indicates. Although the quantity and quality of these objects varies from site to site, the general impression is that a variety of part-time, and perhaps full-time, craft specialists were present throughout the Baluchistan Tradition.

The most impressive craft activity, and a major feature of this tradition, was the ceramic industry. The high quality and rich, decorative diversity of Baluchistan ceramics has few parallels in Bronze Age Central Asia. Most pottery is a red-buff ware, but regionally (Quetta valley, Kachi plain) significant quantities of grey ware are known. Hand-made and mould-made (basket impressed) techniques persist through the tradition, but wheel-made pottery occurs early and rapidly becomes the dominant manufacturing technique. A wide variety of bowl and jar forms are known, some of which are unique to this tradition (e.g. the Nal

5. Since both traditions share many characteristics, the Baluchistan Tradition will be discussed in more detail here to simplify presentation of data.
6. Jarrige and Meadow, 1980.
7. Shaffer, 1978*b*, pp. 112–69.

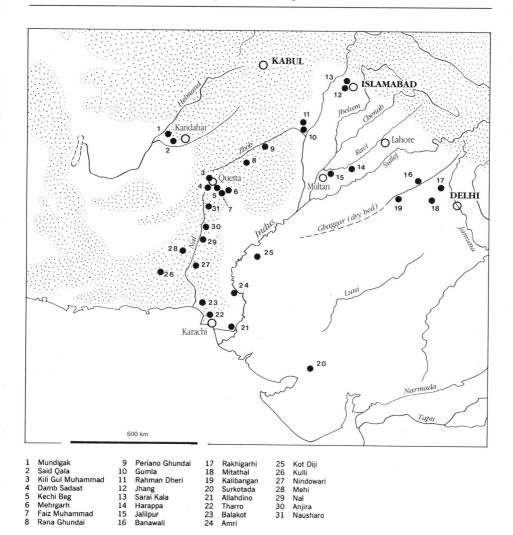

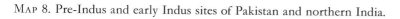

1	Mundigak	9	Periano Ghundai	17	Rakhigarhi	25	Kot Diji
2	Said Qala	10	Gumla	18	Mitathal	26	Kulli
3	Kili Gul Muhammad	11	Rahman Dheri	19	Kalibangan	27	Nindowari
4	Damb Sadaat	12	Jhang	20	Surkotada	28	Mehi
5	Kechi Beg	13	Sarai Kala	21	Allahdino	29	Nal
6	Mehrgarh	14	Harappa	22	Tharro	30	Anjira
7	Faiz Muhammad	15	Jalilpur	23	Balakot	31	Nausharo
8	Rana Ghundai	16	Banawali	24	Amri		

MAP 8. Pre-Indus and early Indus sites of Pakistan and northern India.

249

Phase cannisters). Besides plain surfaces the following modifications are known: (a) basket impressed; (b) red, buff and white slips; (c) a sandy or rusticated slip; and (d) a fine, patterned, textured slip known as 'wet ware'.[8] Painted motifs are applied directly to the surface or on a coloured slipped surface. Most motifs are executed in black or red paint, but a variety of colours are known (brown, white, yellow, blue and green). The predominant decorative scheme is bichrome but polychromes are also produced. Geometric motifs are the most common, but they occur also in combination with zoomorphic and floral motifs. The most important zoomorphic motifs are humped cattle, a gazelle or deer-type animal, fish, dogs, and non-diagnostic birds. The only diagnostic floral motif is the pipal leaf. Grey wares (i.e. Faiz Muhammad grey ware) are very distinctive, being manufactured from a finer paste, turned on a fast wheel, fired to a higher temperature and decorated with red or black motifs painted directly on the surface. The rich stylistic variation definable among this Tradition's ceramics forms the bases for designating the various phases which make up this tradition. Other important terracotta objects include: beads, bangles, biconical balls, animal and human figurines, stamp seals (rare), house models, rattles and buttons.[9]

Limited data precludes thorough discussion of the cultural systems responsible for this tradition's development and maintenance. Although food-production was the economic base, it is evident, judging from the quantity and quality of associated objects, that considerable development of craft activities occurred. For example, Mehrgarh appears to have developed into a regional production centre and it is probable that similar centres were also present in other regions. Existence of such centres implies a level of economic organization capable of coordinating production and distribution of commodities. The efficiency of this economic organization is reflected in the development, distribution and persistence of homogeneous regional ceramic styles. At the same time, distribution of some commodities (marine shell, certain semi-precious stones, and intrusive potsherds) indicate that interregional economic interaction occurred. However, this interregional interaction was never intense enough to integrate the various phases into a homogeneous cultural system. Unlike the Indus Valley Tradition where regional phases were integrated into a single cultural system or phase (i.e. Harappan or Indus Valley Civilization), social groups in Baluchistan maintained a strong regional identity reflected in the persistence of regional ceramic styles.

That some interaction did take place between the Baluchistan and Indus Valley Tradition is indicated by sporadic finds of Harappan artefacts throughout Baluchistan (an exception to this being Dabar Kot).[10] Although Harappan sites are found on the eastern borders of Baluchistan, and a few sites have been located within Baluchistan (in the Kirthar range and Bolan pass), the interaction between traditions appears to be limited. This limited interaction between the two

---

8. Fairservis, 1956, pp. 268–70.
9. Ibid., pp. 263–65.
10. Fairservis, 1959, pp. 308–28; Mughal, 1972a, pp. 137–44.

FIG. 1. Polychrome jar from Mehrgarh IV (3300 B.C.).

traditions may reflect significant cultural differences which inhibited development of the necessary linking networks. In the Quetta valley-Kachi plain area, however, there appears to have been a cultural intrusion, or at least very strong cultural influences, from southern Afghanistan. At present, these intrusive developments appear to have had but small impact on the rest of the Baluchistan Tradition, and the same may be said for the Indus Valley Tradition as well. The reasons and nature of this influence from Afghanistan are at present unknown.

Unfortunately, limited data prevent a discussion of the other cultural systems (e.g. social, political and religious organizations) affecting this tradition. Excavated sites are too few and the scope of excavations too limited to attempt even a preliminary reconstruction of these important cultural systems. Current excavations at Mehrgarh will contribute greatly to our understanding of this complex and interesting tradition, but even when these excavations are completed, comparative data will be needed before comprehensive interpretations can proceed. Given these limitations, the following discussion is tentative and subject to later revision.

The Kili Gul Muhammad No. 1 (hereafter KGM) Phase was preceded by the Mehrgarh Phase represented by Mehrgarh Period I and Kili Gul Muhammad Period I (hereafter a site name followed by Roman numerals indicates occupational periods at that site, e.g. Mehrgarh Period I becomes Mehrgarh I). These important occupations are discussed in Chapter 6 and will not be repeated here.

The Kechi Beg (hereafter KB) Phase dates from the middle to the end of the fourth millennium B.C. (3500–3200 B.C.). Besides the major sites of Kili Gul Muhammad and Mehrgarh, KB Phase occupations have been identified at Surab III,[11] Sur Jangal III (the final occupation), Rana Ghundai III–IV, and *possibly* at Dabar Kot and Periano Ghundai (knowledge of these northern Baluchistan sites is limited). Again, this phase was originally discovered by Fairservis[12] at Kili Gul Muhammad IV–Damb Sadaat I, but our most extensive information comes from Mehrgarh VI–V. At both Mehgarh and Kili Gul Muhammad, the KB Phase demonstrated stratigraphic and cultural continuity with KGM Phase.

The major characteristic of the KB Phase is the introduction of polychrome pottery. However, this introduction was not abrupt since KGM Phase pottery continued to be produced, albeit in a modified style. Mehrgarh IV[13] had three major styles of decorated pottery: (a) monochrome with black motifs; (b) bichrome with motifs in two colours; and (c) polychrome (Fig. 1). Monochrome and bichrome pottery are similar to KGM Phase pottery except that geometric motifs are more intricate and the zoomorphic motifs highly stylized. Polychrome motifs, brown or plum filled with red or white on a pink or creamy surface,

11. Unless specific points of information are discussed, sources of information about particular sites will not be cited after their initial occurrence.
12. Fairservis, 1956, pp. 334–5.
13. Jarrige, 1977; see also all previous references to this site.

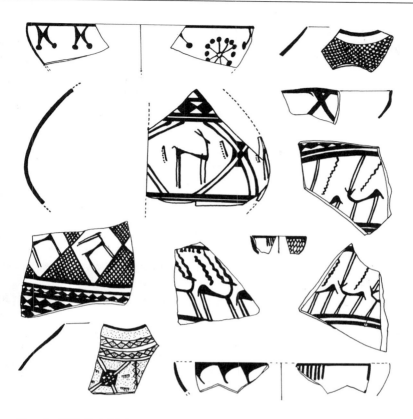

Fig. 2. Kili Gul Muhammad Phase decorated pottery from Mehrgarh (Period III).

involve complex geometric patterns covering large vessel areas. This stylistic diversity contrasts significantly with the more homogeneous style encountered in Mehrgarh II–III (Fig. 2). The greenish-grey wet wares are now found in quantity including fragile goblets and carinated jars. Jars and bowls with a sculptured snake motif were also made in this ware.

In Mehrgarh V several progressive changes can be detected in the polychrome pottery. Geometric motifs become bolder and are limited to bowls and small vessels. The decorative scheme usually involves an upper band of black diamonds against a white background, and a lower area of wide large squares or chevrons in black, filled with white, on a red background. Bichrome pottery is gradually replaced by monochromes with increasingly stylized motifs. Improved firing technology in Mehrgarh V allowed production of more homogeneous red and reddish-grey wares. On the reddish-grey wares, there is an evolution from geometric to more naturalistic elements such as fish and pipal leaves and anticipates the pottery which characterizes Mehrgarh VI–VII.

Among other terracotta objects, the only significant changes involve female figurines. A complete Mehrgarh IV female figurine has a tubular head with pinched nose, pendulous breasts, no arms, heavy hips and joined legs tapering at the end. This seated figurine appears to represent a further development of the KGM Phase figurines. Mehrgarh V female figurines are similar except that they have applied curly hair on the head. Stamp seals with geometric motifs appear for the first time in the KB Phase; two were of terracotta, and bone and steatite examples were also found. Lithic cutting implements decrease in frequency, which Jarrige[14] attributes to the increasing importance of metal tools, though only copper/bronze chisels, pins or rods were found.

Significant structures were defined only in Mehrgarh IV. Unlike KGM Phase structures these were made with modelled mud-bricks, and some had clay plastered floors. The structure(s) appears to represent a complex series of rooms and open areas associated with habitation activities such as food storage and preparation. Workshop areas have not been found as yet, but must exist at the site. Plant and animal remains from this phase have not been reported so far, but no drastic differences from the KGM Phase are expected.

The Faiz Muhammad Phase is defined only at Mehrgarh VI–VII. It seems to represent an evolutionary development from the KB Phase. The Faiz Muhammad (hereafter FM) Phase does, however, share many characteristics with the Damb Sadaat Phase defined for the Quetta valley. It is treated here as a separate phase for two reasons. First, the early Mehrgarh VI ceramic characteristics, including continued production of polychromes, overlap with those of Mehrgarh V. Second, although Quetta black-on-buff pottery (the diagnostic Damb Sadaat Phase pottery) is found in limited quantities at Mehrgarh, and despite resemblances in decorative style, the excavators[15] maintain that Mehrgarh ceramics are distinct from those found at Quetta. Thus, the FM Phase is treated separately here.

Chronologically, at Mehrgarh, the FM Phase spans the first half of the third millennium B.C. (3000–2600 B.C.). The terminal date for this phase may, however, extend into the last half of the third millennium B.C. Quetta black-on-buff and the Damb Sadaat Phase in the Quetta valley date to the middle and last half of the third millennium B.C. This pottery is also the major diagnostic type found at Said Qala, Deh Morasi Ghundai, Mundigak III–IV, and Shahr-i Sokhta I–III, all of which date to the last half of the third millennium B.C.[16] Although no diagnostic Harappan Phase artefacts were found at Mehrgarh, some non-diagnostic artefacts were located that may suggest a Harappan affiliation.[17] Moreover, at Nausharo, a Harappan Phase site 6 km south of Mehrgarh, artefacts of a Mehrgarh VII affiliation were found on the surface. Although the Harappan Phase may date as early as the mid-third millennium B.C. the extensive series of dates

14. Jarrige, 1981, p. 111.
15. Jarrige and Lechevallier, 1979, p. 507.
16. Shaffer, 1978a, p. 76.
17. Jarrige and Lechevallier, 1979, pp. 528–30.

Fɪɢ. 3. Faiz Muhammad Phase decorated grey ware from Mehrgarh VII (2800–2600 B.C.).

from Kalibangan[18] indicates a primary chronology spanning the later part of the last half of the third millennium B.C. Mehrgarh may have been abandoned by 2600 B.C.[19] But the FM Phase may have persisted for some time at such sites as Nausharo. Clearly, data are too limited to draw precise chronological boundaries for this phase.

Ceramically, the major feature of the FM Phase was the production of fine decorated grey wares, although fine red wares were quantitatively dominant. The improved firing techniques and the fine red and reddish grey wares of Meghrgarh V were forerunners of these developments. Mehrgarh V polychromes continue to be produced in early Mehrgarh VI, but eventually disappear. Most painted pottery is the monochrome red ware, whose motifs represent further developments of those in Mehrgarh V despite the presence of a few Quetta motifs. The previous tendency towards naturalistic motifs continues, and elaborate friezes of zoomorphic (humped cattle, fish, caprids, birds) and floral (pipal leaves, palm fronds) motifs in a hatched style are found. Grey wares are fired at higher tem-

18. Shaffer, 1978*a*, p. 76.
19. Jarrige and Meadow, 1980, p. 110.

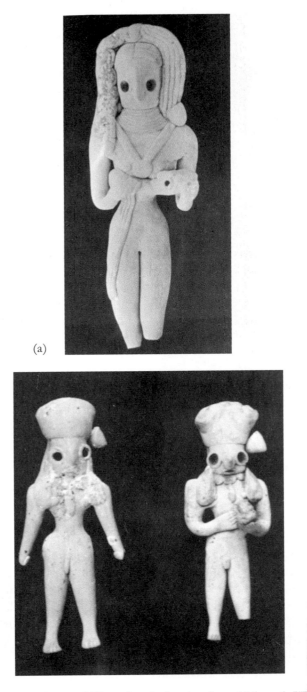

(a)

(b)

FIG. 4. (a) Faiz Muhammad Phase female figurine from Mehrgarh VII (2800–2600 B.C.); (b) Faiz Muhammad Phase male figurines from Mehrgarh VII (2800–2600 B.C.).

peratures and have elaborate naturalistic and geometric motifs in black. A much wider range of vessel forms is found among both red and grey wares.

During Mehrgarh VII, the site became a ceramic production centre as evidenced by extensive kiln remains.[20] Pottery for everyday use and luxury-type vessels were mass produced in a variety of vessel forms (brandy-shaped glasses, tulip-shaped goblets, plates of various sizes). Large storage jars with collared rims and tapering lower parts are comparable to Harappan Phase jars. On monochrome red ware the pipal leaf remained a popular motif on open bowls. A 'buff' ware was made in a variety of vessel forms (tulip-shaped, goblets, small globular pots, and carinated bowls) and decorated with 'Quetta' style geometric motifs similar to those found in Damb Sadaat III. The most spectacular pottery was the black painted grey ware which was fired to a very high temperature. Grey ware motifs have been described as follows:

> Animal, vegetal and geometrical designs are quite often remarkable for their quality and variety. Running caprids on a background of pipal leaves, fish sometimes swimming among aquatic plants, combinations of finely painted geometric motifs represent some of the best decorations ever met on potteries found in Baluchistan. . . . Besides, rather stereotyped 'Quetta' motifs occur on open bowls.[21]

This grey ware corresponds to what Fairservis[22] called Faiz Muhammad grey ware in the Quetta valley, though the range of variation in vessel shape and decoration is much more extensive (Fig. 3). Manufacture of wet wares also continued but in limited quantities.

Another major characteristic of the ceramic industry was the massive production of human figurines. The figurines, like painted pottery motifs, demonstrate a stylistic evolution towards more naturalistic representations. In Mehrgarh VI female figurines are still seated with tapered legs, but now have a coiffure of large coils flanking the head, modelled arms clasped below pendulous breasts, and multistrand necklaces. In Mehrgarh VII, both male and female figurines (Fig. 4 (a) (b)) are mass-produced but the arms and legs are separated from the body and both have protruding eyes and beak-like noses. The female coiffure is draped along the head and and shoulders and often painted, as is the appliqué necklace. Males are depicted with a 'turban' and appliqué necklaces. The females now resemble the so-called 'Zhob mother-goddesses' found throughout Baluchistan. Humped cattle, bird and pig terracotta figurines are also found in some numbers. Compartmented square and circular terracotta stamp seals with geometric motifs and one with a zoomorphic motif were found.

The lapidary industry demonstrates continuity with previous Mehrgarh periods and includes beads of semi-precious stones (a few lapis lazuli and tur-

20. Jarrige and Audouze, 1980.
21. Jarrige and Lechevallier, 1979, p. 520.
22. Fairservis, 1956, pp. 263–5.

quoise), a few flint points, and steatite stamp seals. Copper or bronze objects were rare but included a chisel, flat axe and decorative pin.

Mehrgarh VI architectural remains are badly eroded but a series of habitation rooms and open work areas have been found. Also associated with this period were extensive kiln remains, indicating that Mehrgarh was a major centre for the ceramic industry. Mehrgarh VII had the first example of public/monumental architecture, a large mud-brick platform. North of this platform was a narrow mud-brick wall with regularly spaced pilasters attached to a room complex. A complex series of mud-brick rectangular rooms was found in an area overlooking the platform. These rooms appear to have been habitations some containing basements with large numbers of ceramic vessels. In a corridor separating two rooms, an adult burial in a clay box was found. It was oriented east–west, flexed and faced north. Grave-goods included two plates (one below the hands), and a necklace and bracelet (beads of kaolin, carnelian and lapis lazuli). In deposits above Mehrgarh VII, a series of infant burials in clay boxes were found, some of which were associated with a limited number of grave-goods. A large number of adult graves and cenotaphs have been reported from Mehrgarh, which are associated with grave-goods that appear to be Central Asian in origin, but their stratigraphic affiliation is not published yet.

The presence of finished lapis lazuli and turquoise beads suggests interaction with social groups outside the Baluchistan Tradition to the west. Interaction with other Baluchistan Phases is indicated by intrusive Quetta type pottery of the Damb Sadaat Phase and Nal polychrome pottery associated with the Nal Phase. The presence of a few Harappan Phase type artefacts may also indicate interaction with Harappan or Kot Dijian Phases of the Indus Valley Tradition. The presence of these intrusive objects, and of evidence suggesting that Mehrgarh was a regional centre for ceramic production, may indicate that interregional interaction intensified during this phase.

The agricultural economic base for the FM Phase is similar to that of other phases with one important exception: Meadow's[23] preliminary analysis indicates that the economic importance of cattle was not as great as it was earlier.

The Damb Sadaat (hereafter DS) Phase is known only from the Quetta valley, where it is represented by Damb Sadaat II–III in Fairservis's[24] sequence. It is stratigraphically later than the KB Phase, but cultural relationships between the two Phases are problematic at present. Although the site of Dam Sadaat is continuously occupied, the diagnostic pottery, Quetta ware, is significantly different from anything in the KB Phase. Moreover, this pottery is dramatically similar to that found at Mundigak III 5–6, IV, Said Qala Tepe I–IV, Deh Morasi Ghundai I–III, and Shahr-i Sokhta I–IV, all of which are located in the Helmand region to the west. At present the DS Phase appears to represent an intrusive cultural

---

23. Meadow, 1987.
24. Fairservis, 1956, pp. 334–5.

influence from these regions. The few available dates indicate the second half of the third millennium B.C. (2500–2000 B.C.) for this phase. It is important to note that this DS Phase chronology implies that the KB Phase may have persisted longer in the Quetta valley than it did elsewhere in Baluchistan.

The diagnostic pottery, Quetta ware, is a red-buff ware decorated with black (sometimes red) motifs executed on a white-cream coloured slip, or sometimes applied directly to the vessel's surface.[25] In the initial stages (i.e. Damb Sadaat II) emphasis is placed on solid geometric motifs and occasional use of zoomorphic (humped cattle) and floral (pipal leaf) motifs with hatching. Later stages, such as Damb Sadaat III, however, emphasize more linear geometric motifs with curved elements. A wide variety of bowl and jar forms have been identified, including pedestal and stemmed vessels. Faiz Muhammad grey wares (shallow bowls) and wet wares (large jars) are also found in limited quantities. Other important terracotta objects include: beads, bangles, rattles, compartmented stamp seals, house models, animal and human figurines. The female figurines are similar to those of the FM Phase – the Zhob style.

Stone tools are found, as well as beads made from semi-precious stones (carnelian, lapis lazuli and turquoise) and fragments of alabaster bowls. Only a few small copper or bronze objects are found. The limited nature of Fairservis's excavations makes it difficult to assess the material culture of the DS Phase in detail.

A series of rectangular mud-brick habitation structures were found in Damb Sadaat II. In Damb Sadaat III a large mud-brick platform represents the only example of public architecture. Rough limestone block drains and a mud-brick bench were associated with the platform which also had spur walls connecting it with other areas of the site. Below the main platform wall a small hollow contained a human skull, and in the immediate vicinity several examples of female figurines were found.

Quetta ware, Faiz Muhammad grey and wet wares are identified in both FM and DS Phases, indicating cultural interaction between the two phases. More intense interaction with groups in south-eastern Afghanistan is indicated by the extreme similarity of ceramics at those sites and ceramics of the DS Phase. The nature of this interaction is unknown at present.

Nal Phase occupation is found mainly in southern Baluchistan, and present knowledge about it is restricted almost entirely to its distinctive ceramics. No direct radiocarbon dates are available, and statigraphic information is limited to N. de Cardi's[26] Surab sequence. Nal Phase pottery (Fig. 5) is associated with KB Phase pottery in Surab III and is the dominant pottery in Surab IV. Hargreaves[27] at Sohr Damb located a Nal Phase occupation and cemetery below extensive Kulli Phase (see below) deposits, but methodological problems make it difficult

25. Ibid., pp. 255–6, 259–61, 321–6.
26. De Cardi, 1965.
27. Hargreaves, 1929.

FIG. 5. Nal Phase decorated pottery.

to use this data. At Niai Buthi I Fairservis[28] found Nal Phase pottery associated with what he calls early Kulli. Niai Buthi II is a Kulli Phase occupation dated to the first half of the second millennium B.C. Stratigraphically the Nal Phase appears to be 'sandwiched' between the KB and Kulli Phases. Associated with Surab IV were a few sherds of Quetta ware, Faiz Muhammad grey and wet wares suggesting some interaction and contemporaneity with the DS Phase. Nal pottery has been found in the FM Phase at Mehrgarh, and in DS Phase related occupations at Said Qala[29] dating to the early second millenium B.C. While the Nal Phase may be as early as the late fourth millennium B.C., its main chronological span seems to be the last half of the third to the early second millennium B.C. (2500–1800 B.C.).

28. Fairservis, 1975, pp. 189–94.
29. Shaffer, 1978a, pp. 157–8.

Fɪɢ. 6. Kulli Phase decorated pottery.

Our knowledge of this phase is rectricted almost exclusively to its distinctive decorated pottery. Fairservis has given this succint description of it:

> These include wheel-made canisters, bowls with inward-turned rims, and flat-sided bowls – all with ring bases. It is the decoration which makes this ware the most distinctive in Baluchistan. . . . The Nal ceramic style is basically the repetition of a motif or pattern by multiplying its outline, often in concentric fashion. Red, blue or yellow pigment is often applied to the spaces between outlines or to fill out a motif, many of which occur in northern Baluchistan. Animals and plants also occur. In the case of these motifs, techniques of hatching and rather precise geometric drawing were used.[30]

At Sohr Damb, H. Hargreaves located a series of rectangular, mud-brick with stone foundation structures associated with Nal Phase pottery. Also associated with these structure was a variety of copper or bronze objects (points, celts, chisels, pins), stone tools (including celts and pots) and several types of beads (agate and lapis lazuli). However, most of the Nal Phase pottery was associated with a series of fractional burials which may have been later than this occupation. Fairservis[31] has associated water-control systems involving dams with Nal Phase occupations in southern Baluchistan. Until more extensive excavations are conducted, not much more can be said of the Nal Phase of the Baluchistan Tradition.

Information about the Kulli Phase is also very limited. Stein's[32] early work at Mehi is interesting but of limited value. Fairservis's[33] work in the Lasbela area is important, but was limited to a survey and small excavations. Casal[34] undertook major excavations at Nindowari, but these remain unpublished. It is difficult to assess fully this phase of the Baluchistan Tradition without more data.

Kulli Phase occupations are found throughout the south-eastern and southern fringes of Baluchistan. At Sohr Damb, Niai Buthi II, and perhaps Nindowari, the Kulli Phase is stratigraphically later than the Nal Phase. However, in Niai Buthi I, Kulli and Nal Phase potteries were found in association indicating some degree of overlap. Stylistic parallels exist between some Kulli Phase artefacts and those of the Harappan Phase, and some intrusive Harappan artefacts have been found at Kulli Phase sites. Single radiocarbon dates from Nindowari and Niai Buthi II suggest a chronology spanning the last half of the third to the early part of second millennium B.C. (2500–1800 B.C.).

Kulli Phase pottery (Fig. 6) is a wheel-made red-buff ware. Although black-on-buff slip decoration occurs in early stages (Niai Buthi I), the diagnostic decorative scheme is black-on-red slip. The major decorative characteristic is a central frieze of naturalistic animals (mainly humped cattle, but other animals are

30. Fairservis, 1975, pp. 158–9.
31. Ibid., pp. 171–2.
32. Stein, 1931.
33. Fairservis, 1975, pp. 185–202.
34. Casal, 1966.

FIG. 7. Periano Phase decorated pottery.

also depicted) and plants. This frieze has two animals (sometimes male and female) with elongated hatched bodies, exaggerated eyes, usually tethered to some undefined object. Plant motifs separate the animals and the remaining area is cluttered with smaller motifs. A variety of jar and bowl forms are found, the most important being the dish-on-stand and a straight-sided collared jar which has affinities with the Nal cannister. Other terracotta objects include beads, bangles, toy cart-frames and wheels, animal and human figurines. Human figurines have elaborately moulded coiffures, necklaces and pinched facial features, but most lack diagnostic sexual features.

Besides the usual stone tools, semi-precious stone beads and alabaster stone bowls have been found. At Mehi, Stein found examples of carved steatite stone bowls. Shell bangles are present. Copper or bronze objects include points, pins, celts, bangles and mirrors.

Little is known about Kulli Phase habitation structures. However, at Las-bela[35] and Nindowari large complex units of public architecture were found. These included large architectural complexes with a stepped profile and asso-ciated ramps of stairways. The construction of large walls also appears associated with these complexes. Building materials included large river boulders, mud and fired bricks, and clay plaster. These complexes were not used for habitation, and their precise function is unknown.

Until the Nindowari excavations are published, the Kulli Phase remains indeterminant. Some degree of interaction between the Kulli and Harappan Phases took place, as evidenced by the intrusive artefacts and certain stylistic similarities. Decorative similarities also exist between the Kulli and FM Phase potteries. Likewise, Kulli Phase sites near the Iranian border have pottery similar to that found by N. de Cardi[36] in the Bampur sequence. The Kulli Phase is one of the most intriguing phases of the Baluchistan Tradition, but too little is known for any definitive interpretations about it.

The Periano Phase (Fig. 7) is known only sketchily from areas north of the Quetta valley, and most information is restricted to pottery. At Rana Ghundai,[37] Periano Phase pottery is found in Periods III–IV suggesting an overlap with the KB Phase. However, Fairservis's[38] reanalysis of the Rana Ghundai sequence indi-cates that Periano Phase pottery was the dominant ceramic type in his Level C, implying that the Periano Phase is later than the KB Phase and possibly contem-porary with the DS Phase. At the same time, the black-on-red slip decorative scheme of the Periano Phase suggests continuity with the KGM Phase pottery. At Periano Ghundai and Dabar Kot, Periano Phase pottery was associated with Harappan pottery indicating a degree of contemporaneity and perhaps interac-tion with that phase of the Indus Valley Tradition. Chronologically, it appears that the Periano Phase may date between the mid-third and early second millen-nia B.C. (2500–1800 B.C.).

The diagnostic pottery of this phase corresponds to what Fairservis[39] defines as Periano and Faiz Muhammad painted ware for the Zhob and Loralai regions. Black-on-red slip decorations characterize Periano painted ware, and black-on-grey characterize Faiz Muhammad painted ware. Geometric motifs pre-dominate and are similar to those on Faiz Muhammad and Quetta ware potteries of the DS Phase. The ceramic evidence suggests a cultural connection between the Periano and DS Phases. At the same time, the presence of Harappan artefacts and stylistic traits (e.g. Periano Phase pottery with a double or flanged rim) also indicate interaction with the Indus Valley Tradition. At present the data are

35. Fairservis, 1975, pp. 195–205.
36. De Cardi, 1970.
37. Ross, 1946.
38. Fairservis, 1959, pp. 302–6.
39. Ibid., pp. 367–9, 373–4.

insufficient to determine the cultural role(s) played by the Periano Phase in the Baluchistan Tradition.

The Indus Valley Tradition

Many basic technologies and adaptive strategies of this tradition are similar to those of the Baluchistan Tradition and need not be repeated here. Instead, a brief review will include those characteristics which distinguish the Indus Valley Tradition from the Baluchistan Tradition.

The agricultural economies of the two traditions are very similar, including the emphasis on cattle and probable pastoral nomadism. Craft activities are highly developed indicating the presence of full and/or part-time specialists. The potter's craft was highly developed and stylistic variations define the various phases. These phases cover larger geographical areas probably reflecting the region's alluvial plain topography. Pottery was basically a red-buff ware, with grey ware production more limited than in Baluchistan. Many vessel forms of the two traditions are similar, but the Indus Valley Tradition is distinguished by the dish-on-stand, pot lids, and vessels with double or flanged rims. Other distinguishing terracotta objects are toy cartframes and wheels, triangular cakes, and a higher frequency of beads, bangles and animal figurines.

Except for the large flint blades, stone tools are very similar to the Baluchistan Tradition. Stone beads and vessels are found manufactured from many of the same materials. The shell industry is more developed and a greater variety and frequency of shell objects characterize this tradition. Examples of stone or terracotta stamp seals are not present until the later Harappan Phase. Copper or bronze objects of various types are found and increase dramatically in the Harappan Phase.

The overall impression is that craft activities were more intense in the Indus Valley Tradition, but this may reflect simply a larger sample size. There does appear to be more movement of craft objects and/or commodities throughout the region. Presence of intrusive potsherds and objects made from commodities with limited sources of origins (e.g. marine shells, semi-precious stones, metals) not immediately available in the locale of many settlements suggests more intense and regular interaction between social groups of this tradition. This interaction involved more than the simple movement of objects, as indicated by the widespread occurrence of script characters foreshadowing the development of the Harrapan script. The nature and structure of this interaction remain obscure, but it intensified and eventually integrated various regional phases of this tradition into a single cultural phase – the Harrapan or Indus Valley Civilization. A comparable stage of cultural integration was never achieved in the Baluchistan Tradition, and it is the Harappan Phase that yields many of the most diagnostic characteristics distinguishing the Indus Valley Tradition from the Baluchistan Tradition (see Chapter 12).

Although most Indus Valley Tradition sites are small agricultural settlements or temporary camp sites, industrial sites and urban centres are known. Moreover, at least one urban centre, Kalibangan in the Kot Diji Phase, has been excavated. This site diversity reflects our greater knowledge of the Indus Valley Tradition, and similar sites will no doubt eventually be found in Baluchistan. Still, no Baluchistan Tradition site is yet known which approaches the magnitude and complexity of Mohenjo-daro and Harappa, associated with the later Harappan Phase.

While the Harappan Phase is the most diagnostic of the Indus Valley Tradition, a full account of it is beyond the scope of this chapter. Instead the focus will be on the four phases that clearly formed the foundation for the Indus Valley Tradition. Our data for these phases are still limited, but the phases laid the cultural foundations for one of the most spectacular Bronze Age civilizations in the whole of Central and South Asia.

Like the KGM Phase the Hakra Phase was preceded by early agricultural groups, probably similar to Mehrgarh I (see Chapter 6). Unlike the KGM Phase, however, the cultural, stratigraphic and chronological relationships between the Hakra Phase and these early agriculturalists are ill-defined. The existence of this phase has only recently been recognized due to Mughal's[40] Bahawalpur survey. It seems that the occupations of Sarai Kala[41] and Jalilpur[42] are affiliated with the Hakra Phase. Unfortunately, excavated materials from these sites provide no connection with the Mehrgarh sequence.

The Balakot Phase is known only from excavations at Balakot[43] on the coast near Karachi. Three radiocarbon dates from later occupations of this phase suggest a late-fourth-millennium date (3500–3000 B.C.).

Pottery was all wheel-made red ware, except for some hand-made storage jars. The most diagnostic vessel form was again the globular jar with short everted rim. Other vessel forms include a variety of jar forms, angular walled bowls, and dish-on-stand. The most common decorative scheme was a series of widely spaced horizontal, sometimes wavy, bands executed in black or brown paint on a cream/white surface. Complex floral and zoomorphic motifs were found, executed in a style similar to Nal Phase pottery in the Baluchistan Tradition. Sometimes these motifs were filled in with red or green paint producing a polychrome effect. On the other hand, later Balakot Phase pottery closely resembles that from the Amri Phase (see below). Originally, on the bases of the ceramics, Dales[44] proposed a close affiliation between the Nal and Balakot materials, but more recently[45] he maintains the Balakot material should be treated indepen-

40. Mughal, 1981, 1982.
41. Halim, 1972, pp. 1–32; Mughal, 1972*b*.
42. Mughal, 1972*a*, 1974.
43. Dales, 1974, 1979, 1981.
44. Dales, 1974.
45. Dales, 1979.

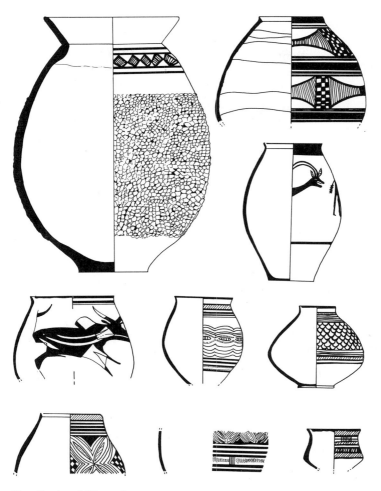

Fɪɢ. 8. Amri Phase decorated pottery.

dently, as it is considered here. Other terracotta objects include beads, cattle figurines and a scoop.

The small-scale excavations limit data collected about other objects but the following artefacts were found: grinding implements, flint blades, semi-precious stone beads (including lapis lazuli), shell beads, and a few amorphous copper or bronze objects. Likewise, knowledge about architectural features is limited, but multi-room, rectangular, mud-brick habitation structures as well as large paved areas of mud-bricks (platforms?) were found. Faunal analysis[46] indicates that although domestic sheep and goat and wild gazelle were present, domestic cattle provided the bulk of the diet. Shellfish were also exploited and domestic barley was present.

46. Meadow, 1979.

Part- or full-time craft specialists are certainly indicated by the pottery and perhaps by the other craft objects. The degree of interaction with other social groups is somewhat difficult to determine since many necessary commodities for craft production may have been available locally. Certainly the similarities with Nal and Amri Phase potteries suggest some awareness of other social groups in both the Baluchistan and Indus Valley Traditions. Furthermore, Hakra Phase pottery present in the Amri Phase may indicate some degree of interaction with that phase. Finally, painted and incised script characters on Balakot Phase pottery are similar to those found on Amri and Kot Diji Phase potteries, suggesting that various kinds of cultural interaction were taking place and providing a connection with the later Harappan Phase.

Surveys have located numerous Amri Phase settlements in the southern Indus valley,[47] but most information comes from Casal's[48] excavations at Amri itself. Hakra Phase style pottery was located in the earliest occupations at Amri (Amri IA), and Kot Diji Phase style pottery has also been identified in Amri IA and ID.[49] The Amri Phase, then, seems to have maintained interaction with, or chronologically overlapped with, all three phases. The two radiocarbon dates from Amri ID date to the first half of the third millennium (3000–2500 B.C.). It should be noted that there is a possibility that the Amri Phase, like the Kot Diji Phase, may have lasted longer in some localities.

Amri Phase pottery is a red-buff ware, mainly hand-made, and included such vessel forms as angular-walled and hemispherical bowls, dish-on-stand (rare), and most commonly S-shaped jars. Black, brown and red paint were applied to the vessel's surface or to a cream or buff slip or wash in monochrome or bichrome schemes. Decorative schemes emphasized geometric motifs in horizontal bands with frequent use of 'checkerboard' and 'sigma' motifs (Fig. 8). In Amri ID, motifs become more complicated and involve the use of intersecting circles, 'fish-scale' motifs, zoomorphic motifs and the rare use of red slip. Other terracotta objects include beads, bangles, humped cattle figurines, and circular, square and triangular cakes.

Stone tools are similar to other phases except that, like the Hakra Phase, there was an emphasis on geometric microliths.[50] Only the following additional type objects have been identified: carnelian beads (rare), shell bangles, bone points and bangles, a steatite rod and a copper blade. Certainly ceramic craft specialists were present, but it is difficult now to establish certainly other types of full- or part-time specialists.

In Amri IB, several small, contiguous, rectangular mud-brick houses divided into small rooms were found. Two types of structures were identified in Amri IC–D. One type was a large, rectangular mud-brick house with lateral

47. Flam, 1981*b*, 1982; Deva and McCown, 1949; Majumdar, 1934; Mughal, 1972*a*, pp. 133–7.
48. Casal, 1964.
49. Mughal, 1970, pp. 84–7.
50. Cleland, 1977, pp. 82–92.

doorways. The other was large rectangular mud-brick structures divided into small units similar to those found in the KGM Phase at Mehrgarh, which may have had a storage function.[51] Stone was also used in construction but probably as a foundation for mud-brick. Public architectural units (enclosing walls) have been noted only at unexcavated sites.

Hunting and fishing may have been more important in the Amri Phase, though the economy was still based on domesticated plants and animals (especially humped cattle). Some Amri Phase sites seem associated with large shell middens, and at Amri Casal found large quantities of gazelle as well as other wild animals. Fairservis[52] has also noticed a slightly more varied settlement pattern involving two settlement types – dispersed (single or small clusters of houses) and nucleated (larger settlements with multiple structures and units of public architecture). This more varied settlement pattern may reflect the larger economic role of hunting and fishing.

This part of the Indus valley region is poor in mineral and semi-precious stone deposits. The presence of semi-precious stones and metal artefacts in the Amri Phase therefore indicates some interaction with other social groups in the Indus Valley and/or Baluchistan Traditions. Some degree of interaction is also suggested by Amri Phase style pottery in the Balakot Phase and Kot Diji Phase pottery located at Amri. Moreover, the presence of similar script characters on the pottery of all these phases suggests that the communication networks linking these phases involved more than just the simple movement of commodities.

Besides the site of Kot Diji,[53] occupations belonging to Kot Diji Phase have been identified at Sarai Kala II, Jalilpur II, Gumla I–III,[54] Rahman Dheri,[55] Siswal,[56] Kalibangan,[57] and at various sites in Bahawalpur.[58] At Sarai Kala IA–early II and Jalilpur I–II, Kot Diji (hereafter KD) Phase and Hakra Phase potteries overlapped. Limited examples of KD Phase pottery were found at Hakra Phase sites in Bahawalpur. At several sites, KD Phase occupations, or pottery, were stratigraphically earlier than those of the subsequent Harappan Phase (e.g. Kot Diji, Gumla, Harappa), and Kalibangan I has consistently dated earlier than the Harappan Phase Kalibangan II occupation. KD Phase pottery at Amri suggests that these two phases are at least partially contemporary. Present evidence suggests that the KD Phase which succeeds the Hakra Phase, is contemporary with the Amri Phase, and precedes the Harappan Phase. Radiocarbon determinations date the KD Phase to the first half of the third millennium B.C. (3100/3000–2500

51. Jarrige 1981, p. 105.
52. Fairservis, 1975, pp. 208–16.
53. Khan, 1965.
54. Dani, 1970/71.
55. Durrani, 1981; Khan, 1979.
56. Suraj Bhan, 1975; See also Shaffer, 1981, for an extensive summary of this material.
57. Fairservis, 1975, pp. 182–3, 340, 352.
58. Mughal, 1982.

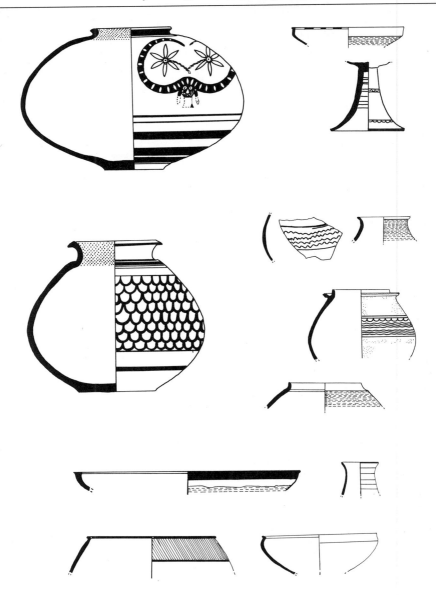

Fig. 9. Kot Diji Phase decorated pottery.

B.C.). It is very important to note that in the eastern Punjab, KD Phase occupations (Siswal) were found to be contemporary with and even post-date the Harappan Phase.[59] Therefore, some degree of regional chronological variation exists and must be considered when discussing this phase.

Likewise, a great deal of regional variation exists in what is called KD Phase pottery (Fig. 9). Indeed, future research may warrant establishment of subphases or even new phases. The most diagnostic vessel is a wheel-made red-ware globular jar with everted or flanged/double rim. Everted rim jars are found in three varieties: (a) simple jars with black or brown horizontal bands painted on the surface; (b) jars with black or brown motifs (geometric and naturalistic) on a red slip; and (c) decorated jars with a fluted surface or with a mud or sandy slip on the lower areas. Flanged-rim jars tend to have complex motifs involving geometric (intersecting circles, 'fish-scales', and others), zoomorphic (fish, bovines, caprids, turtles and the horned deity) and floral (pipal leaves) designs. These complex motifs are done in black or brown paint applied directly to the surface or on a red slip. White paint is also used either as a background or to fill in these complex motifs. Another characteristic vessel is an angular-walled bowl, with incised interior motifs similar to those found in the Hakra Phase. Other important vessel forms include collared and S-shaped jars, dish-on-stand, small carinated bowls with parallel walls (often decorated), and pot lids.

Additional terracotta objects of significance were bangles, beads, balls, toy cart-frames and wheels, triangular cakes, animal and human figurines. Two varieties of female figurines are found: (a) bent and extended legs with modeled buttocks and occasionally mounted on a pedestal stand; and (b) a flat stylized torso with a forward extension which functioned as a stand. Facial features are pinched, arms are raised or extented to the front, and some have elaborate coiffures.

Stone tools include flint blades, a few leaf-shaped points, and, at Sarai Kala II, significant numbers of stone celts. The lapidary industry was well developed as evidenced by the variety of beads made from semi-precious stones (including lapis lazuli) and steatite. The shell industry is reflected in numerous fragments of beads, bangles and rings. A variety of copper or bronze tools and items of personal adornment (pins, rings, bangles, etc.) have been located at many KD Phase sites. It seems that most craft activities were highly developed, with part or full-time specialists present.

Rectangular mud-brick structures have been found at most sites, but complete architectural units have been defined only at Kalibangan.[60] At Kalibangan I large rectangular structures were divided into rooms arranged around central courtyards which contained ovens and storage pits. Buildings were oriented towards cardinal directions and arranged along streets. A large mud-brick wall

59. See Shaffer, 1981, for a summary discussion of this eastern Punjab sequence.
60. Lal, 1979.

with exterior buttresses enclosed the entire settlement. Drains made of red brick were also found at Kalibangan. The magnitude and complexity of Kalibangan I suggests it may have been an urban centre.

In Bahawalpur, Mughal[61] associates a significant increase in the total number of sites with the KD Phase, and notes a particular increase in the number of sites associated with industrial activities. Moreover, the differential site size categories may indicate that various social and economic activities were not uniformly distributed among settlements, strengthening the argument for the presence of urban centres.

Floral remains from KD Phase sites have yet to be published, but the presence of a ploughed field at Kalibangan indicates the importance of agriculture. In Jalilpur II cattle were the dominant domestic animal,[62] more importantly, these cattle lived longer and were larger than contemporary populations elsewhere, suggesting they may have been kept for dairy products, traction and breeding. Sheep and goats, on the other hand, were apparently kept mainly as a meat source.

The data indicate that not only were ceramic craft specialists present, but that local ceramic production centres existed. A similar situation may hold for other craft activities. Existence of local production centres implies the presence of interaction networks linking various communities for the distribution of their surplus production. There is also indirect evidence of more extensive interaction networks linking the KD Phase with social groups in other traditions and geographical areas. KD Phase sites are located mainly in the central Indus valley region, which is poor in deposits of semi-precious stones and minerals, and with non-existent marine shells. The presence of these commodities in KD Phase sites implies the presence of such an extensive interaction network. Moreover, KD Phase pottery has been found in the Amri Phase and sporadically in Baluchistan, Kashmir and southern Afghanistan, suggesting diverse sources of supply for these commodities. Furthermore, location of KD Phase (Siswal) settlements in the eastern Punjab may have provided access to the rich mineral deposits in Rajasthan and the Himalayas. It is increasingly apparent that KD Phase interaction networks played a crucial role in procurement, processing and distribution of these commodities both within the Indus Valley Tradition and beyond. Once again, the presence of script characters on KD Phase pottery similar to those found in other phases suggests that such interaction networks involved more than just commodity exchanges; An interesting aspect of this interaction and distribution network may be indicated by a canopied cart and driver motif painted on a KD Phase pot from Banawali I.[63] This motif, the presence of ceramic toy cart-frames and wheels, and bull figurines, along with Meadow's suggestion that

61. Mughal, 1982.
62. Meadow, 1988.
63. Bisht and Asthana, 1979.

cattle may have been used for traction, suggest that land transport was important for these interaction networks.

The KD Phase clearly was critical in the development of the Harappan Phase, or Indus Valley Civilization.[64] The basic technologies and the social and economic structural framework of the Harappan Phase were established by the KD Phase, if not before. While the Harappan Phase is distinguished by its own particular style in the production of many artefacts, the majority do not radically differ from the KD Phase. For the most part, artefact changes associated with the Harappan Phase appear more quantitative than qualitative. The homogeneity in Harappan Phase characteristics over such a broad geographical area suggests that the changes involved in its development focused on an intensification of the KD Phase's interaction networks. This homogeneity in Harappan Phase artefacts also suggests that production became more centralized which, in turn, would have been aided by more intense and regular interaction networks. Another indication that interaction networks intensified is the appearance of stamp seals and cubical stone weights, artefacts usually associated with the regular movement of commodities between social groups. How or why this intensification occurred, and its impact upon various other cultural systems (social, political, religious) remain unknown. However, the recent rediscovery[65] of a camel burial at Mohenjo-daro may provide a clue for the mechanism of this intensification. Camels can carry or pull a large load more efficiently (i.e. needing water less frequently and having more versatile foraging capacity) than cattle. If the camel, as a beast of burden, was introduced from Central Asia sometime during the late KD Phase or early Harappan Phase, the economic impact would have been very significant for many aspects of cultural development.

The Early Bronze sites situated in India are marked by similar traits. Particularly in the river Ghaggar basin, the settlements culturally near to Kot Diji Phase are located.

As a result of exploration in Rajasthan, Haryana, Punjab and Gujarat in India, over 400 Harappan and late Harappan sites have been freshly discovered. This area of spread falls broadly into two geographical regions, called 'eastern' and 'southern', divided essentially by the Thar desert. The former affording wide flood plains is drained by the Ghaggar-Sarasvati system, including the Sutlej and the Beas, of which the vast aggradational surface shows topographical changes associated with numerous shifts and divisions of the rivers. The neighbourhoods of this region, especially the Aravalis, are rich in copper and other raw material. The latter region, marked by a littoral on one side and dissected plateaux, scarps and estuarine plains on the other, is drained by the Luni, Banas, Bhadar, Savarmati, Mahi, Narmada, Kim, Tapti and Godavari rivers, all unrelated to one another. Within these regions, 'pre' or 'early' Harappan settlements have been

64. Mughal, 1973.
65. Meadow, 1984.

located only in the eastern, principally on the Ghaggar (ancient Sarasvati) and Chautang (ancient Drishadvati), being an extension of the pattern in Cholistan across the border in Pakistan,[66] noteworthy sites being Kalibangan, Sothi, Banawali, Rakhigarhi, Siswal and Balu. Besides these, another site of the same genre, Mitathal, was located on the dried-up old course of Jamuna, which at one time is reported to have contributed to the Ghaggar system. Excepting Sothi, at each of the sites a stratified or cultural relationship between the pre-Harappan and Harappan cultures has been determined.

We may now turn to the principal sites, starting with Kalibangan. The name Kalibangan means literally 'black bangles' from the sight of countless fragments of weather-stained terracotta bangles strewn over the surface of the site. It lies some 310 km north-west of Delhi along the left bank of the now-dry river Ghaggar (ancient Sarasvati) in the northern part of Rajasthan. It comprises two mounds, with the smaller one (KLB–1) located on the west and the larger (KLB–2) to the east, recalling identical disposition of mounds at Mohenjo-daro and Harappa. The excavation (1961–69) revealed a sequence of two periods of occupation, of which the upper belonged to the Indus civilization (see Chapter 12) and the lower to the antecedent phase termed, albeit loosely, as 'pre' or 'early' Harappan. In the present stage of research, however, a more appropriate name would be Kalibangan I.[67]

The settlement was situated on the bend of the river beyond the active flood-plain and was a parallelogram some 250 m from north to south and 180 m from east to west. It was found to have been fortified from the very beginning of the occupation. The fortification wall was made of mud-bricks (30 × 20 × 10 cm) and, in its extant portion, showed two structural phases. In the earlier phase, the basal width was 1.9 m, while in the latter it measured 3–4 m – the extra thickness being added on the inner side. Both the inner and outer faces of the wall seem to have been originally plastered with mud, patches of which were found preserved at many places.

Within the walled area, the houses were built of mud-bricks of the same size as those used in the fortification wall, the masonry being in the English bonding. The use of baked brick was attested by a drain, the size of bricks being the same as that of mud-bricks. The excavation also brought to light part of a 1.5 m wide lane running in an east–west direction. Interesting evidence regarding cooking practices was revealed by the presence, inside the house, of ovens of both underground and overground varieties closely resembling the present-day *tandurs* in the region. Equally noteworthy was the existence of cylindrical pits lined with lime-plaster, possibly for storing drinking water. The alignment of the houses as also the size of the bricks used was significantly different from those of the Harappans.

66. Mughal, 1981.
67. Thapar, 1975.

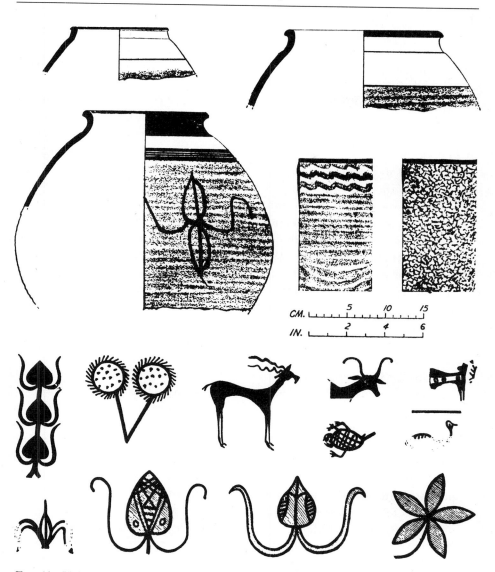

CM.
IN.

FIG. 10. Kalibangan pottery from Fabric B and painted designs.

The distinctive trait of this period, however, was the pottery,[68] which was characterized by six fabrics, labelled for convenience as Fabrics A to F.

Fabric A was marked by an individuality that isolates it from other fabrics. The vessels of this fabric, though made on the wheel, were carelessly potted, showing unskilled handling with tell-tale traces of irregular striations. Comparatively light and thin in section and red to pinkish in colour, most of the vessels were painted in black, combined at times with white over a dull red surface, the field of decoration being confined to the portion above the girth. The design elements drawn in free-style included: (a) horizontal bands, sometimes as thick as the height of the neck; (b) loops fringed below or enclosed by horizontal bands; (c) grouped converting lines forming opposite triangles or rhombs; (d) segments or scallops with fillers; (e) pendant latticed leaves bordered above by horizontal bands; (f) moustache-like bifold scroll within wavy verticals; (g) pendant latticed leaves; (h) symmetrically joined semi-circles with intervening space giving the effect of pendant concave-side triangles; and so on. Various motifs such as radiating lines ending in solid discs, four-petalled flowers, squares with radiating flowers at the corners, cactus-like plants were used as fillers. The range of shapes was, however, limited and comprised vases with out-turned and out-curved rims with disc or ring bases and bowls with tapering or convex sides. Of unusual interest were a vase with a pedestal base and another with a holemouth.

Fabric B was distinguished primarily by its paste, texture and surface treatment. The vessels (Fig. 10) of this fabric were carefully potted on the wheel and were treated with a red slip up to the shoulder, the slipped area being decorated with black painted horizontal bands of varying thickness. The remaining surface of the pot was covered with a thin clayey solution often mixed with sand, and, while wet, roughened by horizontal or wavy combings or by tortoise-shell or dendritic impressions. Over this rusticated surface, naturalistic designs – floral, animal and bird – were painted in black, complemented at times with the ancillary white. Only one shape, namely, a globular jar, was represented in this fabric.

Fabric C was marked by a finer-textured paste and all-over smooth-slipped surface in shades of red and plum or purple-red. The repertory of painted designs included, besides the recurrent carefully ruled horizontal bands or loops or criss-cross borders of plants, fish-scale, metopes, pendant triangles, panelled butterfly or double axe, etc. The shapes represented in this fabric comprised globular or ovoid vases with disc bases, lids, straight-sided bowls, dishes and offering stands.

Fabric D was characterized by vessels with thick sturdy section and slipped red surface. Common shapes included heavy jars, bowls, troughs or basins. The last named, however, was the most characteristic of this fabric. Such basins with ring bases were decorated internally on the sides with sharp-ridged incisions of varying patterns, including grouped wavy lines and on the outside with single or

---

68. Thapar, 1969, 1973.

multiple rows or cord impressions. Besides, black painted horizontal bands and loops were not infrequent.

Fabric E comprised vessels with a buff or reddish buff slip. Common shapes included: large and medium-sized jars, including those with a flange round the rim, lids, bowls, offering stands and dishes, including a small chalice. The painted decoration (in black sometimes tending to purplish and occasionally white) consisted of ubiquitous rim bands, oblique lines with fronds, sigmas, borders of scales, latticed or plain scallops, multi-petalled flowers, fish, double-axe or butterfly within wavy verticals.

Fabric F is related to the grey-coloured pottery and was represented in forms commonly met with in other fabrics, namely dish-on-stand, basins, bowls, vases, etc. For decoration the use of both black and white pigment was current.

Among Fabrics E and F, the difference was more apparent than real and lay in the colour of the surface-dressing (respectively buff and grey), some of the forms being common to other fabrics. In frequency, Fabric A showed the highest percentage, followed in a regression by Fabrics B, C, D, E and F, the last-mentioned two being somewhat uncommon. Being current throughout the occupation, these fabrics did not represent any evolutionary series or different ethnic endogamous groups, but may have resulted from specific uses or demands. The classification of these fabrics is essentially based on purely technical characteristics.

Among the other finds of this period, the more noteworthy were small-sized blades of chalcedony and agate, sometimes serrated or backed; beads, variously of steatite (disc), shell, carnelian, terracotta and copper, shell bangles, terracotta objects comprising a fragmentary bull, a toy-cart wheel with single-sided hub, an annular ring, bangles, both of rectangular (single or subjoined) and circular section; a quern stone with mullers; a bone point, and copper objects, comprissing a celt, a bangle, a nondescript cutting tool, and a few other fragmentary pieces. No figurine of the mother goddess or any other deity have been obtained from the excavation.

A significant discovery of the excavation was a ploughed field situated to the south-east of the settlement, outside the town wall.[69] It showed a grid of furrows with one set more closely spaced (about 30 cm apart) running east–west and the other, widely spaced (about 1.9 m apart) running north–south. Curiously enough this pattern shows a remarkable similarity to modern ploughing in the neighbourhood wherein two types of crops are grown simultaneously, the combination being conditioned by the size and growth behaviour of the respective plants. No remains of a plough, ploughshare or coulter have so far been obtained from the site.

The occupation endured through five structural phases, rising to a height of 1.6 m above the natural soil, when is was brought to a close by a catastrophe

---

69. Lal, 1971; Thapar, 1975.

(perhaps seismic), as indicated by the occurrence of displaced (faulted) strata and subsided walls in different parts of the excavated area. Thereafter the site seems to have been abandoned, albeit temporarily, and a thin layer of sand, largely infertile and wind-blown, accumulated over the ruins.

Siswal, another settlement of this epoch is situated 26 km west of Hissar on the left bank of the now dry Chautang (ancient Drishadvati). A small-scale excavation, conducted in the autumn of 1970, revealed in a 1.25 m thick occupation-strata a succession of two cultures, labelled here as Siswal A and Siswal B,[70] the classification being based on ceramic industries. No structures were found in the limited area of the excavated trench. Siswal A is distinguished by the occurrence of all the six fabrics in use in Kalibangan Period I, with the elaboration that the design repertoire at Siswal shows lesser variety, and the decoration particularly of Fabric D troughs is inferior in execution. Some of these troughs also show rusticated surface on the lower portion. Siswal B, although retaining all the fabrics of A, is marked by an austerity both in shape and design, particularly the absence of the use of white pigment in painting. It also shows a limited though hesitant contact with the typical Harappan ware exemplified by the occurrence of such forms as S-shaped jars, dish-on-stand, perforated cylindrical jars, etc. It may be recalled that a similar assemblage was also met with at Mitathal in Period I. No other finds were obtained from the excavation. However, an assortment of finds collected from the surface included saddle querns and pestles, terracotta bangles, sling balls and terracotta triangular cakes.

Rakhigarhi lies on the old course of the Chautang (Drishadvati) river some 190 km east of Kalibangan in district Hissar and consists of two mounds, the smaller to the west and the larger to the east; recalling the lay-out plan at Kalibangan. A closer observation supplemented by a section scraping, undertaken in 1973, revealed that the lower levels of the smaller mound represented the occupation of the 'pre' or 'early' Harappans, as indicated by the occurrence of all the six fabrics enumerated at Kalibangan. The twin-mound layout of the settlement with the smaller mound used as a citadel and the larger as the lower city was developed by the Harappans to suit their pattern.[71]

Banawali, situated on the Sarasvati, almost midway between Kalibangan and Rakhigarhi (being 80 km from the latter) in District Hissar is another site where remains of a 'pre' or 'early' Harappan occupation have been found stratified below those of the Harappan (see Chapter 12). The former was charcaterized by the occurrence of all the six fabrics recorded at Kalibangan.[72] The structures were made of mud-bricks of standard sizes, conforming to the ratio 3:2:1 ($30 \times 20 \times 10$ cm, or $36 \times 24 \times 12$ cm, or $39 \times 26 \times 13$ cm). In addition, there was an aberrant size ($24 \times 24 \times 2$ cm). Kiln-burnt bricks were also used. Noteworthy structures exposed by the excavations consisted of (a) a 2m-wide brick-on-edge pave-

70. Suraj Bhan, 1975.
71. Ibid.
72. Bisht and Asthana, 1979, pp. 225–6.

ment and (b) a partially excavated house, showing several hearths, fire-pits, etc., pointing perhaps to its use as a metalsmith's workshop. Another interesting find was the existence of circular pits neatly dug into the house-floors containing fine bluish ash mixed with charred grains. Among other finds obtained from the deposits of this occupation are points and awls of bone, microblades of chalcedony, terracotta bangles, beads of gold, semi-precious stone, steatite (disc), faience, bone and clay; bangles of shell, faience and copper and terracotta animal figurines. A noteworthy find, however, is a painted sherd depicting a canopied cart having spoked wheels. In the upper levels of this occupation there is evidence for the intrusive appearance, in a limited way, of the Harappan ware recalling the phenomena at Siswal and Mitathal. The full import and nature of this transitional phase still remains to be ascertained.

Two more sites where a similar cultural sequence has been attested by excavation are Balu in District Jind, Haryana[73] and Rohira in District Sangrur, Punjab.

Among the sites mentioned above only Kalibangan has been sampled for radiocarbon dating (five from the early, one from the middle and three from the late levels). Except for one, the dates are all consistent and indicate an inclusive time-range of 2370–1820 B.C. (without MASCA calibration). As the excavated cuttings from which samples have been obtained lie on the slopes of the mound with very little soil-cover, the dangers of humus contamination cannot be overlooked, especially in respect of samples belonging to the late levels of the period which show a range between 1965 and 1820 B.C. The duration of Period I at Kalibangan may in fact have been much shorter, and, on the above showing, is estimated to be 2500–2300 B.C. without MASCA calibration (calibrated equivalents would be 2900–2700 B.C.). The five structural phases, of which the upper three were large rebuildings, would fully support this postulate.

Coming to comparative study we find that in Pakistan five sites – Amri, Harappa, Kot Diji, Balakot and Gumla[74] – have furnished evidence of the existence of an occupation, yielding alien ceramics stratified below the Harappan strata. In addition, comparable material is also available from Sarai Kala, Rahman Dheri,[75] Jalilpur[76] and sites in Baluchistan and Iranian Sistan. At the outset it may be stated that as an assemblage comprising six fabrics, the pottery of Kalibangan I remains unparalleled. Among fabrics this is particularly true of Fabric A, which is the dominant ceramic of the period. The recently explored sites at Cholistan, however, afford some parallels particularly in Fabrics B and D. The surface decoration of Fabric B resembles that of the so-called wet wares of Baluchistan (Sur Jangal, Dabar Kot, Periano Ghundai) and is also available at Amri[77] and Kot Diji in Sind. Fabric C is commonly met with at Amri, Harappa (prefe-

73. Bisht, 1976, 1978, 1984.
74. Dani, 1970/71.
75. Durrani, 1981.
76. Mughal, 1974.
77. Casal, 1964; Dales, 1981.

rence deposits), Kot Diji, Sarai Kala and perhaps also at Rahman Dheri and Gumla. Fabric D, showing *inter alia* an exclusive decorative element of sharp-ridged incisions of various patterns including wavy, criss-cross, etc. is paralleled at Amri and perhaps also at Kot Diji.[78] Fabrics E and F were distinguished more by their surface colour than by any other technical characteristics. However, the occurrence of buff and grey fabrics is reported from sites of pre-Harappan affiliation in Baluchistan and Sind.

Coming to shapes, of which the range in the whole assemblage is limited, we find that short-necked globular vases, dishes-on-stands, pedestal bowls or chalices, bowls with tapering or convex sides, heavy jars with ledged or flanged rims and wide basins are known variously at Amri, Harappa, Kot Diji, Sarai Kala, Gumla, etc. Similarly, in ornamentation quite a few designs occurring on the pottery of Kalibangan I correspond to those on the pottery of the above-mentioned sites including those in Baluchistan, Mundigak in the Helmand basin of Afghanistan and Shahr-i Sokhta in Iranian Sistan, for example, thick bands, pendant loops, symmetrically joined semicircles, latticed triangles, dot-tipped hanging triangles, radiating lines ending in solid discs, double-axe or butterfly motif, depiction of fish, humped cattle, ibex, etc. In fact, the painted designs on the pottery of these sites are regional variations of basic motifs common to the fourth- and early-third-millennia B.C. pottery of the regions. On the basis of comparison of the material equipment of Kalibangan I with that of corresponding sites in Pakistan, it is seen that while these village/town cultures share a common level of economic subsistence, they are marked by regionalization with an uneven development and differing ceramic traditions. At some stage they were also anticipating some of the Harappan traits. The correlation of the above-mentioned assemblages indicates that the pre-Harappan communities appeared in Rajasthan somewhat later than in Sind as though reflecting a sloping horizon of cultural level, from west to east. The available radiocarbon dates of the comparable strata at Amri, Kot Diji, Rahman Dheri and Kalibangan would support this postulate. One of the characteristic types of Fabric D of Kalibangan I is found to be closely paralleled in Amri IIB,[79] thus providing a datable correlation between the two cultures on a common time-scale. On the strength of a radiocarbon date Amri IC is dated to 2600 B.C. Amri IIB, therefore, would be around 2500 B.C. which agrees with the date proposed above for the beginning of Kalibangan I. Confirmatory evidence about the terminal time-bracket of Kalibangan I is forthcoming from layer 5 at Kot Diji, representing the late phase of Kot Diji culture and dated to 2300 B.C. On the other Indian sites, the pre-Harappan culture seems to have staggered on still later, developing on its own lines within the life-time of the Indus Valley Civilization itself.

78. Khan, 1965.
79. Casal, 1964.

Summary

Both Baluchistan and Indus Valley Traditions developed from an early agricultural society at present known only from the early occupations at Mehrgarh. By the fourth millennium B.C. distinctive phases in each tradition can be defined on the bases of ceramic stylistic variations. Intrusive artefacts and commodities indicate that a degree of interaction existed between phases and to a lesser extent between traditions, but the cultural impact of these interactions was limited. During the third millennium B.C. several distinct cultural phases persisted in the Baluchistan Tradition, with the degree of interaction remaining limited but constant. The only exception to this is the Damb Sadaat Phase which came under direct influence of social groups in southern Afghanistan. However, in the Indus Valley Tradition the degree of interaction between phases seems to have intensified. This intensification is reflected in intrusive artefacts and commodities as well as in ceramic stylistic similarities and identification of common script characters. Finally, in the late third millennium B.C. this interaction is further intensified, reflected by a single cultural phase, the Harappan, identifiable in most areas of the Indus Valley Tradition. Interaction between the Baluchistan and Indus valley Traditions continued to occur, but with the possible exception of the introduction of the camel from middle Asia, the cultural impact of these interactions appears to have been minimal. Although interaction with groups to the west probably occurred in both Traditions, such interaction seems culturally important only for the DS Phase. Both traditions reflect indigenous cultural development, and the Indus Valley Tradition witnessed the development of a major Old World civilization during the Harappan Phase discussed in the next chapter.

Thus various groups of the pre-Harappan population both in Baluchistan and the Indus valley show a further cultural progress in the course of the Chalcolithic and Bronze Ages.[80] There occurred a multifaceted development of a new mode of life which accompanied the advent of the agricultural epoch; the efflorescence of the artistic culture was particularly remarkable in the development of painted pottery and terracotta sculpture. The population growth and the craft specialization created socio-economic prerequisites for the emergence of Harappan Civilization. Cultural and trade links became more intense and regular within the Central Asian region. At a number of Baluchistan sites, links with southern Turkmenistan are particularly obvious in the painted pottery. The vessels imported from Baluchistan decorated in the Nal style were discovered in wealthy graves of an important early urban centre of Shahr-i Sokhta in the Iranian province of Sistan.

---

80. Mughal, 1970.

THE INDUS CIVILIZATION[1]

A. H. Dani and B. K. Thapar

T HE Indus Civilization represents the earliest manifestation of urban development in the plains of the Indus valley and its extension along the Arabian sea-coast. The four principal settlements so far excavated provide the material to reconstruct the cultural content of the civilization. Two lie in Pakistan: Harappa,[2] usually identified with Hariyupiya[3] of the Rigveda, is situated on an old bed (*sukhrawa*) of the river Ravi in Sahiwal District of Punjab, and Mohenjo-daro[4] (literally 'mound of the dead') is on the right bank of the Indus river in Larkana District of Sind. The other two sites are in western India; Lothal[5] is situated on the Sabarmati river at the head of the gulf of Cambay on the west coast of India, and Kalibangan[6] (literally 'black bangles') lies some 310 km north-west of Delhi along the left bank of the now-dry Ghaggar (old Sarasvati) river in northern Rajasthan.

The antecedents of this urban civilization have been described earlier, in Chapter 11, but it is not clear how and under what conditions a transition of the urban development took place. Trade through land connections across Afghanistan with eastern Iran and Turkmenistan was noted in the previous cultures. The Indus Civilization, for the first time, also established overseas trade. The advantaged gained through new mechanics of trade may have enabled an adventurous community to make a bid for the mastery of their resources and lay the foundation of a political system that imposed their supremacy over the entire Indus zone. Such is the case from the available evidence at Harappa, where a new citadel complex[7] had been imposed on an earlier village settlement. The Kalibangan[8]

1. See Map 9.
2. Vats, 1940.
3. Dani, 1950.
4. Marshall, 1931.
5. Rao, 1973.
6. Thapar, B. K., 1975.
7. Wheeler, 1947.
8. Thapar, B. K., 1975.

evidence again shows a new pattern of urban planning on an earlier fortified settlement. Such a sudden change is also noticed at Amri,[9] Balakot[10] and Kot Diji.[11]
It is the Kot Diji cultural type that is widely spread as evidenced by the excavations at Sarai Kala,[12] Gumla,[13] Rahman Dheri,[14] on the Indus plain, near Dera
Ismail Khan, and several other places in the Punjab.[15] It is only Mohenjo-daro[16]
which still holds the mystery, as its earlier levels have not yet been excavated
because of the rise of the water table in the present century. These levels are likely
to reveal a Kot Dijian cultural complex, or an admixture with other early cultural
elements known in Sind and Baluchistan. Yet the new urban development shows
a basic difference in its cultural features, which, though based on local geography
and ecology, needed a motivational inspiration not evidenced in the archaeological data so far recovered. Hence the origin of the Indus Civilization yet remains
unknown and is a matter of several theoretical speculations.[17]

While the earlier phases of the Bronze Age cultural complex show varying
patterns in the different geographical regions of Pakistan and western India, the
Indus Civilization imposes a certain uniformity in its basic cultural manifestation
and hence there is little difficulty in identifying the urban pattern associated with
it. This pattern is confined to a restricted geographical area and adheres mainly to
the alluvial plains of the Indus, east of the Jhelum river. Hence it belongs to the
Indus system, and therefore the name Indus Civilization is appropriate, but it also
extends along a wide coastal stretch from the mouths of the Narmada and Tapti
rivers in the east to Sutkagen Dor[18] in the west. The last-named is one of the four
major port sites, the other three being Balakot[19] and Sotkakoh in Baluchistan, and
Lothal[20] in Gujarat. The discovery of six mounds in the vicinity of Shortugai[21] in
the Kunduz province of north-eastern Afghanistan appears to be a case of an isolated colonial settlement probably acting as a trading depot. The northern limit
of the Indus zone has been extended to Manda,[22] Akhnor, located on the right
bank of the Chenab, about 28 km north-west of Jammu, while the easternmost
site being Alamgirpur on the banks of the Hindan, a tributary of the Jamuna, is
about 45 km north-east of Delhi. Whereas the western hilly regions continued

9. Casal, 1964.
10. Dales, 1981.
11. Khan, 1965.
12. Halim, 1972*a*, 1972*b*.
13. Dani, 1970/71.
14. Durrani, 1981.
15. Mughal, 1981.
16. Dales, 1965.
17. Fairservis, 1961.
18. Dales, 1962.
19. Dales, 1981.
20. Rao, 1973.
21. Francfort and Pottier, 1978.
22. Thapar, B. K., 1981.

with their own older cultural variations and survived side by side with the new urban development sites such as Kulli[23] and Dabar Kot[24] in Baluchistan and Gumla and Hishamdheri in the Gomal plain have shown the impact of the Indus Civilization. On the other hand a far-off place like Daimabad[25] on the Godavari has produced late Harappan material. In brief, among all civilizations of the ancient world that of the Indus spread over the widest territorial limit.

This vast territorial region of the Indus Civilization remains unnamed because of the failure to decipher the contemporary writings on the Indus seals. However, Mesopotamian contact, direct or indirect, has produced some relevant evidence. The contemporary documents there speak of ships coming from Dilmun, Makan and Meluha or Melukhkha;[26] Sargon the Great boasts:

> The ships from Meluha
> The ships from Makan
> The ships from Dilmun
> He made tie up up alongside the quay of Agade.

Dilmun or Tilmun, which is usually identified with the island of Bahrain,[27] is supposed to be the clearing-house for goods bound for Sumer from the east. From Makan and Meluha the ships brought copper ingots and implements in huge quantities – carnelian, ivory, shell, lapis lazuli, pearls, spices, etc. – materials specific to the Indus Civilization. On these grounds Makan and Meluha have been taken to mean 'Indus country'. Particularly Meluha or Melukhkha, which suggestively resembles the much later Prakrit 'Milakkha' or Sanskrit 'Mlechchha'[28] – a name meaning 'a stranger of ill-pronounced speech', and applied to foreigners in Sanskrit literature – has the strongest possibility to be the oldest name of the Indus country. Makan could be a western coastal region, which still bears the name of Makran.

The Indus country, or the ancient Meluha, lies within 25° and 35° N. latitude – a range which also covers the oldest civilizations of Mesopotamia and Egypt, the areas which today have almost desert climatic conditions and which would have been complete deserts but for the great rivers that bring seasonal floods to revivify the parched lands that have themselves been built up by silt deposits. These areas are supposed to have been subjected to severe Post-Pleistocene desiccation. However, recent studies present a different postulate: 'that the degraded environment in these regions is more probably due to man's over-

---

23. Piggott, 1950, pp. 98–116.
24. Fairservis, 1975, p. 153.
25. Thapar, B. K., 1981.
26. Kramer, 1964; Thapar, R., 1975.
27. Possibility of its identification with the Oman coast cannot be ruled out as M. Tosi's excavations at Ra's al-Junayz have been very significant, producing also Indus writing on potsherds. (Personal communication.)
28. Parpola and Parpola, 1975.

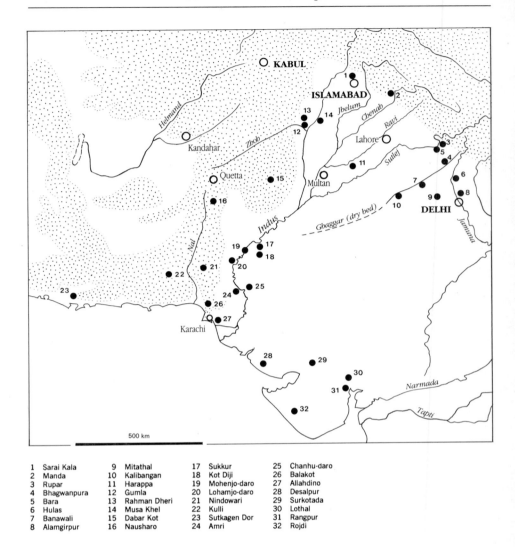

MAP 9. Distribution of Indus Civilization.

1	Sarai Kala	9	Mitathal	17	Sukkur	25	Chanhu-daro
2	Manda	10	Kalibangan	18	Kot Diji	26	Balakot
3	Rupar	11	Harappa	19	Mohenjo-daro	27	Allahdino
4	Bhagwanpura	12	Gumla	20	Lohamjo-daro	28	Desalpur
5	Bara	13	Rahman Dheri	21	Nindowari	29	Surkotada
6	Hulas	14	Musa Khel	22	Kulli	30	Lothal
7	Banawali	15	Dabar Kot	23	Sutkagen Dor	31	Rangpur
8	Alamgirpur	16	Nausharo	24	Amri	32	Rojdi

exploitation than to variation in rainfall and temperature regimes'.[29] On the other hand pollen analysis from Rajasthan lakes carried out by Gurdip Singh[30] and meteorological considerations by C. Ramaswamy[31] have enabled them to reconfirm the earlier opinion of Sir John Marshall, and suggest that there was a period of somewhat higher rainfall in Pakistan and western India between 3000 and 2000 B.C., although Ramaswamy would like to bring the date of the wet period down to 500 B.C. There is little doubt that some of the rivers, such as the Sarasvati and Drishadvati, known to the Rigvedic Aryans, are now dried up and are represented by the Ghaggar of Hakra. This drying process may be the result of less and less precipitation in the post-Indus period. R. L. Raikes and others have, however, explained this drying process by supposing some tectonic activity in the northern Punjab, which bifurcated the water of the Himalayas from the western drainage system of the Indus to the eastern drainage system of the Ganges. Under these conflicting opinions it is difficult to be dogmatic on the actual climatic conditions. However, animals like the elephant, rhinoceros and tiger, which during the last few centuries have become extinct in the region, were known to the Indus people. They took measures to protect the exposed walls by baked bricks, and were also extremely punctilious in providing drains and conduits in their cities for easy flow of excess water. The Indus valley does receive a moderate rainfall from 125 to 625 mm a year. The precipitation in the northern hills is much higher resulting in the forested belt of the hilly regions. The hill slopes have grass lands which support sheep, goats and cattle. The flooded plains have produced various kind of wheat, barley and oats. While sheep and goats dominate in the old civilizations of western Asia, cattle are the hallmark of the Indus. The Indus valley has a character of its own that is derived from the build of the Himalayan chains which throw their off-shoots towards the Arabian Sea, thus providing a cultural context south of the Hindu Kush and between the deserts of Iran and India. Such a wide cultural zone shows variations in climate from extreme cold winters in the north to more mild temperatures along the sea-coast.

The urban development in the Indus valley introduced the pattern of the earliest urbanization in this part. Two things are clear: the first is the surplus food-production in the fertile soil of the river-irrigated plains, mainly yielding wheat and barley and cotton as the cash crop. The surplus was stored in granaries, two of which have been exposed, one at Mohenjo-daro and another at Harappa. Whether there was any centralized cotton-manufacturing industry or handlooms were used in the villages is difficult to say. In any case cotton fabrics, including those of printed designs, appear to have been produced. The second aspect of urban life was craft specialization and industrialization of the cities. Copper, which was available from Baluchistan and neighbouring Rajasthan, was the basic metal for industrial and commercial development. There is little doubt

29. Raikes and Dyson, 1961.
30. Singh, 1971.
31. Ramaswamy, 1968.

that timber, probably from the *deodar* tree was obtained in the northern hills, as in the excavations at Mohenjo-daro[32] timber beams are known to have been used in brick masonry. Carpenter's tools are evidence of skill in carpentry. These three items – copper, cotton and timber – appear to have been the mainstay of urban prosperity. For luxury goods, shell, ivory, lapis lazuli, carnelian and other precious stones as well as gold and silver were obtained to manufacture articles of common taste. A bead-making craft was well established. The painted pottery tradition speaks of another specialized craft. Two kinds of stones were profusely used: steatite probably from the neighbourhood of Tepe-Yahya[33] in eastern Iran was used for making seals, and alabaster for cups and vessels. Limestone statues, musical instruments, dancing figures tell of the development of fine arts in the cities. Except for the last few items, others were already in use in the pre-Indus cultures but in this period there is an acceleration and standardization of these products. The source of surplus food is not clear, as no information is available on irrigation. Mining, exploitation of forests and import of raw materials from distant places indicate an intensification of trade. The sea provided an outlet to overseas markets. There is nothing in this economic exploitation that needed foreign influence. Material evolution from indigenous sources is well documented.

It is only when we turn to the other aspects of culture that the Indus Civilization shows no precedents, but they are again so individualistic and rooted in the local fauna and flora that, as far as material content is concerned, it wholly derives from the local elements. However, an extremely interesting development is the production of steatite seals which have no earlier precedents, but depict local art and writing. The purpose of these seals is not at all clear. However, if they were meant as signet seals for stamping on commercial goods, pots[34] and other objects, they may have had administrative significance.[35] On the other hand, the standardization of goods, enforcement of a definite system of weights and measures, and above all formulation and execution of municipal rules in the cities, speak of the emergence of a political system that must be credited to a determined community of people whose main support lay in the surplus of the Indus plain, but whose prosperity depended on the growth of the industrial urban centres and a peaceful atmosphere for overseas trade and commerce. Such an enterprising people must have felt the need to develop a system of writing to meet their commercial and administrative requirements. As will be explained below, there is no earlier beginning of writing except for some symbols found at random on potsherds.[36] On the other hand, the seals themselves provide us with many animal figures and human scenes that apparently had religious and myth-

32. Dales, 1965.
33. Lamberg-Karlowsky, 1972.
34. Wheeler, 1968, Plate XXXIV, B.
35. Fairservis, 1976.
36. Fairservis, 1975, p. 281.

ological significance. There is little doubt that some pedestalled emblems and actual figures were objects of worship. Such a use of religious symbols in connection with commercial transactions suggests a religion-oriented society, though little evidence has been recovered for institutionalized religion in the architectural remains of the city. Our option for the western Asian model of a temple-dominated social structure has so far been unproved in the Indus Civilization. Some of the features of the religion can be derived from the earlier rural-based social system. In the vast expanse of the Indus system that practice was likely to persist and even influence new urban beliefs and rituals. In other words, the rural Indus had a major role to play in the make-up of the Indus Civilization. On the other hand, the urban centres must have sprung up as cultural foci to serve administrative purposes for the convenience of a determined group of people who laid the foundation of new cities unparalleled in the ancient Orient.

These cities show a twin-settlement pattern – a 'citadel' and a 'lower town', as can be seen in the excavated remains of sites in Pakistan at Mohenjo-daro, Harappa and Sutkagen Dor. Although Thapar[37] seeks the origin of the citadel or high mound from the 'ziggurat' model of Mesopotamia, the two formations are entirely different in concept. In the case of Kalibangan this higher citadel ground is due to an earlier occupation below. But in the case of Harappa and Sutkagen Dor the two sites are deliberately divided. At Mohenjo-daro they are separated by a wide gap between the two, the gap at one time being certainly flooded and hence R. E. M. Wheeler conceives of a canal[38] or a branch of the Indus in between them. It is possible that the two sites were simultaneously occupied on either side of a channel. It is principally at the citadel mound that a mud-brick platform has been traced. Out of seven successive phases excavated at Mohenjo-daro, Marshall located the platform between the lower sixth and seventh – an interval of 6 m built almost entirely by crude brick and alluvial mud. The same platform was identified by Wheeler in his 1950 excavation, underlying a huge granary contemporary with it, and he assigns it to the 'intermediate period' of Marshall's chronology. Still below lie older buildings and phases to an unexplored depth. These unexcavated phases continue to a depth of 12 m below the plain. Wheeler believed that the building of the citadel corresponded with no break in the cultural sequence, yet the material of the lower levels remains to be salvaged, analysed and properly studied. The exposed structures on this high mound are all later than the granary and hence appear on a higher level than the 'lower town'. The purpose of this high mound is not at all clear, as main buildings still remain unrelated. On the other hand, several adjacent areas of the eastern 'lower mounds' have been partly excavated. All through this lower mound a wide, straight street has been traced running north and south. A second possible north–south street has also been located at some distance. The long cross streets

37. Thapar, B. K., 1970; Jansen, 1979.
38. Wheeler, 1968, p. 47.

as shown by Wheeler,[39] still remain hypothetical because the suggested lines follow only the contour of the mound but they remain to be proved by excavation. It is therefore not at all clear whether the two settlement sites were planned on one grid pattern, as is generally assumed. The grid system has not been proved in any of these Indus Civilization sites. If this grid presumption is set aside, the growth of the city plan of Mohenjo-daro can be reached with reasonable understanding on the basis of an earlier continued occupation of the two sites on either side of a small channel – an experience that led to the Indus concept of twin settlements – a 'citadel' and a 'lower town' as we like to call them. B. B. Lal[40] has attributed religious significance to at least half the portion of the citadel mound at Kalibangan but so far no such idea has been proposed for the other city sites.

The Indus cities are unique in their conception. The north–south alignment of long thoroughfares at such an early period is unparalleled in history. The only other site where such a planning appears to have been preceded is surmised from the aerial photograph of Rahman Dheri.[41] Such planning was followed by a straight alignment of house walls along the streets, and of still greater significance are the long covered public drains built through the middle of the wide streets, with manholes in between for the ultimate removal of rubbish. Such drains were properly connected with private drains and water chutes coming from private houses which had a highly developed system of brick-on-edge flooring in the bathrooms. The long thoroughfares appear to have been dictated by wind direction. The street patterning was designed to catch the fresh breeze by those who were familiar with the local climate and environment and, probably for the same purpose, the house ventilations were opened on the side of the main streets. This arrangement and the high sense of sanitation and strict observance of the rules of regularity suggest a community of people who were certainly disciplinary and punctilious in their behaviour patterns at least during the mature phase of the Indus Civilization.

Mohenjo-daro

The two cities of Mohenjo-daro and Harappa (Fig. 1) are preserved disproportionately. The ruins of the former city present a grand view from the riverside, the Indus river of today being at a remove of 5 km. A brick-built embankment,[42] apparently old, protects the city. From a distance the round stupa of the later Buddhists appears crowning the older protohistoric ruins of the citadel mound. What is buried beneath the stupa yet remains to be excavated. A lane west of the stupa has been named 'Divinity Street' from associated religious antiques. From

39. Wheeler, 1968, Fig. 6.
40. Lal, 1981.
41. Dani, 1970/71, Plate IVb.
42. Wheeler, 1968, p. 37.

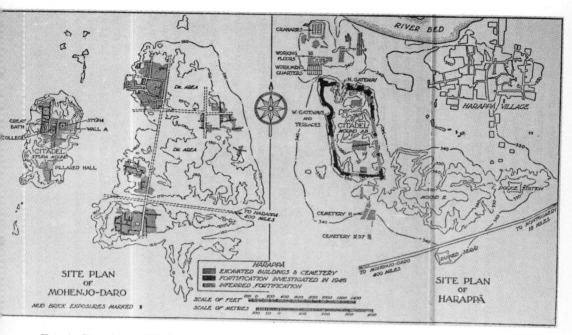

FIG. 1. Site plans of Mohenjo-daro and Harappa.

this street five doorways lead onto a massive structure on the west, which measures 70 × 23 m. Its nucleus consists of an open court of 10 m², with verandas on three sides facing rooms behind. Many of the rooms are carefully faced with bricks, and there are at least two staircases. It is an imposing building of unusual importance and generally referred to as an educational institution. But the most unique building, farther to the west, beyond another lane, is the Great Bath (Fig. 2), consisting of a tank, 12 m long north to south, 7 m broad and 2.5 m deep, with steps leading down to the floor from two sides, built of fine bricks rubbed and carefully made watertight by using gypsum mortar. Furthermore, precaution has been taken by putting a 2.5-cm-thick damp-proof course of bitumen held by a further wall of brick and retained by mud-bricks. All around the tank is a corridor which opens through ranges of brick pier or jambs. Behind them on one side there are other rooms, one of which contains a large well which apparently supplied water to the tank. Near the south-western corner an outlet, a corbel-arched drain about a man's height, was provided. Farther away to the north is a block containing eight smaller bathrooms, each about 3 × 2 m, carefully and solidly built, with finely jointed brick floors, and disposed, on either side of a passage, in a fashion ensuring that none of the doors opened opposite any other. These bathrooms appear to have an upper storey, supposed to have been residential in nature. This whole complex of the Great Bath and smaller bathrooms has a meaning beyond proper comprehension at present. Its public character can be easily guessed but the attribution of any other concept may well be premature.

FIG. 2. Mohenjo-daro: the Great Bath.

Immediately to the west of the Great Bath is the Granary, standing on a massive brick-work podium with a loading platform on its northern side. As the corbelled drain of the Great Bath cuts the eastern end of this platform the original granary is earlier in date than the bath. The Granary consists of a series of brick plinths, rectangular or square in plan, each separated by air passages. It is on these plinths that granary stores were built, some with wooden supports. A later addition to the Granary on the south was made contemporarily and in line with the Great Bath, and both of them opened on to a southern lane. On this side Wheeler further identified a grand staircase leading from the level of the plain to the top of the platform, where stood a small bathroom. It is the battered walls of the outer side of the high podium of the Granary that led to the idea of a citadel at Mohenjo-daro. But strictly speaking, Mohenjo-daro has not as yet produced evidence of any continuous city wall around this high mound, which is almost a parallelogram in shape. However, the south-west corner does show a salient that looks as though it is concealing a tower. A series of towers were actually found in the south-east corner of the 1950 excavations. These square towers, which are of solid brick, except the earliest which showed slots for timber beams, were meant to strengthen this corner. But the walls on the north and the west do not continue to any great length. What was taken to be a 'parapet wall' by Wheeler may be a curtain wall between two towers. Further to the north the later floods penetrated deep into the mound and partly separated the northern half from the southern. In the southern half one important building has been exposed. It consists of a pillared hall with a platform on the southern side corresponding to a later Iranian type of *apadana*.

Harappa

The buildings of the citadel mound of Mohenjo-daro can be compared with what remains at the citadel of Harappa, where the fortification walls were traced in the 1946 excavation.[43] Unfortunately the structures within the citadel are poorly preserved but outside to the north three types of buildings were found. The first is a granary consisting of a series of six storerooms in two rows on either side of a corridor. To its south is another group of circular platforms meant for threshing corn. Still further is a series of two-roomed houses of utilitarian type and hence taken to be workmen's quarters. These buildings at Harappa make a different setting from what we have seen at Mohenjo-daro.

As far as the 'lower town' is concerned, Mohenjo-daro presents a good example, where S. Piggott built up a pattern of a series of blocks of houses arranged in a grid-iron system. The idea of such blocks can be easily conceived from the system of housing units, which have a central open courtyard with living rooms along the sides in the oriental style, the main door opening on to a lane with a wall provided near the door. The houses, which are simple and plastered with mud, also had second storeys. Some had latrines with seats on the ground floor. Attempts have been made to recognize in the structure some temple, palace, inn and industrial quarters. But except for the potter's area of a later period, recognition of quarters for specialized crafts has so far not been successful.

Social stratification has been difficult to determine even on the basis of burials discovered at Harappa, Kalibangan and Lothal. The material from cemetery R–37 at Harappa enabled Wheeler to speak of one single system of inhumation practised by the Indus people, though other sites have produced other types as well. The Harappan burials are all of humble folk and do not show any great variation. Here the skeletons lie extended in the north–south direction accompanied by grave furniture consisting of some fifteen to twenty pots, personal ornaments like shell bangles, necklaces and anklets of steatite or paste beads as well as toilet objects such as a copper mirror, mother-of-pearl shells, an antimony rod and a shell spoon. Only two graves show some special features; one was outlined internally with mud-bricks, suggesting a structural coffin, and the other was buried in a wooden coffin, the wood being *deodar*.

43. Wheeler, 1947.

(a)

(b)

(c)

(d)

FIG. 3. (a) Harappa: a seal showing a birth scene; (b) Mohenjo-daro: a seal showing a tree with two chimerical heads; (c) Mohenjo-daro: a seal showing a tree deity and other figures; (d) Mohenjo-daro: a seal showing a horned deity in a yogic posture.

From burial practices we may go on to examine religious rituals and beliefs and seek to understand the pattern of the Indus society. Although no structural evidence for a temple can be definitely cited, other objects suggest a multiplicity of religious ideas. While J. Marshall has tried to trace many of the later Indian practices to these ideas, others prefer to confine themselves to building the great religious tradition of the Indus people with which the little traditions of various communities became integrated. On this consideration the Great Tradition could be attributed to the nature of the urban set-up and the Little Traditions may appertain to the mass of the village population who must have subsisted side by side with their own humble beliefs.

For an agricultural society of this type the concept of the fertility cult must have exerted a great influence. The discoveries of a large number of terracotta figurines of an almost nude female has suggested the idea of a village mother goddess. With them are associated terracotta figurines of pregnant women with children. There is a remarkable scene (Fig. 3a) depicted on a seal from Harappa that shows a birth scene. The seal bears an inscription of six characters not yet deciphered. On one side two genii are standing, on the other a male is standing with a cutting instrument in his right hand. Before him is a seated lady with her hands raised up and hair dishevelled in distraught mood. The top scene apparently shows the same female upside down with something emerging from her female organ – obviously a representation of childbirth. What the idea is behind such a scene cannot be exactly stated but here certainly some fertility idea has attracted the attention and found expression in this remarkable sealing. Marshall would also like to attribute his recognition of the phallus (lingam) and ringstones to similar beliefs. The second great element in the popular beliefs is seen in the many animals represented on the seals. Some of the animals are multi-headed and some multi-bodied, and some are no doubt mythological in so far as they combine in a single figure the attributes of several animals. Among these animals the bull certainly predominates. The appearance of the unicorn on a large number of seals still remains enigmatic. Even if these animals were not actually worshipped, an animal spirit appears to have been a component part of religious beliefs and may be seen in the figure of many horned deities.

Another popular idea can be traced in the depiction of trees or tree-trunks on the seals. A tree within a railing is a common feature. These by themselves may not be of any great significance, but combined with the appearance of a pipal leaf motif, noted on several painted pots or carved on seals, they begin to acquire some meaning. One seal (Fig. 3b) actually shows two heads coming out of a tree suggesting an idea of a living spirit of the tree. The concept of a tree deity is obtained from other seals where a horned figure stands within a tree motif (Fig. 3c). Here the humble tradition of village folk has become integrated in a ceremonious performance that speaks of urban sophistication.

The tree deity, who is horned and has a pigtail hanging down to one side, stands within a leafy pedestalled bowl. Before her a horned personage kneels down in a supplicating mood and appears to invoke the deity through the intermediary of a mythological animal standing behind. On the lower row stand seven plumed and pig-tailed figures probably awaiting their own chance. Whether these secondary figures are meant for worship or for sacrifice is difficult to say. But the whole scene is a remarkable representation of an intensely emotional ceremony. Such tree deities are also depicted alone. In another example the kneeling man, with a sharp-edged knife in his hand, is pushing a deer before the deity as if in the act of sacrifice. Many of the seals depict a 'standard' below the mouth of the unicorn. The emblematic nature of this object is clear from another seal where it is carried in combination with a bull on an altar in the middle with a fluttering flag in front. From Harappa comes another seal,[44] which shows two scenes besides some writing. The lower one has a horned bull to the left with a standing man in between facing a structure, probably wooden, a square in two storeys with pinnacle tops and a vestibule in front. The upper row depicts two growling tigers on either side of a remarkable human figure sitting on a high-legged seat on his heels, with his toes touching the seat and his knees doubled; his bangled hands rest on his knees, and his head, which is not very distinct, is apparently horned. In another seal the same horned man in a similar pose is being worshipped with folded hands by two men, one on each side. These worshippers have cobra hoods behind them, recalling *naga devas* (serpent deities) of a later period. The pose of the seated deity is more simple. Marshall proposed to see in it a *yogic* posture. The deity has a remarkable history and can be traced back to the horned deities seen in the painted sherds of the pre-Indus period. The iconography of the figure reveals the various composite elements. On a clay tablet from Kalibangan the figure is crowned by a simple tree. On a seal from Mohenjo-daro the crown is horned. But a more stylized figure appears on another seal (Fig. 3d). Here the seated deity has an erect male organ and is multifaced, the horned crown has a stylized stump in the middle and a series of torques around the neck. Below the seat are two ibexes. Four animals are round the seated figure who appears to be motionless in a trance. Out of the four animals the elephant is receding while a tiger, a rhinoceros and a bull are in an aggressive mood. Marshall sees in him a 'prototype of Śiva' a concept which is biased towards modern Indian beliefs. On the other hand, the different component elements are already there in contemporary beliefs. The representation here is an integrated concept of a sophisticated type that must have evolved in the urban setting of the Indus Civilization.

There are some extraneous elements, like the figures of Gilgamesh and Enkidu, also appearing in Indus seals. But the religious repertoire would not be complete without mentioning the limestone statues. In one example there is a bearded figure with half-closed eyes. In a second example the man is seated in a half-kneeling position with his hands on his knees and a *shawl* over the body with

---

44. Vats, 1940, Plate XCIII, No. 303.

FIG. 4. Mohenjo-daro: stone bust of a 'priest-king'.

(a)

Fig. 5.
(a) Mohenjo-daro:
bronze figurine of a
dancing girl;
(b) Mohenjo-daro:
terracotta female
figurine.

(b)

298

the right shoulder bare. The third is a highly sophisticated bust of a man (Fig. 4), with his beard trimmed, upper lip shaven, half-closed eyes looking at the tip of a sharp nose, hair combed and held by a gold fillet, ears imitating a shell design, a ring armlet on his right arm, and a *shawl* over his body except for the right shoulder. The *shawl* is decorated with the trefoil design. It is this statue that has been taken to be a 'priest king' though we have no evidence of any priestly dominance in the Indus Civilization.

The statuettes, seals, terracotta figurines and several other decorative objects also reveal the artistic trends of the time. A total number of eleven stone statuettes have been recovered at Mohenjo-daro, nine of which are human or parts of human figures and two are animals. One human is made of steatite, two humans are of alabaster and the remainder are of limestone. One animal is clearly a ram but another is a composite animal with ram's horns and an elephant's trunk. These figures are all drawn in a conventional style and show a tendency that leaves very little choice for freedom. In physical depictions they have an individuality of their own though it is possible to detect some correspondence with Mesopotamian figures, for example, in the shaven upper lip, sturdy neck, trefoil design on the *shawl*, and the use of inlay for the eyes. All the figures are modelled and belong to a tradition hieratic in origin. On the other hand, there are two other statuettes found at Harappa which belong to an entirely different school.

The first is a young *danseuse* in grey stone, who is headless with parts of her legs broken, showing remarkable movement as reconstructed by Marshall. The second figure, which is also headless with its arms and legs missing, is modelled in red sandstone and shows the use of tubular drills for the attachment of arms. The muscles are depicted in a superb and naturalistic fashion. Such a naturalistic representation is seen in the case of animals and seals. Particularly, the drawing of the two-horned bull shows a power of keen observation. It is here that Indus art is seen to be far removed from the general run of Indian art, which is generally stylized and over-burdened with iconographic details. The Indus art, as seen in the seals, is steeped in naturalism and the scenes represented on the sealings are derived from the usual activities of man. Unfortunately the sculptures are confined to small figurines. There is nothing to compare with the huge statues of the Egyptian civilization.

A remarkable figure in the round is of a bronze dancing girl (Fig. 5a) which is highly emotional. Although her feet are broken, her remaining bent leg still speaks of the free movement associated with dancers. Her bangled left hand appears to produce a ringing musical sound when striking her wrist on her thigh, while her lips, which are thick and protruding, are open to a soft tune of a song. The figure, which is totally nude, has its hair drawn stylistically to one side. It has been compared to the temple girls of a later period. In physiognomy it is different from other figures but in the free movement of its limbs it carries the agile spirit of the time.

Fɪɢ. 6. Mohenjo-daro: terracotta toy-cart.

The terracotta figurines, both human and animal, represent the folk art of the time. Among them cattle are preponderant, generally humped bulls, but short-horned ones and buffalo also occur. The cow is not depicted at all. Other animals include dogs, sheep, elephants, rhinoceros, pigs, monkeys, turtles and birds. The human figurines are mostly females in different activities or postures. The standing female figurines (Fig. 5b) are very common, with a loincloth held by a girdle, a series of beaded necklaces, ear paniers and a fan-shaped head-dress. All these figurines are hand-modelled with appliqué technique used for attachments. Some are very appealing, suggesting that they are more than ordinary toys. However, there was no scarcity of toys, which included bird whistles, wheeled carts (Fig. 6) and animals with holed legs to be drawn by children. Terracotta was the poor man's medium of expression. This was also used for utilitarian objects like feeder bottles, rattles, bangles for ladies, cubical or tabular discs, spoons, mousetraps, flesh rubbers, etc. The most abundant are the carrot-shaped cones of plain terracotta, terracotta cakes of triangular shape and rounded missiles. The cones look like carrots and are assumed to be used as styli and the cakes as oven stands or for toilet purposes.

Faience is another material used for modelling animals or for making other objects like bracelets, finger rings, studs, buttons and inlays for caskets and furniture. The faience was composed of crushed steatite pressed and modelled to produce the object desired. It was then coated with a glaze and fused in a kiln. The colour as seen today is light blue or green. Faience materials are normally small, yielding tiny figurines of sheep, monkeys, dogs and squirrels.

Faience was also used for making beads, barrel-shaped or convex-bicone, and they were carved with a trefoil design cut with a drill. The bead-making craft was highly developed in the Indus Civilization. Besides faience, other materials include gold, silver, copper, steatite, semi-precious stones, shell and pottery. E. J. Mackay[45] gives the detail of a bead-maker's shop from his excavations at Chanhu-daro, where the processes of sawing, flaking, grinding and boring the stone beads are well illustrated. A series of gold beads was included in a hoard of jewellery found at Mohenjo-daro. The silver beads are mostly globular or barrel-shaped. Another significant type of faience is the segmented bead. Decorated carnelian and etched beads are well known. The trefoil design seen on the beads is the same as that seen in the *shawl*. At Harappa a great mass of jewellery of gold and semi-precious stones was found underneath the workmen's quarters. There were nearly 500 pieces of gold, ranging from armlets to beads and many complete necklaces made up of multiple strings of beads and metal.

Two other materials used by the Indus people for preparing decorated designs are lapis lazuli and shell. The lapis, which was imported from Badakhshan, was sparingly used, but shell was plentifully available on the sea-coast. It was used for making various types of bangles, studs, cones and cut into different designs for decorative purposes. The shell industry was highly developed.

The metal industry of the Indus people shows many curious and interesting features. S. Piggot[46] has commented that the metalsmiths were manufacturing objects in copper, either crude or refined, in bronze (copper with approximately 10 per cent of tin deliberately or accidently added); and in copper-arsenic alloy, almost certainly accidental but one which gave an added hardness to the metal. The commonest techniques used in metallurgy included casting and forging. Casting was done by pouring molten metal into a mould. As this process required special care to avoid bubbles, by the addition of a small percentage of tin or arsenic, it appears to have been used very sparingly. However, the lost-wax method must have given good results. It is by this method that the dancing girl statuette was made. But other tools of copper or bronze were cast by the simple technique. These included simple flat-type axes, tanged spearheads, barbed harpoons, arrowheads, razors, knives, handled mirrors and, occasionally, shaft-hole axes. Copper or bronze was abundantly used for making metal pots, pans, bowls, cups, dishes and small bottles. The find of spindle-whorls and many cloth impressions in the Indus cities is evidence of the growth of textile manufacture out of the good-quality cotton produced in the Indus plains.

For means of transport the Indus people used carts with solid wheels that were tied to the axle and which turned round along with the axle, a type of small

---

45. Mackay, 1943, pp. 180, 210.
46. Piggott, 1950, p. 196.

cart that is still in use in the villages of Sind. Two types of river-going ships have been noted. One depicted on a seal shows the high prow, central cabin and double steering oar. Before the cabin are poles apparently to hold the standard. At Lothal other terracotta ship models have also been found.

Although a few stone vessels have been found, pottery was the basic manufacture. Potter's kilns, about six in number, have been found in the latest phase of Mohenjo-daro. They are circular, with a stokehole and furnace beneath a perforated floor originally covered by a domed roof. The pottery from the Indus is for the most part plain, mass produced for utilitarian purposes. The vessels, which have thick sides, are well baked and produce a ringing sound when beaten with the fingers. The commonest type is an offering stand with narrow tapering base, probably a development of the pedestalled bowls of the earlier period. Other types include beakers, pointed-base goblets, handled cups, jar stands, perforated cylindrical vessels and varieties of vases, pans and plates. Specialized types are knobbed-ware pottery and perforated vessels. The great bulk of material is wheel-turned, but some hand-made vessels have been recovered from lower levels. Goblets with pointed bottoms and scored exteriors are found in great numbers in the later levels. Some of them bear a short stamped inscription. Most of the pottery is of pinkish ware made of alluvial river-clay mixed with other ingredients. It is coated with bright red slip. The decorated pottery has designs painted in black on a red background. The designs are equally divided between geometric and naturalistic with trees, birds, fish and animals.

The Indus pottery is heavy, well made and sharply contrasts with the delicate vessels of the pre-Indus cultures. Among the distinctive patterns the intersecting circle motif, the pipal leaf, the chequer design and the kidney-shaped motif occur in a mass of foliage and tendrils. Among birds the peacock takes its place. Some of the painted sherds also show human figures. A painted sherd from Harappa shows a fisherman, carrying two nets suspended from a pole across his shoulders with a fish and turtle near his feet. Another sherd shows a doe suckling her kid, with two birds, a fish and a star in the upper part of the panel and secondly a man with one hand raised and the other touching his head, and a child with upraised arms along with fishes and a cock in the field. Wheeler noted that painted decoration is of better quality in the lower levels so far explored at Mohenjo-daro.

Such a diverse paraphernalia of urban civilization could hardly be controlled without a system of writing. It is therefore not surprising that the Indus people adopted a system of writing to suit their purposes. However, this written system has been found in a fully developed form as seen in the many steatite seals and sealings, copper tablets and some stamped on pots and other objects. In the absence of its earlier evolutionary process the beginning of the writing remains unknown, though we have been able to trace some pot marks[47] which bear some

47. Fairservis, 1975.

resemblance to symbols used in the Indus writing. The inscriptions so far discovered are limited to a few signs on the seals and there is a lack of longer inscriptions with the result that great difficulty is faced in the structural analysis of the writing. However, attempts have been made to make a full list of the inscriptions,[48] draw up a comparative chart and to break the sign lists into suffixes, main stem, accent marks and numerals.[49] There have also been attempts to decipher[50] them on the basis of analogies and on the supposed basis of the language being some form of proto-Dravidian or some other language. Failing in these deciphering attempts, some scholars[51] have tried to interpret them directly on the basis of their own understanding of the cultural pattern. But in the absence of bilingual inscriptions there is no check to the phonetic value given to different symbols. So far the Indus writing has remained undeciphered as it is written in an unknown script and an unknown language. The system of writing is neither pictographic nor alphabetic. It is in the intermediate stage, referred to as logographic or logo-syllabic,[52] and it appears to have been limited to a class of literati who managed the professional control concerned primarily with the urban set-up. As the writing started full blown in the Indus Civilization, it did not leave behind any trace of the post-urban scene that developed in this part after its decline.

This literate urban civilization of the Indus valley, although rooted in the maximum exploitation of the fertility of the Indus alluvium on the basis of the available knowledge of technology, flourished at a time when there was the greatest amount of sea-faring activity in the Arabian Sea, between the older civilizations of Mesopotamia and the Indus region and along the littoral of Makran and southern Iran. In terms of the Mesopotamia chronology[53] it coincides with the old Akkadian and Ur III phases. The decline of this sea-trading activity coincides favourably with the latter part of the Mesopotamian Isin-Larsa period. In terms of C14 dates the beginning of the mature phase of the Indus Civilization cannot be placed earlier than 2500 B.C. in round figures and the end should be placed somewhat about 1900 B.C.

In the last phase the city of Mohenjo-daro shows a slackness in the observance of rules regarding the alignment of walls, which are now found to intrude into the streets. Some more squat type of loose construction using older bricks was also noted by Wheeler in his excavations at Mohenjo-daro and Harappa. The old urban set-up appears to have collapsed in a way that has not left sufficient evidence for proper analysis. The Mesopotamian evidence does show that there was a break in the overseas trade and this break must have deeply affected the economic base of the state. On the other hand, the Indus floods, which were recur-

48. Koskenniemi and Parpola, 1973; Mahadevan, 1977.
49. Ross, 1938.
50. Pande, 1969.
51. Meriggi, 1934.
52. Zide, 1970.
53. Dales, 1973.

ring phenomena, must have created further difficulties by the over deposit of silt and mud. Whatever may be the reason, this urban pattern crashed to a degree that did not leave behind those distinguishing features that characterized the urban nature of the civilization, and what remained later was a continuity in the rural survival of the older life.

The above description of the Indus Civilization is derived mainly from the sites in the Indus valley. But now the geographical horizon of this civilization is greatly widened.

Within about four years of the partition of the subcontinent, planned surveys were undertaken in India to locate more Indus Civilization sites in the regions contiguous to the frontiers of Pakistan – in Rajasthan and Punjab for an eastward extension and in Gujarat for the southward. The exploration of the Ghaggar valley, conducted in 1951/52, resulted in the discovery of as many as twenty-five Harappan sites within the present-day borders of India in the region beginning right from the Pakistan border (eastwards) up to mid-way between Hanumangarh and Suratgarh in the Sarasvati valley and about 22 km east of Bhadra in the Drishadvati valley.[54] Noteworthy among these sites was also Kalibangan, which has been subjected to large-scale excavation the findings of which remain still to be fully published. During 1952–55, excavation was undertaken at Rupar, not very far from Kotla Nihang Khan, where the Harappan remains were found for the first time stratified between the deposit yielding the painted grey ware and the natural soil.[55] Three years later a similar sequence was identified at Alamgirpur, some 45 km north of Delhi on the Hindan, a tributary of the Jamuna, and recently again at Hulas across the Jamuna. Further explorations in Rajasthan, Haryana, Punjab, Jammu and Kashmir and in Meerut and Saharanpur districts of Uttar Pradesh added more Harappan and late Harappan sites in this (eastern) region. With these discoveries the eastern limit of the Indus Civilization now extends to Alamgirpur, across the Indo-Gangetic divide, and the northern limit to Manda, located on the right bank of the Chenab in the foothills of the Pir Panjal range, 28 km west of Jammu.

As regards the distribution pattern, no mature Harappan sites have so far been located in the present-day valleys of the Sutlej and Beas with the singular exception of Kotla Nihang Khan and Rupar situated on the left bank of the Sutlej in the foothills of the Siwaliks. On the other hand, there is a chain of pre-Harappan and Harappan sites in the valleys of various streams like Sirhind Nadi Sarasvati, Markanda, Patialvi, including Chautang (ancient Drishadvati), all contributing to the Ghaggar (ancient Sarasvati) system. Late Harappan settlements are, however, found both in the Ghaggar-Sarasvati system and in the Sutlej basin. Among the excavated sites in this region, Rupar and Manda, located in the foothills, represent the limit of the ecological zone which the pre-Harappans or

54. Gosh, 1952; Anon., 1955; Sankalia and Deo, 1979; Pandya, 1958, 1959; Deshpande, 1959; Sali, 1981; Soundara Rajan, 1967; Joshi, 1979, 1980; Dikshit, 1981.
55. Sharma, 1956.

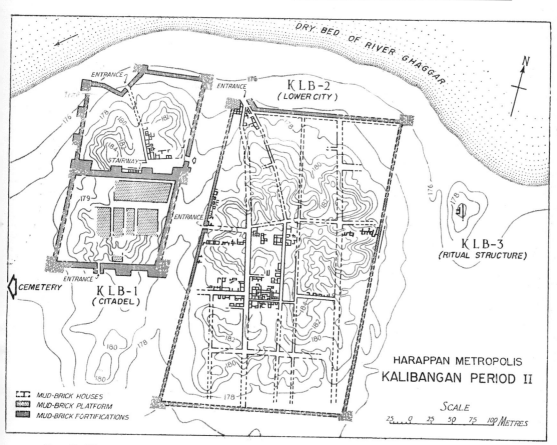

FIG. 7. Plan of Kalibangan.

Harappans could exploit, besides being important centres for supplying teak to the settlements in the valleys below. Similarly, Alamgirpur and Hulas located across the divide of the Indus and Jamuna systems, mark the eastern limit of the ecological zone, beyond which lay the real Indian monsoon-fed jungle which the Indus people found difficult to civilize without an ample supply of metal (perhaps iron).

On the southern side, excavations were resumed at Rangpur in 1947[56] and again in 1953.[57] Thereafter large areas in Gujarat, including Kutch and Kathiawad, were extensively explored, resulting in the location of several Harappan and late Harappan sites, the southernmost being situated on the estuary of the Kim.[58] Recent excavations at Daimabad, located on the Pravara, a tributary of the Godavari, has now extended the limit of the Indus Civilization further south up to almost the latitude of Bombay in the Ahmadnagar District of Maharashatra.

56. Dikshit, 1950.
57. Rao, 1962/63, 1973, 1978a.
58. Rao, 1963; Possehl, 1979a; Raikes, 1968.

As regards the distribution pattern, we find that the spread of the Indus Civilization was not uniform in this southern region, being conditioned by areas of attraction, namely coastal flats, fertile river valleys, estuarine plains, routes of communication, etc. No mature Harappan sites have so far been located in the narrow corridor connecting the Kutch and Kathiawad peninsula with the mainland. The Harappan expansion to Gujarat may perhaps be explained by the urge to search for raw materials (timber, ivory, carnelian) and ports. Among the excavated sites in this region Lothal, Prabhas Patan and Bhagatrav were located on the coast, indicating coastal movement of the Harappans, and Surkotada on the possible land route connecting Lower Sind with Kutch and the estuarine plains of north-western parts of Gujarat. We may now turn to the principal sites *seriatim*.

Kalibangan and other eastern sites

Kalibangan, a site of considerable importance in the Ghaggar valley with a two-fold culture sequence, has already been referred to in Chapter 11 wherein the characteristics of its pre-Indus and early Indus occupations were discussed.[59] The Harappan metropolis at this site consisted of two principal parts: the citadel on the west, represented by a smaller mound (KLB I); and the lower city towards the east, represented by a fairly extensive mound (KLB 2). The former was situated atop the remains of the preceding occupation to gain an eminence over the lower city which was laid out towards the east, leaving a gap of over 40 m.

The citadel complex is roughly a parallelogram, some 240 m from north to south and 120 m from east to west consisting of two almost equal but separately patterned parts, rhomboid on plan, with a bipartite wall in between and reinforced at intervals with rectangular bastions (Fig. 7). The fortifications were built throughout of mud-bricks of two sizes (40 × 20 × 10 cm and 30 × 15 × 7.5 cm) representing two principal phases of construction, the larger one in the earlier phase and the smaller one in the later. On the north and west, the fortification wall overlies that of the preceding period, while on the east and south including the bipartite portion, it was built on the ruins of the earlier occupation, obviously to achieve the proportion of 1:2.

The southern half of the citadel was more heavily fortified not only with corner bastions but also with rectangular salients along the southern and northern (bipartite wall) sides, the latter projecting imposingly into the areas of the northern half, indicating thereby that the southern half formed the main part of the citadel complex. The enclosed area contained some five to six massive platforms of mud and mud-bricks. Of these, the complete outline of one (50 × 25 m) and sizeable portions of four have so far been exposed. Access to the working floors of platforms was by means of steps which rose from the passage. Of the buildings that stood upon these platforms, no intelligible plans are available,

59. Thapar, B. K., 1973*a*, 1973*b*, 1975, 1978, 1981, 1982; Vats, 1937.

FIG. 8. Kalibangan: excavated street in the northern part of the citadel.

being obscured by the depredations of brick-robbers. Nevertheless the available remains do indicate that these might have been used for religious or ritual purposes of a public character. On the only one with a surviving complete plan, besides a well and a fire altar, a rectangular pit (1.24 × 1 m) was built with baked bricks and contained bovine bones and antler representing perhaps a sacrifice; on top of another was noticed a row of seven rectangular fire-altars aligned in north–south axis. A short distance away on the same platform was a well with some bath-pavements. Baked brick drains ran through the passages carrying ablution water.

The entrances to this part of the citadel were located on the south and north. The southern one was situated between the central salient and the north-western corner bastion. The passage, which has been extensively ransacked for bricks, seems to have been a stepped one fronting the fortification wall. The northern entrance comprised a mud-brick stairway, which running along the outer face of the bipartite fortification wall, between the two centrally located salients, led up to the required height at which passage across the fortification wall was provided. From the locations of the entrances it is surmised that the

307

southern may have been the main one intended for the general public from the 'lower city' and the northern that for the dwellers in the residential annexe (i.e. the northern half) of the citadel. The structural features of both these entrances precluded the possibility of any vehicular traffic within the southern half of the citadel.

The northern half, which was also fortified, contained residential buildings, perhaps of the élite, including the priestly class. A complete street plan of this part of the citadel has not been exposed. Meanwhile, a thoroughfare running north–south has been partially explored (Fig. 8). Starting from the easterly of the two salients of the partition fortification wall it ran obliquely in the direction of the entrance on the north. There were three entrances to this part of the citadel on the eastern, northern and western sides, none of which were of the ramp or stairway type.

The 'lower city' was also a parallelogram, some 240 m from east to west and 360 m from north to south and lay to the east beyond a broad space of 40 m. It was also found to be enclosed by a fortification wall. Within it there was a gridiron or irregular net plan of streets running north to south and east to west, dividing the area into blocks. The existence of four arterial thoroughfares running north to south and three (with an indication for the fourth in the northern part) running east to west was established by excavation. Besides, there were quite a few lanes that served only one or two blocks. The streets do not seem to lead to any important building or open public space. The width of the thoroughfares seems to have been maintained throughout the occupation, the only structural encroachments into the thoroughfares being rectangular platforms immediately outside some of the houses which may have represented semi-public spaces serving as bazars or for sitting and gossiping. The streets, except in the late phase were unmetalled. No evidence of regular street-drains has so far been encountered: house-drains discharged themselves into soakage jars buried under street floors.

Two entrances to the walled area were exposed by excavation. Of these, one was located on the west and the other in the north-western angle. From the location of these two entrances, it could be inferred that the western one was used by the city-dwellers for communicating with the citadel and the northern one for the city's commercial river traffic. It is likely that there may have been other entrances particularly on the east and south. From the very beginning of the occupation, the houses were built of mud-bricks (30 × 15 × 17.5 cm), the use of baked bricks (both of the same size and of wedge-shaped type) being confined mostly to drains, wells, sills and bathing-pavements. Some of the houses had a 'fire altar' in one of the rooms, intended for private ritual.

Besides the above two principal parts of the metropolis, there was also a third one, namely a modest structure situated upwards of 80 m east of the lower city. The structure, of which the complete outline could not be recovered, consisted of an impressive wall enclosing a room containing four to five 'fire altars' located individually. The absence of any normal occupation on this mound suggests that the lonely structure with the fire altars was used for ritual purposes.

The cemetery of the Harappans was located upwards of 300 m west-south-west of the citadel. Three types of burials were attested: (a) extended inhumation in rectangular or oval graves along with pottery and other funerary objects; (b) pot-burials in a circular pit; and (c) rectangular or oval graves containing only funerary furnishings. The latter two methods were unassociated with any skeletal remains.

The finds including pottery obtained from the occupation of this period were all characteristic of the Indus Civilization. Among these the following deserve special mention: (a) a cylinder seal; (b) a terracotta cake incised on the obverse with a horned human figurine and on the reverse with a human figure pulling an obscure object (perhaps an animal); (c) a terracotta human head; (d) a copper bull showing the dynamic mood of the animal; (e) a terracotta graduated scale; and (f) an ivory comb.

Environmental studies have indicated that one of the compelling reasons for the abandonment of Kalibangan was the drying up of the Ghaggar river.

Banawali is situated along the ancient bank of the Sarasvati river (now merely a storm-water drain known as Rangoi), some 220 km north-west of Delhi. A threefold sequence of cultures has been identified at this site, of which the upper one belongs to the late Harappan, the middle one to the Harappan and the lower one to the pre-Harappan occupation. During the Harappan occupation, the settlement was fortified, showing two subjoined parts, with a bipartite wall, the south-western quarters perhaps used as a citadel and the remaining part as a residential annexe. The former, as at Kalibangan, was located on top of the pre-Harappan occupational strata to gain an eminence. An intercommunicating entrance reinforced by a massive square salient seems to have been provided in the mid-portion of the partition wall. No structures within the citadel have so far been exposed. The residential part was found, however, to be subdivided into an irregular plan, and not a complete chessboard. The houses were made of mud-bricks of average size, 30 × 15 × 7.5 cm. As at Kalibangan, larger-sized bricks of average size 40 × 20 × 10 cm were used for the fortification walls. The typical finds recovered from the deposits of this period include cubical weights, seals bearing the Indus script, long chert blades, copper or bronze arrow- and spear-heads, fish hooks, bangles, a double spiral-headed pin, gold beads, including one of copper with a gold foil and painted pottery. Noteworthy among these finds, however, are two examples of terracotta mother-goddess figurines with characteristic head-dress. It may be recalled that this type, though commonly found at Harappa and Mohenjo-daro, is completely absent in the southern and eastern regions, even at the extensively excavated sites of Kalibangan and Lothal.

The late Harappan occupation, the remains of which were found outside the walled town on the east, was attested by a number of pits containing pottery which was different alike in fabric and decoration from the Harappan.

Mitathal lies some 118 km north-west of Delhi along the dried-up former course of the Jamuna.[60] The site attracted the attention of archaeologists through chance finds, while ploughing, of two copper harpoons and, through canal digging, of thirteen copper rings. Excavation revealed a twofold sequence of cultures of which the latter was further divided into two sub-periods, labelled Period I, Sub-period IIA and Sub-period IIB. Of these, Period I represented a stage when both the pre-Harappans and Harappans lived together, though with a larger bias towards the former, as indicated by the pottery. The structures were built of mudbricks $30 \times 20 \times 10$ cm in size as prevalent at Kalibangan in Period I. Sub-period IIA is characterized by the typical Indus equipment including pottery, household objects and architecture. The pre-Harappan element (labelled here as Siswal B), continued in a lesser degree. The houses were made of mud-bricks $40 \times 20 \times 10$ or $36 \times 18 \times 9$ cm in size. Cubical agate weights, a few long blades also of chert, triangular terracotta cakes and toy-cart wheels, faience and terracotta bangles and pottery confirm the Harappan affiliation of the site. Sub-period IIB is distinguished by a general deterioration and impoverishment of the material culture of the Harappans. The pottery shows degeneration in treatment and decoration apart from introduction of new forms. The surface find of the harpoons in all likelihood may have belonged to this phase.

Manda is situated 28 km west of Jammu on the right bank of the Chenab river, in the foothills of the Pir Panjal range.[61] The excavation revealed a 9-m-thick occupation deposit, a threefold sequence of cultures with two sub-periods in the earliest. Sub-period IA is marked by the occupation of the Harappans. Besides the typical Harappan pottery and terracotta cakes, sherds of pre-Harappan fabric were also found in the deposits belonging to this sub-period. Perforated jars were conspicuously absent in this assemblage. A noteworthy find, however, was a double spiral-headed pin of copper. Sub-period IB shows two distinct ceramic traditions, namely Harappan red ware and the plain grey ware, usually associated with the well-known painted grey ware. Periods II and III belong to the historical period.

Hulas is situated some 140 km north-east of Delhi across the Jamuna river in Saharanpur District. The excavation[62] yielded a fivefold sequence of cultures of which the earliest belonged to the Harappan culture and the remaining to the historical. A seal bearing Indus characteristics confirms the Harappan affiliation of the site.

Bara lies some 8 km south of Rupar. The excavation[63] revealed an occupation of over 4 m thick, in which such typical forms as Indus goblets or terracotta cakes were rare, confined to the lower levels. The antecedents of this culture are

60. Suraj Bhan, 1975, 1976.
61. Joshi and Bala, 1982; see *IAR*, 1978–80.
62. Sali, 1981.
63. Sharma, 1976.

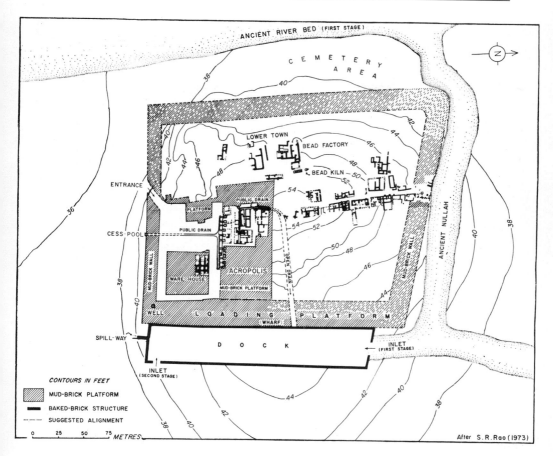

Fig. 9. Plan of Lothal.

traceable to a pre-Harappan tradition. Harappan elements are also represented in this assemblage albeit in a transformed manner.

Bhagwanpura is situated on the right bank of the Sarasvati. The excavations[64] revealed, in a 2.7-m-thick occupation stratum, a twofold sequence of cultures of which the earlier was represented by the late Harappan and the later, which was found interlocked with the preceding one, by the painted grey ware culture. This evidence purports to fill the earlier gap between the two cultures. A noteworthy find from the overlapped phase was a terracotta seal, bearing incised Indus characters. An identical culture sequence was also observed at Dadheri in the Sutlej valley.

64. Joshi, 1979.

FIG. 10. Lothal: Brick structure, known as a dockyard, with a spillway in the foreground.

Lothal and other southern sites

Lothal is situated on the coastal flats at the head of the Gulf of Cambay[65] 80 km south-west of Ahmedabad. Being located only 16 km north-west of the junction of Sabarmati and Bhogawo rivers it was subjected to frequent floods. At the same time it had the advantage of commanding the navigable estuaries of both these rivers. The settlement, therefore, had to be reinforced with mud and mud-bricks against flooding on more than one occasion. The excavations revealed five phases of continuous occupation, of which the first four labelled Lothal A, are Harappan and the fifth, labelled Lothal B, variant or sub-Indus, representing a late or degenerate phase. While the ceramics belonging to Lothal A show all the essential elements of the Indus Civilization in the substantive sense, there are two which are not met with on the sites in the Indus valley proper and the eastern region and as such require our attention: the micaceous red ware and the black-and-red ware, both showing painted decoration.[66] The former was represented by round-bottomed bulbous jars and bowls, the type fossil being the convex-sided bowl with stud handle. This type was also adopted by the Harappans. A pre-Harappan horizon yielding the above-mentioned ceramics has, however, not been recorded at the site, though it would be reasonable to argue for the existence of a settlement near by using these ceramics. Among the other noteworthy ceramics of Lothal A is the reserved slip ware which indicates its connections

65. Rao, 1979.
66. Ibid., 1979, pp. 28–33.

with Mohenjo-daro. The painted decorations on the Harappan pottery include, besides the typical patterns like the pipal leaf, intersecting circles, fish-scale, peacocks, etc., free-style painting of cranes and fish-eating storks as well as depictions of caprids etc., which indicate a provincial style. Other finds were characteristically Indus, like the seals, cubical weights, chert blades, disc beads, copper fish-hooks, etc. Coming to the settlement plan (Fig. 9), we find that Lothal was a fortified settlement oriented to cardinal directions some 300 m from north to south and 225 m from east to west, a trapezoidal south-eastern part of which was intended to serve as a citadel or acropolis, being separated from the remaining part of the city by high plinths made of mud, and a mud-brick platform. The prominent structures located on the acropolis included what the excavator terms the 'ruler's residence', the regimented series of rooms each with a brick-paved bath, a remarkable system of underground drains and a warehouse. On the eastern flank of the settlement was an oblong enclosure (Fig. 10) measuring some 225 m in length (north–south) and some 36 m in width (east–west) and perhaps 4.15 m in depth (the extant height of the embankment in the south-west corner of the basin being 3.3 m, with forty-two extant courses of bricks), claimed to have been a dock for shipping; this interpretation, however, is disputed by some scholars.[67] Both the dock and warehouse coupled with the discovery of a Persian Gulf style seal[68] at the site are indicative of the maritime trade of this coastal site. To the west of the city lay the cemetery, where as many as sixteen graves were excavated. Of these, thirteen contained one skeleton each and three, two. While extended inhumation along with funerary objects seems to have been the normal burial practice, simultaneous inhumation of two bodies has not been met with at any other Harappan site except at Damb Buthi.[69]

The Lothal B Phase was marked by certain changes in ceramics; the goblet beaker and perforated jars became scarcer; the dish-on-stand became squattish; concave-sided bowls became concavo-convex in profile; the complicated crisp geometrical designs were replaced by groups of horizontal and wavy lines, loops, fronds, triangles, volutes, panels, stylized peacocks and birds drawn in a free style on a limited surface of the pot; terracotta bangles were completely replaced by those of conch shell, cubicle chert weights by spheroid-shaped ones of schist and sandstone and long ribbon flakes by the short blades. A significant change in the seals was the absence of the animal motifs and other pictures.

Rangpur, long recognized as the southern outpost of the Indus Civilization, is situated on the river Sukha Bhadar, a sluggish stream which disappears in the salty waste farther down the ancient site. The excavation revealed a threefold sequence of cultures, the earliest of which was marked by crude microliths of jasper and agate without pottery. The succeeding culture, termed Period II, represents the Harappan occupation showing three phases, IIA, IIB and IIC, denoting

---

67. Ratnagar, 1981.
68. Rao, 1963.
69. Majumdar, 1934.

respectively the mature, the decadent and the transition stages of the Indus Civilization. In Sub-period IIA, the pottery is impeccably Harappan and also includes the micaceous red ware and the black-and-red ware of Lothal affiliation; in Sub-period IIB the fabric of the pottery becomes coarser, and forms like beakers and goblets, already scarce in the preceding sub-period, were almost discarded. In Sub-period IIC new forms and fabrics were introduced. The last cultural period at the site is marked by the dominant use of the lustrous red ware which in fact began to be made in Sub-period IIC itself. The ware was often painted in black with less ambitious designs and animals like bulls, running deer, rows of birds, etc. Among the noteworthy finds was a terracotta figurine of a horse. Faience and steatite were almost unknown in the period.

Prabhas Patan is situated on the south-western coast of Saurashatra at the mouth of the Haranya river near the port town of Vereval.[70] The excavation revealed a fivefold sequence of cultures of which the earlier three are Chalcolithic. These were marked by the use of what is termed Prabhas ware – a mossy grey-coloured pottery, painted in purple or dark brown with a design ornament usually set in panels or registers. The most predominant shape is a sub-spherical bowl which occurs in all sizes. Among the Harappan forms were the dish-on-stand and the stud-handled bowl. Late Harappan pottery of Rangpur Sub-period IIB was also in use, but there were no beakers, goblets or terracotta cakes. In the later phases, the lustrous red ware also came to be used. They used blades of chalcedony and even imported a few of obsidian. Besides they also used cubical chert weights and segmented faience beads. A unique seal amulet of steatite, obtained from levels ascribable to the later half of the second millennium B.C. and engraved on one side with seven stylized deer and on the other with five, deserves special mention.

Rojdi is situated on the left bank of the Bhadar river about 55 km south of Rajkot.[71] The ancient site is thought to have been girt with a fortification wall built with large boulders. The excavations provided a sequence of two phases, of which the earlier was Harappan and the latter showed links with Prabhas, Rangpur IIB and IIC. An important evidence of the Harappan connection was the discovery of a convex-sided bowl inscribed with four Indus characters.

Desalpur is located on the northern bank of the one depredatory stream Bamu-chels in Kutch.[72] The excavation revealed a 3-m-deep cultural deposit, of which the upper 75 cm belonged to the early historic period and the remaining 2.25 m to the Chalcolithic, further divided into Sub-period IA as mature Harappan and Sub-period IB as late Harappan. The Harappan settlement, measuring 130 × 100 m, was contained by a fortification wall built of partially dressed stones and reinforced with rectangular salients. A partially exposed structure in the central part of the settlement may have served as a partition wall separating the cita-

70. Pandya, 1957.
71. Pandya, 1958.
72. Soundara Rajan, 1967.

FIG. 11. Seals from Surkodata, Lothal, Kalibangan and Desalpur.

del part from the residential area. In Sub-period IA, besides the typical Harappan pottery and other finds, sherds of the so-called reserved slip ware were also found. In Sub-period IB the white-painted black-and-red ware of the Ahar genre and cream-slipped bichrome ware were introduced. The excavation confirmed the Harappan affiliation of the site by the find of two script-bearing seals (Fig. 11), one in steatite and the other in copper, and a lettered terracotta sealing and segmented beads of faience.

Surkotada, situated some 160 km north-east of Bhuj in Kutch[73] provides much useful evidence relating to the diffusion of the Indus Civilization from the lower Indus valley to Gujarat by the land route. The excavation brought light to a sequence of three cultural phases of the Harappa culture. From the very beginning of the occupation (Sub-period IA) the settlement was fortified on a rectangular plan (approximately 130 × 65 m, with east–west as the larger axis) divided into two parts: the western half was used as a citadel while the eastern half was residential. The fortification wall was made of mud with a veneer of rubble masonry. Some of the structures were made of mud-bricks (size 40 × 20 × 10 cm). The finds obtained from the deposits of this sub-period included a typical steatite seal, sherds bearing painted Indus characters, long chert blades, etc. Besides the characteristic Harappan pottery a cream-slipped bichrome ware showing painted designs in brown and purplish red or black and the so-called reserved slip ware were also found. The cemetery area lay to the north-west of the

73. Joshi, 1972, 1973, 1974.

settlement. The people practised urn-burial as one of the modes of the disposal of the dead. In Sub-period IB, the Indus elements become less pronounced with the appearance of a new ceramic tradition of coarse red ware. The upper levels yielded sherds of white-painted black and red ware. In Sub-period IC the Harappan pottery tradition had further waned, the dominant ceramic being the white-painted black-and-red ware. The fortifications were reconstructed in rubble masonry. Noteworthy finds included a terracotta seal bearing signs in the Indus script, chert weights, etc. The presence of the horse is indicated by the discovery of horse bones in deposits of this sub-period.

Daimabad is situated on the Pravara, a tributary of the Godavari in Ahmadnagar District, Maharashatra. The site had attracted the attention of the archaeologists through the find of a cache of four solid bronze objects; an elephant, a rhinoceros, a buffalo and a chariot yoked to a pair of bulls and driven by a standing human figure, all weighing 65 kg. A closely observed excavation[74] at the site revealed a fivefold sequence of cultures labelled as: Period I – Sawalda culture; Period II – late Harappan culture; Period III – buff- and cream-ware culture; Period IV – Malwa culture; and Period V – Jorwe culture. Of these, the Sawalda culture takes its name from the site of the Tapti valley where it was first encountered and is characterized by a wheel-made painted pottery of medium-to-coarse fabric. The thick slip coat on this pottery often shows crazing and has turned red, pink, greyish brown or chocolate in colour and is painted in black or red, or in both colours. The types represented include the dish-on-stand, high-necked jar, basin, etc. Along with this ware burnished grey and thick coarse wares were also in use. Period II is distinguished by a sturdy red ware of late Harappan tradition, painted with simple designs like cross-hatched triangles, groups of vertical or wavy lines, chains, loops sometimes interlaced, etc. The types represented in this ware are the dish-on-stand vase with collared rim, dish and bowl. Associated with this was also a bichrome ware. Other objects included copper/bronze celt, small-sized blades and microliths. The burial practice of the people was evidenced by the discovery of a grave (within the habitation area itself), showing an extended articulated inhumation with the head towards the north, the body being covered with fibrous material like hemp, the sides of the grave being lined with mud-bricks $32 \times 16 \times 8$ and $28 \times 14 \times 7$ cm in size. The continuing sequence in Periods II, IV and V ties up the site with the Chalcolithic culture of central India and provides the Indus Civilization with a rational sequel.

The problem of the chronology of the wide territories of the Indus Civilization requires some measure of circumspection. Within its widely distributed area, the spread of the civilization from the nuclear to the peripheral regions was obviously conditioned by the urge to seek out familiar environments and to search for resource material and trading ports. The spread would thus show a sloping horizon for the civilization in terms of time and space. The evidence at

74. Rao, 1978

present available both from the eastern and the southern regions indicates that such was indeed the fact.

It has already been postulated that the nuclear cities of the Indus Civilization were founded some time before 2400 B.C. and that they endured in some shape to the eighteenth century B.C.[75] (These and all other data mentioned in the remainder of this chapter are without MASCA calibration.) In the eastern region five sites, namely Kalibangan, Banawali, Mitathal, Sanghol and Bara have been radiocarbon dated. Among these, Kalibangan, which is located nearest to the nuclear region of the civilization, was sampled very extensively (six from the early, nine from the middle and nine from the late levels), showing an inclusive time-bracket of 2300–1700 B.C. (or, with MASCA calibration, 2850–2060 B.C.) for the Harappan occupation with a margin on the earlier side. Banawali, which lies some 120 km east of Kalibangan on the same river, namely Sarasvati, seems to have been occupied by the Harappans around 2250 B.C., middle levels of the occupation being radiocarbon dated to *circa* 1950 B.C. (MASCA calibrated 2200 B.C.). Mitathal, which is situated some 110 km farther south-east of Banawali along the dried up course of the Jamuna, shows a still later beginning of the Harappan occupation at the site as indicated by the radiocarbon dates (around 1800 B.C.) for the middle levels of the occupation. However, it is likely that sites like Rupar and Manda, due to their proximity to the source of timber, which was an essential requirement, would have been occupied by the Harappans not much later than Kalibangan. Of these Harappan sites, Banawali and Mitathal also show late Harappan occupations, for which no absolute dates are available. However, from Sanghol, located along the ancient bed of the Sutlej, where a distinct late Harappan occupation was attested with cultural equipment comparable to that of Banawali and Mitathal, five radiocarbon dates have been obtained. Of these, excepting the one aberrant determination, the remaining four indicate a range of 1750–1500 B.C. (MASCA calibrated 2110–1690 B.C.). The late Harappan occupation at Bhagwanpura, which shares some of the characteristics of those of Mitathal and Sanghol, also falls broadly within the same range, with perhaps a margin on the younger side as shown by the scatter of thermoluminescence dates obtained from the samples of pottery. Bara which lies close to Rupar did not have any Harappan occupation in a substantive sense, but instead shows an effete culture with some of its antecedents traceable to the pre-Harappan tradition, and having limited contacts with the Harappans. The four radiocarbon dates obtained from this site indicate a time-bracket of *circa* 1900–1000 B.C. (MASCA calibrated 2180–1100 B.C.), which responds consistently to the current evidence discussed above.

Turning to the southern region we find that the picture is somewhat different; unlike the eastern region the spread of the civilization did not follow a single directional course. Four sites, namely Lothal, Surkotada, Prabhas Patan and

75. Wheeler, 1968, pp. 110–26.

Rojdi have been radiocarbon dated. Of these, Lothal, which was a port town, is amply, though inadequately, sampled, on the basis of which, as also of other factors, Phase A (mature Harappan) may be dated to 2300–1900 B.C. (MASCA calibrated 2850–2180 B.C.) and Phase B (sub- or late Harappan) to 1900–1600 B.C. (MASCA calibrated 2180–1800 B.C.). Surkotada which was on the land route connecting southern Sind with northern Gujarat, was founded almost at the same time as Lothal, if not somewhat earlier. Rojdi which was located inland north of Lothal was occupied by the Harappans a century or so later, resulting from the movement of people from flood-prone Lothal. The C14 dates for Period IB (1970 $\pm$ 115 and 1745 $\pm$ 105 B.C.) (MASCA calibrated 2190 B.C. and 2110 B.C.) fully support this premise. Prabhas Patan, with its individualistic pottery was in the main contemporary with Rojdi, notwithstanding the two early dates around 2400 B.C. which seem to be inconsistent with the general chronology of the region. The so-called late Harappan phase in this region is represented, besides the sites discussed above, at Rangpur (Period III), Daimabad (Period II) and Desalpur (Period II) and carries the sequence to the middle of the second millennium B.C. or a little later.

From the foregoing it would be seen that in the two regions the spread of the civilization varied both in pattern and content. In the eastern region, the settlements had an advantage of the alluvial plains, while in the southern regions, the settlements conform to areas of attraction namely coastal flats, routes of migration, fertile hinterland plains, etc. There is thus an apparent uniformity in the cultural manifestation in the former region and regional diversities in the latter. The diverging trends are more prominent in the later phase of the Indus Civilization. At Kathiawad, Prabhas and the lustrous red ware are the two distinct ceramic industries which overtake the Indus Civilization; at Kutch it is the white-painted black-and-red ware of Ahar genre; and at other sites in Gujarat it is the sturdy red ware painted with elementary designs. As compared with this the late Harappan phase in the eastern region is represented by an amalgam, consisting of distant traditions of pre-Harappan, Harappan and Bara cultures resulting from interaction and communication of these cultures over a long period when the former cultures were becoming impoverished. Thus in the southern region it was a case of transmutation while in the eastern it was one of cultural fragmentation.

The Bronze Age in eastern parts of Central Asia[1]

An Zhimin

I N contrast to the Neolithic, which is fairly uniform in the whole of western China, Bronze Age cultures show important local variations. There existed an interchange between these cultures which influenced each other and were in contact also with neighbouring regions lying farther east. Because of the wide scope of such cultural exchanges and the influence on them of the nomadic cultures of the steppe, these cultures have often been mentioned in archaeological works. Unfortunately, as a result of an imbalance in archaeological research, there are gaps in our knowledge of the area. Because of this limitation only a brief introduction to the material available can be presented here.

Early cultural remains in Gansu province

THE QIJIA CULTURE

The Qijia culture is so named because it was discovered in 1924 at Qijiaping in Guanghe county, Gansu province. A total of over 350 sites of the Qijia culture have been found superimposed on the Majiayao culture. Moreover, quite a large quantity of metal ware, mostly copper objects, including some bronzes, have been excavated from various sites in Gansu province and at Gamatai in Qinghai province. They belong to the transition period from the Chalcolithic to the Bronze Age. The C14 dates give a range of 2200–1600 B.C. (calculated according to the 5730 half-life, similarly hereinafter, or 2630–1800 B.C. with MASCA calibration). The Qijia culture is contemporary with, or later than, the Longshan culture of the Yellow river. Characterized by painted pottery, it originated possibly from the Longshan culture in Shaanxi province. As the Qijia culture kept expanding westward, it inherited certain features, such as the making of painted pottery of the Majiayao culture.

1. See Map 10.

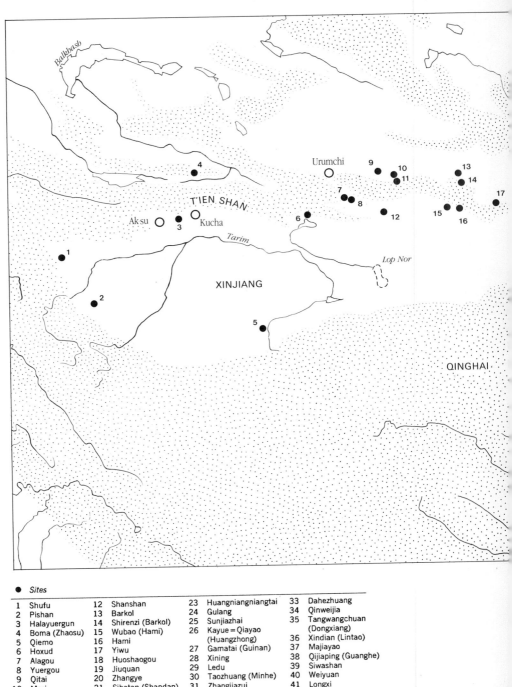

MAP 10. Bronze Age sites in eastern parts of Central Asia.

● Sites

1	Shufu	12	Shanshan	23	Huangniangniangtai	33 Dahezhuang
2	Pishan	13	Barkol	24	Gulang	34 Qinweijia
3	Halayuergun	14	Shirenzi (Barkol)	25	Sunjiazhai	35 Tangwangchuan
4	Boma (Zhaosu)	15	Wubao (Hami)	26	Kayue = Qiayao	(Dongxiang)
5	Qiemo	16	Hami		(Huangzhong)	36 Xindian (Lintao)
6	Hoxud	17	Yiwu	27	Gamatai (Guinan)	37 Majiayao
7	Alagou	18	Huoshaogou	28	Xining	38 Qijiaping (Guanghe)
8	Yuergou	19	Jiuquan	29	Ledu	39 Siwashan
9	Qitai	20	Zhangye	30	Taozhuang (Minhe)	40 Weiyuan
10	Mori	21	Sibatan (Shandan)	31	Zhangjiazui	41 Longxi
11	Sidaogou	22	Shajing (Minqin)	32	Jijiachuan	42 Zhuyuangou (Baoji)
						43 Anyang

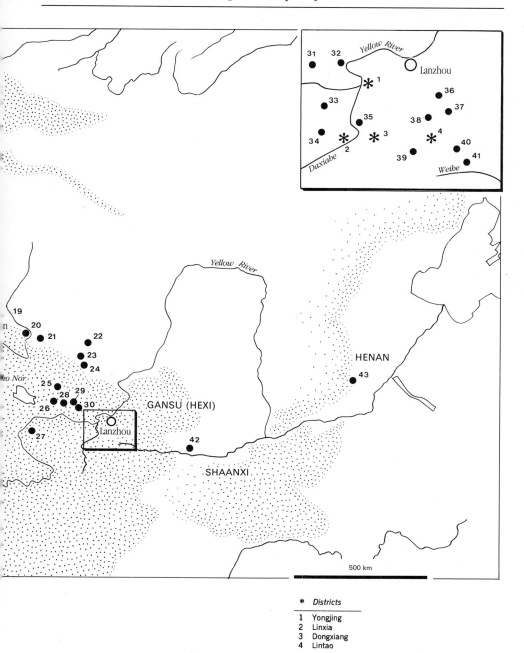

Yellow River

31 32 Yellow River ○ Lanzhou

* 1

33 36

34 35 37

38

Daxiahe * 2 * 3 * 4 40

39 41

Weihe

19

20 n

21 22

23

24

eo Nor

25 29

28

26 30 GANSU (HEXI)

27 ○ Lanzhou

HENAN

43

42

SHAANXI

500 km

* Districts

1 Yongjing
2 Linxia
3 Dongxiang
4 Lintao

The emergence of metallurgical technology is an outstanding achievement of the Qijia culture. The remains at Huangniangniangtai, Dahezhuang, Qinwei-jia, Qijiaping and Xiping in Gansu province and at Gamatai in Qinghai province, have yielded some fifty small pieces of bronze, such as knives, chisels, axes, awls, mirrors, finger-rings and other ornaments. Analysis of twenty-five pieces shows that they differ from each other in terms of metal elements and metallurgical treatment. Among the twenty-five pieces, those made from copper are the most numerous, accounting for 64 per cent of the total. There are alloys of copper and lead, the lead content being 5 per cent, of copper and tin, the tin content being 10 per cent, and of copper, lead and tin, though the number of artefacts made of these alloys is not great – only three, accounting for 12 per cent of the total. Copper objects such as knives, awls, chisels, finger-rings and round decorative ornaments were forged. Hammering impressions can be clearly seen on these artefacts. Some of the knives and axes were cast in open moulds, while bar-ornaments with designs on them, socketed axes, and mirrors as well as some bronzes were cast in more advanced composite moulds. Forging and open-mould casting are technical features of the copper objects, suggesting that although metallurgical treatment had begun to take shape, it still remained primitive. On the other hand, the socketed axes and mirrors cast with composite moulds – a more advanced technology – might prove that the later period of the Qijia culture had already entered into the Bronze Age. Of particular interest is a bronze mirror from Tomb No. 25 at Gamatai. The mirror was found *in situ* under the chest of a skeleton in a facedown position. The handle of the mirror is incomplete but there are two small holes drilled on its rim; it was probably used as a pendant. The mirror has a diameter of 9 cm, and is 0.4 cm thick. With a smooth and even surface, the mirror has its back mounted within the raised periphery of its concentric circle. The back is decorated with triangular patterns formed by oblique fine threads. The casting, shape and decorative patterns of the mirror are signs of advanced workmanship, bearing a close resemblance to the Shang bronze mirrors unearthed from the Fuaho tomb in Anyang, Henan province.

Techniques of pottery-making are marked by a fine red ware and a coarse reddish-brown ware. There are also a few pieces of grey ware. They are hand-made, there being no evidence of wheel-made ware. The surface of most pottery vessels was rubbed smooth by wetted hands and only a small number of pieces were burnished. In some cases, the fine ware has a white slip. Besides undec-orated pottery, the decorations mainly include cord and basket-impressions. In a few cases, they are decorated with applied ornaments and comb-marks. Painted pottery is rarely seen. Only the double-handled *guan* vases are painted with trian-gular designs consisting of lines and checks, which, though plain and simple, retain obvious influence of the Majiayao culture. The shapes include *pen* basin, bowl, cup, stemmed *dou* vessel, double-handled *guan* vase, sometimes with a long neck, and others like *li* tripod and *he* vessel. Though the Qijia culture has its own stylistic characteristics, it has very much in common with the Longshan culture in Shaanxi. For example, the *li* tripod and *he* vessel as well as cord impressions, have basket impressions. The regional features of the Qijia culture, however, followed the elements of the Majiayao culture.

THE SIBA CULTURE

The Siba culture was discovered in 1984 at Sibatan in Shandan county, Gansu province. It is so named because the 'Siba-type' pottery vessels unearthed here are different from those excavated at other sites in Gansu. Pottery of this kind is found mainly to the west of the Gansu corridor, in places like Yongchang, Shandan, Minyue, Zhanye, Jiuquan, and Yumen counties. The area of distribution of the Siba culture is bordered on the east by that of the Qijia culture, identical with the later period of that culture. The Siba culture is a separate entity that developed independently. Only a little excavation of remains of the Siba culture has yet been done, and we may take the site at Huoshaogou in Yumen, particularly grains of millet stored in large pottery jars found in the tombs, and the presence of pigs, all direct proof of activities of agricultural production. Remains of sheep, numerous though they are, among those of domestic animals, suggest a developed animal husbandry but the economy was based on agriculture.

Judging by the features of human skeletons, the population was of Mongoloid race, and similar in physique and build to people of the Neolithic Age in Gansu and Qinghai provinces.

Mortuary objects from the Huoshaogou tombs can be divided into three groups, each belonging to the early, middle or late period, according to their stratigraphic overlaps and pottery styles. The small double-handled *guan* vases of the painted pottery are commonly seen among those of the early period. Big double-handled *guan* vases belong to the middle period and the single-handled painted pottery *guan* vases belong to the late period. The C14 date available indicates that tomb No. 84 dates to 1500 $\pm$ 700 B.C. (or 1700 B.C. with MASCA calibration) and House No. 42 to 1390 $\pm$ 100 B.C. (or 1600 B.C. with MASCA calibration). Both are contemporaneous with the Shang Dynasty of the central plains. Therefore, exchange between the two cultures cannot be ruled out.

Later cultural remains in Gansu and Qinghai provinces

THE XINDIAN CULTURE

The Xindian culture is so named because of its being discovered in 1924 at Xindian in Lintao county, Gansu province. Soon after its discovery, because of a series of new finds, the Xindian culture was divided into two sections, A and B. These sections differ from each other in cultural style as well as in geographical distribution. Even when they border each other, they show different stylistic features. Of particular interest is that in Section B there are associated pottery vessels of the Tangwang-type. Therefore, Sections A and B do not seem to be variants of the same culture. The latter should be classified into the Tangwang culture. Our discussions here will only be limited to Section A.

The Xindian culture appears in Gansu in the lower reaches of the Taohe, Daxiahe and Huangshui rivers, all tributaries of the Yellow river. It extends westward to the east of Ledu county, Qinghai province, and its remains are found also in Weiyuan and Longxi counties in the upper reaches of the Weihe river.

Remains of the Xindian culture have been found in eighty to ninety places, but systematic excavations have been conducted only at Jijiachuan in Yongjing county. The site covers an area of about 10,000 m², overlying the Qijia culture. Only one dwelling site has been found. It is a rectangular semi-subterranean structure, with a sloping doorway on the wesern side and a round fireplace at the centre. The dwelling site is on the whole similar in shape to that of the Qijia culture. A total of forty-one storage pits have been unearthed, most of which are round. An oblong shaft, earthen pit-tomb has also been found. The skeleton, identified as male, lies in a flexed sideways position. Near the head are a pottery *pen* basin, a pottery *guan* vase and the skeleton of a sheep. Tombs have also been excavated with other remains, but the burial rites vary. For instance, there are extended supine and secondary burials.

Pottery vessels are all hand-made and coarse. Most of them consist of reddish-brown ware with sand-powdered potsherds. There are also a few red and grey sherds. The decorations mainly include cord impressions and many sherds are decorated with coloured paintings. However, they are coarsely polished. In some cases, paint is applied directly to the cord impressions. It was a usual practice to apply a white slip to pottery vessels before painting. Most of the vessels are painted black and some are painted in both black and red. Designs commonly used are composed of broad bands, zigzags, double-hooks or meanders. Some vessels were first painted with red bands on which decorations were then applied. In some cases, in between the bands, they were painted with sun patterns, human figures and animals such as dogs and deer. Vessels are characterized by their round concave bases, and include one-eared cups and double-handled *guan* vases as well as *li* tripods and vessel covers with handles. A few double-handled *guan* vases are saddle-shaped, similar to pottery vessels of the Siba culture.

Stone implements have been discovered in large quantities, mostly chipped, including discs, axes, spades, adzes, chisels, knives, mortars and pestels, spindle-whorls, and net weights. Some of these implements are both chipped and polished, most of them being stone knives with notched ends.

Among bone implements, spades made from the shoulder-blades of animals are the most numerous. Others include awls, needles and arrowheads. Most of the above-mentioned implements are farm tools, indicating that the economy was based on agriculture. Among the bones found, those of sheep are the most numerous, followed by those of pigs. There are also bones of other animals such as oxen and deer. All this, together with arrowheads and net weights, indicates that animal husbandry, fishing and hunting still played a certain role in the over-all economy.

Some small bronzes have been discovered at Huizui in Lintao county. They include knives, awls and buttons. The shape and make of the knives has improved, an indication that this culture belongs to the Bronze Age.

Stratigraphic evidence shows that the Xindian culture is preceded by the Qijia culture. Its pottery *li* tripods and bronze knives are very similar, in shape and make, to implements of the Western Zhou dynasty. The meanders on the painted pottery of the Xindian culture bear a close resemblance to the decoration of the bronzes of the Western Zhou dynasty. As for the pottery with a dropping mouth, it might have been influenced by the Siba culture, whereas the shape of other vessels and the decorative patterns on the painted pottery reveal correlations with the Tangwang culture (for example, Section B of the Xindian culture). All these cultures belong almost to the same period. In short, the remains represented by the Xindian culture are those of a minor group who might have been the descendants of a branch of the ancient Qiang people, who lived in Gansu and Qinghai at the time of the Western Zhou and with whom they entertained relations.

THE TANGWANG CULTURE

The Tangwang culture was discovered in 1956 at Tangwangchuan in Dongxiang autonomous county, Gansu province. Pottery first discovered here falls into two groups. One is marked by the painted pottery with a purplish-red slip and whorl patterns, known as the Tangwang-type pottery. The other is painted with a white slip and with decorations similar to those of the Xindian culture. Similarities between the two types of vessel were noticed at the time of their discovery. Because of the lack of stratigraphic evidence, for a time the two were treated differently, as if they belonged to two different cultures. The Tangwang-type pottery was first discovered as early as the 1920s, but it was at that time mistakenly regarded as belonging to the Machang-type pottery of the Majiayao culture and was not recognized as of special significance.

The Tangwang culture is distributed mainly along the Yellow river where Gansu and Qinghai provinces meet, along the Huangshui river and on the lower reaches of the Daxiahe and Taohe rivers. Specifically, its range of distribution extends to the Dongxiang autonomous county and westward to Ledu county, Qinghai province. Within this area, the Tangwang-type pottery appeared associated with Section-B pottery of the Xindian culture. In the area between the west of Ledu county and Xining, Tangwang is found associated with pottery of the Kayue type, thus creating a new complex. The two might be two different types of the same culture and could be named Zhangjiazui-type and upper Sunjiazhai-type respectively.

Stratigraphic evidence obtained at Zhangjiazui in Yongjing county, Gansu province, reveals that the Tangwang culture is later than the Qijia culture. Tomb No. 333 at upper Sunjiazhai has yielded a C14 date indicating that the Tangwang culture dates back to 990 $\pm$ 90 B.C. (or 1110 B.C. with MASCA calibration), the time of the Western Zhou dynasty. This has also been proved by a number of cultural relics.

Dwelling sites can be represented by the Zhangjiazui remains, covering an area of 10,000 m². The cultural deposits are more than 1 m thick. A total of 165 storage pits have been unearthed, all crowded together suggesting a stable settlement. A large quantity of farming implements made of stone or bone; bones of sheep, oxen, pigs, dogs, horses and other animals have been discovered. All this indicates that the economy was one based on agriculture. The presence of bones of deer show that the animal was intensively hunted. Tombs are represented by those unearthed at upper Sunjiazhai. Of all the 200-odd tombs excavated here, most are shaft earthen pits. There are also some catacombs. Large tombs are over 3 m long. There are morticed wooden coffins, rectangular and trapezoidal in shape. Secondary burials are commonly seen, skeletons being put together at one side of the tomb. Only a few of the dead lie in an extended, supine position. Mortuary objects are mainly pottery, but include stone and bone implements and bronze. Relics unearthed also include gold ear-rings, gold and stone replicas of cowrie shells, agate and turquoise beads. Tombs of the Zhangjiazui-type were unearthed at Taozhuang in Minhe county, Qinghai province. They are similar in structure to those at upper Sunjiazhai, but extended supine burials predominate, while secondary burials are quite rare. Burial objects consist mainly of pottery, but also include a few stone tools and bone implements. The four tombs unearthed at Yatou in Dongxiang autonomous county, Gansu province, are also of extended supine burials.

Among vessels, painted pottery is the most distinctive, being mostly coarse red ware with powdered sherds as a temper. They have a burnished surface and a slip. They are classified into two different kinds according to their decoration and shape. One is known as the Tangwang-type pottery, which is coated with a purplish-red slip, painted in black, and decorated mainly with spirals, occasionally interspersed with S-, N- or X-shaped designs, as well as parallel lines on the belly. The forms of these decorations are peculiar to this group and are rarely seen in other cultures. The other type is known as Section-B pottery of the Xindian culture. Vessels of this group are made from fine paste, and their surface is not glossy, though burnished. Some of the cord impressions are not even rubbed smooth. The vessels are generally coated with a white slip. Decorations are basically painted in black – sometimes in black and red – and are simple, consisting of bands, hyperbola patterns, N- and X-shape motifs, suns and crosses. The decorations and shapes of this type of pottery are in a way similar to those of the Xindian culture.

Chipped-stone implements include discs and knives. Polished implements include axes, knives, sickles, mortars, pestles and spindle-whorls. The T-shaped stone axe with a raised ridge, in particular, is typical. Bone implements include arrowheads, awls, needles, chisels, spades and combs. The spades are made of shoulder blades or mandibles of oxen or horses. Bone tubes carved with exquisite designs and bone plates marked with circlets have been found, but their usage is still unknown.

Bronze casting was quite developed. Archaeologists have found at Zhangjiazui fragments of the mouth and belly of a bronze container, an incomplete spearhead with an oblong socket, as well as some slag, which has been identified as bronze with a content of tin and lead.

Prismatic *ge* daggers, mirrors and animal-shaped castings have been unearthed at upper Sunjiazhai. An intact bronze *li* tripod has been found at Baojiazhai in Xining city, Qinghai province. It might have been cast during this phase of the Tangwang culture.

The formation of the Tangwang culture is indeed a new discovery. Further studies are needed to determine its character and category. But it is evident that it is closely related with the Xindian and Kayue cultures. As tombs of the Tangwang culture have been excavated above those of the Kayue culture, and its pottery vessels absorbed certain elements of the latter, the Tangwang culture is probably posterior to the early period of the Kayue culture. The fact that the areas of the Tangwang and Xindian cultures overlap and that pottery vessels of both bear certain similarities, suggests either the correlation or the coexistence of the two. The decorations on the Tangwang-type painted pottery exerted certain influence on the painted pottery in Xinjiang.

THE SIWA CULTURE

The Siwa culture, discovered in 1924 at Siwa Shan in Lintao county, Gansu province, is divided into two types – Siwa and Anguo. The former is distributed along the Taohe river and the latter along the Weihe river. Apart from the difference in their geographical location the two might also represent different timespans, the Siwa-type identical with or being slightly earlier than the Western Zhou dynasty while the Anguo-type being more or less contemporaneous with it. Archaeological investigations are confined only to the excavation of large sites covering an area of 30,000 to 40,000 m². The cultural layer is over 3 m deep at its thickest point. Of the relics collected, chipped-stone implements are predominant. Axes and knives are similar to those of the Xindian culture. The settlements seem to have been stable, their economy based on agriculture. Sheep bones unearthed from tombs show the importance of animal husbandry in the overall economy.

Excavated tombs are quite numerous, totalling more than 120. Most are small-sized shaft-pit graves, some provided with niches. There are also vestiges of outer coffins in a few large tombs. The tombs contain extended supine burials, secondary burials and cremation burials.

As far as cremation is concerned, the ashes of the dead are contained in pottery urns covered with stone slabs. Traces of human sacrifice have been found in a few large tombs. Burial objects are mainly pottery vessels, varying in number from one or two to four or five and even to as many as over seventy pieces in a few instances. Some tombs have no mortuary objects at all. In small tombs, there are stone axes, stone knives, pottery spindle-whorls and bronze bracelets. In large tombs, there are also bronze weapons and ornaments, and turquoise and agate beads. Most of the pottery is of coarse red ware. Powdered sherds are frequently used as the temper for paste. There are also a few pieces of coarse grey ware. Pottery of the Siwa-type is marked by its plain surface and poor burnish, some vessels being decorated with applied ornaments. No painted pottery has yet been discovered. Pottery of the Anguo-type is also marked by its plain surface, some being burnished, some with cord impressions or traces of flattened cord impressions. The shapes of pottery vessels of both the Siwa- and Anguo-types are plain and simple, but differ from each other. For instance, *ding* tripods and lids for vessels of the Siwa type are not found among the vessels of the Anguo type; while *gui* vessels and stemmed *dou* vessels of the Anguo type are not seen among vessels of the Siwa type. Again the double-handled *guan* vases with drooping mouths, *hu* vases and *li* tripods, which are shared by both types, are not exactly the same as regards shape. Therefore, it is likely that pottery vessels of the two types belong to two different cultures; further study is needed.

The only bronze artefacts of the Siwa-type are bracelets made of long thin strips of sheet bronze. Bronze artefacts of the Anguo-type are quite numerous. They include *ge* daggers, spears, arrowheads, knives, bells and buttons. Weapons are identical in shape with those of the Western Zhou dynasty, from whence indeed some might have been imported directly.

The Siwa culture is distributed across an area bordering both the Xindian culture and the Western Zhou culture, thus facilitating cultural interflow between the three. For example, the stone implements and pottery vessels with drooping mouths of the Xindian culture are quite similar in shape to those of the Siwa-type, suggesting that they should belong to the remains of the two co-existing cultures. The discovery of pottery of the Anguo-type in the tombs at Zhuyuangou in Baoji city, Shaanxi province, and of bronze weapons in tombs of the Anguo-type at Xujianian in Zhuanglang county, Gansu province, not only reveals the close ties between the two cultures, but also provides convincing evidence for the determination of the date of the Siwa culture.

The practice of cremation in the Siwa culture is a notable phenomenon. Literary records of the pre-Qin period all refer to such a practice by the Qiang. Considering the geographical distribution of the Siwa culture, we may infer that it had some connections with the Qiang.

THE KAYUE CULTURE

The Kayue culture discovered in 1924 in Huangzhong county, Qinghai province, was once classified under the Siwa culture. But new finds have identified it as a separate cultural system. Its remains are centred on the middle and lower reaches of the Huangshui river, extending eastward to the banks of the Yellow river in the border region of Gansu and Qinghai provinces. They have been found even around Lake Qinghai in the west. Over 200 early dwelling sites have been discovered in this area. Most have not yet been excavated. The basic conditions of Kayue culture are similar to other bronze cultures in Gansu province. Over 600 tombs have been excavated. That at Sunjiazhai in Datong county, Qinghai province, is the richest in finds. Most of the tombs are oblong shaft-pit graves. Some are shaft catacombs. Burial rites vary, including extended supine burials, secondary burials, prone burials and joint burials of mother and child, as well as children's urn burials. The sizes of the tombs vary. The shaft catacombs are big and rich in mortuary objects, and wooden poles were used to seal up the entrance. The ordinary tombs are small with a few narrow chambers and a few mortuary objects. The difference between rich and poor is distinct.

Among burial pottery, coarse grey ware predominates while red ware made of fine clay is rare. As for the coarse ware, powdered sherds were frequently used as a temper. Most have red slip on the outside surface and inside the neck. Painted vessels are few. The decorations are simple and include stripes, meanders and triangles, all in red colour. They mostly have a small concave base with a ring-foot. It is assumed that the base was made first and the ring-foot attached later. This is a prominent characteristic of the Kayue culture. The pottery consists mainly of double-handled *guan* vases, but also some with two or four large handles. The *guan* vases with two large handles clearly show the influence of the Qijia culture.

Stone tools are mostly polished, including axes, knives, pestles and mortars. The bone implements include spades, needles, tubes, arrowheads and spindle-whorls. The bronzes include *ge* daggers, axes, knives, awls, arrowheads, rings, bells and buttons. Among the *ge* daggers with a socket, the two-winged arrowheads, and the plain-surface mirrors are similar to their Western Zhou counterparts. Buttons have distinct characteristics, some are round and others are in clusters. They were probably used for decoration on clothes. Buttons are also found in the Shajing culture along the Gansu corridor. Other ornaments include turquoise, agate and amber beads, cowrie shells, stone and bone replicas of cowrie shells.

The remains of the Kayue culture are often superimposed on the Majiayao or Qijia cultures. This indicates its more recent date. Its bronzes are reminiscent of the Western Zhou, and provide good evidence of dating. Its relations with the Xindian and Tangwang cultures are not clear.

Kayue culture was probably contemporary with the later two. Since its duration was relatively long, they may not be similar in date and geographical distribution. For instance, at upper Sunjiazhai, tombs of the Kayue culture are overlain by those of the Tangwang culture, showing their sequent relations. The Kayue culture, therefore, appears to be slightly earlier, being identical roughly with a period between the Western Zhou and Shang dynasties on the central plains. As far as the people living here are concerned, they also belonged to the ancient Qiang people.

THE SHAJING CULTURE

The Shajing culture discovered in 1923 at Minqin, Gansu province, is confined to an area from Gulang, Minqin, Yongchang to Zhangye in the Gansu corridor. Its remains are superimposed on those of the Machang type of the Majiayao culture. Red pottery is rare and stone tools are found to be associated with bronzes.

Remains and tombs are all found in the desert. Because of drifting sand, relics are mostly exposed above the ground. Liuhudong site in Minqin can be regarded as representative of this culture. Very little of the ash stratum is left. At some places, the ash layer exposed is 30 cm deep. Few tombs have been found. At this site, there is a citadel with an area of 50 × 50 m. Sandstone rocks were used for the foundation of the wall above which earthern walls were built. The height of the surviving walls is 1.5 m.

At Liuhudong forty-seven shaft-pit tombs have been found. Most contain extended supine burials. In some cases, the dead are found lying sideways in a flexed position with the head pointing to the north. Only one or two pieces of funerary pottery were found. Other burial objects include bronze knives and stone rings, turquoise pendants, cowrie shells and gold ear-rings. In one of the tombs a bronze arrowhead was found stuck into a vertebra showing that its owner died from battle wounds. Not far from the cemetery are the remains of a triangular citadel, with walls built of heavy sandstone rocks, in which Shajing relics were discovered. It is clear that the cemetery is close to the dwelling site. Among the pottery, coarse red ware predominates. Some vessels are burnished on the surface, but traces of cord impressions and cloth patterns are still visible on the lower parts. Cord impressions are most commonly seen. There are also comb marks and incised impressions. As for painted pottery, vessels are generally coated with a red slip first and then painted in red. The decorations are simple, consisting mainly of parallel or criss-cross stripes and vertical triangles. There are also designs of diamonds, zigzags and birds. The typical vessels are round-bottomed *guan* vases with one or two handles and cylindrical mugs. There are also flat-bottomed *guan* vases and *li* tripods.

Stone tools, both chipped and polished, are roughly made. Stone axes, knives and arrowheads are also found. Bronze objects have been discovered in great number. The bronze ornaments, buttons with decorations, ornamental plates and tubes bear a close resemblance to their counterparts, characteristic of

FIG. 1. Stone sickle from Aktala in Shufu County, Xinjiang.

the nomadic population of the Inner Mongolian grasslands, a clear distinction of the cultural interflow and relations between the peoples of Shajing and the steppe. The relics collected also include axes, knives, two-winged arrowheads, prismatic arrowheads and undecorated mirrors.

The cultural characterization of the Shajing and Siwa cultures is similar, but the former is quite late in date. It is C14 dated to 560 ± 90 B.C. (780 B.C. with MASCA calibration), indicating that its absolute date as the lower limit is rather late, and this has been roughly born out by its relics. The citadel, used for defence, shows that the people of Shajing lead a sedentary life. The discovery of an oblong perforated stone knife fits in with the agricultural settlements of the time, at least suggesting that an agrarian economy already existed. Essentially agricultural, animal husbandry was still an important part of the economy. Skeleton identification demonstrates that the Shajing people were Mongoloid.

Cultural remains of Xinjiang

Cultural remains of the Bronze Age distributed in Xinjiang are divided into two groups: one is represented by pebble tools, the other by painted pottery, which mistakenly used to be ascribed to the Neolithic. Remains of the two groups may probably belong to different cultural systems and should be dated differently.

Remains of the pebble-stone culture are mainly distributed at the eastern foot of the Congling mountains in western Xinjiang, and around the area of Shufu and Aksu south of the T'ien Shan mountains. Rivers once flowed by the area, which now has been turned into a wasteland of sand-dunes. Because of wind erosion, stone tools and potsherds are mostly exposed on the ground. Occasionally a cultural layer of about 1 m deep can be found. This shows that the sites belong to settlements. Moreover, the natural environment of that time may have been superior to that of today. Thus agriculture was the main form of production, supplemented by fishing and hunting. Stone tools are mostly made from pebbles. The chipped stone tools are rather coarse and simple in shape, including discs and net weights with notches on both ends. Polished stone implements, exquisitely made, are found in great numbers. Among them, sickles (Fig. 1) and crescent knives used for cutting crops are most common. The crescent-shaped

FIG. 2. Stone hoe from Kuktala in Shufu County, Xinjiang.

knives without any perforations show regional characteristics. Objects of this kind are seldom seen in other parts of Xinjiang. Although only one battle-axe has been found, its significance should not be overlooked. Mortars and pestles, balls and spindle-whorls have also been found. Only one bone arrowhead was found, finely made and with a sharp blade. The sites at Aksu, Shufu and Halayuergun have yielded copper objects – a knife and a circlet respectively. The pottery is of coarse sandy ware. Most vessels are undecorated, but in some cases they are decorated with incising, applied ornaments and basket impressions and, usually round the rim of the vessel, is a cluster of small holes. Pottery includes examples of *guan* vase, *fu* cauldron, *pen* basin, *pan* plate, bowl and cup, of which the round-bottomed vessels are most common, while flat-bottomed and ring-footed vessels are seldom seen. As sites of this type are rare it is very difficult to determine their date. Considering the discovery of copper objects, the similarities to stone tools of Shang and Zhou times and the lack of painted pottery, the objects in question probably belong to the tenth century B.C.

Cultural remains represented by the painted pottery have a wide distribution. They are centred on northern Xinjiang, for instance, the counties of Yiwu, Barkol, Mori, Qitai and around the cities of Urumchi and Yining at the northern foot of the T'ien Shan and in the counties of Hami, Shanshan, Hoxud and Kucha at the southern foot of the T'ien Shan; they are even found in south Xianjiang's Qiemo, Pishan, and around Lop Nor in the Tarim basin. Basically these remains belong to Bronze Age. In view of their wide distribution in space and time, Xinjiang's cultural remains probably comprise different cultural systems. But the lack of research and the fact that most data have not yet been published, prevent further analysis.

The excavated sites and cemeteries are divided into two groups. Dwelling sites are generally located on mounds close to rivers. Several sites north of the T'ien Shan are located on terraces halfway up the hillsides or on hilltops. Usually, a river or a dried-up river bed can be found near by. Generally, each site is around 10,000 m² in area. The thickness of the cultural layers ranges from 1 to 2 m. Some foundations are found to be built of rocks or mud-bricks. Buildings were usually square. A large quantity of stone tools, pottery and small quantity of bronze objects have been unearthed at the sites. A large metre-long stone mortar has

FIG. 3. A tomb unearthed at Wubao in Hami County, Xinjiang.

been found not far from the dwelling sites. Carbonized wheat grains have been found at Shirenzi in Barkol, showing that these were sedentary settlements and that the inhabitants engaged mainly in agriculture. Stone tools are mostly polished, including axes, battle-axes, adzes, pestles and mortars. Of particular interest is a heavy axe with a perforation. When fixed to a handle, it was probably used as a hoe (Fig. 2). Also found are bowls, mugs and other stone containers. Chipped tools, such as discs and choppers, exquisitely made, are often seen. Typical microblades have been found at Sidaogou in Mori county, indicating that some microliths must have remained in use during that period. Bronze socketed axes, knives, awls, arrowheads and ornaments are all of quite advanced quality.

On the whole the pottery is sandy-red coarse ware. Black ware is rarely found. Pottery vessels usually have a plain surface and rough burnish. Their colours in the patterns are quite noticeable. Incised impressions and comb marks are rarely seen. It is notable that there are also clusters of holes along the rims of some vessels, closely resembling those found at Shufu county in western Xinjiang. Vessels of painted pottery were first coated with red slip, then painted in black or red. Usually the two colours were not used together, and the decorations

FIG. 4. Painted pottery *guan* vase from Yuergou
in Urumchi County, Xinjiang.

are not clear. The designs are quite simple, including triangles, stripes, zigzags, wavy lines, impressed checks and whorls. Triangles or triangular designs predominate. The rim or the belly of the vessel is often decorated with designs and interspersed with multiple zigzags and wavy lines between parallel stripes, used as ornamental bands. The inside of the rim is decorated with triangles, a unique stylistic feature of these vessels, with parallels in the Shajing culture of Gansu. The whorl pattern is similar to that of the Tangwang culture. The handles, especially of the painted pottery unearthed at Sidaogou in Mori, are decorated with a stylized S-motif, almost the same as that appearing in the Tangwang culture. The shapes are simple, consisting mainly of *guan* vase, *hu* vase, *fu* cauldron, *pen* basin, *pan* plate, bowl and mug. Most vessels have one or two handles, many of them having a round base. The paste and decoration of the painted pottery fully show that the Xinjiang material is closely related to the bronze cultures of the Gansu-Qinghai region.

Cemeteries of this period can be represented by those found at Wubao in Hami and at Yuergou and Alagou in Urumchi. The latter include some tombs of a later date. Twenty-nine closely clustered oblong, round-cornered, shaft-pit tombs have been excavated at Wubao (Fig. 3) in Hami. They are 1.4 m long, 0.8 m wide and about 1 m deep. The bodies lying on their side in a flexed position were covered with wood or mud-bricks. Apart from a few personal belongings made of leather and wool, mortuary objects are quite poor.

In the areas of Yuergou and Alagou in the city of Urumchi seventy-eight tombs have been discovered. All are shaft pits with stone chamber walls built of pebbles and covered with poles. The number of skeletons in each tomb varies from a few to dozens. They lie layer upon layer. Sometimes there are three or four layers of skeletons. Both extended supine burials and fractional burials are found in the tombs, together with bones of horses and sheep. The people buried had long hair coiled and put in silk hair-nets. The skeletons are partly Mongoloid and partly Caucasian. However, further study is needed to discover the relationship between them. Among the mortuary objects pottery, mostly of the painted type, predominates (Fig. 4). Most vessels were first coated with a red slip and then painted in black or red. Their designs include triangles, triangular checkers and whorls, also geometrical designs made up of parallel vertical lines or parallel slanted short lines. There are also stone tools, cowrie shells, bone carvings, strings of stone and bone beads and small bronze articles. A few later tombs have yielded small iron objects. The mortuary objects vary greatly in composition and shape. For instance, painted pottery is seldom or not at all found in the later tombs. Instead, there appear stemmed pottery *dou* vessels, lacquer-ware, and silk articles originating in the central plains. The early tombs are contemporary with the Spring and Autumn period, while the later tombs are contemporary with the Warring States period.

Remains represented by painted pottery can be further confirmed by C14 dating. For instance, the two C14 dates available for the Sidaogou finds at Mori give a range of about 900–600 B.C. (or 950–740 B.C. with MASCA calibration). The five C14 dates for the Wubao cemetery in Hami range between 1200–900 B.C. (1380–950 B.C. with MASCA calibration). The two C14 dates available for the two early tombs of Yuergou in Urumchi indicate a date of 700 B.C. (800 B.C. with MASCA calibration). But the absolute date for the lower limit of Xinjiang's painted pottery is quite late. Vessels of painted pottery appear not only in tombs at Yuergou and Alagou during the Warring States period, but extended to early Han times, as in the tombs of Wu-sun at Boma in Zhaosu county. It is evident that the painted pottery in Xinjiang was in use for a long time and is shared by different cultural systems. The tombs reveal distinctly different burial rites and mortuary objects. By no means can they be totally defined by means of painted pottery. The different physical features of the human skeletons show a rather complex racial situation in Xinjiang.

The Bronze Age in the western parts of China has been illustrated by the above-mentioned finds in Gansu, Qinghai and Xinjiang. Owing to lack of suffi-cient finds belonging to this period, the cases of Tibet and the western part of Inner Mongolia had to be omitted here. The archaeological data available have fully proved that during the period from the Chalcolithic Age to the Bronze Age, different cultures in this area possessed their own characteristics. They too had contacts with and influence upon one another.

The Bronze Age in the western regions was first represented by the Qijia culture. A great number of primitive copper articles have been found there. The upper limit of the absolute date is roughly identical with that of the late Longshan culture of the central plains. This can be confirmed directly by its characteristics and C14 dates. However, the Qijia culture lasted a long time. Thus a bronze mirror unearthed at Gamatai in Guinan, Qinghai province, closely resembles in shape and decoration its Shang counterparts from the Fu Hao Tomb in Anyang, Henan province. This shows that they are not only identical in date, but also constitute direct evidence of cultural interflow. The Siba culture is contemporary with the Qijia culture, but slightly later, being a regional culture. Other cultures such as Xindian, Tangwang, Siwa, Kayue and Shajing, all represent tribal variants in different areas. Whether early or late, they belong intrinsically to the same stage of development and are identical with, or slightly later than, the Western Zhou of the central plains. The bronze weapons, such as knives, *ge* daggers and arrowheads are similar in shape to those of the Western Zhou. The typical *li* tripods of the central plains culture have also been discovered among other cultures. A primitive bronze tripod has been unearthed at Xining in Qinghai province. It shows that the bronze culture in the Gansu-Qinghai region is closely connected with that of the central plains area. Remains found in Xinjiang possess an outstanding regional style. But the prevalent painted pottery had close links with the Gansu-Qinghai region.

The cremation rites of the Siwa culture are similar to those of the ancient Qiang people. Other cultures in the Gansu-Qinghai region may also be related to the Qiang people. The young woman with golden hair, discovered in the tomb at Wubao in Hami county in Xinjiang, obviously suggests a Caucasian origin. The discovery of Mongolian and Caucasian skeletons in the same cemetery at Alagou in Urumchi city demonstrates the complexity of the racial situation in Xinjiang from earliest times. As noted in historical records, the tribes of Xinjiang were often on the move and were subject to dramatic changes. For instance, the nomadic tribes of the Ta Yüeh-chih and Wu-sun, who used to live in the Gansu corridor prior to the Qin and Han dynasties, under pressure by the Hsiung-nu moved to Xinjiang and farther west.

Archaeological research has proved that the peoples of Qijia, Siba and Shajing enjoyed a settled life, with agriculture as their main economic basis obviously different from the nomadic life of the Ta Yüeh-chih and the Wu-sun. Nevertheless the reliability of the historical records needs to be confirmed by future work in archaeology.

The decline of the Bronze Age civilization and movements of the tribes[1]

V. M. Masson

I N the second millennium B.C. there were major shifts in the development of society over a wide area of Central Asia, and the whole picture of ethnocultural development changed. In the first place – and it is to this that attention has primarily been paid by all investigators – the former centres of a highly developed sedentary culture fell into decline and became scattered. Thus in the Indus valley the immense capitals of Harappan culture, Mohenjo-daro and Harappa, became deserted, and life declined in most of the other centres of habitation. At almost the same time in north-eastern Iran Tepe Hissar and Turang-tepe were depopulated, and the same thing happened on the plain adjoining the Kopet Dag range in two local centres – Namazga-depe and Altyn-depe. However, this whole phenomenon is most striking when the materials are first studied. Further excavations and archaeological discoveries have shown that the real picture was much more complicated. Along with the decline and disintegration we find some traditions suggesting that there was transformation of culture rather than a break.[2] The decay of old centres was followed by the cultivation of new lands. For example, the abandonment of Altyn-depe and Namazga on the northern Kopet Dag plain was followed by a simultaneous organized movement of groups of communities to the east into the Murghab deltaic regions and the subsequent cultivation of fertile lands along the middle course of the Amu Darya, the region that later came to be known as Bactria. No less important changes occurred in the steppe zone of Soviet Central Asia. Here the cultures of hunters and fishermen, who practised some form of productive economy, were replaced during the second millennium B.C. by herdsmen from the steppes and semi-deserts, who left behind them remains of the so-called steppe bronze. This radically altered the whole historical situation. The mobile, energetic and resourceful herdsmen, using light war-chariots drawn by horses, advanced in many dif-

1. See Map 11.
2. Dani, 1981a.

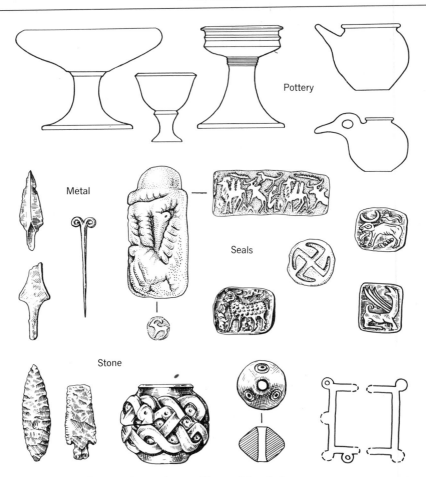

Fɪɢ. 1. Late Bronze Age culture of lower Murghab.

ferent directions. In the south we have indisputable evidence of their active contacts with those who built the sedentary civilizations, in whose destinies they played a major role. Thus historical development during the second millennium B.C. was marked by a complex pattern of migratory movements, transformations and cultural interactions.

In the civilization in the oasis adjacent to the Kopet Dag range, which shows the displacement of the traditional centres, there is evidence of indisputable decline in the middle of the second millennium B.C. by comparison with the preceding period. Altyn-depe and a considerable part of Namazga-depe lay in ruins, and these ancient urban centres gave way to small settlements with an area not exceeding 1–2 ha. Some of these settlements came into being on new sites (Tekkem-depe, Elken-depe), while others occupied the same site as settlements of the preceding period (the Namazga-depe 'watch tower', the south mound at Anau, Ulug-depe). The Altyn-depe area as a whole became completely derelict, and the development of an agricultural culture came to a temporary halt in this

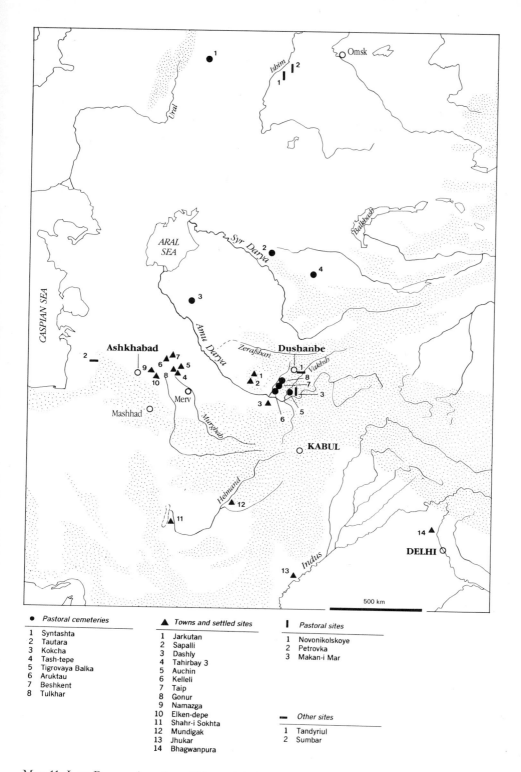

MAP 11. Late Bronze Age sites of Central Asia.

Pastoral cemeteries

1 Syntashta
2 Tautara
3 Kokcha
4 Tash-tepe
5 Tigrovaya Balka
6 Aruktau
7 Beshkent
8 Tulkhar

Towns and settled sites

1 Jarkutan
2 Sapalli
3 Dashly
4 Tahirbay 3
5 Auchin
6 Kelleli
7 Taip
8 Gonur
9 Namazga
10 Elken-depe
11 Shahr-i Sokhta
12 Mundigak
13 Jhukar
14 Bhagwanpura

Pastoral sites

1 Novonikolskoye
2 Petrovka
3 Makan-i Mar

Other sites

1 Tandyriul
2 Sumbar

339

area. Cemeteries began to be sited outside the settlement (Yandi-kala), whereas in the preceding period burials mostly took place within the settlement. The excavations at Tekkem-depe and Namazga-depe have shown that, despite the decrease in the absolute size of the settlements, the traditions of developed unbaked-brick architecture are, on the whole, preserved: the settlements consist of solidly built houses with several rooms, separated by narrow alleyways. The forms of ceramics become coarse, female terracotta figurines come to an end or become fewer and seals are comparatively rare.

This picture of definite decay and provincialism is in striking contrast to what we find in the lower Murghab (Margiana), where some 100 remains from the second millennium B.C. have been discovered.[3] These are the remains of ancient settlements spread along the banks of the former Murghab delta which is now situated in the zone of sandy strata of the Kara Kum desert. The settlements are arranged in groups, corresponding to the ancient oases, and eight such groups are at present known. The oldest, the Kelleli group, is still related to the closing stages of developed bronze and is dated to the beginning of the second millennium B.C. This period saw the arrival, from the belt flanking the mountains, of a number of communities who brought with them all the main forms of material culture, from pots to clay figurines, which the ancient craftsmen began to make directly where they settled. In the Late Bronze Age, when the belt flanking the mountains was the scene of decline and decay, in the Murghab region on the contrary there was an increase in the number of oases and a further rise in culture, with the range of cultural items expanded to include, in particular, flat stone seal-amulets with artistic representation of mythological scenes and cylindrical seals of Mesopotamian type. All in all, the nerve-centre for the development of southern Turkmenistan society shifts at this time from the belt flanking the mountains to the region of Margiana (Fig. 1).

The Late Bronze Age monuments of Margiana relate to the middle and second half of the second millennium B.C. and fall into two chronological groups – the earlier Auchin group and the later Tahirbay group. The Auchin period in the Murghab delta coincided with a marked increase in the inhabited area, which now embraced six oases, each containing settlements of different types. The oases centred round large settlements covering more than 5 ha in area and normally consisted of a roughly square fortress with round towers at the corners and an extensive adjoining mound of amorphous features. These settlements also included special artisans' quarters, where there were ovens for firing ceramics and where clay pots, and also seemingly metallic goods, were manufactured. Of this kind, for instance, was the Taip I settlement with a total area of 12 ha and a square fortress. This site is notable for the richness of its culture; four cylindrical seals were discovered here, as well as impressions from two more on a clay pot. The largest settlement in the Murghab delta, possibly even a sort of local capital,

3. Masson, 1959; Sarianidi, 1981a, 1981b; Masimov, 1981a, 1981b.

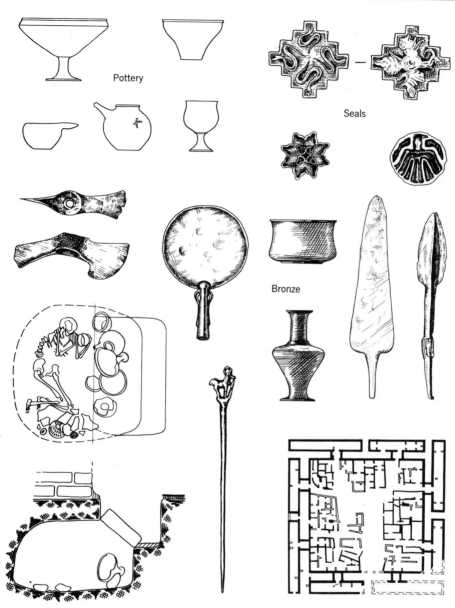

Pottery

Seals

Bronze

Plan of the site of Sapalli

FIG. 2. The Sapalli culture.

was the settlement of Gonur, centre of the oasis of the same name. It covered 28 ha and here too there is a fortress measuring 135 × 125 m. Many of the ancient settlements are small, covering from 0.5 to 3 ha, and do not usually present traces of intense commercial activity. It is mainly the large centres that should be regarded as settlements of urban type, and the oasis as the initial substratum of a social unit which turns into the organism we know as the city-state. However, there is still no evidence that this level of political and social development had been attained in Late Bronze Age of Margiana. In fact, during the Auchin period the Murghab settlements themselves as well as the outlying area furnish roughly modelled pottery with simply incised ornamentation, ware that is very similar to that of the steppe bronze tribes – clear evidence of population movement. Wheel-made pots show some new forms, but the earlier traditions are mainly preserved. There are also some changes in the types of female figurines though their number is greatly decreased. Human figurines executed in schematic fashion also become widespread. They are used to build up, on the rims of cult vessels, whole scenes in which snakes and four-legged animals take part. However, the most impressive innovation without doubt is the stone seals. Flat and usually square-shaped, they have figurines on both sides with a hole for a cord. Most depict wild beasts, but there is also one seal depicting a mighty hero who is gripping two prostrate beasts. This iconographic motif clearly calls to mind the favourite hero of Meso-potamian epic, Gilgamesh. There are numerous scenes of animals fighting, espe-cially bulls and dragons, which are depicted as horned snakes. Similar subjects are also reproduced on the cylindrical seals where we see another hero fighting with a wild beast, birds in flight, a lion and a bull standing on either side of a tree and a complex scene with human figures, camels and other animals.[4] Above all, these images reproduce mythological subjects dear to the sedentary agricultural tribes of Margiana.

In the concluding stage of development of the Late Bronze Age settlements in the Murghab delta there is some decrease in the number of oases and some changes are also observed in the material culture, where the tradition of making terracotta statuettes of human figures and animals is gradually extinguished. What we find more and more frequently in the settlements is roughly modelled ware, usually without ornamentation. Of the new ceramic forms encountered mention should be made of vessels with elongated tapering spouts.

Colonization of the Murghab delta by sedentary agricultural communities was only the prelude to the further development of new areas. In the middle of the second millennium B.C. permanent settlements with a culture differing little in practice from the Murghab culture made their appearance along the middle reaches of the Amu Darya, on both the right bank, in the area of Uzbekistan and Tajikistan, and the left bank, in Afghanistan. The remains found on the right bank have been studied in detail by Soviet archaeologists and are attributed by

4. Masimov, 1981*b*.

them to the Sapalli culture (Fig. 2).[5] In this region the permanent settlements occupy mainly the strip along the foot of the Kugitangtau and Baisuntau ranges, clustering near the streams and tributaries that flow down from them. The earliest Sapalli settlement lies to the south of this area, some miles from the channel of the Amu Darya, from where the communities gradually spread northwards along the Surkhan Darya valley. Individual groups even penetrated to the Vakhsh valley in Tajikistan, where a cemetery of the Sapalli culture has been found near Nurek. Unquestionably, the waters of the lesser streams flowing down from the mountains were used to irrigate the fields, since the rainfall in this region is insufficient for permanent cultivation without watering. There was a fairly wide range of crops – two kinds of wheat, barley, millet and grapes. Remains of what seems to be gruel have been found on a number of dishes placed in the ancient graves, and the fact that the teeth of the Sapalli culture people are but little worn down shows that leguminous and milky foods predominated in their diet, though it is true that alongside the vegetal products, they placed in the graves parts of sheep carcasses, of which either the hind legs or the shoulder with a few ribs are preserved. About one third of the Sapalli people's livestock consisted of a small strain of cattle, most of the remainder being sheep. There are also isolated bones of camels, pigs and, seemingly, asses. The pastoral/agricultural economy is organically combined with a developed commerce. The pottery is wheel-made and fired in twin-bed furnaces. Exceptionally numerous are metallic objects, including notably weapons – especially battle-axes with cross-guards and tanged spearheads – and a variety of toilet articles, ranging from mirrors to pins, bracelets and rings. The working of stone attains a considerable degree of professionalism, with wide use of steatite. It was also used to make pots, beads and seal-amulets identical to those made in the Murghab.

Typical of the settlements of this time is Sapalli itself, which has been completely excavated over several seasons. The centre of the settlement was a square fortress measuring 82 × 82 m, surrounded by a mud-brick wall with oval towers. Along each wall ran two narrow corridor-like rooms. In the centre of the fortress was an open area, a kind of square, along the four sides of which were situated the working and living complexes, consisting of a number of small buildings, each complex having a uniform type of hearth. The number of people living in this fortified settlement can be roughly estimated at 230–250. Graves here were inside the settlement, being arranged in special catacombs beneath the floors and, in some cases, beneath the walls of buildings. Adjoining the fortress is a small mound of ill-defined shape, where there were evidently other constructions of various kinds. The Sapalli community, like the other settlements of this culture, was distinguished by its high material level. This is attested by the copious inventory of objects found in the graves: sometimes they contain as many as thirty pieces of earthenware and ten objects made of bronze and copper. These funerary

5. Askarov, 1973, 1977, 1981.

gifts are extremely varied in type; among those that have come down to us there are four types of wooden vessels, basketware and leather goods, including a leather cap and footwear. One of the bodies was placed in a wooden coffin. Culturally Sapalli is in practice almost indistinguishable from settlements of the Auchin type in the Murghab, and evidently is one of the earliest on the right bank of the Amu Darya. When the sedentary farming communities spread out to the north another settlement was founded, namely Jarkutan. This also has a square fortress, but a larger one, covering about 4 ha. Outside this fortified nucleus there were the working and living complexes and an extensive necropolis, where about 900 graves have been uncovered. Jarkutan's life-span was longer than that of Sapalli and it was the largest centre in that part of Bactria along the right bank of the river. As at Sapalli there are cenotaphs among the graves, though more are found in later complexes. One of the cenotaphs at Sapalli was found to contain a bronze axe and pike, which seems to point to the fact that it was erected to commemorate a warrior who had been killed somewhere close by. It indicates that the cenotaphs on the whole contain a more plentiful inventory than the average number of articles placed in a tomb. It is possible that the increase in the number of cenotaphs points to an intensification of intertribal conflicts, in which notables and well-to-do warriors took an active part. For the later period of development of Sapalli culture archaeologists differentiate a number of stages which as a whole belong to the second half of the second millennium B.C., and correspond in point of time to the monuments of Tahirbay type in the Murghab.

The close links between the remains of the Sapalli culture and the Murghab settlements are manifest not only in the types of fortified sites but also in the range of the main ceramic forms and the flat seal-amulets. As in the Murghab, terracotta figurines are extremely rare in Bactria and soon disappear entirely. As also in the Murghab there are resplendent specimens of artistic handiwork, especially again the seals. Here for example we find representations of a camel or an eagle with outstretched wings; on one seal, in the form of a serrated cross, the bordering of intertwined snakes enfolds medallions of four animals – a mountain goat, a boar, a lion and another carnivorous beast of the feline family. Highly original are the mirrors with a handle depicting a human figure with arms akimbo, especially a woman whose head is replaced by the mirror.

The similarity of the Sapalli and Murghab remains is a clear pointer to the genetic link between them and the fact that they derive from a single source. In this connection different opinions have been expressed. Some investigators suppose the centre of the new type of culture to have been somewhere in Iranian Khorasan, from whence the tribes spread out both in the direction of the Murghab delta and into the middle reaches of the Amu Darya.[6] Other authors take the view that in both cases this was the result of the movement of groups of

---

6. Sarianidi, 1981*a*, pp. 189–92.

communities from the belt along the foot of the Kopet Dag mountains.[7] And indeed the principal components of the Sapalli and Murghab cultures directly recall the civilization of Altyn-depe, and the Kelleli oasis describes the first stage in its subsequent movement towards the east. The finest specimens of the new type of artefact that made their appearance in the Late Bronze Age are the flat seal-amulets and cylindrical seals and also, as far as materials from the left bank of the Amu Darya are concerned, individual types of bronze artefacts. The actual form of seals is in the final analysis highly original, but a number of subjects as well as the stylistic features indicate intensified contacts with western Asia and especially Mesopotamia. These contacts could have come about either through closer trade relations or the movement of individual groups or tribes, who became intermingled with the inhabitants of the Murghab and middle Amu Darya and assimilated by the local cultural environment. There are also a number of analogies further to the south. In particular, mirrors with a handle in human shape come from southern Baluchistan. But hardly less important is the evidence of contacts in the opposite direction, towards the north.

In many permanent settlements in the belt adjoining the Kopet Dag range, in the Murghab delta and along the middle course of the Amu Darya we find utensils that are quite different from the high-quality pottery produced in these centres. The vessels in question are modelled and decorated with simple incised motifs. These finds are clear evidence of the mutual interaction of two cultural worlds – the sedentary civilizations of the Bronze Age and the steppe tribes of herdsmen/farmers. It was in fact in the second millennium B.C. that the Early Iron Age culture of the steppe tribes took shape, though the origins of the process extend back to the third millennium, as can be seen from the remains of the Afanasievo culture, which has been the subject of study in southern Siberia.[8] These communities already kept all the main domestic animals – cattle, sheep and goats, as well as horses. Some of their artefacts – ornaments, awls and small knives – were made of beaten bronze, but there are also ornaments made of gold and silver. It is true that these represented only first steps in metallurgy in the steppe zone of Asia, and many large objects, including axes and pike heads, were still made of stone. The pottery was brittle as it was not fired in special ovens but on a charcoal bed, and the decoration consisted of simple incised patterns. The Afanasievo people's sites themselves are still unknown, but to judge from the size of the burial-grounds they were small, consisting of eight to eleven small families.

Unlike what happened in the southern zone of the earliest farmers and herdsmen, the spread of stock-raising in the steppe belt was closely linked to the primary foci for the domestication of animals. While sheep and goats apparently came from the south, specialists in the matter do not exclude the possibility that cattle were developed in many foci, since wild oxen were widely distributed in

---

7. Askarov, 1977, pp. 106–8.
8. Gryaznov, 1969.

(a)

(b)

FIG. 3. (a) Syntashta cemetery – parts of chariots;
(b) Syntashta cemetery – horse burials.

the steppes of the Asian continent. The camel, too, was domesticated in the zone of the southern cultivators, apparently already in the fourth millennium B.C. The situation was different with the horse. Studies made by zoologists show that the domestic horse probably derives from the wild horse that inhabited eastern Europe. In that case the domestic horse spread from west to east, from the steppes along the Caspian Sea with the Afanasievo culture into Mongolia and China. In the oases along the base of the Kopet Dag and in Transoxania this purely steppe animal was still unknown in the tamed state during the third millennium B.C. and even at the beginning of the second millennium B.C.

The monuments of the Afanasievo culture were only the first forerunner of the decisive changes that occurred in the steppe and semi-desert zone. These changes are linked to three main phenomena – the spread of bronze metallurgy, the use of horses for drawing war-chariots and the universal consolidation of a type of economy combining animal husbandry and land cultivation. Above their burial-places the steppe-dwellers began to erect special tumuli and more complicated constructions, today clearly visible in open areas as barrows. Mound burials are typical of steppe pastoralists as well as the early nomads who succeeded them.

The most striking materials characterizing the initial stage of this process come from the region adjoining the Urals and western Kazakhstan, where a number of extremely interesting settlements and burial-sites dating from the seventeenth to sixteenth centuries B.C. have been discovered. Typical of these is the cemetery at Syntashta I.[9] The excavations here have centred on mounds covering large burial-pits, lined on the inside with logs held in place by vertical posts. The tombs themselves were roofed with timber. In five such burial-places were found remains of light war-chariots with wheels having a diameter up to 1 m with ten spokes each. This was no longer a cumbersome cart with four wheels cut out of pieces of wood but a two-wheeled equipage, mobile and light. Naturally, the animals used to draw it were not slow-moving oxen or, as was the practice in the oases along the foot of the Kopet Dag, camels, but fiery horses. Skulls and indeed whole skeletons of these animals have been found in these burial-sites, whither also the chariots were brought (Fig. 3a). In one such tomb were found the skulls and lower parts of the legs of two horses (Fig. 3b); it is possible that the horses' hides were placed here too. Above the wooden canopy covering the tomb were piled up the bodies of the horses, usually in twos or fours, though in one case there were as many as seven. Of the harness, the bits made of bone have been preserved. Within the burial-site there were also cult buildings where the skulls of horses, oxen and sheep were laid in pits alongside vessels containing grave-gifts of various kinds. Above the tomb an earth mound was heaped up and the funeral pyre was lit, reddening the earth. Weapons have also been discovered in the graves – bronze pikes with cross-guards and drop-hafted axes as well as maces made of stone. Ornaments are also found here – copper bracelets, rings and tem-

---

9. Gening, 1977; Kuz'mina and Smirnoff, 1977.

ple bands sometimes decorated over the copper with gold leaf. In one case fragments of a silverplate breastpiece have come to light. At the same time the earthenware found in these tombs is inferior to the pottery of the southern cases; it is hand-thrown, frequently on a mould, and embellished with simple motifs of zigzags, triangles and representations of fir trees.

The settlements of this time consist of a semi-torus of several dozen frame dwellings slightly sunk into the ground; they are rectangular in plan and measure 60 × 95 or 70 × 120 m. To be noted is the special concern with defence: the sites are surrounded by twin walls and a ditch (Novonikolskoye I, Petrovka II). At most of the settlements there are also traces of metallurgical production – copper slag, casting moulds and sometimes also metal castings.

Remains of the Syntashta-type (archaeologists sometimes also call it the Novopetrovo or Novokumaksk-type) reveal links with the culture of eastern Europe in very many respects. For instance several forms of ornamented vessel call to mind the pottery of the Abashev culture, and many bronze artefacts have markedly western analogies. Western influences evidently played a definite role in forming this Bronze Age steppe complex. The result is a new type of culture and society, in which the group of warrior-charioteers plays an important part. The period in which this new type came into being was one of tension, and even small settlements hastened in vain to defend themselves against the uninvited newcomers. But the new type of culture quickly spread far enough, apparently as a result of migration and also possibly of hostilities, when the local tribes defeated by an invader took over the cultural complex brought by their conquerors. In the middle of the second millennium B.C. a whole extensive area of Kazakhstan, southern Siberia and the lands along the Syr Darya as well as the lower reaches of the Amu Darya and Zerafshan, were occupied by tribes at similar levels of cultural development. By convention, the remains left by them are referred to as steppe bronze cultures. Even in the Vakhsh valley in Tajikistan a seasonal abode of these roving pastoralists has been discovered, and individual potsherds and pots are also known in northern Afghanistan.

The economy of these tribes was originally primarily a mixture of animal husbandry and land cultivation, with cattle predominating among the livestock, and the settlements were situated in depressions and river valleys, where there were favourable conditions for feeding the livestock. Even so about a third of the livestock was made up of horses. In the course of time the role of horses and sheep increased, and a breed of fine-woolled sheep became widespread, which were capable, like horses, of foraging in winter from beneath the snow. In consequence, the area of cultivated land increased, and settlements came into existence on the open steppe, where water was obtained from wells, now known from excavations at a number of sites. All the evidence indicates that transhumance developed in the semi-desert and arid steppe regions. In Central Asia steppe bronze cemeteries have been found in high mountain districts in the T'ien Shan and Pamir ranges, where the herds were evidently taken to graze during summer.

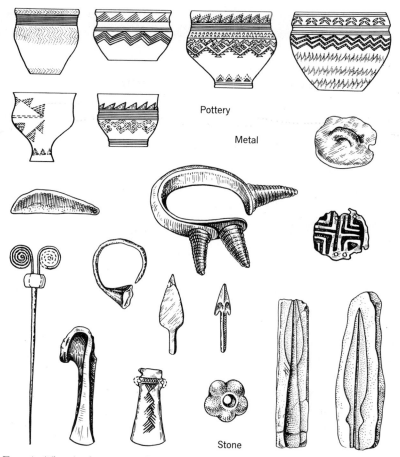

FIG. 4. The Andronovo culture.

While the culture of the steppe bronze tribes is uniform in comparison with the highly developed oases of the south, it has a number of local features associated with other cultures. For example, the remains of the Andronovo type (Fig. 4), which cover a vast territory from the middle Yenisey to western Kazakhstan, form a distinct category. Their pottery is decorated in a particularly artistic manner with a design of, notably, meanders, occasionally with swastika motifs. There are indeed links between the culture of the western Kazakhstan remains and the other major steppe bronze cultural type, namely the timber-grave culture of eastern Europe. Here graves, too, provide evidence of a different people. While the settlers on the Yenisey and in eastern and central Kazakhstan represent the so-called Andronovo variant of the proto-European race, in the lands along the Volga and western Kazakhstan we find a dolichocephalic Europoid population of the so-called eastern Mediterranean type. Local cultural and economic peculiarities are also evident in the Andronovo culture. Thus in eastern, and to some extent also, in central Kazakhstan there are remains of the Fedorovo type, similar to those of the wooded steppe zone of southern Siberia. Among the cemeteries that have been investigated on the Yenisey and the Ob rivers some of the dead have been buried but others have been cremated, and the actual remains are preserved in stone chests. No settlements have as yet been found here, and these were evidently the temporary abodes of a stock-raising population. During the Andronovo period there was in Kazakhstan active exploitation of the metallic ore deposits — copper, tin and gold. In the Dzhezkazgan region alone tens of thousands of tons of copper ore were smelted in the ancient foundries.

The southward movement of the tribes is linked with both cultural regions. Along the lower Amu Darya, in the vicinity of Khorezm, the second half of the second millennium B.C. saw the spread of the Tazabagyab culture (Kokcha cemetery), which is related both to the world of the timber-grave tribes and to the remains in western Kazakhstan. Here we know of about fifty settlements, usually small in size and consisting, as a rule, of two or three large rectangular houses of pillar design, slightly sunk into the ground. The average number of people living on such sites was about 100.[10] They included metal-working craftsmen – in the house of one of such craftsman was found a stone mould for casting pikes with cross-guards. In the conditions obtaining in the former Amu Darya delta the Tazabagyab people developed irrigated agriculture leading small canals off the gradually shrinking watercourses to water the fields. A similar culture also spread around the lower reaches of the Zerafshan. Specifically, timber-grave tribes also advanced southwards. At any rate a number of timber-grave burial-sites have been found on the west of the plain adjoining the Kopet Dag range.[11]

Kirghizia and the Ferghana valley, on the other hand, experienced the incursion of tribes of the Andronovo culture, who brought with them the northern tradition of carrying out burials in cemeteries situated apart in stone enclosures or under barrows formed by bringing in earth or a mixture of earth and stone. Of this kind is the Tautara cemetery on the northern slopes of the Karatau chain. The pottery includes forms not found in more northern regions and imitating in particular the commercial vessels produced in the settled oases of the south.

The T'ien Shan tribes are characterized by the ceremonial use of vessels containing foodstuffs and other substances in cremations. For example, one of the graves in the Tash-tepe cemetery was found to contain more than 100 bronze and silver vessels, glass beads and nearly 1,200 antimony ear-rings. In the course of their peregrinations the tribes of steppe pastoralists came right up to the borders of the oases of Bactria and Margiana, and possibly themselves became the residents of permanent settlements. In a number of cases mixed-type cultures emerged, combining features pertaining to the sedentary land-tillers of the south and the steppe-dwellers of the north (Beshkent and Vakhsh cultures in southern

10. Itina, 1977.
11. Mandel'shtam, 1966, pp. 239–42.

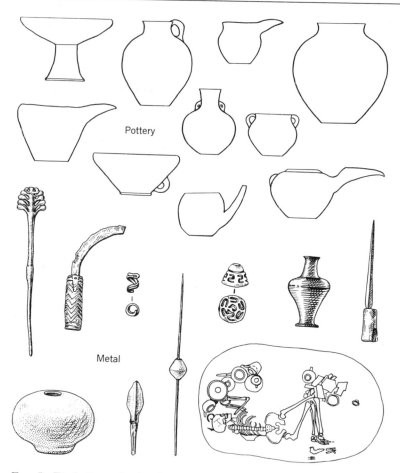

Pottery

Metal

FIG. 5. Finds from the Sumbar cemetery.

Tajikistan). The culture of the settled oases in turn acquires the domestic horse, previously unknown there, and to judge from the models of vehicles, chariots with light-spoked wheels. Ethnic assimilation also possibly begins. At any event, excavations at the Murghab settlement Tahirbay–3 have brought to light, alongside the interments typical of a sedentary farming population, partial cremation, and those who were actually interred include an anthropological type similar to the Andronovo type. In the designs traced on the vessels we find a motif previously unknown in the oases along the base of the Kopet Dag, namely the swastika. It is possible that the sharp increase in the number of oases on the Murghab delta in the middle of the second millennium B.C. is partly due to the fact that newcomers from the steppes had been incorporated in the local sedentary population. A similar interaction is a characteristic feature of the settled cultures of the Murghab and Transoxania in the second half of the second millennium B.C.

For north-eastern Iran, where the outstanding Hissar-Turang-tepe culture flourished during the developed bronze period, no data are yet available to show what happened to the society after these large centres were depopulated at the beginning of the second millennium B.C. However, all the evidence indicates that there was no complete break in the local tradition, which is typified by a liking for grey and black pottery. At any rate two cemeteries have been excavated in the western Kopet Dag in the Sumbar valley, relating to the late bronze period (apparently the second half of the second millennium B.C.) and the materials used in them can be regarded as developing on the basis of a culture of the Tepe-Hissar-Shah-tepe type.[12] The cemeteries are located outside the limits of the settlement and consist of catacombs, whose entry was sealed off by stones or mud-bricks once the burial had been completed. Among the numerous vessels placed in the tomb, which by their very abundance recall the customs of Sapalli, there are vases on tall stems, teapots with beaks, and other pots with great heavy beaks tapering to long spouts (Fig. 5). Both the shape and the grey colour of most of the articles are closely linked to the cultural traditions practised earlier in the south-eastern Caspian region. There are daggers and tanged spear- and arrowheads, as well as ground stone pins. There is also a great abundance of ornaments – pendants, fillets, cornets and beads of carnelian and lazurite. Particular interest attaches to a faience seal of conical form bearing a schematic image of a tree. Other settlements of that time have not yet been found in the immediate vicinity, but the high quality ware made for trade purposes and unbaked bricks are clear evidence that the traditions of a sedentary agricultural community had been preserved.

Unlike the regions of southern Turkmenistan and Transoxania, for southern Afghanistan and south-eastern Iran there is as yet no evidence that the sedentary farming communities brought new areas under cultivation during the second millennium B.C. Development continued in the traditional centres, and, as on the plain adjoining, the Kopet Dag is marked by features of decline. In Sistan at Shahr-i Sokhta the inhabited area at the beginning of the second millennium B.C. shrank from 80 to 5 ha; instead of an early urban centre we have before us an ordinary settlement, which moreover very soon fell into total decay. Similarly, in the Kandahar district there is a marked reduction in the size of the Mundigak settlements. The Mundigak V complex, which relates to the second millennium B.C.,[13] is distinguished, on the one hand, by the still glowing traditions of an earlier civilization but on the other, by features of definite cultural decay. Continuity is preserved in the field of construction – on the main elevation in the Mundigak V stratum excavations have uncovered a massive structure of unbaked bricks. But by this time the greater part of the settlement lay in ruin, and in any event no new constructions were erected on the foundations. The most noticeable changes are in the earthenware, which unlike the earlier Mundigak complexes is here hand-thrown. The decoration, consisting of a limited repertoire of geometrical motifs, is in black paint on a red background. Schematic representa-

12. Khlopin, 1973.
13. Biscione, 1981.

FIG. 6. Bhagwanpura: site and terracotta animal figurine.

tions of animals or parts of animals are comparatively rare – for example, a border of goat's horns continuing on from the animal-style motifs used in the decorated pottery from Mundigak IV. In many respects the origin of the Mundigak V culture remains unclear. J. M. Casal has suggested that tribes having the decorated pottery of the Chust culture which existed in the Ferghana valley moved outward,[14] but as in Ferghana this pottery dates from a later period than in Mundigak. At any rate the preservation of a certain cultural continuity goes hand in hand with a departure from craft traditions – for example, hand-turned ware replaces pottery made using a potter's wheel.

There is more evidence available as to what happened to the Harappan civilization. At a late stage in its existence there were already traces of cultural distinctiveness in the different regions, and these were intensified during the period of decline and depopulation. Thus the Punjab is typified by complexes of the Cemetery-H type in Harappa itself, Sind by remains of the Jhukar culture and Gujarat by a local form of late, or 'decadent', Harappan. In all three regions high-quality decorated pottery continued to be produced, carrying on what were specifically Harappan traditions in regard to both form and ornamentation. At the same time a large number of distinctive Harappan elements disappeared, in particular the square steatite seals with inscriptions and the main types of metal instruments.[15]

An extremely interesting picture of the cultural transformation that took place during the second millennium B.C. has been compiled by Indian archaeologists for the Punjab and Haryana regions.[16] The results of the excavations of the Bhagwanpura site in Haryana are especially striking. This settlement was founded in the late Harappan period, when the first settlers erected their habitations directly on the alluvial deposits of the Sarasvati (Ghaggar) river (Fig. 6). In the uppermost layers there is already evidence of considerable cultural changes: pottery of late Harappan type called painted grey ware, which was more typical of the Early Iron Age in northern India. It seems probable that Bhagwanpura is the earliest known complex having this type of ware. It is significant that in some of its forms it reflects Harappan specimens, showing the close connections that existed between the two traditions. The ornamental motifs used in the painted grey ware are, it is true, highly distinctive, comprising rosettes and solar circles; there is also a Maltese cross inscribed in a lozenge.

An interesting evolution is evident in the architectural style of this post-Harappan culture. These settlers initially lived in oval and semi-oval framework dwellings made of wood or bamboo and generally thatched. These relatively short-lived structures are then replaced by houses with clay-daubed walls and the development culminates in houses with many rooms and walls made of rectangular mud-bricks. Thus, to begin with, a sharp break is observable in the architectu-

14. Casal, 1961, Vol. I, p. 119.
15. Mughal, 1981, p. 37.
16. Joshi, 1978*a*, 1978*b*.

ral sphere with the Harappan style of house construction and only gradually did the population revert to the former architectural traditions, interrupted but not forgotten. The same picture can be seen at other sites, for example at Dadhar and Nagar. There is thus every reason to conclude that new inhabitants arrived in northern India who were evidently unacquainted with clay-daub architecture and had possibly followed a nomadic style of life. Cultural assimilation gradually took place and the newcomers adopted building techniques previously developed by the Harappan civilization.

Comparison of Harappan and non-Harappan features can be traced in a whole series of material artefacts. There are, for example, a considerable number of terracotta figurines of animals – dogs, birds, sheep, including figures mounted on chariots. However, unlike the Harappan culture, the figures themselves are decorated with engraved lines, and among the animals depicted, pride of place goes to the sheep. Ornaments are of many different kinds – terracotta beads, pins for elaborate coiffure made of copper, shells and faience. The copper artefacts are few in number, but some of them, such as a pin with a double-spiral head, are manifestly in line with the casting traditions of the sedentary agricultural centres of Iran and the plain bordering the Kopet Dag range. The inhabitants of Bhagwanpura and other settlements of this type were engaged in farming, as is evidenced from the finds of stone pestles and grindstones, and also raised cattle, sheep and goats. Of particular interest is the find of the skeleton of a horse and it is possible that it was already used for draught purposes. At any rate we are confronted with clear evidence of the formation in northern India of a new type of culture organically combining traditions of the local Bronze Age civilization with new features clearly connected with the incursion of some new population. Subsequent development of these new elements gives birth to the Early Iron Age painted grey ware culture, which may well coincide with the culture of the first Aryan princedoms.

All the evidence suggests that the causes of the events that occurred in Central Asia during the second millennium B.C. were numerous, and it would hardly be justified to reduce them to a single common factor, as was done previously. For example, Mortimer Wheeler painted a striking picture of the collapse of the Harappan civilization as the result of the Aryan invasion,[17] while more than one investigator has reverted to views linking the decline of the cities of the Indus valley to climatic changes,[18] and more recently the reasons for decline, in regard to Shahr-i Sokhta, for example, have been attributed to changes in types of demographic movement and socio-economic processes.[19] It is probable that what we have here is a whole complex pattern of interrelated factors which ended up by undermining the already none too stable systems constituting the Bronze Age civilization in Central Asia. Thus the movement of the steppe bronze tribes far

17. Wheeler, 1959.
18. Raikes, 1964; Dales, 1966.
19. Basaglia, 1977, p. 111.

southwards right up to the middle reaches of the Amu Darya is indisputable, yet there are no traces whatever of a violent incursion by warlike steppe-dwellers into the ancient cities. The tribal movements that have been identified by investigators were not a simultaneous act but a lengthy process involving the gradual migration of tribal groups who mingled with the local population as they went along. In the course of their long journeyings they left scattered behind them the burial-places of deceased tribesmen, which are now assiduously studied by archaeologists.

Some climatic changes in the direction of greater aridity for Transoxania are evident at the end of the third and the first half of the second millennium B.C.; up to this period there was in the inner regions of the Kyzyl Kum more plentiful ground cover of bushes and shrubs, with groundwater condensation.[20] At Altyn-depe during the same period there is a decrease in the proportion of cattle and a sharp increase in the number of sheep, which are less dependent on abundant pasture. In the area of the main centres of Harappan civilization the period 1800–1500 B.C. saw some increase in aridity, which expert opinion is inclined to link, it must be said, with the impact exerted by society itself on the environment.

In the northern Kopet Dag plain it is possible that the decline of the local Bronze Age towns was due in part to the exhaustion and salinification of lands that had been continuously parcelled out for irrigated cultivation for nearly four millennia.

Be that as it may, the second millennium B.C. brought a change in the historic geographical pattern and new centres of highly developed settled culture came into being in Margiana and Bactria. But almost everywhere the new cultural traits observable in the area of Bronze Age civilization in the second millennium B.C. were the result not only of internal processes but also of the manifest arrival of new inhabitants linked for the most part with the world of the steppe pastoralists. This results in a cultural synthesis, traits typical of the highly developed Bronze Age civilizations being combined with elements traceable to more archaic cultures. This can be clearly seen in India, as illustrated in a complex of the Bhagwanpura type. It was by such complex mechanisms of interaction and assimilation that the new ethnic societies came into being, linked for the most part with the Indo-Iranian linguistic community.

20. Vinogradov, 1981, pp. 28–9.

The emergence of the Indo-Iranians: the Indo-Iranian languages

J. Harmatta

Among the numerous idioms of present-day India and Pakistan there exists a series of important tongues (as Hindī, Urdu, Hindustānī, Bengālī, Panjābī, Sindhī, Gujarātī, Marāthī, Kaśmīrī, Naipālī, Bihārī, Uriyā, Āsāmī) which belong to the Indo-European family of languages and are called (Modern) 'Indian' in a specific sense of this term. Modern Indian languages are the descendants of the Prakrit (from Old Indian *prākṛta-* 'natural, popular') idioms of medieval India which are partly known by inscriptions and literary texts (Pālī, Māgadhī, Śaurasenī, Gāndhārī, Paiśācī, Mahārāṣṭrī, etc.). The rise of the Prakrit languages dates back to the middle of the second millennium B.C. when they existed as spoken idioms beside Vedic Sanskrit (from Old Indian *saṃskṛta* – 'artistically composed, prepared') and later, parallel with Epic and Classical Sanskrit, both highly developed literary languages. Besides the 'Indian' languages in a specific sense, there exist also a group of Dardic and another of Kāfirī, also called Nūristānī, languages genetically related to the 'Indian' tongues but separated from them at an early epoch. The Dardic idioms (such as Shina, Indus Kohistānī, Khowar, Kalasha, Pashai, Tirahī) became isolated from the 'Indian' ones before the rise of prakritisms and the Kāfirī languages (Kati, Waigali, Ashkun, Prasun) still earlier. Thus, on the territory of the Indian subcontinent, from the second half of the second millennium B.C., there existed groups of respectively 'Indian', Dardic and Kāfirī dialects all belonging to the Indo-European family of languages.

On the territory of Iran, Afghanistan, the Soviet Union and Pakistan again another group of languages (Persian, Tājik, Pashtō, Ossetic, Baluchī, Shugnāni, Yidgha-Munjī, Wakhī, Yaghnōbī, etc.) is known, belonging also to the same family of languages but termed (Modern) 'Iranian' in a specific sense of the word. Modern Iranian languages also have their medieval antecedents called 'Middle Iranian' languages (Middle Persian, Parthian, Sogdian, Bactrian, Khorezmian, Saka, Alan, etc.) as well as their forerunners in Antiquity termed 'Old Iranian' (Old Persian, Avestan, etc.).

With the help of an abundance of linguistic and literary monuments it was easy to prove genetic relationship between the Indo-Dardic, Kāfīrī and Iranian languages. In fact, the farther we go back in time in studying the monuments of these languages, the closer they come to one another. In Antiquity, for example, Avesta stood so near to Vedic Sanskrit that by making use of the phonetic correspondences between the two we can transpose whole Avestan sentences word by word, sound by sound, into Vedic Sanksrit. Genetic relationship between the Indo-Dardic, Kāfīrī and Iranian languages means that they formed a common system of communication (a linguistic unity in other terms) in an earlier period. Linguistic research created, therefore, the term Indo-Kāfīrī-Iranian to denote the common idiom once spoken by the ancestors of both Indians (Dards), Kafirs and Iranians. The ancient tribes speaking Indo-Kāfīrī-Iranian (or Proto-Indo-Iranian) are called in prehistory Proto-Indo-Kāfīrī-Iranians. To avoid this clumsy term, in this chapter we shall simply use the term Proto-Indo-Iranian(s) (PII). Besides the term 'Indo-Iranians', the name 'Aryans' is also used in scholarship because both the Indians and the Iranians called themselves *'ārya-'*; this word denoted originally the tribal aristocracy of these peoples.

The original homeland of the Indo-Iranians

The earlier existence of the Indo-Iranians and of an Indo-Iranian linguistic community presupposes an area and a period in which they were living. The earliest literary evidence attesting the presence of Indians in the territory of southern Asia dates back at least to the middle of the second millennium B.C. At the same time they are attested indirectly by Indian names and terms appearing in the kingdom of Mitanni and elsewhere in Mesopotamia beginning with the sixteenth century B.C. or perhaps even earlier. At that time the territory occupied by the ancient Indian tribes in India was restricted mainly to the north-western part of the subcontinent. As regards the Iranians, according to linguistic and historical evidence, they appeared south of Lake Urmia in the course of the ninth century B.C. Both Indians and Iranians moved towards the south and east and slowly occupied their later territories. There are no direct linguistic or historical data concerning the migrations of the eastern Iranians but, on the basis of historical considerations and later evidence, it seems probable that their immigration took place more or less simultaneously with the spread of the western Iranians.

From the structure of these movements it becomes clear that Indians, Dards, Kafirs and Iranians had already separated from one another at the time when they migrated to Iran and the Indian subcontinent from the north and the north-west. Consequently, we have to look for their ancient home in the territories lying to the north of the Iranian plateau and India. Arriving at this logical conclusion, we have to search for the traces of the Indo-Iranians outside Iran and India in the northern territories of Central Asia or even Eurasia. From the first millennium B.C., we have abundant historical, archaeological and linguistic sources for the location of the territory inhabited by the Iranian peoples. In this period the territory of the northern Iranians, they being equestrian nomads, extended over the whole zone of the steppes and the wooded steppes and even the semi-deserts from the Great Hungarian Plain to the Ordos in northern China. This fact was taken into consideration by both important theories on the 'original' (it would be more correct to say 'earlier') home of the Proto-Indo-Iranians.

One of these theories regards Central Asia (in a narrower sense)[1] and the territory north of it as the earliest area of the Proto-Indo-Iranians while the other attempt to determine their earlier home locates it in the steppes of eastern Europe. Obviously, these two conceptions do not exclude one another entirely. If we presume that the earlier area of habitation of the Proto-Indo-Iranians was the zone of the steppes and wooded steppes in eastern Europe, this assumption does not prevent us from regarding Central Asia (in a narrower sense) as an intermediate stage of their migrations towards the east, south-east and south. Theoretically, we could, of course, also think of a reverse succession of these two stages in the migrations of the Proto-Indo-Iranians but in this case the great detour (Central Asia–eastern Europe–Caucasus–Mesopotamia–Iranian plateau–Indian subcontinent) would require a specific justification.

The choice between the two alternatives depends on the position taken by Proto-Indo-Iranian among the Indo-European languages. According to recent linguistic and archaeological investigations, Indo-European represented already a widely ramified group of languages at the very beginning of the Neolithic. The separation of the Indo-European groups of languages had to take place at a time when agriculture began to develop in eastern Europe, that is, in the beginning of the sixth millennium B.C. as shown by the fact that the western Indo-Europeans and the eastern group (represented mainly by the Indo-Iranians) have no common agricultural terminology. At the present level of linguistic and archaeological research, the following Indo-European groups could be distinguished on the territory of central and eastern Europe in the Early Neolithic:

Anatolian group, included Thracian and Pelasgian, represented in Europe by the Körös-Starchevo-Sesklo culture.

Proto-Greek-Macedonian-Phrygian group, represented by the Central European Linear Pottery Cultures.

Daco-Mysian group, represented by the Cucuteni-Tripolye culture.

Baltic group, represented by the Dniepr-Donets culture.

Proto-Indo-Iranian group, represented by the eastern European Kurgan culture (Sredniy Stog II and Pit-Grave cultures).

The geographical area inhabited by the Proto-Indo-Iranians before their migrations towards Central Asia can be established with the help of isoglosses linking them to other Indo-European languages on the one hand and by means of loan-

1. For which the Russian name *Svednyaya Aziya*, or Soviet Central Asia, is frequently used.

words borrowed from Proto-Indo-Iranian by the neighbouring peoples on the other. It seems that the Proto-Indo-Iranians, the Baltic tribes and the Daco-Mysians remained in contact with each other even after the disintegration of the Indo-European linguistic community. The isogloss PIE *n̥ – m̥ > a* shows the presence of the Proto-Indo-Iranians in a vast linguistic area comprising, beside them, the Daco-Mysian, Proto-Greek, Proto-Macedonian, Proto-Phrygian, Armenian, Venetian, Illyrian, and one part of Celtic, that is, languages which all take part in this phonemic change. The isogloss PIE *o > a* testifies, however, the successive change of the linguistic zone. Beside Proto-Indo-Iranian, the latter phonemic change also comprises Daco-Mysian, Baltic, Germanic, Albanian. Its starting point might have been in the Proto-Indo-Iranian linguistic area because later the phonemic change PIE *ō > PII ā* also took place there. It seems that the formerly coherent linguistic zone extending from western Europe to the eastern European steppes was interrupted by the movement of the Proto-Greeks towards the south.

In any case, the isogloss PIE *o > a* bears witness to the contacts of the Proto-Indo-Iranians with Balts and Daco-Mysians, that is, to a process which fully corresponds to the geographical position of these Indo-European language groups. Unlike the Balts, however, the Protoslavs had no immediate contact with the Proto-Indo-Iranians because their habitats at that time can be localized between the middle course of the Vistula, the Pripet' river, the Dniepr and the Carpathian mountains. Later, when the Balts began to move towards the north and the Slavs advanced towards the east and south-east, they also got in touch with the Proto-Indo-Iranians.

One of the most important isoglosses, shared by the latter with the Balts, the Slavs and the Daco-Mysians, was the first palatalization: PIE *k̂ ĝ ĝh* became PII *ć j́ j́h* in the first phase, and Proto-Iranian *ś ź źh*, Proto-Kāfīrī *ć j́ j́h*, Proto-Indian *ś j́ j́h* in the second phase. At this stage of phonemic development we can observe the progressive separation of the Proto-Iranians from the Proto-Kāfirs and Proto-Indians which began by the phonemic change PIE *l > r* in Proto-Iranian earlier, while the Proto-Indian linguistic area was not fully included in this isogloss. Proto-Baltic and Daco-Mysian also shared in the development PIE *kʷ gʷ gʷh > k g gh* with Proto-Indo-Iranian but the further palatalization of the PIE labiovelars (= second palatalization) did not take place in Proto-Baltic. The weakening of Proto-Baltic and Proto-Indo-Iranian contacts is well-illustrated also by the fact that the phonemic change PIE *s > š* after *i u r k* was not fully shared by the Balts; it was only in Lithuanian that this development took place and even in it only following *r*.

The successive dissolution of the Proto-Indo-Iranian linguistic community is clearly marked by the exclusion of the Proto-Indians from the isogloss PIE *bh dh gh > b d g* while the Proto-Kāfirs shared in the loss of aspiration. This phonemic change extended over a broad linguistic territory comprising beside Proto-Iranian also Baltic, Slavic, Daco-Mysian, Germanic, Illyrian, Macedonian and

Celtic. Comparing this linguistic zone with that of the isoglosses PIE *n̥ m̥* > *a* and PIE *o* > *a*, we can clearly establish the gradual displacement of all these languages. Afterwards, the isoglosses PIE *ō* > *ā* and PIE *kʷe gʷe* > *k̂e ĝe* > *ć ȷ* (= second palatalization) obviously indicate an intensive linguistic contact between Proto-Slavs and Proto-Iranians.

A similar picture is offered by the innovations in the vocabulary. There are some lexical elements which also attest Proto-Baltic and Proto-Indo-Iranian contact, as for example the following:

vīros (as against Western IE *viros*): OInd. *vīra-*, Oīr. *vīra-*, Lith. *výras*, Lett. *vīrs*, OPruss. *wijrs* 'man, hero'.

vēyu-: OInd. *vāyu-*, OIr. *vāyu-*, Lith. *vejas* 'wind'.

ǵhosto-: OInd. *hasta-*, Av. *zasta-*, OP *dasta-* 'hand', Lith. *pažastē* 'armpit'.

yevo-: OInd. *yava-* 'grain, barley, millet', Av. *yava-* 'grain', Lith. *javaĩ* (Pl.) 'grain'. There exists again a group of words bearing witness to linguistic contacts between Proto-Baltic, Proto-Slavic and Proto-Iranian, for example:

tek̂- 'to flow': Av. *tač-*, Lith. *tek-*, SbKr. *tèč-*.

kvento- 'holy, sacred': Av. *spanta-*, Lith. *šveñtas* , OChSl. *svętŭ*.

The contacts between Slavs and Iranians continued even after the separation of the Proto-Iranians, during the Old Iranian and Middle Iranian epochs. Similarly, the Daco-Mysians were in contact with the Proto-Indo-Iranians, later with the Proto-Iranians and the Iranians from the Neolithic, at least up to the end of the Late Iron Age. They shared almost in the same isoglosses as did the Balts and Slavs, and were considerably influenced by the nomadic culture of the Indo-Iranians. According to recent studies, the horse was first domesticated in the southern Ukraine about the middle of the fourth millennium B.C. or perhaps even earlier. The domestication of the horse, together with the invention of two- and four-wheeled vehicles, had an enormous import on the development and spread of the Proto-Indo-Iranians. On the one hand, through horse-breeding they could better develop their economy while, on the other, they acquired a means that allowed them unprecedented movement on a large scale. In fact, they began to make incursions into the neighbouring territories and arrived, for example, in the course of the Copper Age, also on the plains of eastern Hungary. Thus, their contacts with the neighbouring peoples became more intensive and they exerted considerable influence on their economic and social development. This process was also reflected by the loan-words borrowed by these peoples from Proto-Indo-Iranian and Proto-Iranian.

Such borrowings may be for example OPruss. *aswinan dadan*, 'horse milk', from PIr *aśva-* 'horse', and *dadi-* 'milk', or OPruss. *ape* 'river' (as against Lith. *upe*, Lett *upe*), from PIr *āp-*, *āpi-* 'water'. It seems that some important terms were borrowed by the Daco-Mysians, too, for example, DM *az-* 'goat' (as against *aiz-* 'goat'), from PIr *aža-* 'goat', DM *āpa* 'water' (as against *upa* 'river'), from PIr *āp-* 'water', DM *sara-* 'brook', 'river' (as against *serā-* 'brook', 'river'), from PIr *sara-* 'brook', DM *ude* 'water', from PIr (or OIr.) *uda-* 'water', DM *esp, asp* 'horse', from

OIr *aspa-* 'horse'. The name for 'horse' was taken over even by the Thracians in the form *asp*.

But the Proto-Indo-Iranians also exerted great influence on the Finno-Ugrian tribes living to the north of them in the forest zone. The linguistic contacts between Finno-Ugrians and Indo-Iranians (or Proto-Iranians and Iranians) lasted roughly from the fifth millennium B.C. up to the invasion by the Huns of eastern Europe at the end of the fourth century A.D. During this long period the Finno-Ugrians adopted a large number of loan-words from Indo-Iranian and Iranian and a considerable part of these borrowings are from the Indo-Iranian and Proto-Iranian epochs. With the help of these loan-words, it will be possible to follow the development of Proto-Indo-Iranian, its split into different dialects or languages, and to establish the succession and relative chronology of some linguistic changes and even to give some hint concerning their absolute chronology. In the final analysis, within the Proto-Indo-Iranian and Proto-Iranian period, eleven stages of phonemic development can be established comprising three-and-a-half millennia.

FIRST STAGE: 4500–4100 B.C.

Change in the phonemic system

PIE η m > PII $a(n)$, $a(m)$, PIE o > PII a , PIE $\acute{k}e$ $\acute{k}a$ $\acute{g}e$ $\acute{g}a$ $\acute{g}he$ $\acute{g}ha$ ke ka ge ga ghe gha $k^{u}e$ $k^{u}a$ $g^{u}e$ $g^{u}a$ $g^{u}he$ $g^{u}ha$ remained still unchanged, PIE l > PIR r (but l was partly preserved in Proto-Indo-Dardic and Proto-Kāfīrī).

Loan-word

FU **aja-* 'to drive, hunt' < PII **aǵ-a-*

SECOND STAGE: 4100–3800 B.C.

Change in the phonemic system

PIE $\acute{k}$ $\acute{g}$ $\acute{g}h$ > PII $\acute{c}$ j jh

Loan-words

FU **orpas*, **orwas* 'orphan' < PII **arbhas*
FU **pakas* 'god' < PII **bhagas*
FU **tarwas* 'sickle' < PII **dharvas*
FU **martas* 'dead' < PII **mṛtas*
FU **porćas* 'piglet' < PII **parćas*
FU **taivas* 'heaven' < PII **daivas* 'heavenly being'
FU **werkas* 'wolf' < PII **vṛkas*

THIRD STAGE: 3800–3500 B.C.

Change in the phonemic system

PII *-as -is -us* > PII < *-aḥ -iḥ -uḥ* > (in absolute word ending)

Loan-words

FU *oćtara* 'whip' < PII *aćtrā
FU *ońća* 'part' < PII *anćaḥ
FU *ońćura* 'tusk' < PII *anćurah
FU *ćaka* 'goat' < PII *ćāgaḥ, *ćāgā
FU *kać* 'to look' < PII *kać-
FU *mańća* (< *manuća) 'man' < PII *manujaḥ
FU *arwa* '*present given or received by the guest' < PII *arg^whaḥ

FOURTH STAGE: 3500–3200 B.C.

Changes in the phonemic system

PII *ć j jh* > PIr *ś ź źh* (Proto-Indian *ś j jh*, Proto-Kāfīrī *ć j, jh* >
PIE *k^we g^we g^whe* > PII *ke ǵe ǵhe*

Loan-word

FU *ońśa* 'part' < PIr *anśaḥ

FIFTH STAGE: 3200–2900 B.C.

Changes in the phonemic system

PIE *bh dh gh* > PIr *b d g* (PInd *bh dh gh*, PKāf *b d g*)
PIE *ke ǵe* > PIr PInd PKāf *ć j*
PIE *ō* > PII *ā*

Loan-words

FU *tǟjine* 'cow' < PIr *de^xinuḥ
FU *tǟδ´e* 'milk' < PIr *dedi
FU *peδ´* 'to milk' < PIr *pe^xy-
FU *sasar* 'younger sister' < PIr *svesār

SIXTH STAGE: 2900–2600 B.C.

Changes in the phonemic system

PIE *p t k* + *X* > PII *ph th kh*
PIr *-ār -an* > *ā*, PIr *-ēr -en* > *ē*

Loan-words

FU *śum- 'strap' < PIr *syumē
FU *erśe 'male, man' < PIr *ṛśyaḥ
FU *warsa 'foal, colt' < PIr *vṛsaḥ
FU *säptä 'seven' < PIr *septa
FU *teśe 'ten' < PIr *deśa
FU *śata 'hundred' < PIr *śata Pl. N.
FU *sew- 'to eat' < PIr *ksev-
FU *reśme 'strap, cord' < PIr *reśmiḥ
FU *sone 'tendon' < PIr *snēvē
FU *kota 'house' < PIr *kataḥ

SEVENTH STAGE: 2600–2300 B.C.

Change in the phonemic system

PII *rs ks* > PIr [*rš kš*]

Loan-words

FU *mekše 'honey-bee' < PIr *mekšī
FU *mete 'honey' < PIr *medu
FU *kar- 'to dig, plough' < PIr *kar-
FU *jewä 'corn' < PIr *yevaḥ
FU *repe, *ropa 'fox' < PIr *reupaḥ
FU *repeśe, *ropaśa < PIr *reupāśaḥ 'fox'

EIGHTH STAGE: 2300–2000 B.C.

Changes in the phonemic system

PIE *e* > PII *a*, PIE *əi* > PII *ai*, PIE *ə* > PII *i*
PIr *-is+d* > *-izd*, PIr *-us+d* > *-uzd*

Loan-words

FU *asura 'lord' < PIr *asuraḥ
FU *sara 'flood' < PIr *saraḥ
FU *säre 'vein' < PIr *sariḥ
FU *sura 'beer, wine' < PIr *surā
FU *sejte 'bridge' < PIr *saituḥ
FU *śasra 'thousand' < PIr *źasra Pl. N.
FU *śeŋke 'wooden wedge' < PIr *śankuḥ

364

FU *śorwa 'horn' < PIr *śruvā
FU *śuka 'barb of corn' < PIr *śūkaḥ
FU *wos- 'to buy' < PIr *vas-
FU *waśara 'axe' < PIr *važraḥ
FU *woraśa 'wild-boar' < PIr *varāźaḥ

NINTH STAGE: 2000–1700 B.C.

Change in the phonemic system

PIE -*is* > PII -*iś*, PIE -*us* > PII -*uś* (but Kāfīrī -*us* > -*us*)

Loan-words

FU *saś-, *soś-, 'to become dry' < PIr *sauś-
FU *śäre 'brooklet, rill' < PIr *ksaraḥ

TENTH STAGE: 1700–1400 B.C.

Changes in the phonemic system

PII *st zd* > [*št žd*] (before 1600 B.C.)
PII -*iś* > [-*iš*], PII -*uś* > [-*uš*] (but Kāfīrī -*us* > -*us*)
PII *tst dzd* > PII *st zd*

Loan-words

FU *wiša 'anger, hatred, hate' < PIr *viš, *višam
FU *ora 'awl' < PIr *ārā
FU *punta 'soil, earth' < PIr *bundaḥ

ELEVENTH STAGE: 1400–1000 B.C.

Changes in the phonemic system

PIr /b d g/ > [b- d- -g] + [-β- -δ- -γ-]
PIr *ph th kh* > *fθx*

Loan-words

FU *oŋke 'hook' < PIr *ankaḥ
FU *śere 'clan, custom' < PIr *śarδaḥ
With the help of Proto-Indian lexical elements in Hurrian, we can state that the
seventeenth to sixteenth centuries B.C. fall within the limits of the tenth stage of

Proto-Iranian linguistic chronology. On the basis of this chronological evidence it seems that an average of about 300 years may be attributed to each stage. Surely, this schematic chronological system may not correspond to reality because the rhythm of linguistic change is not necessarily constant. However, this chronological scheme may serve as a starting point for prehistory, in search of the ethnic background of archaeological cultures, and it may be adjusted with the help of additional, such as archaeological, evidence, by later research.

On the basis of these PII and PIr lexical elements adopted by Finno-Ugrian languages, we can reconstruct not only the phonemic development of Proto-Indo-Iranian and Proto-Iranian, but by examining contacts between Proto-Finno-Ugrian and Proto-Indo-Iranian we are even able to sketch the development of economy and society of the Proto-Indo-Iranians. The PII loan-words of Proto-Finno-Ugrian can be grouped as follows:

1. Food-gathering, fishing, hunting: *aǵ-* 'to drive, to hunt', *ankah* 'hook', *mekšī* 'honey-bee', *medu* 'honey, *anćurah* 'tusk', *reupah* 'fox', *reupāśah* 'fox', *śruvā* 'horn', *varāźah* 'wild boar', *vr̥kas* 'wolf'.
2. Animal husbandry: *aćtrā* 'whip', *ćāgah* 'goat', *dedi* 'milk', *deˣinuh* 'cow', *parćas, parśas* 'piglet', *peˣy-* 'to milk', *vr̥sah* 'foal, colt'.
3. Tillage: *bundah* 'soil, earth', *dharvas* 'sickle', *kar-* 'to dig, to plough', *śūkāh* 'barb of corn', *yevah* 'corn'.
4. Handicrafts: *ārā* 'awl', *reśmih* 'strap, cord', *syume* 'strap', *śankuh* 'wooden wedge', *vaźrah* 'axe'.
5. Social relations: *arbhas* 'orphan', *argʷhah* '*present given or received by the guest', *anćah* 'part', *asurah* 'lord', *manujah* 'man', *mr̥tas* 'dead', *r̥śyah* 'male, man', *svesār* 'younger sister', *śarδah* 'clan', *was-* 'to buy'.
6. Intellectual life: *bhagas* 'god', *daivas* 'heavenly being', *kać* 'to look', *viš* 'anger, hatred, hate', *septa* 'seven', *deśa* 'ten', *śata* (Pl. N.) 'hundred', *źasra* (Pl. N.) 'thousand'.
7. Human body, dwelling, habitation, alimentation: *katah* 'house', *ksev-* 'to eat', *sarih* 'vein', *snēve* 'tendon', *surā* 'beer, wine'.
8. Nature: *kšarah* 'brooklet, rill', *saituh* 'bridge', *sarah* 'flood', *sauś-* 'to become dry'. This arrangement of the PII loan-words borrowed by Proto-Finno-Ugrian, together with the chronology given above, may clearly show the development of both populations in the course of their contacts and the dynamic process implied by it.

The contacts between Proto-Indo-Iranians and Proto-Finno-Ugrians began by the practice of hospitality, characteristic of tribal society. The term *argʷhah,* 'contact, friendly welcome, gift given or received by guest, price', points to the beginnings of exchange of goods in the form of mutual presents given by guest and host to one another. Mutual hospitality led to marriage relations already in an early period. By that time Proto-Finno-Ugrian groups could have adopted the beating for game in the hunt and the driving of domesticated animals, the knowledge of some games, the keeping of small cattle, some terms concerning hunting and animal husbandry as well as important notions in the field of society and religion.

Later on, one of the Proto-Finno-Ugrian tribes also adopted the keeping of large cattle to exploit in various ways. In the same epoch, as a result of their contacts with the Proto-Iranians, knowledge of the higher numerals and the construction of semi-subterranean houses spread among the Proto-Finno-Ugrians.

In the following period one group of Finno-Ugrians already acquired some primitive forms of agriculture and the practice of gathering honey. The final periods of contact between Proto-Iranians and Finno-Ugrians were characterized by the general widening of their relations to encompass the whole field of production and material culture, excepting that of animal husbandry. The social differentiation of ethnic contacts is well-illustrated by the borrowing of an important social term, *asuraḥ*, 'lord', meaning originally perhaps 'head of the clan'. Towards the end of the PIr period the clan itself as a form of social organization appeared in Proto-Iranian–Finno-Ugrian ethnic relations.

The importance of Proto-Indo-Iranian and Proto-Finno-Ugrian linguistic contacts is obvious. With the help of these well-studied linguistic data we can also draw interesting analogical conclusions concerning the relations of Proto-Indo-Iranians with other peoples and tribes of eastern Europe and western Asia for which, in consequence of the disappearance of whole groups of languages, we dispose only of very fragmentary and scant linguistic evidence.

Spread of the Indo-Iranians

The economic and social development of the Proto-Indo-Iranians took place in three phases. The first begins with the rise of animal husbandry including cattle, sheep, goats, pigs and dogs. Economy was, therefore, mainly pastoral. The two- or four-wheeled vehicle appeared at this phase but, being drawn by oxen, it could not revolutionize economy and communication.

The second phase is marked by the domestication of the horse, about 3500 B.C. – an event which fundamentally changed the scope of animal husbandry and the development of economic life. Economic and social changes were accelerated and, towards the end of this phase, in the period immediately preceding the Bronze Age, horse-breeding became predominant. The great stock of horses, together with the invention of the spoked-wheeled light vehicle, made possible the development of communications to a degree unforeseen before, and the introduction of the war chariot as an important innovation in warfare. Also, a further important consequence, social differentiation was strengthened, royal clans and the classes of war charioteers and warriors developed and, if formerly a slow infiltration of the Proto-Indo-Iranians could only take place into the neighbouring territories, now expeditions and invasions on a larger scale were directed against the rich territories of the south and south-east where a highly developed urban civilization was flourishing.

The third phase is characterized by the acquisition of the practice of horse-riding which enabled the Proto-Indo-Iranians (or more correctly the Proto-Iranians because the Proto-Indians had already left for the south-east at the end of the second phase) to develop nomadic horse-breeding and to organize great armies of cavalrymen. They became equestrian nomads, compelled by their great herds of horses to change pastures regularly and driven by their one-sided economy to establish economic ties with the neighbouring agricultural peoples either through trade or through robberies and invasions. Climatic changes often forced the nomads to look for new pastures, thus causing great ethnic movements. All these factors gave an important impulse to Proto-Iranian society, strengthened the formation of social classes (priests, warriors, craftsmen and peasants), forced the class of warriors to invade neighbouring lands and in the long run led to the rise of a state organization and conquest of vast territories.

On the basis of what has been said, it becomes clear that the migrations of the Proto-Indo-Iranians may have taken place in at least three successive periods and that they were of very different character.

The first type of migration was represented by the slow infiltration of small cattle-breeding groups who, in general, established friendly relations with the local population of food-gatherers, fishers or hunters.

The second type was the movement of greater groups, clans or tribes, headed by a well-organized army of charioteers and warriors who wanted to settle as leading social groups in new territories but, instead, often adapted themselves to the existing society and state organization.

Finally, the third type may be characterized by the massive movements of equestrian nomads who, together with their livestock, either looked for new pastures or wanted to conquer agricultural territories to supplement their own one-sided economy with their products.

Of course, there also existed some other, transitional types of migrations, but for the understanding of the Proto-Indo-Iranian movements, the forms just mentioned had the greatest historic importance.

The Proto-Indo-Iranians came into contact with the tribes of the Caucasus at an early epoch when animal husbandry in general and horse-breeding in particular began to develop in the steppes of eastern Europe.

The earliest trace of these contacts may be represented by Udi *ekʿ* 'horse' which could only be borrowed from PII **ekva-* before the first palatalization took place, perhaps at about 4000 B.C. according to the chronological scheme elaborated above on the basis of PII and PIr loan-words in Finno-Ugrian. Thus, perhaps, the word was adopted before the domestication of the horse as a term for the wild species.

But there exists probably yet another linguistic proof of the most ancient cultural contacts between the Proto-Indo-Iranians and the peoples settled on Ciscausian and Transcaucasian territories. Assyrian sources preserved the Lullubean word *kiurum* 'god' which can be regarded as an adoption of PII **kūra-* (cf. OInd

368

śūra-, Avestan *sūra-*), the Old Indian and Old Iranian correspondents of which were still applied to denote some gods in Vedic and Avestan times.

Besides these terms, however, other names for the horse and other domesticated animals were also taken over by the Caucasian languages from Proto-Indo-Iranian and Proto-Iranian. We can quote the following examples:

1. Circassian *šə*, Kabardian *šə* 'horse', Abkhaz *a-čə* 'the horse'; Georgian *ačuča* 'horse (in children's language)', Akhvakhian *ičwa* 'horse', Andian *iča*, Lak *č'u*, Khinalug *pšə* , (< *b-šə*) 'horse'.
2. Circassian *ača*, Kabardian *aza* 'goat for breeding'.
3. Chechen *gaɣr*, Ingush *goɣr* 'horse'.
4. Khinalug *spa* 'ass colt'.
5. Abkhaz *gu* 'pinfold'.

Of these terms *ačua, ičwa, iča, č'u, čə, šə, šə* may go back to PII **ečva-, *ešva-, *ašva-* because the initial vowel might have been understood as a demonstrative element in north-western Caucasian languages (cf. Abkhaz *a-čə* 'the horse'). The adoption of the word by the Caucasian languages might have taken place at different epochs. The earliest form could have been **ečva-* which may represent the third stage of the phonemic development of Proto-Indo-Iranian at about 3500 B.C. if the borrowing dates back to the period of the first domestication of the horse.

The second loan-word *ača, aza* obviously represents PII **aja-, *aža* 'goat' (cf. MP *azak* 'goat'), the phonemic forms of which would correspond to the third and fourth stages.

The term *gaɣr, goɣr* can apparently be connected with Persian *gōr* 'wild ass', which probably goes back to a PII prototype **gʷōɣra-*, but the borrowed form already speaks for **gaɣra-* representing the fifth stage or even a later period (after *gʷ-* > *g-* and *ō* > *ā*).

Khinalug *spa*, 'ass colt', can be regarded, of course, as an adoption of Old Northern Iranian *aspa-* and offers a valuable testimony for the long-lasting influence of Iranian horse-breeding in the Caucasus.

Finally, Abkhaz *gu*, 'pinfold', being an important term of cattle breeding, may be the adoption of PIr or OIr **gava-* 'pinfold' which only survived in the Avestan name of land *Gava-* and in the Ossetic *γäu, qäu* 'village' later.

From among the numerous Iranian loan-words of north-western and south-eastern Caucasian languages some may be of Proto-Iranian or even Proto-Indian origin. Thus, Kürin *γab*, 'handful', is obviously an archaic borrowing from PInd or PIr **gabha-* (cf. OInd *gabhasti-*) while Batsian *ḥač-*, 'to see', may go back to PII **kač -*, 'to see', reflecting the third stage of Proto-Indo-Iranian phonemic development, that is, approximately the end of the fourth millennium B.C. Chechen and Ingush *mār*, 'husband', may also be an ancient Proto-Indian or Proto-Iranian borrowing of the well-known term **marya-*.

In spite of the poverty of the linguistic evidence, these ancient Proto-Indian or Proto-Iranian loan-words occurring in Caucasian languages offer a valuable testimony for the advance of Proto-Indo-Iranian tribes towards the Caucasus which might have caused some ethnic movement there. If the ancient home of the Gutians ($^{KUR}gu\text{-}ti\text{-}um^{KI}$) can really be sought on the territory of later Media, then we may think of the possibility that the impulse to their invasion into Mesopotamia – which overthrew the dynasty of Agade, at the end of the third millennium B.C. – was given by the beginning of migrations of the Proto-Indian groups towards the Caucasus, the Caspian and Aral Seas.

Movements of Proto-Indians and Proto-Iranians and their migration routes

Be that as it may, in any case the following great ethnic movement, the invasion of Babylonia by the Kassites – which caused the fall of the first Babylonian dynasty – was already obviously connected with the migrations of the Proto-Indians. In spite of some scholarly efforts, the ethnic origin and the language of the Kassites are obscure but generally this people is regarded as a part of a widely spread population bearing slightly differing, though probably identical, names in the literary sources. Thus, the Greek name *Kaspioi*, Middle Iranian *Kǎsp* seems to be the outcome of an ancient form **Kǎśva-* which may be reflected also by Akkadian *Kaśśu*. The latter name was identified with Kassite *galzu/galdu*, assumed on the basis of the name *^mKurgalzu* explained by *^mRe'ikaśśi* 'shepherd of the Kassites' in the *List of Kassite Names*. This theory, however, is to be rejected because the phonemic change *lz/ld* > *śś* cannot be proved and even the sporadic development *lś* > *śś* occurs only in Middle- and Neo-Babylonian.

The development of the name **Kǎśva-* might have been similar to that of PIr **aśva-* which yielded *aspa-* in Median and Avestan, *asa-* in Old Persian, and **aśśa-* in Saka. Thus, the Iranians became acquainted with the name at the Proto-Iranian epoch in the form **Kǎśva-*, which developed into **Kǎspa-* in Median, into **Kǎspa-* in Old Bactrian and into **Kǎśśa-* in Old Saka. It is, therefore, not surprising if Herodotus lists among the peoples of the Old Persian satrapies a tribe *Kaspioi* located in the neighbourhood of the Caspian Sea, and also another tribe of the same name, *Kaspioi*, living in north-eastern Iran. If the original form of the name really was **Kǎśva-*, then we could have expected in fact the form **Kǎspa-* both in the north-west and the north-east of the Old Persian empire.

To explain the existence of the two peoples bearing the name *Kǎspa-* but who settled at a great distance from one another, historic research presumed that we have to do with the remnants of the same population, spread once from the Caspian sea to the north-eastern part of the Old Persian empire. One may doubt the probability of this assumption but there exists some additional evidence in its favour. Further to the north-east of the boundaries of the Old Persian empire, within the Saka language area, we find a land named *Kǎś* in Parthian, *Kasia, Kas* in Greek, *Kǎś* in Sogdian and **K'aṣa* in ancient Chinese. The name survives later as *Kǎśγar*. All these forms of the name may reflect the Saka development *Kāś(ś)a-, (> Kāśa-) of *Kāśva- and attest the presence of this ancient ethnic element even in Kashgaria.

Without doubt, the historical data and their linguistic interpretation speak in favour of the presumption that the Kassites (*Kaššu*) represent a part of a population which, at an earlier epoch, spread from the Caspian sea to Kashgaria and which was cut in two and pushed by the massive migrations of Proto-Indians and Proto-Iranians towards the east on the one hand and towards the west on the other, and therefore survived up to the Old Persian epoch only on the western and the eastern fringes of its former territory.

Attempts were made to regard the *Kaššu, Kăsp, Kăś* as an ancient population speaking Burushaski, which was thought to belong to the Caucasian languages. There can be no doubt that the language area of Burushaski once had a much greater extension than it has today. It is, however, impossible to admit the spread of the Burushaski population as far as the Caspian Sea in the Neolithic and Eneolithic because archaeological research has clearly shown the existence of three great cultures on the territory stretching from the Caspian Sea to the Pamir. These are the Jeitun culture (the territory of the Kopet Dag), the Kelteminar culture comprising a vast territory around the Aral sea from the Caspian Sea up to Tajikistan, and the Hissar culture in Tajikistan and in neighbouring territories. Of these three the settlements of the Kopet Dag can possibly be ascribed to a Dravidian population and in this case they may mark the northernmost extension of Proto-Dravidians living on the Iranian plateau before the arrival of the Indo-Iranians. As for the Kelteminar culture, it covers a vast territory, much greater than the ancient area which by any stretch of imagination may be attributed to the ancient extension of the Burushaski population. At the same time, however, the geographical horizon of the Kelteminar culture could well correspond to the area inhabited by the *Kaśu-, *Kaśva- (Kaššu, Kăsp, Kăś, etc.) population towards the end of the third millennium B.C. If, however, the identification of the Kelteminar culture with the *Kaśu-, *Kaśva- peoples proves to be correct, then the Burushaski tribes may be considered bearers of the Hissar culture.

The first infiltration of the Proto-Indian tillers and shepherds into the territory of the Kelteminar culture might have accelerated the economic and social development of the western *Kaśva- tribes, while their second wave, the great movement of the Proto-Indian war-charioteers, induced the most developed part of the *Kaśva- population to invade Babylonian Mesopotamia. Finally, the massive migrations of the Proto-Iranian equestrian nomads (Syntashta and Andronovo cultures), that is, the third wave of the Indo-Iranians, compelled the less developed *Kaśva- tribes to withdraw either into the hardly accessible mountainous districts or into the northern wooded steppes and the taiga zone. Later on, in the course of complicated ethnogenetic processes which led to the rise of the Samoyed peoples, they might have had some ethnic contacts with the Nenets (Yurak-Samoyeds), Enets (Tawgi-Samoyeds), Nganasans (Yenisey-Samoyeds) and Sayan-Samoyeds denoting themselves by the term *kaśa 'man', which can be the continuation of the ancient term **Kaśva-* > **Kaśśa-* > **Kaśa-* once used by the Kelteminar tribes as a self-appellation.

In the scanty linguistic material of the Kassites three important terms denoting deities occur: *Šuriyaš*, *Maruttaš* and *Bugaš*, corresponding to the Old Indian names of gods *Sūrya-*, *Marut-* and *Bhaga-*. *Sūrya-* and *Marut* are unknown in Old Iranian; this fact clearly points to the borrowing by the Kassites of these names from Proto-Indian. Thus, linguistic evidence speaks clearly for the assumption that the people of war-charioteers, which had induced the Kassites to invade Babylonia, belonged to the Proto-Indians. Because of the paucity of Kassite linguistic data, it is difficult to give a realistic assessment of the number of Proto-Indian elements in Kassite. However, the presence in Kassite of the names of three important Proto-Indian deities clearly indicates that ethnic contacts between the tribal aristocracies (the class of war-charioteers) of the two peoples must have been lively and that the new elements of culture introduced by the Proto-Indian war-charioteers deeply transformed the economic and social life of the Kassites.

It seems very likely that simultaneously with the movements of the Kassites – and in any case before 1700 B.C. at the latest, or perhaps even earlier, at the end of the third millennium B.C. – the immigration of Proto-Indian groups into Hurrian territory began, led by the class of war-charioteers (*maryannu*). They brought with them a new species of horse, more suitable for the war-chariot, a new method for horse-training, described by Kikkuli, the man of Hurri, in a treatise written in Hittite, and a perfected form of the chariot. Through these important elements of their civilization the Proto-Indians gave an impetus to the development of Hurrian society and to the organization of the Mitanni kingdom, many kings of which bore Proto-Indian names. The Proto-Indian tribal aristocracy spread also to Syria and Palestine where it brought about the formation of stage organization based on the class of war-charioteers. Proto-Indian linguistic influence was considerable on the vocabulary of horse-breeding, horse-training, social life and religion as shown by the following list of Proto-Indian terms borrowed by the Hurrians and other peoples of western Asia:[2]

Horse-breeding and horse-training

aśva-nī- 'horse-driver'; *aśva-* 'horse'. This term was borrowed by Hieroglyphic Hittite in the form *aśuwa-*, by Hebrew in the form of the radical *s-w-s* (< **aśvas*) becoming *sūs* and by Akkadian with metathesis **aśwas s-w-s* > *s-s-w* giving *sisû*.

*važhanasya Gen. 'ground', *vartani-* 'round', *babhru-* 'brown', *palita-* 'grey', *piṅgala-* 'red', **aika-* 'one', *tri-* 'three', *pañca* 'five', *sapta* 'seven', *nava* 'nine', *vart-* 'to turn', *rathya-* 'part of the chariot'.

2. Phonetic forms which are earlier than Vedic Indian are marked with an asterisk. All the other words are given in their Old Indian form and not in their cuneiform spellings.

Social life: marya- 'member of the charioteer-aristocracy', *miždhā- 'wage', magha-
  'gift, present', maṇi- 'necklace', rukmá- 'jewel', khādi- 'bracelet'.
Religion: Mitra-, Varuna-, Indra-, Nāsatyā-, Agni- (in Hittite ritual texts) 'names of
  gods'.

Also many personal names are known; they enlarge considerably our knowledge
of the Proto-Indian vocabulary. There were heated debates about the extent and
importance of Proto-Indian ethnic elements in Mesopotamia. In the present writer's opinion recent research tends to underestimate or even to deny the role
played by the Proto-Indians in Mesopotamia in general and in the Mitanni kingdom in particular. The objective historic evaluation of the Proto-Indian elements
in Mesopotamian texts must take into account the fact that our knowledge of
Ḥurrian is very limited, insufficient to give comprehensive information about
the strength of the Proto-Indian immigration into western Asia. It would be a
mistake to form an idea about the strength and importance of a population,
which did not have its own script and left behind no historical documents, on the
basis of the fragmentary evidence at our disposal. Yet the adoption by the
Ḥurrians of numerous Proto-Indian terms and their use of a great number of
Proto-Indian names, even in their royal family, show clearly the important role
the Proto-Indians played in the Mitanni kingdom and elsewhere in western Asia.

The lack of written sources compels us to try to establish the chronology
and the routes of the Proto-Indian movements with the help of archaeological
finds. It was observed that at three important sites lying to the south-east of the
Caspian Sea, namely, Shah-tepe, Turang-tepe and Tepe Hissar in the Gorgan valley, a black pottery (also called grey pottery) – unknown earlier in Iran – began to
appear towards the end of the fourth millennium B.C. The same black pottery was
found in the great Ḥurrian centres of Chagar Bazar and Alalaḥ. The recently
recognized identity of the black/grey pottery of the Gorgan valley and that of the
Ḥurrian sites calls for an historical interpretation.

It can be assumed that the Proto-Indians moving in the third millennium
B.C. from the steppes of eastern Europe between the Aral and the Caspian Seas to
the south, conquered the Gorgan valley and brought about the rise and spread of
the black/grey pottery independently of its origin. At the sites in the Gorgan valley a great number of horse skeletons were found, indicating the growing importance of horse-breeding. The signal horns made of gold and silver, from Tepe
Hissar and Turang-tepe, may well reflect the organization of war-charioteer
troops for the command of which the signals given by these were indispensable.
Advancing from the Gorgan valley farther to the west, the Proto-Indians pro-
moted the spread of many important elements of their culture: highly developed
horse-breeding and horse-training, the new tactic of war-charioteers, the black/
grey pottery, the social layer of *maryannu*, and their religion. In this historical process they did not act as a separate ethnic body. On the contrary, they became a
constituent of Ḥurrian society even though, for a long time, they still preserved

their language. The occurence in Hurrian of inflected Proto-Indian words clearly proves that for many centuries Proto-Indian was a living language on Hurrian territory.

Doubts have been expressed as to the correctness of this theory which attempts to connect the spread of the black/grey pottery with the Proto-Indian movements. In fact, the relationship between elements of a material culture and a population is never simple and obvious. The ethnic factor and the migration of ethnic groups represent only one among other elements that can give impulse to the rise and spread of several elements of material culture. Even if the black/grey pottery had not been invented and produced by the Proto-Indians, its appearance and spread could still be connected with their movements. Pastoral peoples invading a territory with a sedentary culture easily adopt many elements of the indigenous craft skills and thereby create a new material culture, different from their former one. There can hardly be any doubt about the possible or even probable justification of the theory which sees a connection between the rise of the black/grey pottery and the movements of the Proto-Indians. In general, pottery cannot be regarded as an ethnic identification mark, but it can well reflect even large-scale historical processes.

Chronological arguments have also been used against the theory of a Proto-Indian background to the spread of the black/grey pottery. According to these, the emergence of black pottery in the sites of the Gorgan valley may have been much earlier than the arrival of the Proto-Indians. This opinion is based on the theory of the late disintegration of the Indo-European linguistic community, which is now no longer acceptable. However, on the basis of the linguistic evidence discussed above and the relative and absolute chronology resulting from it, the beginnings of the Proto-Indo-Iranian movements can be dated to the first half of the fourth millennium B.C. The separation of Proto-Indian from Proto-Iranian and Proto-Kāfīrī possibly began around the middle of the fourth millennium B.C. simultaneously with the domestication of the horse in the steppes of eastern Europe. Accordingly, infiltration and migration of the Proto-Indians could begin towards the end of the same millennium and even the second phase of their advance towards the south might have taken place around the middle of the third millennium B.C., at a time when the first linguistic traces of the Proto-Indians may appear in ancient west Asia. Towards the end of the third millennium B.C. two names, namely *A-ri-si-* (< *sa'*)-*en* (**Arisaina-* = OInd **Arisena-*, to be distinguished from the Hurrian name *Arišen* < *Aripšen*), king of Urkiš and Nawar and *Sa-um-si-* (< *sa'*)-*en* (**Sauma-saina-* = OInd **Somasena-*), occur on a tablet dating from the time of the dynasty of Agade. Thus the spread of the Proto-Indians towards Mesopotamia and their amalgamation with the Hurrian population must have begun between 2300–2100 B.C.

It follows from this chronology that the main bulk of the Proto-Indians could arrive through Margiana and Bactria, that is, the northern route, in Gandhāra and create there the 'Gandhāra Grave Culture' around the seventeenth century B.C. The early advance of Proto-Indians on this route towards the Dravidian language area and the Indian subcontinent may be seen from the earliest traces of linguistic contacts between the two populations. In spite of the difficulty caused by the poverty of the Dravidian consonantal system, and particularly that of consonant clusters, insufficient to establish the phonological basis of the most ancient contacts between Proto-Indian and Proto-Dravidian, we can surmise that Dravidian words such as *cāy-* 'to incline, to lie down', *cari-* 'to roll', *cantam* 'beauty, pleasure, happiness', *cati-* 'to destroy, kill' could go back to the respective Proto-Indian forms *ćay-* (Skr. *śete*), *ćar-* (Skr. *car-*), *ćāntam* (Skr. *śānta-*, *śānti-*), and *ćāt-* (Skr. *śātayati*). In any case, even though Proto-Dravidian possessed only one initial affricate to render Indian initial *c-*, *s-*, *ś-*, the words cited can be postulated for Proto-Dravidian, that is, for a rather early chronological level of Dravidian prehistory. For such a date of Proto-Indian and Proto-Dravidian contacts speaks also the fact that one of the Dardic languages, namely, Tirahī, borrowed the word *kuzǝra* from Dravidian (cf. Tamil *kutirai*).

Early linguistic contacts between Proto-Indian and Proto-Dravidian groups may have been established through the Dravidian settlements of the Kopet Dag, which had lively relations with Mesopotamia. The territory of the Kopet Dag can possibly be identified with the golden land *Ḫarali* (later *Arali*, *Arallu*) of the Sumerian hymn on the trade with Tilmun, situated beyond Tukriš in the far north-east. The name *Ḫarali* (*Arali*) may be of Dravidian origin (cf. Tamil *aṟal* 'to burn, shine', *arali* 'fire', *aṟalōn*, 'Agni, sun'), and its meaning could be the same as that of Khorezm, going back to Old Iranian *Xvāra-zmi-* 'Land of the Sun'. Thus, if this identification proves to be correct, we have direct linguistic evidence for the existence of a Dravidian population in the Kopet Dag settlements. In the sites of this territory, particularly in Namazga IV (dated to the second half of the third millennium B.C.) and V, VI, the black/grey pottery and clay models of vehicles also appeared. This phenomenon may indicate the immigration to the Kopet Dag of one group of Proto-Indian pastoral tribes.

In this epoch another important centre of the Dravidian population might have been Shahr-i Sokhta. It is now generally assumed that Shahr-i Sokhta can be identified with the land *Aratta* mentioned in Sumerian literature. Once again linguistic evidence can be cited in support of this identification. The name *Aratta* can probably be explained by the Dravidian name of the Tamils, namely, *Arava* 'Tamil man', *Araviti* 'Tamil woman'. Thus, *Aratta* (shortened perhaps from *Aravata*) might have meant 'Tamil settlement' or 'Tamil land', directly attesting the Dravidian language of the population of Shahr-i Sokhta.

Very likely, the migration of the bulk of the Proto-Indians eastward and southward also compelled one part of the Dravidians to leave their settlements and to move in the direction of the Indian subcontinent. But in view of the slim evidence of linguistic contacts between Proto-Indians and Proto-Dravidians (most of the Dravidian loan-words in Indian and of the Indian ones in Dravidian belong to later epochs), one cannot speak of a general movement of the Dravidian population, already living on the territory of Iran at that time. The presence in Baluchistan of the Brāhui, belonging to the Dravidian languages, speaks for the Dravidian immigration into India by the southern route and at a later date, while the Proto-Indians could use the northern route, across the Khyber and other passes, some centuries earlier. Therefore, the massive immigration into India of the Dravidians could have taken place simultaneously with the latest phase of Proto-Indian and Proto-Kāfirī movements perhaps under the pressure of the Proto-Iranian tribes occupying their later territories.

The spread and migrations of the Proto-Iranians probably took place in three groups and in three directions. The separation of the Iranian languages into three great groups, namely, western, eastern and northern, clearly speaks in favour of such an assumption. These movements followed the migrations of the Proto-Indians and the spread of the eastern Iranian branch of the Proto-Iranians closely connected with the advance to Gandhāra of the Proto-Indians.

Most probably, the western group of Proto-Iranians moved across the pass of Derbend; they appear under the name *Baršua* (in Urartian) and *Parsua* (in Assyrian) in the neighbourhood of Lake Urmia in the ninth century B.C. Their movement may have started in the second half of the second millennium B.C.. The eastern Iranian group of the Proto-Iranians appeared somewhat earlier following in the footsteps of the Proto-Indians and Proto-Kāfirs in Margiana and Bactria. The Bronze Age culture of Bactria can probably be ascribed to the eastern group of Proto-Iranians who later also spread to Transoxania, and to the Proto-Kāfirs.

The question now arises: which was the language of the population which inhabited the territory before the arrival of the Indo-Iranians? We have already mentioned that the Hissar culture may belong to the ancient Burushaski population, which in the third millennium B.C. inhabited a much larger area than it does today. Some linguistic evidence suggests the ancient extension of the Burushaski population towards the west. According to Tacitus (*Ann.* X10), the Parthian Vardanes conquered all the peoples as far as the river *Sindes* which separates the *Dahae* from the *Arii*. On the basis of this passage, the river *Sindes* can be identified either with the Murghab or with the Tedzhen. Whichever river might have been identical with the Sindes, the latter name is remarkable from a linguistic point of view.

The name *Sindes* has been viewed as a linguistic trace of Indians who had remained in *Areia* after the majority of the Proto-Indians moved to the Indian subcontinent. Tempting though this theory may be, two arguments speak strongly against it. Indian settlements on the territory of Iran were numerous but all had names of the type *Hindugān, Hinduvān*. This can be explained by the Iranians' ability to identify the Indians on the basis of their language. It is therefore unlikely that the Iranians should have preserved an Indian river name *Sindhu*, for them easily recognizable as *Hindu*. On the other hand, a second argument against linking the name *Sindes* with the Indians relates to the question when the Iranians conquered the territory of *Areia*. If this happened before the change *s* > *h*, that is, before 800 B.C., the approximate date of the conquest, then the Iranians could only have preserved the name in the form *Hindu*. Besides, the Latin form *Sindes* (going back to a Greek source) could better reflect a foreign prototype *Sinda* than a form *Sindhu*.

Thus, the river name *Sindes* < *Sinda* can probably be explained by the Burushaski word *sinda* 'river' and can be regarded as a sign of the earlier presence of the Burushaski population on the northern border of *Areia*. There they could have maintained some contacts with the Proto-Dravidian population of Iran and even with the tribes of the Caucasus, a hypothesis that would explain the presence of some common elements in the respective vocabularies of the Burushaski and the Caucasian languages (e.g. Burushaski *har* 'ox' ~ Georgian *hari*). The relationship of the Sapalli culture with the sedentary civilization of the Kopet Dag and with the territory of Murghab becomes well understandable if we admit the presence of Burushaski ethnic elements reaching from the Sinda river to northern Bactria.

The advance of the Proto-Indians into the Gorgan valley, and the territory of Murghab and further east at the end of the third millennium B.C. set in motion only one part of the sedentary population and did not replace at once all the earlier inhabitants. Most probably the indigenous ethnic elements maintained themselves for a long time, even until the Proto-Iranian immigration in the second half of the second millennium B.C., and preserved their language and toponyms up to the Old Iranian epoch.

Perhaps there exists another linguistic trace of the ancient Burushaski population of Central Asia. Pliny the Elder mentions (*Natural History* VI. 49) that the Scythians used the name *Sil(is)* for the *Iaxartes* river. The latter being of Iranian origin, *Sil(is)* may be the name given to the river by the ancient pre-Iranian population. Thus, it can probably be explained by Burushaski *ts.hil* 'water' and in a slightly Iranized form (*Sil* > *Sir*) it survives in modern *Sir Darya*.

The beginnings of the move of the northern Proto-Iranians towards southern Siberia can be set into an even earlier period. The Syntashta culture may already represent a later phase of their migrations. If we look for this spread towards the east, we have to state that no clear linguistic trace has been found of direct contact between Proto-Iranians and Samoyeds. The reason for this may be that a belt of tribes, speaking Ket, Kott, Arin, Assan and other related languages and reaching from the Iset' river up to the Yenisey in ancient times, separated the Proto-Iranians from them. Unfortunately, the Kets excepted, the overwhelming majority of these tribes, together with their languages, completely disappeared. Nevertheless, some traces of their ancient linguistic contacts with Proto-Iranians can still be recognized. Thus, Kott *art'a*, 'true, veritable', may go back to Proto-Iranian **ṛta-*, Kott *ćâk* 'force', *ćaga* 'strong' may reflect Proto-Iranian **ćak-* (cf. OInd *śaknoti*) and Kott *ćak* 'to pass down' could be an adoption of Proto-Iranian **ćak-* 'to pass' (cf. OIr *sak-*). All these forms may represent the third stage of

Proto-Iranian development, that is, a rather early period. Perhaps Ket *kuos* 'cow', if it goes back to Proto-Iranian *$g^w\bar{a}us$*, reflects the same stage.

These loan-words may speak in favour of a rather ancient linguistic contact between Proto-Iranian and Ket. Some loans penetrated also into the Turkic languages (cf. Turkic *čaq* 'force', *čaq* 'time') which probably adopted some Proto-Iranian terms independently from the Ket languages. If these loan-words did not come into Turkic through the intermediary of some unknown, now disappeared languages, one may think of an early advance of Proto-Iranians as far as the northern zones of Central Asia.

Finally the question arises how is the spatial position of Proto-Iranian, Proto-Kāfīrī and Proto-Indian to be reconstructed before the migration of the Proto-Indian tribes to Gandhāra. The linguistic features of Kāfīrī (namely PII *$*\acute{z}h$, *$*jh$ > Kāfīrī *z* (*dz*), *ž* (*ǰ*) but > OInd *h*, PII *$*\acute{c}$ > Kāfīrī *ts* but > OInd *ś*) can be explained only by the twofold assumption that Proto-Kāfīrī occupied a fringe position within the Indo-Iranian linguistic area and that it had a closer contact with Proto-Iranian. These two statements can only be harmonized if the original position of Proto-Iranian and Proto-Indian was not along a north–south axis but was, at least partly, parallel in this direction and Proto-Kāfīrī took the northern fringe of Proto-Indian. Thus, by the movement of the Proto-Indians towards the south-east, the Proto-Kāfīrs found themselves between them and the Proto-Iranians, a spatial position which has remained unchanged up to now.

PASTORAL TRIBES OF THE BRONZE AGE IN THE OXUS VALLEY (BACTRIA)[1]

B. A. Litvinsky and L. T. P'yankova

THE migration of tribes and the resettlement of large numbers of people, evidence of which is provided by Indo-Iranian linguistics, necessarily produced changes in the pattern of ancient cultures. In some cases, as in Margiana and Sapalli in southern Uzbekistan, new features appeared in the midst of highly developed settled cultures: innovations in burial rites or new themes in the visual arts. At the same time, there appeared in Soviet Central Asia tribes of herdsmen whose culture contained features going back to the traditions of settled civilizations, though these features were far from dominant. More is known of the migratory herding tribes from their burial grounds than from their settlements, since they spent too short a time in the latter to leave substantial cultural deposits. An entire series of such archaeological assemblages was discovered in the middle reaches of the Amu Darya (Oxus).

The cemeteries in the Oxus valley (in Bactria), located both outside and within settlements, present a different picture. The appearance of cemeteries situated outside settlements become typical from the time of Namazga VI; in other words, during the period when most of the Bactrian cemeteries considered here were built. The cemeteries are spread over three regions – northern Afghanistan, southern Tajikistan and southern Uzbekistan.

The Bronze Age cemeteries in northern Afghanistan were discovered by a Soviet-Afghan archaeological expedition. The most extensive work was done in the Dashly oasis, beginning in 1970. The cemeteries were excavated and the research published by V. I. Sarianidi.

A series of Bronze Age remains were found in a valley running southwards from the Amu Darya. In one of them, in the Farukhabad oasis, now a desert, there are a number of settlements. A feature of the central settlement, Farukhabad I, is that a large cemetery is situated in its centre and three others along its periphery. The graves had been plundered.

---

1. See Map 11 on page 339.

In the Dashly oasis, 30 km south of the Amu Darya, in a broad steppe setting, watered in Antiquity by the delta channels of the Balkhab river, a large number of Bronze Age remains were found. The Dashly 1 cemetery is situated on the ruins of a derelict fortified settlement of the same name. This is not an isolated, compact cemetery but is situated on the actual site of the settlement. Altogether ten graves have been uncovered. Some 3 km away is the Dashly 3 settlement, with the ruins of a temple. Here a scattered burial ground containing five graves has been found, as well as a cemetery built in the ruins of the temple and containing eighty-seven graves. The upper parts of the graves have been destroyed by erosion. The actual graves are rectangular in shape, with rounded corners, measuring 1.7 × 1 m, or more seldom circular or oval. They were frequently lined with mud-bricks, and it is possible they were also covered over in the same way. When the graves were built on unused or derelict sites, tunnel-like recesses were let into the walls. Children were sometimes buried in large containers. In addition to burials with entire skeletons (which are in majority) there are others with only part of the skeleton placed in the grave, but with extensive grave goods. The latter are fractional burials. Mention should also be made of the ritual burials of sheep, also with grave goods. In one such sheep burial food for the deceased was placed in the grave too – the front portion of a sheep's flank.

In the Dashly 18 and 19 sites large cemeteries were found, though unfortunately they had been plundered. The graves were of the recess and catacomb type. In one of them a horse was buried. The majority of the graves are single burials. The body is crouched lying either on the left or the right side; in a few cases it is laid on its back or stomach. Generally speaking, the burials tend to be oriented towards the north. As food for the deceased, joints of sheep were placed in the grave. The grave goods are rich and varied, and consist for the most part of pottery, between one or two and fifteen or twenty items in each tomb. About 90 per cent of the items have been turned on the potter's wheel. The principal forms are vases with and without stems, as well as pots, jars, goblets, basins, vessels in the form of teapots with spouts, etc. Among the metal artefacts mention should be made of bronze mirrors, bracelets, pots, pins, fillets (bandeaux) and daggers. Other items placed in the graves included stoneware and woven baskets. The graves, including the plundered ones, have also produced numerous seals.

From 1965 to 1969, A. M. Mandel'shtam investigated two Bronze Age cemeteries in the low country of the Kafirnigan river, in the narrow intramontane Beshkent valley. These cemeteries – early Tulkhar, with seventy-five graves, and early Aruktau, with twelve tumuli – represent a new type of Bronze Age cultural complex (Fig. 1), exhibiting various burial techniques and different kinds of graves. Some of the burials (fifty-four, all in the early Tulkhar cemetery) showed a departure from the normal pattern by the standard nature of the ceremonial and grave goods, and were related by Mandel'shtam to the Beshkent culture.[2]

2. Mandel'shtam, 1968.

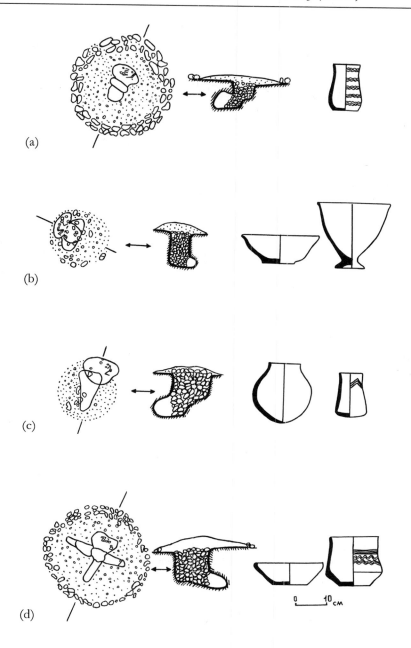

(a)

(b)

(c)

(d)

FIG. 1. Southern Tajikistan: Early Tulkhar burial grounds.
Main types of burials: (a) hole with a slope (Beshkent culture); (b) grave
with cremated corpse; (c) catacomb (Vakhsh culture); (d) burial of bones of
a dismembered skeleton in a stone box. (After A. M. Mandel'shtam.)

In the 1960s a number of Bronze Age kurgan burial-sites (tumuli) along the lower reaches of the Vakhsh and Kyzyl-su rivers were investigated under the supervision of B. A. Litvinsky. Five sites were investigated in full or in part: Vakhsh 1, Tigrovaya Balka, Oikul, Jara-Kul (in the lower reaches of the right bank of the Vakhsh) and Makan-i Mar (in the lower reaches of the right bank of the Kyzul-su). In all, 233 tumuli were excavated. A feature of all the sites is the uniform mode of interment and the identical composition of the grave goods. Litvinsky relates them to the Vakhsh culture.[3] In 1981 a new burial site of this culture was discovered – Sarband in the neighbourhood of the village of Kyzyl-kala, in the middle portion of the Vakhsh valley, on the right bank of the river. A number of other single graves have been found there in southern Tajikistan.

In 1973 a study of the Beshkent valley cemeteries was continued. Three cemeteries were excavated: Beshkent I (BM I), which by the design of the burial structures resembles the cemeteries of the Vakhsh culture; Beshkent II (BM II), which consists of structures of the steppe type; and Beshkent III (BM III), in which only commemorative structures are represented.[4]

During the 1970s a number of Bronze Age cemeteries were investigated along the northern border of the Afghan-Tajik depression: Tandyriul and Zarka-mar in the Hissar valley, and two cemeteries near the town of Nurek. They relate to the late Molali period of the Sapalli culture.[5]

The cemeteries on the right bank of the Panj and Amu Darya rivers include complexes representing various cultures. The largest number of remains are of the Vakhsh culture (Fig. 2). Cemeteries of this culture are sited on the upper loess river terraces, on land leading up to low mountain ridges. The largest site is situated in Tigrovaya Balka. It measures 680 × 800 m, and contains 130 tumuli, 116 of which have been excavated. Vakhsh 1 measures 180 × 200 m (fifty tumuli, forty excavated), Oikul 220 × 260 m (fifty-two tumuli, all excavated), Jarkul 240 × 250 m (eighty tumuli, thirteen excavated) and Makan-i Mar 200 × 300 m (forty tumuli, twelve excavated).

Burial sites of the Vakhsh culture are visible on the surface by means of low mound-like artificial barrows (0.1 to 1.1 m high), circular or slightly oval in shape, made of loess, sometimes with the addition of pebbles or stones. Most of the barrows are surrounded at the base by a ring of stones lying horizontally in one to four rows. Sometimes the ring is situated up the slope of the barrow. Some tumuli are ringed by a further outer circle of stones, between 9.5 and 30 m, beyond the base of the barrow. With few exceptions the graves are of the niche-recess or catacomb type. The entrance passage leading down is sealed by large cobble-stones, the interstices between which are filled with friable loess. The burial chambers are niches cut into the soil on one or other side of the passage. In accordance with the terminology most widely used in Central Asian archaeology

3. Litvinsky, 1964, p. 158.
4. Litvinsky et al., 1977, p. 76–92.
5. Antonova and Vinogradova, 1979; P'yankova, 1979.

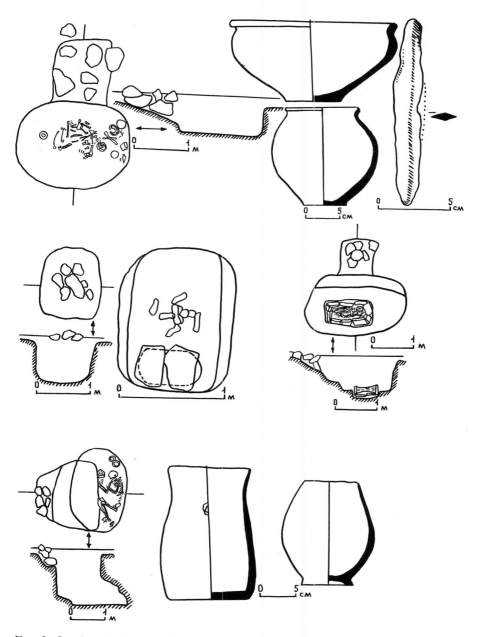

FIG. 2. Southern Tajikistan: Main types of burials of Vakhsh culture. 'Tiger Gorge' burial ground.

for similar tombs in later historic periods, we shall call the chambers hollowed out in the long wall of the passages, niches, and those in the short wall, catacombs. The structures have various forms of entrance passage and, taking also into account the particular type of chamber, fall into the following categories:

1. Tombs with an oval or rectangular passage and a catacomb burial chamber.
2. Tombs with an oval or rectangular passage and niche burial chamber.
3. Tombs with a trapezoidal passage and a catacomb burial chamber.
4. Tombs with a T-shaped passage and niche chamber.
5. Tombs with an arc-shaped passage and a niche chamber.
6. Multiple burials in simple pits form a separate type.
7. Individual cases of tombs with a U- or L-shaped passage and burials at former ground-level under the soil used for the barrow.

Most typical of the Vakhsh culture are tombs of Types 1 (about 43 per cent) and 2 (about 30 per cent). The other designs are not common. No regular pattern is observable in regard to the orientation of the passage or the burial chambers relative to the cardinal points.

In cemeteries of the Vakhsh culture the bodies were invariably placed in a crouching position on their side (in a few cases on their backs or stomachs), the arms being folded at the elbow and the legs at the knee. The skeletons are lying directly on the floor of the chambers, the depth below the original ground level varying from 0.8 to 3 m. In some cases the skulls are resting on rectangular clay 'pillows'. The orientation of the bodies varies, but most frequently it is towards the north (about 30 per cent) and least frequently towards the south. Most of the burials are single, though there are also double burials (of one sex or both sexes), and in some cases a woman was buried with a child. Some of the couples were buried at the same time, others at different times. In the Oikul and Makan-i Mar cemeteries a few cases have been identified where two to three graves are found beneath each barrow. For single male burials, except in isolated cases, the body was typically placed on its right side, facing the entrance to the burial chamber. The female skeletons are placed in various positions: the commonest is on the left side (about 50 per cent), facing the entrance to the chamber. The people of the Vakhsh cemeteries are related to a Europoid, dolichocephalic, leptomorphic type.[6]

The grave goods are made up primarily of pottery, there being very few metal artefacts (from all the tumuli excavated only fourteen have daggers, mirrors and knives). Several stone and bone artefacts were also found. In the cemeteries along the Vakhsh the number of items found in each grave is from one to six (usually one or two). The burials at Makan-i Mar are accompanied by a larger number of objects – from two to eight in single graves (generally four to five) and from eight to fourteen in double burials (most commonly eight to nine).

Over 70 per cent of the pottery is hand-made. In many cases hand-made and wheel-turned ware are identical in shape and even in dimensions. Generally

6. Kiyatkina, 1976, p. 25.

speaking, pottery of the Vakhsh culture relates to the range of designs commonly found among sedentary agricultural populations in Soviet Central Asia and contiguous territories during the Late Bronze Age. Some of the designs are widely distributed throughout the region. The closest analogies can be found in the sedentary agricultural remains of ancient Bactria, practically all types of Vakhsh pottery (except for round-bottomed kitchen pots) being comparable with the ware produced by the sedentary agriculturalists of northern Afghanistan.[7]

The pottery found among the southern Bactrian remains also has analogies with all types of vessels specific to the range of materials produced by the Vakhsh culture – egg-shaped, biconical and jar-shaped. These types are not found among the northern Bactrian remains of the Sapalli culture. Close analogies are also to be found in northern Afghanistan for the stemmed goblet and the vase on a tall hollow stem which are unique specimens as far as the Vakhsh culture is concerned. The collections of pottery found in southern Bactria also include types of vessel that could serve as genetic prototypes for the Vakhsh ware. All metallic and other artefacts of the Vakhsh culture are related to types commonly encountered among agricultural cultures. The burial arrangements were also those of the agricultural population living in the Bactrian region.

The origin of the Vakhsh culture is in probability linked to the northward movement of one part of the tribes from southern Bactria. These people, at the close of the Bronze Age, went over predominantly to animal husbandry, which, along with land tillage, constituted a developed branch of the economy among the early agricultural societies of the Bactrian region. A factor conducive to this switch was the favourable natural conditions they encountered. It is possible that their constant contacts with steppe bronze tribes also contributed to this process. At the end of the second millennium B.C. there is evidence of a strong incursion by these northern tribes into Soviet Central Asia, right up to the borders of the sedentary-agricultural oases. In southern Tajikistan, steppe bronze sites and individual finds of steppe-type pottery have come to light in the immediate vicinity of the areas where the Vakhsh culture occurred. The possibility that new arrivals from the steppes took part in the formation of the Vakhsh culture is supported by the design on some cooking pots and also by certain details in the design of burial structures, such as the ring of stones surrounding a barrow. To judge from the sheep bones found in many Vakhsh culture graves, its bearers were primarily engaged in pasturing and rearing sheep and goats.

The burial remains bear witness to a number of cults connected with funeral rites. That most clearly evinced is the cult of fire, to which 25 per cent of all Vakhsh culture graves bear witness, represented in the tombs by: (a) charcoal and embers from braziers consisting of three small pebbles with a kitchen pot standing on them (in no case, however, are there any signs of a fire being lit in the passage of the chambers, the charcoal must have been brought into the tombs from a

7. Sarianidi, 1977; Francfort and Pottier, 1978.

funeral pyre outside); (b) a funeral pyre at the original ground-level, before the soil was brought in to form the barrow; and, (c) in the case of two chiefs buried in the Tigrovaya Balka cemetery, round each tomb a ring of funeral pyres (in one case numbering forty-one, in the other twenty) which burned for several days. The Vakhsh tribes also typically had a cult of the deceased and ancestors, as is evident from the construction of many commemorative structures. The Vakhsh culture dates from the last centuries of the second millennium B.C.

The Beshkent valley graves reflect a variety of cultural traditions. The most numerous group is made up of graves of the Beshkent culture (early Tulkhar). The burial structures are uniform: quasi-rectangular or rounded pits with an inclined descent or shaft from the former ground level. Externally such structures are visible as a covering of stones. The pits are filled with loess, and stones are found only in the upper portion of the descent. In most cases the long axis of the pits extends in a west–east direction. The orientation of the descents relative to the cardinal points varies. The bodies are laid on their sides, hunched up, with arms bent at the elbow and legs at the knee. Most of the burials are single, but there are eight pair-burials, all of different sexes, some buried at the same time, others at different times. Four of the tombs were found to contain multiple child burials, the children's necropolis being situated at some distance from the adult cemetery.

All the men buried at early Tulkhar in pits with an inclined descent are laid on their right side, facing the descent, while the women are laid on their left side, either facing the descent or with their backs to it. In pair-burials (whether at the same or different times) the woman always lies with her back to the entrance and facing the man. The corpses are not oriented uniformly, except in the case of pair-burials, where both the dead lie with their heads to the east.

Anthropologically the early Tulkhar population falls into the category of southern proto-Mediterranean types, though morphologically speaking it is not closely related to the people of the Vakhsh culture and the sedentary agricultural remains of Bactria. The group of skulls from early Tulkhar stand out among other craniological series for their exceptional size in all dimensions.

The Beshkent culture grave goods consist of pottery and metal and stone artefacts. About 70 per cent of the pottery is hand-made. The main forms of ware are pots, dishes and basins. The metal products include foliated knives, usually with the end of the blade curved outwards and sometimes with a midrib, daggers, 'razors', adzes, round mirrors with a lateral handle and pins. Stone objects are represented by a few flint arrowheads and also various forms of bead, mainly barrel-shaped. Economically the Beshkent culture was based on animal husbandry.

Early Tulkhar also contains a group of graves where the bodies have been cremated (nine tombs). Externally, they are visible by means of a covering of seven stones. The burial structures are shallow pits usually extending from north to south. At the bottom of the southern part of such pits an oval depression has been hollowed out and covered with flagstone chips or elongated stones. On its floor lie fine calcined human bones, ashes and charcoal. The pit is laid with stones, giving the form of a swastika or a circle with four 'spokes'. These pits also occasionally yield small fragments of modelled, ill-fired pottery. It is not possible to reconstruct the shape of the pots. Seven burials at early Tulkhar were carried out in catacomb-like tombs. They contain typical Vakhsh grave goods and can be attributed to this culture.

A small group of burials (three graves) also in pits with an inclined entrance reflect fundamentally different funeral arrangements. In these graves a rectangular depression has been hollowed out in the centre of the base of the pit, its floor and walls being lined with flagstone chippings to form a box. In this miniature stone box are buried the bones of the dismembered skeleton, the skull being always laid in the eastern part of the box, the leg-bones in the western part, the arm-bones between them and the remaining bones underneath them. This open box was then covered over with reeds. There are no grave goods.

A final type of burial structure in the early Tulkhar cemetery consists of stone surrounds enclosing a pit. There are two such cases. The surrounds are roughly square-shaped, and the corner-stones are extremely large. The burial pits are oval. The bodies were laid in the graves on their sides in a hunched-up position (the man on the right, the woman on the left). Around the skull of each of the deceased is a narrow band of ashes and charcoal chips, which indicates that a fire was lit in the tomb for ritual purposes of some kind or another. The grave goods consist of vessels, round mirrors and sheep bones. In the man's grave there is also the skeleton of a lamb (but without the skull).

In the early Aruktau cemetery we find two types of burial structures. The first consists of round or rectangular stone surrounds, sometimes paired. The bodies were buried at the original ground level, and stones strewed above (eleven graves). Within each surround the graves are identical. All the skeletons are lying on the right side, hunched up, with the head towards the north or north-east. The grave goods consist of bronze sickles, ornaments, sheep bones and pottery similar to that found in the Beshkent graves. The second consists of a pit beneath a stone cairn (one grave). The pit is rectangular and extends from west to east. The body is that of a girl lying on her left, hunched up, with her head to the east. The grave goods consist of pottery (also similar to the Beshkent pottery), bronze mirrors and ear-rings.

The Beshkent I cemetery comprises two types of structure: (a) catacomb-type tombs with a trapezoidal passage (nineteen cases); and (b) commemorative structures, consisting of stones laid out in the form of a ring (seven cases). The Beshkent II cemetery also consists of actual burials and structures of a commemorative character. The Beshkent III cemetery consists entirely of commemorative structures (six), made of circles of stones enclosing areas of paving made of flagstones laid flat on the ground.

To judge from the materials found in the burial complexes, the ethnic situation in the Beshkent valley area, as reflected in the cemeteries, would appear to be fairly complicated in relation to the size of the area, which is not large. For the early Tulkhar cemetery, A. M. Mandel'shtam proposed a date of the fourteenth to eighth centuries B.C., including the thirteenth to eleventh centuries B.C. for the Beshkent culture itself. We can now identify with certainty the centre from which the pottery found in the Beshkent valley cemeteries comes – these are remains from the late Molali stage of the Sapalli culture (Fig. 3), such as have now been found both in southern Uzbekistan and southern Tajikistan.

Thanks to the comparative chronology worked out by Uzbek archaeologists for remains of the Sapalli culture, materials of the Molali period can today be dated unambiguously to the eleventh to tenth centuries B.C. The presence of pottery from the north Bactrian sedentary agricultural area among the materials that have come down to us from the Beshkent culture makes it possible to say something about where this culture took shape. Of the population groups taking part in forming the Beshkent valley complexes was one belonging to the late stage of the Sapalli culture; this was in line with a process that was characteristic of the economy of the agricultural tribes of Bactria during the final Bronze Age, namely that whereby some of the tribes switched to animal husbandry as their principal occupation. As has been seen from the example of the Vakhsh culture, this process occurred concurrently in northern and southern Bactria, though the formation of the pastoralist complexes in the Beshkent valley involved a greater degree of participation by the steppe bronze tribes. Traces of the incursion of such tribes into the Beshkent valley are documented both by the finds of pottery (BM III) and metal artefacts typical of steppe cultures (in the early Tulkhar pits with entrance ramps investigators have found a dagger of eastern Kazakhstan type and two knives similar to classic specimens of the timber grave (*srubnaya kul'tura* and Andronovo culture) and by the burial arrangements typical of a steppe population (graves with cremation in early Tulkhar, stone boxes in BM II). The marked degree of mixing of the population here probably explains the emergence of the distinctive anthropological type that characterizes the Beshkent culture. The appearance of catacombs with typical Vakhsh-culture grave goods in early Tulkhar is evidently linked to the direct incursion of some group of the bearers of this culture into the Beshkent valley.

From the materials found in the cemeteries along the lower reaches of the Kafirnigan it is also possible to trace a certain transformation in the kind of representations associated with the burial ritual. The Beshkent culture is characterized by the mandatory standardized appearance of the fire cult for each and every burial, as evinced by the construction of the distinctive small hearths in the graves. In male burials the hearths are square and made of pieces of broken flagstone, while in female burials they are circular hollows. When the body was interred, a fire was lit in these hearths. As has been said above, for the Vakhsh culture manifestations of the fire cult varied from one burial to another and were not mandatory. In the catacomb tombs of early Tulkhar a fire ritual accompanies each burial (this being the pre-eminent link with Beshkent culture burials), but it

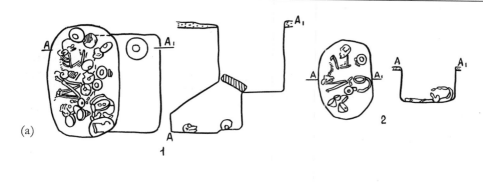

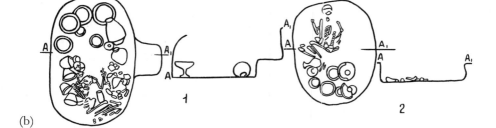

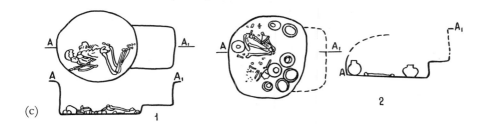

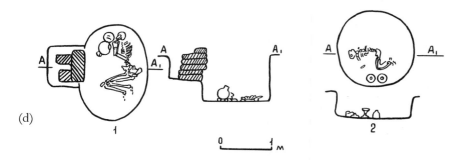

Fig. 3. Southern Uzbekistan: Burial grounds of Sapalli culture:
(a) Sapalli stage; (b) Jarkutan stage; (c) Kuzalinksi stage; (d) Molali stage.
(After A. A. Askarov and B. N. Abdulaev.)

is different in form: there are no standard hearths but a small funeral pyre is lit on the top step of the entrance shaft, while the charcoal and ashes are carried into the chamber in ready form on a shaving of flagstone or a fragment of a pottery (ideological influence of the Vakhsh culture). Tribes of the Vakhsh culture as well as those of the Beshkent culture took part in forming the Beshkent I complex. The BM I cemetery contains in addition a large group of commemorative structures, a characteristic feature of Vakhsh complexes.

Cemeteries from the Molali stage of the Sapalli culture have been found in the Hissar valley and in the area of Nurek. In the Tandyriul cemetery thirty-four graves have been excavated, one in Zarkamar, and sixteen in one of the Nurek cemeteries. The main type of burial structure is a pit in the ground, identified on the surface by a number of stones. In Tandyriul a number of catacomb tombs have also been discovered. The bodies were buried hunched up, lying on their sides. The skeletons are very poorly preserved. In the Nurek cemetery they have been almost completely destroyed through leaching by salty gypsum.

The grave goods comprise pottery, almost exclusively wheel-turned and of high quality, with white slip and burnish (principally pots, vases and basins), though there are also modelled articles (jugs, pots and dishes). Metal items at Tandyriul are represented by bronze votive knives, and cylindrical beads. A bell-mouthed pendant of typical Andronovo design has also been found here. In the Nurek cemetery excavations have brought to light a fragment of a bronze knife-blade with the tip drawn backwards and a golden fillet with five protuberances into one of which is inserted a piece of turquoise. Both cemeteries have yielded lazurite and azurite beads in the shape of miniature axes.

The origin of these complexes is associated with the migration of bearers of the Sapalli culture in its late stage to the north-east, up the Surkhan Darya valley where it joins the Hissar valley. In its material appearance, however, the Tandyriul cemetery is closer to the remains of the Molali stage in Uzbekistan. In the Nurek cemetery the proportion of hand-made ware is higher, most of the pots having a biconical body, untypical of the pottery collections found in Uzbekistan, and among the materials found here there is one modelled basin decorated in the manner of Kuchuk-tepe, Tillya-tepe and similar sites. All this suggests that the Nurek cemetery is somewhat, though not a great deal, later than Tandyriul.

Historical evolution

We have described above the interrelationship of the various local and chronological variants of the Bronze Age Bactrian culture, of which cemeteries provided the main evidence.

The problem of the origin of this culture as a whole has aroused lengthy discussion. Immediately after having excavated the Bronze Age cemeteries in the Beshkent valley, A. M. Mandel'shtam raised (1966 and 1968) the question of the genesis of the culture he had discovered. In this connection he put forward the view that it was appropriate, above all, to start from two fundamental premises, that of the culture's pastoral character and the manifest evidence of its being affected by other population groups of Bactria or contiguous countries. He laid special stress on the northern links, analysing in a somewhat one-sided fashion the grave goods and, to some extent, the burial rites, and paying attention principally to the links and similarities with the zone of steppe cultures. In this connection he emphasized that 'we do not have available any materials that would enable us to posit a local origin for the Beshkent culture'. The conclusion drawn from all this was that 'the earlier but probably not original places of residence of the bearers of the Beshkent culture must be sought somewhere to the north of Bactria'. One possible alternative put forward was the steppe region to the north of the Syr Darya, though the possibility of this region's lying to the south of the Syr Darya was not ruled out. The tribe that left the Beshkent cemeteries, he writes elsewhere, moved 'southward', but from where it came remained a mystery for Mandel'shtam. He simply pointed out in this respect that attention should be paid to the Tazabagyab culture and other steppe bronze cultures allied to it.[8]

This concept was supported and developed by E. E. Kuz'mina who suggested that 'a new archaeological culture took shape in Central Asia as a result of the crossing of two groups of pastoralists – descendants of the Zamanbaba and Andronovo peoples', none other than the culture of the people who built the southern Tajikistan cemeteries. Since the same period had seen publication of the data concerning the sedentary agricultural remains of Bactria, the fact that the grave goods included many objects of a sedentary agricultural type was explained as the consequence of an exchange between steppe dwellers who had come down from the north and the inhabitants of southern agricultural settlements.[9] This hypothesis has proved to be incorrect.

Another hypothesis was advanced by B. A. Litvinsky.[10] He drew attention to the close similarity – in some cases identity – with the culture of southern Turkmenistan of Namazga VI, especially its Murghab variant, while recognizing the influence of steppe bronze cultures. It was suggested that the advent of these cemeteries is linked to the movement of tribes from south-western Turkmenistan.[11] Subsequently he modified this hypothesis,[12] which is also currently accepted by A. Askarov.

The hypothesis is now formulated as follows. In the central and eastern part of southern Turkmenistan in the second half of the second millennium B.C. there were settlements of an archaeological culture known as Namazga VI with

8. Mandel'shtam, 1966, pp. 256–9.
9. Kuz'mina, 1972*b*, pp. 120–1.
10. Litvinsky, 1964, pp. 157–8.
11. Ibid.
12. Litvinsky, 1967, pp. 121–7, 1973, pp. 9–13, 1981, pp. 155–6.

its eastern, Murghab variant.[13] Settlements and cemeteries of a very similar (and in some points identical) culture (especially by comparison with the 'Murghab' variant) have been investigated, as had been indicated, in the Bactrian region. All these settlements and cemeteries, separated from one another (from east to west) by nearly 1,000 km, were left behind by communities with a single life-style. At the same time the nature of the settlements, the tribes' movement from one small oasis to another around centrally fortified settlements, the mode of construction, the planning, the form taken by the material culture were likewise similar, notwithstanding certain regional differences. This also relates to the anthropological aspect of the population. All this points to the existence of a huge historico-cultural area of Central Asia, on the territory of what was to become Parthia, Margiana and Bactria. Here in the middle and second half of the second millennium B.C. lived closely related tribes who had moved eastwards from the western foci of this culture at the beginning of the second millennium B.C. By the middle of the millennium Margiana and Bactria were densely populated.

Whence came the colonizing wave? Obviously one of the basic foci was the oases of southern Turkmenistan as a whole, the leading role of the Ahaltekin and Etek centres being taken, after their population declined, by the centres of Margiana as well as those of Iranian Khorasan. Iranian Khorasan is in fact regarded by V. I. Sarianidi as the original focus of migration, but the arguments in support of this hypothesis are insufficient.

On arriving in Bactria, these tribes initially continued to preserve their own economic and cultural patterns. This was facilitated by the fact that Bactria, or those parts of it where they initially settled, offered comparable ecological conditions. Peoples with a traditional mud architecture, an economy based on primitive irrigated tillage with a considerable admixture of stock-raising, a high level of craftsmanship, in particular the potter's craft, the products of which developed and varied the Anau tradition, such were the characteristic features of the Bactrian population. The spiritual culture also by and large retained initially its original features. However, the ecological conditions were not wholly identical. Moreover the newcomers did not live in a vacuum: they were subject to the influence of the local substrate population as well as the steppe tribes, and intermingled with them. As a result of their severance from the original foci and the above-mentioned factors, the paths of development were not absolutely identical, and there were gradual but fairly marked changes both in production and also in the material and spiritual culture. Typical are the existence of catacomb burials under the floors of the houses, and the ritual burials of sheep.

Part of the population continued to migrate. In particular, large groups from northern Afghanistan and, subsequently, from southern Uzbekistan pushed forward into the valleys and hills of southern Tajikistan. Coming upon ecological conditions that were not propitious for a primitive agricultural economy, they

13. Litvinsky, 1952; Masimov, 1976.

switched to one based primarily on stockraising. This transition was facilitated by their continual contacts with the 'steppe-dwellers'. This group of newcomers from the area of agricultural cultures (which is represented by the cemeteries of southern Tajikistan) underwent certain changes in their economic arrangements and cultures. There were also major changes in their burial rites; for instance, they began to erect over the tombs structures of a type borrowed from the bearers of the steppe cultures. There were a number of ethnographic population groups who led a semi-sedentary life-style, raising herds they had driven away from their natural pastures.

The links between the Bactrian Bronze Age culture and other cultures were directed primarily towards the west. It must be said that investigators differ in assessing the relative importance of the various westward links. A. Askarov and B. A. Litvinsky give priority to the links between Bactria and Margiana; V. I. Sarianidi, while not denying their importance (he even speaks of the Margiana-Bactria archaeological complex), stresses the special significance of the Iranian links.[14] Detailed attention is also being paid to links further westwards, as far as Mesopotamia.

On the other hand, there are evident links and points of correspondence in certain directions with the Bronze Age culture of the Swat valley (Pakistan). Drawing attention to these points of correspondence (on the basis of materials from the cemeteries in southern Tajikistan), Litvinsky noted that the material from the Swat cemeteries is more closely related to Iran and the Caucasus.[15]

Another point of view was expressed by E. E. Kuz'mina who argued that the cemeteries of southern Tajikistan and Swat were identical in most of their features, that there was cultural affinity between them, and that the question of the origin of the Swat cemeteries must be solved taking this identity into account.[16] However, as detailed analysis has shown, this similarity is of a general character, and there are not so many specific points where the two coincide.[17] Moreover, the excavations of other remains in Bactria, especially in northern Afghanistan, have shown that in fact the culture of these sites has a much more evident link with the cultures of the Swat valley.[18] Kuz'mina's idea of a genetic link between the Swat cemeteries and those of southern Tajikistan must accordingly be rejected; all that can be said is that there are 'common sources to these cultures.'[19] For the location of these common sources we are referred either to north-eastern Iran[20] or to southern Turkmenia – to the culture of Namazga VI

14. Sarianidi, 1977.
15. Litvinsky, 1967, pp. 122–4, 127.
16. Kuz'mina, 1972*a*.
17. Antonini, 1973.
18. Ibid.; Sarianidi, 1977, pp. 146–7.
19. Litvinksy, 1973, p. 12.
20. Sarianidi, 1977, p. 147; Stacul, 1979, p. 242.

and its local variants in Margiana and Bactria.[21] In our view, the two suggestions may possibly be combined. Complex historic, cultural and ethnic processes ultimately led to the establishment in the Bactrian region of an eastern Iranian ethnos, known as the Bactrian.[22]

Such is the complex nature of the problem of the people of the Bactrian cemeteries. In the Beshkent cemeteries we have cremation rites; ritual hearths were built in the graves; and swastikas were used in marking the site. In the Vakhsh cemeteries funeral pyres were lit around the grave of a leader. A number of beliefs and cult practices that can be reconstructed from the materials found in the Vakhsh cemeteries recall common Indo-European rites and beliefs or specifically Indo-Iranian ones. Moreover the genetic link between the material and spiritual culture of the final stage of the Bactrian culture and the Bactrian culture of Achaemenid times point to cultural and also linguistic continuity. The language of the Bactrians of Achaemenid and later periods was Iranian or, more precisely, eastern Iranian. Thus the hypothesis can be advanced that the ethnic character of Bactrian Bronze Age culture was predominantly Proto-Iranian.

Taking account the hypothesis put forward by Gray and Burrow,[23] we can reconstruct this process as follows. The 'aryanization' of Central Asia began at the end of the third and during the first half of the second millennium B.C., when it was connected with the Proto-Indo-Aryan wave. The process became much more intense in the second half of the second millennium B.C., when it acquired a 'Proto-Iranian' hue. The process by which Iranian-speaking tribes came into existence was exceedingly complicated, a proto-Iranian wave being superimposed on the local substrate and its aryanized component. This was accompanied by cultural synthesis and a synthesis of socio-economic structures. This process lasted a considerable time.[24]

21. Antonini, 1973, pp. 242–4.
22. In Swat, where the substrata were different and another wave of Aryan tribes had entered the land, the people who left the cemeteries took shape as a proto-Dard population. Litvinsky, 1967, p. 127, n. 30; Tucci, 1977, pp. 34–8.
23. Burrow, 1973.
24. Litvinsky, 1981, pp. 160–1.

Pastoral-agricultural tribes of Pakistan in the post-Indus period[1]

A. H. Dani

THE tribes discussed in this chapter probably had some cultural links with those described in the previous chapters, but in Pakistan they had abandoned their pastoral ways of living and fully adopted the life of agricultural settlers in small rural units at a time when the centralized urbanism of the Indus Civilization had faded away. It is these tribes who, with their tribal society and equipped with bronze and later iron tools and weapons, contributed a new element to this region's history. The evidence for these people first came from graves excavated in the region of Gandhāra, and hence their culture was termed the 'Gandhāra Grave Culture'; it has also been referred to as 'Protohistoric Culture', and others have related it to Dardic-speaking people. Today this culture is also known from the excavations of the settlement sites at Aligrama in Swat and Hathial at Taxila.[2] This is the culture of the people who became powerful in north-western Pakistan in the post-Indus period. That period continued to the beginning of the historical cities of Takshasilā (Taxila) and Pushkalāvati (Peucelaotis) – the two cities of Gandhāra that heralded a second urban phase in southern Asia, and played a definitive role in the periods of the Achaemenids and Alexander the Great.[3] They more or less fill the gap that earlier appeared to exist between the end of the urban phase of the Indus Civilization and the beginning of the historical period. The Indus region is characterized by widely differing environmental conditions and these cultures assume different forms and characters in different parts of the country. Human cultures, after all, originate from life-styles adopted in response to the traditional, material and technological problems peculiar to different parts. It is natural that the hill zones of Pakistan, mostly lying to the west and north of the Indus river, should exhibit features that may be described as a hill pattern as opposed to the fertile valleys and plains where the advantage of natural river inundation and the annual refertilization of

1. See Map 12.
2. Dani, 1967; Allchin, 1982.
3. Marshall, 1951; Wheeler, 1962; Dani, 1965/66.

the soil by silt deposits enabled man to develop settled intensive agricultural systems. Even within the fertile plains variations are seen between the irrigated areas of Punjab and deltaic Sind, separated as they are by the great Indus gorge at Sakkhar and connected with the neighbouring countries of the west and the east through their own particular passes and channels of communication. There is again a variety of cultural forms in the hill zone: (a) the northern areas of Pakistan drained mainly by the Indus river, showing isolated cultural growth; (b) the western frontier region, which is characterized by a number of small valleys of the Swat, Panjkora, Kabul, Kurrum and Gomal rivers, with varying cultural patterns; and (c) the Baluchistan plateau, with its inner desert, marginal hills and coastline, and its own rural system.

As a result the highly developed technical tradition of agriculture, as seen in the Indus Civilization, continued on the plains while the less developed hill zone was overridden by the new invaders who could force their systems upon comparatively small, isolated cultural pockets. When such people moved from the hills to the plains, they could not but take advantage of the available facilities in the local system and adapt themselves to the varying conditions of living obtaining in different areas. Hence the cultures of this period in the Indus valley are not uniform. Their multiple facets only emphasize the multiplicity of human groups who responded differently as the circumstances demanded. If analogous cultures are compared outside the Indus valley, the differences assume far greater proportions. It is only remote parallelism that dimly points to a common bond of uniting factors. However remote the parallels may be in the contemporary cultures of the Oxus, Indus and Ganges valleys and the intermediate regions, there is a remarkable coincidence in the historical circumstances that appear at the end of the ancient world civilization and introduce a new era, where the horse replaces the ass, the chariot the old-fashioned cart and the double-edged sword adds to the fighting capacity of a new population itself divided but distinct from others. The break-up of the older urbanization, as seen in different areas, does not lead to a discontinuity in human living, but it speaks of a change in socio-economic organization from a pattern of centralized control to a diffused rural set-up where small communities reorganize themselves and evolve their own particular patterns. It is these multiple patterns that characterize the post-Indus phase in the Indus valley as well as in other areas of Central Asia.

This kind of change was first noted by E. J. H. Mackay[4] in his excavations at Chanhu-daro, in the post-Harappan, Jhukar[5] and Jhangar[6] periods. The recent French excavation at Pirak[7] at the mouth of the Bolan pass in the Kachi plain of Baluchistan has identified a 'Pirak Culture' with three different periods, that fills the gap between 1800 B.C. and the historical period in this region. In 1946, Sir

4. Mackay, 1943.
5. Majumdar, 1934.
6. Ibid.
7. Jarrige and Santoni, 1979.

Mortimer Wheeler[8] produced stratigraphic evidence to separate chronologically the culture represented by Cemetery-H at Harappa, and where recently M. R. Mughal[9] has traced its extent in the Bahawalpur region along the Hakra river. In 1971, in Gomal valley,[10] a new type of burial was discovered, a type also found at Taxila in the Iron Age graves of Sarai Kala,[11] and thus added a new variant on either side of the Indus river. But even greater in significance and wider was the discovery of further different types of graves in the north-western parts of Pakistan, extending from the Pakistan-Afghan border in Bajaur to beyond the Indus at Taxila on the Hathial site. This new material has been termed the 'Gandhāra Grave Culture' by A. H. Dani[12] and is attributed to the Dardic people by G. Tucci.[13]

This material has been found not only in graves but also in settlement sites. Typologically the graves have been classified into three main groups, and on the basis of stratigraphy they have been referred to three periods, ranging respectively from 1700 to 1400 B.C., from 1400 to 1000 B.C., and from 1000 to 500 B.C. These are hereafter referred to as Periods I, II, and III. To these main periods three earlier phases have been added by G. Stacul on the basis of his excavations in the the Ghaligai cave.[14] And, finally, Stacul also recognizes the last phase, ranging from 500 to 300 B.C., referred to here as Period IV. Thus, according to the periodization proposed by Stacul for the Swat valley there are seven periods in all. This sequence covers a time-span to which has been ascribed the emergence of the Indo-Iranians (see Chapter 15). The geographical distribution of such cultural material lies within the region where the Aryans, as reconstructed from the earliest Vedic literature, are considered to have lived. But actually the Vedic geography is much wider and embraces not only the whole of the Indus valley but also those parts that verge on the Jamuna-Ganges system where the 'painted grey ware' culture (see Chapter 18) has been identified. Westward, the cultural material shows still greater variety. Such a multiplicity of cultures speaks of the past inheritance of this period, in which new people, who could harness horses and ride on chariots, dominated the scene and dictated the future trends of events. Archaeology does not provide their names but they used the horse as a great source of energy and power.

The Cemetery-H culture is no longer an isolated phenomenon in the Indus valley. Until 1968,[15] it was known mainly from the type site at Harappa and further recognized at two sites, Lurewata and Ratta Theri in Bahawalpur region,

8. Wheeler, 1947, pp. 84–6.
9. Mughal, 1981.
10. Dani, 1970/71.
11. Halim, 1972.
12. Dani, 1967.
13. Tucci, 1977.
14. Stacul, 1967*b*, 1969*b*.
15. Wheeler, 1968, pp. 69–70; Piggott, 1950, pp. 229–35.

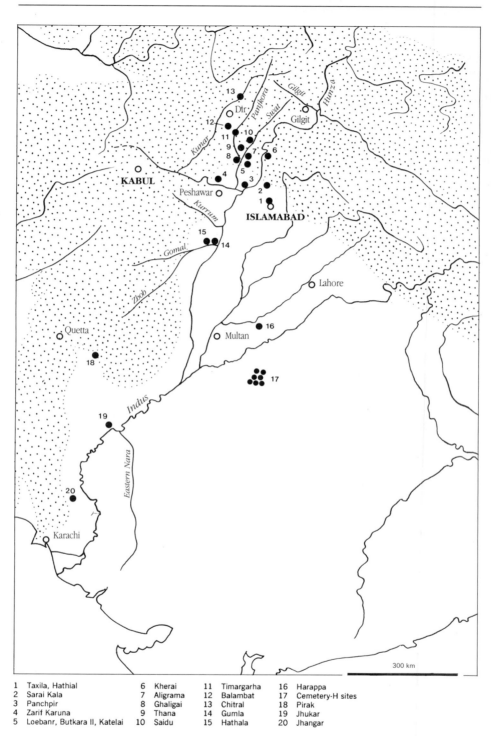

MAP 12. Distribution of prehistoric graves in the post-Indus period.

1	Taxila, Hathial	6	Kherai	11	Timargarha	16	Harappa
2	Sarai Kala	7	Aligrama	12	Balambat	17	Cemetery-H sites
3	Panchpir	8	Ghaligai	13	Chitral	18	Pirak
4	Zarif Karuna	9	Thana	14	Gumla	19	Jhukar
5	Loebanr, Butkara II, Katelai	10	Saidu	15	Hathala	20	Jhangar

but today 'Bahawalpur has revealed an impressive number of seventy-two sites containing Cemetery-H related materials'.[16] The culture thus appears to have extended to the central Indus valley, with one of the important centres being Harappa, generally identified with Hariyupiya,[17] mentioned in the *Rigveda,* which speaks of Indra's destruction of the Dasa tribe, called Varchin (actually Vrichivants and their children), at this place. Two periods of graves have been noted at Harappa. A lower and earlier, with burials, about 2 m below the present ground-level, has revealed two dozen extended inhumations, normally lying north-east and south-west, with the legs slightly flexed. They were accompanied with food offerings in pots peculiar to this period. In one grave an entire dismembered goat was laid with the corpse. Another grave yielded a gold bangle on the wrist of a woman, and a third grave had gold wire looped round three loose teeth. The upper and latter period had fractional burials, the skull and a few large bones being deposited in large urns along with pieces of burnt bones. Only infants were placed in the urns complete, in the embryonic position. These urns were covered by lids or fragments of pots. The pottery from both types of graves is distinctive. Although it is red ware and has red slip applied to it, the painted designs, black-on-red, make for a new cultural departure and the technique of firing speaks of the use of an advanced kiln. Characteristic motifs are stars of various kinds, stylized plant forms, ring-and-dot designs, groups of lines, and frequent representations of cattle, goats, peacocks and fishes. But the most expressive are the continuous scenes (Fig. 1) which encircle the vase, sometimes in panels or in roundels, placed at the lower side of the circular pot covers. It is from these symbolic representations that we can infer the ideas that must have moved the makers of the pots at least with respect to burial rites. Here we get a series of peacocks between motifs, the belly showing a roundel with a standing human figure. Another panel depicts a complicated scene – a double peacock followed by a standing man holding a horned bull on either side, with a barking dog behind, separated by a mythological bull supporting on his horns a series of three-pronged symbols and again a man with bulls. It seems that the peacock, along with other birds, bulls and deer, played a special role in burial customs – a subject of unusual interest, which was attributed to the Aryans, as illustrating their practices, by the excavator M. S. Vats. Whether they can really be attributed to any particular linguistic group or not, they do show a type of cultural milieu, the meaning of which was not clear at the time of excavation, but when seen today in a wider perspective of numerous graves of the period, builds up a picture consistent with other material.

Further different types of graves have been found in the excavations in the Gomal valley,[18] which may be assigned to a 'Gomal Grave Culture', as it was first recognized from the graves of this region. They have been noted at Hathala, Gumla and Marha Sharif in the Gomal plain and across the Indus river, graves of

16. Mughal, 1981, p. 37.
17. Dani, 1950.
18. Dani, 1970/71, pp. 50–3, 56–9.

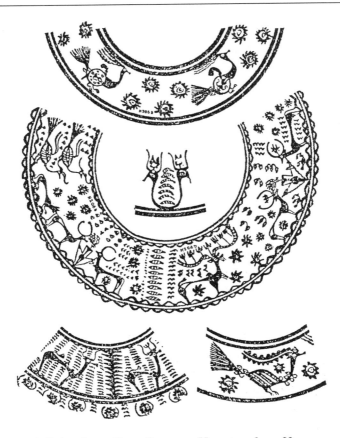

FIG. 1. Painted motifs on Cemetery-H pottery from Harappa.

Period III of Sarai Kala bearing a close resemblance. Gumla and Hathala have produced stratigraphic evidence for placing the graves into two periods. The lower and earlier graves show burnt material. The ritual, as disclosed in the excavations, presents a unique practice. Originally a circular grave pit was dug to a depth of about 1.5 m from the original ground-level. At the bottom, on the virgin soil and over a scatter of what was probably a pile of wood, the animals, supposedly killed or sacrificed, were placed in the middle of the pit. They were again covered by a pile of wood and loose earth, leaving a fire chute at one end. The whole was then filled with clay. On the top of this clay filling and, again over a pile of wood, the body was placed along with a scatter of other objects. It is very difficult to say whether the antiquities were part and parcel of the ritual or not. The whole was sealed by clay. It seems that a fire was lit later, after the grave was sealed, and it was not opened again. As such we may take the grave as a burial as well as a funeral pyre.[19] Inside the grave the funerary material consists of terracotta bangles, female figurines and horses, and tiny saucers, flesh rubbers of

19. Dani,1970/71, pp. 51–2.

stone, hubbed wheels, clay bulls and microlithic flakes. The upper and later burial includes the whole skeleton (Fig. 2). The body was aligned north–south with the head towards the north. The upper part of the body, from shoulder to hip, lay flat down on the ground but the head was slightly tilted to the left and the legs were flexed, the left leg being crossed over the right leg. The right hand lay straight by the side of the body while the left hand went across the body towards the right palm. The mouth was wide open. A single terracotta bull was found below the hip. Generally such burials are not accompanied by any funerary material.

Far away at Sarai Kala, on the bank of Kala rivulet, near Taxila, two types of graves have been excavated on the top of a mound which bears Early Bronze Age (Kot Diji) material. Both these types of graves belong to the Iron Age and are not accompanied by any funerary material, except for the discovery of two iron finger rings and some fragments of paste bracelets. The method of burial with wide-open mouth puts them in close similarity with the later graves of the Gomal plain, which also belong to the Iron Age. They bear no similarity at all to those seen in the Gandhāra Grave Culture, as is surmised by the excavator. The distinction between the two types at Sarai Kala rests purely on the two methods of grave construction. The first type, which had its top flush with the ground, was marked by two stones, one at the head and another at the foot. The second type was secured and sealed with large and medium-sized river pebbles. The grave floor was generally hardened. Fifty-seven graves of the first type were excavated and, of the second type, sixty-five were exposed. M. A. Halim describes the burial custom thus:

> All the skeletons exposed so far were found laid on the back. The heads, with gaping mouths, rest either on the right or the left cheek facing north or south and sometimes on the occiput facing skyward. The arms of the dead are placed in different positions according to sex and age. It should be pointed out that sex played an important role in the nature of burial customs of the age. We have already stated that the men and women were buried in separate rows, and in different postures, so that male and female burials can be distinguished with some certainty. Women of different age-groups were buried in different postures and great care was taken in their disposal, perhaps, because woman was regarded as the member of society most to be respected. From the postures of the female burials and the insufficient depth of grave pits, it appears that the dead were buried naked and for observing the sanctity of womanhood, the hands were placed in the pelvic region and on the breasts to cover the sources of fertility. People of different sex and age were buried in the following postures. Adult males in an east–west direction lay on their backs with arms stretched parallel to the body. Young boys of different age-groups were buried with arms stretched parallel to the body. One leg, right or left, was slightly bent so that the foot touched the ankle. Adult females were also buried in the same direction as their male counterparts but their hands were placed in the pelvic region. In most of the cases the left or right hand was placed in the pelvic region while the other arm was stretched parallel to the body. Young girls, perhaps unmarried, were buried

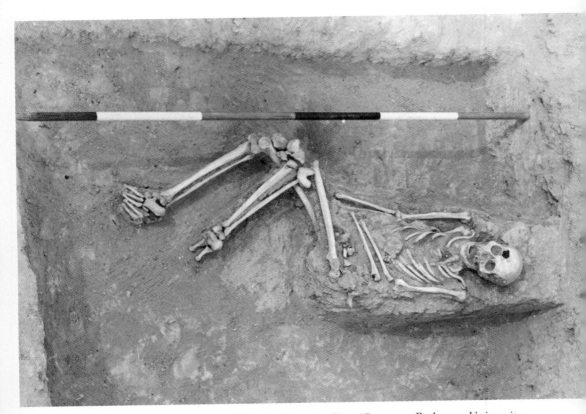

Fɪɢ. 2. Iron Age grave from Hathala, Gomal valley. (Courtesy, Peshawar University, Department of Archaeology.)

with one hand in the pelvic region and other crossed over the navel and holding the first hand on the opposite side. In the other cases one hand was placed in the usual manner in the pelvic region and the other lay on the opposite shoulder covering the breast. Teenage girls were buried in the same position as boys but with the above variation of hand positions. In all cases of girls one hand was invariably placed in the pelvic region. Children were buried with one leg slightly bent so that one foot touched the other leg.[20]

The link of the Sarai Kala grave material with the Gomal Grave Culture is established entirely on the mode of burial practice. The way in which the head is placed so as to leave the mouth gaping or wide open is the common feature of Iron Age graves. They are not accompanied by any domestic furniture. The recognition of this Gomal Grave Culture presents a new cultural complex that had hitherto remained unnoticed.

The last group consists of graves belonging to the Gandhāra Grave Culture, so named because it was first recognized in many localities in Gandhāra.

20. Halim, 1972, pp. 61–3.

The culture spreads from the Pakistan-Afghan border in the west through Bajaur, Dir, Chitral, Swat, Buner, Peshawar valleys, Indus Kohistan and beyond the Indus river at Basham and Taxila on the Hathial ridge. G. Tucci[21] makes a geographic distinction between Gandhāra and Dard country, seeking to identify the latter with Dadicae of the Greek historian, embracing, according to him, the hill region north of the Peshawar valley. As the Grave Culture has been found, to a large extent, in this hilly part, he attributes this culture to the Dards. However, the modern burial practice among the Kalash Kāfirs, known to belong to the Dardic group, is different from that found in the 'Protohistoric cemeteries in the Chitral valley'.[22] Similarly the old graves, as seen by the author, in Punyal valley, Cakuch and Ishkomen – the area where another Dardic language, Shina, is spoken – are also different. In fact Gandhāra, in Sanskrit literature, is a wide geographic territory which embraces both the valleys and the hilly areas, and its twin capitals of Pushkalāvati (Peucelaotis), on the confluence of the Swat and Kabul rivers, and Takshasilā (Taxila) are well documented. The hilly part north of the Peshawar valley has been the hinterland of Pushkalāvati, and the hilly region in Hazara and beyond has a direct link with Taxila. It is therefore natural to expect the culture to have spread all over this region.

This culture, which was originally identified as consisting of different types of graves, has now been traced in several settlement sites at Loebanr III,[23] Ali-grama[24] and Birkot-ghundai (Barikot)[25] in Swat district; at Balambat[26] near Timargarha in Dir district; and at Hathial, Taxila.[27] Some cultural material related to graves has also been found in the Ghaligai cave[28] in Swat. Unfortunately, in the absence of an extensive horizontal excavation of the settlement sites, information about the culture is still limited. We know more about the dead than about the living people who built this culture.

As its geographical extent is well attested, so is its chronology well defined by C14 dating, comparative study of the material with other cultures and by internal stratigraphic excavations. On the whole the settlements have revealed a stone masonry, consisting of rough stone blocks or river pebbles, sometimes held together by small chips, seen in all periods from beginning to end. But no important building has so far been excavated. It is only at Loebanr III that pit dwellings have been identified. The same type of stone masonry is also seen in the construction of stone-built graves. From the architectural point of view at least it is legitimate to infer that the whole material refers to one cultural continuum. On the

21. Tucci, 1977.
22. Stacul, 1969*a*.
23. Stacul, 1976, 1977*a*.
24. Stacul, 1977*b*; Stacul and Tusa, 1975, 1977.
25. Stacul, 1978.
26. Dani, 1967, pp. 235–88.
27. Allchin, 1982; the site is under excavation by Gulzar Mohammad Khan – see Khan, 1983.
28. Stacul, 1967*b*, 1969*b*.

other hand, the pottery tradition shows three distinct trends: the first is the black-on-red painted ware, seen in the lowest levels at the Ghaligai cave and at Loebanr III and Birkot-ghundai; the second is the black-grey ware and brown gritty ware, sometimes with mat impressions at the base of the pots, seen in almost all the settlement sites, and perhaps continuing in the plain black-grey ware seen in many graves; the third is the plain, sometimes burnished, red ware, which has many forms, and is later characterized by incised decorations, sometimes paint, handles and pedestalled stands. The continuity of red ware throughout is uncontested. It is only the meagre painted sherds that are almost certainly intrusive. Similarly, the large quantity of black-grey pottery appears to belong to new arrivals. The painted tradition has been viewed by Stacul in the background of the Early Bronze Age cultures of Turkmenistan, Mundigak and the Indus valley, where painting of pots had a long history. At what particular time and from what source the local hill people could have derived a few such pots is difficult to say. But the black-grey ware is a trait that imposes itself on the older red-ware tradition and the two then continued side by side, black-grey ware dominating in some places and red ware in others. There is a technical difference also, some pottery being hand-made and the other wheel-made, but the two techniques are so intermixed that it is difficult to be positive about their chronology. Under these circumstances the only possible inference can be of two main cultural traditions: the first and earlier of hand-made pottery, red or black, sometimes burnished or gritty, with black-on-red painted intrusions, and the second and later sturdy black-grey and red-ware pots, which are almost all plain, and invariably associated with graves and a characteristic type of architecture. It is the second category that belongs to the Gandhāra Grave Culture. The first must be taken to be an earlier cultural tradition of this backward hilly region, contemporary with a later phase of the Indus Civilization, and may have some remote connection with the material culture of Burzahom in Kashmir. But the main character of that tradition needs to be defined in the context of the local geography by explaining the integral parts of the various elements.

As far as the internal chronology of the Gandhāra Grave Culture is concerned, it is divisible into two main technical periods – the first belonging to the Late Bronze Age (Fig. 3) and the second to the Iron Age. Underneath these two technically distinct phases there are cultural trends of different kinds which need to be categorized as a whole so that the main cultural group may be reconstructed from a combination of traits. Three traits may be viewed together: burial rites, pottery tradition and small finds. Stacul has placed the extended burial graves of Kherai in the Gorband valley in the earliest group, mainly because of the pot forms and potting technique. The same type of extended burial has been placed in the earliest category by Dani from his evidence of Timargarha. And Khan has now produced stratigraphic evidence at Zarif Karuna[29] to show that the extended

---

29. Khan, 1979, p. 12.

FIG. 3. Pottery forms of Period I of the Gandhāra
Grave Culture.

burial type was the earliest in the sequence. Thus, what has been described at
Kherai as graves containing fragmentary bones are actually fractional burials but,
because of the limited excavation and the nature of the site, this was not at first
recognized. On the other hand, at Timargarha and Zarif Karuna, fractional
burials are associated only with iron. The same is true in Swat. A study of the
associated pottery and small finds also suggests fundamental cultural differences.
However, the commonest ritual practised was cremation, which did not entirely
replace extended burial but which increasingly became more common. It is in
this type of cremated grave that varieties of pot forms (Fig. 4) are found that were
part of the ritual of burning and disposing of the burnt bones and ashes. When
we find the practice of burning continuing into the historical period, obviously
fractional burial must be understood as an intrusive phenomenon by a people
who introduced iron. The cremated burials are seen to belong mainly with

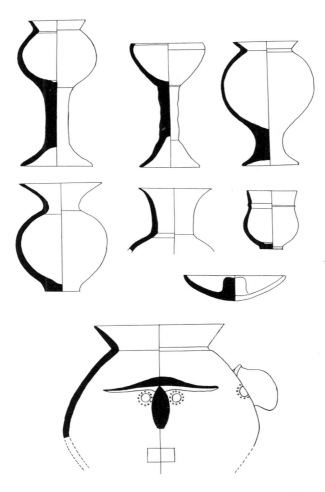

FIG. 4. Pottery forms of Period II of the Gandhāra
Grave Culture.

bronze technology in this context. Along with the fractional type we also get
multiple burials. Thus three cultural divisions are made on the basis of the totality of cultural traits and they are assigned to three different periods on a stratigraphic basis. It is only in Swat and Balambat that two subdivisions are made in
the Iron Age, the second subdivision being assigned to Period IV. C14 dating has
extended the time-span for the earliest graves from the eighteenth to the seventeenth century B.C. and for the latest graves from the fourth to the third century
B.C. As has been noted earlier, these burials continue into the historical period.
But the end of the earliest period should be determined by the time when the diffusion of black-grey ware started at such type sites as Tepe Hissar in north-eastern
Iran, somewhere towards the close of the third or the beginning of the second

millennium B.C. It is to this part of Central Asia, to the east of the Caspian Sea, that comparative material points to a possible link. It is to the same region that the source of iron technology should be referred because, *inter alia,* the characteristic channel-spouted vase, found in some graves, is also common there. Outside such groups it is difficult to rely on any one pot form or material object.

The anthropological analysis has led W. Bernhard to say that the skeletal remains do not belong to a homogeneous anthropological group. Although there were only twenty-five skulls at our disposal for morphological and metrical analysis, we could at least distinguish five different main morphological types, which could also be metrically differentiated. The most common type is the *Leptodolichomorph* (Mediterranean type), including its subtypes, such as the Transcaspian type or the Khorasan type.[30]

Burial rites played a significant part in the life of these people. Although the rites are uniformly observed all over the area, yet there is a variation in the construction of the graves, as noted in different places. The variation is seen probably because of the local conditions and more probably because the graves are badly preserved, and hence the descriptions vary from one excavator to another. It is only at Timargarha that a complete constructional principle is noted. All the graves of Period I have a larger, upper pit, circular or oval at Timargarha and rectangular at Zarif Karuna. This upper pit is filled with either rammed earth or stones. At Timargarha the ground surface is marked by a circle of stone boulders (Fig. 5). Underneath this upper pit, there is a smaller rectangular grave chamber, which, in the case of Timargarha and Zarif Karuna, is sometimes lined with dry-stone masonry, but at Thana no such masonry is seen. This lower chamber is sealed by flat stones on the top. At Kherai there is no upper pit and the lower grave chamber is lined on each side with orthostatic stones placed at right angles, thus making a box-like grave – a type also noted in some examples at Timargarha in the third period. On the floor, which is generally of beaten earth or, as at Thana, a flat schist slab, the skeleton lies on its back (Fig. 6), the head generally placed on the north-east, the face turned to the west, and the legs flexed, the hands bent and placed on one side, generally a drinking vessel near the hand, and the remaining funerary pots either at the feet or on one side. Usually three pots are seen in the graves of this period; a hand-made rippled-rim cooking pot, a drinking vessel and a bowl-on-stand, probably used as an offering stand. At Kherai the pot varieties are very limited, being a bowl-on-stand, or only a bowl and a small water vessel (*lotā*).

The second type of cremated burial is more widespread (Fig. 7). In this case, too, the same kind of grave pit is dug. In some cases it is circular, sometimes enclosing a big jar. In these graves burnt bones and ashes are placed mostly in jars of different kinds: a tub-shaped urn, which is open at the top and later covered by another pot, with either three or six holes in the sides; a visage urn, which

30. Dani, 1967, pp. 371–5.

FIG. 5. Timargarha: circle of stones bounding the upper pit. (Courtesy, Peshawar University, Department of Archaeology.)

imitates a human face by representing the nose, two eyes and a mouth on the body of the jar, covered by a handled lid, placed upside down; a similar globular jar with everted rim, again having holes to indicate a human face, and covered by a simple saucer-like lid; in other cases the jars have no holes at all. All these jars were placed inside the burial pit along with other pots, copper pins, beads and gold ornaments. In one grave (No. 122) at Timargarha twenty-four funerary pots, one broken copper pin, one copper antimony rod, one gold ring, one bead of semi-precious stone, and one copper hooked rod with a blade at one end, were found.

The third period (Fig. 8) makes a definite change in the cultural tradition but no change in grave construction. Timargarha has produced evidence that in several cases the older graves were reopened, bones disturbed, and new bones deposited along with ritual pots and other materials. On the other hand, in the graves of Swat complete burials are reported in this period.[31] Similarly at Chitral[32] the one properly excavated grave showed only a fractional burial. A tanged and barbed arrowhead was found, with a flat-topped copper pin along with etched carnelian beads, barrel-shaped, dumbell-shaped and globular beads. The long

31. Antonini and Stacul, 1972.
32. Stacul, 1969*a*.

408

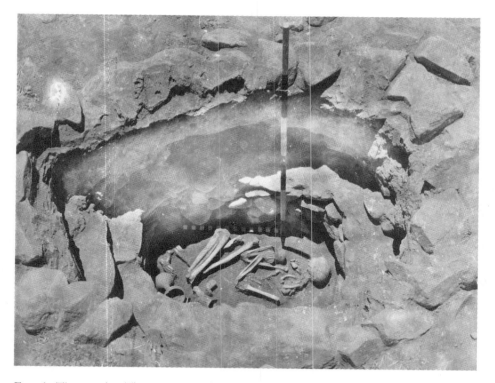

Fig. 6. Timargarha: The upper circular pit and the lower structurally made rectangular pit with extended burial of Period I. (Courtesy, Peshawar University, Department of Archaeology.)

bottle-necked jars belong to this grave period. In Buner again, except for one cremated burial found in a jar, others are all fractional. A spearhead and a javelin-head were found there, both made of iron. The position in Timargarha may thus be summed up:

> The people who practised this type of burial, sometimes reopened the earlier graves and after moving the earlier bones to a corner, put in their own dead according to their own ritual. As no complete skeleton has been found in this type of burial, the term 'fractional' is applied to it. However, the term need not imply that only some or particular parts of the bones were picked up and buried. In some cases only a small portion of the bones is missing while in others very little is preserved. In some graves multiple burial is also seen, in which the bones of one skeleton are properly disposed of, while the others are collected and jumbled up. This practice suggests the re-use of the grave by the same people for subsequent burials. It is possible that such a practice among these people led to the re-opening of the different types of graves, in which cremation or complete burial was observed. The partial collection of the bones in these graves suggests that the dead body was probably earlier exposed and then the bones were later collected and placed in the graves. Only such a supposition can account for the variation in the proportion of bones. However, within

409

Fɪɢ. 7. Timargarha: cremated bones along with funerary vessels inside a structural grave. (Courtesy, Peshawar University, Department of Archaeology.)

the graves, whatever bones were available, they were placed in the same fashion as in the case of complete burial. Here also we have graves of adults lying deeper in the earth and those of children which are at a higher level. These are described separately . . . [as] some mixed burials showing an earlier complete burial with a later fractional burial.[33]

In Swat the story is somewhat different and the chronology is built on the basis of the typology of pots and other materials. The differences may also be due to various groups of people practising different burial rites. The chart,[34] published by S. Salvatori, about his analysis of Swat material, shows that inhumation persists all through the periods, but cremation peters out in the late periods. Only two examples are shown in the later periods. However, as Stacul states,

On the basis of the typology of the vases and the other furnishings, the chronological and cultural classification of the graves under examination show that those without or almost without bones mainly belong to the most ancient period of util-

33. Dani, 1967, p. 81.
34. Salvatori, 1975, pp. 335–6.

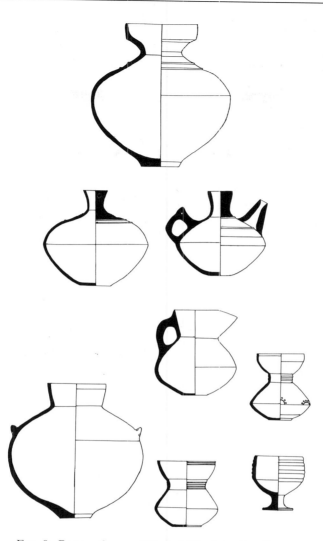

Fɪɢ. 8. Pottery forms of Period III of the Gandhāra
Grave Culture.

ization of the aforementioned graveyards [i.e. Period II in the chronological terminology adopted here], with only a few examples in the following period [Period III]
and in the late one [Period IV]. Graves containing only one fractional burial are
found dating from both period V [Period II in the present terminology] (4.4 per
cent in comparison with the graves ascribed to this period) and even more frequently, from the subsequent period VI [Period III] (6.3 per cent) while there is no
evidence of them in period VII [Period IV].[35]

35. Stacul, 1975, pp. 325–6.

In Zarif Karuna the excavator observes:

> In the graves of Period III, unburnt fractional bones of one or more persons were found placed in the anatomical order in inflexed position. Sometimes fractional bones have also been found heaped in the middle of a grave along with the grave furniture. In one grave two fractional skeletons were found in reconstructed position facing each other. Here it may be suggested that, in case of multiple fractional burials, the graves were reopened for the subsequent burials or two dead persons perhaps belonging to one family were buried together in one grave.[36]

These fractional burials, in which skeletal remains of more than one person are sometimes found are the richest in so far as grave furniture is concerned. In one grave (No. 149) at Timargarha twenty-six funerary vessels were found. One pot had an iron spoon. The pot varieties also increase in number. The important feature to note is the disc-based pots of the earlier periods. Here in Period III we get a preponderance of flat-bottomed vases, with painting and incised decorations on some of them. Long bottle-necked jars and several varieties of bottles, some on pedestals, are seen mainly in this period. One important type is the hour-glass vase, which is so extremely thin and light that it was probably moulded. Two new varieties are the channel-spouted vase and triple bowls-on-stand, both found in Swat. There is also an increase in the number of small jars, miniature vases, saucers and lids of all kinds. One lid found in Swat has a horse-handle on top. Spouted and pinched-mouthed vases, and large water jars with straight-collared rims are seen. However, it should be noted that not all varieties of pots are found in all graves everywhere. What should be noted is the new technique of manufacturing pots: first, the new method of using moulds; second, the increased frequency of flat-bottomed vases; third, the increase of red ware; and, lastly, the increase of several varieties of bottles and miniature vases.

Whatever little material has so far been excavated on the Hathial range at Taxila is also instructive, mainly through the study of the pottery. On this site three main periods have been detected. The earliest belongs to what is called the 'Later Kot Kiji Culture' of the Early Bronze Age, almost similar to the cultural material of this period found at Sarai Kala and later dated at both sites by C14 to 2100 B.C. (calibrated). The second cultural phase is introduced by the typical material of the Gandhāra Grave Culture. The predominance of flat-bottomed, red burnished pottery so far observed over other materials suggests that this cultural phase probably belongs to Period III when iron had already come into use. The last phase belongs to the historical period. In this connection the evidence from Balambat is very significant, where two structural periods of stone masonry wall, along with storage or rubbish pits above earlier graves, have also been found. The pits are of the same type as those found at Loebanr III and Aligrama. The stone walls of the first period at Balambat are in one alignment, the longer

---

36. Khan, 1979, p. 16.

arms being from north-west to south-east. They make up large rectangular halls probably used for residence. Contemporary with them are two circular stone rooms. As the materials include iron and copper objects, ground-stone celts, ring stones and terracotta human figurines, this is dated to Period III of the graves. The end of this structural period was abrupt. The newcomers ignored the alignment of the older houses. The new structures, which cut through the walls of the earlier period, have their walls running north–south and east–west and thus provide firm evidence of their later dating. It is in these new structures that we get the most advanced pottery along with improved iron objects, and fireplaces in every room. For the first time diaper stone masonry is seen in the walls. Hence this second structural phase is dated to the sixth to the fourth century B.C. and the first structural phase to the first half of the first millennium B.C.

At Loebanr III, Stacul recognized a very significant single-period settlement below the superficial upper layers, which showed some river-pebble constructions. Human figurines and bulls of terracotta were found on the surface, obviously of a later date. The human figurines have pinched noses and flat bases while the bulls are of the same type as those found in Zarif Karuna III. The main settlement revealed two large-sized pit dwellings, oval in plan, and several small pits of different shapes. One large pit showed a step or a bench. Some hearths and fireplaces were also found. Similar but much deeper pit dwellings have been noted at Burzahom in Kashmir and shallower dwelling pits occur at Sarai Kala at the opening of Period II. It is natural to find them in this colder region of the north. Here metal objects were rare. Only one piece of twisted copper was found. An iron arrowhead has been recently recognized as intrusive from the upper surface. Other small finds from the main settlement include two green jade beads, two polished stone axes, a ring stone, a schist pendant, bone tools and hairpins, including two double-headed pins. However, the most instructive are the pottery forms and ware, among which, after the first season of excavation in 1968, it is recorded that 60 per cent was black-grey burnished ware and less than 2 per cent red ware. The first ware has been rightly recognized as an intrusion from the west. The pot forms include large and medium-sized jars, flat-based or mat-impressed bowls, *lotās* (water vessels) and *thalis* (eating vessels). Stacul has compared these pots, particularly the mat-impressed ones, with those found at Burzahom and at Sarai Kala in Period I, but the Sarai Kala material is very early, as it is found in the pre-Kot Diji period.

Birkot-ghundai, as published in 1978, has been stratigraphically divided into four periods.[37] The last is relegated to Period IV of the scheme adopted here. It has yielded miniature vases and an iron spearhead. Although the excavator does not make a gap, the penultimate occupation, associated with a wall built of large and middle-sized stones, is referred to Period II of the scheme adopted here. It is in this period that a human and an animal figurine, both of terracotta, have

37. Stacul, 1978, p. 139.

been found along with seventeen spindle whorls and two copper pins. This is preceded by a phase that is said to be 'almost barren' but has produced 'disconnected bones of two human skeletons (scattered bones consisting of the skulls and parts of the upper and lower limbs)'. The lowest occupation is associated with the earliest wall built of river pebbles. It is here that a faience spacer-bead bone hair pin, bone and faience beads and a terracotta bull of the same type, as has been noted in other places, have been discovered. This is the first time that a terracotta bull has been reported from such a great depth. The pottery is very instructive. Besides grey-burnished and gritty ware, the most important are the painted black-on-red sherds. The painted designs show, among others, a peacock, a bull, a star, a four-petalled flower and chequer – some of the motifs known in the Indus Civilization pottery. Although the motifs are obviously derived, yet it is not clear whether the pottery is of the Indus type or not. In the Ghaligai cave the painted pottery is found in Period II. It appears that in this backward region the painting tradition survived longer, as noted here in the earliest occupation, just as the horned deity painted on a grooved pot of the Kot Diji type is seen much later in Burzahom Period II.[38]

At Aligrama several trenches were laid to understand the settlement pattern.[39] In Trench A two circular pits and several walls built of irregularly shaped blocks of stone, set in pebbles, were found. Some of them made up rectangular rooms and were associated with floors. The pits were lined with dry-stone masonry. In Trench B the superimposed structures belonged to three phases. They were covered by alluvial deposits of the upper levels. Five pits 'for the storage of food-stuffs or other things' were also found, four of them also lined with stones. The settlement is supposed to have been ended by fire. Five inhumation burials, with legs flexed, were also found here. One of them in Phase II is associated with miniature pedestalled vases and four are placed in Phase III 'at the end of the life of the settlement'. Here spherical bowls and one iron pin were found. Phase II was the high point of occupation. Two main periods have been distinguished on the basis of finds associated with different strata, the earliest containing a funnel-shaped vase, a mat-impressed jar and tall drinking vases. It is the first time that mat-impressed pottery has been found in so late a layer. The second, which was the main occupation, has produced pedestalled bowls and cups, a bowl-on-stand, miniature vases and a four-legged theriomorphic vessel along with copper and iron pins, an iron arrowhead, beads and terracotta bulls. This second Phase is relegated to Period III of the scheme adopted here. Subsequent excavations at Aligrama provided more detail. Out of the new trenches laid, Trench F was limited to a small area available for excavation. Although five floor levels have been recognized by the excavator, he places all of them in the main period, equivalent to Period III of the scheme adopted here, though no iron

38. Sankalia, 1974, p. 303.
39. Stacul and Tusa, 1975, p. 298.

material has been found here. The pottery types are all later, except a few survivals from the earlier period. Significant small finds are a bull, a toy wheel and a human figurine with pinched nose – all in terracotta. Trench K belongs to the historical period, dating from the fourth century B.C. to the fourth century A.D. The main evidence comes from Trench E, where the excavator divides his material into eight phases, later classified into three periods, in the last of which is a recent construction. It is only Phase I that is relegated to the first building period and is almost depleted of cultural material in the succeeding phase. This is followed by a long-lasting cultural Period II, to which Phases II–VI are relegated. Six C14 dates were obtained from Pennsylvania University laboratory. Four of them give the following results: Period I (of our scheme) 1400 ± 40 B.C. and 1500 ± 50 B.C. (1600 and 1690 with MASCA calibration); Period II (of our scheme) 1460 ± 60 B.C. and 1140 ± 40 B.C. (1680 and 1300 with MASCA calibration).

Whatever the tests may be worth, it is difficult to rely on their basis for the exact dating of the different periods. As the main long occupation is referred to Period II, its cultural data are solid and hence relevant. The material published shows that here we have two sub-periods, upper and lower. No metal object is reported in this trench. One significant terracotta figurine has been found in upper layer 4. This has rows of pricked decorations on the chest, representing a necklace. Such terracotta figurines have been found at Balambat in the first structural period. This pricking technique is also known in the case of Iron Age pottery. Ringstones and saddle-querns have also been found here. If the material is divided into upper and lower sub-periods, the lower will give an early date. The lowest occupation phase has produced beads or spindle-whorls and a broken ringstone or macehead. The pottery is divided into black-grey ware, showing jars with everted rims, and brown-grey gritty ware, showing jars with outturned rims and bowls, either carinated or having a bulging belly.

Still more important than chronology is the extension of the knowledge of the cultural area. So far only three aspects have been noted. The first is the settlement pattern which, leaving aside a single cave at Ghaligai which is marginal to the main context, shows settlements on hill-tops or slopes, generally not far from the river bank. The settlements are in the form of either pit dwellings, as at Loebanr III, or stone-built rectangular rooms, again characterized by several storage pits. The second aspect is the three types of burial rites, which, as is natural, vary in different places in the sequence. The third feature is the large number of pot forms, varying from hand-made pottery to grey and red wheel-made pots, sometimes burnished and mat-impressed, and very occasionally painted. The pot forms show many variations, like cooking vessels, *thalis* (eating plates), bowls, drinking vessels, bowls-on-stands, pedestalled bowls and cups, bottles, water pitchers, globular jars, handled vessels, jars with pinched mouths as well as ritual pots like visage urns and burial tubs. These pot forms show a pattern of life materially differing from that of the Indus Civilization and more related to a rural setting than to what follows in the second period of urbanization in the early historical context.

The next important item is the presence of terracotta human and animal figurines. As noted in the case of Timargarha graves and the settlement at Balambat, they played a significant part in life. The figurines in the graves appear to have played a ritual part. Both at Timargarha and Zarif Karuna they have been found in the context of Iron Age graves or settlement sites. It is only at Katalai and Loebanr in Swat that human figurines are said to have been found in all types of graves, inhumation, cremation, double inhumation and burial with no traces of bones. However, a typological study is very instructive. The human figurines are all hand-modelled, with the face pinched, eyes and ornaments shown by pricking, the back of the head pressed by the thumb, the hands being only extended stumps. They are both male and female, the female breast being shown by a ball-like swelling. No appliqué technique is used as in the terracotta figurines of the Indus Civilization. One major type has the two legs apart, as in the examples from Timargarha and Swat. A Timargarha example has a crossband (*Chhanavīra*) across the body and the female figurines from Swat have necklaces shown by the pricking technique. This type is also shown from Balambat settlement site. The second major type has the legs joined. One example from Zarif Karuna and others from Swat. The Zarif Karuna specimen has a curved head-dress, described as 'fan-shaped', but it does not bear any similarity to the female figurines with fan-shaped head-dress from the Indus Civilization. On the other hand, the Swat examples have broad hips and are exactly of the same type as figurines from Taxila.[40] There is a third variety from Swat, which has a flat base, also found from settlement sites.

The only animal terracotta type is the four-legged bull found in Zarif Karuna and Swat. It has a prominent hump, its horns point straight forward and it has a short tail between its legs. This hand-modelled example is robust but it shows no detail of the muscles or the folds of the skin at the neck, as we find in the bulls of the Indus Civilization. The Zarif Karuna examples, all found in the graves of Period III (Iron Age), vary in size and present remarkably excellent specimens. In Swat the bulls, as for example at Birkot-ghundai, have also been found in the earlier period. As these bulls were found in the graves, they were probably cult objects.

An important ritual object discovered from a Period III grave at Zarif Karuna[41] is an alabaster figure of an Eye goddess with a flat base, showing a circle for the navel, the sideways swelling for breast distinguished by two circles, the mouth shown again by two circles and nose by one, but the two eyes are represented by two large holes on a broad head, which is slightly depressed on the middle top. The goddess has been compared by the excavator to similar examples

40. Marshall, 1951, Plate 132, n. 1.
41. Khan, 1979, Plate XIXA, p. 85.

from Mesopotamia.[42] This type of goddess never became popular in this part, appearing to be an import from the west.

Other objects found are in bronze, iron, bone, ivory, stone, jade, faience and gold and relate to household goods, tools and weapons. Two jade beads from Loebanr III have already been referred to. The most numerous are the long pins with varying tops in bronze, ivory and bone. From Zarif Karuna only bronze pins have been reported. As they are quite long and in some cases associated with female skeletons, they are thought to be hairpins. From the point of view of varieties they have been classified on the basis of their heads: (a) globular showing a globule below flat top; (b) globular showing a globule below convex or umbrella-shaped top; (c) pins having a conical top with no globule below; (d) pins having a looped head; and (e) pins having a pyramidal shape. Zarif Karuna examples, being in bone, do not show the globule but have a flattened base below the top of the head. The two bone pins from Loebanr III have a double-headed top on a stem which, in one case, tapers and, in the other, is concave. The second form has led the excavator to recognize in it an anthropomorphic shape and hence made him compare it to an example from a Shang layer at Cheng-Chom.[43] But when we remember that almost all types of pins are derived from those known in Hissar, it is reasonable to look for these examples to the same source. What has been described as a copper wand,[44] which shows double figures on the top, could as well inspire the present type. Copper needles, antimony rods of copper and ivory, pendants of bone and copper, ear-rings and finger-rings of both copper and gold have been found. In one example an ear-ring has bead-like attachments, and the finger-rings are all made in coils.

Several types of beads of different kinds of stones have been reported, and a spacer-bead in faience has been found at Birkot-ghundai. The most common bead is barrel-shaped in quartz, agate or carnelian. There are also cylindrical and dumb-bell-shaped beads. From Chitral come carnelian beads with white etching on the surface, as well as large-holed, biconical bead-shaped objects, described as net-sinkers or spindle-whorls. Copper and shell bangles with twisted bands have been reported from settlement sites. Two green jade beads of biconical shape from Loebanr III and a curved jade pendant from the Ghaligai cave are important comparable material. The Ghaligai specimen is ascribed to Period I of our chronology by Stacul. He compares the pendant to Japanese *magatama* of the last centuries B.C. and connects it with an earlier Chinese prototype. But such curved pendants are also known in Hissar, though no jade has been found there.

The most important of the tools is the copper hoe from the Ghaligai cave, where a copper spearhead with long blade was also found. A number of stone tools, including stone celts, saddle-querns and ring-stones are known in this culture. A copper chisel was found at Aligrama in Trench F. There are two types of

42. Mallowan, 1947, Plate XXVI, nn. 3 and 4.
43. Cheng, 1960, p. 36, Fig. 9.
44. Schmidt, 1937, p. 196, Fig. 117; also Plate XLVIII, H. 4885.

bone arrowhead reported from the Ghaligai cave – one with two barbs and another with a hollow base. The same cave also yielded several bone awls or points and spatula. These bone tools have been compared to those found at Sarai Kala and Burzahom. But these types are also known in Hissar, from where so much cultural material is known to have been derived.

There are several types of iron objects, the most common being flat-topped nails. No iron has been found at Zarif Karuna. Timargarha graves have produced a leaf-shaped spearhead and a ladle with a scooped cup at one end and, at the other, a double loop, as well as an iron cheek-piece from a bridle. From Balambat settlement site several objects have been recovered, all hailing from the last occupational period. They include thick loop-headed needles, a nail, a three-flanged arrowhead, a finger-ring of one coil, a hollow fire-blower, a chisel with a tang and socket at one end and flat working edges at the other, a hooked carpenter's tool, a knife-blade, and sheep shears made of a flat iron bar hammered into two broad blades. It is natural that we should expect more material from the settlement site than from the graves. From a Chitral grave a tanged and barbed arrowhead is reported. From Buner came a leaf-shaped arrowhead having a tang at one end, a quadrangular javelin-head and an iron pin. From the top layer of Loebanr III comes an iron arrowhead.

The iron cheek-piece from a Timargarha grave of Period III has three holes in the middle. K. Jettmar writes:

> It is clear that it belongs typologically to those groups which played a great role in the Steppe belt between the tenth and sixth centuries B.C. Its shape is rather similar to late pieces in Eastern Europe (sixth century B.C.), also in iron, but this could be due to a parallel evolution, i.e. a simplification caused by the use of the new metal. So a more exact dating depends still upon the question when iron arrived in the Indian subcontinent. Today the trend is to assume that it came earlier than in the steppes.[45]

In this connection it is pertinent to quote the evidence of horse burials found along with graves in Swat and also of a series of rock carvings found at Gogdara I in Swat.[46] The study made by Brentjes places the carvings 'within a period of time going from the second millennium B.C. to the beginning of the first millennium B.C.'. The excavator adds:

> Some stylistic details, such as the representation of carts drawn by animals, suggest the hypothesis that, at least for a certain period of time, the authors of the petroglyphs belonged to a group stably installed in this area. In such a perspective it might be possible to assume a connection with the population who left the graveyard of Butkara, Loebanr, and the site of Aligrama (second millennium B.C.).

Brentjes further comments:

45. Jettmar, 1967, p. 207.
46. Brentjes, 1977, pp. 92–3.

We can also get to this datation through analogies with similar images, since we are dealing with the repeatedly documented reproduction of two-wheeled battle-carts or race-carts with a driver, in the same way as they are represented in the late Bronze Age in a large area going from China up to Sweden, and to North Africa. . . . From the historical background, the general view of the images coming from Gogdara I must be placed in the period of the 'war-chariots' that lasted up to the beginning of the first millennium B.C. and in this way the datation resulting from the tombs would be confirmed.

If this dating is accepted, the attribution of the 'battle-cart' to the grave people may be plausible, and such an attribution will throw light on another aspect of the pattern of life of these people. However, such chariots were also used by the Achaemenian emperors for hunting.[47] In any case the presence of war chariots in a context of the early centuries B.C. itself is important in so far as it represents a type of war machine so well attested in Sanskrit literature.

To sum up, the whole material presents a new cultural horizon that marks a new stage of socio-ethnological change in the entire zone of Central Asia, that must be distinguished from the Early Bronze Age Civilizations ending with the collapse of the old urban setting. The social change is fundamental and should be understood in the new framework of a widespread cultural movement affecting the life of the people at large who were isolated in hill pockets and survived with their traditional pattern of food-production. Although the new change did not accelerate the process of production, it did bring about a change in the general set-up of the rural population and brought them closer together in a way of living that was economically not much better but socially and culturally far different from their earlier experience. This new life, in which the horse and chariot played a definitive role, had more leaning towards the hilly north and west than towards the distant plains of China or India. The hills of the west hold the key to unlocking the secrets of these people. A few stray materials, like jade, which appear to have come from China, cannot disturb the concept of this cultural zone. Similarly, some painting, which may have borrowed some motifs from the Indus Civilization, should be understood in the wider setting of the material from the west. Thus the cultures, which were originally found in the graves but are now traced in several settlement sites, provide the material base from which the literary evidence of the period should be understood.

47. Frye, 1963, Plate 89.

The Painted Grey Ware Culture of the Iron Age[1]

B. B. Lal

HE period between the end of the Indus Civilization (*c.* 1500 B.C.) and the beginning of the historical period (*c.* 600 B.C.) was formerly regarded as the 'Dark Ages' of India's past. The present author undertook exploration of sites referred to in ancient Indian texts, such as Hastinapura, Mathura, Kurukshetra, Indraprastha, etc. Encouraged by the results, he published a paper highlighting the importance of the Painted Grey Ware.[2] Thereafter a systematic excavation was undertaken at Hastinapura during 1950–52, as a result of which the identity of what is now well known as the Painted Grey Ware Culture was established.[3] On the basis of comparative stratigraphy, the Painted Grey Ware settlement at Hastinapura was dated to 1100–800 B.C.

As a result of exploration as many as 650 sites of this culture have so far been discovered. While the main concentration of sites is in Indian Punjab, Haryana, north-eastern Rajasthan and the upper Ganges-Jamuna basin in Uttar Pradesh, the occurrence of some sites has been reported from as far west as Lakhiyo Pir[4] in Sind and Harappa[5] in southern Punjab, both in Pakistan. Sites along the dry bed of the Ghaggar in the Bahawalpur region of Pakistan have already been referred to and it is likely that Painted Grey Ware may also be found in the Ravi-Jhelum valleys of Pakistan Punjab, since Gharinda[6] near the Indo-Pakistan border has yielded it. The easternmost site to have yielded this pottery is Sravasti[7] in Uttar Pradesh, where, however, it is intermixed with the Northern Black Polished Ware. Ujjain[8] in Madhya Pradesh is the southernmost site, though, here

1. See Map 13.
2. Lal, 1950.
3. Lal, 1954/55.
4. The material is in the Central Antiquity Section, Archaeological Survey of India, New Delhi.
5. Allchin and Allchin, 1968, p. 210.
6. Joshi, 1977.
7. Sinha, 1967.
8. Banerjee, 1957, p. 24.

again, the ware did not occur in an independent horizon. However, the most interesting is the recent discovery at Thapli[9] on the bank of the Alaknanda in District Tehri, Uttar Pradesh. It takes the Painted Grey Ware Culture right into the Himalayas, the significance of which will be discussed later. To bring into a sharper focus the extent of distribution of this ware, it may be pointed out that from Lakhiyo Pir in Sind to Sravasti in Uttar Pradesh it is about 1,400 km, and from Gharinda in Punjab to Ujjain in Madhya Pradesh, about 900 km, a span which compares with that of the Indus Civilization.

The sites of this culture are located along river-banks, the average distance from one site to another being about 10 to 12 km. However, in a favourable ecological environment it could be as little as 5 km.[10] These settlements were mostly small villages. In northern Haryana where an intensive survey has been made, they have been found to cover as small an area as 1,570 m², and as large as 96,193 m².[11]

Another very interesting feature emerges from Mughal's survey in Bahawalpur.[12] Of the fourteen sites discovered by him, as many as seven range between 1.1 and 2.1 ha, which would be regarded as the normal run of the sites. Further, while three are less than 1 ha, three others fall between 3 and 4 ha. However, the most noteworthy point is that only one of these fourteen sites is unusually large, namely 13.7 ha. This clearly shows the emergence of a chief town amidst smaller villages – a pattern which in due course gave rise to local 'capitals'.

It is proposed first to discuss the factual data about house construction, agriculture, technology of iron, copper, etc., and then to reconstruct the life-style of the Painted Grey Ware period. To date, the only site where a reasonably large portion of the settlement has been dug horizontally is Bhagwanpura and thus we shall deal with it in detail, supplementing the information from other sites.

At Bhagwanpura, J. P. Joshi reports three kinds of construction. One of these is a round hut, indicated by the arrangement of twenty-three post-holes. It covered an overall area of 4.25 × 6.85 m. On its floor lay four saddle-querns and a variety of pestles. Joshi is inclined to think that the hut belonged to a corn-grinder.[13] If this is so, it would indicate that some people were specially engaged in this activity and not that each family ground its own corn. Although further details have not been given about the nature of the construction of the hut walls, evidence from other sites, such as Hastinapura, Atranjikhera, etc., throws valuable light on it. In these post-holes were inserted wooden poles or, more probably, thick bamboos, charred fibres of which have been met with at several sites. Furthermore, at most of these sites we come across mud plaster bearing impressions

9. Nautiyal, 1981.
10. Agrawala and Kumar, 1976, p. 240 (map).
11. Suraj Bhan and Shaffer, 1978, p. 62.
12. Mughal, 1981, p. 38.
13. Joshi, 1977.

of the material over which the plaster was applied. An examination of samples of the plaster has revealed the use of wild cane which was evidently put in between the posts, both horizontally and vertically. The cane-frames and bamboos must have been tied with string, of which some impressions (though not very clear) have been noted. This framework of cane-and-bamboo was then plastered over on both the inner and outer surfaces with mud, strengthened with the addition of rice-husks. R. C. Gaur states that he found fine sand in some of the post-holes and suggests that this was deliberately put there to protect the posts from white ants.[14] On the basis of the disposition of the post-holes Gaur thinks that some of the wattle-and-daub houses were also rectangular or square in plan.

At Atranjikhera domestic hearths have been identified. These were U-shaped in plan. The sides had a slight inward taper and further curved in at the top. The size of these hearths (sometimes as much as 50 cm in length and 25–35 cm in height) indicates that large cooking vessels were placed on them, which in turn, suggests the existence of large families, evidently joint families, as has long been the pattern in India.

Attention here may also be drawn to certain circular pits discovered in the early and middle phases of the Painted Grey Ware period at Atranjikhera. These contained ash, charcoal, grains and a few small fragments of animal bones. Gaur suggests that these might have been sacrificial fire-pits.[15]

The second kind of construction was that of mud walls. Sometimes mud-bricks have also been reported; but not their size. At Bhagwanpura a house plan has been identified. The occurrence of Painted Grey Ware dishes and bowls on the floor of this house leaves no doubt that it belongs to this period. It had as many as thirteen rooms, their sizes varying from 1.6 × 1.6 m to 3.35 × 4.2 m.[16] The smaller rooms may have been stores, while the bigger were evidently meant for living. In between two sets of rooms a corridor was noted, and on the eastern side a courtyard. Maybe the person owning this big house in a central part of the settlement was the village chief.

The third kind of constructional material encountered at Bhagwanpura relates to kiln-burnt bricks. It is said that owing to the subsequent ploughing away of the site, no clear-cut structures were identified, but bricks of the following sizes were met with: 20 × 20 × 8 cm; 12 × 12 × 8 cm; 20 × 30 × 8 cm; 16 × 12 × 4 cm; and 29 × 22–12.5 × 7 cm.[17] The first two sizes represent clear squares, while the last one is wedge-shaped. It is known that bricks used in walls are generally rectangular not square. On this basis, it would appear that the square bricks had been used in some other kind of construction – maybe a squarish ritualistic altar or some similar structure. The wedge-shaped bricks may have been used in a circular structure. Evidence of burnt bricks also comes from Dadheri where the

14. Gaur, 1983, p. 127.
15. Ibid.
16. Joshi, 1978, p. 98.
17. Ibid., pp. 99–100.

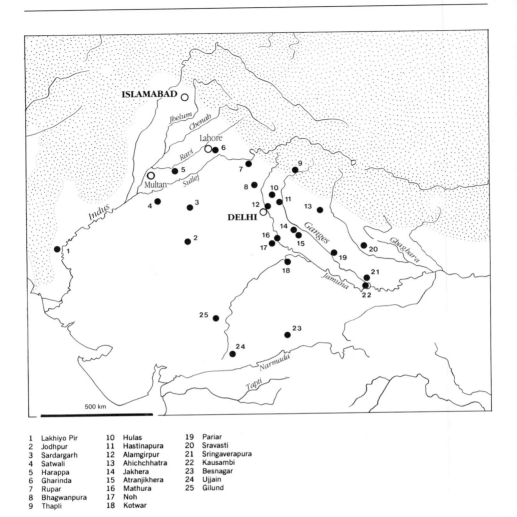

MAP 13. Distribution of Painted Grey Ware sites.

1	Lakhiyo Pir	10	Hulas	19	Pariar
2	Jodhpur	11	Hastinapura	20	Sravasti
3	Sardargarh	12	Alamgirpur	21	Sringaverapura
4	Satwali	13	Ahichchhatra	22	Kausambi
5	Harappa	14	Jakhera	23	Besnagar
6	Gharinda	15	Atranjikhera	24	Ujjain
7	Rupar	16	Mathura	25	Gilund
8	Bhagwanpura	17	Noh		
9	Thapli	18	Kotwar		

sizes are 12 × 12 × 7 cm and 25 × 20 × 5 cm.[18] Use of burnt bricks is also attested at Hastinapura, Atranjikhera, Ahichchhatra, Noh, etc., but the pieces are too fragmentary to indicate the complete size.

Although no idea of the lay-out of a settlement can be had form the available meagre data, interest is attached to the construction of a mud bund at Atranjikhera to protect the settlement from the flooding of the river. Its surviving height and length, evidently reduced owing to subsequent erosion, were 1.45 and 35 m respectively. At Jakhera, too, a mud embankment, with a basal width of 4.8 m and extant height of 1.2 m, was observed. Sahi feels it may have circumscribed the settlement.[19] Such constructions as these would evidently have involved community effort.

The credit of bringing the upper Ganges-Jamuna valley under large-scale cultivation goes to the Painted Grey Ware people. They could achieve this mainly because of their iron technology to which a detailed reference will be made later. They cleared the heavy jungle with the help of iron axes. Of the ploughshare no example has so far been found from this period, though the subsequent period has yielded examples. However, a hoe has been reported from Jakhera. Very scanty evidence is available regarding irrigation. Gaur refers to unlined wells in the vicinity of Atranjikhera, which he thinks were used for irrigation.[20] Sickles found at Jakhera, for example,[21] may have been used for reaping the harvest.

The excavations at Hastinapura brought to light the remains of rice (*Oryza* sp.); the same was the case at Noh. Thus, it was thought for some time that the people did not cultivate wheat. However, Atranjikhera has made the position very clear. Here, besides rice (*Oryza sativa* L.), wheat (*Triticum compactum* Host.) and barley (*Hordeum vulgare* L., hulled, six row) have been found.[22] The presence of both rice and wheat, which are, respectively, summer and winter crops would indicate that the people had begun to grow two crops a year as is the practice even today.

Although pollens of *Pinus* were found at Hastinapura, actual wood was not. K. A. Chowdhury and his colleagues have now identified the remains of Chir wood (*Pinus roxburghii*) in the Painted Grey Ware levels at Atranjikhera.[23] The occurrence of this wood is significant, since it does not grow on the Ganges plains but in the Himalayan region. Thus the inhabitants of Atranjikhera in particular and of the Painted Grey Ware people in general, must have been in contact with that region. This has indeed now been established with the discovery of the Painted Grey Ware site of Thapli in District Tehri in the Himalayan region

18. Gaur, 1983, p. 100.
19. Sahi, 1978, p. 102.
20. Gaur, 1983, p. 123.
21. Sahi, 1978, p. 103.
22. Chowdhury et al., 1977.
23. Ibid., p. 66.

of Uttar Pradesh. The site of Thapli contains a fairly thick deposit of the Painted Grey Ware, indicating that it was not a case of mere contact but actual occupation by the Painted Grey Ware people themselves, who in the course of their expansion must have penetrated this Himalayan region either along the Ganges valley from Hardwar upwards or through some other convenient pass on the south.

Some charcoal from Hastinapura has been identified as that of sissoo (*Dalbergia sisso*).[24] It is one of the important varieties constituting the deciduous forest and is found in the sub-Himalayan region but not far from Hastinapura and even grows down along the large rivers in north-western Uttar Pradesh. It is good timber and is likely to have been used for household furniture etc. though for climatic reasons no articles of furniture have survived. Interest is also attached to the identification of wild cane (*Saccharum spontaneum*),[25] which, as mentioned above, was used for constructing wattle-and-daub houses.

Next to agriculture, the people depended for their subsistence on domesticated animals. Cattle (*Bos indicus* Linnaeus) accounted for the largest number among the domesticated animals. While the cows supplied milk, from which curds, cheese and butter were made, the bullocks were used as draught animals and for ploughing. The other animals identified at Hastinapura were sheep (*ovis vignei* Blyth, race *domesticus*), buffalo (Bos (*Bubalus*) *bubalis* Linnaeus), pig (*Sus cristatus* Wagner var. *domesticus* Rolleston), and horse (*Equus caballus* Linnaeus).[26] A large number of bones of cattle, sheep, buffalo and pig had incision marks made with a sharp instrument, and were charred, indicating that these animals were slaughtered for food. From Atranjikhera comes additional evidence in regard to the domestication of the goat (*Capra hircus aegagrus* Erxleben) and the dog (*Canis familiaris* Linnaeus) of which the former added mutton to the diet. Besides, fish, river-turtle, varanus, bivalves and fowl were also consumed.[27] Special interest is attached to the presence of the horse, evidence of which has been found not only at Hastinapura, but also at Atranjikhera[28] and Bhagwanpura.[29]

There is enough evidence to show that the Painted Grey Ware people engaged in fishing and hunting, for which the surroundings were quite suitable. Most of the Painted Grey Ware sites were located on river-banks and, as new ground was cleared, jungle was left in the neighbouring areas. Fishing was done with the help of fish-hooks of which examples both of copper and iron have been found. Ramie-fibre nets were also used, to which terracotta sinkers were attached to make them effective.

While Hastinapura reveals evidence of the presence of the stag (*barasingha*),

24. Chowdhury and Gosh, 1954/55, p. 134.
25. Ibid.
26. Nath, 1954/55, pp. 107–20.
27. Gaur, 1983, p. 124.
28. Ibid.
29. Joshi, 1977.

from Atranjikhera comes additional evidence of the *nilgai* and leopard, indicating that hunting of wild animals was resorted to. Spear- and arrowheads of iron, copper and of antler itself, of which ample examples have been found, must have been used for hunting.

The most distinctive pottery of the period is the very one on the basis of which the culture itself has been christened, namely the Painted Grey Ware. As the name indicates, it is a grey ware with designs painted on it, usually in black pigment. Made of well-levigated clay, the pots are usually fine-grained, though somewhat coarser and thickish examples are not lacking. By and large the pots were wheel-thrown, though a few hand-made examples also occur. On the exterior of the bottom of some pots a series of indentations can be seen. How exactly these came into being is difficult to say. After the pots had been dried in the sun, they were painted. K. T. M. Hegde, who has re-created samples of this ware under laboratory conditions, states that red ochre ground in water was the pigment used for these decorations. The painted designs range from a simple band round the rim through a variety of oblique and criss-cross lines, to more specialized designs such as a row of sigmas, a chain of short spirals, concentric circles and semi-circles, intersecting circles, maltese squares, swastikas, etc. (Fig. 1). There are, however, no human or animal figures.

The more common shapes in this ware are the dish and bowl, the former usually with convex sides and base, and the latter with either vertical or convex sides or even a flat base. Besides bowls and dishes, there are examples of vases for holding drinking water. Among vessels special mention may be made of the following: corrugated stems, from Hastinapura, Ahichchhatra, etc., which constituted the lower part of a dish-on-stand or cup-on-stand (unfortunately no complete example has yet been found); a strap handle with painting on it from Sardargarh, which, judging from a handled pot in dull-red ware, would appear to have formed a part of a vase with a flaring rim, and somewhat bulging body.

Although the culture is designated after the Painted Grey Ware, it should be mentioned that this pottery constituted only about 10 to 15 per cent of the total ceramic assemblage. It was evidently highly valued as a luxury ware.

But by far the majority of the pottery was of red ware, some slipped but mostly unslipped. In most cases husks and mica ware were used as *degraissants*. It is the red-ware pots that met most of the people's needs – for fetching and storing water, for storing cereals and for cooking.

At Atranjikhera a kiln has been discovered.[30] Oval in plan, it was a about 1 m deep, with the longer axis measuring 2.35 m. Within it were encountered alternate layers of pots and fuel, the latter consisting primarily of cakes of animal dung. Towards the top were placed heaps of reeds and twigs and the kiln was finally sealed with mud-plaster.

Those who preceded the Painted Grey Ware people in the upper Ganges

30. Gaur, 1983, p. 128.

FIG. 1. Some designs on the Painted Grey Ware. (Courtesy of the Archaeological Survey of India.)

valley did not use iron; for example, the Harappans at Alamgirpur and Hulas; the Ochre Colour Ware people at Hastinapura and the black-and-red ware people at Atranjikhera and Jakhera. However, since the Ganges valley has hard alluvial soil and there is evidence suggesting that in ancient times it was deeply forested, substantial use of iron would appear to be a logical necessity to overcome these ecological handicaps in order to put the region under large-scale sedentary occupation.

That the Painted Grey Ware people were skilled in the manufacture of iron objects is evidenced by as many as 135 specimens from a relatively small dig at Atranjikhera. From Jodhpur, comes the evidence of two furnaces from an early phase of the Painted Grey Ware period. These furnaces were of the open type and provided with bellows as indicated by the presence of holes.

Very little work has been done to identify the sources from which the people obtained iron ore. Source material, however, exists in varying degrees in the neighbouring Himalayan regions of Kangara, Mandi Almora, Garhwal, etc., in the Aravalli terrain of Alwar, Jaipur, Bharatpur, etc., in Rajasthan and in the Gwalior region immediately south of the Chambal. Later, however, when the Northern Black Polished Ware stage was reached, the Bihar ores, very much richer in content, were exploited, which gave a great boost to the iron industry, resulting both in profusion and new varieties of implements.

The iron objects used by the Painted Grey Ware people fall under four broad categories: (a) household objects; (b) tools for agriculture; (c) other craft tools; and (d) weapons used for warfare or hunting. Under the first category come such objects as nails, pins, hooks, needles, knives, which are reported from various sites, and a pair of tongs found so far only at Atranjikhera (Fig. 2). Although this site has not yielded any specific agricultural tools, a sickle and a hoe was found at Jakhera.[31] Chisels, borers, clamps, nails and hooks may have been used in carpentry. Arrowheads, mounted on cane shafts and projected from wooden bows, could have been used in warfare as well as in hunting. The arrowheads are found in simple forms as well as barbed, and have a tang that is sometimes socketed. Spearheads, sometimes as long as 25 cm, were evidently mounted on bamboo shafts. Unlike arrows, which were used for long-distance attacks, whether on an enemy or a wild animal, the spear could be used only at a close range. There is so far no evidence of any defensive armour.

While discussing the use of iron, it should be mentioned that at Bhagwanpura, Dadheri and Nagar, Joshi found no iron at all in the levels of this culture, though copper objects were met with.[32] Such evidence tends to suggest that during Painted Grey Ware times, there may have been an early stage when only copper was used but no iron. However, before the point can be taken as fully established, evidence from a few more sites would be a desideratum.

Although iron had come into use during the Painted Grey Ware period, copper was still an indispensable metal. While the two specimens from Hastinapura which were chemically examined showed no evidence of any alloy, of the three objects examined from Atranjikhera, one showed the inclusion of tin, lead and zinc to the extent of 11.68 per cent and another of tin and zinc as much as 20.72 and 16.2 per cent respectively. The third one was unalloyed. Furthermore, iron was present in all the Atranjikhera samples, varying from 1.23 to as much as 9.7 per cent. The source of the metal could thus be iron chalchopyrite and the retention of iron in the samples should be ascribed to inadequate melting of the ore.[33]

In this culture, there are no copper swords such as, for example, we have in the copper hoards. This may perhaps be explained by the fact that weapons of war were by then manufactured from iron, which is decidedly more suitable for the purpose. However, copper arrowheads have been found at Hastinapura and

31. Sahi, 1978, p. 103.
32. Joshi, 1978, pp. 98–100.
33. Agrawal, 1983, p. 490.

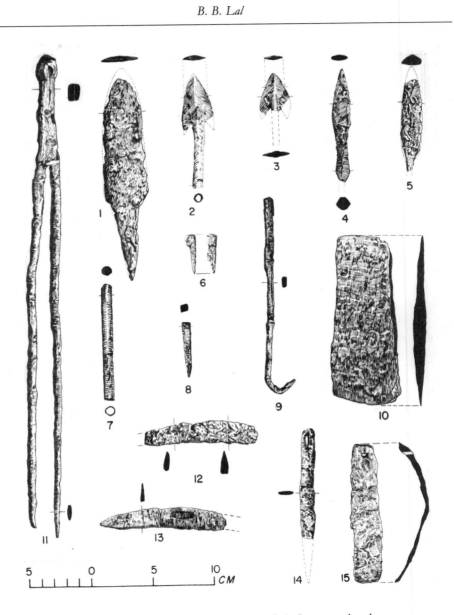

F<small>IG</small>. 2 Atranjikhera: iron objects: 1 – spearhead; 2–5 – arrowheads; 6 and 8 – nails; 7 – shaft; 9 – hook; 10 – axe; 11 – pair of tongs; 12–13 – knives; 14 – large needle (?); 15 – clamp.

Allahpur. Very likely these were used primarily for hunting, though their use in warfare cannot be excluded.

Among tools and other objects of copper which were used for cutting or in the manufacturing of goods, mention may be made of the axe, chisel, borer, pin and clamp. Toilet objects included the antimony rod, nailparer, antimony-rod-cum-nailparer and toothpick. The find of a needle indicated stitching, most likely of clothes. Among ornaments, rings and bangles deserve mention. That there was no paucity of copper is attested by the discovery of a dish, with a diameter of 17 cm, from Atranjikhera.[34]

A very remarkable contribution of this period is that of glass technology. The discovery of two specimens of glass bangles from Painted Grey Ware levels at Hastinapura came as a significant addition to our knowledge of ancient Indian glass technology. Of the two glass bangles from Hastinapura, one is brown and the other black, resulting in both cases from the presence of iron. In both, the typical conchoidal fracture of glass is unmistakable. Besides bangles, glass beads have also been found. These come from Allahpur and Alamgirpur. From Atranjikhera comes a piece of glass of dark green colour, which formed a part of a bottle or some other receptacle.[35]

By far the majority of the bone objects found in the levels of this culture are made of antler. The objects include arrowheads, both barbed and unbarbed, the tang being with or without a socket. Some of the barbed arrowheads from Atranjikhera and Jakhera bear the design of an incised circle with a central dot. Some of the specimens are pointed at both ends and may have been used for knitting or weaving. A long spacer from Jakhera, with a hole at each extremity, may also have been used in weaving. Sometimes the pointed tools are taken as styluses for writing. Since, however, no inscription has so far been recovered from the Painted Grey Ware levels, there is little to confirm the hypothesis. There were also bone ear-studs, usually cylindrical in shape, and combs (Fig. 3), and from Jakhera comes a carved hollow handle, in which the tang of a polished copper mirror may have been inserted.

Jakhera has brought to light three human terracotta figurines. Made of well-levigated clay, they are all hand-modelled. Of these figures, two, depicting a male and a female, were found together. These have an ovalish-to-circular hollow behind the head, stumpy arms, relatively thin waist and broad hips (Fig. 4). A characteristic feature of these figurines is the incised decoration over the body which in one case is rather heavy. The third figure, found separately in a lower level, is somewhat different in its execution. The face is pinched and the disposition of the nostrils leads one to suspect that it may be of some animal (Fig. 5). The body, however, is human. Could this figure be of some animal-headed

---

34. Gaur, 1983, p. 231.
35. Agrawal, 1983, p. 490.

Fig. 3. Jakhera: Bone combs used by the Painted Grey Ware people. (Courtesy of Aligarh Muslim University.)

female deity? The position, however, is uncertain, and the case can be established only if clearly identifiable examples of the kind are obtained in future.

Dull to bright red in colour, the terracotta animal figurines are also hand-made. These include the humped bull, horse and ram. While the bull and horse are not decorated, the ram invariably bears incised lines on the body. The ram has been found not only at Alamgirpur and Bhagwanpura, where some Harappan 'mix-up' might be suspected, but also at Jakhera were there is no Harappan or even late Harappan substratum. The occurrence of the terracotta horse, in addition to the presence of skeletal remains, reinforces the belief that it was one of the favourite animals of the Painted Grey Ware people.

That these people were skilled in various branches of technology – ceramics, iron, copper, glass, bone, etc. – must be amply clear from the foregoing pages. There are, however, some objects that throw valuable light on their knowledge of geometry. From Jakhera come four flattish pieces of terracotta, which may be classified under two categories. In one case there are three sides of which two are straight, joining each other at a right angle, while the third one (i.e. the hypotenuse) is an arc of a circle. In the other case, there are four sides, of which three are straight with intermediary angles of 90 degrees, while the fourth one is an arc of a circle. All these demonstrate some knowledge of the concept of the circle, quadrant, rectangle, etc. That these people also used scientific instruments such as the divider is clearly indicated by the intersecting circles incised on a potsherd found at Jakhera. The point where one of the arms of the divider was fixed to draw the circles concerned is clearly visible as a pin-hole.

FIG. 4. Jakhera: Grey terracotta figure of the Painted Grey Ware people. It is to be noted for its archaic features and notched decoration. (Courtesy of Aligarh Muslim University.)

Although it may entail a partial repetition of some of the data given above, it would be well worth while to visualize how the Painted Grey Ware people actually lived.

The settlements were mostly along the rivers, the average intermediary distance being 10 to 12 km. To begin with, these settlements were small but, as time passed, they increased in size, but at no stage did a 'city', with all that it implies, come into being. Because of the lack of horizontal excavation it is not known whether there was any apportioning of areas for craftsmen of certain categories, such as potters, ironsmiths, etc., though such a possibility cannot altogether be ruled out. The economy, however, was essentially rural. Agriculture was the mainstay of the people who produced wheat, barley and rice. Iron axes helped in felling trees and making the land cultivable, which must have been ploughed with the help of bullocks.

Agriculture was supplemented by cattle-breeding which provided the people with milk and its derivatives, namely curds, ghee, buttermilk, cheese, etc.

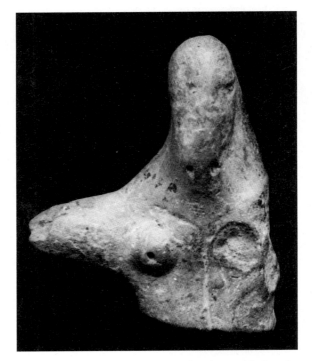

FIG. 5. Jakhera: Grey terracotta figurine, with female
human body and animal (?) head. (Courtesy of
Aligarh Muslim University.)

Several other animals, such as the buffalo, dog, pig, ram, horse, etc., were also domesticated. Dogs would have kept watch over the fields, farms and even the houses, pigs would have done the scavenging while horses would have been used for riding, and perhaps for drawing chariots, though admittedly no evidence of this has yet been found.

The nature of the houses varied: while the lowlier members of the community lived in round or rectangular huts of modest size, constructed essentially of wattle-and-daub, the more well-to-do lived in sizable houses with mud-walls, sometimes having as many as a dozen rooms. Burnt bricks do not appear to have been used for house construction, though their presence is duly attested. Generally squarish, these may have been used in religious structures like altars, etc.

Vegetarian as well as non-vegetarian food was consumed. While rice may have been boiled and eaten, wheat and barley were ground with mortar and pestle. From the ground floor, one may imagine, *chapatis* were prepared on a U-shaped hearth as is done today. To the diet were also added mutton, pork, beef and venison. Likewise, fowls, river-turtles and bivalves were also consumed. The food was eaten from the luxury Painted Grey Ware dishes and bowls (Fig. 6).

Very little evidence is available about the dress of the people. That cloth

Fɪɢ. 6. A typical dinner set in the Painted Grey Ware consisting of the *thali* (dish), *katora* (bowl) and *lota* (drinking vessel). It highlights the tradition followed, even today, in an average Indian household.

was woven is indirectly attested to by the impressions found on potsherds. But whether the cloth was just draped around the body or sown into garments is a matter for conjecture. The discovery of needles, however, suggests that certain garments were indeed stitched.

Women bedecked themselves with jewellery which seems to have included necklaces made variously of beads of semi-precious stone like agate, jasper, etched carnelian, etc. From Atranjikhera comes a soapstone mould in which probably gold jewellery was cast (Fig. 7). There is evidence of the use of bangles, finger-rings and ear-studs. The hair was duly combed and collyrium applied to the eyes.

Hunting and fishing may have been resorted to partly for augmenting food supplies and partly as a sport. But one of the pastimes of the adults seems to have been gambling. This is attested to by the discovery of a die from Alamgirpur and of gamesmen from Noh and Mathura. Made of bone (or some kind of wood – the material has not been thoroughly examined), the die is oblong, the cross-section being rectangular. On its four faces there are broad pin-holes numbering 1, 2, 3 and 4, in an arrangement in which 3 is opposite 1 and 4 opposite 2. Flat at the bottom and having a somewhat parabolic elevation, the Noh gamesman is of the same material as the Painted Grey Ware one, and it even bears black paintings. The Mathura specimens are in two wares, grey as well as red, and may be assumed to have been used by two opposite parties. The dice and gamesmen are similar to those used in the game of *chaupar* even to this day (Fig. 8). Horse-racing could have been another diversion.

435

Fig. 7. Atranjikhera: Soapstone mould used by the Painted Grey Ware people probably for making jewellery. (Courtesy of Aligarh Muslim University.)

The children played hopscotch with circular pieces made by trimming broken pottery. Sometimes these circular pottery pieces have one or two holes. It is likely that, as at present, the children then put a thread through the holes and played by twisting the thread backwards and forwards. The terracotta ram found at Alamgirpur has holes in the lower part of the legs. This would indicate the use of wheeled toys by children.

The fireplaces at Atranjikhera found associated with charred rice and bones may indicate some kind of sacrifice. Terracotta discs with a variety of incised designs have also been found at most of the sites (Fig. 9). Gaur believes that these may have had some religious significance.

There is not much evidence of large-scale trade and commerce. None the less iron ores, of which tools were manufactured locally at various sites, must have been brought through trade. Likewise, semi-precious stones for beads would imply some sort of trade. However, barter must have been the means of exchange of goods and services, since there was no system of coinage.

The dating of the Painted Grey Ware period at Hastinapura had originally to be carried out on the basis of its relative stratigraphic horizon. On the one hand, it overlay the remains of the Ochre Colour Ware and, on the other, it was itself overlain by Northern Black Polished Ware deposits. There was a break of occupation between each of these three successive periods. The chronological horizon of the Northern Black Polished Ware had been approximately indicated at Taxila where the majority of the specimens of this ware preceded the level yielding coins of Alexander (c. 300 B.C.) and went down to a further depth of 2.15 m below that level. On a rough computation, therefore, the Northern Black Polished Ware was thought to have appeared at Taxila some time in the sixth century B.C. Since there was a break of occupation between the Painted Grey

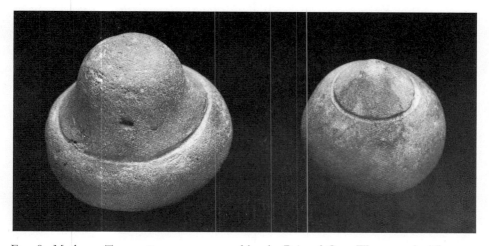

FIG. 8. Mathura; Terracotta gamesmen used by the Painted Grey Ware people. The one on the left is in red ware and that on the right in grey ware, the colour difference being for allocation of two opposite parties. These gamesmen are similar to the ones used in the game of *chaupar*. (Courtesy of Archaeological Survey of India.)

Ware and Northern Polished Ware periods at Hastinapura, with substantial changes in the material culture from one to the other (such as the appearance of burnt-brick structures, a system of coinage, weights, etc.) it was thought that the end of the Painted Grey Ware period at Hastinapura may have come around 800 B.C. In view of the 2.5 m thickness of the Painted Grey Ware deposits, it was estimated that the beginning of the settlement of this culture at Hastinapura may have been around 1100 B.C. It was also postulated that the Painted Grey Ware may have continued later at other sites and may have even overlapped with the Northern Black Polished Ware. Later when the radio-carbon method came into vogue, samples from Hastinapura itself and from other sites like Rupar, Atranjikhera, Noh, etc., were put to the test. As a result, there is a good evidence to say that the beginning of the Painted Grey Ware at the iron-using sites such as Noh and Atranjikhera and derivatively at Hastinapura and Mathura too, is in no case later than 1000 B.C. It may well be much earlier. The Painted Grey Ware levels in the iron-using sites of the upper Ganges-Jamuna basin may broadly be dated between the limits of 1100 and 700 B.C. and the Painted Grey Ware/Northern Black Polished Ware overlap between 700 and 500 B.C. The pre-Iron phase of this culture which has yet to be firmly established may well antedate 1100 B.C.

This archaeological evidence about the Painted Grey Ware Culture may be understood in the background of the Vedic material. The general consensus of scholarly opinion puts the Rigvedic period broadly between 1500 and 1200 B.C. and the later Brahmanic-cum-Upanishadic period between 800 and 500 B.C.

Then there is the 'space' factor. From the geographical data available in these texts, it would appear that the Rigvedic locale was primarily that of the Sap-

FIG. 9. Atranjikhera: A terracotta disc. On its two sides are incised designs which may have had some religious significance. (Courtesy of Aligarh Muslim University.)

tasindhu, that is, the rivers of the Indus system including the easterly ones such as the Sarasvati and Drishadvati, though Jamuna and Ganges are also referred to. In terms of modern political division, this would cover the northern part of Pakistan as well as Punjab, north-eastern Rajasthan and contiguous parts of Haryana in India. During the later Vedic-cum-early Brahmanic period the main focus was on what was known as the Madhyadesa, corresponding to the upper Ganges-Jamuna valley, to which could be added some areas west of the Jamuna itself. Finally, during the later Brahmanic-cum-Upanishadic period the scene shifted to eastern Uttar Pradesh and even northern Bihar.

Put together, the 'time' and 'space' factors would seem to indicate a fair amount of concordance between the three periods of Vedic literature as propounded by Max Muller, i.e. the Rigvedic, the late Vedic, and the period of Sutras (Velit I–III) on the one hand, and Painted Grey Ware (PGW I–III), on the other. Indeed, it would be too much to expect more than that, for literary changes need not necessarily keep full pace with changes in the material culture or vice versa.

We may now go into some details of the 'content' factor. To recapitulate, people in both Velit I and Velit II were essentially at a rural stage and so were those in PGW I and II. It is only towards the end of Velit III that the signs of urbanization become discernible, and the same is the situation towards the end of PGW III. In Velit I and II the houses were made of wattle-and-daub, as were the houses in PGW I and II. While no data are available regarding the cereals of PGW I, those of PGW II, namely rice, wheat and barley, compare well with the cereals of Velit II.

The horse, making its appearance right from Velit I, occurs in PGW I (Bhagwanpura) and PGW II (Hastinapura and Atranjikhera). Knowledge of iron in Velit I is doubtful; and neither has PGW I yielded any iron so far (Bhagwan-pura, Dadheri, etc.). Iron occurs in Velit II as well as in PGW II. Likewise, glass referred to in Velit II, is also found in PGW II.

Writing seems to have been unknown to Velit I and II, as it was in PGW I and II. It is only towards the end of Velit III that a knowledge of writing is indi-cated. More or less the same may be the position towards the end of PGW III.

The evidence regarding the use of dice from Velit I onwards compares pos-itively to that obtained so far from PGW II (the Alamgirpur specimen bears 4, 3, 2 and 1 markings).

Finally, we come to the disposal of the dead. Although negative evidence should never be overstressed, it may well be that cremation was the practice in PGW II as it was in Velit II. The burials at Bhagwanpura may be of either Harap-pan or of Painted Grey Ware people, because it was a period of overlap. Thus, it is difficult to say anything positive about the disposal of the dead in PGW I, much less to compare it to the *anagnidagdha* method of Velit I.

From the foregoing it becomes amply clear that there is an overall concor-dance between Velit II and PGW II; namely between the later Vedic-cum-early Brahmanic period, on the one hand, and the upper Ganges-Jamuna valley stage of the PGW culture, on the other.[36] Likewise, new features such as urbanization, writing, etc., discernible towards the end of Velit II (i.e. later Brahmanic-cum-Upanishadic period), are also met with towards the end of PGW III (i.e. towards the end of the Painted Grey Ware/Northern Black Polished Ware overlap[37]).

The equation between Velit I (the Rigvedic period) and PGW I (the north-ern Pakistan to north-eastern Rajasthan stage of the Painted Grey Ware Culture) is, however, not so secure. What is needed now is more evidence of the pre-Iron stage of the culture in this area. In this context we may pin some hope on what A. H. Dani says when discussing the Aryan problem in relation to the Gandhāra Grave Culture and the Painted Grey Ware Culture:

> But we have seen in our region how there had been two main periods of invasion of these Grey Ware people. While the earlier date of Lal tallies with the first invasion in our region, we have so far no evidence for extending this invasion into East Pan-jab and the upper Ganges valley. But the second invasion came about the same time when the Painted Grey Ware Culture is seen in upper India. Could we, therefore, not see the spread of this latter culture as a result of the second invasion from the West? *A definite answer to this question will be provided only when our investigations are extended into Panjab east of the river Indus.*[38]

36. Here we may draw attention to a very good paper by Sharma (1978). The date adopted in this paper for the Painted Grey Ware Culture was *c*. 800–400 B.C., presumably on the basis of the date suggested by Agrawal and Kusumgar (1974). However, Sharma (1980, p. 48) has accepted 1000–500 B.C. as the date of the iron-using Painted Grey Ware sites.
37. Although to-date no inscription prior to the Mauryan times has been found, there is a reasonable possibility of writing having come into being somewhat earlier.
38. Dani, 1967, pp. 54–5 (my italics).

This is, however, not to say that the Painted Grey Ware Culture alone would fill the bill for the entire Rigvedic stage. There could be other cognate cultures too, for the terrain from the Sarasvati in Rajasthan back to the Kubha (Kabul) in Afghanistan is a long and varied one.

Conclusion

In the foregoing pages we have presented the characteristic features of a protohistoric culture. No doubt the Indus Civilization was great in many respects, but not much of it ultimately survived. For reasons still not fully known to us, the Indus Civilization withered away. But the authors of the Painted Grey Ware Culture, clearly identifiable with the later Vedic Aryans (if not yet with the Rigvedic Aryans as well), are the ones who provided the seeds of philosophic thought for which India is known all over the world. And it was not mere spirituality that they bequeathed. Their contribution to material life is no less significant. The Painted Grey Ware people, with their iron technology, are the first to have brought about a revolution in the settlement pattern in the Ganges-Jamuna basin – the Madhyadesa of old. Their predecessors in this region, namely, the copper-hoard people, seem to have been merely sporadic occupants, leaving hardly any mark on the civilization to be. Further, it is the Painted Grey Ware period that brought northern India to the threshold of what is known as the second urbanization. The glory lost through the fall of the Indus Civilization was regained after a lapse of nearly 1,000 years by the immediate descendants of the Painted Grey Ware people, namely the Northern Black Polished Ware people. On the solid foundation laid by the Painted Grey Ware people arose the superstructure in which during the sixth and fifth centuries B.C. there flourished not only the legendary Mahajanapadas ruled by kings like Udayana, Prasenjit and Bimbisara, but also the great religious teachers, Mahavira and Buddha.

THE BEGINNING OF THE IRON AGE IN TRANSOXANIA[1]

A. Askarov

T HE discovery of iron triggered off one of the greatest technological revolutions in the history of mankind. But iron implements were slow to come into general use; the metal was at first reserved mainly for ornament. Ferrous metallurgy became widespread after the discovery of the process whereby the metal is produced directly from the ore at a temperature of 900 °C. Molten iron cannot be obtained at less than 1,530 °C which at that time was unattainable. Unlike copper and bronze, iron was a universally accessible, cheap metal with sound qualities. But forging iron implements involved considerably more labour than did the casting of bronze. The new technology was mastered slowly.

At the very start of the Iron Age, what are known as bronze-and-iron tools and weapons, those with an iron blade and a bronze handle, became widespread in Middle Asia (Soviet Central Asia). Iron soon made its way into all fields of warfare and daily life. It increased labour productivity dramatically, led to a full-scale technological revolution, and played a crucial part in the development of arable farming and crafts. The spread of iron transformed the whole of society.

Archaeological investigations of Early Iron Age sites have shown that as in the preceding period, the territory of Soviet Central Asia was made up of two broad zones: one peopled by steppe tribes whose livelihood revolved primarily around stockbreeding, and the other settled by communities with a deeply-rooted, advanced arable-farming culture of the ancient Oriental type. The cultures of those two zones developed unequally. The cultural and economic tradition of the advanced southern communities gradually permeated the stockbreeding population of the steppes. The two were always, as archaeological evidence shows, in close contact and passed on their cultural and economic achievements to each other. As a result of these intercultural and interethnic links, Early Iron Age society developed further and more intensively.

1. See Map 14.

The cultural and economic achievements of either zone were undoubtedly subject to external influences, likewise thereby influencing the cultural development of their neighbours. All this could come about either by peaceful cultural and intertribal relations, by penetration or by conquest. In the final analysis, the overall result of contacts between settled and pastoral tribes was that society advanced and progressed further. Among the main features of that progress in the Early Iron Age was that agriculture and the crafts took a leap forward. This was directly bound up with the development of artificial irrigation systems, with the change from a herding and tilling life-style to a transhumant, stockbreeding and semi-nomadic way of life. The adoption of the new economy was the decisive factor in the further development of the new economic and cultural forms, which is vividly reflected in the material culture of the Soviet Central Asian Early Iron Age.

The Amirabad culture

The most interesting Early Iron Age culture of ancient Khorezm was that of Amirabad in the tenth to eighth centuries B.C.[2] Dozens more settlements were found in the lower reaches of the former channels of Akcha Darya, the ancient delta of the Amu Darya. The most interesting was Yakka-Parsan II, alongside which were found ancient fields, and the remnants of an Amirabad-period irrigation system (Fig. 1). The old channel passed near by, its banks being reinforced with dykes.

Two rows of semi-dugout houses – some twenty in all – were found in the Yakka-Parsan II settlement. Large numbers of storage pits were found around the houses, and the entire site is rich in animal bones, pottery, grain-querns and so on. The houses stood between two canals that merged to the south, all the doors giving on to the canals. Rectangular in ground-plan, the houses were 90 to 110 m^2 in area and had two or three rooms. The interiors contained many storage pits and post-holes, each with a long fireplace in the centre. The major finds were pottery, hand-made with a darkish brown, red or greyish slip, the shoulders of the bowls being decorated with small crosses, lattice-work or 'fir-trees'. According to S. P. Tolstov, the Amirabad culture was genetically akin to the Kaundy complex and dates from the ninth to eighth centuries B.C. It should be observed that the pottery shows more obvious traces of Karasuk influence, the commonest shapes being similar to the ceramics of the latter; this entitles us to date its origins to a somewhat earlier period – the tenth century B.C. Other finds include bronze artefacts – a needle with an eye, a sickle with a shaped handle, a bronze arrowhead with a shaft – and stone moulds for casting shaft-hole arrowheads and sickles. A bronze sickle, large numbers of grain-querns and the advanced irrigation network and fields together show that agriculture was widely practised,

2. Tolstov, 1962.

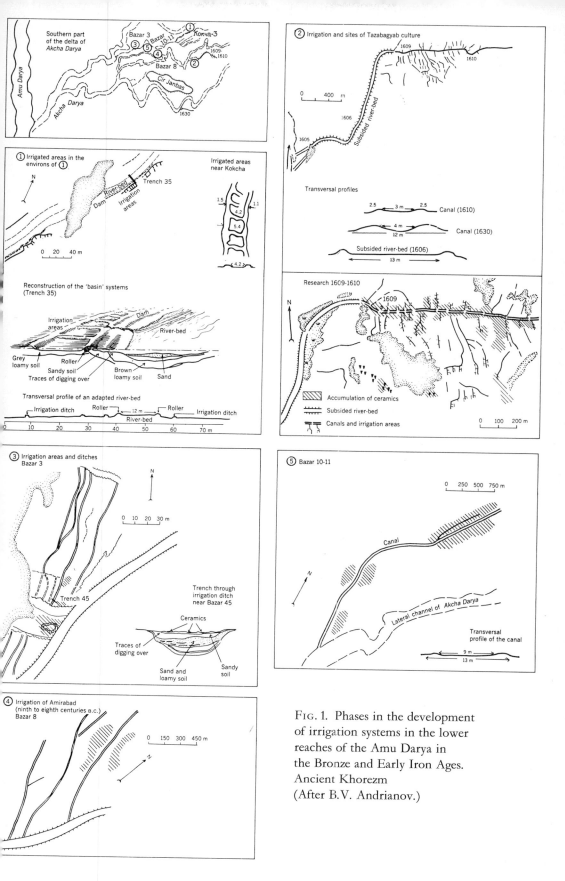

Fig. 1. Phases in the development of irrigation systems in the lower reaches of the Amu Darya in the Bronze and Early Iron Ages. Ancient Khorezm (After B.V. Andrianov.)

while the bone finds further indicate that the population was engaged in stock-breeding.[3]

The culture of the northern Tagisken tribes

The most striking view of the Early Iron Age of Transoxania is afforded by the tenth-to-eighth-century-B.C. mausoleums of the northern Tagisken plateau to the east of the Aral Sea. The Tagisken mausoleums are outstanding monuments of the Early Iron Age and a testimony to the advanced standard of cult architecture and building techniques among the ancient stockbreeders of the region to the east of the Aral Sea.

The Tagisken sepulchres take the shape of tumuli and number over seventy. They fall into northern and southern groups. The early tumuli are time-worn ruins of large mausoleums built of rectangular raw bricks measuring 54 × 28 × 10–12 or 48 × 32 × 10–12 cm, and surrounded by small tombs of various shapes and sizes but chiefly of the enclosure kind, annexed to them or grouped around them. At one large mausoleum seven tombs were found, at a second, six and, at another, three. The cemetery apparently consisted of several large mausoleums and a number of smaller tombs surrounding and between them.[4] The central chamber of the mausoleums and inner corridor contained burial goods such as pottery, bronze implements, bronze or gold ornaments. One aspect of the ritual was that parts of animals were buried with the dead.

Ritual cremation appears to have been practised on the Tagisken and at the culmination the entire building was set ablaze. It is unlikely that it was left in its ruined state; it may be that the mausoleum was again roofed over after the cremation, where the brick columns were used to support the roof.[5] Another hypothesis, however, is that all the mausoleums have been plundered and set on fire. M. P. Gryaznov suggests that the plundering preceded the burning, prompting the thought that it was done long ago, possibly by the contemporary builders, who then fired the structures to cover their tracks, since the walls and the structure proper were not disturbed and the fire left its marks on the floors of the mausoleums.[6]

The tombs annexed to the mausoleums were rectangular enclosures, also of raw bricks, where the leader's kin and close friends were buried. A particular place among these structures goes to a complex built on to the north wall of one of the large mausoleums. Its central chamber contained the remains of a woman together with an assortment of vessels and ornaments – gold and carnelian beads, a massive gold ear-ring and a bronze pin. To the west was a chamber in which some forty vessels of various shapes and sizes stood around a fireplace.

3. Itina, 1977*a*, pp. 147–72.
4. Tolstov, 1962; Tolstov et al., 1963, pp. 3–90.
5. Itina, 1977*b*.
6. Gryaznov, 1966.

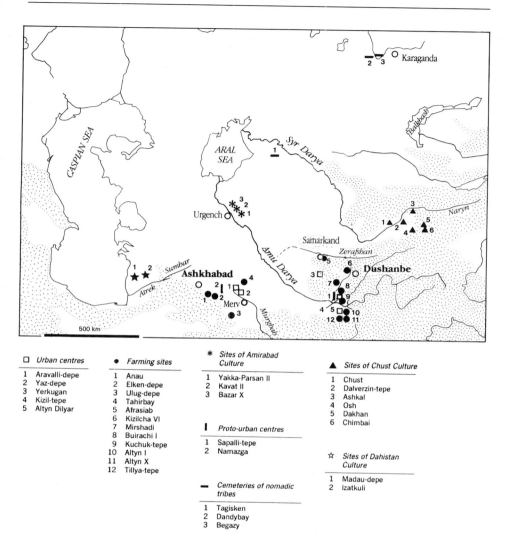

MAP 14. Early Iron Age sites of Central Asia.

☐	*Urban centres*	●	*Farming sites*	*	*Sites of Amirabad Culture*	▲	*Sites of Chust Culture*
1	Aravalli-depe	1	Anau	1	Yakka-Parsan II	1	Chust
2	Yaz-depe	2	Elken-depe	2	Kavat II	2	Dalverzin-tepe
3	Yerkugan	3	Ulug-depe	3	Bazar X	3	Ashkal
4	Kizil-tepe	4	Tahirbay			4	Osh
5	Altyn Dilyar	5	Afrasiab			5	Dakhan
		6	Kizilcha VI			6	Chimbai
		7	Mirshadi	▮	*Proto-urban centres*		
		8	Buirachi I	1	Sapalli-tepe		
		9	Kuchuk-tepe	2	Namazga	☆	*Sites of Dahistan Culture*
		10	Altyn I			1	Madau-depe
		11	Altyn X			2	Izatkuli
		12	Tillya-tepe	—	*Cemeteries of nomadic tribes*		
				1	Tagisken		
				2	Dandybay		
				3	Begazy		

There is another group of structures from the same period as the annexes. Also built of brick, they were considerably simpler in ground-plan than the mausoleums, but retained all the basic principles of their construction. The outer wall was not square but round, and between it and the rectangular chamber was a circular corridor. The entrance was again on the east side and the same system of post-holes was used, but there were no columns and the beams were an integral part of the design here.

The largest mausoleum on the Tagisken is No. 6, the ruins of a rounded sepulchre some 25 m in diameter (Fig. 2). The inner walls of the burial chamber were faced with a thick layer of wicker and twigs and – judging by the 100 or more bronze nails that were found – hung with carpets. In the corners were groups of vessels which clearly stood there for a purpose. Sickle-shaped bronze knives, bronze needles and gold articles were found. This mausoleum was found to contain a rich collection of vessels, numbering over sixty. One was even adorned with four small gold scrolls on the rim (Fig. 3).

The hand-made pottery, with its slip and white incrustation, is similar in shape and decoration to Karasuk ceramics. The cultural resemblance of Tagisken to Dandybay-Begazy in central Kazakhstan or the Karasuk culture of southern Siberia is obvious. Tagisken pottery, however, differs in its wider range of shapes, the elegance and lavishness of its decoration and the presence of wheel-pitchers, spherical jugs with narrow, pool-shaped necks. These vessels are closely paralleled in the Bronze Age pottery of the southern oases.[7] Some traditions of the Andronovo culture may be clearly seen in the mausoleum complexes of the northern Tagisken.

The Tagisken mausoleums are reminiscent of similar structures in central Kazakhstan, though the cyclopean stonework of the latter is replaced by unburnt brick. The farming cultures of southern Soviet Central Asia had used this material for a long time, and the builders of the Tagisken mausoleums must be supposed to have been familiar with their southern neighbours' practices, and to have borrowed certain structural techniques from them, primarily the manufacture of unburnt brick. And so the architectural design of the mausoleums was based on a ground-plan akin to the monuments of Dandybay-Begazy, but executed in different materials. What is more, the technique by which the square structure was topped by a round drum – using brick columns in the inner corners of the square outer walls – appears to pre-date the pendentive. The same technique is known in Begazy, though there the columns are of stone. We are therefore faced with architectural skills of a fairly high order for which there is no known analogy in the Central Asian steppe zones. The southern component appears in the rounded ceramic pitchers, though the large range of hand-made vessels found with them resemble known objects used by the steppe tribes.

7. Askarov, 1977.

FIG. 2. Northern Tagisken: Mausoleum No. 6.

The Chust culture

More advanced cultures are represented in the northern regions of Soviet Central Asia. One of them is that of the Chust culture. In the late second and early first millennium B.C., a distinctive sedentary farming culture, named after the first settlement to be studied, Chust,[8] sprang up in the ancient Ferghana valley. Its characteristics included hand-made and decorated pottery, an advanced bronze metallurgy and a varied range of secondary stone artefacts. An important field for the study of the Late Bronze and Early Iron Ages in the region, it was largely confined to the northern and eastern parts of the valley. While over eighty sites are now known, only the settlements of Chimbai, Chust, Ashkal and Osh, and the ancient town of Dalverzin-tepe have been fully investigated.

Chust culture sites were located in the valleys of small streams running down from the northern Ferghana range, or near the sources and tributaries of the Kara Darya in the east of the valley. They were grouped in the lowland plains, where they are known in fifteen distinct areas, most being clan settlements or relatively large fortified towns. The larger of them – Chust with an area of 4 ha, Dakhan about 5 ha and Ashkal over 10 ha – came to acquire defensive walls, while the central towns, such as the 25 ha Dalverzin-tepe, also had citadels of some kind. These became important at a later stage of the Chust culture, at the time when iron artefacts appeared there.

In the early stage, the chief form of housing was the dugout or pit dwelling with large numbers of grain-storage pits. In the later stage, houses were built above ground-level using rectangular raw unburnt brick. The dead were buried chiefly outside the settlements in the desert or in ruined houses. At Chust and Dalverzin-tepe, several graves have been studied in which the dead lay doubled-up or on their sides in pits, with no consistent orientation. In the upper strata of the settlement, some were buried alone on their backs, usually without burial goods. Dismembered and disordered human bones and skulls have also been found, frequently in storage pits in the open fields, together with animal bones, and bearing the marks of fire.

The crafts were fully developed, particularly that of casting bronze, as is

8. Zadneprovsky, 1962.

447

Fig. 3. Northern Tagisken: pottery from Mausoleum No. 6.

clear from the many finds of stone or clay moulds for casting small-handled mirrors, sickles or knives, and clay crucibles. The range of bronze Chust artefacts is quite wide, including tools, armaments, horse harnesses, ornaments, personal requisites and so on (Fig. 4). While bronze metallurgy remained widespread, this was the time when the first signs appeared that the population of Ferghana valley was familiar with iron, a fragment of an iron knife and iron ore slag having been found at Dalverzin-tepe. Stone objects such as sickle-shaped knives, grain querns,

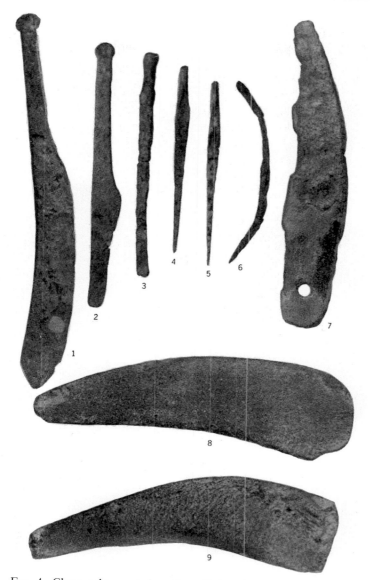

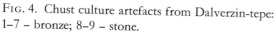

FIG. 4. Chust culture artefacts from Dalverzin-tepe:
1–7 – bronze; 8–9 – stone.

picks, hoes, etc., were commonplace, and many tools were made of bone, including such varied articles as combs and shuttles for weaving, awls, three-holed bridle cheek-pieces of horn, arrowheads, etc. Pottery accounted for the bulk of the household goods. Hand-made and of various shape, it had a surface slip in colours ranging from light brown to black. Only a small proportion was decorated. The commonest vessels were round-bottomed jugs, flat-based bowls, basins, cups and pouring vessels (Fig. 5).

449

Fɪɢ. 5. Chust culture clay vessels from Dalverzin-tepe.

The defensive fortifications in the larger settlements and the finds of bridles, cheek-pieces and iron objects, chiefly in the upper strata, place the late stage of the Chust culture in the Early Iron Age.

Analysis of the evidence to date suggests that the Chust-type decorated pottery cultures in Soviet Central Asia originated and developed locally. In other words, former steppe tribes, influenced by the cultural attainments of their southern and eastern neighbours, gradually adopted a sedentary life-style.

The Chust culture is linked by a number of features to Bronze Age sites in Xinjiang. These features include, in particular, stone sickles and various kinds of decorated ceramics. This obviously suggests that the establishment of a settled culture in the territories of the Ferghana valley in the Bronze Age followed a common pattern with a major contribution from a component connected with Bronze Age steppe cultures. Chust-like hand-made and decorated ceramics from the Early Iron Age have in recent years been recorded in the lower strata of Afrasiab (now Samarkand) and Yerkurgan in the Karshi oasis. The pottery and other evidence suggest that the Chust culture people were in close cultural contact with the tribes living in the Early Iron Age in the southern regions of Soviet Central Asia.

In the light of the latest discoveries, ten geographical regions characterized by the spread of late painted pottery have been identified in the territory of Soviet Central Asia, in Yaz I in Turkmenistan and Kuchuk in Uzbekistan. They were virtually contemporary and occupied all the major farming oases in Transoxania. The similarity of their economies and cultures is marked; it appears above all in their identical decorated pottery.

Settlements in southern Soviet Central Asia and northern Afghanistan

Late decorated pottery culture developed rather differently in the south and north of Soviet Central Asia. Immediately before this period, the region had been occupied by tribes with an advanced proto-urban culture (the late Namazga IV in southern Turkmenistan and the Sapalli culture in southern Uzbekistan); these exerted a tremendous influence on the late decorated pottery tribes, who borrowed many of their cultural and economic traditions. In the south, the economy and domestic architecture of the late decorated pottery culture were identical with those of the Sapalli and late Namazga IV cultures. The chief occupations were arable farming and stockbreeding, and domestic architecture was monumental – a marked contrast with the Chust culture. Together with hand-made and decorated vessels, an old tradition survived of wheel-thrown pottery, which was completely lacking in the Chust or similar cultures of northern Soviet Central Asia.

Historical and topographical studies of sites in the south of Soviet Central Asia have revealed that there were then two types of settlement. The sites belonging to the first type are generally large in area with remains of citadels, while the other type consists of small mounds of various sizes with no citadels and with considerable variations in ground-plan. Several settlements of the second type have recently been discovered and investigated in northern Bactria. Examples are Kuchuk-tepe, Maida-tepe, Mirshadi, the upper stratum of Buirachi I, Buirachi II, Bezymyannoye (Nameless) Tepe, the lower stratum of Kizil-tepe and the lower stratum of Kizilcha VI, which were located mainly in the Sherabad, Band-

Khan and Shurchi irrigated oases of northern Bactria.[9] Excavations have shown that some of these settlements, such as Kuchuk-tepe and Maida-tepe, were farmsteads built on brick platforms several metres thick and surrounded by walls; inside was a dense pattern of residential, religious and farm buildings. Iron artefacts were found at two sites, Kuchuk-tepe and Kizilcha VI.

Late decorated pottery culture has also been identified in southern Bactria, now the territory of Afghanistan. The studies of these cultures are based on the material of Tillya-tepe in Shiberghan oasis.[10] Tillya-tepe covers an area of around 1 ha, and stands on a high platform. The lowest levels, Tillya-tepe I and Tillya-tepe II, belong to the Early Iron Age, with a mixture of wheel-thrown pots with wing-shaped lips and decorated, hand-made pottery; there were two-bladed shaft-hole arrowheads and iron artefacts from the time of the Yaz I complex. Sites with similar archaeological complexes were found in the Naimabad and Farukhabad oases of north Afghanistan. V. I. Sarianidi, who carried out this field research, considers that, regardless of current thinking as to how Soviet Central Asia's late decorated pottery culture arose, it was probably Iranian in origin. After studying the way the people of this culture moved eastwards, he suggests that there was an earlier centre in Afghanistan from which it subsequently spread throughout northern Bactria.[11]

Sites of this period are to be found in three parts of ancient Margiana: the central district around Yaz-depe, the west around Aravalli-depe, and the eastern or Tahirbay group.[12] The last two groups are archaeologically 'sterile' and contain no remains from a later period than the Yaz-depe complexes. The largest settlement of the 'metropolitan' type in the eastern group was Tahirbay I where the remains of a small, rectangular keep were found. To the west were small eroded mounds – the remains of the settlement itself. The western group of the Murghab oasis sites were located in the lower basin of the Guni-yab, where there were some ten settlements of which the largest, and apparently the ancient capital, was Aravalli-depe, some seven hectares in area, with a citadel 10 m high occupying the centre.

The metropolitan part of Margiana was then the central district of the oasis and the large settlement of Yaz-depe, 1 ha in extent, stood on an unburnt brick platform 8 m high. Several stratigraphic excavations have been carried out over an area of 200 m², and the remains of houses dating from the Yaz III period (450–350 B.C.) and levels of the Yaz II complex (650–450 B.C.) and the Yaz I complex (900–650 B.C.) were discovered. The Yaz I stratum represented the late decorated-pottery period.

Like similar complexes in northern Bactria, the Yaz I complex is characterized by a predominance of hand-made and sometimes decorated pottery, by the

9. Askarov and Al'baum, 1979.
10. Sarianidi, 1972.
11. Sarianidi, 1977.
12. Masson, 1959.

appearance of the first iron artefacts and two-bladed shaft-hole arrowheads made of bronze; but also, as noted above, by the development of large settlements centred around keeps built on massive platforms. Additionally, the Yaz-depe excavations failed to locate the early phases corresponding to the transition from the Late Bronze Age, such as late Namazga VI. Such phases would appear to have been found at Kuchuk-tepe, Ulug-tepe, Maida-tepe and Buirachi I. Analysis of the evidence of the transitional period fully corresponds with the proposition that the late decorated pottery culture of southern Soviet Central Asia and northern Afghanistan grew out of two components – the local population with its proto-urban tradition and former steppe tribes coming from northern Soviet Central Asia.

A group of hand-made decorated-pottery sites of the Yaz I type has been investigated in the foothill zone of southern Turkmenistan, the homeland of the earliest Soviet Central Asian farmers. At the start of the first millennium B.C., this region may be termed northern Parthia.[13] Yaz I type strata have been found in Parthia at Elken-depe, Ulug-depe and the northern mound at Anau. Furthermore, at all these settlements the Yaz I complexes overlie Namazga VI type Late Bronze Age strata. Here, too, small settlements sprang up at new places. Unlike the Bronze Age centres, the large settlements in the foothill zone had keeps, and their inhabited areas were larger. A case in point is Elken-depe, where the Early Iron Age inhabited area was as much as 12 ha,[14] in places where the Yaz I strata, which are 2–2.5 m thick, lie on the subsoil. The settlement was ringed with ramparts, while the citadel stood on a 6 m platform. The possibility cannot be excluded that Elken-depe was then the capital of northern Parthia.

The Dahistan culture

In contrast with the late decorated-pottery culture is the advanced sedentary farming culture of the Soviet Central Asian Early Iron Age – the grey-pottery culture of the region once known as Dahistan. It differed in several respects from that of the Chust community, since its agriculture was the most advanced of its day and it had developed what were then Soviet Central Asia's largest settlements, with powerful defensive fortifications and citadels.

The Dahistan culture was largely confined to the Misrian plain; its characteristic small settlements and extensive burial grounds have also been found in the Sumbar valley and in the western foothill range near Kyzyl-Arvat, Bami and Beurme.[15] Two types of settlement have been found on the Misrian plain: hamlets of some 5,000 m² and large settlements with strong citadels the ruins of which spread over several dozen hectares. The biggest – Izatkuli – is around 50 ha

13. Masson, 1966.
14. Marushenko, 1959, pp. 54–109.
15. Masson, 1955, pp. 385–458; Khlopin, 1983.

in area and has a pentagonal central keep around which lie the remains of houses in the form of degraded hillocks. The remains of potter's wheels have been found at several points on the outskirts. A broadly similar ground-plan is presented by another site, Madau-depe, where the degraded mound of the central keep is as much as 13 m high. Part of a house with several rooms has been excavated, and a 6.5 m cultural deposit has been stratigraphically studied.

It has been established that at the time when the Dahistan culture flourished, the southern Misrian plain was irrigated by a system of canals as much as 50 to 60 km long, leading from the Atrek river.[16] The remains of such canals have been discovered near Izatkuli and Madau-depe, where fields were irrigated by a network of ditches.

Pieces of iron slag were found in the settlements, as were bronze, leaf-shaped and twin-bladed, conical or three-bladed and hafted arrowheads, and others that were twin-bladed with a shaft-socket. In Madau-depe there was even a bronze sword with a square grip and a slight rib along the blade. All these bronze artefacts lay together with flint flakes used as blades for composite sickles.

The distinctive flavour of ancient Dahistan appears clearly in its pottery. All the tableware and fine vessels, but not the cooking pots, were wheel-thrown; the bulk was of high-quality grey clay, often covered with a black slip, the commonest type being a cup with three feet. A variety of pots – cups and beakers – had spouts, and there were bowls on saucers with long, curving spouts. Others again had open handles attached by luting, instances being goblets and cups with one handle, or ceramic strainers and rectangular bowls with hanging handles decorated with point ornament. Of particular quality is a censer with a spherical body on a tall, hollow foot. The specific set of pottery, together with a range of other, chiefly metal artefacts, the advanced irrigation system and other factors place the Dahistan culture at the end of the second and the first quarter of the first millennium B.C.[17] The sites of Dahistan culture constitute, through their archaeological materials, a distinctive cultural complex that differs sharply from that of the foothill zone and the Murghab delta in southern Turkmenistan. The individuality of this culture is due to its origin in, and kinship ties with, the neighbouring Caspian regions of Iran, and is rooted in that country's Shah-tepe and Turang-tepe archaeological culture.

Integrated studies by archaeologists, geomorphologists and soil specialists have established that agriculture based on canal-fed artificial irrigation arose in Soviet Central Asia in the Chalcolithic period. This early form used small channels leading from mountain streams or river deltas, and is known as Geoksiur farming, from the name of the first simple irrigation system.[18] The Geoksiur basin system of irrigation, which allowed fields to be flooded several times,

---

16. Kes' et al., 1980.
17. Masson, 1955, pp. 388–458.
18. Lisitsyna, 1978.

became common particularly during the Bronze Age in the Murghab oasis and ancient Bactria,[19] the lower reaches of the Zerafshan[20] and ancient Khorezm.[21]

In B. V. Andrianov's view the small lateral channels, no more than a few dozen or at most a few hundred metres long, which were used in the lower Amu Darya irrigation system in the mid-second millennium B.C., were replaced in the early first millennium B.C. by longer main canals.

The former sinking or silting basin channels, or disused river-beds, gradually came, through subsequent dredging, to be flow-fed main canals. This advance took place in the Amirabad period. From that time, completely man-made main canals, 3 km or more in length, have been identified and studied near the Amirabad settlements of Kavat II, Yakka-Parsan II, Bazar X and others. Thus a new link appeared in the system for supplying water from the river to the fields.[22] All this defined the standard of the Early Iron Age irrigation system, providing the foundation for the construction of the very large canals of Antiquity.

In 1951–53 and 1969, V. M. Masson studied the archaeological sites and ancient irrigation network of Dahistan where he recorded the remains of major man-made canals 50–60 km long, leading from the Atrek river. Subsequent thorough investigations by geomorphologists, soil scientists and archaeologists, during which a large number of trenches were dug in the irrigation dykes and canals of the Dahistan period, demonstrated[23] that the main Shah-duz canal branched off into complex irrigation systems and into the large Akhura and Izatkuli canals. The waterways in those systems may be subdivided by dimension and structure into primary and secondary channels and a dense network of ditches which were developed from the corresponding old channels.

The main canals of ancient Dahistan – those of Akhura and Izatkuli – were artificial constructions dating from the late second or early first millennia B.C., and in their central parts they had large tail-runs. The canals were 5–8 m wide and 2.3–2.7 m deep; the primary irrigation channels were 1.5–3 m wide and 1.2–1.65 m deep; the secondary channels were 0.8–1.3 m wide and 0.8–1 m deep, while the ditches were 0.5–0.7 m wide and 0.4–0.5 m deep.

A broadly similar picture emerges in respect to irrigation systems in the Murghab oasis, in ancient Bactria, the lower reaches of the Zerafshan and the Amu Darya delta. The Late Bronze and Early Iron Age canals generally followed the edges of the main channels of the local deltas; they were built along commanding features of the terrain, usually the tops of the channel banks or dykes, and could thus supply large areas of farmland on the gentler slopes of these features. That is why both the irrigation channels and the canals were flow-fed. This

---

19. Ibid., pp. 212–14.
20. Gulyamov, 1966; Gulyamov and Mukhamedzhanov, 1975, pp. 133–52.
21. Andrianov, 1969.
22. Ibid.; Itina, 1977a.
23. Kes' et al., 1980.

was the initial phase in the development of irrigation systems, when special devices began to be built to control the heads of the main canals.

To build large canals of dozens of kilometres long was beyond the capability of isolated clans or tribal communities. The economic change triggered off in the late second and early first millennia B.C. by the gradual expansion of irrigated farming led, in the final analysis, to a turning point in the social and political affairs of the local peoples, resulting in the establishment of military democracies controlled by aristocracies or tribal chiefs (chiefdoms). The capitals would appear to have been Izatkuli and Madau-depe in northern Parthia, Yaz-depe in Margiana, Altyn-depe I and Altyn-Dilyar in Bactria and Dalverzin-tepe in the Ferghana. With their powerful citadels standing on high platforms, these early townships, at first exclusively agrarian in vocation, gradually became craft centres. The administrative and political authority they exercised appears to have been that of a military democracy, and the area they governed was no greater than an oasis, thus they were not capable of public works such as the irrigation schemes of later Antiquity. The construction and upkeep of large canals called for a colossal outlay of labour, several times exceeding that involved in the smaller-scale irrigation systems of the times.[24] Discussing the problems of pre-Achaemenian Khorezm, S. P. Tolstov considered that this ancient realm was a tribal confederation of chiefdoms that gradually evolved into a state.[25] M. M. D'yakonov, matching archaeological findings with literary tradition, accepts that there was a centralized state in ancient Bactria and ascribes it to the second quarter of the first millennium B.C.[26] The recent expansion of archaeological investigations has furnished additional proofs of D'yakonov's thesis of the existence of an early organized state in Soviet Central Asia.

As a result of his studies of several archaeological sites in the Murghab oasis, V. M. Masson[27] noted the presence of two important factors in the life of the early states established in Margiana – the construction of large irrigation systems and the development of citadels. He also concluded that there was in Bactria a major political unit that extended its influences to Margiana and, possibly, to Aria and Sogdiana. The existence of a pre-Achaemenian Bactrian empire has been archaeologically proved through studies of the northern Afghanistan settlements of Altyn-Dilyar-depe, with its lofty citadel ringed with ramparts and bastions, Altyn-depe I with its keep, and Altyn-depe X with its summer and winter palaces.[28] With their tall citadels raised on platforms and their defensive walls, such heavily fortified settlements as Altyn-Dilyar in the Farukhabad oasis or Altyn-depe in that of Dashly, contrast sharply with the hand-made decorated

24. Gulyamov and Mukhamedzhanov, 1975.
25. Tolstov, 1948, p. 135.
26. D'yakonov, 1954.
27. Masson, 1959, p. 135.
28. Sarianidi, 1977.

pottery. This means that the culture originated at the latest in the mid-eighth century B.C. Consequently, in the case of Bactria and possibly of Margiana, it would not be correct to ascribe Achaemenian-type pottery to the period from the sixth to fourth centuries B.C. Thus the pottery complex erroneously described as Achaemenian must now be called ancient Bactrian, following M. M. D'yakonov's suggestions,[29] on the basis of the Kobadian I archaeological assemblage. Ancient Bactria-type sites yielding sixth-to-fourth-century-B.C. pottery are now known in the Karshi oasis, in the Yerkurgan IA strata, and in ancient Samarkand in the settlements of Lalazar and Kurgan-shah, which share the early urban material culture of pre-Achaemenian Soviet Central Asia.

At the turn of the second and first millennia B.C., the populations of Soviet Central Asia held a number of religious concepts and beliefs, the commonest in the Early Iron Age being the cult of fire, which incorporated the symbol of divine justice. In archaeological terms, that cult manifested itself in the shape of temple buildings that contained the remains of small altars.

This was the period when the beliefs reflected in the writings of the Avesta were becoming widespread in the settled oases. The image of the goddess Aredvi Sura Anahita, which can be traced back directly to the fertility deities of the early agricultural period, is represented here. The powerful god Mithra, who is usually depicted as a magnificent armed warrior driving a chariot, enjoyed great popularity. This image was completely in keeping with a period of armed conflicts that left clear traces in the archaeological material in the form of formidable fortifications and armaments. However, other aspects or beliefs are poorly represented in the archaeological evidence. Furthermore, there is an almost complete absence of clay figurines depicting people and animals that could be connected with certain requirements of orthodox Zoroastrianism.

Conclusion

This first third of the first millennium B.C. – the Early Iron Age – was associated in southern Soviet Central Asia with considerable economic progress. New oases based on irrigated cultivation appeared in a number of areas, including Khorezm and the Caspian Sea region. At the centres of these oases on massive platforms citadels were built which were, judging by all the evidence, rulers' residences. But specific paths of cultural and historical development were quite complex. In Khorezm, in the lower reaches of the Amu Darya, a settled culture was formed on the basis of Bronze Age traditions in the steppes. The origins of the Chust culture were also multiple. Cultural transformation in the main oases of Parthia, Margiana and Bactria occurred within a clear-cut continuation of local traditions in an area of economics and, to a certain extent, culture. The construction of

29. D'yakonov, 1954.

monumental mausoleums for the local aristocracy in the southern Aral Sea region at Tagisken is particularly instructive as regards cultural links; the principal construction techniques and standards here are clearly southern in origin. While the settled oases of the south display an overall cultural unity, there are glimpses of original local features that anticipate the cultural features of such ancient people as the Parthians, the Khorezmians and the Bactrians.

Pastoral and Nomadic Tribes at the Beginning of the First Millennium B.C.

A. Askarov, V. Volkov and N. Ser-Odjav

As early as the Bronze Age, pastoral tribes in the northern regions of Central Asia established original cultures reflecting their own way of life and new areas of activity. This development gradually transformed the economy and culture in the direction of greater specialization. Nomads in the full sense of the term made their appearance, the renowned nomads of Asia who played such a considerable role in world history. While they differed in their economic habits and life-styles, adoption of a semi-nomadic or nomadic way of life caused them to acquire, somewhere around the late eighth or seventh century B.C., many common cultural traits, regardless of the region in which they lived, and this has created the impression that all nomads shared a similar culture. The change to new technology was the key to the development of progressive economic and cultural forms and rejection of earlier forms. It is in this transformation that the Early Iron Age is rooted, and with that is closely related the rise of chiefdoms in the territory of present Soviet Central Asia. This is well-illustrated in the contributions of the Karasuk tribe of the new historical epoch.

Many monuments in the northern regions of Central Asia are chronologically close to the Karasuk tombs and are viewed by certain authors, such as M. P. Gryaznov, as coming within the orbit of the Karasuk culture. The late phase of this south Siberian culture may also be ascribed to the initial phase of the Early Iron Age. Much time has passed since then, and a large number of Karasuk-period sites have been studied both in southern Siberia and over a wide area of Kazakhstan[1] and Mongolia.[2] It has thus proved possible to divide the sites into two periods, the Karasuk proper and that of Kamennîy Log. The first dates from the thirteenth to eleventh centuries B.C. and belongs to the Bronze Age, while the second, Kamennîy Log, dates from the tenth to eighth centuries B.C. We have ascribed it to the initial phase of the Early Iron Age.

1. Gryaznov, 1956.
2. Volkov, 1967.

The commonest monuments of the Karasuk period are graveyards. The graves contained stone coffins, trapezoid in shape, made of thin slabs. The skeletons in them were either flexed or lay full-length on their backs: the head was normally in the broad part of the coffin, which was closed with slabs and covered with earth. Around the graves square or occasionally round enclosures were built of flagstones or rubble; they were often built up against each other, and double or triple enclosures may be found. Where, as in the Ob region, there was no stone, other materials were used. Most of the graves were occupied singly, but some contained a couple or a woman and children. The funeral inventory was quite varied: one or two bowls of food were usually placed at the head and meat at the feet. The bulk of the graves were poor in objects and many were empty, with only a sherd of pottery left among the disturbed bones of the dead; but some contained a considerable range of artefacts – beads and clay vessels or bronze tools and weapons.

Karasuk vessels are spherical with a rounded or sometimes flat base. All are hand-made; some have a fine slip and others burnished walls. They are decorated predominantly with zigzags, rhomboids or equilateral triangles and combinations thereof; one frequent pattern consists of chevrons and meanders. Some bear several tiers of geometric decoration encrusted with a white paste, often on a black, glassy ground. M. P. Gryaznov feels that they betray contacts with the steppe Bronze Age of the north Caucasus and of Soviet Central Asia, and concludes that the Bronze Age and Early Iron Age pastoral tribes had similar economies and life-styles and that inter-tribal contacts were extensive.

The commonest tool of the Karasuk period was the bronze dagger, hooked, convex, concave or straight.[3] Cast in stone or clay moulds, the knives had massive handles with pommels shaped in a ring – often with three knobs – a mushroom, an animal head or an entire animal figure.

The chief occupation in this culture was stockbreeding, and during the Kamennîy Log stage the proportion of sheep and goats rose considerably. Excavations have revealed that this was when the first, still primitive, bridle with bone cheek-pieces for the bit appeared. The riding horse brought the possibility of rapid movement to individual groups.

From his studies of Karasuk-type sites over an extensive area of Siberia and Kazakhstan, M. P. Gryaznov was able to identify ten local variants of this culture,[4] noting in each case certain particular features in the economy and life-style, individual styles of bronze artefacts and differences in the shape and decoration of the vessels. He also drew attention, however, to the striking resemblances between their material cultures. Knives, daggers or ornaments completely identical with those of Karasuk are spread widely in the wide area extending from the Volga to An-Yang in China.[5] This stemmed from the greater mobility the riding

3. Kiselev, 1951.
4. Gryaznov, 1956.
5. Gryaznov, 1952.

horse conferred on the population and the consequent stimulus to more extensive cultural exchange. A clear indication of the period's inter-tribal contacts is
that many of the same bronze objects, which none the less have local features,
may be found in very different areas. These local peculiarities have been crucial
both in clarifying the chronology of the Karasuk culture and in the study of its
origins, which to this day give rise to some controversy.[6]

On careful study, the bronze knives characteristic of the Yin period in An-
yang are massive tools with a broad, straight-backed blade and a slightly curved
tip. At the junction of the blade and the handle there is a sharp shoulder, and they
have no tenon as do those of Karasuk. Some have distinctive ornamental details
completely unknown in Karasuk artefacts. There is a second group of knives in
An-yang identical with those of the Yenisey, and a third group that combines the
features of the other two. Crucially, the second group of knives – the Siberian
type – are found in the earliest Yin period tombs in An-yang, and what is more,
no precursors of them are to be found. It should likewise be noted that the first
group – that typical of Yin China – become rarer as we move north-west from
An-yang: even in Mongolia they are found only in the southern regions bordering on China, and beyond Lake Baikal, in Buriatia, they are unknown.

Culturally and ethnically, the roots of Karasuk lay in southern Siberia and
the steppes of Kazakhstan. During the Dandybay-Begazy period of the tenth to
eighth centuries B.C. the culture of the Kazakhstan steppe tribes covers a large
part of that vast area. The sedentary tribes of the previous period there, developing their pastoral and agricultural economy, gradually turned to transhumant
stockbreeding and the semi-nomadic way of life that went with it. They left with
their herds each spring for the summer pastures after sowing the small fields
around their settlements, returning in autumn to gather the harvest and to winter
there. They built their winter homes in the winter grazing areas and had summer
settlements in the summer pastures.

These tangible changes in the economy and way of life of the Karasuk people led to considerable changes in their life-style, to some redistribution of family
and tribal pastures and, possibly, to tribal regroupings and migrations to new
parts; and this gave rise, in a relatively brief time, to the formation of a new culture, which, however, was not homogeneous. Thus the fundamental features of
the Karasuk culture as a whole must have developed not in one small district, but
over a very large area in which there had previously been some kind of culture
that was itself highly advanced. The Andronovo culture was just such a medium
for the rise of the Karasuk culture over a wide area.

The genetic links between the Karasuk tribes and those of Andronovo may
be seen primarily in the shapes and decoration of the pottery. The bath-shaped
Karasuk vessels have close analogies in the Andronovo pottery. The lavish geometrical decoration of Karasuk ceramics is a development of the Andronovo

6. Kiselev, 1951, 1960.

style. Strikingly, the mirrors, palmate pendants, rings, arabesques and tubular pendants of Karasuk are virtually exact replicas of those of Andronovo. The burial structures of the Karasuk stage proper still use Andronovo building techniques, particularly the stone coffins and the round burial enclosures. It is germane that Karasuk-type pottery is not found east of the Yenisey and that there are no burial structures of the Karasuk-type there.

The early phase has been studied through the Aksu-Ayuly II burial complex, the structures of which were typically enclosed by a double well and a perimeter gallery, and contained a massive coffin covered with stone slabs. The inner compartments still had the stepped, pyramidal beam frames that once supported the roofs. In the Aksu-Ayuly II tumulus, a layer of charred beams and ashes suggests that, as in the Tagisken mausoleums to the east of the Aral Sea, the wooden roofs were ritually fired. The stone coffin in the large tumulus contained a skeleton lying full-length and pottery of a Late Andronovo type. There were very many domestic animal bones, and even sacrificed animals had special coffins.

To the mature phase of Dandybay-Begazy belong the necropolises of Begazy, Aibas-Darasy, Akkoitas, Dandybay, Ortau II, Sangru I and III, and the settlements of Ulutau, Shortandy-Bulak, Karkaraly I–III and Yar.[7] Both residential and religious buildings at these sites were architecturally and structurally advanced, and a new range of spherical pottery was found there. Particularly noteworthy are the tombs of Begazy which are built of enormous granite slabs weighing up to 3 tonnes.

The Begazy mausoleums were of mixed construction with an entrance corridor, a perimeter gallery and a stone support pier set in the ground to a depth of 1.2 m. They were square structures with sides facing the points of the compass, and contained one or two chambers. In one of the Begazy mausoleums there was an internal shelf 2 m high with a carefully smoothed surface on which were fragments of fine-walled vessels. Above were the massive outlines of the granite slabs with which the outer walls were faced. Together with the roofing of the inner chamber they formed a gallery running completely round the building. All the walls were supported by rows of rectangular pillars. The roof was made of slabs corresponding in size to the span of the interior, which was divided by rows of stone pillars into two 3 m areas because of the need to cover a 6 m span with 3 m slabs.

A peculiarity of the Begazy mausoleums is that they contained altars to hold ritual objects and for sacrifice. One of the altars took the shape of an earthern table cut out when the foundation pit was dug. Three stone pillars were set into it, and the surface of the table around them became drenched with fat and littered with organic remains. Another sign of sacrifice and feasting was a large

7. Margulan et al., 1977.

heap of mutton bones. On the table were large numbers of clay vessels, together with household objects, ornaments and weapons.

In its later phase, when the way of life became nomadic, the high culture of Dandybay-Begazy entered a new phase. With its original culture, the population of this period was a distinctive ethnic and cultural formation that sprang up in the steppes of Early Iron Age in Kazakhstan. These tribes developed in close contact with their kinsmen in the eastern Aral region, ancient Khorezm, south-western Siberia, the Altai and the Yenisey whose cultures were of the Karasuk type. Despite the great distances that separate these regions, the archaeological complexes are very similar, confirming that the ancient tribes maintained close cultural and economic ties. In this cultural interchange, the primitive metallurgy of Kazakhstan – copper, tin and gold – figured prominently as an important instrument of inter-tribal commerce.

From what is known of the semi-nomadic tribal cultures of the eastern Aral and central Kazakhstan, it may be concluded that the increase in property inequalities coincided with the emergence of a tribal élite. This was especially true of the chiefs, whose prominence is very clear from the monumental sepulchres of Dandybay and Begazy and the mausoleums of Tagisken. And this in turn denotes the start of the new age, the Early Iron Age, even though the sites of this period in the steppes of Kazakhstan and ancient Khorezm contain no iron artefacts for use in day-to-day life or production.

In connection with this aspect of the history of the eastern part of Central Asia, the turning point was the transition from the Late Bronze to the Early Iron Ages, or as it is sometimes called, the 'Age of the Early Nomads' (the Scythian Age). It is precisely in that period that the territory of Mongolia, along with most of the other regions of the Eurasian steppe belt, saw the final establishment of nomadic pastoralism along with all of its technological achievements. It was then also that the nomadic-pastoral way of life developed and that the striking and highly expressive art of the nomads grew up. Improvements in means of transport, first and foremost the extensive use of the saddle-horse, together with the mobility that their economy called for, fostered the establishment of contacts between various tribes and peoples whose homelands lay vast distances apart. The proliferation of such ties led in turn to the cultural integration of the pastoral tribes and sometimes to the formation of enormous historico-cultural communities, one of these being the Scytho-Siberian group. This was characterized by the so-called 'Scythian triad' comprising weapons, horse equipage (bridles, saddles and saddle-cloths) and art in the animal style (Fig. 1), whose closely related forms became widespread among nomadic cultures throughout the Eurasian steppes all the way from the Danube in the west to the upper reaches of the Amur in the east.

Needless to say, not everything about the Scytho-Siberian community can be explained by reference to cultural contact: it was a complex phenomenon, shaped and conditioned by many factors. An important role in the cultural inte-

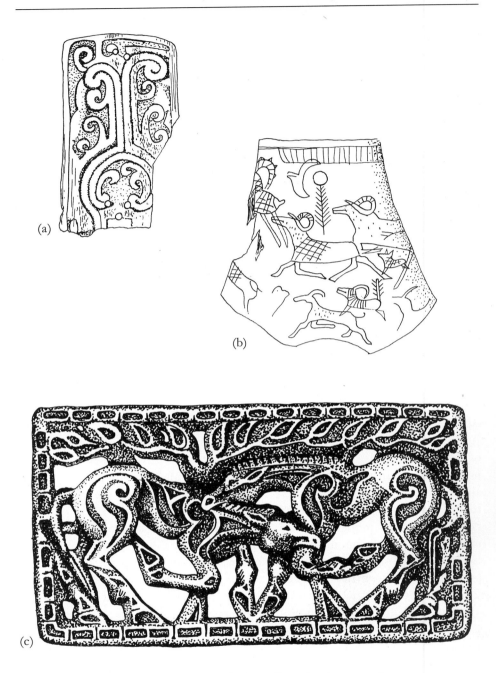

FIG. 1. Eastern and central Mongolia: a–b – bone; c – bronze.

gration of the Eurasian pastoralists was certainly played by the similarity of their habitats (the vast open spaces of the steppes and semi-desert ranges); the fact that they practised the same type of economic activity (nomadic cattle-raising); the nomadic existence as such; a roughly similar level of societal development marked by considerable internal differentiation based on property and social standing and by the emergence of a steppe aristocracy; a similar ideology determined in large measure by similar economic and social factors (as reflected in common religious cults and forms of artistic representation); and, last but not least, a certain ethnic unity consequent upon the fact that the tribes who migrated into and eventually mastered the steppe *oikoumene* were of Indo-Iranian stock, which is usually considered to include both the Scythians of the Black Sea and the Sakas of Central Asia.

Many areas in the eastern part of Central Asia have not yet received sufficient study by archaeologists. This is why it is still difficult to establish fully and reliably the place of the cultures of this region in relation to the many other Scythian-period cultures in Eurasia and to elucidate their role in shaping the Scytho-Siberian historico-cultural community. Nevertheless, archaeological investigations in Mongolia, Tuva, Gorno-Altai (High Altai) and Kazakhstan have shown that these regions lay not on the periphery of the Scythian world but rather the contrary, that is, that they constituted the centre of a traditional pastoral and nomadic culture which was the very well-spring of the forms that culture took throughout the entire Eurasian steppe.

In the first millennium B.C., bronze cultures in the vast steppes and semi-deserts of Mongolia and in many other parts of the Eurasian steppeland were supplanted by those of the Early Iron Age. The process of mastering the new metal was relatively slow in Mongolia, and it was only in the middle of the first millennium B.C. that iron began to be used on a mass scale for the production of implements and weapons.

The history of Mongolia and adjacent regions in the second and beginning of the first millennia B.C. is first and foremost the history of pastoral tribes, the story of the lives of nomadic herdsmen and their relations with the agricultural peoples to the east and west. Originating in an area bordering on one of the major centres of ancient civilization, that of Yin (Chang) China, the pastoral communities soon became a significant economic and political force and a powerful external stimulus to the consolidation of the Yin and Zhou kingdoms of ancient China. The stockbreeding herdsmen who inhabited Mongolia and other areas north of the Great Wall in the second millennium B.C. differed from the Chinese in their economy, their way of life and their original and distinctive art. Moreover, they constituted a distinct ethnic entity, to which they owed many of the specific features of their culture.

One of the principal cultures of the Early Iron Age in Mongolia was that of the slab grave. Like many other nomadic cultures, it is represented largely by burial complexes. The graves are marked by small walls made of vertically placed stone slabs arranged in a square. Hence the term 'slab grave'. Most of the slab graves date back to Scythian times (from the seventh to the third centuries B.C.), but some of them are evidently from much earlier.

The slab-grave culture flourished over most of Mongolia. The western boundary of this culture probably ran along the Great Lake basin which divides Mongolia in a north–south direction. Only isolated smaller groups of slab graves have been discovered further west, in the Gobi Altai foothills. On the other hand, there are no slab graves at all in the Gorno-Altai and Tuva, and none has been discovered in those parts of Mongolia that border on these regions. Here, during the first millennium B.C. we find stone kurgans and *kereksurs* apparently similar to those of the Sayan-Altai region. Slab graves are rare in southern Mongolia. However, slab enclosure walls, including 'figured' ones, have been noted by Maringer and Bergman in Inner Mongolia. Sites closely resembling slab graves have been reported in areas still farther south in northern Tibet. Slab walls are also known to occur outside the borders of Mongolia, to the north in Transbaikal, while slab graves of a later date have been discovered in the Lake Baikal area as well.[8] The slab graves of Mongolia are identical with those of Transbaikal, suggesting that in the first millennium B.C. the steppes of central and eastern Mongolia and Transbaikal constituted a single ethno-cultural domain.

The origin of this slab-grave culture is not definitely known. The ornamentation and shape of various bronze objects and especially the technology and stylistic methods used in the making of artistic bronzes found in the slab graves have led scholars to attribute at least some of them to the Karasuk period.[9] At the same time it appears that the slab-grave culture shares some features with the Karasuk culture of southern Siberia.[10]

In the first millennium B.C. and possibly much earlier, north-western Mongolia, more precisely the area lying next to the Sayan and Altai mountains, saw the emergence of another distinct ethno-cultural zone coinciding with a distribution of stone kurgans of the Pazyryk and Uyuk types. The sites in question have hardly been studied. The only kurgans to have been investigated lie in neighbouring Tuva. Notwithstanding differences in the arrangement of the structures of the graves (stone kurgans with various types of fencing), the funeral rites were on the whole the same. At centre of the mound is a stone coffin or cist-like structure made of large stone slabs with a skeleton, lying on its side with knees flexed and head pointing either westwards or north-westwards, buried along with burial furniture in a very shallow pit.

The skulls found in cist kurgans are those of Europoids with a slight Mongoloid admixture. They resemble most closely the skulls from the Karasuk and Okunevo burials of southern Siberia and analogous sites in Tuva, as well as those

---

8. Dikov, 1958.
9. Ibid.; Okladnikov and Zaporozhskaya, 1969, p. 89.
10. Volkov, 1967, p. 44.

of the Saka-Wu-sun graves of Kazakhstan and Kirghizia.[11] Scholars attribute the cist kurgans of Tuva to the earliest stage of the Uyuk culture dating back to the seventh and sixth centuries B.C.,[12] or take them to be a distinct Mongun-Taiga culture. Kurgan burials may belong to Karasuk times.[13]

The Ulangom site has multiple burials in timber-lined pits and single or double burials in stone sarcophagi, with profuse ceramic vessels, decorated with black paint and a large hoard of bronze and iron objects, including weapons as well as a wealth of ornaments of all kinds. The Ulangom burial ground can be attributed to the late stage of the Uyuk culture found in Tuva and in north-western Mongolia.

Both the cist kurgans and the Ulangom burials differ radically from the slab graves in respect of rites, grave goods (especially ceramics) and the anthropological type of their dead. Whereas the slab-grave culture belonged to typical Mongoloids of the northern branch of that race, the people of both Mongun-Taiga and Ulangom were of Europoid type, with only traces of Mongoloid features.

Early local nomad monuments had some common cultural traits (Fig. 2). They have similar Scythian prototype arrowheads; bridle gear like horse-bits and cheek-pieces; applied arts common with Black Sea Scythians and with Saka tribes of Central Asia, some recalling the Karasuk tradition; and finally deer-stones with carved representations. These deer-stones are widespread in eastern Mongolia and Transbaikal. In the west they form part of architectural complexes and in Tuva they stand besides kurgans. They are found as far as Chita, also in Kirghizia, Kazakhstan and the southern Urals. A variation of the deer-stones is reported from the Caucasus, and on some stele from ancient Olbia on the Black Sea and along the banks of the Dniepr river.

The deer-stones fall into two major groups: stele that represent only animals and those that do not yet display all other features usually appearing on such stones, such as necklaces, narrow belts and weapons. The former subgroup is in turn subdivided into two main types; stele with ornamentally stylized animal representations and those showing naturalistically depicted animals. Stele devoid of animal representations predominate in the west but also occur with some frequency in the eastern part of their distribution. This subgroup of stones might tentatively be referred to as 'Eurasian'. An appropriate term for stele featuring ornamentally stylized figures would then be 'Mongolo-Transbaikalian', since this type of deer-stone is prevalent in both Mongolia and Transbaikal.

Finally, the third variety of deer-stone (Fig. 3), the one presenting naturalistic animal figures, might well be called the 'Sayan-Altai' type. The animal pictures on the stele of the second and third types conform to the traditions of the Scytho-Siberian animal style. Despite certain differences in form and stylistic

11. Alekseev, 1974, pp. 370–90.
12. Kyzlasov, 1961.
13. Grach, 1965.

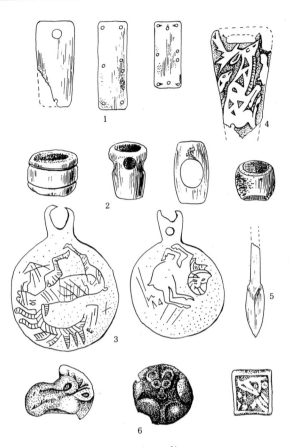

Fig. 2. North-western Mongolia:
1, 2, 4 and 5 – stone implements;
3 and 6 – bronze implements.

idiosyncrasies, an anthropomorphic image invariably underlies the drawings seen on deer-stones of all types. Deer-stones are in fact a variety of anthropomorphic sculpture in which the human figure is rendered in a highly conventionalized and schematic form. As a rule, it is only the details that are realistically depicted, for example, pendants, bead necklaces and battle or ceremonial belts hung with weapons. It is the pictures of weapons that show detail. The weapons include daggers with mushroom-shaped annulate pommels, sometimes in the form of animal heads (goats, horses and wild-cats), bows, battle-axes, as well as those indispensable attributes of the steppeland warrior, the knife and whetstone. Particularly notable is the Karasuk aspect of most of the objects depicted.

These deer-stones with figures of animals in the Scytho-Siberian animal style appeared in Mongolia, Tuva and the Altai region as early as the ninth or eighth century B.C., whereas stele without animal pictures may be still earlier.

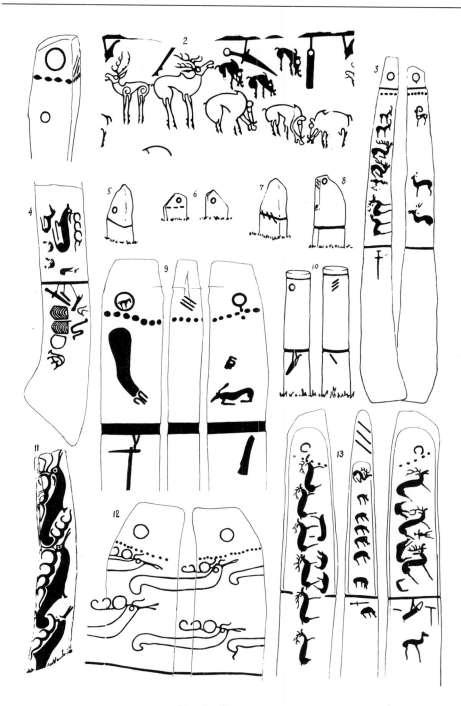

Fɪɢ. 3. Deer-stones.

Additional supporting evidence may be seen in a deer-stone fragment unearthed in the barrow of Arjan-kurgan in Tuva, and a stela found in a pre-Scythian complex of the Chernayagora stage in the Crimea.

As far as the east is concerned, deer-stones with zoomorphic drawings in the Scytho-Siberian animal style certainly belong to the early stages of the development of cultures of the Scythian type. It would perhaps be simpler to attribute the western deer-stones to the Scythians. But this would raise the problem of why the deer-stones of the Black Sea region should have given way in the sixth century B.C. to the genetically unrelated Scythian *babas*.

One of the best examples of early nomad monuments is the Arjan barrow, located in the mountainous area of Tuva (Fig. 4). It is the monumental tomb of an important leader, or even king, of the early nomadic tribes, in the form of a gigantic stone circle with a diameter of roughly 120 m. At the centre of the enclosure was a frame containing the main burial, which has been destroyed by looters. Around the periphery were sections constructed of massive logs, containing the bodies of several people and dozens of fully caparisoned sacrificial horses. The horses were of different colours and accordingly grouped in separate sections. The details and components of their harnesses also varied. M. P. Gryaznov, who excavated this magnificent tomb, believed that the sacrificial gifts of the various tribes subject to the buried ruler could be distinguished in this way. At Arjan, even after looting, there remained a number of artistic bronze artefacts illustrating the initial period of the so-called Scythian animal style. Judging by the entire assemblage, Arjan may be dated to the ninth or eighth century B.C. (Fig. 5).

The Arjan-kurgan is in any case considerably older than the generally recognized Scythian culture remains in the southern parts of eastern Europe; and no less ancient than the tomb of an ancient lord Ziviya (Zawiyeh) in Iran (the Sakkiz treasure) in which some investigators have perceived the sources of Scytho-Siberian art. All of this confronts the scholar with the need to reassess certain concepts. The evidence of the deer-stones undoubtedly strengthens the position of those who argue for the eastern, Central Asian origin of the animal style and of the entire Scythian culture.

Conclusion

The Bronze Age pastoralists in the steppes completed the transition to various forms of nomadism at the beginning of the first millennium B.C. in the northern areas of Central Asia. This was a fundamental, qualitative leap comparable in its economic, cultural and political consequences with the so-called urban revolution in the settled oases of the southern regions. The wide-scale introduction of metallurgy contributed to the development of specialized branches of manufacture, including weapon-making. The accumulation of wealth and military con-

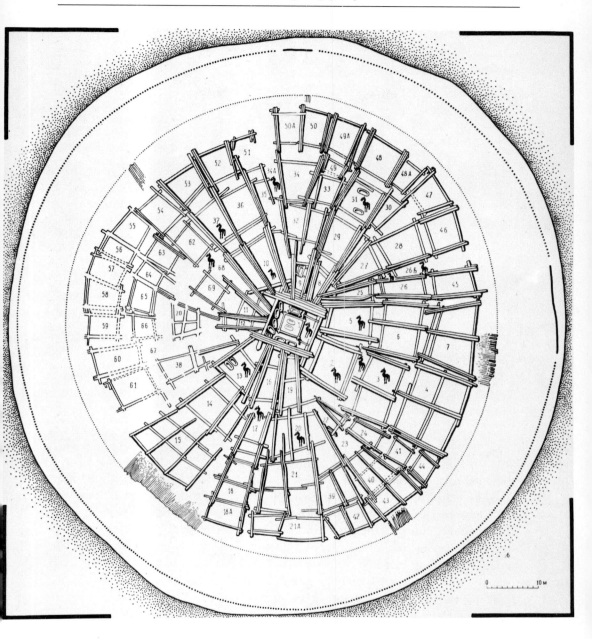

FIG. 4. Arjan: plan of a royal tomb.

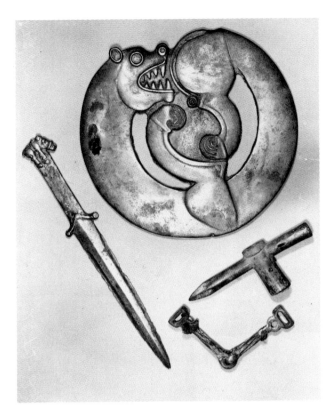

FIG. 5. Arjan: bronze artefacts called 'Scythian animal style'.

flicts led to the institutionalization of power, and tribal leaders developed into absolute petty rulers. On the ideological level, these processes were reflected in the appearance of monumental tombs for these members of the developing élite. Interregional contacts increased sharply, particularly with the acquisition of horse-riding. Spiritual and material values thus spread rapidly over great distances. A striking example of this is provided by the so-called deer-stones decorated with artistic reliefs, which are known over an enormous area from Mongolia to Bulgaria. The transition to nomadism was also responsible for a fundamental change in the mode of life: the armed rider became the symbol of the new period and we encounter his equipment in burials and in the arts. On this foundation, powerful groups of early nomadic tribes were formed around the middle of the first millennium B.C. A new force as powerful as the ancient States of the Orient entered the arena of world history.

CONCLUSION

The Editors

THE materials presented in this book throw light on the history of Central Asia, defined for the first time as one geographical, historical and cultural unit, covering its prehistoric and protohistoric periods. The beginning of human history in this part of the world, which is treated in this volume, has been reconstructed entirely through archaeological material – artefacts of daily use, tools and weapons, pots and pans, toys and playthings, dress and ornaments, furniture and fabrications of all sorts, objects of and for worship as well as many other items that constitute human culture or cultures. Through the evolutionary process, they integrated with each other by human genius and led man towards the creation of great civilizations such as that of the Indus and the Oxus. These mute objects bear witness to the path of human progress. There are many items lost along this path, leaving wide gaps in human history, and there are still insuperable difficulties in deciphering some of the writing, such as that of the Indus, the first of its kind to be found in these parts. Hence, it is the dead objects alone that, as studied by scientists of many countries, speak of the past lives of the Central Asian peoples – a part of humanity that still persists in the great traditions it has inherited. The *History* recaptures many forgotten peoples and tribes, whose names we may not know but regarding whom sustained research has reconstructed a solid base for the understanding of the origin of man and his culture in Central Asia.

Sufficient evidence has been presented above to show the importance of Central Asia as an independent centre of creative human cultures. It can no longer be regarded as a marginal area for it lies within the hub of great civilizations as much as it is itself the home of ancient civilization. More than a million years ago mankind, as in other regions of the Old World, started out on the road to progress. Siberia and the far northern regions were populated by people coming from Central Asia. Right from the Palaeolithic period, man has exploited the resources of the various geographical subareas of Central Asia from the high mountains up to the steppes and semi-deserts, and contributed to the evolution of

473

economic patterns and to building up an intellectual heritage. In Mousterian times, about 100,000 years ago, human imagination soared beyond the immediate needs of the present, as can be learnt from the practice of burying dead kinsmen in special graves decorated with the horns of the mountain goat, sure evidence of the animal cult.

The discovery of expressive cave paintings in Mongolia and the Urals has added to the stock of this human art so far known only in France and Spain, and has enabled us to understand new aesthetic canons about man's artistic advance in different parts of the world almost simultaneously.

From food gathering, so far noted in the Early Stone Age, to food production, as seen in the Neolithic period, man took a great step in his march towards civilization. This period, which has been significantly designated as the period of 'Neolithic revolution', is marked by two productive systems, one of agriculture and another of cattle-breeding, both leading to the most important framework for economic and cultural progress in society. The new archaeological discoveries in Central Asia mark out the areas as important centres of production. The various forms of transition are well illustrated by the cultures developed in Central Asia, some centring around agriculture and others around cattle-breeding. The early agricultural communities were responsible for laying the foundations of the first civilizations. The whole process of development is reflected in the archaeological material known from different parts of Central Asia and together they present a whole plethora of ancient oriental civilizations culminating in the well-known Harappan civilization, one of the greatest creations of the ancient world, in the rich Indus valley, south of Soviet Central Asia and east of Iran and Afghanistan. In the latter zone, local civilizations assumed different forms, which, from the later geographical name of this subregion, may be called the proto-Bactrian phase. To this subregion may be added the achievements of the peoples and tribes who inhabited the steppes and semi-deserts and whose cattle-breeding led to stable cultural and economic patterns. It is here in this last sub-area that horses were first saddled and used for transport and from the same sub-region are traceable the origins of the proto-Indo-Iranian languages as a specific linguistic group.

The cultural plurality seen in Central Asia does not speak of isolated developments of various cultures. These cultural manifestations, as known from archaeological discoveries, underlie human contacts, cultural inter-relationships and the exchange of ideas, materials of consumption and items of luxury and comfort. They all point to the complexity of human development: the long and tedious process of man's endeavour for better living conditions in which the whole of humanity has participated with a sharing of knowledge and skills – a historical process reflecting complex dialectics and not all smooth sailing, but with periods of crisis, interruption and economic and cultural changes. Being unaware of the social laws of development, the ancient societies faced periods of stagnation and disintegration, as is illustrated in the progressive decay and transformation of the Harappan civilization. Simultaneous change is seen in the proto-Bactrian subregion in the late third and early second millennia B.C.

All these transformations are not yet fully explained by the available archaeological data. Future discoveries may provide further evidence to build a still better historical framework, but the present material is suggestive and relevant to a rationale of development that the authors of the present book have tried to follow. The conclusion is certainly revealing. It strengthens the picture of diversity and complexity of modern historical reality, as reflected in the affairs and work of numerous peoples who had their own traditions, customs and ideas. We have in reality a picture of the co-existence and interaction of different local cultures and civilizations beginning in Palaeolithic times. The specific features of each culture are being studied by scholars from all over the world. The present book is an attempt to give a synthetic picture of all these cultural features so as to show the peculiarities common to the peoples and tribes of the region as a whole. Historical progress is the result of the interaction and mutual enrichment of cultures. There are cases of the slowing down of the process of development; there are also examples of the loss of values. In the cases of low growth, societies are seen to become easy prey to active and energetic neighbours. Archaeology provides us with excellent examples of cultural interaction of the peoples of Central Asia with the civilizations of Mesopotamia and Elam at one side and the Chinese civilization at the other. The intermediate region, as for example the Persian Gulf region, felt the impact of cultural interchange and became centres of cultural development, and in the steppes of Kazakhstan there developed a social and military élite with chariots as their symbol. Thus the persistent efforts of scientists have enabled us to reconstruct a continuous history of civilizations in Central Asia as an inseparable part of the great heritage of mankind.

Appendix:
A note on the meaning of the term 'Central Asia' as used in this book[1]

L. I. Miroshnikov

The use of the term 'Central Asia' in scientific literature has a long history of its own. First it was used simply as a synonym of the terms 'High Asia', *'la Haute Tartarie'* or *'l'Asie intérieure'* and some others, widely used in European literature on Asian history and geography or in travel stories – to denote the central regions of the continent with no references to the geographical boundaries of the area concerned. It was Alexander von Humboldt, the well-known German geographer and traveller in the first half of the nineteenth century who first attempted to define the boundaries of Central Asia. In his major work *Asie centrale*, published in Paris in 1843,[2] Humboldt proposed to include in Central Asia a vast area lying between 5° N. and 5° S. of latitude 44.5° N., which he considered to be the middle parallel of the entire Asian mainland. There were no definite indications in Humboldt's proposal concerning the western and eastern limits of Central Asia, but after a careful reading of his study it can be understood that the plateau of Ustyurt and Greater Khingan mountains might be regarded as boundaries.

Nevertheless, while using the term 'Central Asia' to denote conveniently the inner regions of the Asian mainland, not all scholars were in agreement with the geographical boundaries proposed for Central Asia by Humboldt, while others rejected the very method used by him in defining these boundaries. Nicolay Khanykoff,[3] Russian orientalist and explorer of Central Asia, was the first to state that the method used by Humboldt did not fulfil the requirements of geography and that in defining boundaries of Central Asia one should be guided by common physical features. Furthermore, he suggested that the absence of flow of water into the open sea might be considered as a good criterium for establishing the boundaries of Central Asia. His own view of Central Asia was therefore broader than that proposed by Humboldt. More specifically, Khanykoff included into the

---

1. The opinions expressed in this text are those of the author – Ed.
2. Humboldt, 1843.
3. Khanykoff, 1862.

477

area the entire region of eastern Iran and Afghanistan, lying beyond the southern limit of Humboldt's Central Asia.

In less than two decades the concept of Central Asia and its geographical limits were again thoroughly examined, this time by Ferdinand Richthofen, another German geographer. In his major work *China*,[4] he analysed all definitions of Central Asia and, considering them unsatisfactory, he proposed one of his own. Richthofen divided Asia into two types of natural region, 'central' and 'peripheral', differing from each other by their physical character and geological origin.[5] By Central Asia he meant all the regions of Inner Asia characterized by their hydrographical system (i.e. having no flow of water to the open sea). The boundaries proposed were to be the Altai mountains in the north, Tibet in the south, the Pamirs in the west and the Khingan mountain range in the east.

In Russian scientific literature of the last quarter of the nineteenth century the meaning of the term 'Central Asia' was most significantly discussed in the book *Turkestan* by Ivan Mushketov, a prominent geologist and traveller.[6] He acknowledged Richthofen's contribution and stated that this term 'became more precise than it had ever been before'. He also stated, however, that the German geographer had no sufficient grounds for narrowing the meaning of the term. Basing his arguments on the results of his own explorations in Central Asia and on studies by other scholars, he came to the conclusion that the eastern and western parts of Inner Asia have so much in common in their geological origin and natural features, that to relate one of them to the category of 'central' and the other to 'peripheral' (or even 'transitional'), as had been done by Richthofen, did not have much sense.

Mushketov believed that in dividing the Asian continent into natural regions one must 'strictly adhere to main principle based on the absence or presence of the flow of water into the open sea and also on the prevalence of aeolian or water agents in the area concerned'. Basing his arguments on these criteria, he suggested a division of the Asian continent into two principal parts: Peripheral (or Outlying) and Inner (or Middle) Asia, which sharply differed from each other in their location, physical features and origin. By 'Inner' Asia Mushketov meant the aggregate of 'all the land-locked regions of Asian mainland, having no flow of water into open sea and possessing the features of Khan-Khai'.

While differing from Richthofen on the geographical limits of Inner Asia, Mushketov was, however, in favour of retaining the name 'Central Asia' for the eastern part of the area (i.e. for Richthofen's Central Asia). For greater Central Asia he suggested two names: either 'Inner Asia' which was only used sporadically earlier, or 'Middle Asia',[7] the term which, before Richthofen's definition,

---

4. Richthofen, 1877.
5. Richthofen recognized also the existence of so-called 'transitional regions', that is, the areas either losing their 'central' features or 'going to be central'.
6. Mushketov, 1886.
7. *Srednyaya Azya* in Russian.

was widely used in nineteenth-century Russian literature as a synonym for Central Asia.

Mushketov's *Turkestan* summed up an almost century-long discussion on the definition of the term 'Central Asia'. But the controversy on this point did not cease and the term itself continued to be understood and used differently. Moreover, a noticeable tendency manifested itself in the last quarter of the nineteenth century and beginning of the twentieth century, in using this term mainly as a general title for the eastern part of Inner Asia within the boundaries proposed for Central Asia by Richthofen. This, perhaps, was explicable at that time, when this part of 'unknown' Central Asia became a principle area of geographical exploration and a convenient term for this area was therefore necessary.

On the other hand a tradition to use the name of Central Asia for denoting greater geographical area continued. It manifested itself mainly in geographical and ethnographical studies.

In this connection, we would like to recall that by Central Asia we mean, in the context of the present study, the whole interior of Asian continent which largely coincides with greater Central Asia within geographical limits proposed by Humboldt and Mushketov. Thus, we follow the tradition of Central Asian historical and cultural studies developed in the preceding century. The term 'Central Asia' as used in the title of the book may also be considered as synonym of 'Inner Asia', which was increasingly used in the studies on the history of peoples inhabiting inland Asia.

Here we approach an important question, namely the existence of a certain coincidence of geographical (or natural) limits of Central Asia with those proposed by historians, and this coincidence is not fortuitous. The fact that human history is inseparable from natural history is generally accepted in the historical sciences. Even if we are not inclined to attach undue importance to the geographical factor, we believe that analogous natural conditions cannot but favour the birth of analogous modes of production as well as the appearance of similar cultures. These observations might be fully applied to Central Asia.

The meaning of the term 'Central Asia' has been the subject of discussions at various scholarly meetings held in the framework of the UNESCO Central Asian Project. The first international meeting of experts on the study of civilizations of Central Asia, organized at UNESCO Headquarters, in April 1967, admitted that this term 'may be understood in different ways' and that 'any attempt to define it would remain controversial'. But it was stated, nevertheless, that the geographical area defined for the project by the General Conference of UNESCO 'corresponds to a cultural and historical reality'.

Further discussion on the geographical limits for UNESCO's activities on Central Asian Studies took place a decade later at Dushanbe, in connection with the preparation of the *History of Civilizations of Central Asia*. Considering that in various periods of its history, Central Asia had different geographical limits, the Working Group for the preparation of a framework for the *History* admitted that the definition of Central Asia adopted earlier by UNESCO for its pilot project would correctly reflect the historico-cultural and geographial scope of the publication to be prepared.

The Meeting of Experts on the preparation of a History of Civilization of Central Asia, held at UNESCO Headquarters in Paris in October 1978, fully agreed with the statement made at Dushanbe. It clearly stated that 'the delimitation of modern Central Asia should be that accepted by previous UNESCO sponsored conferences'. To avoid any misunderstanding concerning the cultural definition of Central Asia, the Final Report of this Meeting reads that the area in question covers 'territories lying at present within the boundaries of Afghanistan, the western part of China, northern India, north-eastern Iran, Mongolia, Pakistan and the Central Asian Republics of the USSR'.[8]

However,while delimiting various parts and regions of Central Asia it should be remembered that the history of the peoples and the civilizations they created is the main subject of the present study, and geographical boundaries proposed here should not be regarded as something rigid.

8. Meeting of Experts for the Preparation of a History of Civilizations of Central Asia (UNESCO Headquarters, Paris, 9–11 October 1978). Final Report (CC–78/CONF. 636/3), Paris, 12 Feburary 1979. For the Final Report of the Working Group of the symposium in Dushanbe, see Annex II of the same document. In connection with the UNESCO project, the meaning of the term 'Central Asia' has been discussed in the following works: Miroshnikov, 1971; Gafurov and Miroshnikov, 1976; Miroshnikov, 1987.

BIBLIOGRAPHY AND REFERENCES

ABBREVIATIONS OF PERIODICALS

AA = *Arts asiatiques* (Paris)

AAn = *American Anthropologist* (Washington)

Acta Ant. Hung. = *Acta antiqua Academiae scientiarium hungaricae*

Af = *Afghanistan*

AIn = *Ancient India* (New Delhi)

AP = *Asian Perspectives* (Honolulu)

APk = *Ancient Pakistan* (Peshawar)

Annali IUON = *Annali dell'Istituto Universitario Orientale di Napoli*, Naples

ART = *Arkheologicheskiye raboti v Tajikistane* (Dushanbe)

BGSCh = *Bulletin of the Geological Society of China*

CAn = *Current Anthropology* (Chicago)

CHM = *Cahiers d'histoire mondiale/Journal of World History*

EW = *East and West* (Rome)

Ex = *Expedition* (Philadelphia)

GJ = *The Geographical Journal*

IAR = *Indian Archaeology – A Review* (New Delhi)

IB = *Information Bulletin of the International Association for the Study of Cultures of Central Asia*

ICnp = *Indus Civilization: New Perspectives* (ed. A. H. Dani), Islamabad, 1981

IMKUz = *Istoriya material'noy kul'turî Uzbekistana*, Tashkent

IrAn = *Iranica Antiqua*

IsMeo.RM = *Istituto italiano per il Medio ed Estremo Oriente. Reports and Memoirs*, Rome

IzSO = *Izvestiya sibirskogo otdeleniya Akademii nauk SSSR*, Novosibirsk

JAOS = *Journal of the American Oriental Society*

JCA = *Journal of Central Asia* (Islamabad)

JESHO = *Journal of the Economic and Social History of the Orient*

JRAS = *Journal of the Royal Asiatic Society*

KSIA = *Kratkiye soobshcheniya Instituta Arkheologii Akademii nauk SSSR*

KSIE = *Kratkiye soobshcheniya Instituta Etnografii Akademii nauk SSSR*

KSIIMK = *Kratkiye soobshcheniya Instituta Istorii Material'noy Kul'turî*

MASI = *Memoirs of the Archaeological Survey of India*

481

MDAFA = *Mémoires de la délégation archéologique française en Afghanistan*, Paris, Librairie
    C. Klincksieck

ME = *Man and Environment* (Ahmedabad)

MIA = *Materialî i Issledovaniya po Arkheologii* (Moscow/Leningrad)

MSFOu = *Mémoires de la Société Finno-Ougrienne* (Helsinki)

ÖAW = *Österreichische Akademie der Wissenschaften*

PA = *Pakistan Archaeology* (Karachi)

PS = *Palaeontologia sinica*

PSB = *Palestinskiy sbornik*

Pt = *Puratattva* (New Delhi)

SA = *Sovetskaya arkheologiya*

SAA = *South Asian Archaeology*

  = *1977* (ed. M. Taddei), Naples, Istituto Universitario Orientale

  = *1979* (ed. H. Härtel), Berlin, Dietrich Reimer Verlag

  = *1981* (ed. B. Allchin), Cambridge, Cambridge University Press

SAm = *Scientific American*

SAI = *Arkheologiya SSSR. Svod Arkheologicheskikh Istochnikov*, Moscow/Leningrad

SAS = *South Asian Studies*

SE = *Sovetskaya Etnografiya*

SM = *Studi Mongolici*

SO = *Studia Orientalia*

Trudî KhAEE = *Trudî Khorezmskoy arkheologo-etnograficheskoy ekspeditsii*, Moscow

Trudî SamGU = *Trudî Samarkandskogo gosudarstvennogo universiteta*

Trudî YuTAKE = *Trudî yuzhno-turkmenistanskoy arkheologicheskoy ekspeditsii*, Leningrad

USA = *Uspekhi Sredneaziatskoy Arkheologii*

VDI = *Vestnik drevney istorii*

VPA = *Vertebrata PalAsiatique*

WKBL = *Wiener Beiträge zur Kulturgeschichte und Linguistik*

ZDMG = *Zeitschrift der deutschen morgenländischen Gesellschaft*

INTRODUCTION

ALEKSEEV, V. P. 1978. *Paleoantropologiya zemnogo shara i formirovaniye chelovecheskikh ras. Paleolit.*
    Moscow, Izdatel'stvo Nauka.

——. 1985. *Geograficheskiye ochagi formirovaniya chelovecheskikh ras.* Moscow, Izdatl'stov Nauka.

AMIET, P. 1986. *L'Age des échanges inter-Iraniens 3500–1700 av. J.-C.* Paris, Éditions de la
    Réunion des Musées Nationaux.

BARTHOLD, W. 1968. *Turkestan Down to the Mongol Invasion.* 3rd ed. London, Luzac & Co.

——. 1971. Istoriko-geograficheskiy obzor Irana. *Sochineniya* (Moscow), Vol. VII.

DANI, A. H. 1983*a*. *Chilas, The City of Nanga Parvat (Dyamar).* Islamabad.

——. 1983*b*. *Human Records on the Karakorum Highway.* Islamabad.

DE TERRA, H.; Patterson, T. T. 1939. *Studies on the Ice Age in India and Associated Human Cul-*
    tures. Washington, D.C., Carnegie Institution of Washington.

DUTTA, P. 1972. The Bronze Age Harappans: A Reexamination of Skulls in the Context of
    the Population Concept. *American Journal of Physical Anthropology*, Vol. 36, pp. 391–6.

GAFUROV, B. G.; MIROSHNIKOV, L. I. 1976. *Izucheniye tsivilizatsii Tsentral'noy Azii. Opît mezh-dunarodnogo sotrudnichestva po proektu UNESCO.* Moscow, Nauka.

GARDINER, K. H. J. 1982. Yarkand in the First Century A.D. In: S. N. Mukherjee (ed.), *India: History and Thought. Essays in Honour of A. L. Basham,* pp. 42–70. Calcutta, Sub-arnarekha.

HUMBOLDT, A. DE. 1843. *Asie centrale. Recherches sur les chaînes de montagnes et la climatologie com-parée,* Vols. I–III. Paris.

JARRIGE, J.-F.; MEADOW, R. H. 1980. The Antecedents of Civilization in the Indus Valley. *SAm,* Vol. 243, No. 2, pp. 122–33.

JETTMAR, K. 1979. Bolor – A Contribution to the Political and Ethnic Geography of North Pakistan. *JCA,* Vol. 2, pp. 39–70.

KHANYKOFF, N. DE. 1862. *Mémoire sur la partie méridionale de l'Asie centrale.* Paris.

KLIMBURG-SALTER, D. E. 1982. *The Silk Route and the Diamond Path: Esoteric Buddhist Art on the Trans-Himalayan Trade Routes.* Los Angeles, Frederick S. Wright Art Gallery.

LE STRANGE, G. 1930. *The Land of the Eastern Caliphate: Mesopotamia, Persia, and Central Asia, From the Moslem Conquest to the Time of Timur.* Cambridge, Cambridge University Press.

MAJUMDAR, R. C. (ed.). 1951. *The Vedic Age.* London, Allen & Unwin.

MASSON, V. M. 1981. Seals of a Proto-Indian Type from Altyn-depe. In: P. L. Kohl (ed.), *The Bronze Age Civilization of Central Asia: Recent Discoveries,* pp. 149–62. Armonk, N.Y., M. E. Sharp.

——. 1983. A New Type Culture Formation Leading to Food Production and Social Pro-gress. *JCA,* Vol. 6, pp. 65–72.

MILLER, K. J. 1982. *Continents in Collision.* London, G. Philip.

MINORSKY, V. 1970. *Hudud al-'Alam, The Regions of the World. A Persian Geography 372 A.H. – 982 A.D.* London, Luzac & Co.

MIROSHNIKOV, L. 1971. Les civilisations d'Asie centrale et leur étude. *CHM.* Vol. 13, No. 2. Neuchâtel.

——. 1987. Tsentral'naya Aziya: k voprosu o geograficheskikh granitsakh istoriko-kul'tur-nogo regiona. *IB* (special issue).

MOVIUS, H. S. 1944. Early Man and Pleistocene Stratigraphy in Southern and Eastern Asia. *Papers of the Peabody Museum of American Archaeology,* Vol. 19, No. 3.

MUSHKETOV, I. V. 1886. *Turkestan. Geologicheskoye i orograficheskoye opisanie po dannîm, sobrannîm vo vryemya puteshestviy s 1884 do 1880 goda,* Vol. I. St Petersburg.

NADVI, S. 1930. *Arab va Hind ke ta'lugat.* Azamdagh.

OBRUCHEV, V. A. 1951. *Izbrannîe rabotî po geografii Azii,* Vols. I–III. Moscow.

PARPOLA, A.; KOSKENNIEMI, S.; PARPOLA, S.; AALTO, P. 1969. *Decipherment of the Proto-Dravidian Inscriptions of the Indus Civilization.* Copenhagen, Scandinavian Institute of Asian Studies.

RICHARDS, F. J. 1933. Geographical Factors in Indian Archaeology. *Indian Antiquity,* Vol. 62, pp. 235–43.

RICHTHOFEN, F. VON. 1877. *China. Ergebnisse eigener Reisen und darauf gegründeter Studien.* Vol. I. Berlin.

SHAHRANI, M. N. M. 1979. *The Kirghiz and Wakhi of Afghanistan,* Seattle/London, Uni-versity of Washington Press.

SHARMA, G. R. 1983. Beginnings of Agriculture: New Light on Transformation from Hunting and Food Gathering to the Domestication of Plants and Animals: India, A Primary and Nuclear Center. *JCA,* Vol. 6, pp. 51–64.

483

SINITSIN, V. M. 1959. *Tsentral'naya Aziya.* Moscow.

SPATE, O. K. H. 1954. *India and Pakistan, A General and Regional Geography.* London, Methuen.

STEIN, M. A. 1977. *Ancient Geography of Kashmir.* Calcutta.

SUBBARAO, B. 1958. *Personality of India; Pre- and Proto-historic Foundation of India and Pakistan,* 2nd ed. Baroda, Faculty of Arts, Maharaja Sayajirao, University of Baroda.

UNESCO INTERNATIONAL SCIENTIFIC COMMITTEE FOR THE DRAFTING OF A GENERAL HISTORY OF AFRICA. 1981–85. *General History of Africa.* Paris/London/Berkeley, Calif., UNESCO/Heinemann Educational Books/University of California Press.

WHEELER, R. E. M. 1968. *The Indus Civilization,* 3rd ed. Cambridge, Cambridge University Press.

CHAPTER I

ARMAND, D. L., et al. 1956. *Zarubezhnaya Aziya, Fizicheskaya geografiya.* Moscow.

BOBRINSKY, N. A. 1951. *Geografiya zhivotníkh.* Moscow.

CHOU SHAO-TAN. 1953. *Geografiya novogo Kitaya.* Moscow.

DALES, G. F. 1965. Civilization and Floods in the Indus Valley. *Ex,* Vol. 7, pp. 10–19.

DANI, A. H. 1975. Origins of Bronze Age Cultures in the Indus Basin – A Geographic Perspective. *Ex,* Vol. 17, pp. 12–18.

DE TERRA, H.; PATTERSON, T. T. 1939. *Studies on the Ice Age in India and Associated Human Cultures.* Washington, D.C., Carnegie Institution of Washington. (Carnegie Institute Publications, No. 493.)

DOLUKHANOV, P. M. 1979. *Ecology and Economy in Neolithic Eastern Europe.* London, Duckworth.

GEPTNER, V. G. 1936. *Obshchaya zoogeografiya.* Moscow/Leningrad.

GOSH, R. N. 1977. Protogeological Studies on the Ancient Water Regimes of Rajasthan Rivers. In: D. P. Agrawal and B. M. Pande (eds.), *Ecology and Archaeology of Western India,* pp. 157–66. Delhi, Concept Publishing Co.

KOHL, P. 1975. Carved Chlorite Vessels: A Trade in Finished Commodities in the Mid-third Millennium. *Ex,* Vol. 18, pp. 18–31.

KOSTENKO, N. I. 1963. *Osnoví stratigrafii antropogena Kazakhstana.* Alma-Ata.

MASSON, V. M. 1977. Pustînya i obshchestvo: dinamika vzaimodeistviya v istoricheskom aspekte. *Problemí osvoeniya pustîni,* Vol. 6, pp. 3–10.

MURZAEV, E. M. 1952. *Mongol'skaya Narodnaya Respublika. Fiziko-geograficheskoye opisaniye.* Moscow.

OBRUCHEV, V. A. 1951. Izmeneniye vzglyadov na rel'ef i stroyeniye Tsentral'noy Azii ot A. Gumbol'dta do Ed. Zyussa. *Izbranníe rabotî po geografii Azii,* Vol. 1, pp. 331–54.

RAIKES, R. L.; DYSON, R. H. 1961. The Prehistoric Climate of Baluchistan and the Indus Valley. *AAn,* Vol. 63, pp. 265–81.

RYABCHIKOV, A. M. (ed.). 1976. *Prirodníye resursí zarubezhníkh territoriy Evropî i Azii.* Moscow.

SANKALIA, H. D. 1974. *Prehistory and Protohistory of India and Pakistan.* 2nd ed. Poona, Deccan College, Postgraduate and Research Institute.

SHARMA, G. R.; Clark, J. D. 1982. Palaeo-environments and Prehistory in the Middle Son Valley, Northern Madhya Pradesh. *ME,* Vol. 6, pp. 56–62.

SINGH, G. 1971. The Indus Valley Culture. *Archaeology and Physical Anthropology in Oceania*, Vol. 6, pp. 177–89.

SPATE, O. H. K. 1954. *India and Pakistan; A General and Regional Geography*. London, Methuen.

SUBBARAO, B. 1958. *The Personality of India, Pre- and Proto-historic Foundation of India and Pakistan*. 2nd ed. Baroda, Faculty of Arts, Maharaja Sayajirao University of Baroda.

VAVILOV, N. I. 1967a. Rol' Tsentral'noy Azii v proiskhozhdenii kul'turnîkh rasteniy. In: N. I. Vavilov (ed.), *Izbranniye proizvedniya v dvukh tomakh*, Vol. 1, pp. 203–24. Leningrad.

——. 1967b. Tsentrî proiskhozhdeniya kult'turnîkh rasteniy. In: N. I. Vavilov (ed.), *Izbranniye proizvedniya v dvukh tomakh*, Vol. 1, pp. 88–202. Leningrad.

VINOGRADOV, A. V. 1981. *Drevniye okhotniki i rîbolovî sredneaziatskogo mezhdurechiya*. Moscow.

VAN ZEIST, W. 1967. Late Quaternary Vegetarian History of Western Iran. *Review of Palaeobotany and Palynology*, Vol. 2, pp. 301–11.

CHAPTER 2

ALLCHIN, B. 1986. Earliest Traces of Man in the Potwar Plateau, Pakistan: A Report of the British Archaeological Mission to Pakistan. *SAS*, Vol. 2, pp. 69–83.

ARARI, A.; THIBAULT, C. n.d. Nouvelles précisions à propos de l'outillage palaéolithique ancien sur galets du Khorassan (Iran). (Unpublished MS.)

DAVIS, R. S. 1978. The Palaeolithic. In: F. R. Allchin and N. Hammond (eds.), *The Archaeology of Afghanistan from the Earliest Times to the Timurid Period*, pp. 37–70. London, Academic Press.

DENNELL, R. W. 1984. The Importance of the Potwar Plateau, Pakistan, to Studies of Early Man. *SAA 1981*, pp. 10–19.

DE TERRA, H.; PATERSON, T. T. 1939. *Studies on the Ice Age in India and Associated Human Cultures*. Washington, D.C., Carnegie Institution of Washington.

DORJ, D.; TSEVEENDORZH. 1978. *The Palaeolithic Period of Mongolia*. Ulan Bator. (In Mongolian.)

GHOSH, A. 1976. Pleistocene Man and his Cultures in Central, East, South and Southeast Asia, An Appraisal. In: A. K. Gosh (ed.), *Le Paléolithique inférieur et moyen en Inde, en Asie Centrale, en Chine et dans le Sud-est Asiatique*, pp. 200–36. Ninth UISPP Congress. Nice, UNESCO. (Col. VII.)

HUME, G. W. 1976. *The Ladizian: An Industry of the Asian Chopper-Chopping Tool Complex in Iranian Baluchistan*. Philadelphia, Dorrance & Co.

JAYASWAL, V. 1978. *Palaeohistory of India, A Study of the Prepared Core Technique*. Delhi, Agam Kala Prakashan.

JIA LAN-PO. 1950. *Primitive Man of China*. Long-Men United Book Co.

LI YAN-XIAN; JI HONGO-XIANG. 1981. Discussion of the Natural Environment and its Changes at the Time of Peking Man. *VPA*, Vol. 19.

MOVIUS, H. L. 1944. Early Man and Pleistocene Stratigraphy in Southern and Eastern Asia. *Papers of the Peabody Museum of American Archaeology and Ethnology*, Vol. 19, No. 3, pp. 1–125.

OKLADNIKOV, A. P. 1972a. K istorii pervonachal'nogo osvoyeniya chelovekom Tsentral'noy Azii. *Tsentral'naya Aziya i Tibet. Istoriya i kul'tura Vostoka Azii*, Vol. 1, pp. 17–21. Novosibirsk.

OLADNIKOV, A. P. 1972*b*. Ulalinka – drevnepaleoliticheskiy pamyatnik Sibiri. In: Z. A. Abramova and N. D. Praslov (eds.), *Paleolit i neolit SSR*, Vol. 7, pp. 7–19. Leningrad, Izdatel'stvo Nauka.

——. 1973. Vnutrennyaya Aziya v kamennom veke, nizhnem i srednem paleolite. *SM*, Vol. 1, pp. 149–53.

——. 1978. The Palaeolithic of Mongolia. In: Fumiko Ikawa-Smith (ed.), *Early Palaeolithic in South and East Asia*. The Hague/Paris, Mouton.

PATERSON, T. T.; DRUMMOND, H. J. H. 1962. *Soan – The Palaeolithic of Pakistan*. Karachi, Government of Pakistan, Department of Archaeology.

PEI WEN-CHUNG. 1962. The Living Environment of China's Primitive Man. *VPA*, Vol. 2.

PEI WEN-CHUNG; ZHANG SEN-SHUI. 1979. Research into the Stone Tools of China's Primitive Man. *Some Essays from the Commemoratory Meeting of the Fiftieth Anniversary of the Discovery of the First Skull of Peking Man*. Peking, Chinese Academy of Sciences, Institute of Vertebrate Palaeontology and Palaeoanthropology.

RAGOZIN, L. A. 1982. K drevneyshemu poseleniyu Sibiri – 1,5 milliona let! *Priroda*, Vol. 1, pp. 119–21.

RANOV, V. A. 1980. Drevnepaleoliticheskiye nakhodki v lessakh yuzhnogo Tajikistana. In: K. V. Nikiforova and A. E. Dodonov (eds.), *Granitsa neogena i chetvertichnoyi sistemî*, pp. 202–07. Moscow.

RANOV, V. A.; DAVIS, R. S. 1979. Toward a New Outline of the Soviet Central Asian Palaeolithic. *CAn*, Vol. 20, pp. 252–6.

RENDELL, H. 1984. The Pleistocene sequence in the Soan Valley, Northern Pakistan. *SAA 1981*, pp. 3–9.

RENDELL, H.; DENNELL, R. W. 1985. Dated Lower Palaeolithic Artefacts from Northern Pakistan. *CAn*, Vol. 26, No. 3, p. 393.

SADEK-KOOROS, H. 1976. Early Hominid Traces in East Azerbaijan. In: *Proceedings of the Fourth Annual Symposium on Archaeological Research in Iran*, reprint ed., pp. 1–5. Tehran.

SANKALIA, H. D. 1974. *Prehistory and Protohistory of India and Pakistan*. 2nd ed. Poona, Deccan College, Postgraduate and Research Institute.

STILES, D. 1978. Palaeolithic Artefacts in Siwalik and Post Siwalik Deposits of Northern Pakistan. *Kroeber Anthropological Society Papers*, Vol. 53–4, pp. 129–48.

TEILHARD DE CHARDIN, P.; WENG CHUNG. 1932. The Lithic Industry of Sinanthropus Deposits. *Bulletin of the Chinese Geological Society*, Vol. 11.

WEIDENREICH, F. 1941. The Extremity Bones of *Sinanthropus Pekinensis*. *PS*, New Series D, No. 5, p. 116.

——. 1943. The Skull of *Sinanthropus Pekinensis:* A Comparative Study on a Primitive Hominid Skull. *PS*, New Series D, No. 10, p. 127.

WOO JU-KANG; JIA LAN-PO. 1954. The Fossils of China's Primitive Man Newly Discovered at Choukoutien. *Acta Paleontologica Sinica*, Vol. 2.

CHAPTER 3

AGRAWAL, D. P. 1982. *The Archaeology of India*. London, Curzon. (Scandinavian Institute of Asian Studies, Monograph Series, 46.)

ALLCHIN, B. 1959. The Indian Middle Stone Age: Some New Sites in Central and Southern India. *Bulletin of the Institute of Archaeology*, Vol. 2, pp. 1–36.

——. 1973. Blade and Burin Industries of West Pakistan and Western India. In: N. Hammond (ed.), *SAA*, pp. 39–50. London, Duckworth.

——. 1976. The Discovery of Palaeolithic Sites in the Plains of Sind and their Geographical Implications. *GJ*, Vol. 142, Part 3, pp. 471–89.

——. 1981. The Palaeolithic of the Potwar Plateau, Punjab, Pakistan: A Fresh Approach. *Paléorient*, Vol. 7, No. 1, pp. 123–34.

ALLCHIN, B.; GOUDIE, A.; HEDGE, K. T. M. 1978. *The Prehistory and Palaeogeography of the Great Indian Desert*. London/New York, Academic Press.

ALLCHIN, F. R. 1953. A Flake Tool from the Oxus. *Proceedings of the Prehistoric Society*, Vol. 19, p. 226.

ANGEL, J. L. 1972. A Middle Palaeolithic Temporal Bone from Darra-i-Kur, Afghanistan. In: L. Dupree (ed.), *Prehistoric Research in Afghanistan (1959–1966)*, pp. 54–7. Philadelphia, American Philosophical Society.

COON, C. S. 1951. *Cave Explorations in Iran, 1949*. Monograph of the University of Pennsylvania Museum. Philadelphia, University Museum.

——. 1957. *Seven Caves: Archaeological Explorations in the Middle East*. London, Jonathan Cape.

DANI, A. H. 1964. Sanghao Cave Excavation: The First Season, 1963. *APk*, Vol. 1, pp. 1–50.

DAVIS, R. S. 1978. The Palaeolithic. In: F. R. Allchin and N. Hammond (eds.), *The Archaeology of Afghanistan from the Earliest Times to the Timurid Period*, pp. 37–68. London/New York, Academic Press.

DAVIS, R. S.; DUPREE, L. 1977. Prehistoric Survey in Central Afghanistan. *Journal of Field Archaeology*, Vol. 4, pp. 139–48.

DE TERRA, H.; PATERSON, T. T. 1939. *Studies on the Ice Age in India and Associated Human Cultures*. Washington, D.C., Carnegie Institution of Washington.

DUPREE, L.; DAVIS, R. S. 1972. The Lithic and Bone Specimens from Aq Kupruk and Darra-i-Kur. In: L. Dupree (ed.), *Prehistoric Research in Afghanistan (1959–1966)*, pp. 14–32. Philadelphia, American Philosophical Society.

GREMYATSKY, M. A. (ed.). 1979. *Teshik-Tash. Paleoliticheskiy chelovek. Sbornik statey*. Moscow, Trudî Nauchno-issledovatel'skogo Instituta Antropologii.

JOSHI, R. V. 1966. Acheulian Succession in Central India. *AP*, Vol. 8, No. 1, pp. 150–63.

KHAN, A. R. 1979. Palaeolithic Sites Discovered in Lower Sind and their Significance in the Prehistory of the Country. *Grassroots*, Vol. 3, No. 2, pp. 80–3.

McBURNEY, C. B. M. 1972. Report of an Archaeological Survey in Northern Afghanistan, July–August, 1971. *Af*, Vol. 25, No. 3, pp. 22–32.

MISRA, V. N. 1968. Middle Stone Age in Rajasthan. In: *La Préhistoire. Problèmes et tendances*, pp. 295–302. Paris.

RANOV, V. A.; DAVIS, R. S. 1979. Toward a New Outline of the Soviet Central Asian Palaeolithic. *CAn*, Vol. 20, No. 2, pp. 249–70.

RENDELL, H. 1984. The Pleistocene Sequence in the Soan Valley, Northern Pakistan. *SAA 1981*, pp. 3–9.

SANKALIA, H. D. 1964. Middle Stone Age Culture in India and Pakistan. *Science*, Vol. 146, No. 3642, pp. 365–75.

SHARMA, G. R.; MANDAL, D.; RAI, G. K. 1980. *History to Prehistory. Contribution of the Department to the Archaeology of the Ganges Valley and the Vindhyas*. Allahabad, Department of Ancient History, Culture and Archaeology.

SOLEKI, R. S. 1971. *Shanidar. The Humanity of Neanderthal Man*. London, Allen Lane.

UNESCO. 1964. *Preservation of the Monument of Moenjodaro, Pakistan.* Paris, UNESCO.

CHAPTER 4

ABRAMOVA, Z. A.; ERISYAN, B. G.; ERMOLOVA. 1976. Novîy must'erskiy pamyatnik Yuzhnoy Sibiri. *Arkheologicheskiye otkrîtiya 1975 goda.* pp. 211–12.

ALEKSEEV, V. P. 1981. *Paleantropologiya zemnogo shara.* Moscow.

ALLCHIN, B. 1986. Earliest Traces of Man in the Potwar Plateau, Pakistan: A Report of the British Archeological Mission to Pakistan. *SAS,* Vol. 2, pp. 69–83.

ANISYUTKIN, N. K.; ASTAKHOV, S. N. 1970. K voprosu o drevneyshikh pamyatnikakh Altaya. *Drevnyaya Sibir',* Vol. 3, pp. 27–33.

CULTURAL WORK TEAM OF INNER MONGOLIA AUTONOMOUS REGION. 1963. *A Selection of Objects Unearthed in Inner Mongolia.* Wenwu Publishing Co.

DANI, A. H. 1964. Sanghao Cave Excavation: The First Season, 1963. *APk,* Vol. 1, pp. 1–50.

DEREVYANKO, A. P. 1980. V poiskakh olenya Zolotîye roga. *Sovetskaya Rossiya,* (Moscow), pp. 219–29.

DEREVYANKO, A. P.; OKLADNIKOV, A. P. 1969. Drevniye kul'turî Vostochnîkh rayonov MNR. *SA,* No. 4, pp. 141–3.

DUPREE, L.; DAVIS, R. S. 1972. The Lithic and Bone Specimens from Aq Kupruk and Darra-i-Kur. In: L. Dupree (ed.), *Prehistoric Research in Afghanistan (1956–66),* pp. 14–32. Philadelphia, American Philosophical Society.

DZHURAKULOV, M. D.; KHOLYUSHKIN, Y. P.; KHOLYUSHKINA, V. A.; BATYROV, B. K. 1980. Samarkandskaya stoyanka i eë mesto v pozdnem paleolite Sredney Azii. In: *Paleolit Sredney i Vostochnoy Azii.* Novosibirsk.

GINZBURG, V. V.; GOKHMAN, I. I. 1974. Kostnîye ostatki cheloveka iz Samarkandskoy stoyanki. In: *Problemî êtnicheskoy antropologii i morfologii cheloveka.* Leningrad.

JIA LAN-PO. 1953. *Hetao Man.* Longman United Book Co.

JIA LAN-PO; GAI PEI; LI YANG-XIANG. 1964. New Evidence from the Palaeolithic Site of Shuidonggou. *VPA,* Vol. 8, No. 1.

KASYMOV, M. R. 1972. Mnogosloynaya paleoliticheskaya stoyanka Kul'bulak v Uzbekistane (Predvaritel'nîye itogi issledovaniya). *MIA,* Vol. 185, pp. 111–19.

KHOLYUSHKIN, Y. P. 1981. *Problemî korrelyatsii pozdnepaleoliticheskikh industriyi Sibiri i Sredney Azii.* Novosibirsk.

LAZYUKOV, G. I. (ed.). 1981. *Priroda i drevniy chelovek (osnovnîye êtapî razvitiya prirodî, paleoliticheskogo cheloveka i ego kul'turî na territorii SSSR v pleyistotsene.* Moscow.

LEV, D. N. 1964. Poseleniye drevnekamennogo veka v Samarkande. Issledovaniya 1958 1960gg. *Trudî SamGU,* (new series), Vol. 135, pp. 102–207.

MARSHACK, A. 1972. Aq Kupruk: Art and Symbols. In: L. Dupree (ed.), *Prehistoric Research in Afghanistan,* pp. 66–72. Philadelphia, American Philosophical Society.

NESMEYANOV, S. A. 1980. Geologicheskoye stroyeniye Samarkandskoy verkhne-paleoliticheskoy stoyanki. In: *Paleolit Sredney i Vostochnoy Azii.* Novosibirsk.

OKLADNIKOV, A. P. 1959. *Kamennîy vek Tajikistana. Itogi i problemî. Materialî II soveshchaniya arkheologov i êtnografov Sredney Azii.* Moscow/Leningrad.

——. 1962. Novoye v izuchenii drevneyshîkh kul'tur Mongolii. *SE,* Vol. 1, pp. 83–90.

——. 1964. Pervobîtnaya Mongolia. *Studia Archaeologica* (Ulan Bator), Vol. 3, No. 8–10, pp. 3–23.

——. 1972. *Tsentral'noaziatskiy ochag pervobítnogo iskusstva.* Novosibirsk.

——. 1974. Poseleniye kamennogo veka na gore Khere-Uul (Vostochnaya Mongoliya) i dokeramicheskiye kul'turî Yaponii. *Istoriko-filologicheskiye issledovaniya,* pp. 332–7. Moscow.

——. 1981. *Paleolit Tsentral'noy Azii. Moiltyn am (Mongoliya).* Novosibirsk.

OKLADNIKOV, A. P.; ISLAMOV, R. I. 1961. Palaeolitcheskiye nakhodki v Urochische Shuralitay. *IMKUz,* Vol. 2, pp. 119–29.

OKLADNIKOV, A. P.; LARICHEV, V. E. 1963. Arkheologicheskiye issledovaniya v Mongolii v 1961–62 gg. *IzSO* (seria obshchestvennîkh nauk), No. 1, Part 1, pp. 78–89. Novosibirsk.

OKLADNIKOV, A. P.; MURATOV, V. M.; OVODOV, N. D.; FRIDENBERG, E. O. 1973. Peshchera Strashnaya. Novîy pamyatnik paleolita Altaya. *Material po arkheologii Sibiri i Dal'nego Vostoka* (Novosibirsk), Part 2, pp. 3–54.

OKLADNIKOV, A. P.; TROITSKIY, S. L. 1967. K izucheniyu chetvertichnîkh otlozheniy paleolita Mongolii. *Byulleten' Komissii po izucheniyu chetvertichnogo perioda* (Moscow), Vol. 33, pp. 3–30.

PEI WEN-CHUNG. 1960. The Environment of Primitive Man in China. *VPA.*

PEI WEN-CHUNG; LI YOU-HENG. 1964. Preliminary Investigations of the Salawusu River System. *VPA,* Vol. 8.

QI GUO-QIN. 1975. Mammal Fossils of the Quaternary Epoch in the Valley of the Salawusu River in Inner Mongolia. *VPA,* Vol. 13.

RANOV, V. A. 1960. Raskopki paleoliticheskoy peshchernoy stoyanki v Afganistane. *Izvestiya otdeleniya obshchestvennîkh nauk AN TajSSR,* Part 1 (22), pp. 145–50.

——. 1965. O vozmozhnosti vîdeleniya lokal'nîkh kul'tur v paleolite Sredney Azii. *Izvestiya AN TajSSR,* Otdeleniye obshchestvennîkh nauk, Dushanbe. Vol. 3 (53), p. 10.

——. 1972. Srednyaya Aziya i Indiya v êpokhu paleolita. (Opît sravneniya arkheologicheskikh periodizatsii). *Stranî i narodî Vostoka.* Moscow.

——. 1973. Shugnou-mnogosloynaya paleoliticheskaya stoyanka v verkhov'yakh r. Jakhsu. 1970. In: *ART,* Vol. X, pp. 42–61.

RANOV, V. A.; NESMEYANOV, S. A. 1973. *Paleolit i stratigrafiya antropogena Sredney Azii.* Dushanbe.

RUDENKO, S. I. 1960. Ust' Kanskaya peshchernaya paleoliticheskaya stoyanka. *Paleolit i neolit SSSR* (Moscow/Leningrad); *MIA,* Vol. 4, No. 79, pp. 104–25.

SULEYMANOV, R. K. 1972. *Statisticheskoye izucheniye kul'turî grota Obi-Rakhmat.* Tashkent.

TASHKENBAEV, N. K. 1975. Ob issledovanii paleoliticheskoy stoyanki Kuturbulak. *IMKUz.*

TASHKENBAEV, N. K.; SULEIMANOV, R. K. 1980. *Kul'tura drevnekamennogo veka dolinî Zerafshana.* Tashkent.

WANG YU-PING. 1953. A Preliminary Report on Excavations in the Sjaro-osso-gol Valley in Ikechzhao Province. *Wenwu,* Vol. 4.

——. 1957. Short Report of Archaeological Survey at Salawusu River in Yi League. *Wenwucankaozilia,* Vol. 4.

——. 1962. The Paleolithic Site of Shuidonggou Village. *Kaogu,* Vol. 11.

WEIDENREICH, F. 1943. The Skull of *Sinanthropus Pekinensis*: A Comparative Study on a Primitive Hominid Skull. *PS,* New Series D, No. 10, p. 127.

WO RU-KANG. 1958. A Skull and Femur Fossil of Hetao Man. In: *VPA,* Vol. 8, No. 2.

ZHOU MING-ZHEN. 1955. The Natural Environment of the Life of Chinese Fossil Man As

It Can Be Seen from Vertebrate Fossils. *The Discovery and Study of Human Fossils in China.* Science Publishing Co.

UZHUKAN, U.; CHEBOKSAROV, N. P. 1959. O neprerîvnosti razvitiya fizicheskogo tipa khozyaystvennoy deyatel'nosti i kul'turî lyudey drevnekamennogo veka na territorii Kitaya. *SE,* Vol. 4, pp. 3–25.

CHAPTER 5

BERDYEV, O. 1969. *Drevneyshîye zemledel'tsî yuzhnogo Turkmenistana.* Ashkhabad.

BRAIDWOOD, R. J. 1952. *The Near East and the Foundation for Civilization. An Essay in Appraisal of the General Evidence.* Eugene, Ore., Oregon State System of Higher Education.

BRAIDWOOD, R. J.; HOWE, B. 1960. *Prehistoric Investigations in Iraqi Kurdistan.* Chicago, University of Chicago Oriental Institute.

CASAL, J.-M. 1961. *Fouilles de Mundigak.* 2 Vols. *MDAFA,* No. 17.

CHILDE, V. G. 1941. *Man Makes Himself.* London, Watt & Co.

COON, C. 1951. *Cave Exploration in Iran, 1949.* Philadelphia, University Museum, University of Pennsylvania.

DESHAYES, J. 1967. Céramiques peintes de Tureng Tepe. *Iran,* Vol. 5, pp. 123–31.

DUPREE, L. (ed.). 1972. Prehistoric Research in Afghanistan. *Transactions of the American Philosophical Society,* Vol. 62, Part 4. Philadelphia, American Philosophical Society.

McBURNEY, C. M. B. 1968. The Cave of Ali Tappeh and the Epi-Palaeolithic in N.E. Iran. *Proceedings of the Prehistoric Society,* Vol. 34, pp. 385–413.

MASSON, V. M. 1971. Poseleniye Dzheytun. *MIA,* No. 180.

MASUDA, S. 1974. Tepe Sang-i Chakmak. *Iran,* Vol. 12, pp. 222–3.

MELLAART, J. 1975. *Neolithic of the Near East.* London, Thames & Hudson.

VAVILOV, N. I. 1967. *Izbrannîye proizvedeniya,* Vol. 1. Leningrad.

VAVILOV, N. I.; BUKINICH, D. D. 1929. *Zemledel'cheskiy Afganistan.* Moscow.

VINOGRADOV, A. V. 1981. *Drevniye okhotniki i rîbolovî Sredneaziatskogo Mezhdurechiya.* Moscow. *Trudî KhAEE,* Vol. 13.

CHAPTER 6

AGRAWAL, D. P. 1981. Multidisciplinary Investigations in Kashmir: 1979–1980: A Report. *ME,* Vol. 5, pp. 87–91.

ALLCHIN, B.; ALLCHIN, F. R. 1982. *The Rise of Civilization in India and Pakistan.* Cambridge, Cambridge University Press.

BASU, A.; PAL, A. 1980. *Human Remains from Burzahom.* Calcutta, Anthropological Survey of India.

CHANG, K. C. 1968. *The Archaeology of Ancient China.* 2nd ed. New Haven, Yale University Press.

——. 1977. *The Archaeology of Ancient China.* 3rd ed. New Haven, Yale University Press.

CHENG, T. K. 1959. *Archaeology in China.* Cambridge, Heffer & Sons.

COSTANTINI, L. 1984. The Beginning of Agriculture in the Kachi Plain: The Evidence of Mehrgarh. *SAA 1981,* pp. 29–33.

DANI, A. H. 1970/71. Excavations in the Gomal Valley. *APk,* Vol. 5, pp. 1–77.

DE TERRA, H. 1942. The Megaliths of Burzahom, Kashmir. A New Prehistoric Civilization from India. *Proceedings of the American Philosophical Society,* Vol. 42, pp. 483–504.

DE TERRA, H.; PATERSON, T. T. 1939. *Studies on the Ice Age in India and Associated Human Cultures.* Washington, D.C., Carnegie Institution of Washington.

DIKSHIT, K. N. 1982. The Neolithic Cultural Frontiers of Kashmir. *ME,* Vol. 6, pp. 30–6.

FAIRSERVIS, W. A. 1956. Excavations in the Quetta Valley, West Pakistan. *Anthropological Papers of the American Museum of Natural History,* Vol. 45, Part 2, pp. 169–402.

GRAZIOSI, P. 1964. *Prehistoric Research in North Western Pakistan. Anthropological Research in Chitral.* Leiden, E. J. Brill.

HALIM, M. A. 1972*a*. Excavations at Sarai Khola, Part I. *PA,* Vol. 7, pp. 23–89.

——. 1972*b*. Excavations at Sarai Khola, Part II. *PA,* Vol. 8, pp. 1–112.

JARRIGE, J.-F. 1981. Economy and Society in the Early Chalcolithic/Bronze Age of Baluchistan: New Perspectives from Recent Excavations at Mehrgarh. *SAA 1979,* pp. 93–114.

——. 1984. Chronology of the Earlier Period of the Greater Indus As Seen from Mehrgarh, Pakistan. *SAA 1981,* pp. 21–8.

JARRIGE, J.-F.; LECHEVALLIER, M. 1979. Excavations at Mehrgarh, Baluchistan: Their Significance in the Prehistorical Context of the Indo-Pakistan Border-lands. *SAA 1977,* pp. 463–535.

JARRIGE, J.-F.; MEADOW, R. H. 1980. The Antecedents of Civilization in the Indus Valley. *SAm,* Vol. 243, No. 2, pp. 122–33.

KHAN, F. A. 1965. Excavations at Kot Diji. *PA,* Vol. 2, pp. 11–85.

KHAZANCHI, T. N. 1976. Pit Dwellers of Burzahom. *The Illustrated Weekly of India,* Vol. 97, No. 36, pp. 25–7.

——. 1977. North-western Neolithic Cultures of India. *News Letter,* Nos. 7 and 8. Simla, Indian Institute of Advanced Study.

KHAZANCHI, T. N.; DIKSHIT, K. N. 1980. The Grey Ware Culture of Northern Pakistan, Jammu and Kashmir and Punjab. *Pt,* Vol. 9, pp. 47–51.

LECHEVALLIER, M. 1984. The Flint Industry of Mehrgarh. *SAA 1981,* pp. 41–51.

LECHEVALLIER, M.; QUIVRON, G. 1981. The Neolithic in Baluchistan: New Evidences from Mehrgarh. *SAA 1979,* pp. 71–91.

MEADOW, R. H. 1984. Notes on the Faunal Remains from Mehrgarh, With a Focus on Cattle (*Bos*). *SAA 1981,* pp. 34–40.

MUGHAL, M. R. 1970. The Early Harappan Period in the Greater Indus Valley and Northern Baluchistan (ca. 3000–2400 B.C.). Ann Arbor, Michigan University of Pennsylvania. (Ph.D. thesis.)

——. 1972. Excavation at Jalilpur, Pakistan. *Archaeology,* Vol. 8, pp. 117–24.

——. 1974. New Evidence of the Early Harappan Culture from Jalilpur, Pakistan. *Archaeology,* Vol. 27, No. 2, pp. 106–18.

MUGHAL, M. R.; HALIM, M. A. 1972. The Pottery. *PA,* Vol. 8, pp. 33–110.

PANDE, B. M. 1972. A Neolithic 'Tectiform' from Burzahom, District Srinagar, Kashmir. *Indian Anthropological Society Journal,* Vol. 7, No. 2, pp. 175–7.

——. 1973. Neolithic Hunting Scene in a Stone-slab from Burzahom, District Srinagar, Kashmir. *AP,* Vol. 14, pp. 134–8.

PANT, R. K.; AGRAWAL, D. P.; KRISHNAMURTHY. 1978. Scanning Electron Microscope and Other Studies on the Karewa Beds of Kashmir, India. In: W. B. Whalley (ed.), *Scanning Electron Microscopy in the Study of Sediments,* pp. 275–82. Norwich, Geo Abstracts.

PANT, R. K.; GAILLARD, C.; NAUTIYAL, V.; GAUR , C. S.; SHALI, S. L. 1982. Some New Lithic and Ceramic Industries from Kashmir. *ME,* Vol. 6, pp. 37–40.

PATERSON, T. T.; DRUMMOND, H. J. H. 1962. *Soan. The Palaeolithic of Pakistan.* Karachi, Department of Archaeology, Government of Pakistan.

SANKALIA, H. D. 1974. *Prehistory and Protohistory of India and Pakistan.* 2nd ed. Poona, Deccan College, Postgraduate and Research Institute.

SHARMA, A. K. 1967. Neolithic Human Burials from Burzahom, Kashmir. *Journal of the Oriental Institute* (Baroda), Vol. 16, pp. 239–42.

SHARMA, G. R. 1983. Beginnings of Agriculture: New Light on Transformation from Hunting and Food Gathering to the Domestication of Plants: India, a Primary and Nuclear Centre. *JCA,* Vol. 6, pp. 51–64.

SHARMA, G. R.; MISRA, V. D.; MANDAL, D.; MISRA, B. B.; PAL, J. N. 1980. *Beginnings of Agriculture.* Allahabad, Abinash Prakashan.

SINGH, G. 1964. A Preliminary Survey of the Post-glacial Vegetation History of Kashmir Valley. *Palaeobotanist,* Vol. 12, No. 1, pp. 72–108.

STACUL, G. 1967. Excavations in a Rock Shelter Near Ghaligai (Swat, West Pakistan). Preliminary Report. *EW,* Vol. 17, pp. 185–219.

——. 1969. Excavation Near Ghaligai (1968) and Chronological Sequence of Protohistorical Cultures in the Swat Valley. *EW,* Vol. 19, pp. 44–91.

——. 1976. Excavation at Loebanr III (Swat, Pakistan). *EW,* Vol. 26, pp. 13–30.

——. 1977. Dwelling and Storage-pits at Loebanr III (Swat, Pakistan), 1976. Excavation Report. *EW,* Vol. 27, pp. 227–53.

THAPAR, B. K. 1964. Neolithic Problems in India. In: V. N. Mishra and M. S. Mate (eds.), *Indian Prehistory,* pp. 87–142. Poona, Deccan College, Postgraduate and Research Institute.

——. 1974. Problems of the Neolithic Cultures of India: A Retrospect. *Pt,* Vol. 7, pp. 61–5.

——. 1978. Early Farming Communities in India. *Journal of Human Evolution,* Vol. 7, pp. 11–22.

——. 1984. Fresh Light on the Neolithic Culture of India. *JCA,* Vol. 7, pp. 191–206.

THOMAS, K. D.; ALLCHIN, F. R. 1986. Radiocarbon Dating of Some Early Sites in N.W. Pakistan. *SAS,* Vol. 2, pp. 37–44.

VISHNU-MITTRE. 1968. Proto-historic Records of Agriculture in India. *Transactions of the Bose Research Institute,* Vol. 31, No. 3, pp. 87–106.

CHAPTER 7

AN ZHIMIN. 1978. Mesolithic Remains at Hailar in Heilungkiang Province – With Notes on the Origin of the Microlithic Tradition. *Kaogu Xuebao,* No. 3, pp. 289–315. (English summary, p. 316.)

——. 1979*a*. A Brief Survey on the Neolithic in China Since Liberation. *Kaogu,* No. 5, pp. 393–403.

——. 1979*b*. Peiligang, Cishan and Yangshao. An Exploration of the Origin and Development of Neolithic Culture on the Central Plains. *Kaogu,* No. 4.

AN ZHIMIN; YIN ZESHENG; LI BINGYUAN. 1979. Palaeolithics and Microlithics at Shenja (Xainza) and Shuanghu in Northern Tibet. *Kaogu,* No. 6.

ANDERSON, J. G. 1943. Researches into the Prehistory of the Chinese. *Bulletin of the Museum of Far Eastern Antiquities,* Vol. 15.

BERGMAN, F. 1939. *Archaeological Researches in Sinkiang*, Stockholm, Bokförlage Aktiebolaget Thule.

COMMITTEE OF THE TIBET AUTONOMOUS REGION. 1979. A Brief Report on the Trial Diggings at Karuo Changdu, Tibet. *Wenwu*, No. 9, pp. 22–8.

DADIWAN EXCAVATION TEAM OF THE GANSU PROVINCIAL MUSEUM AND THE QINAN COUNTY CULTURAL CENTRE. 1981. Early Neolithic Remains at Dadiwan in Qinan County, Gansu Province. *Kaogu*, No. 4.

DAI ERJIAN. 1972. Stone Tools Found at Nyalam County in Tibet. *Kaogu*, No. 1.

DANI, A. H. 1962. *Prehistory and Protohistory of Eastern India*. Calcutta, Firma K. L. Mukhopadhyay.

GANSU PROVINCIAL MUSEUM. 1979. *Painted Pottery from Gansu*. Gansu Provincial Museum.

GUPTA, S. P. 1979. *Archaeology of Soviet Central Asia and the Indian Borderlands*. Vol. 2. Delhi, B. R. Publishing Corp.

HUANG, W. 1948. *Explorations Round Lob Nor*. Beijing.

——. 1958. *Exploration Round the Tarim Basin*. Beijing.

MARINGER, J. 1950. *Contribution to the Preshistory of Mongolia*. Stockholm, The Sino-Swedish Expedition. (Publication 34.)

MASSON, V. M. 1964. Istoricheskoye mesto Sredneaziatskoy tsivilizatsii. *SA*, No. 1, pp. 12–25.

PEI, W. 1948. *Prehistoric Northwest China*. Beijing.

QINGHAI PROVINCIAL ARCHAEOLOGICAL TEAM. 1980. *Painted Pottery from Qinghai*.

RANOV, V. A. 1975. Pamir i problema zaseleniya vîsokogoriyi Azii chelovekom kamennogo veka. *Stranî i narodî Vostoka*, Vol. 17, pp. 136–57.

TEILHARD DE CHARDIN, P.; Young, C. C. 1932. On Some Neolithic (and Possibly Palaeolithic) Finds in Mongolia, Sinkiang and West China. *BGSCh*, Vol. 12, No. 1.

WAN HENGJIE. 1975. A Neolithic Site Found at Nyingchi County in Tibet Autonomous Region. *Kaogu*, No. 5, pp. 310–15.

WU ZHEN. 1964. Some Neolithic Sites in Eastern Xinjiang. *Kaogu*, No. 7, pp. 333–45.

XIA NAI. 1977. Carbon-14 Dating and Chinese Prehistory. *Kaogu*, No. 4, pp. 217–32.

THE XIAN BANPO MUSEUM AND THE LINTONG COUNTY CULTURAL CENTRE. 1980. A Summary of the 4th-11th Seasons of Excavations at Jiangzhai Site, Lintong County. *Wenwu yu Kaogu*. No. 3.

ZHANG XUEZHENG; ZHANG PENGCHUAN; GUO DEYONG. 1979/80. On the Periodization and Interrelationships of the Majiayao, Banshan and Machang Types. *A Collection of Treaties of the First Annual Conference of the Chinese Society of Archaeology*.

CHAPTER 8

CHALAYA, L. A. 1972. Ozernîye stoyanki Pavlodarskoy oblasti Pen'ki 1 i 2. *Poiski i raskopki v Kazakhstane*, pp. 163–81. Alma Ata.

CHERNIKOV, S. S. 1959. Robotî Vostochno-Kazakhtanskoy arkheologicheskoy expeditsii v 1956g. *Kratkiye soobshcheniya. Instituta istorii material'noy kul'turî Ak. nauk*, No. 73, pp. 99–106. Moscow.

DEREVYANKO, A. P.; OKLADNIKOV, A. P. 1969. Drevniye kul'turi Vostochnikh rayonov Mongolskoy Narodnoy Respubliki. *SA*, Vol. 4, pp. 156–71.

DORJ, D. 1971. *Neolit vostochnoy Mongolii*. Ulan Bator.

DORJ, D. 1974. Tamsa-Bulagskaya kul'tura i eë mesto v drevneyshey istorii Tsentral'noy Azii. *Rol' kochevîkh narodov v Tsivilizatsii Tsentral'noy Azii*, pp. 127–31. Ulan Bator.

DORJ, D.; DEREVYANKO, A. P. 1970. Novîye materiali dlya izucheniya nêolita Vostochnoy Mongolii. *Izvestiya Akademii Nauk Mongol'skoy Narodnoy Respubliki*, pp. 43–56.

Istoriya Kazakhskoy SSR. 1977. Alma Ata.

KOROBKOVA, G. T. 1969. Orudiya truda i khozyaystvo neoliticheskikh plemën Sredney Azii. *MIA*, No. 158. Leningrad.

MARINGER, I. 1930. *Contribution to the Prehistory of Mongolia.* Stockholm, The Sino-Swedish Expedition. (Publication 34.)

MURZAEV, E. M. 1952. *Mongol'skaya Narodnaya Respublika.* Moscow.

NELSON, N. C. 1926a. The Dune Dwellers of the Gobi. *Natural History*, Vol. 28, pp. 305–8.

——. 1926b. Prehistoric Archaeology of the Gobi Desert. *American Museum Novitates*, No. 222, pp. 10–16.

OKLADNIKOV, A. P.; DEREVYANKO, A. P. 1970. Tamsa-Bulagskaya neoliticheskaya kul'tura Vostochnoy Mongolii. *Materialî po istorii i filologii Tsentral'noy Azii*, Vol. 5, pp. 3–20.

ZAYBERT, V. F.; POTEMKINA, T. M. 1981. K voprosu o mezolite lesostepnoy chasti Tobolo-Irtîsheskogo mezhdurechya. *SA*, Vol. 3, pp. 107–29.

CHAPTER 9

ADAMS, R. M. C. 1972. The Origin of Cities. *Foundations for Civilization.* San Francisco.

AMIET, P. 1983. The Archaic Glyptic of Shahr-i Sokhta (Period I). Prehistoric Sistan. *IsMeo.RM.* Vol. 19, No. 1, pp. 199–210.

AMIET, P.; TOSI, M. 1978. Phase 10 at Shahr-i Sokhta: Excavations in Square XDV and the Late Fourth Millennium B.C. Assemblage of Sistan. *EW*, Vol. 28, pp. 9–32.

BASAGLIA, P. (ed.). 1977. *La città bruciata del deserto salato.* Venice, Enzzo Editor.

BISCIONE, R. 1977. The Crisis of Central Asian Urbanization in the Third Millennium B.C. and Villages as an Alternative System. In: J. Deshayes (ed.), *Le Plateau iranien et l'Asie Centrale des origines à la conquête islamique*, pp. 113–27. Paris.

——. 1984. Baluchistan Presence in the Ceramic Assemblage of Period I at Shahr-i Sokhta. *SAA 1981*, pp. 69–80.

BISCIONE, R.; TOSI, M. 1979. *Protostoria degli stati Turanici.* Supplement 20 of *Annali IUON*, Vol. 39, p. 3.

BULGARELLI, G. M. 1979. The Lithic Industry of Tepe Hissar at the Light of Recent Excavation. *SAA 1977*, pp. 39–54.

BULGARELLI, G. M.; TOSI, M. 1977. La lavorazione ed il commercio delle pietre semipreziose nelle città dell'Iran protostorico (3200–1800 a.C.). *Geo-Archeologia*, Vol. 1/2, pp. 37–50.

CALDWELL, J. R. 1967. *Investigations at Tal-i Iblis.* Springfield, Illinois State Museum. (Illinois State Museum Preliminary Report, 9.).

CASAL, J.-M. 1961. *Fouilles de Mundigak.* 2 vols. *MDAFA*, No. 17.

CASSOLI, P. 1977. L'Avifauna, AA.VV. In: P. Basaglia (ed.), *La città bruciata del deserto salato*, pp. 159–71. Venice, Enzzo Editore.

CIARLA, R. 1981. A Preliminary Analysis of the Manufacture of Alabaster Vessels at Shahr-i Sokhta and Mundigak in the Third Millennium B.C. *SAA 1979*, pp. 45–64.

494

CLEUZIOU, S.; COSTANTINI, L. 1981. Premiers éléments sur l'agriculture protohistorique de l'Arabie orientale. *Paléorient,* Vol. 6, pp. 245–51.

COMPAGNONI, B. 1978*a*. The Bone Remains of *Equus Hemionus* from Shahr-i Sokhta. In: R. H. Meadow and M. A. Zeder (eds.), *Approaches to Faunal Analysis in the Middle East,* pp. 105–18. Cambridge, Mass., Peabody Museum of Archaeology and Ethnology. (Peabody Museum Bulletin, 2.)

——. 1978*b*. The Bone Remains of *Gazella subqutturosa* from Shahr-i Sokhta. In: R. H. Meadow and M. A. Zeder (eds.), *Approaches to Faunal Analysis in the Middle East,* pp. 119–28. Cambridge, Mass., Peabody Museum of Archaeology and Ethnology. (Peabody Museum Bulletin, 2.)

COMPAGNONI, B.; CALOI, L. 1977. I mammiferi. In: P. Basaglia (ed.), *La città bruciata del deserto salato,* pp. 183–213. Venice, Enzzo Editore.

COMPAGNONI, B.; TOSI, M. 1978. The Camel: Its Distribution and State of Domestication in the Middle East During the Third Millennium B.C. in Light of Finds from Shahr-i Sokhta. In: R. H. Meadows and M. A. Zeder (eds.), *Approaches to Faunal Analysis in the Middle East,* pp. 91–103. Cambridge, Mass., Peabody Museum of Archaeology and Ethnology. (Peabody Museum Bulletin, 2.)

COSTANTINI, L. 1977. Le piante nella vita della città. In: P. Basaglia (ed.), *La città bruciata del deserto salato,* pp. 159–71. Venice, Enzzo Editore.

——. 1979. Plant Remains from Pirak. In: J.-F. Jarrige and M. Santoni (eds.), *Fouilles de PiraK,* Vol. 1, pp. 326–33. Paris, Diffusion de Boccard.

——. 1984*a*. The Beginning of Agriculture in the Kachi Plain: The Evidence of Mehrgarh. *SAA 1981,* pp. 29–33.

——. 1984*b*. Palaeoethnobotanical Studies of Prehistoric Settlements in Soghun and Dowlatabad Valleys, Iran. Preliminary manuscript prepared for C. C. Lamberg-Karlovsky, Department of Anthropology, Harvard University.

COSTANTINI, L.; TOSI, M. 1977. Popolamento e risorse naturali del Sistan preistorico. In: P. Basaglia (ed.), *La città bruciata del deserto salato,* pp. 277–93. Venice, Enzzo Editore.

DE CARDI, B. 1965. Excavations and Reconnaissance in Kalat, West Pakistan – The Prehistoric Sequence of the Surab Region. *PA,* Vol. 2, pp. 86–182.

——. 1970. Excavations at Bampur, A Third Millennium Settlement in Persian Baluchistan. *Anthropological Papers of the American Museum of Natural History,* Vol. 51, pp. 231–355.

DESHAYES, J. 1974. Cachets susiens et chronologie iranienne. *Syria,* Vol. 51, No. 3–4, pp. 253–64.

——. 1975. Les fouilles récentes de Tureng-Tepe: la terrasse haute de la fin du IIIème millénaire. *Comptes rendus de l'Académie des Inscriptions et Belles-lettres,* pp. 522–30. Paris, Académie des Inscriptions et Belles-lettres.

——. 1977. A propos des terrasses hautes de la fin du IIIème millénaire en Iran et en Asie Centrale. In: J. Deshayes (ed.), *Le plateau iranien et l'Asie Centrale des origines à la conquête islamique,* pp. 108–11. Paris, CNRS.

DUPREE, L. 1963. Deh Morasi Ghundai: A Chalcolithic Site in South-Central Afghanistan. *Anthropological Papers of the American Museum of Natural History,* Vol. 50, Part 2.

DYSON, R. H.; HOWARD, S. M. (eds.). 1989. Tappeh Hesar. *Reports of the Restudy Project, 1976.* Florence, Casa Editrice le Lettere. (Monografie di Mesopotamia II.)

EGAMI, N.; MASUDA, S. 1962. *Marv-Dasht.* Vol. 1: *The Excavation at Tall-i-Bakun.* Tokyo, Yamakawa Publishing Co.

FAIRSERVIS, W. A. 1956. Excavations in the Quetta Valley, West Pakistan. *Anthropological Papers of the American Museum of Natural History*, Vol. 45, Part 2, pp. 169–402.

GENITO, B. 1982. Hearths of the Iranian Area: A Typological Analysis. *Annali IUON*, Vol. 42, pp. 195–245.

GHIRSHMAN, R. 1938. *Fouilles de Sialk, près de Kashan 1933, 1934, 1937.* Paris, Librairie Orientaliste Paul Geuthner. 2 Vols.

HAKEMI. A. A. 1972. *Catalogue de l'exposition Lut Xabis (Shahdad).* Tehran, Department of Archaeology.

JARRIGE, C.; TOSI, M. 1981. The Natural Resources of Mundigak – Some Observations on the Location of the Site in Relation to its Economical Space. *SAA 1979*, pp. 115–42.

JARRIGE, J.-F.; MEADOW, R. H. 1980. The Antecedents of the Indus Civilization. *SAm*, Vol. 243, No. 2, pp. 122–32.

KAMILLI, D. C.; LAMBERG-KARLOVSKY, C. C. 1979. Petrographic and Electron Micro-probe Analysis of Ceramics from Tepe Yahya, Iran. *Archaeometry*, Vol. 21, No. 1, pp. 47–59.

KOHL, P. L. 1975. Carved Chlorite Vessels: A Trade in Finished Commodities in the Mid-Third Millennium. *Ex*, Vol. 18, pp. 18–31.

LAMBERG-KARLOVSKY, C. C. 1973. Urban Interactions on the Iranian Plateau: Excavations at Tepe Yahya 1967–1973. *Proceedings of the British Academy*, Vol. 59, pp. 283–319.

——. 1978. The Proto-Elamites on the Iranian Plateau. *Antiquity*, Vol. 52, pp. 114–20.

LAMBERG-KARLOVSKY, C. C.; TOSI, M. 1973. Shahr-i Sokhta and Tepe Yayha: Tracks on the Earliest History on the Iranian Plateau. *EW*, Vol. 23, No. 1/2, pp. 21–57.

LECHEVALLIER, M.; MEADOW, R. H.; QUIVRON, G. 1982. Dépôts d'animaux dans les sépultures néolithiques de Mehrgarh, Pakistan. *Paléorient*, Vol. 8, pp. 99–106.

LECHEVALLIER, M.; QUIVRON, G. 1981. The Neolithic in Baluchistan: New Evidence from Mehrgarh. *SAA 1979*, pp. 71–92.

LISITSYNA, G. N. 1965. *Oroshayemoye zemledeliye êpokhi êneolita na yuge Turkmenii.* Moscow.

——. 1970. Osnovnîye êtapi istorii oroshayemogo zemledeliya na yuge Sredney Azii i Blizhnem Vostoke. *KSIA*, Vol. 122, pp. 114–17.

——. 1972. Istoriya oroshayemogo zemledeliya v yuzhnoy Turkmenii. *USA*, Vol. 1, pp. 11–16.

MAJIDZADEH, Y. 1982. Lapis Lazuli and the Great Khorasan Road. *Paléorient*, Vol. 8, pp. 59–69.

MARIANI, L. 1984. Craftsmen's Quarters in the Proto-urban Settlement of the Middle East: The Surface Analysis. *SAA 1981*, pp. 118–23.

MASSON, V. M. 1962. Eneolit yuzhnîkh oblastey Sredney Azii, Pamyatniki razvitogo êneolita yugo-zapadnogo Turkmenii. *SAI*, Fasc. B3–8.

——. 1967. Protogorodskaya Tsivilizatsiya yuga Sredney Azii. *SA*, pp. 165–90.

——. 1968. The Urban Revolution in Southern Turkmenia. *Antiquity*, Vol. 42, pp. 1782–7.

——. 1970. Raskopki na Altyn-Depe v 1969 g. *Materialî YuTAKE*, Vol. 3, pp. 5–24. Ashkhabad.

——. 1971. Poseleniye Dzheytun. *MIA*, No. 180.

——. 1977. Altyn-Depe v êpokhu êneolita. *SA*, No. 3, pp. 164–88.

——. 1981. Altyn-Depe. *Trudî YuTAKE*, Vol. 18.

MASUDA, S. 1976. Report on the Archaeological Investigations at Shahrud 1979. *Proceedings of the IVth Annual Symposium on Archaeological Research in Iran*, pp. 63–70. Tehran.

MEADOW, R. H. 1983. The Equids of Mehrgarh, Sibri and Pirak: An Osteological Evidence for the Introduction of the Horse to South Asia. Paper presented at the seventh Conference of South Asian Archaeology, Brussels, 4–8 July 1983.

McCOWN, D. E. 1942. *The Comparative Stratigraphy of Early Iran.* Chicago, University of Chicago Press. (Studies in Ancient Civilizations, 23.)

MEDER, O. G. 1979. *Klimaökologie und Siedlungsgang auf dem Hochland von Iran in vor- und frühgeschichtlicher Zeit.* Marburg, Lahn. (Marburger Geographische Schriften, 80.)

MERIGGI. 1971/72. *La scrittura protoelamica,* Vols. 1–3. Rome.

MUSCARELLA, O. W. 1977. Unexcavated Objects and Ancient Near Eastern Art. In: L. D. Levine and T. C. Young (eds.), *Mountains and Lowlands: Essays in the Archaeology of Greater Mesopotamia,* pp. 153–207. Malibu, Undens Publications.

PIGGOTT, S. 1947. A New Prehistoric Ceramic from Baluchistan. *AIn,* Vol. 3, pp. 131–42.

PIPERNO, M. 1976. Grave 77 at Shahr-i Sokhta: Further Evidence of Technological Specialization in the Third Millennium B.C. *EW,* Vol. 26, pp. 9–12.

——. 1977. La necropoli, AA.VV. In: P. Basaglia (ed.), *La città bruciata del deserto salato,* pp. 113–48. Venice, Enzzo Editore.

——. 1979. Socio-economic Implications from the Graveyard of Shahr-i Sokhta. *SAA 1977,* pp. 123–39.

PIPERNO, M.; SALVATORI, S. 1983. Recent Results and New Perspectives from the Research of the Graveyard of Shahr-i Sokhta, Sistan, Iran. *Annali IUON,* Vol. 13, pp. 174–91.

PIPERNO, M.; TOSI, M. 1975. The Graveyard of Shahr-i Sokhta, Iran. *Archaeology,* Vol. 28, pp. 186–97.

PRICKETT, M. 1976. Settlement and the Development of Agriculture in the Rud-i Gusk Drainage Dams. In: *Zusammenfassungen der für den VII Internationalen Kongress für iranische Kunst und Archäeologie vorgenommenen Vörträge.* Munich.

PUMPELLY, R. 1908. *Explorations in Turkestan. Expedition of 1904. Prehistoric Civilizations of Anau. Origins, Growth and Influence of Environment.* Washington, D.C., Carnegie Institute of Washington. 2 vols.

SALVATORI, S. 1979. Sequential Analysis and Architectural Remains in the Central Quarters of Shahr-i Sokhta. *SAA 1977,* pp. 141–8.

SALVATORI, S.; VIDALE, M. 1982. A Brief Survey of the Protohistoric Site of Shahdad (Kerman, Iran): Preliminary Report. *Rivista di Archeologia,* Vol. 6, pp. 5–10.

SARIANIDI, V. I. 1959. Novîy tip drevnikh pogrebal'nikh sooruzheniy yuzhnoy Turkmenii. *SA,* Vol. 2, pp. 253–8.

SCHMIDT, E. F. 1937. *Excavations at Tepe Hissar Damghan.* Philadelphia, University of Pennsylvania Press.

SHAFFER, J. G. 1971. Preliminary Field Report on Excavations at Said-Kala-tepe. *Af,* Vol. 2/3, pp. 89–127.

SNEAD, R. E. 1978. Geomorphic History of the Mundigak Valley. *Af,* Vol. 5, No. 2, pp. 59–69.

SPRÖDE, K. 1977. Morphologische Untersuchungen an Vogeleierschalen von Shahr-i Sokhta in Sistan (Iran) aus dem 3. Jahrtausend v. Ch. Bonn, Rheinischen Friedrich-Wilhelms-Universität. (Unpublished thesis.)

STEIN, A. 1937. *Archaeological Reconnaissance in Northwestern India and Southeastern Iran.* London, Macmillan.

Tosi, M. 1974*a*. Some Data for the Study of Prehistoric Cultural Areas on the Persian Gulf. *Proceedings of the Seminar for Arabian Studies,* Vol. 4, pp. 145–71.

——. 1974*b*. The Problems of Turquoise in the Third Millennium B.C. Trade Across the Iranian Plateau. *Memorie dell'Istituto Italiano di Paleontologia Umana,* Vol. 2, pp. 147–62.

——. 1976. A Topographical and Stratigraphical Periplus of Šar-e Suxteh. *Proceedings of the IVth Annual Symposium on Archaeological Research in Iran,* pp. 130–58. Tehran.

——. 1977. The Archaeological Evidence for Protostate Structures in Eastern Iran and Central Asia at the End of the Third Millennium B.C. In: J. Deshayes (ed.), *Le plateau iranien et l'Asie centrale des origines à la conquête islamique,* pp. 45–66. Paris, CNRS.

——. 1983. Excavations at Shahr-i Sokhta 1969–70. In: M. Tosi (ed.), *Prehistoric Sistan I,* pp. 73–125. *IsMeo.RM,* Vol. 19, No. 1.

——. 1984. The Notion of Craft Specialization and its Representation in the Archaeological Record of the Early States in the Turanian Basin. In: M. Spriggs (ed.), *Marxist Approaches in Archaeology.* Cambridge, Cambridge University Press.

Tosi, M.; Biscione, R. 1981. *Conchiglie. Il commercio e la lavorazione della conchiglie marine del medio oriente dal VI e II millenio a.C.* Rome, De Luca Editore.

Tosi, M.; Piperno, M. 1973. Lithic Technology Behind the Ancient Lapis Lazuli Trade. *Ex,* Vol. 16, pp. 15–23.

Vanden Berghe, L. 1959. *Archéologie de l'Iran ancien.* Leiden, E. J. Brill.

Vidale, M. 1984. The Pear-shaped Beaker of Shahr-i Sokhta: Evolution of a Ceramic Morphotype During the Third Millennium B.C. *SAA 1981,* pp. 81–97.

Weiss, H.; Young, T. C. 1975. The Merchants of Susa, Godin V and Plateau-lowland Relations in the Late Fourth Millennium B.C. *Iran,* Vol. 13, pp. 1–17.

Zangsdorff, A.; McCorn, D. E. 1942. *Tall-i-Bakun H. Season of 1932.* Oriental Institute Publications, Vol. 59. Chicago.

Chapter 10

Agrawal, D. P. 1971. *The Copper Bronze Age in India.* New Delhi, Munshiram Manoharlal.

Biscione, R. 1973. Dynamics of an Early South Asian Urbanism: First Period of Shahr-i Sokhta and its Connections with Southern Turkmenia. In: N. Hammond (ed.), *SAA,* pp. 105–18. London, Duckworth.

Bovington, C. H.; Dyson, R. H. Mahdavi, A.; Masoumi, R. 1974. The Radiocarbon Evidence for the Terminal Date of the Hissar III Culture. *Iran,* Vol. 12, pp. 195–9.

Dyson, R. H. 1965. Problems in the Relative Chronology of Iran 6000–2000 B.C. In: R. W. Ehrich (ed.), *Chronologies in Old World Archaeology,* pp. 215–56. Chicago/London, University of Chicago Press.

Ermolova, N. M. 1970. Novîye materialî po izucheniyu ostatkov mlekopitayushchikh iz drevnikh poseleniy Turkmenii. *Karakumskiye drevnosti,* Vol. 3, pp. 205–32.

Gulyamov, G.; Islamov, U. I.; Askarov, A. 1966. *Pervobîtnaya kul'tura i vozniknoveniye oroshayemogo zemledeliya v nizov'yakh Zarafshana.* Tashkent.

Gupta, S. P. 1979. *Archaeology of Soviet Central Asia and Iranian Borderlands.* Delhi, B. R. Publishing Corp. 2 vols.

Khlopin, I. N. 1963. Eneolit yuzhnîkh oblastey Sredney Azii. *SAI,* Fasc. B3–8, Part I.

——. 1964. *Geoksyurskaya gruppa poselenii êpokhi êneolita.* Leningrad, Nauka.

——. 1969. Pamyatniki razvitogo êneolita yugo-vostochnoy Turkmenii. *SAI,* Fasc. B3–8, Part 3.

KOHL, P. L. (ed.). 1981. *The Bronze Age Civilization of Central Asia: Recent Soviet Discoveries.* New York, M. E. Sharp.

KOROBKOVA, G. F. 1981. *Khozyaystvennîye kompleksî rannikh zemledel'chesko-skotovodcheskikh obshchestv yuga SSSR.* Moscow.

KUZ'MINA, E. E. 1966. Metallicheskiye izdeliya êpokhi êneolita i bronzovogo veka Sredney Azii. *SAI,* Fasc. B4–9.

LAMBERG-KARLOVSKY, C. C.; TOSI, M. 1973. Shahr-i Sokhta and Tepe Yahya: Tracks on the Earliest History of the Iranian Plateau. *EW,* Vol. 23, No. 1/2, pp. 21–57.

LISITSYNA, G. N. 1978. *Stanovleniye i razvitiye oroshayemogo zemledeliya v yuzhnoy Turkmenii.* Moscow.

MASIMOV, I. S. 1976. *Keramicheskoye proizvodstvo êpokhi bronzî v yuzhnom Turkmenistane.* Ashkhabad.

——. 1979. Izucheniye pamyatnikov êpokhi bronzî nizov'ev Murgaba. *SA,* Vol. 1, pp. 111–31.

MASSON, V. M. 1960. Kara-depe u Artîkha. *Trudî YuTAKE,* Vol. 10, pp. 319–463.

——. 1962. Eneolit uzhnîkh oblastey Sredney Azii. *SAI,* Fasc. B3–8, Part 2.

——. 1964. *Srednyaya Aziya i Drevniy Vostok.* Moscow/Leningrad.

——. 1976. The Art of Altin-depe: The Artistic Traditions of the Urbanized Cultures Between Sumer and India. In: J. V. S. Megaw (ed.), *To Illustrate the Monuments. Essays on Archaeology Presented to Stuart Piggott,* pp. 253–62. London, Thames & Hudson.

——. 1981*a*. Altyn-depe. *Trudî YuTAKE,* Vol. 18.

——. 1981*b*. Altyn-depe during the Aeneolithic Period. In: P. Kohl (ed.), *The Bronze Age Civilization of Central Asia: Recent Soviet Discoveries,* pp. 63–95. New York, M. E. Sharp.

MASSON, V. M.; SARIANIDI, V. I. 1972. *Central Asia: Turkmenia before the Achaemenids.* London, Thames & Hudson.

——. 1973. *Sredneaziyatskaya terrakota êpokhi bronzî.* Moscow.

PUMPELLY, R. 1908. *Explorations in Turkistan. Expedition of 1904. Prehistoric Civilizations of Anau. Origins, Growth and Influence of Environment.* Washington, D.C., Carnegie Institute of Washington. 2 vols.

SARIANIDI, V. I. 1965. Pamyatniki pozdnego êneolita Yugo-Vostochnoy Turkmenii. *SAI,* Fasc. B3–8, Part 4.

——. 1976. Yuzhnîy Turkmenistan v êpokhu bronzî. *Pervobîtnîy Turkmenistan,* pp. 82–111. Ashkhabad.

CHAPTER II

BISHT, R. S. 1976. *Banawali.* Chandigarh, Public Relations Department, Government of Haryana.

——. 1978. Banawali, A New Harappan Site in Haryana. *ME,* Vol. 2, pp. 86–8.

——. 1984. Structural Remains and Town Planning of Banawali. In: B. B. Lal and S. P. Gupta (eds.), *Frontiers of the Indus Civilization. Sir Mortimer Wheeler Commermoration Volume,* pp. 89–97. Delhi, Books and Books, for the Indian Archaeological Society.

BISHT, R. S.; ASTHANA, S. 1979. Banawali and Some Other Recently Excavated Harappan Sites in India. *SAA 1977,* pp. 223–4.

CASAL, J.-M. 1964. *Fouilles d'Amri*. Paris, Commission des Fouilles Archéologiques/Librairie C. Klincksieck. 2 vols.

——. 1966. Nindowari – A Chalcolithic Site of Western Baluchistan. *PA*, Vol. 3, pp. 10–21.

CLELAND, J. H. 1977. Chalcolithic and Bronze Age Chipped Stone Industries of the Indus Region: An Analysis of Variability and Change. Charlottesville, University of Virginia. (Ph.D. thesis.)

DALES, G. F. 1974. Excavations at Balakot, Pakistan – 1973. *Journal of Field Archaeology*, Vol. 1, pp. 3–22.

——. 1979. The Balakot Project: Summary of Four Years' Excavations in Pakistan. *SAA 1977*, pp. 241–74.

——. 1981. Reflections on Four Years of Excavations at Balakot. *ICnp*, pp. 25–32.

DANI, A. H. 1970–71. Excavations in the Gomal Valley. *APk*, Vol. 5, pp. 1–177.

DE CARDI, B. 1965. Excavations and Reconnaissance in Kalat, West Pakistan – The Prehistoric Sequence in the Surab Region. *PA*, Vol. 2, pp. 86–182.

——. 1970. Excavations at Rampur, A Third Millennium Settlement in Persian Baluchistan – 1966. *Anthropological Papers of the American Museum of Natural History*, Vol. 51, pp. 231–355.

DEVA, K.; McCOWN, D. E. 1949. Further Explorations in Sind: 1938. *AIn*, Vol. 5, pp. 12–30.

DURRANI, F. A. 1981. Indus Civilization: Evidence West of Indus. *ICnp*, pp. 133–8.

FAIRSERVIS, W. A. 1956. Excavations in the Quetta Valley, West Pakistan. *Anthropological Papers of the American Museum of Natural History*, Vol. 45, Part 2, pp. 169–402.

——. 1959. Archeological Surveys in the Zhob and Loralai Districts, West Pakistan. *Anthropological Papers of the American Museum of Natural History*, Vol. 47, Part 2, pp. 273–448.

——. 1975. *The Roots of Ancient India. The Archaeology of Early Indian Civilization*. 2nd ed. Chicago, University of Chicago Press.

FLAM, L. 1981*a*. The Paleogeography and Prehistoric Settlement Patterns in Sind, Pakistan (*c.* 4000–2000 B.C.). Philadelphia, University of Pennsylvania. (Ph.D. thesis.)

——. 1981*b*. Towards an Ecological Analysis of Prehistoric Settlement Patterns in Sind, Pakistan. *ME*, Vol. 5, pp. 52–8.

——. 1982. Suggested Archaeological Evidence for Complex Social Organizations in Prehistoric Sind. In: S. Pastner and L. Flam (eds.), *Anthropology in Pakistan*, pp. 219–30.

HALIM, M. A. 1972. Excavations at Sarai Khola, Part II. *PA*, Vol. 8, pp. 1–112.

HARGREAVES, H. 1929. Excavations in Baluchistan 1925: Sampur Mound, Mastang and Sohr Damb, Nal. *MASI*, Vol. 35.

JARRIGE, C.; AUDOUZE, F. 1980. Etude d'une aire de cuisson de jarres au IIIe millénaire: comparaison avec des techniques contemporaines de la plaine de Kachi, Baluchistan. *L'archéologie de l'Iraq du début de l'époque Néolithique à 333 avant notre ère*, pp. 85–98. Paris, Editions du CNRS. (Colloques internationaux du Centre National de la Recherche Scientifique, 580.)

JARRIGE, J.-F. 1977. Nouvelles recherches archéologiques au Baluchistan: les fouilles de Mehrgarh. In: J. Deshayes (ed.), *Le plateau iranien et l'Asie Centrale des origines à la conquête islamique*, pp. 74–94. Paris, Editions du CNRS. (Colloques internationaux du Centre National de la Recherche Scientifique, 567.)

——. 1981. Economy and Society in the Early Chalcolithic Bronze Age of Baluchistan: New Perspectives from Recent Excavations at Mehrgarh. *SAA 1979*, pp. 93–114.

JARRIGE, J.-F.; LECHEVALLIER, M. 1979. Excavations at Mehrgarh, Baluchistan: Their Significance in the Prehistorical Context of the Indo-Pakistan Borderlands. *SAA 1977*, pp. 463–535.

JARRIGE, J.-F.; MEADOW, R. H. 1980. The Antecedents of Civilization in the Indus Valley. *SAm*, Vol. 243, No. 2, pp. 122–33.

KHAN, F. 1979. A Preliminary Report on the Microlithic Blade Industry from Rahman Dheri. *SAA 1977*, pp. 374–404.

KHAN, F. A. 1965. Excavations at Kot-Diji. *PA*, Vol. 2, pp. 11–85.

LAL, B. B. 1971. Perhaps the Earliest Ploughed Field So Far Excavated Anywhere in the World. *Pt*, Vol. 4, pp. 1–3.

——. 1979. Kalibangan and the Indus Civilization. In: D. P. Agrawal and D. K. Chakrabarti (eds.), *Essays in Indian Protohistory*, pp. 65–97. Delhi, B. R. Publishing Corp.

MAJUMDAR, N. D. 1934. Explorations in Sind. *MASI*, Vol. 48.

MEADOW, R. H. 1979. Prehistoric Subsistence at Balakot: Initial Consideration of the Faunal Remains. *SAA 1977*, pp. 275–315.

——. 1984. A Camel Skeleton from Mohenjo-Daro. In: B. B. Lal and S. P. Gupta (eds.), *Frontiers of the Indus Civilization. Sir Mortimer Wheeler Commemoration Volume*, pp. 133–9. Delhi, Books and Books, for the Indian Archaeological Society.

——. 1987. Faunal Exploitation Patterns in Eastern Iran and Baluchistan: A Review of Recent Investigations. In: G. Gnoli, L. Lanciotti (eds.), *Orientalia Iosephi Tucci Memoriae Dicata*, Vol. 2, pp. 881–916. Rome, Istituto Italiano per il Medio ed Estremo Oriente.

——. 1988. The Faunal Remains from Jalipur. *PA*, Vol. 23, pp. 204–20.

MUGHAL, M. R. 1970. The Early Harappan Period in the Greater Indus Valley and Northern Baluchistan (*c.* 3000–2400 B.C.). Philadelphia, University of Pennsylvania. (Ph.D. thesis.)

——. 1972*a*. A Summary of Excavations and Explorations in Pakistan. *PA*, Vol. 8, pp. 113–58.

——. 1972*b*. The Sarai Khola Pottery Types of the Early Periods I and II. In Excavations at Sarai Khola, Part II. *PA*, Vol. 8, pp. 40–76.

——. 1973. *The Present State of Research on the Indus Valley Civilization*. International Symposium on Mohenjo-daro, pp. 1–28. Karachi, National Book Trust.

——. 1974. New Evidence of the Early Harappan Culture from Jalilpur, Pakistan. *Archaeology*, Vol. 27, No. 2, pp. 106–13.

——. 1981. New Archaeological Evidence from Bahawalpur. *ICnp*, pp. 33–42.

——. 1982. *Archaeological Surveys in Bahawalpur*. Karachi, Department of Archaeology and Museums, Government of Pakistan.

POSSEHL, G. L. 1980. *Indus Civilization in Saurashtra*. Delhi, B. R. Publishing Corp.

ROSS, E. J. 1946. A Chalcolithic Site in Northern Baluchistan. *Journal of Near Eastern Studies*, Vol. 5, pp. 291–315.

SHAFFER, J. G. 1978*a*. The Later Prehistoric Periods. In: F. R. Allchin and N. Hammond (eds.), *The Archaeology of Afghanistan from Earliest Times to the Timurid Period*, pp. 71–186. London, Academic Press.

——. 1978*b*. *Prehistoric Baluchistan (with Excavation Report on Said Qala Tepe)*. Delhi, B. R. Publishing Corp.

SHAFFER, J. G. 1981. The Protohistoric Period in the Eastern Punjab: A Preliminary Assessment. *ICnp,* pp. 65–102.

STEIN, A. 1931. An Archaeological Tour in Gedrosia. *MASI,* Vol. 43.

SURAJ BHAN. 1971/72. Siswal: A Pre-Harappan Site on the Drishadvati Valley. *Pt,* Vol. 5, pp. 44–6.

———. 1975. *Excavations at Mitathal (1968) and Other Explorations in the Sutlej-Yamuna Divide.* Kurukshetra, Kurukshetra University.

THAPAR, B. K. 1969. The Pre-Harappan Pottery of Kalibangan: An Appraisal of its Inter-relationship. In: B. P. Sinha (ed.), *Potteries in Ancient India,* pp. 251–6. Patna, Patna University, Department of Ancient History and Archaeology.

———. 1973. New Traits of the Indus Civilization at Kalibangan: An Appraisal. In: N. Hammond (ed.), *SAA,* pp. 85–104. London, Duckworth.

———. 1975. Kalibangan: A Harappan Metropolis Beyond the Indus Valley. *Ex,* Vol. 17, No. 2, pp. 19–32.

WILLEY, G. R.; PHILIPS, P. 1958. *Method and Theory in American Archaeology,* Chicago, University of Chicago Press.

CHAPTER 12

AGRAWAL, D. P.; KUSUMGAR, S. 1974. *Prehistoric Chronology and Radiocarbon Dating in India.* New Delhi, Munshiram Manoharlal.

ALLCHIN, B.; ALLCHIN, R. 1968. *The Birth of Indian Civilization.* Harmondsworth, Penguin.

ANON. 1955. Bara and Salaura, District Ambala. *IAR,* 1954/55, pp. 9–10.

BIBBY, G. 1958. The Ancient Indian Style Seals from Bahrain. *Antiquity,* Vol. 32, pp. 243–6.

BISHT, R. S. 1976a. Transformation of the Harappa Culture in Punjab with Special Reference to the Excavations at Sanghol and Chandigarh. In: U. V. Singh (ed.), *Archaeological Congress and Seminar, 1972,* pp. 16–22. Kurukshetra, Kurukshetra University.

———. 1976b. *Banawali.* Chandigarh, Public Relations Department, Government of Haryana.

———. 1978. Banawali: A New Harappan Site in Haryana. *ME,* Vol. 2, pp. 86–8.

BISHT, R. S.; ASTHANA, S. 1979. Banawali and Some Other Recently Excavated Harappan Sites in India. *SAA 1977,* pp. 223–41.

BOSE, N. K.; GOSH, A.; DATTA, J. M.; GUPTA , P.; DUTTA, P. C.; BASU, A. 1962. *Human Skeletal Remains from Harappa.* Calcutta, Anthropological Survey of India. (Memoir No. 9.)

BRUNSWIG, R. H. 1974. A Comprehensive Bibliography of the Indus Civilization and Related Subjects and Areas. *AP,* Vol. 16, pp. 75–111.

CASAL, J.-M. 1961. *Fouilles de Mundigak.* 2 vols. *MDAFA,* Vol. 17.

———. 1964. *Fouilles d'Amri.* Paris, Commission des Fouilles Archéologiques/Librairie C. Klincksieck. 2 vols.

DALES, G. F. 1962. Harappan Outposts on the Makran Coast. *Antiquity,* Vol. 36, pp. 86–92.

———. 1965. New Investigations at Mohenjo Daro. *Archaeology,* Vol. 18, No. 2, pp. 145–50.

———. 1973. Archaeological and Radiocarbon Chronologies for Protohistoric South Asia. In: N. Hammond (ed.), *SAA,* pp. 157–69. London, Duckworth.

——. 1981. Reflections on Four Years of Excavations at Balakot. *ICnp*, pp. 25–32.

DANI, A. H. 1950. Hariyupiya in the Rigveda. *Varendra Research Society Monograph*, Vol. 8, pp. 17–24.

——. 1970/71. Excavations in the Gomal Valley. *APk*, Vol. 5, pp. 1–177.

——(ed.). 1981. *Indus Civilizations: New Perspectives (ICnp)*. Islamabad.

DESHPANDE, M. N. 1959. Excavation at Daimabad, District Ahmednagar. *IAR*, 1958/59, pp. 15–18.

DIKSHIT, K. N. 1981. Excavation at Hulas, District Saharanpur. *IAR*, 1978/79, pp. 60-1.

DIKSHIT, M. G. 1950. Excavations at Rangpur: 1947. *Bulletin of the Deccan College Research Institute*, Vol. 11, pp. 3–55.

DURRANI, F. A. 1981. Indus Civilization: Evidence West of Indus. *ICnp*, pp. 133–8.

EHRICH, R. W. (ed.). 1965. *Chronologies in Old World Archaeology*. Chicago, University of Chicago Press.

FAIRSERVIS, W. A. 1961. The Harappan Civilization: New Evidence and More Theory. *Novitates*, No. 2055, pp. 1–35.

——. 1975. *The Roots of Ancient India*. 2nd ed. Chicago, University of Chicago Press.

——. 1976. *Excavation at Allahdino. I: Seals and Inscribed Material. Papers of the Allahdino expedition*. New York, American Museum of Natural History.

FRANCFORT, H.-P.; POTTIER, M. H. 1978. Sondage préliminaire sur l'établissement proto-historique harappéen et post-harappéen de Shortugaï (Afghanistan du N.-E.). *AA*, Vol. 34, pp. 29–65.

GADD, C. J. 1933. *Seals of Ancient Indian Style Found at Ur*. London, H. Milford.

GHOSH, A. 1952. The Rajputana Desert – Its Archaeological Aspect. *Bulletin of the National Institute of Sciences of India*, Vol. 1, pp. 37–42.

GORDON, D. H. 1953. *The Prehistoric Background of Indian Culture*. Bombay.

HALIM, M. A. 1972*a*. Excavations at Sarai Khola, Part I. *PA*, Vol. 7, pp. 23–89.

——. 1972*b*. Excavations at Sarai Khola, Part II. *PA*, Vol. 8, pp. 1–112.

JANSEN, M. 1978. City Planning in the Harappa Culture. *Arts and Archaeology Research Papers*, Vol. 14.

——. 1979. Architectural Problems of the Harappan Culture. *SAA 1977*, pp. 405–32.

——. 1980. Public Spaces in the Urban Settlements of the Harappa Culture. *Arts and Archaeology Research Papers*, Vol. 17, pp. 11–19.

——. 1981. Settlement Pattern in the Harappan Culture. *SAA 1979*, pp. 251–69.

JOSHI, J. P. 1972. Exploration in Kutch and Excavation at Surkotada and New Light on Harappan Migration. *Journal of the Oriental Institute*, Vol. 22, No. 1–2, pp. 98–144.

——. 1973. Excavation at Surkotada. In: D. P. Agrawal and A. Ghosh (eds.), *Radio-carbon and Indian Archaeology*, pp. 173–81. Bombay, Tata Institute of Fundamental Research.

——. 1974. Surkotada: A Chronological Assessment. *Pt*, Vol. 7, pp. 34–8.

——. 1978. A Note on the Excavation at Bhagwanpura. *Pt*, Vol. 8, pp. 178–80.

——. 1979. Excavation at Bhagwanpura, District Kurukshetra. *IAR*, 1975/76, pp. 16–17.

——. 1980. Excavation at Manda, District Jammu. *IAR*, 1976/77, pp. 19–21.

JOSHI, J. P.; BALA, M. 1982. Manda, A Harappan Site in Jamnu and Kashmir. In: G. L. Possehl (ed.), *Harappan Civilization: A Contemporary Perspective*, pp. 185–95. Delhi, Oxford/IBH Publishing Co.

KHAN, F. A. 1964. *The Indus Valley and Early Iran*, Karachi, Pakistan Department of Archaeology.

——. 1965. Excavations at Kot-Diji. *PA*, Vol. 2, pp. 11-85.

KING, D. F. 1975. *A Comprehensive Bibliography of Pakistan Archaeology: Paleolithic to Historic Times*. East Lansing, Michigan State University. (South Asian Series, Occasional Paper, 24.)

KOSKENNIEMI, S.; PARPOLA, A. 1973. *Material for the Study of the Indus Script*. Helsinki, Helsinki University.

——. 1979. *Corpus of Texts in the Indus Script*. Helsinki, Helsinki University.

——. 1980. *Documentation and Duplicates of the Texts in the Indus Script*. Helsinki, Helsinki University.

KRAMER, S. N. 1964. The Indus Civilization and Dilmun: The Sumerian Paradise Land. *Ex*, Vol. 6, No. 3, pp. 44–52.

LAL, B. B. 1981. Some Reflections on the Structural Remains at Kalibangan. *ICnp*, pp. 47–54.

LAL, B. B.; THAPAR, B. K. 1967. Excavations at Kalibangan: New Light on the Indus Civilization. *Cultural Forum*, Vol. 9, pp. 78–88.

LAMBERG-KARLOVSKY, C. C. 1972. Trade Mechanism in Indus-Mesopotamian Interrelations. *JAOS*, Vol. 92, No. 2, pp. 222–9.

Leshnik, L. 1968. The Harappan 'Port' at Lothal: Another View. *AA*, Vol. 70, No. 5, pp. 911–22.

MACKAY, E. J. H. 1935. *Early Indus Civilization*. London, Clay & Sons.

——. 1938. *Further Excavations at Mohenjo-Daro*. Delhi, Government of India. 2 vols.

——. 1943. *Chanhu-daro Excavations, 1935–36*. American Oriental Series, Vol. 20. Boston, Museum of Fine Arts.

MAJUMDAR, N. G. 1934. Explorations of Sind. *MASI*, Vol. 48.

MARSHALL, J. 1931. *Mohenjo-Daro and the Indus Civilization*. London, A. Probsthain. 3 vols.

MERIGGI, P. 1934. Zur Indus Schrift. *ZDMG*, Vol. 12, pp. 198–241.

MUGHAL, M. R. 1973. The Present State of Research on the Indus Valley Civilization. In: A. N. Khan (ed.), *International Symposium on Mohenjodaro*, pp. 1–28. Karachi, National Book Trust.

——. 1974. New Evidence of the Early Harappan Culture from Jalilpur, Pakistan. *Archaeology*, Vol. 27, No. 2, pp. 106–13.

——. 1978. The Origin of Indus Civilization. *Sindhological Studies*, Vol. 1, No. 1, pp. 1–10.

——. 1981. New Archaeological Evidence from Bahawalpur. *ICnp*, pp. 33–42.

PANDE, H. C. (ed.). 1969. *Soviet Studies on Harappan Script*. Florida, Field Research Project. (Occasional Paper, 6.)

PANDYA, P. P. 1957. Excavation at Prabhas Patan, District Sorath. *IAR*, 1956/57, pp. 16–17.

——. 1958. Exploration in District Gohilwad, Halar, Jhalawar, Madhya Saurashtra and Sorath. *IAR*, 1957/58, pp. 18–20.

——. 1959. Excavation at Rojdi, District Madhya Saurashtra. *IAR*, 1958/59, pp. 19–20.

PARPOLA, A.; PARPALO, S. 1975. On the Relationship of the Sumerian Toponym Meluhha and Sanskrit Mleccha. *SO*, Vol. 46, pp. 205–38.

PIGGOTT, S. 1950. *Prehistoric India*. Harmondsworth, Penguin.

POSSEHL, G. L. (ed.). 1979*a*. *Ancient Cities of the Indus*. New Delhi, Vikas Publishing House.

——. 1979*b*. Pastoral Nomadism in the Indus Civilization: A Hypothesis. *SAA 1977*, pp. 537–51.

RAIKES, R. L. 1968. Kalibangan: Death from Natural Causes. *Antiquity*, Vol. 42, pp. 286–91.

RAIKES, R. L.; DYSON, R. H. 1961. The Prehistoric Climate of Baluchistan and the Indus Valley. *AA*, Vol. 63, pp. 265–81.

RAMASWAMY, C. 1968. Monsoon Over the Indus Valley During the Harappan Period. *Nature*, Vol. 217, No. 5129, pp. 628–9.

RAO, S. R. 1962/63. Excavations at Rangpur and Other Explorations in Gujarat. *AIn*, Vol. 18–19, pp. 5–207.

——. 1963. A 'Persian Gulf' Seal from Lothal. *Antiquity*, Vol. 37, pp. 96–9.

——. 1973. *Lothal and the Indus Civilization.* New York.

——. 1978a. Bronzes from the Indus Valley. *Illustrated London News*, March, pp. 62–3.

——. 1978b. Late Harappan Daimabad. *Illustrated London News*, April, pp. 74–5.

——. 1979. Lothal. A Harappan Port Town. *MASI*, Vol. 78.

RATNAGAR, S. 1981. *Encounters. The Westerly Trade of the Harappan Civilization.* Delhi, Oxford University Press.

ROSS, A. S. C. 1938. The Numeral Signs of the Mohenjo-Daro Script. *MASI*, Vol. 57.

SALI, S. A. 1981. Excavation at Daimabad, District Ahmednagar. *IAR*, 1978/79, pp. 46–52.

SANKALIA, H. D. 1974. *Prehistory and Protohistory of India and Pakistan.* 2nd ed. Poona, Deccan College, Postgraduate and Research Institute.

SANKALIA, H. D.; DEO, S. B. 1979. Excavation at Prabhas Patan, District Junagadh. *IAR*, 1975/76, p. 13.

SHARMA, Y. D. 1956. Past Patterns in Living as Unfolded by Excavations at Rupar. *Lalit Kala*, Vol. 1–2, pp. 121–9.

——. 1976. Transformation of the Harappan Culture in the Punjab. In: Udai Vir Singh (ed.), *Archaelogical Congress and Seminar*, 1972, pp. 5–15. Kurukshetra.

SINGH, G. 1971. The Indus Valley Culture. *Archaeology and Physical Anthropology in Oceania*, Vol. 6, No. 2, pp. 177–89.

SOUNDARA RAJAN, K. V. 1967. Excavation at Desalpur (Gunthli), District Kutch. *IAR*, 1963/64, pp. 10–12.

SURAJ BHAN. 1975. *Excavation at Mitathal (1968) and Other Explorations in the Sutlej-Yamuna Divide.* Kurukshetra, Kurukshetra University.

——. 1976. Transformation of Harappa Culture in Haryana. In: Udai Vir Singh (ed.), *Archaeological Congress and Seminar, 1972*, pp. 23–30. Kurukshetra, Kurukshetra University.

THAPAR, B. K. 1970. The Concept of the Citadel in the Indus Civilization. Paper read at the thirtieth International Congress of Human Sciences in Asia and North Africa, Mexico City.

——. 1973a. New Traits of the Indus Civilization at Kalibangan: An Appraisal. In: N. Hammond (ed.), *SAA*, pp. 85–104. London, Duckworth.

——. 1973b. Synthesis of the Multiple Data as Obtained from Kalibangan. In: D. P. Agrawal and A. Gosh (eds.), *Radiocarbon and Indian Archaeology*, pp. 264–71. Bombay, Tata Institute of Fundamental Research.

——. 1975. Kalibangan: A Harappan Metropolis beyond the Indus Valley. *Ex*, Vol. 17, No. 2, pp. 19–32.

——. 1978. Editorial. *Pt*, Vol. 8, pp. 1–2.

——. 1981. The Mosaic of the Indus Civilization beyond the Indus Valley. *ICnp*, pp. 55–64.

——. 1982. The Harappan Civilization: Some Reflections on its Environments and

Resources and their Exploitation. In: G. L. Possehl (ed.), *Harappan Civilization. A Contemporary Perspective*, pp. 3–13. Delhi, Oxford/IBH Publishing Co.

THAPAR, B. K. 1984. Six Decades of Indus Studies. In: B. B. Lal and S. P. Gupta (eds.), *Frontiers of the Indus Civilization. Sir Mortimer Wheeler Commemoration Volume*, pp. 1–25. Delhi, Books and Books, for the Indian Archaeological Society.

THAPAR, R. 1975. A Possible Identification of Meluhha, Dilmun and Makan. *JESHO*, Vol. 18, Part 1, pp. 1–42.

VATS, M. S. 1937. Trial Excavations at Rangpur, Limbdi State, Kathiawas. *Annual Report of the Archaeological Survey of India, 1934–35*, pp. 34–8.

——. 1940. *Excavations at Harappa*. Delhi, Government of India. 2 vols.

WHEELER, R. E. M. 1947. Harappa 1946: The Defences and Cemetery R-37. *AIn*, Vol. 3, pp. 58–130.

——. 1968. *The Indus Civilization*. 3rd ed. Cambridge, Cambridge University Press.

ZIDE, A. R. K. 1970. A Brief Survey of Work to Date on the Indus Valley Script. *Journal of Tamil Studies*, Vol. 2, pp. 1–12.

CHAPTER 13

AN ZHIMIN. 1956. Ancient Cultures in Gansu and Some Problems Concerned. *Kaogu Tonxuan*, No. 6.

——. 1957. Painted Pottery from Tangwangchuan in Dongxiang Regions. *Kaogu Xuebao*, No. 2.

——. 1959. The Neolithic Site at Sibatan in Shandan County. *Kaogu Xuebao*, No. 3.

——. 1980. Two Grotesque Bronze Weapons of the Western Zhou: Brief Discussions of the Relationships Between the Shang – Zhou Civilizations. *Wenwu Jikan*, No. 2.

——. 1981. China's Early Copper and Bronze Artefacts. *Kaogu Xuebao*, No. 3.

ANDERSON, J. G. 1943. Researches into the Prehistory of the Chinese. *Bulletin of the Museum of Far Eastern Antiquities*.

ARCHAEOLOGICAL TEAM OF THE GANSU MUSEUM. 1981. Excavation Report of the Tomb Finds of the Xindian (Hsintian) Culture at Yatou Dongxiang County, Gansu Province. *Wenwu*, No. 4, pp. 16–20.

ARCHAEOLOGICAL TEAM OF THE MUSEUM OF XINJIANG UIGHUR AUTONOMOUS REGION. 1977. Reconnaissance of Neolithic Sites of Aketala in Shufu County, Xinjiang. *Kaogu*, No. 2.

ARCHAEOMETALLURGY OF BEIJING INSTITUTE OF IRON AND STEEL TECHNOLOGY. 1981. A Preliminary Study of Early Chinese Copper and Bronze Artefacts. *Kaogu Xuebao*, No. 3.

BERGMAN, F. 1939. *Archaeological Researches in Sinkiang*. Stockholm, Bokfölage Aktiebolaget Thule.

CPAM OF QINGHAI, QINGHAI PROVINCE AND THE QINGHAI ARCHAEOLOGICAL TEAM, IOA ACADEMIA SINICA. 1963. Reconnaissance and Trial Diggings at Talitaliha, Nuomuhong, in Tula, Qinghai. *Kaogu Xuebao*, No. 1.

EDITORIAL BOARD OF WENWU. 1979. *Thirty Years of Archaeological Work*.

GANSU PROVINCIAL MUSEUM. 1981. Cultural Relics from Gansu. *Kaogu Xuebao*, No. 3.

HUANG WENBI. 1932. *Collection of Potsherds from Gaoshang*.

LI YUCHUN. 1959. Painted Pottery Discovered in Xinjiang. *Kaogu*, No. 3.

MUSEUM OF XINJIANG UIGHUR AUTONOMOUS REGION. 1975. *Archaeological Finds Unearthed in Xinjiang.*

PEI WENCHONG. 1948. Archaeological Reconnaissance in Kansu Corridor and in Kokonor Region in Northwest China. *Contributions from the Institute of Geology*, No. 8.

QINGHAI ARCHAEOLOGICAL TEAM. 1980. *Painted Pottery from Qinghai.*

CHAPTER 14

ASKAROV, A. 1973. *Sapalli tepa.* Tashkent.

——. 1977. *Drevnezemledel'cheskaya kul'tura êpokhi bronzî yuga Uzbekistana.* Tashkent.

——. 1981. Southern Uzbekistan in the Second Millennium B.C. In: Philip Kohl (ed.), *The Bronze Age Civilization of Central Asia: Recent Soviet Discoveries*, pp. 256–72. New York, M. E. Sharp.

BASAGLIA, P. (ed.). 1977. *La città brucilata del deserto salato.* Venice, Enzzo Editore.

BISCIONE, R. 1981. Centre and Periphery in Late Protohistoric Turan: The Settlement Pattern. *SAA 1979*, pp. 203–13.

CASAL, J.-M. 1961. *Fouilles de Mundigak*, 2 Vols. *MDAFA*, Vol. 17.

DALES, G. F. 1966. The Decline of the Harappans. *SAm*, Vol. 214, No. 5, pp. 92–100.

DANI, A. H. 1981. The Indus Civilization: New Perspectives. *ICnp*, pp. 3–14.

GANSU ARCHAEOLOGICAL TEAM OF IASS. 1975. Excavation of Chichia Culture Cemeteries at Chinweichis in Yongjing, Gansu. *Kaogu Xuebao*, No. 2.

GANSU PROVINCIAL MUSEUM. 1960. Excavation of a Neolithic Site at Huangniangliangtai in Wuwei County, Gansu Province. *Kaogu Xuebao*, No. 2, pp. 53–70. (English summary, pp. 70–1.)

——. 1978. Excavations of the Fourth Season (1975) at the Site of Huangniangniangtai in Wuwei County. *Kaogu Xuebao*, No. 4, pp. 421–47. (English summary, p. 448.)

GENING, V. F. 1977. Mogil'nik Sintashta i problemî rannikh indoiranskikh plemën. *SA*, No. 4, pp. 53–73.

GRYAZNOV, M. P. 1969. *Southern Siberia.* Geneva/Paris/Munich, Nagel Publishers.

ITINA, M. A. 1977. *Istoriya stepnîkh plemën yuzhnogo Prialral'ya (vtoroye nachalo pervogo tîsyacheletiya do n.ê).* Trudî KhAEE, Vol. 13.

JOSHI, J. P. 1978a. Interlocking of Late Harappan Culture and Painted Grey Ware Culture in the Light of Recent Excavations. *ME*, Vol. 2, pp. 98–101.

——. 1978b. A Note on the Excavations at Bhagwanpura. *Pt*, Vol. 8, pp. 178–80.

Istoriya Kazakhskoy SSR I. 1977. Alma-Ata.

KHLOPIN, I. N. 1973. Denkmäler der Bronzezeit im Tal des Flusses Sumbar (Südturkmenien). *IrAn*, Vol. 10.

KUZ'MINA, E. E.; SMIRNOV, K. F. 1977. Proiskhozhdeniye indoirantsev v svete noveyshîkh arkheologicheskikh dannîkh. *Mezhdunarodnîy simpozium po etnicheskim problemam drevney istorii Tsentral'noy Azii, 'Tezisî dokladov sovetskikh uchënikh'*, pp. 19–22. Moscow.

LAMBRICK, H. T. 1967. The Indus Flood Plain and the 'Indus' Civilization. *GJ*, Vol. 133, Pt. 4, pp. 483–95.

MANDEL'SHTAM, A. M. 1966. Pamyatniki stepnogo kruga êpokhi bronzî na yuge Sredney Azii. In: V. M. Masson (ed.), *Sredneyaya Aziya v êpokhu kamnya i bronzî*, pp. 239–49. Moscow/Leningrad.

MASIMOV, I. S. 1981a. The Study of Bronze Age Sites in the Lower Murgab. In: P. Kohl (ed.), *The Bronze Age Civilization of Central Asia: Recent Soviet Discoveries*, pp. 194–220. New York, M. E. Sharp.

——. 1981*b*. Novîye nakhodki pechatey êpokhi bronzî s nizovîy Murgaba. *SA*, No. 2, pp. 132–50.

MASSON, V. M. 1959. Drevnezemledel'cheskaya kul'tura Margianî. *MIA*, No. 73.

MUGHAL, M. R. 1981. New Archaeological Evidence from Bahawalpur. *ICnp*, pp. 33–42.

RAIKES, R. L. 1964. The End of the Ancient Cities of Indus. *AA*, Vol. 66, No. 2, pp. 284–99.

SARIANIDI, V. I. 1981*a*. Margiana in the Bronze Age. In: P. Kohl (ed.), *The Bronze Age Civilization of Central Asia: Recent Soviet Discoveries*, pp. 165–93. New York, M. E. Sharp.

——. 1981*b*. Seal-amulets of the Murgab Style. In: P. Kohl (ed.), *The Bronze Age Civilization of Central Asia: Recent Soviet Discoveries*, pp. 221–55. New York, M. E. Sharp.

SINGH, S. 1971. The Indus Valley Culture (Palaeobotanical Study of Climatic Changes). *Pt*, Vol. 4, pp. 68–76.

TEILHARD DE CHARDIN, P.; YOUNG, C. C. 1932. On Some Neolithic (and Possibly Palaeolithic) Finds in Mongolia, Sinkiang and West China. *BGSCh*, Vol. 12, No. 1.

VINOGRADOV, A. V. 1981. Drevniye okhotniki i rîbolovî sredneaziatskogo mezhdurechya. *Trudî YuTAKE*, Vol. 13.

WHEELER, R. F. M. 1959. *Early India and Pakistan to Ashoka*. New York, Praeger.

CHAPTER 15

ANTONOVA, K.; BONGARD-LEVIN, G.; KOTOVSKY, G. 1979. *A History of India*. Moscow.

ASIMOV, M. S. 1978. Ethnic History of Central Asia in the Second Millennium B.C. *JCA*, Vol. 1, pp. 1–11.

ASIMOV, M. S.; GAFUROV, B. G.; ABAEV, V. I.; KUZMINA, Y. Y.; ALIEV, I.; POGREBOVA, M. N.; GHIRSHMAN, R.; LITVINSKY, B. A.; ASKAROV, A. A.; SARIANIDI, V. I.; GRANTOVSKIY, E. A.; LAL, B. B.; THAPAR, B. K.; GAUR, R. C.; ALLCHIN, F. R. 1981. *Ethnic Problems of the History of Central Asia in the Early Period (Second Millennium B.C.)*. Moscow.

BERGER, H. 1985. A Survey of Burushaski Studies. *JCA*, Vol. 8, pp. 33–7.

BIRNBAUM, H.; PUHVEL, J. (eds.). 1966. *Ancient Indo-European Dialects*. Berkeley, Calif., University of California Press.

BLEICHSTEINER, R. 1930. Die Werschikisch-burischkische Sprache im Pamirgebiet und ihre Stellung zu den Japhetitensprachen des Kaukasus. *WKBL*, Vol. 1, pp. 289–331.

BÖKÖNYI, S. 1974. *History of the Domestic Mammals in Central and Eastern Europe*. Budapest, Akadémiai Kiadó.

——. 1980*a*. The Importance of Horse Domestication in Economy and Transport. In: P. Sörbon (ed.), *Transport Technology and Social Change*, pp. 15–21. Stockholm, Tekniska Museet. (Tekniska Museet Symposia, 2.)

——. 1980*b*. La domestication du cheval. *La recherche*, Vol. 116, pp. 919–26.

BOSCH-GIMPERA, P. 1961. *Les Indo-Européens. Problèmes archéologiques*. Paris, Payot.

BRANDENSTEIN, W. 1936. Die Lebensformen der Indogermanen. *WBKL*, Vol. 4, pp. 231–77.

BURROW, T. 1973. The Proto-Indoaryans. *JRAS*, pp. 123–40.

CARDONA, G.; HOENIGSWALD, H. M.; SENN, A. (eds.). 1970. *Indo-European and Indo-*

Europeans. Papers Presented at the Third Indo-European Conference at the University of Pennsylvania. Philadelphia, University of Pennsylvania Press.

CHATTERJI, S. K. 1960. *Indo-Ayran and Hindi.* 2nd ed. Calcutta, Firma K. L. Mukhopadhyay.

DAFFINA, P. 1982. *Il nomadismo centroasiatico,* Vol. 1. Rome, Istituto di Studi dell'India e dell'Asia Orientale, Università di Roma/Il Bagatto.

D'YAKONOV, I. M. 1982. O prarodine indo-evropeyskikh dialektov. *VDI,* Vol. 3, No. 4, pp. 3–30.

DANI, A. H. 1978*a*. Movements of Peoples in Inner Asia in the Pre-Achaemenid Period. *JCA,* Vol. 1, pp. 12–20.

——. 1978*b*. Gandhara Grave Culture and the Aryan Problem. *JCA,* Vol. 1, pp. 42–55.

DEBETS, G. F. 1947. Sel'kupî. Antropologicheskiy ocherk. *Trudî Instituta Etnografii,* Vol. 2, pp. 103–45.

DESHPANDE, M. M.; HOOK, P. E. (eds.). 1979. *Aryan and Non-Aryan in India.* Ann Arbor, Center for South and Southeast Asian Studies, University of Michigan. (Michigan Papers on South and Southeast Asia, 14.)

DUL'ZON, A. P. 1960. *Etnitcheskiy sostav drevnego naseleniya Zapadnoy Sibiri po dannîm toponimiki.*

——. 1968. *Ketskiy yazîk.* Tomsk.

EMENEAU, M. B. 1966. The Dialects of Old Indo-Aryan. In: H. Birnbaum and J. Puhvel (eds.), *Ancient Indo-European Dialects,* pp. 123–38. Berkeley, Calif., University of California Press.

EHRICH, R. W. 1970. Some Indo-European Speaking Groups of the Middle Danube and the Balkans: Their Boundaries as Related to Cultural Geography through Times. In: G. Cardona, H. M. Hoenigswald and A. Senn (eds.) *Indo-European and Indo-Europeans. Papers Presented at the Third Indo-European Conference at the University of Pennsylania,* pp. 217–51. Philadelphia, University of Pennsylvania Press.

FRYE, R. N. 1984. *The History of Ancient Iran,* pp. 45–64. Munich, C. H. Beck'sche Verlagsbuchhandlung.

GAFUROV, B. G.; LITVINSKY, B. A. 1963. *Istoriya tadzhikskogo naroda,* Vol. 1. Moscow.

GAMKRELIDZE, T. V.; IVANOV, V. V. 1980. *Drevnyaya Perednyaya Aziya i indoevropeyskaya problema. VDI,* Vol. 3, pp. 3–27.

——. 1981. Migratsii plemën – nositeley indo-evropeyskikh dialektov – s pervonachal'noy territorii rasseleniya na Blijnem vostoke v istoricheskiye mesta ikh obitaniya Evrazii. *VDI,* Vol. 2, pp. 11–33.

——. 1984. K probleme prarodini nositeley rodstvennîkh dialektov i metodam eë ustanovleniya. *VDI,* Vol. 2, pp. 107–22.

GEIGER, W. 1882. *Ostiranische Kultur im Altertum.* Erlangen, Verlag von Andreas Deichert.

GEORGIEV, V. I. 1966. *Introduzione alla storia delle lingue indoeuropee.* Rome.

GHIRSHMAN, R. 1977. *L'Iran et la migration des Indo-Aryens et des Iraniens.* Leiden, E. J. Brill.

GIMBUTAS, M. 1963. The Indoeuropeans: Archaeological Problems. *AAn,* Vol. 65, pp. 815–36.

——. 1970. Proto-Indo-European Culture: The Kurgan Culture during the Fifth, Fourth, and Third Millennia B.C.. In: G. Cardona, H. M. Hoenigswald and A. Senn (eds.), *Indo-European and Indo-Europeans. Papers Presented at the Third Indo-European Conference at the University of Pennsylvania,* pp. 155–97. Philadelphia, University of Pennsylvania Press.

GOODENOUGH, W. H. 1970. The Evolution of Pastoralism and Indo-European Origins.In: G. Cardona, H. M. Hoenigswald and A. Senn (eds.), *Indo-European and Indo-Europeans. Papers Presented at the Third Indo-European Conference at the University of Pennsylvania*, pp. 253–65. Philadelphia, University of Pennsylvania Press.

GRANTOVSKIY, E. A. 1970. *Rannyaya istoriya iranskikh plemën Peredney Azii*. Moscow.

HARMATTA, J. 1972. Az indoeurópai népek régi településterületei és vándorlásai [Early Homes and Migrations of Indo-European Peoples]. *Magyar Tudományos Akadémia I osztályának Közleményei*, Vol. 27, pp. 309–24.

——. 1977. Irániak és finnugorok, irániak és magyarok [Iranians and Finno-Ugrians, Iranians and Hungarians]. *Magyar östörténeti tanulmányok*, pp. 167–82.

——. 1978. Migrations of the Indo-Iranian Tribes. *Acta Ant. Hung.*, Vol. 20, pp. 185–94.

HAUSCHILD. 1962. Über die frühesten Arier im Alten Orient. *Berichte über die Verhandlungen der sächsischen Akademie der Wissenschaft zu Leipzig, Phil.-hist. Kl.*, Vol. 106. Berlin.

HEINE-GELDERN, R. 1964. Das Dravidaproblem. *ÖAW*, Vol. 101, pp. 187–201.

HENCKEN, H. 1955. Indo-European Languages and Archaeology. *AA*, Vol. 57, No. 6, Pt. 3. Memoir No. 84.

HERZFELD, E. 1968. *The Persian Empire. Studies in Geography and Ethnography of the Ancient Near East*. Wiesbaden, Franz Steiner Verlag.

JOKI, A. J. 1952. Die Lehnwörter des Sajansamojedischen. *MSFOu*, Vol. 103.

——. 1973. Uralier und Indogermanen. *MSFOu*, Vol. 151.

KAMMENHUBER, A. 1968. *Die Arier im Vorderen Orient*. Heidelberg.

KORENCHY, E. 1972. *Iranische Lehnwörter in den obugrischen Sprachen*. Budapest, Akadémiai Kiadó.

KUZ'MINA, E. E.; SMIRNOV, K. F. 1977. Proiskhozhdeniye indoirantsev v svete noveyshîkh arkheologicheskikh dannîkh. *Mezhdunarodnîy simpozium po etnicheskim problemam drevney istorii Tsentral'noy Azii, Tezisî dokladov*, pp. 19–22. Moscow.

LELEKOV, L. A. 1982. K noveyshemu resheniyu indoevropeyskoy problemî. *VDI*, Vol. 3, pp. 31–57.

McALPIN, D. W. 1979. Linguistic Prehistory: The Dravidian Situation. In: M. M. Deshpande and P. E. Hook (eds.), *Aryan and Non-Aryan in India*, pp. 176–89. Ann Arbor, Center for South and Southeast Asian Studies, University of Michigan.

MARQUART, J. 1896, 1905. *Untersuchungen zur Geschichte von Eran*. Göttingen, Dietrich'sche Verlagsbuchhandlung.

MASSON, V. M. 1981. Altyn-Tepe. *Trudî YuTAKE*, Vol. 18.

MAYERHOFER, M. 1966. *Die Indo-Arier im Alten Vorderasien*. Wiesbaden.

——. 1974. *Die Arier im Vorderen Orient – Ein Mythos?* Vienna.

——. 1983. Lassen sich Vorstufen des Uriranischen nachweisen? *ÖAW*, Vol. 120, pp. 249–55.

MORGENSTIERNE, G. 1973. Die Stellung der Kafirsprachen. *Irano-Dardica*, pp. 326–43. Wiesbaden, Dr Ludwig Reichert Verlag.

ORANSKY, I. M. 1960. *Vvedenie v iranskuyu filologiyu*. Moscow.

P'YANKOV, I. V. 1979. K voprosu o putyakh proniknoveniya iranoyazîchnîkh plemën v Perednyuyu Aziyu. *PSB*, Vol. 3, pp. 193–207.

PORZIS, W. 1954. *Die Gliederung des Indogermanischen Sprachgebiets*. Heidelberg.

SMIRNOV, K. F.; KUZ'MINA, E. E. 1977. *Proiskhozhdeniye indoirantsev v svete noveishîkh arkheologicheskikh otkrîtiy*. Moscow.

SOUTHWORTH, F. C. 1979. Lexical Evidence for Early Contacts between Indo-Aryan and

Dravidian. In: M. M. Deshpande and P. E. Hook (eds.), *Aryan and Non-Aryan in India*, pp. 192–233. Ann Arbor, Center for South and Southeast Asian Studies, Unversity of Michigan.

SZEMERENYI, O. 1964. Structuralism and Substratum. Indo-Europeans and Aryans in the Ancient Near East. *Lingua*, Vol. 13, pp. 1–29.

THOMAS, H. L. 1970. New Evidence for Dating the Indo-European Dispersal in Europe. In: G. Cardona, H. M. Hoenigswald and A. Senn (eds.), *Indo-European and Indo-Europeans. Papers Presented at the Third Indo-European Conference at the University of Pennsylvania*, pp. 199–215. Philadelphia, University of Pennsylvania Press.

TRUBACHEV, O. N. 1967. Iz slavyano-iranskikh leksicheskikh otnosheniy. *Etimologiya 1965*, pp. 3–81. Moscow.

TYLER, S. A. 1968. Dravidian and Uralian: The Lexical Evidence. *Language*, Vol. 44, pp. 798–812.

WIESNER, J. 1939. Fahren und Reiten in Alteuropa und im Alten Orient. *Der Alte Orient* (Leipzig), Vol. 38, Parts 2–4.

ZIMMER, H. 1879. *Altindisches Leben. Die Kultur der vedischen Arier*. Berlin.

CHAPTER 16

ABDULLAEV, B. N. 1979. Mogil'nik Dzharkutan. *IMKUz*, No. 15.

——. 1980. *Kul'tura drevnezemledel'cheskikh plemën êpokhi pozdney bronzî Severnoy Baktrii (po materialam mogil'nika Dzharkutan)*. Novosibirsk.

——. 1981. Novîye dannîye o kul'ture Sapalli. *IMKUz*, No. 16.

AMIET, P. 1977. Bactriane proto-historique. *Syria*, Vol. 14, No. 1–2, pp. 89–121.

——. 1978. Antiquités de Bactriane. *La revue du Louvre et des Musées de France*, Vol. 28.

ANTONINI, C. S. 1973. More about Swat and Central Asia. *EW*, Vol. 23, No. 3/4, pp. 235–44.

ANTONOVA, E. V.; VINOGRADOVA, N. M. 1979. O letnikh i osennikh razvedkakh v Rergarskom rayone v 1974. *ART*, No. 14.

ASKAROV, A. 1973. *Sapallitepa*. Tashkent.

——. 1977. *Drevnezemledel'cheskaya kul'tura êpokhi bronzî yuga Uzbekistana*. Tashkent.

BELYAEVA, T. V.; KHAKIMOV, Z. A. 1973. Drevnebaktriyskiye pamyatniki Mirshade. *Iz istorii antichnoy kul'turî Uzbekistana*. Tashkent.

BURROW, T. 1973. The Proto-Indoaryans. *JRAS*, No. 2, pp. 123–40.

FRANCFORT, H.-P. 1981. The Late Periods of Shortugai and the Problem of the Bishkent Culture (Middle and Late Bronze Age in Bactria). *SAA 1977*, pp. 191–202.

FRANCFORT, H.-P.; POTTIER, M. H. 1978. Sondage préliminaire sur l'établissement proto-historique harappéen et post-harappéen de Shortugaï (Afghanistan du N.-E.). *AA*, Vol. 34, pp. 29–65.

KHODZHAYEV, T. K. 1981. *Paleoantropologia Sredney Azii i êtnogeneticheskiye problemî*. Moscow.

KHODZHAYEV, T. K.; KHALILOV, K. 1978. Cherepa êpokhi bronzî iz mogil'nikov Dzharkutan i Bustan (raskopki 1975 g.). *IMKUz*, No. 13.

KIYATKINA, T. P. 1976. *Materialî paleoantropologii Tajikistana*. Dushanbe.

KUZ'MINA, E. E. 1972*a*. Kul'tura Svata i eë svyazi s Severnoy Baktriey. *KSIA*, Vol. 32.

——. 1972*b*. K voprosu o formirovanii kul'turî Severnoy Baktrii ('Baktriyskiy miraj' i arkheologicheskaya deystvitel'nost'). *VDI*, Vol. 1. (English translation in *EW*, Vol. 26, 1976).

LITVINSKY, B. A. 1952. Namazga-tepe po dannîm raskopok 1949–1950. *SE*, No. 4.

——. 1964. Tajikistan i India (primerî drevnikh svyazey i kontaktov). *India v drevnosti*. Moscow.

——. 1967. Arkheologicheskiye otkrîtiya v Tajikistane za godî sovetskoy vlasti i nekotorîye problemî drevney istorii Sredney Azii. *VDI*, Vol. 4.

——. 1973. Arkheologicheskiye rabotî v Tajikistane v 1962–1977. *ART*, Vol. 10, pp. 5–41.

——. 1981. Problemî etnicheskoy istorii Sredney Azii vo II tîsyacheletii do n.ê. *Etnicheskiye problemî istorii Tsentral'noy Azii v drevnosti (II tîsyacheletiye do n.ê)*. Moscow. (English translation in *JCA*, Vol. 4, 1981.)

LITVINSKY, B. A.; ZEIMAL, T. I.; MEDVEDSKAYA, I. N. 1977. Otchët o rabotakh yuzhno-Tajikistanskoy arhkeologicheskoy êkspeditsii v 1973 g. *ART*, Vol. 13.

MANDEL'SHTAM, A. M. 1966. Pamyatniki 'stepnogo' kruga êpokhi bronzî na yuge Sredney Azii. *Srednyaya Aziya v êpokhu kamnya i bronzî*, Moscow/Leningrad.

——. 1968. Pamyatniki êpokhi bronzî v yuzhnom Tajikistane. *MIA*, No. 145.

MASIMOV, I. S. 1976. Material'naya kul'tura yuzhnoy Turkmenii v period razvitoy i pozdney bronzî. *Pervobîtnîy Turkmenistan*. Ashkhabad.

MASSON, V. M. 1959. Drevnezemledel'cheskaya kul'tura Margianî. *MIA*, Vol. 73.

P'YANKOVA, L. T. 1974. Mogil'nik êpokhi bronzî Tigrovaya Balka. *SA*, No. 3.

——. 1979. Otchët o rabote Nureskogo arkheologicheskogo otryada. *ART*, Vol. 14.

——. 1981. South-western Tajikistan in the Bronze Age. *IB*, No. 1, pp. 35–46.

SARIANIDI, V. I. 1976. Issledovaniye pamyatnikov Dashlinskogo oazisa. *Drevnyaya Baktriya*. Moscow.

——. 1977. *Drevniye zemledel'tsî Afghanistana*. Moscow.

——. 1982. Novîy tsentr drevnevostochnogo iskusstva. *Arkheologiya starogo i novogo sveta*. Moscow.

STACUL, G. 1979. The Black-burnished Ware Period in the Swat Valley (*c.* 1700–1500 B.C.). *SAA 1977*, pp. 661–73.

TUCCI, G. 1977. On Swat. The Dards and Connected Problems. *EW*, Vol. 27, pp. 9–103.

CHAPTER 17

ALLCHIN, F. R. 1982. How Old is the City of Taxila? *Antiquity*, Vol. 56, pp. 8–14.

ANTONINI, C. S. 1964. Preliminary Notes on the Excavation of the Necropolises Found in Western Pakistan. *EW*, Vol. 14, pp. 13–26.

ANTONINI, C. S.; STACUL, G. 1972. The Protohistoric Graveyards of Swat. *IsMeo.RM*.

BRENTJES, B. 1977. On the Petroglyphs of Gogdara I in Swat. Appendix II. *EW*, Vol. 27, pp. 92–3.

CHEN TE-K'UN. 1960. *Archaeology in China*. Vol. II: *Shang China*. Cambridge, Heffer & Sons.

DANI, A. H. 1950. Hariyupiya in the Rigveda. *Varendra Research Society Monograph*, Vol. 8, pp. 17–24.

——. 1955/56. Shaikan Dheri Excavation (1963 and 1964 Seasons). *APk*, Vol. 2, pp. 17–214.

——. 1965/66. Excavations at Charsada. *APk*, Vol. 2.

——. 1967. Timargarha and Gandhara Grave Culture. *APk*, Vol. 3.

——. 1968. Gandhara Grave Complex in West Pakistan. *APk*, Vol. 9, pp. 99–110.

———. 1970/71. Excavations in the Gomal Valley. *APk*, Vol. 5, pp. 1–177. (Special number.)

———. 1978. Gandhara Grave Culture and the Aryan Problem. *JCA*, Vol. 1, pp. 42–55.

———. 1980. North-west Frontier Burial Rites in their Wider Archaeological Setting. In: H. H. E. Loofs-Wissowa (ed.), *The Diffusion of Material Culture*, pp. 121–50. Honolulu, Social Sciences Research Institute, University of Hawaii at Manoa.

DANI, A. H.; DURRANI, F. A. 1966. A New Grave Complex in West Pakistan. *AP*, Vol. 8, pp. 164–5.

FRYE, R. N. 1963. *The Heritage of Persia*. New York, World Publishing Co.

HALIM, M. A. 1972. Excavations at Sarai-Khola, Part I. *PA*, Vol. 7, pp. 23–89.

JARRIGE, J.-F.; SANTONI, M. 1979. *Fouilles de Pirak*. Paris, Diffusion de Boccard.

JETTMAR, K. 1967. An Iron Cheek-piece of a Snaffle Found at Timargarha. *APk*, Vol. 3, pp. 203–9.

KHAN, G. M. 1979. Excavations at Zarif Karuna. *PA*, Vol. 9, pp. 1–94.

———. 1983. Hathial Excavation. *JCA*, Vol. 6, No. 2, pp. 35–44.

MACKAY, E. J. H. 1943. *Chanhu-daro Excavations, 1935–6*. Boston, Museum of Fine Arts. (American Oriental Series, 20.)

MAJUMDAR, N. G. 1934. Explorations in Sind. *MASI*, Vol. 48.

MALLOWAN, M. E. L. 1947. Excavations at Brak and Chagar Bazar. *Iraq*, Vol. 9.

MARSHALL, J. 1951. *Taxila, An Illustrated Account of Archaeological Excavations Carried out at Taxila under the Orders of the Government of India between the years 1913 and 1934*. Cambridge, Cambridge University Press.

MUGHAL, M. R. 1981. New Archaeological Evidence from Bahawalpur. *ICnp*, pp. 33–42.

PIGGOTT, S. 1950. *Prehistoric India*. Harmondsworth, Penguin.

SALVATORI, S. 1975. Analysis of the Association of Types in the Protohistoric Graveyards of the Swat Valley (Loebanr I, Katelai I, Butka II). *EW*, Vol. 25, pp. 333–51.

SANKALIA, H. D. 1974. *Prehistory and Protohistory of India and Pakistan*. 2nd ed. Poona, Deccan College, Postgraduate and Research Institute.

SCHMIDT, E. F. 1937. *Excavations at Tepe Hissar, Damghan*. Philadelphia, University of Pennsylvania Press.

STACUL, G. 1966. Notes on the Discovery of a Necropolis near Kherai in the Gorband Valley (Swat, West Pakistan). *EW*, Vol. 16, pp. 261–74.

———. 1967*a*. Discovery of Four Pre-Buddhist Cemeteries near Pacha in Buner (Swat, West Pakistan). *EW*, Vol. 17, pp. 220–32.

———. 1976*b*. Excavations in a Rock Shelter near Ghaligai (Swat, West Pakistan). A Preliminary Report. *EW*, Vol. 17, pp. 185–219.

———. 1969*a*. Discovery of Protohistoric Cemeteries in the Chitral Valley (West Pakistan). *EW*, Vol. 19, pp. 92–9.

———. 1969*b*. Excavations near Ghaligai (1968) and Chronological Sequence of Protohistorical Cultures in the Swat Valley. *EW*, Vol. 19, pp. 44–91.

———. 1970. An Archaeological Survey near Kalam (Swat Kohistan). *EW*, Vol. 20, pp. 87–91.

———. 1975. The Fractional Burial Custom in the Swat Valley and Some Connected Problems. *EW*, Vol. 25, pp. 323–32.

———. 1976. Excavation at Loebanr III (Swat, Pakistan). *EW*, Vol. 26, pp. 13–30.

———. 1977. Dwelling and Storage Pits at Loebanr III (Swat, Pakistan). 1976 Excavation Report. *EW*, Vol. 27, pp. 227–53.

STACUL, G. 1978. Excavation at Bir-kot-ghundai (Swat, Pakistan). *EW*, Vol. 28, pp. 137–50.

——. 1979. The Black-burnished Ware Period in the Swat Valley (*c.* 1700–1500 B.C.). *SAA 1977*, pp. 661–73.

STACUL, G.; TUSA, S. 1975. Report on the Excavations at Aligrama (Swat, Pakistan) 1966, 1972. *EW*, Vol. 25, pp. 291–321.

——. 1977. Report on the Excavations at Aligrama (Swat, Pakistan) 1974. *EW*, Vol. 27, pp. 151–205.

TUCCI, G. 1963. The Tombs of Asvakayana-Assakenoi. *EW*, Vol. 13, pp. 27–8.

——. 1977. On Swat. The Dards and Connected Problems. *EW*, Vol. 27, pp. 9–103.

VATS, V. S. 1940. *Excavations at Harappa.* 2 vols. Delhi, Government of India.

WHEELER, R. E. M. 1947. Harappa, 1946: The Defences and Cemetery R-37. *AIn*, Vol. 3.

——. 1962. *Charsada. A Metropolis on the North-west Frontier. Being a Report on the Excavations of 1958.* London, Oxford University Press.

——. 1968. *The Indus Civilization.* 3rd ed. Cambridge, Cambridge University Press.

CHAPTER 18

AGRAWAL, D. P.; BHANDARI, N.; LAL, B. B.; SINGHVI, A. K. 1981. Thermoluminescence Dating of Pottery from Sringaverapura – A Ramayana Site. *Proceedings of the Indian Academy of Science, Earth and Planetary Sciences*, Vol. 90, No. 2, pp. 161–72.

AGRAWAL, D. P.; KUSUMGAR, S. 1974. *Prehistoric Chronology and Radiocarbon Dating in India.* Delhi, Munshiram Manoharlal.

AGRAWAL, O. P. 1983. Scientific and Technological Examination of Some Objects from Atranjikhera. In: R. C. Gaur (ed.), *Excavations at Atranjikhera. Early Civilization of the Upper Ganga Basin*, pp. 487–98. Delhi, Motilal Banarsidass.

AGRAWALA, R. C.; KUMAR, V. 1976. The Problem of PGW and Iron in North-Eastern Rajasthan. In: S. P. Gupta and K. S. Ramachandran (eds.), *Mahabharata: Myth and Reality. Differing Views*, pp. 241–4. Delhi, Agam Prakashan.

ALLCHIN, B.; ALLCHIN, R. 1968. *The Birth of Indian Civilization.* Harmondsworth, Penguin.

BANERJEE, N. R. 1957. Excavation at Ujjain. *IAR*, 1956/57, pp. 20–8.

CHOWDHURY, K. A.; GHOSH, S. S. 1954/55. Plant Remains. Quoted in: B. B. Lal (ed.), Excavations at Hastinapura and Other Explorations in the Upper Ganga and Sutlej Basins 1950–52: New Light on the Dark Age Between the End of the Harappa Culture and the Early Historical Period. *AIn*, Vol. 10/11, pp. 120–37.

CHOWDHURY, K. A.; SARASWAT, K. S.; BUTH, G. M. 1977. *Ancient Agriculture and Forestry in North India.* Bombay, Asia Publishing House.

DANI, A. H. (ed.). 1967. Timaragarha and Gandhara Grave Culture. *APk*, Vol. 3, pp. 3–64. (Special number.)

DIKSHIT, K. N. 1973. The Allahapur Evidence and the Painted Grey Ware Chronology. In: D. P. Agrawal and A. E. Ghosh (eds.), *Radiocarbon and Indian Archaeology*, pp. 148–53. Bombay, Tata Institute of Fundamental Research.

——. 1981. The Excavations at Hulas and Further Exploration of the Upper Ganga-Yamuna Doab. *ME*, Vol. 5, pp. 70–6.

GAUR, R. C. 1983. *Excavations at Atranjikhera. Early Civilization of the Upper Ganga Basin.* Delhi, Motilal Banarsidass.

GHOSH, A. 1952. The Rajputana Desert – Its Archaeological Aspects. *Bulletin of the National Institute of Sciences of India,* Vol. 1, pp. 37–42.

GHOSH, A.; PANIGRANI, K. C. 1946. The Pottery of Ahichchhatra, District Bareilly, U. P. *AIn,* Vol. 1, pp. 37–59.

HÄRTEL, H. 1976. Some Results of the Excavations at Sonkh. In: Cultural Department of the Embassy of the Federal Republic of Germany (ed.), *German Scholars on India. Contributions to Indian Studies,* Vol. 2, pp. 69–99. Bombay, Nachiketa Publications.

HEGDE, K. T. M. 1975. The Painted Grey Ware of India. *Antiquity,* Vol. 49, pp. 187–90.

JOSHI, J. P. 1977. Overlap of the Late Harappan Culture and Painted Grey Ware Culture in the Light of Recent Excavations in Haryana, Panjab and Jammu. In: B. B. Lal and S. C. Malik (eds.), *Seminar on Indian Civilization: Problems and Issues.* Simla, Indian Institute of Advanced Study.

——. 1978. Interlocking of Late Harappa Culture and Painted Grey Ware Culture in the Light of Recent Excavations. *ME,* Vol. 2, pp. 98–101.

LAL, B. B. 1950. The Painted Grey Ware of the Upper Gangetic Basin. An Approach to the Problems of the Dark Age. *Journal of the Royal Asiatic Society of Bengal (Letters),* Vol. 16, No. 1, pp. 89–102.

—— (ed.). 1954/55. Excavations at Hastinapura and Other Explorations in the Upper Ganga and Sutlej Basins 1950–52: New Light on the Dark Age Between the End of the Harappa Culture and the Early Historical Period. *AIn,* Vol. 10–11, pp. 4–151.

——. 1980. Did the Painted Grey Ware Continue up to the Mauryan Times? *Pt,* Vol. 9, pp. 64–80.

LAL, B. B.; DIKSHIT, K. N. 1981. Sringaverapura: A Key Site for the Protohistory and Early History of the Central Ganga Valley. *Pt,* Vol. 10, pp. 1–7.

LAL, M. 1985. Settlement Patterns of Painted Grey Ware Culture in the Ganga Valley. In: V. N. Misra and P. Bellwood (eds.), *Recent Advances in Indo-Pacific Prehistory,* pp. 373–9. Leiden, E. J. Brill.

MUGHAL, M. R. 1980. New Archaeological Evidence from Bahawalpur. *ME,* Vol. 4, pp. 93–8.

——. 1981. New Archaeological Evidence from Bahawalpur. *ICnp,* pp. 33–42.

NATH, B. 1954/55. Animal Remains. *AIn,* Vol. 10–11, pp. 107–20.

NAUTIYAL, K. P. 1981. Pushing Back the Antiquity of Garhwal: Results of Recent Explorations and Excavations. Paper Presented at Seminar on Regional Historical Writings in India with Special Reference to Western Himalayas, Simla, 22–25 October 1981.

SAHI, M. D. N. 1978. New Light on the Life of the Painted Grey Ware People as Revealed from Excavations at Jakhera (District Etah). *ME,* Vol. 2, pp. 101–3.

SHARMA, R. S. 1978. The Later Vedic Phase and the Painted Grey Ware Culture. *Pt,* Vol. 8, pp. 63–7.

——. 1980. *Sudras in Ancient India. A Social History of the Lower Order Down to Circa A.D. 600.* 2nd ed. Delhi, Motilal Banarsidass.

SHARMA, Y. D. 1955/56. Past Patterns in Living as Unfolded by Excavations at Rupar. *Lalit Kala,* Vol. 1–2, pp. 121–9.

SINHA, K. K. 1967. *Excavations at Sravasti – 1959.* Varanasi, Banares Hindu University.

SURAJ BHAN, J.; SHAFFER, J. G. 1978. New Discoveries in Northern Haryana. *ME,* Vol. 2, pp. 59–68.

TRIPATHI, V. 1976. *The Painted Grey Ware: An Iron Age Culture of Northern India*. Delhi, Concept Publishing Co.

CHAPTER 19

ALEKSEEV, V. P. 1961. Paleoantropologiya Altaye-Sayanskogo nagor'ya êpokhi neolita i bronzî. *Antropologicheskiy sbornik*, Vol. 20.

ANDRIANOV, B. 1969. *Drevniye orositel'nîye sistemî Priaral'ya*. Moscow.

ASKAROV, A. A. 1977. *Drevnezemledel'cheskaya kul'tura êpokhi bronzî yuga Uzbekistana*. Tashkent.

ASKAROV, V.; AL'BAUM, L. I. 1979. *Poseleniye Kuchuktepe*. Tashkent.

CHLENOVA, N. L. 1972. *Khronologiya pamyatnikov karasukskoy êpokhi*. Moscow.

DEBETS, G. F. 1932. Rasovîye tipî naseleniya Minusinskogo kraya v êpokhu rodovogo stroya. *Antropologicheskiy zhurnal*, No. 2.

——. 1948. Paleoantropologiya SSSR. *Trudî Instituta êtnografii Akademii nauk SSSR*, No. 4.

D'YAKONOV, M. M. 1954. Slozheniye klassovogo obshchestva v severnoy Baktrii. *SA*, Vol. 19, pp. 121–40.

ENGELS, F. 1984. Proiskhozhdeniye sem'yi, chastnoy sobstvennosti i gosudarstva. *Izbrannîye proizvedeniya v trëkh tomakh*, Vol. 3. Moscow.

GAFUROV, B. G. 1972. *Tadzhiki*. Drevneyshaya, drevnyaya i srednevekovaya istoriya. Moscow, Vostochnaya Literatura Publications.

GANYALIN, A. F. 1953. Arkheologicheskiye pamyatniki gornîkh rayonov severozapadnogo Kopet-Daga (po dannîm arkheologicheskih razvedok 1952 g). *Izvestiya Akademii nauk Turkmenskoy SSR*, No. 5, pp. 14–20.

GRYAZNOV, M. P. 1947. Pamyatniki Mayemirskogo êtapa rannikh kochevnikov na Altaye. *KSIIMK*, Vol. 55.

——. 1952. Pamyatniki Karasukskogo êtapa v Tsentral'nom Kazakhstane. *SA*, Vol. 16, pp. 129–62.

——. 1956a. K voprosu o kul'turakh êpokhi pozdney bronzî v Sibiri. *KSIIMK*, Vol. 64.

——. 1956b. O chernoloshchenoy keramike Kavkaza, Kazakhstana i Sibiri v êpokhu pozdney bronzî. *KSIIMK*, Vol. 64.

——. 1957. Etapî razvitiya khozyaystva skotovodcheskikh plemën Kazakhstana i yuzhnoy Sibiri v êpokhu bronzî. *KSIE*, Vol. 26, pp. 21–8.

——. 1966. Tagisken – usîpal'nitsa vozhdey. *Srednyaya Aziya v êpokhu kamnya i bronzî*. Moscow/Leningrad.

——. 1980. *Arzhan. Tsarskiy kurgan ranneskifskogo vremeni*. Leningrad.

GRYAZNOV, M. P.; MAKSIMENKOV, G. A.; PYATKIN, B. I. 1980. Karasukskaya kul'tura. *Istoriya Sibiri*, Vol. 1, pp. 180–7. Leningrad.

GULYAMOV, J. G. 1966. Gidrografiya i usloviya vozniknoveniya orosheniya. In: Ja. Gulyamov, U. Islamov and A. Askarov (eds.), *Pervobîtnaya kul'tura v nizov'yakh Zarafshana*, pp. 9–26. Tashkent.

GULYAMOV, J. G.; MUKHAMEDZHANOV, A. R. 1975. Istoriya irrigatsii Uzbekistana s drevneyshikh vremën do seredinnî XIX veka. *Razvitiye irrigatsii v komplekse proizvoditel'nîkh sil Uzbekistana*, Vol. 1, pp. 133–52. Tashkent.

ITINA, M. A. 1977a. *Istoriya stepnîkh plemën yuzhnogo Priaral'ya*. Moscow.

——. 1977b. Kul'tura plemën Priaral'ya. *Istoriya Kazakhskoy SSR s drevneyshikh vremën do nashîkh dney*, Vol. 1. Alma-Ata.

Kes', A. S.; Kostyuchenko, V. P.; Lisitsyna, G. N. 1980. *Istoriya naseleniya i drevniye orosheniye yugo-zapadnoy Turkmenii.* Moscow.

Kiselev, S. V. 1951. *Drevnyaya istoriya yuzhnoy Sibiri.* Moscow.

——. 1960. Neolit i bronzovîy vek Kitaya. *SA,* No. 4.

Khlopin, I. N. 1983. *Yugo-zapadnaya Turkmeniya v êpokhu pozdney bronzî (Po materialam Sumbarskikh mogil'nikov).* Leningrad.

Lipskiy, A. N. 1954. Afanas'evskiye pogrebeniya v nizov'yakh rek Esi i Tei. *KSIIMK,* Vol. 54.

Lisitsyna, G. N. 1978. *Stanovleniye i razvitiye oroshaemogo zemledel'ya v yuzhnoy Turkmenii.* Moscow.

Margulan, A. K.; Akishev, K. A.; Kadyrbaev, M. K. et al. 1966. *Drevnyaya kul'tura Tsentral'nogo Kazakhstana.* Alma-Ata.

Margulan, A. K.; Akishev, K. A.; Kadyrbaev, M. K. 1977. Dandybay-Begazinskaya kul'tura. *Istoriya Kazakhskoy SSR,* Vol. 1. Alma-Ata.

Marushenko, A. A. 1959. Yel'ken-Depe (otchët o raskopkakh 1953, 1955 i 1957 gg). *Trudî Instituta istorii arkheologii i êtnografii Akademii nauk Turkmenskoy SSR,* Vol. 5, pp. 54–109. Ashkhabad.

Masson, V. M. 1955. Pamyatniki kul'turî arkhaicheskogo Dakhistana v yugozapadnoy Turkmenii. *Trudî YuTAKE,* Vol. 7, pp. 385–458.

——. 1956. Pervobîtno-obshchinnîy stroy na territorii Turkmenii. *Trudî YuTAKE,* Vol. 7.

——. 1959. *Drevnezemledel'cheskaya kul'tura Margianî.* Moscow/Leningrad.

——. 1966. Yugo-vostok Sredney Azii. *Srednyaya Aziya v êpokhu kamnya i bronzî.* Moscow/Leningrad.

Novgorodova, E. A. 1970. *Tsentral'naya Aziya i Karasukskaya problema.* Moscow.

Sarianidi, V. I. 1972. *Raskopki Tillya-tepe v Severnom Afganistane.* Moscow.

——. 1977. *Drevniye zemledel'tsî Afganistana.* Moscow.

Teploukhov, S. A. 1927. Drevniye pogrebeniya v Minusinskom kraye. *Materialî po Etnografii,* Vol. 3, No. 2, pp. 57–112. Leningrad.

——. 1929. Opît klassifikatsii drevnikh metallicheskikh kul'tur Minusinskogo kraya. *Materialî po Etnografii,* Vol. 4. Leningrad.

Tolstov, S. P. 1948. *Drevniy Khorezm.* Moscow.

——. 1962. *Po drevnim del'tam Oksa i Yaksarta.* Moscow.

Tolstov, S. P.; Zhdanko, T. A.; Itina, M. A. 1963. Rabotî Khorezmskoy arkheologo-êtnograficheskoy êkspeditsii AN SSSR v 1958–1960 gg. *Trudî KhAEE,* Vol. 6.

Vishnevskaya, O. A. 1973. *Kul'tura sakskikh plemën nizov'yev Syrdar'i.* Moscow.

Volkov, V. V. 1967. *Bronzovîy i rannezheleznîy vek Severnoy Mongolii.* Ulan-Bator.

Zadneprovsky, Y. A. 1962. *Drevnezemledel'cheskaya kul'tura Erganî.* Moscow/Leningrad.

Chapter 20

Alekseev, V. P. 1974. Novîye dannîye o evropoidney rase Tsentral'noy Azii. *Bronzovîy i zheleznîy vek Sibiri.* Novosibirsk.

Chlenova, N. L. 1967. *Proiskhozhdeniye i rannyaya istoriya plemën tagarskoy kul'turî.* Moscow.

Dikov, N. V. 1958. *Bronzovîy vek Zabaykal'ya.* Ulan-Ude.

Dorj, D. 1976. *Neolit Vostochnoy Mongolii.* Ulan-Bator.

Dorsjuren, Ts. 1961. *The Northern Hsiung-nu.* Ulan-Bator. (In Mongolian.)

GRACH, A. D. 1965. Problema sootnosheniya kul'tur skifskogo vremeni Tuvî, Altaya i Minusinskoy kotlovinî v svete noveyshîkh issledovanii. *Materialî sessii, posvyashchennoy itogam arkheologicheskikh i etnograficheskikh issledovaniy,* pp. 86–8. Baku.

——. 1980. *Drevniye kochevniki v tsentre Azii.* Moscow.

GRISHIN, Y. S. 1975. *Bronzovîy i ranniy zheleznîy vek Vostochnogo Zabaykal'ya.* Moscow.

GRYAZNOV, M. P. 1950. *Pervîy Pazîrîkskiy kurgan.* Leningrad.

——. 1952. Pamyatniki Karasukskogo êtapa v Tsentral'nom Kazakhstane. *SA,* Vol. 16, pp. 129–62.

——. 1956. K voprosu o kul'turakh êpokhi pozdney bronzî v Sibiri. *KSIIMK,* Vol. 64, pp. 24–72.

KISELEV, S. V. 1951. *Drevnyaya istoriya yuzhnoy Sibiri.* Moscow.

——. 1960. Neolit i bronzovîy vek Kitaya. *SA,* Vol. 4.

KONOVALOV, P. B. 1976. *Hunnu v Zabaykal'e (pogrebal'nîye pamyatniki).* Ulan-Ude.

KYZLASOV, L. R. 1961. Obzor Trudov Tuvinskoy kompleksnoy arkheologo-êtnograficheskoy êkspeditsii Instituta Etnografii AN SSR. *SE,* No. 4, p. 288.

——. 1979. *Drevnyaya Tuva.* Moscow.

LARICHEV, B. E. 1953. *Proiskhozhdeniye kul'turî plitochnîkh mogil Zabaykal'ya.* Ulan-Ude.

MANNAI-OOL, M. K. 1970. *Tuva v skifskoye vremya (Uyukskaya kul'tura).* Moscow.

MARGULAN, A. K.; AKISHEV, K. A.; KADYRBAEV, M. K. 1977. Dandybay – Begazinskaya kul'tura. *Istoriya Kazakhskoy SSR,* Vol. 1. Alma-Ata.

NAVAAN, D. 1970. *Bronzovîy vek Vostochnoy Mongolii.* Ulan-Bator.

——. 1978. Novîye nakhodki 'Zverinogo stilya' Mongolii. *Arkheologiya i êtnografiya Mongolii,* pp. 118–22. Novosibirsk.

NAVAAN, D.; Dorj, D. 1970. *Mongolyn Khuriinye.* Ulan-Bator. (In Mongolian.)

NOVGORODOVA, E. A. 1980. *Alte Kunst der Mongolei.* Leipzig, E. A. Seemann Verlag.

NOVGORODOVA, E. A.; VOLKOV, V. V.; KORENEVSKIY, S. N.; MAMONOVA, N. N. (Preface by Karl Jettmar). 1982. *Ulangom. Ein skythenzeitliches Gräberfeld in der Mongolei.* Wiesbaden, Otto Harrassowitz. (Asiatische Forschungen, 76.)

OKLADNIKOV, A. P. 1950. Neolit i bronzovîy vek Pribaykal'ya (istoriko-arkheologicheskiye issledovaniya), I–II. *MIA,* Vol. 18.

OKLADNIKOV, A. P.; ZAPOROZHESKAYA, V. A. 1969. *Petroglifî Zabaykal'ya,* Vol. 1. Leningrad.

PERLEE, K. 1961. *Ancient and Medieval Cities and Settlements in the Mongolian People's Republic.* Ulan-Bator. (In Mongolian.)

RUDENKO, S. I. 1960. *Kul'tura naseleniya Tsentral'nogo Altaya v skifskoye vremya.* Moscow/Leningrad.

SAVINOV, D. G.; CHLENOVA, N. L. 1978. Severokavkazskiye olennîye kamni v ryadu olennîkh kamney Evrazii i vopros ob ikh etnicheskoy prinadlezhnosti. *Krupnovskiye chteniya, Tezisî dokladov,* Vol. 7, pp. 59–60. Nal'chik.

SER-ODJAV, N. 1958. *The Ancient History of Mongolia.* Ulan-Bator. (In Mongolian.)

TSEVVENDORJI, D. 1978. Chaman'skaya kul'tura. *Arkheologiya i êtnografiya Mongolii,* pp. 108–17.

VOLKOV, V. V. 1967. *Bronzovîy ranniy zheleznîy vek Severnoy Mongolii.* Ulan-Bator.

——. 1974. Ulangomskiy mogil'nik i nekotorîe voprosî êtnicheskoy istorii Mongolii. *Rol'kochevîkh narodov v tsivilizatsii Tsentral'noy Azii,* pp. 69–72. Ulan-Bator.

——. 1978. Ulangomskiy mogil'nik (po materyalam raskopok 1972). *Arkheologiya i êtnografiya Mongolii,* pp. 101–7.

APPENDIX

HUMBOLDT, A. DE. 1843. *Asie centrale. Recherches sur les chaînes de montagnes et la climatologie comparée*, Vol. 1, pp. xxviii–xxix. Paris.

KHANYKOFF, N. DE. 1862. *Mémoire sur la partie méridionale de l'Asie centrale,* Vol. 13, pp. 205–6. Paris.

MUSHKETOV, I. V. 1886. *Turkestan. Geologitcheskoye i orografitcheskoye opisaniye, po dannîm, sobrannîm vo vryemya puteshestviye s 1844 do 1880,* Vol. 1, pp. 9–11. St Petersburg.

OBRUTCHEV, V. A. 1951. *Izbrannîye rabotî po geografii Azii,* Vol. 1, p. 255. Moscow.

RICHTHOFEN, F. VON. 1877. *China. Ergebnisse eigener Reisen und darauf gegründeter Studien,* Vol. 1 p. 7. Berlin.

SINITSIN, V. M. 1959. *Tsentral'naya Aziya,* pp. 9–10. Moscow.

INDEX

Abashev culture 348
Acheulean culture 49-50, 56
adobe 244-5
Afanasievo culture 345, 347
Afghanistan (Hindu Kush); Baluchistan
  influences 252; Bronze Age 193,
  215-22 (cemeteries 379-82; Deh
  Morasi Ghundai 218; Mundigak
  215-17; Said Qala 217-18); coppper
  metallurgy 193; geography 35-6; Iron
  Age cultures 452-3; Late Bronze Age
  342, 352-4; Middle Palaeolithic 81-2;
  Neolithic sites 124-6; northern
  civilization 219-20, 222; Palaeolithic
  finds 56; Upper Palaeolithic sites
  46-7(map), 94-5
see also Bactria
agriculture, 111(map); Afghanistan
  Chalcolithic 193; Dadiwan Neolithic
  156; Ganges-Jamuna valley 425; Iran
  Chalcolithic 192; Mongolian Neolithic
  180-1; PGW 425, 426, 433-4; ploughed
  field 272, 277; post-Indus 396; Sapalli
  343; Tamsagbulag 174-5; Tangwang
  326; Xindian 324-5; Xinjiang 331,
  333
see also farming
Ak-depe Eneolithic 235, 237
Ak-kupruk 46-7(fig), 94-5, 124-5
Aksu-Ayuly burial complex 462
alabaster 288

Alagou 334-5
Ali-tepe 111(map), 113
Aligrama 414-15
Altyn-depe; decline 243, 338, 340; gold
  ornaments 236(fig); Harrapan
  influence 242; Middle Bronze Age
  237-8; Murghab/Sapalli similarities
  345; temple 233, 237, 239, 241; 3rd
  millenium 233, 235
Amirabad culture 442, 444
Amri 249(map), 267(fig), 269
Amri/Kalibangan connections 279, 280
Amu Darya 33, 33-4, 35, 41; irrigation
  443(fig)
see also Farukhabad; Dashly; Amirabad
  culture
Andronovo culture 349-50, 461-2
Anguo (Siwa) culture 320-1(map), 327-8
animal cult 179-80, 474
animal domestication 110, 113, 141, 175,
  367
animal fossils, Sjara-osso-gol 105
animal paintings 102-3, 262-3
animals; adaptability 38; desert/steppe
  38-9; Samarkand 93; tugai scrub 39
see also specific breed; stockbreeding
annealing of copper 228
anthropological characteristics; Beshkent
  388; Burzahom 146; gracile groups 25;
  Harappa 25; Mongolia 25, 171, 466,
  467; Neolithic 25; Palaeolithic 24-5;

521

1000 km